California
Real Estate
Finance
10th Edition

Fesler · Brady

California Real Estate Finance, Tenth Edition

John Fesler and Mary Ellen Brady

Executive Editor: Sara Glassmeyer

Project Manager: Arlin Kauffman, LEAP Publishing

Product Specialist: Abby Franklin

Cover Design: Chris Dailey

Cover Image: © Shutterstock / f11photo

© 2016, 2011 OnCourse Learning

ALL RIGHTS RESERVED. No part of this work covered by the copyright herein may be reproduced, transmitted, stored, or used in any form or by any means graphic, electronic, or mechanical, including but not limited to photocopying, recording, scanning, digitizing, taping, web distribution, information networks, or information storage and retrieval systems, except as permitted under Section 107 or 108 of the 1976 United States Copyright Act, without the prior written permission of the publisher.

> For product information and technology assistance, contact us at
> **OnCourse Learning and Sales Support, 1-855-733-7239.**
> For permission to use material from this text or product.

Library of Congress Control Number: 2015950563
ISBN-13: 978-1-62980-017-2
ISBN-10: 1629800171

OnCourse Learning
3100 Cumberland Blvd, Suite 1450
Atlanta, GA 30339
USA

Visit us at **www.oncoursepublishing.com**

Printed in the United States of America
1 2 3 4 5 6 7 20 19 18 17 16

BRIEF CONTENTS

Illustrations	*xix*
Preface	*xxi*
Acknowledgments	*xxv*
About the Authors	*xxvi*
Authors' Note	*xxviii*

1	Introduction to Real Estate Finance	2
2	Institutional Lenders	40
3	Noninstitutional Lenders and the California Real Property Loan Law	72
4	Adjustable Rate and Other Alternative Mortgage Instruments	104
5	Conventional Loans	130
6	Government-Backed Financing	162
7	Points, Discounts, and the Secondary Mortgage Market	196
8	Qualifying the Property	222
9	Qualifying the Borrower	264
10	Processing, Closing, and Servicing Real Estate Loans	298
11	Foreclosures and Other Lending Problems	334
12	Construction Loans	370
13	Creative Financing Approaches	400
14	Financing Small Investment Properties	448
15	Basic Mathematics of Real Estate Finance	478
	Appendix A	520
	Answers to Multiple-Choice Questions	528
	Glossary	533
	Index	552

CONTENTS

Illustrations	*xix*
Preface	*xxi*
Acknowledgments	*xxv*
About the Authors	*xxvi*
Authors' Note	*xxviii*

1 Introduction to Real Estate Finance — 2
Overview — 3
1.1 Welcome to the Real World of Real Estate Financing — 3
   A Bit of History — 4
   The Ability to "Fog a Mirror" Was Sufficient to Get a Loan — 4
   The Old Rules Return — 5
   Who to Blame — 5
   Roller-Coaster Ride — 7
   Enter New Regulations — 8
   Disintermediation — 8
1.2 Short Overview of the Mortgage Market — 9
1.3 The Meaning of Money — 9
   How Is Money Created? — 9
   How Is Money Accumulated? — 10
1.4 The Flow of Money and Credit into the Mortgage Market — 11
   Intermediation of Savings — 12
   Disintermediation of Savings — 13
   Reintermediation of Savings — 13
1.5 Federal Control of the Money Supply — 14
   The Federal Reserve System (Monetary Policy) — 14
   A Comment on the Fed — 14
   Reserve Requirements — 15

Quantitative Easing	19
The U.S. Treasury (Fiscal Policy)	19
The Government Dilemma	20
1.6 Cost Characteristics of the Mortgage Market	22
Cost of Mortgage Money	22
What Causes Mortgage Interest Rates to Change?	23
"Tight" versus "Easy" Money	25
The California Mortgage Market	26
1.7 Instruments of Real Estate Finance	27
Promissory Notes	27
Deed of Trust (Trust Deed)	28
Installment Sales Contracts	30
Special Clauses	30
The Language of Real Estate Finance	31
1.8 The Five-Step Financing Process	31
Chapter Summary	32
Important Terms and Concepts	33
Case & Point	37
What Happened and What Is Ahead	37
2 Institutional Lenders	**42**
Overview	43
The Blurring of Bank Identities	43
2.1 Savings Banks/Thrifts	43
What Is a Savings Bank?	43
Lending Characteristics of Savings Banks (Thrifts)	44
2.2 Commercial Banks	46
Commercial Banks	46
Lending Characteristics of Commercial Banks	46
Credit Unions	47
Lending Characteristics of Credit Unions	47
Anticipated Future Impacts on Lending Institutions	48
Community Reinvestment Act (CRA)	49
Home Mortgage Disclosure Act (HMDA)	50
What Is a Life Insurance Company?	51
2.3 Life Insurance Companies	52
Lending Characteristics of Life Insurance Companies	52
Lending Practices of the Life Insurance Industry	53

2.4 Mutual Savings Banks	54
2.5 Depository Institutions and Monetary Control Act	54
2.6 Pension and Retirement Funds	55
Administration and Lending Policies of Pension and Trust Funds	55
Individual Retirement Accounts (IRAs) and Keogh Plans	56
The Past and Present of Lending Regulation	56
2.7 Government Regulatory Agencies	57
Regulation and its Consequences	61
2.8 Trade Associations	62
Chapter Summary	64
Important Terms and Concepts	65
Case & Point	69
The Secure and Fair Enforcement for Mortgage Licensing Act of 2009 (SAFE)	69
3 Noninstitutional Lenders and the California Real Property Loan Law	**72**
Preview	73
3.1 Private Party Lenders	73
Lack of Structure	73
New Qualified Mortgage Rules	74
Types of Private Lenders	74
Sellers as Private Lenders	76
Characteristics of Private Lenders	76
3.2 Usury Law	78
Payday Loans	79
Mortgage Entities	80
Agency Structure & Characteristics	80
Bankers, Brokers, and Other Lenders	81
3.3 Real Property Loan Law	83
Subprime Borrowers and Predatory Lending	**83**
Purpose of the Mortgage Loan Broker Law	84
Exceptions to the Mortgage Loan Broker Law	87
Maximum Commissions	88
Other Costs and Expenses	89
Balloon Payments	89
Insurance	90

3.4 Syndications	90
3.5 Real Estate Investment Trusts and Endowment Funds	91
Types of REITs	91
REITs as a Source of Financing	92
The Ups and Downs of REITs	92
Pension Funds	93
Endowment Funds	93
3.6 Finance Companies	94
3.7 Financial Advisory Role of the Real Estate Broker	94
Computerized Loan Origination	95
Buyer-Borrowers Going Directly Online to Obtain a Real Estate Loan	96
Chapter Summary	96
Important Terms and Concepts	97
Case & Point	101
Yield-Spread Premiums: Good or Bad?	101

4 Adjustable Rate and Other Alternative Mortgage Instruments — 104

Overview	105
4.1 Objectives And Rationale	105
Purpose of Adjustable Rate and Other Alternative Loans	106
4.2 Adjustable Rate Mortgages (ARMs)	107
What Is an Adjustable Rate Mortgage?	107
Some Things to Know About Adjustable Rate Mortgages	107
What Does Today's ARM Loan Look Like?	109
Why Use an Adjustable in a Fixed Rate World?	110
Disclosure Requirements for ARMs	111
4.3 Hybrid Loan Options	114
4.4 Balloon Payment Fixed Rate Loans	115
4.5 Reverse Annuity Mortgage (RAM)	115
General Provisions	115
Program Concerns	117
4.6 Miscellaneous Alternative Plans	119
Fifteen-Year and Twenty-Year Mortgages	119
Biweekly Loan Payments	119
4.7 Epilogue	122

	Chapter Summary	123
	Important Terms and Concepts	124
	Case & Point	127
	Are Negatively Amortized Loans a Thing of the Past?	127
5	**Conventional Loans**	**130**
	Overview	131
	5.1 What Is a Conventional Loan?	131
	Conventional versus Government-Backed Loans	131
	Sources of Conventional Money	135
	5.2 Keeping up with Lender Policies	138
	Note of Interest—Risk Based Pricing	139
	Which Lender to Use?	140
	5.3 Buy-Down Loans	140
	Why the Seller Participates	141
	Temporary Buy-Down Plans	141
	Permanent Buy-Down Plans	142
	5.4 Low Down Payment Conventional Loans	142
	97 Percent Financing Returns	143
	Special Interest Topic	144
	5.5 California Fair Lending Regulations	146
	5.6 Private Mortgage Insurance (PMI)	148
	New Rules Emerge	151
	How Is Mortgage Insurance Obtained?	153
	How Are Claims Handled?	154
	Chapter Summary	154
	Important Terms and Concepts	155
	Case & Point	158
	Consumer Financial Protection Bureau (CFPB)	158
6	**Government-Backed Financing**	**162**
	Overview	163
	6.1 Federal Housing Administration	163
	What Is the FHA?	163
	FHA: Its Role in the Recovery	164
	New Hawk Program Introduced	166
	Why Use FHA Loan?	167
	Calculating FHA Loan Amounts	169
	FHA Programs	169
	What Is Ahead for the FHA?	172

    6.2 U.S. Department of Agriculture (USDA) Loans   175
    6.3 Department of Veterans Affairs   176
        What Is the Department of Veterans Affairs (VA)?   176
        Administration of VA Home Loan Program   176
        VA Loans   177
        Who Is Eligible for a VA-Guaranteed Loan?   179
        Certificate of Eligibility   180
        Reinstatement of Full Entitlement   180
        Partial Entitlements   180
        General Guidelines   181
        Choosing a Lender for FHA and VA Loans   184
    6.4 Cal-Vet Loans   185
        Who Is Eligible for Cal-Vet Loans?   185
        General Information about Cal-Vet Loans   186
        Advantages and Disadvantages of Cal-Vet Loans   188
    6.5 California Housing Finance Agency Program (CALHFA)   188
        Two Main Programs   189
        Various Programs Available   189
    Chapter Summary   190
    Important Terms and Concepts   191
    Case & Point   194
        Risk Based Pricing and What It Means   194

7 Points, Discounts, and the Secondary Mortgage Market   196
    Overview   197
    7.1 Secondary Mortgage Market   197
        Purpose of the Secondary Market   198
        The GSEs Importance   199
        Why and How Are Mortgage Funds Shifted?   200
        The Federal Government's Involvement   201
    7.2 Points and Discounts   201
        Lenders' Use of Discounts   202
        Price and Yield   204
        Where Are Discounts Used?   205
        Mortgage-Backed Securities   207
        Collateralized Mortgage Obligations   211
        Nonconforming Loans   211
        Investment Bankers   212

    Standardization 214
    Mortgage Revenue Bonds 214
  Chapter Summary 215
  Important Terms and Concepts 215
  Case& Point 219
    Fannie/Freddie ... Now and In the Future! 219

8 Qualifying the Property   222

  Overview 223
  8.1 What Does Qualifying the Property Mean? 223
    Lenders' Property Standards 224
    Influence of Freddie Mac and Fannie Mae 224
    FHA and VA Property Standards 225
    Procedure for Qualifying a Property 225
    Conventional Lenders and the Appraisal Process 226
    New Rules Impact Appraisal Time Frames 227
  8.2 Appraising a Property 228
    Location 229
    At the Property 237
  8.3 Using a Standard Appraisal Form 238
    Neighborhood 238
    Property 239
    Valuation 241
  8.4 Underwriting the Appraisal 248
  8.5 Planned Unit Developments and Condominiums 248
  8.6 The Licensing of Real Estate Appraisers 251
  8.7 Working With Appraisers: The Do's And Don'ts 254
  Chapter Summary 255
  Important Terms and Concepts 256
  Case & Point 260
    Appraisals and the New HVCC Rules 260

9 Qualifying the Borrower   264

  Overview 265
  9.1 How Lenders Qualify Prospective Borrowers 266
  9.2 Ability or Capacity to Pay: A Case History 267
    What Does This Case Illustrate? 268
    Why Qualify Borrowers? 268
  9.3 Capacity to Pay 269
    Income Ratios 271
    Debts 272

9.4	Qualifying Under Government-Backed Loans	274
	Department of Veterans Affairs (VA)	274
9.5	What Is Income?	278
	FNMA and FHLMC	278
	Commissioned People and Tradespeople	279
	Overtime and Bonus	279
	Part-Time Work	279
	Spousal/Alimony and Child Support	280
	Pensions and Social Security	280
	Military Personnel	280
	Income from Real Estate	280
	Self-Employment	281
9.6	Co-Borrowing	282
9.7	After Income, What Then?	282
	Stability of Income	282
	Borrower's Assets	283
9.8	Desire to Pay	284
	Past Payment Record	285
	Credit Scoring—FICO	287
	Motivation	288
9.9	Working with Lenders	289
	Chapter Summary	291
	Important Terms and Concepts	292
	Case & Point	295
	TILA-RESPA Integrated Disclosure (TRID) – New Forms Required	295

10 Processing, Closing, and Servicing Real Estate Loans — 298

	Overview	299
10.1	Processing the Loan	299
	Completing Loan Application Forms	309
	Equal Credit Opportunity Act (ECOA)	310
	Real Estate Settlement Procedures Act (RESPA)	311
	The Mortgage Disclosure Improvement Act (MDIA)	311
	Verifying the Information on the Application	312
	Loan Package	313

10.2	How Is a Loan Approved?	314
	Federal Housing Administration (FHA) and Department of Veterans Affairs (VA)	314
	Fair Credit Reporting Act	315
10.3	Closing the Loan	316
	Loan Documents for Escrow	316
	Truth-in-Lending Law (Regulation Z)	319
	Closing Costs	321
10.4	After the Loan: Rights and Responsibilities	324
	Loan Payments	324
	Late Charges	325
	Prepayment Privileges and Penalties	325
10.5	Handling Loan Takeovers	326
	Loan Assumptions/Subject to Transfers	326
	Subject To's	326
Chapter Summary		327
Important Terms and Concepts		328
Case & Point		332
	A Typical Loan Process	332

11 Foreclosures and Other Lending Problems — 334

Overview		335
11.1	Collateral Provisions of Deeds of Trust	335
11.2	Default and Foreclosure	338
	Trustee's Sale	339
	Judicial Sale	346
	Deed in Lieu of Foreclosure	347
11.3	Minimizing Loan Defaults	348
	Impound Accounts	348
	Forbearance	349
	Mortgage Guaranty Insurance	352
	Automatic Payment Plans	355
	Consumer Protection Laws and Regulations	355
11.4	Other Lending Problems	356
	Usury	356
	Redlining	358
	Community Reinvestment Act (CRA)	359
	Home Mortgage Disclosure Act (HMDA)	359

	Short Sales	360
	Web Help and Its Reliability	361
	Chapter Summary	362
	Important Terms and Concepts	363
	Case & Point	366
	Foreclosure and Short Sales: Government Intervention Continues	366
12	**Construction Loans**	**370**
	Overview	371
	12.1 Nature of Construction Loans	371
	Sources of Funds	372
	Kinds of Loans	372
	Loan Costs	374
	12.2 Evaluation and Lending Process	374
	Lender Considerations for a Construction Loan	374
	Lending and Disbursement Procedures	376
	12.3 Take-Out or Permanent Loans	380
	Subordination Clauses	380
	Partial Release Clauses	381
	Rental Achievement Clauses	384
	Mechanic's Liens and Their Impact on Construction Loans	385
	12.4 Public Construction	391
	Chapter Summary	392
	Important Terms and Concepts	393
	Case & Point	396
	Tax Deferred Exchanges	396
	Glossary of Exchange Terms	398
13	**Creative Financing Approaches**	**400**
	Overview	401
	13.1 Secondary Financing Techniques	402
	Second Trust Deeds Carried by the Seller	402
	Collateralizing Junior Loans	403
	Seller Sells the Second Loan	405
	Broker Participation	406
	Combination or Split Junior Liens	409
	13.2 All-Inclusive Trust Deed (AITD)	410
	Definition	410
	Uses for All-Inclusive Trust Deeds	411

Comprehensive Application of AITD 413
Characteristics and Limitations 413
Types of AITDs 414
Benefits to Seller 414
Benefits to Buyer 416
Some Pitfalls of AITDs 417
Procedures in Setting Up an AITD 418
13.3 Installment Sales Contract 419
Lease with Option to Purchase 423
13.4 Lender Participations 425
13.5 Sale-Leaseback 426
Procedure 426
Potential Advantages to Seller 427
Potential Disadvantages to Seller 428
Possible Advantages to Buyer 428
Possible Disadvantages to Buyer 429
13.6 Open-End Trust Deed 430
13.7 Personal Loan 431
13.8 Stock Equity/Pledged Asset Loans 431
13.9 Blended-Rate Loans 432
Benefits of the Blended Rate 433
13.10 Creative Financing Disclosure Act 433
13.11 Imputed Interest 434
Chapter Summary 439
Important Terms and Concepts 440
Case & Point 444
Fraud Enforcement and Recovery Act (FERA) 444

14 Financing Small Investment Properties 448
Overview 449
14.1 The Single-Family House as Income Property 450
Key Characteristics 450
Kinds of Financing Available for Non-owner-Occupied Single-Family Dwellings 450
Interest Rate and Other Loan Terms for Rental Houses 450
Advantages of the Single-Family Home as an Investment Vehicle 451
Disadvantages of the Single-Family Home as an Investment Vehicle 452

14.2 The Two- to Four-Unit Residential
     Income Property **453**
   Key Characteristics 453
   *Kinds of Financing Available on
   Two- to Four-Unit Dwellings* 453
   *Interest Rates and Other Terms on
   Two- to Four-Unit Properties* 454
   *Advantages of Two- to Four-Unit
   Dwellings as Investment Vehicles* 454
   *Disadvantages of Two- to Four-Unit
   Dwellings as Investment Vehicles* 455
14.3 The Five-Plus Unit Residential Income Property ... 455
   Financing Options for Five-Plus Units 456
   Advantages of Investing in Five-Plus Units 457
   Disadvantages of Investing in Five-Plus Units .. 459
14.4 Break-Even Analysis 459
14.5 Financing Starts with the Listing 462
   Why Sell Your Apartment Building? 462
   Obtain Financing Information on the Building ... 463
   Plan for Probable Financing of Sale 463
   *How Market Financing Conditions
   Affect Property Prices* 464
   Economic Principles versus Tax Shelter 465
14.6 Introduction to Commercial and
     Industrial Properties 466
   Commercial Properties 466
   Industrial Properties 467
   Office Parks 467
   *Advantages of Investing in a Commercial or
   Industrial Property* 467
   *Disadvantages of Investing in a Commercial or
   Industrial Property* 468
   Looking Ahead 469
14.7 Debt Coverage Ratio 470
Chapter Summary 471
Important Terms and Concepts 472
Case & Point 476
   Some Things to Know About Investing 476

15 Basic Mathematics of Real Estate Finance — 478

Overview — 479

15.1 Review of the Basic Components of a Real Estate Loan — 479
Review of Promissory Notes — 480
Amortized Loan — 480
How to Compute Amortized Loan Payments — 481
30- Versus 40-Year Amortization — 481

15.2 The Real World of Financial Calculators and Computers — 483

15.3 Illustrated Use of Calculated Industries Qualifier Plus IIIx Real Estate Calculator — 484
Loan Payments — 485
Making Larger Loan Payments — 485
Interest and Principal Allocation — 486
Principal and Interest Allocation for 12 Months — 487
Balloon Payments — 488
More Complicated Calculations — 489
Biweekly Loan Payments — 492

15.4 Annual Percentage Rates — 493
Disclosure of Total Interest Paid — 493
Disclosure of Annual Percentage Rate — 494

Chapter Summary — 495
The Financing Partnership — 496
Loan Pre-Approval Letters — 498
Shopping Rates: A Few Comments — 500
Locking the Rate — 502
Understanding your Credit Report — 504
Credit Scoring: How It Works — 506
Don't Let Closing Costs Be a Surprise — 508
Title Insurance: Basic Information — 512
Various Ways to Hold Title — 513
Internet Lenders: Approach with Caution! — 515
Behavior Accompanying Being Your Best! — 516
Important Terms and Concepts — 518

Appendix A — 520

Answers to Multiple-Choice Questions — 528
Glossary — 533
Index — 552

ILLUSTRATIONS

Figure 1.1	The roller-coaster ride of the housing market.	7
Figure 1.2	Money Is....	10
Figure 1.3	Simplified circular flow of the economy, excluding the impact of foreign trade and savings entering the U.S. economy.	12
Figure 1.4	Discount rate versus prime rate.	17
Figure 1.5	Balancing the interest–inflation conflict.	25
Figure 1.6	The creation of a real estate debt and its payment, using a deed of trust.	29
Figure 2.1	Sources of money in the mortgage market.	42
Figure 2.2	How savings become real estate loans.	42
Figure 3.1	The role of the mortgage broker.	75
Figure 3.2	A loan shark.	78
Figure 3.3	Sample mortgage loan disclosure statement.	85
Figure 4.1	Sample adjustable rate loan rider.	112
Figure 5.1	Fair lending notice.	149
Figure 5.2	Mortgage insurance.	150
Figure 5.3	The difference between private mortgage insurance and credit life insurance.	151
Figure 7.1	The difference between secondary financing and secondary mortgage market.	198
Figure 7.2	Contribution of secondary markets to home loans.	208
Figure 8.1	Residential appraisal report.	231
Figure 8.2	Computing square footage.	242
Figure 8.3	(a) A typical PUD (b) A typical condominium.	250
Figure 8.4	FNMA/FHLMC condominium rider.	252
Figure 8.5	FNMA/FHLMC planned unit development rider.	253

Figure 9.1	Basic information about sample borrowers.	270
Figure 9.2	Summary of qualifying procedure for conventional lenders.	273
Figure 9.3	Summary of VA qualifying procedure.	275
Figure 10.1	FNMA/FHLMC residential loan application.	300
Figure 10.2	Promissory note (partial).	317
Figure 10.3	Deed of trust (partial).	318
Figure 10.4	Sample closing cost.	321
Figure 11.1	Partial deed of trust form.	336
Figure 11.2	Sample notice of default.	341
Figure 11.3	Sample notice of trustee's sale.	343
Figure 11.4	Sample trustee's deed for a foreclosure resale.	344
Figure 11.5	Deeds of trust versus mortgages.	345
Figure 12.1	Sample partial building loan agreement.	378
Figure 12.2	Example of a draw system for a construction loan.	379
Figure 12.3	Sample subordination agreement (partial).	382
Figure 12.4	Sample mechanic's lien.	386
Figure 12.5	Sample notice of completion.	387
Figure 12.6	Sample notice of non-responsibility.	389
Figure 12.7	Sample release of a mechanic's lien.	390
Figure 13.1	Protection devices for sellers.	404
Figure 13.2	Sample assignment of deed of trust.	407
Figure 13.3	Sample installment note.	408
Figure 13.4	Sample all-inclusive deed of trust.	412
Figure 13.5	Installment land sale contract.	421
Figure 13.6	Sample seller financing disclosure statement.	435
Figure 14.1	Argument Against Rent Control.	460
Figure 14.2	Monthly break-even analysis.	462

PREFACE

This tenth edition is prepared to not only refine the readers' understanding of the basic real estate lending practices, but examines the rapid and continuing changes that have occurred in the financial arena during the past several years. When appropriate, the authors have made an attempt to anticipate pending and future changes. The subprime mortgage days of easy money and flexible qualifying guidelines is presented as a backdrop to the continuing changes in rules and regulations designed to rein in the excesses of those heady days, when it seemed that anyone could get a loan.

For the real estate novice, this edition resolves much of the mystery surrounding real estate financing and its terms and basic principles. For the more experienced, the increasingly complicated aspects of real estate lending and the new legislative mandates are made easier to understand. A plus for all readers is the detail given to the new developments in real estate financing that impact not only the real estate practitioner but every real estate buyer and seller.

NEW TO THIS EDITION

This edition is one of the most current and practical textbooks on real estate financing principles and practices in California. An alphabet of acronyms describes the numerous, newly legislated rules and regulations that touch practically every aspect of real estate financing. We have addressed the new regulations and discuss the positive and negative aspects of each.

The Consumer Financial Protection Bureau (CFPB) was created in an effort to combat real estate finance abuses. For some, this legislation and all of its accompanying regulation seems excessive, while for others, it was all too late to avert a financial crisis. As with most new legislation, the CFPB and a host of accompanying regulations continue to be tweaked as the unintended consequences of their enforcement are exposed. As a seller, buyer, or real estate agent, regulations may impact your performance now and in the future.

New details of such forms as the Mortgage Loan Disclosure Statement and the newly required Loan Estimate and Closing Statement are examined as the emphasis on better disclosure remains critical. Changes to the Home Valuation Code of Conduct (HVCC), introduced in the last edition, are detailed as they impact the appraisal process.

The recent introduction of fixed rate mortgage options, the adaptation of the adjustable rate mortgages (ARMs) to the new rules, and the modifications of FHA, which restores it to viability, are all documented.

Additional changes in this tenth edition include:

- **Chapter 1:** A discussion of what happened to create the financial problems of the last decade and a look ahead to the rules and regulations that will likely guide future financing. An introduction to the Consumer Financial Protection Bureau (CFPB) and the Qualified Mortgage (QM) rules and its accompanying Ability to Pay (ATP) calculations.

- **Chapter 2:** A look at the growing role of government regulatory agencies and an expanded review of each agency's goals, rules, and oversight obligations. The expansion of the Home Mortgage Disclosure Act (HMDA) and its impact upon eligible borrowers.

- **Chapter 3:** An explanation of the Mortgage Loan Disclosure Act (MLDA) which identifies new time frames for disclosure information and, in turn, impacts the time required to initiate the appraisal process. An explanation and review of the new Fraud Enforcement and Recovery Act (FERA) regarding its intention and likelihood of controlling fraudulent loan practices. The subject of rebate pricing via the use of Yield Spread Premium and how it assists cash-strapped borrowers is fully discussed in the Case and Point.

- **Chapter 4:** The introduction of the hybrid loan and an enhanced review of the positive and negative aspects of adjustable rate mortgage financing. A necessary look at all the aspects of the reverse mortgage and the impact of the new financial assessment rules on the increasing number of seniors attempting to use this loan option. A thorough explanation of the advantages of biweekly mortgages and how to establish them. Finally, a Case & Point discussing the potential future of Adjustable Rate Financing.

- **Chapter 5:** The modified role of real estate practitioners to keep up with lender policy changes. The emerging new rules around conventional financing resulting in new buyer qualification guidelines, changes in private mortgage insurance (PMI) coverage, and the revised use of buy-down loans. The introduction of a 97% conventional loan option. A detailed explanation of the Stimulus Bill as well as its effect on lending practices into the future.

- **Chapter 6:** A look at the new FHA rules, including what might be expected in 2016 and beyond. A look at the expanding use of the Department of Agriculture USDA loan.
- **Chapter 7:** The current and future role of government-sponsored entities (GSEs) and the continuing role of Fannie Mae and Freddie Mac. Updated changes to Fannie Mae and Freddie Mac as they have adjusted to the new financial climate.
- **Chapter 8:** Full details of the Home Valuation Code of Conduct (HVCC) (its imposition has caused significant changes to the appraisal process). New suggestions to help real estate agents relate to appraisers in this changing environment.
- **Chapter 9:** An introduction of new risk-based qualification and pricing models and how borrowers are impacted by these more restrictive policies. The Case and Point discusses in detail the new required Loan Estimate and Closing Disclosure forms that replace the Good Faith Estimate, the Truth in Lending and HUD 1 forms.
- **Chapter 10:** Introduction of the new Mortgage Disclosure Improvement Act (MDIA). An explanation of how borrowers are impacted by the increased emphasis on disclosure and the resulting increase in documentation. A step by step loan process from loan application to closing the loan is detailed in the Case and Point.
- **Chapter 11:** Expanded information on short sales and foreclosures to reflect their increase during the last several years. An explanation of the government's efforts to restore the housing sector of the economic spectrum both in the past and looking into the future.
- **Chapter 12:** The impact of the state laws surrounding new construction are clarified. The 1031 Tax Deferred Exchange overview is completely new to this edition.
- **Chapter 13:** The installment sale and the lease with option to purchase sections are expanded with new information.
- **Chapter 14:** A new look at the investment potential of real estate following the financial crises. An expansion of the multiple unit section includes an understanding of cap rates as a way to measure a property's value. The Case & Point "Some Things to Know About Investing" looks at four aspects of an investment in determining its viability as an investment property.
- **Chapter 15:** After a brief introduction to the mathematic calculations required in real estate financing, the "tip sheet" section addresses areas of real estate generally not included in financial texts but important to licensees as they embark on a career.

Global Changes: Vocabulary and terms surrounding real estate financing continue to grow with the alphabet soup of the new regulatory agencies and their constantly changing regulations. While the financial language can at first seem complicated, as you progress through the chapters, you will find that the text makes them easier to understand. The glossary will add to your understanding and is a great asset when you need to check the meaning of a word or term.

Case & Point: Recognizing this as a unique period in real estate financing, every chapter includes this feature, which provides insight into past and present financial developments as well as introducing several new topics including the Consumer Financial Protection Bureau and 1031 Tax Deferred Exchanges in considerable detail.

With so much of our lives influenced by the Internet, readers will appreciate the numerous references to helpful websites spread throughout the text. Although some Internet-related resources appear in some chapters, the new Appendix discusses specific uses and groups potential sites based on the information being researched. Over time, some sites are likely to become outdated and irrelevant, and some may try to sell products or services to the public. However, to the extent that they prove useful, they are included throughout the text and in the Appendix. It should be noted that the inclusion of firms promoting their lending policies and products on the Web is not meant to construe endorsement of the firms or their offerings.

Each chapter in the book is self-contained, allowing instructors to adapt the book to various course formats. Instructors and students alike will appreciate the multiple-choice questions and the questions for discussion—both designed for testing, learning, and review of the material covered in each chapter.

SUPPLEMENTS

Instructors who adopt this textbook receive access to additional instructor resources, which can be found on the book page on www.oncoursepublishing.com. These resources include an instructor's manual, sample exams, and a PowerPoint presentation that corresponds with each chapter.

ACKNOWLEDGMENTS

Any book, in its final form, is the result of the time and talents of many individuals. While we cannot acknowledge all of the contributors, we are grateful for their review of information, their insights, and their suggestions, all of which have enhanced this edition. We hope that we have successfully included the information that they so generously provided.

We would like to express our appreciation to Richard Ghidella, Citrus College and Marc Gottlieb, College of San Mateo for reviewing this text and providing insightful comments and valuable suggestions.

Additionally, we would like to thank a former author of this volume, Robert Bond. The passing of Robert Bond closed a rich chapter in the world of real estate finance education. Robert was a fount of information that those preparing finance texts drew upon for years. His expertise in commercial real estate finance was unsurpassed. He was an expert in the HP-C12 calculator, viewed by many commercial real estate licensees as the epitome of the early calculators. In more recent years, Robert focused mostly on preparing the questions contained in texts that complimented the information contained in the texts. Robert's enthusiasm for real estate finance, his quick mind, and easy collaborative style will be very much missed.

ABOUT THE AUTHORS

John Fesler, licensed since 1973, sold real estate, managed a real estate office of some 35 licensees, and owned his own mortgage company, Consultants West Financial Service. He was an Anthony Schools Instructor for the RE license exam prep for six years. He was also a weekend instructor at Hancock Community College for community subjects, including understanding your credit, preparing for a loan, and understanding investment properties. Mr. Fesler was a California Association of REALTORS® (CAR) instructor authorized to teach the state required ethics course. He was also the committee chairman for his local Real Estate Association Long-Range Planning Committee and Grievance Committee and served on the Professional Standards Committee. He is currently chairperson of the Humboldt Association of Realtors Education Committee. He has trained real estate licensees in understanding the FHA, in using the real estate calculator, and in all aspects of real estate financing. Mr. Fesler is currently involved in the educational field as an instructor for real estate finance at College of the Redwoods, Eureka, CA, and is an active mortgage broker as well as the developer and author of the information found at the educational site www.humboldthomeloans.com.

Mary Ellen Brady was licensed as a California real estate salesperson in 1988. In 1992 she became a licensed California real estate broker. Ms. Brady opened her own real estate office in 1999, after working for seven years as a real estate office manager in conjunction with listing and selling residential properties.

In 1993, 1996, and 1997, Ms. Brady was named REALTOR® of the Year by the Downey Association of REALTOR®. She was President of the Women's Council of REALTORS® in 1997and President of the Downey Association of REALTORS® in 1998. Ms. Brady has chaired many committees within and outside of the REALTOR® association.

Ms. Brady received her AA Degrees from Cerritos College in Real Estate and General Studies. She graduated from Azusa Pacific University, with a Bachelor of Science Degree in Organizational Leadership. She also has a Master of Arts in Management from Azusa Pacific University.

Ms. Brady enjoys teaching Real Estate and Business Administration courses full-time at Cerritos College.

AUTHORS' NOTE

The field of real estate financing, by its very nature, is a continuing work in progress and creates a constant challenge to remain current and up-to-date. The information contained herein will hopefully start you on a successful and satisfying journey into this exciting world and encourage your continuing search for the most recent changes. May you increase your knowledge as you travel over each page of this text and in your real estate career.

INTRODUCTION TO REAL ESTATE FINANCE

OVERVIEW

This chapter provides a short overview of real estate finance. After completing this chapter, you will be able to:

- Describe current financing trends in the real estate market.
- Trace the flow of money and credit into the mortgage market.
- Discuss the role of the Federal Reserve System.
- List five characteristics of the California mortgage market.
- Explain and illustrate two basic types of promissory notes.
- Describe the differences among a deed of trust, a mortgage, and an installment sales contract.
- Be familiar with the Consumer Financial Protection Bureau (CFPB) and its effect on recent lending practices.

1.1 WELCOME TO THE REAL WORLD OF REAL ESTATE FINANCING

Great wealth has been created via investment in real estate. But real estate is expensive and few people ever accumulate sufficient savings to pay with cash alone. Most real estate transactions depend, therefore, on a buyer's ability to obtain financing. Without it, most people can't buy the real estate—hence the oft heard phrase, "If you can't finance it, you can't sell it."

Even people who have sufficient funds rarely pay cash for real estate but elect to use other people's money in order to maximize the investment potential of their purchase. Income tax deductions and investment yields (as noted in a later chapter) also encourage purchasing with borrowed funds, called leverage. Thus, whether by necessity or by choice, financing is essential for most real estate transactions.

A Bit of History

Historically, real estate financing had operated within a fairly established set of rules. The guidelines identified down payment, credit, income, and employment requirements. Qualifying ratios based upon a borrower's income compared to the monthly mortgage payments prevailed. Loan guideline flexibility was limited, and potential buyers had to demonstrate an ability to afford the mortgage payments.

Then in 2000 lending regulations were relaxed with an emphasis on assuring that everyone had an opportunity to experience the American dream of home ownership. Investors wanted higher returns on their money and pressured banks to lend money. Increasing home values, coupled with this prevailing attitude that more people should be able to purchase a home, resulted in a relaxation of qualifying requirements and buyers acquiring loans for which they would qualify but, as it turned out, could not afford.

During the next few years, more and more lenient loan options were introduced. So-called liar loans were widely used to allow otherwise unqualified borrowers to purchase homes. The long held tenet of determining a buyer's **ability to repay (ATR)** was largely abandoned. This, in turn, fueled an explosion of home appreciation, based mostly on speculation.

As home values grew, owners were encouraged to tap their growing equity and use the funds for consumer spending. Homeowners were besieged with offers to use their equity for everything from buying a vehicle to taking that dream vacation. Many accepted the fantasy that property values would continue to escalate and that easy borrowing guidelines would continue and prevail. Homeowners refinanced (some more than once), using their equity much like a never-ending line of credit.

The Ability to "Fog a Mirror" Was Sufficient to Get a Loan

It is too often true that a good idea becomes corrupted and abused. Thus was the case with the new loan options designed to help more people buy homes. As these loan options evolved, mortgage brokerage ads proclaim that anyone could obtain a loan.

While not completely true, many of the new loan instruments were seen as requiring borrowers only to prove they were alive by "fogging a mirror."

Interest-only, stated income, 100 percent loans were introduced. Perhaps the most egregious of the new loan options was the negative amortized adjustable rate mortgage, or option ARM. These loans allowed a borrower to qualify and make initial monthly mortgage payments at a low 1 to 2 percent interest rate. The monthly payments in such loans were insufficient to pay even the interest due on the mortgage, resulting in the unpaid amount being added to the loan balance in what are called negative amortized loans. This will be discussed in more detail in Chapter 4.

The Old Rules Return

In hindsight, it seemed inevitable that the uncontrolled escalation of home values accompanied by ever-diminishing guidelines for loan qualification would come to an end. But for many, it seemed their best option to obtain wealth was by buying a home and letting it appreciate exponentially over a short period of time.

As home values adjusted downward and the easy money loan options collapsed, borrowers found themselves with adjusted monthly payments beyond their capacity to pay. Many of the most creative loan instruments were suddenly characterized as toxic, and homeowners found they owed more than their homes were now worth, a situation known as being "underwater." A monetary crisis developed that became a worldwide phenomenon.

Investors became more cautious with a return to more historically sound home loan financing methods. As we examine the basic principles of real estate financing, we will explore its continuously changing landscape as well as the currently available real estate home loan programs. While the main emphasis will be on financing residential real estate, Chapter 14 will discuss the financing of residential income properties.

Who to Blame

The above is merely a brief overview of what preceded and eventually resulted in the financial crises of the early 2000s. The following is a more detailed account of what happened and the inevitable search for someone to blame. The explanation is important because unless we understand what happened, we can easily be seduced into duplicating the mistakes in the future. Admittedly, the following is the authors' hindsight interpretation of the causes of what became known as the Great Recession.

The concept of expanding home ownership capability to a greater number of Americans was, on the surface, a laudable goal. The idea that the poor and lower middle class could be economically elevated by an ability to own a home seemed sensible. This attempt at social engineering, unfortunately, did not work out as anticipated.

For varied reasons, most members of Congress initially agreed that assisting seniors and the less wealthy among us was good campaign rhetoric. Senators Chris Dodd and Barney Frank were instrumental in promoting a relaxation in home loan qualifying standards. Their pressure on Fannie Mae and Freddie Mac (reviewed more extensively in Chapter 5) to reduce underwriting standards in the interest of promoting home ownership resulted in the major lending institutions developing an ever-increasing array of easy qualifying loan options. Investors had money to lend, and borrowers who heretofore had been unable to qualify to purchase eagerly accepted the creative loan instruments. Most chose to ignore the riskiness of this new lending environment.

The sale of this increased volume of loans and the replenishment of capital to keep making loans became critical to the continuation of this real estate boom. The loan instruments themselves became more and more risky, and the process of rating these loans became corrupted as the rating agencies overlooked deficiencies in favor of accumulating huge profits. In retrospect, the banks and the rating agencies share a considerable responsibility for continuing the poor lending practices long after they recognized that the loans were high risk, poorly performing, and unsustainable.

Consumers are not blameless, and real estate speculation grew exponentially. Borrowers accepted loans for which they knew they were unqualified, and lenders were happy to provide them. As the real estate market exploded and annual appreciation rates were at record highs, the fear of never being able to purchase was fueled by some unscrupulous lenders. Borrowers wanted to believe that even if they were unable to make the increased loan payments of the future that, at worst, they could sell their homes for a huge profit. The anticipation of ever-increasing appreciation proved a fantasy when home values eventually declined, leaving many homeowners underwater (owing more than the property was worth).

The breakdown of integrity within the lending process accompanied by an increased greed factor among all participants (lenders, investors, bond raters, and consumers) resulted in the financial crises from which we have yet to fully recover in 2015.

Ironically, it was Senators Dodd and Frank who authored the 2010 legislation known as the **Consumer Financial Protection Bureau** (see Case & Point following Chapter 5) designed to rein in what were then perceived as abusive lending practices.

Roller-Coaster Ride

Real estate in the form of land and improvements comprises a substantial amount of the total net worth of the United States. From 2000 to 2006, skyrocketing appreciation, accompanied by historically low interest rates, encouraged homeowners to tap their equity and use those funds for consumer spending. This in turn helped fuel the economic growth of the United States from 2003 to 2006. In addition, the real estate industry is a major employer, providing billions of dollars in income for millions of American workers and investors. When mortgage funds are scarce, real estate activity and employment decline, and a general hardship is felt throughout the economy. Unfortunately, the housing cycle can be irregular and wild, with great booms followed by disastrous busts, as shown in Figure 1.1.

Several boom times in real estate occurred in the early 1960s, 1971–1973, 1975–1979, 1982–1989, and the late 1990s to mid-2000s.

However, between these periods were some bad years—1966, 1969, 1974, 1980–1981—and a severe housing crash from 1990 to 1996 in many parts of California. But, none as severe as the housing recession that began in 2007 and from which we have not fully recovered in 2015.

During 2006 and 2007, the robust real estate market began to unravel. The usual causes of a bust in the real estate market include

FIGURE 1.1 The roller-coaster ride of the housing market.

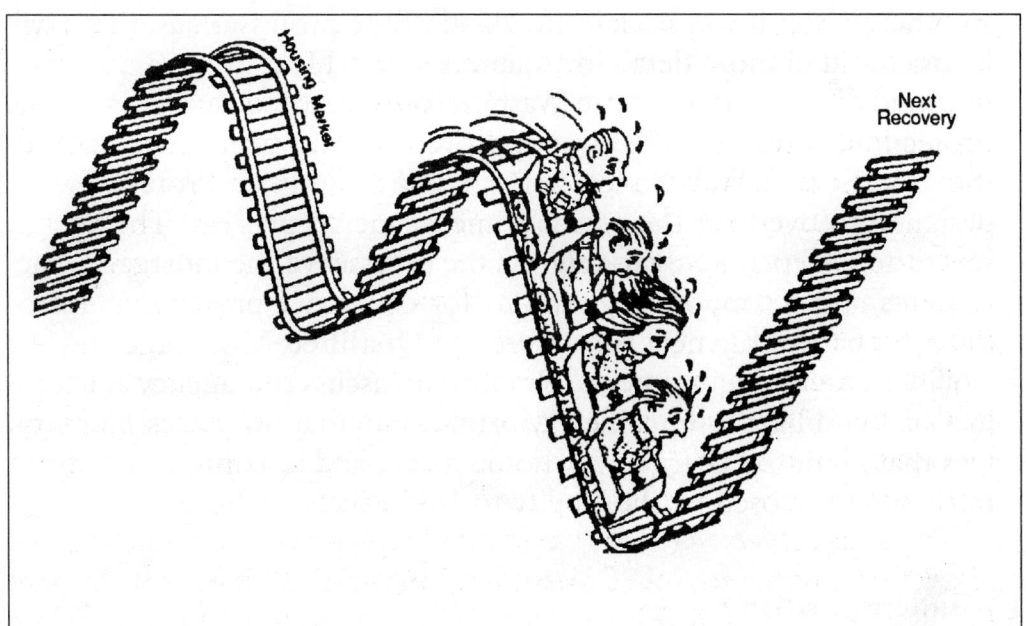

Source: © 2016 OnCourse Learning

high interest rates, government deficits, and better investment opportunities. But the turmoil in the mid-2000s was fueled by several years of greed throughout the finance system and a consistent relaxation of loan requirements that resulted in a complete breakdown of our banking system and a worldwide economic crisis.

Enter New Regulations

In an effort to restore confidence in the housing arena, new regulations were eventually adopted. As is often the case when correcting behavior, the new rules easily became over-burdening. In other words, the financial loan pendulum swung from the "anyone can get a loan" attitude to what seemed like a "we don't want to make a loan to anyone" stance. New regulations included enhanced disclosure requirements, insistence upon assuring that the borrower had the ability to repay, tightening credit standards, and a new licensing process (Nationwide Mortgage Licensing System or NMLS) designed to keep track of mortgage licensees who might have committed fraud or other mortgage lending violations.

While the immediate effect was to create an absence of liquidity or available home mortgage funding, the swindlers who had perpetrated much of the home loan abuses left the business. Mortgage lending had become more difficult and the "fog a mirror, get a loan" days were gone. The remnants of the mortgage arena were left to those practitioners who had never viewed it as a get-rich-quick opportunity. In other words, it was back in the hand of the professionals. (This will be discussed in more detail in Chapters 9 and 11.)

Amid much controversy in Washington, a new Consumer Financial Protection Bureau (CFPB) was approved following the enactment of the Dodd-Frank Wall Street Reform and Consumer Protection Act designed to overhaul the entire home financing process. The agency was to act independently to reign in the excesses of the mortgage practitioners and to impose regulations for consumer protection. Introduced as part of the new rules were the **Qualified Mortgage** and the Ability to Repay requirements. Briefly (we discuss this agency at length in Chapter 11), the Qualified Mortgage stipulation places limits on fees that could be charged for home loans, and maximum qualifying ratios were imposed by the Ability to Pay aspects of the law.

Disintermediation

While major changes to the financial markets fortunately do not occur too frequently, the consequences of even more minor disruptions can cause what is known as **disintermediation**, which is the sudden flow of funds out of thrift institutions (which grant real estate loans) into the general money market (where real estate loans are not common). By 2008, the excesses of the preceding years affected all aspects of the banking world and the lack of liquidity (the lack of funds for real estate loans) reached distressing proportions.

Such drying up of real estate funds wreaks havoc in the housing market. In short, real estate activity is directly tied to the availability and cost of mortgage funds and to the general state of the economy. As these two items shift up and down, so goes the real estate market.

Therefore, an agent's or an investor's success in real estate partially depends on a thorough understanding of trends in the mortgage market. The remainder of this book is devoted to an explanation of real estate finance, including a reduced range of creative and alternative financing techniques used in buying and selling real estate.

1.2 SHORT OVERVIEW OF THE MORTGAGE MARKET

Real estate financing usually requires the buyer to find a new loan at a lending institution, or occasionally the seller is asked to carry paper, or a combination of both. In all cases the interest rate and terms of real estate loans are dictated by the operations of the money and mortgage market. This section is a short primer on the operations of the mortgage market, stressing the functions of money and the role of the **Federal Reserve System**.

1.3 THE MEANING OF MONEY

Money has been defined in a variety of ways: a medium of exchange, a standard of value, a storehouse of value. In general, money is anything that people will accept in exchange for goods and services. Its value lies primarily in the confidence that other people will accept the money in exchange for their goods and services. Contrary to popular belief, money does not have to be a precious metal. Anything that is universally accepted by society can be used as money. Figure 1.2 outlines the many forms of money.

How Is Money Created?

The money supply is usually thought to consist of coins and paper currency issued by the government. But money is comprised of more than the cash that people have in their wallets and purses. Indeed, the bulk of what is called the money supply is in the form of checking

FIGURE 1.2 Money Is....

Money is commonly considered to be:

1. Coins.
2. Paper currency.
3. Checking accounts, technically called demand deposits.
4. Negotiable orders of withdrawal accounts, or NOW for short.
5. Money market accounts issued by financial institutions.

Near money consists of assets that can be quickly converted to cash, such as:

1. Savings accounts, technically called time deposits.
2. U.S. government bonds.
3. Cash value of life insurance.
4. Preferred and common stocks on organized exchanges.
5. Money market mutual funds.

The following items operate like money but are forms of **credit**:

1. Personal credit cards ("electronic IOUs"). Not debit cards, which are merely a way to access funds in a checking account.
2. Bank-allowed overdrafts (ODs).
3. Credit reserves.
4. Home equity lines of credit, personal loans from 401k or retirement accounts.

Money and credit are frequently used interchangeably—but they are not the same. *Money* means currency and checking accounts, while *credit* consists of loan funds or savings that a saver or lender makes available to a borrower. Both money and credit can be used to purchase real property; that is why both terms are frequently used in the real estate business.

Source: © 2016 OnCourse Learning

accounts—that is, money that individuals and businesses have deposited into checking accounts, plus the money "created" by the banking system under what is called **fractional reserve banking**. This will be explained and illustrated later in this chapter.

How Is Money Accumulated?

Money accumulates in many ways. The principal method is through savings—that is, spending less than one earns. Money is earned in one of four ways:

1. Wages, fees, and commissions in exchange for labor and services.
2. Interest and dividends in exchange for the use of capital.

3. Profits in exchange for management and entrepreneurship.
4. Rents in exchange for real and personal property usage.

Savings are accumulated funds not needed at the time that they are earned. Savings represent surplus money put aside for future use. There are many ways to save money, and where those savings will ultimately accumulate depends upon the needs, degrees of risk, and personal preferences of individuals. Although it is not necessary to explain the various methods of saving, it is important to recognize that the *ultimate source of funds for borrowing is savings*. In other words, one person's savings becomes another person's source for borrowing. If people spent all of their income, there would not be any funds for borrowing! The greater the rate of savings inflows, the greater the reservoir for borrowing.

At the beginning of 2009, the American savings rate had reduced to near zero and remains so low that there is little incentive to use bank savings or CD accounts. The loans made during the preceding several years through a lack of adequate qualifying standards were beginning to default. Homeowners had used their home equity as piggy banks or large checking accounts and found themselves largely over encumbered. The scene was set for what was to become known as a financial meltdown.

The global economy expanded during this time, and other countries sustained our economy by lending our nation money. That a borrower could be from one country and the saver or lender from another was not uncommon before the meltdown, but the public was mostly unaware of this phenomenon during this extraordinary time of borrowing. As the financial crises grew, so did concern over the amount of debt owed other countries as they continued to finance our borrowing appetite. In subsequent chapters this situation and its effect on our financial industry will be discussed in more detail.

1.4 THE FLOW OF MONEY AND CREDIT INTO THE MORTGAGE MARKET

If the source of all loans, including mortgage loans, is ultimately savings, how do savings via money and credit flow into the mortgage market? Stated differently, how does capital for real estate financing accumulate? This occurs through a process called the *circular flow of the economy*. Do not be troubled by this section, which appears to be heavy stuff! Stated here are some basic economic facts, but the information can still be daunting. Read the following as a brief economic review regarding the flow of money, which will lead into the next section dealing with the Federal Reserve. This section will get into the nitty-gritty of how money is created to finance real estate transactions.

As noted in Figure 1.3, the production of goods and services requires that money be paid for the use of labor, raw materials, entrepreneurship, and capital. This money is called personal income, and all or some of it may be taxed, spent on goods and services, or saved. That which is saved is usually deposited in financial intermediaries, which in turn pump funds back into production.

Figure 1.3 is a simplified model of how U.S. savings accumulate to become the reservoir for future loans. Carefully trace this circular flow until you understand that individuals own land, labor, capital, and entrepreneurship (the supply components), and that businesses need these supply components to produce. Thus, businesses buy land, labor, and capital from individuals, thereby giving individuals income in the form of wages, rents, interest, and profits. This personal income is then taxed, spent, or saved. That which is saved becomes capital for borrowing.

Intermediation of Savings

According to the circular flow of the economy, income that is not taxed away or consumed in the marketplace represents savings.

FIGURE 1.3 Simplified circular flow of the economy, excluding the impact of foreign trade and savings entering the U.S. economy.

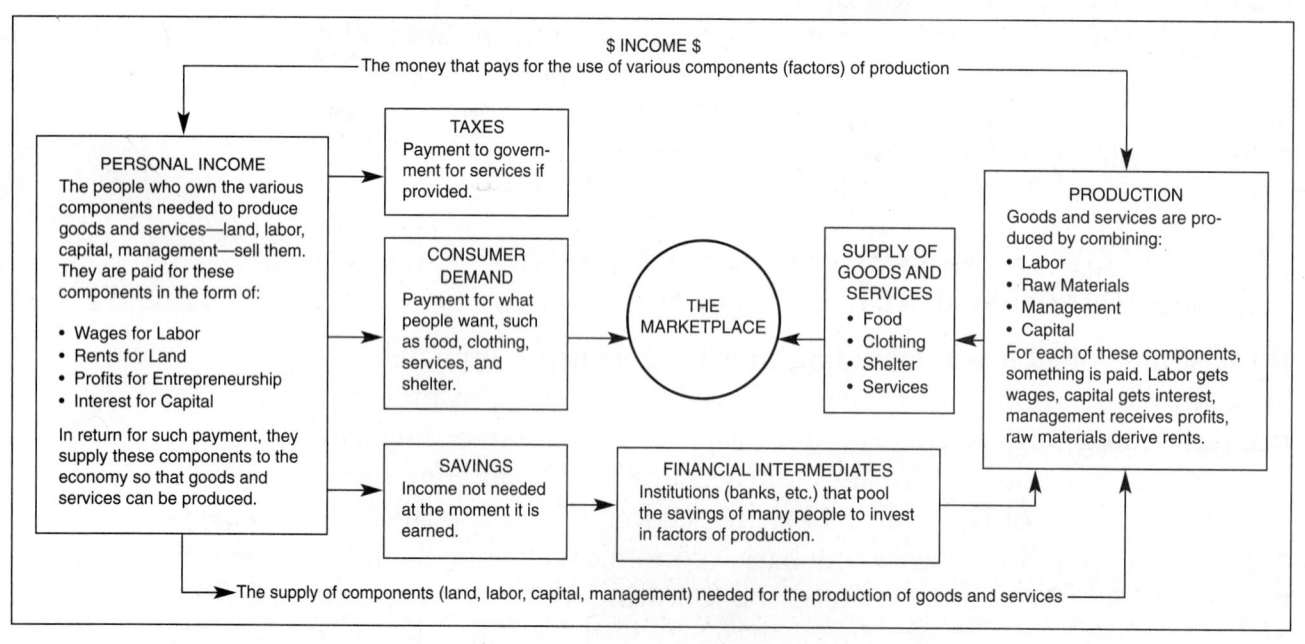

Source: © 2016 OnCourse Learning

Where these savings go depends largely on the kinds of returns desired by the saver. Many dollars flow into savings or commercial bank accounts, certificates of deposit (CDs), credit unions, life insurance premiums, and so on.

Savings or commercial banks, credit unions, life insurance companies, and other financial institutions are referred to as "intermediaries," since they are wedged between the saver and the ultimate investment outlet into which the money will be placed. Pooling the savings of many people is called **intermediation**, or acting as a go-between for saver-depositors and borrowers on home loans.

Many of the dollars saved through intermediaries are loaned to real estate borrowers, builders, developers, and investors. This in turn stimulates the real estate market and generates income and profits for sellers, real estate agents, loan brokers, and lending institutions. At the same time, this process makes it possible for people to buy homes and investors to acquire income property.

Disintermediation of Savings

Where savers place their funds depends on convenience and on how much depositories or investment outlets are willing to pay in interest. It can be said that a bidding process takes place, with savings going to the highest bidder, commensurate with safety and other criteria laid out by the saver. Money may be deposited with virtually absolute safety, up to designated dollar amounts, in an insured savings account in a bank or other thrift institution. However, when opportunities for greater returns present themselves, people withdraw part or all of their deposits and seek higher returns elsewhere. Since banks and thrift institutions frequently place their funds into real estate loans, the withdrawal of deposits is referred to as disintermediation—that is, deposits are removed from the institutions that act as intermediaries. When such withdrawals occur on a massive scale, the impact on the real estate market can be drastic. If people suddenly withdraw their savings and buy government notes and money market funds, the supply of mortgage money declines and the real estate market can enter into a slump.

Reintermediation of Savings

When the flow of savings again returns to the thrift institutions that act as intermediaries for the placement of mortgage loans, the process is referred to as **reintermediation**. If yields on government bonds plunge or the stock market crashes, money may reenter banks and thrift institutions in search of safety. As money returns to thrift institutions, the funds available for real estate loans increase, interest rates soften, more buyers can qualify for loans, and the housing market begins to pick up.

Thus the processes of intermediation, disintermediation, and reintermediation all have a dramatic impact on the real estate market. To understand this process fully, the role of the Federal Reserve System and the U.S. Treasury must be examined.

1.5 FEDERAL CONTROL OF THE MONEY SUPPLY

Although some economists disagree, most believe that manipulating the supply and cost of money and credit helps to achieve economic balance. To this end, the Federal Reserve System and the U.S. Treasury are each involved in efforts to balance the national economy. Though not always successful, these agencies have a profound effect on the financing of real estate. In this section the Federal Reserve System and the U.S. Treasury are discussed in detail.

The Federal Reserve System (Monetary Policy)

The Federal Reserve System (often called the Fed) is sometimes viewed as the "fourth branch" of the U.S. government. It is charged with maintaining sound credit conditions to help counteract inflation and deflation, to encourage high employment, and to safeguard the purchasing power of the dollar.

The Federal Reserve System contains 12 districts located throughout the United States. Each district is served by a regional Federal Reserve Bank that is coordinated and directed by a seven-member board of governors appointed by the president. The Fed has control over all banks and thrift institutions.

The Fed performs numerous functions, including the issuance of currency. However, this section is concerned only with its ability to influence the money supply. After all, money is the key to real estate transactions without which real estate activities would come to a grinding halt. This ability to control the supply and cost of money and credit is referred to as **monetary policy**. The principal ways in which the Fed exerts its influence on the money supply are through **reserve requirements**, **open-market operations**, and **discount rates**.

A Comment on the Fed

The Fed, under the guidance of Ben Bernanke during the troublesome years beginning in 2007 and since mid-2014 under the direction of Janet Yellen, is largely credited with keeping the housing recession from becoming much worse via the manipulation of home mortgage interest rates. By retaining historically low interest rates for years with which to stimulate home buying, the housing industry was slowly able to recover.

Reserve Requirements

All banks and thrift institutions must set aside reserve funds in order to protect depositors. Even more important than the security, the Fed is able to manipulate the amount of money in circulation by adjusting the reserve rate up or down. For example, if the reserve requirement is 20 percent, banks would need $200 in reserves for every $1,000 of deposits. (In reality, reserve requirements vary with the size of the institution and form of account—the 20 percent used here is illustrative only.) Any money beyond the required reserves may be lent out at a ratio, in this case, of 5 to 1. In other words, the banks may then create $5 of credit for every excess reserve dollar.

To see how banks actually create money, let us return to our example of a $1,000 deposit. Assume that bank policy requires that 20 percent of each deposit in checking accounts must be kept as a reserve against withdrawals. The remaining 80 percent can be used to create a loan.

Now let us assume that $1,000 is deposited into Bank A. Bank A will put $200 in reserve and loan out $800 to Mr. X. Mr. X will take the $800 and spend it. The receiver of this money will probably deposit the funds into Bank B. Bank B now has an $800 deposit, of which $160—20 percent—is kept in reserve, and $640 is lent to Ms. Y. She spends the $640 and the receiver deposits the money into Bank C. Bank C now has a $640 deposit, of which $128 is kept in reserve and $512 is lent to others. In theory, this process continues until all funds are exhausted. Table 1.1 illustrates this process.

TABLE 1.1 How banks create money.

Banks	Deposits	Reserves (@20%)	Loans ("Debt Fiat")
Bank A	$1,000.00	$200.00	$800.00
Bank B	800.00	160.00	640.00
Bank C	640.00	128.00	512.00
Bank D	512.00	102.40	409.60
Bank E	409.60	81.92	327.68
Plus all others	1,638.40	327.68	1,310.72
Totals	$5,000.00	$1,000.00	$4,000.00

Source: © 2016 OnCourse Learning

A single $1,000 deposit under a 20 percent reserve requirement can expand to become a $5,000 deposit, $4,000 of which is loaned out.

In essence, the banking system has created additional purchasing power through demand deposits. This has the same effect on spending as increasing the amount of coin and paper money.

In the real world, does this creation of bank money always occur at a constant, smooth rate? Not usually. Some banks differ in their reserve policy and each bank varies in the amount of loans available from each deposit. In addition, leakage occurs when people fail to deposit money in banks. Referring to Table 1.1, what would happen if the borrower of the $640 from Bank B buys merchandise and the store owners put the $640 under their mattress instead of depositing the money in Bank C?

Change in the Reserve Requirements

All banks that are members of the Federal Reserve System are required to keep a certain percentage of each deposit as reserves. These reserves are kept at the regional Federal Reserve Bank. If the Fed feels that easy money and credit are feeding inflation, it can raise the reserve requirements, which will force banks to restrict their lending, as money must be diverted from loans to cover the shortage in reserves. This action is designed to decrease the amount of money in circulation, drive up interest rates, and eventually lessen inflation by slowing down spending.

What will happen if the Fed decreases the reserve requirements? Will this increase or decrease the money supply? Will this raise or lower interest rates? Trace the steps that were outlined above to check your understanding.

Open-Market Operations

As part of its money-management tools, the Fed is allowed to buy and sell government securities, called *open-market* operations. Banks must buy them, but the public, consisting of private citizens and *financial institutions*, also may buy and sell government securities as a form of investment. When the Fed buys government securities from the public, the seller of these securities (the public) receives the Fed's check, which the seller then deposits in a local bank. The local bank forwards the check to the Fed for payment. When the Fed receives its own check, it increases the amount being held in reserve of the local bank by the amount of that check. The local bank now has more reserves than are required and therefore can grant more loans. *Thus, when the Fed buys government securities from the public, it increases the money supply by increasing bank reserves, which in turn will support more loans.*

What happens to the money supply when the Fed sells government securities to the public? The money supply tightens up, which increases interest rates and discourages borrowing.

To review, trace what happens when the Fed sells government securities. When government securities are sold, the public purchases them by writing checks on their local bank. The Fed receives the buyer's check and subtracts it from the reserve account of the local bank. The local bank now has less in reserve and therefore must constrict its lending. *So when the Fed sells government securities, it decreases bank reserves, which in turn decreases the bank's ability to grant loans.*

Once again we notice that the ultimate effect is a change in the money supply by manipulating bank reserves. But the Fed still has another important tool—changes in the discount rate.

Discount Rates

Banks borrow from each other via the Federal Reserve Bank's lending facility known as the "discount window." Primary borrowing is usually for the purpose of avoiding having a bank's reserves dip below the required minimum. The rate charged for this overnight borrowing is called the *discount rate*. The term "banker's bank" is used to describe the relationship of the Federal Reserve Bank to a member bank. The discount rate is not to be confused with the so-called **prime rate** (rate given to a bank's most favored corporate borrowers) that is charged by commercial banks. The two are compared in Figure 1.4.

The higher the Fed's discount rate charged to the bank, the more likely a higher interest rate will be charged by the bank to the real estate borrower. A higher discount rate generally indicates a more restrictive monetary policy is being adopted. Over time, the discount rate tends

FIGURE 1.4 Discount rate versus prime rate.

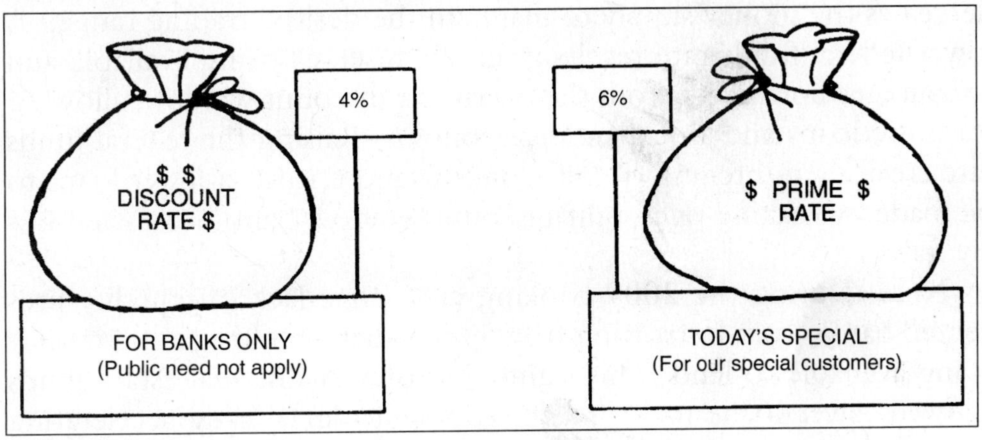

Source: © 2016 OnCourse Learning

to adjust fairly closely with other short-term interest rates. While a change in the discount rate can affect long-term home mortgages, it tends to most immediately affect short-term lending options. For this reason, consumers can be confused when a reduction in the discount rate does not immediately affect long-term mortgage rates.

Ultimately, an upward adjustment in the discount rate is likely to translate into higher home mortgage rates. Any increase in rates can have a dampening effect on potential buyers of real estate. Many prospective home buyers will simply postpone the purchase of a home, for example, in the hope that interest rates will soon come down.

The reverse is also true. The lower the discount rate, the lower the potential rate of interest charged by the bank to real estate borrowers. A greater demand for loans is expected to follow, and the number of real estate loans actually placed will increase.

Federal Funds Rate

Although not technically listed as a major tool of the Fed, the **federal funds rate** is one of the most closely watched indicators as to the current thinking of the Federal Reserve managers. What is the federal funds rate? When one bank is at a maximum loan-to-reserve requirement, it cannot grant additional loans to expand business until its reserves are increased. Or if the bank has granted too many loans relative to its existing reserves, it must, by law, either call in some loans or increase its reserves. One way to solve these problems is to borrow excess reserves from another bank that currently is not granting additional loans. The federal funds rate, then, is the rate of interest one bank charges another for the overnight use of excess reserves. This alternative source of temporary funds can be used instead of borrowing from the Federal Reserve noted above.

The Federal Reserve, in its efforts to fight inflation or recession, sets a federal funds target rate, which they influence via increases or decreases the money supply to maintain the desired trading range. A lower federal funds rate results in excess reserves being available and encourages borrowing from the overnight discount window, allowing for more loans and an expanding economy. Raising the federal funds rate creates a tightening of the economy and results in fewer loans to be made by making overnight discount window bank borrowing less favorable.

Note: During the 2009 banking crises, the lack of liquidity prevented banks from borrowing from each other, resulting in no money being available to lend. This tightening of available real estate funds allowed fewer loans to be made, adding to an already accelerating housing crisis.

Summary of the Major Federal Reserve Tools*

Changes in the reserve requirements, open-market operations, and changes in the discount rate all help the Fed control the supply of bank money. Of these tools, the most commonly used is open-market operations. To increase the money supply, the Fed will decrease the reserve requirement, buy government securities, decrease the discount rate, or use some combination of all three.

To decrease the money supply, the Fed will increase the reserve requirement, sell government securities, increase the discount rate, or use some combination of all three. In addition, the Fed will keep a close eye on the federal funds rate and attempt to raise or lower this rate, depending on its economic goals.

Quantitative Easing

Housing rebound has traditionally led the nation out of past recessions, but as the housing market collapse begun in late 2007 remained stubbornly unresponsive to the typical market stimuli the Fed introduced in 2010 a new program called quantitative easing (QE). The plan was to introduce funds into the economy by having the government purchase mortgage-backed bonds, accompanied by the government's guarantee of repayment. The program's intent was to keep interest rates low and slow the decline in housing prices. In a short period of time, the Fed printed the money and bought over $1.26 trillion worth of mortgage-backed bonds.

In December of 2013, the Fed began to taper or gradually reduce its monthly bond purchases that had grown to as much as $85 billion a month, ending the program in September 2014. There is no consensus regarding whether QE worked as the housing market remained somewhat sluggish through 2014.

The U.S. Treasury (Fiscal Policy)

Whereas the Federal Reserve Board determines monetary policy, the U.S. Treasury, under the direction of Congress and the president, acts as the nation's fiscal agent, managing the federal government's enormous debt. The government's spending and taxing policy is referred to as **fiscal policy**, in contrast to the monetary policy of the Fed. How much the federal government spends, and how much it takes in through taxation, will decidedly affect real estate financing. For example, if

---

* *The Essentials of Real Estate Economics*, 5th ed., Dennis J. McKenzie and Richard Betts, OnCourse Learning, 2006.

the U.S. Treasury decides to issue long-term debt instruments called treasury certificates, consisting of notes and bonds, to help finance government spending, more money is therefore siphoned off from mortgage investments. The impact is similar to the Fed's increasing the reserve requirement. Fewer homes would be constructed and purchased because of the reduction in available capital. This is called the "crowding out" effect. The opposite, of course, is also true. If the government decides to curtail or reduce its spending, more money is made available for the capital markets, including the financing of real estate.

During the late 1990s and early 2000s, the crowding out effect had a minimal impact on housing because of the massive amount of U.S. government notes, bonds, mortgages, and other securities purchased by foreign countries and their citizens.

The Treasury is more than just the supplier of funds for federal spending. It has long been involved in the initial funding of new programs designed to bolster the economy. It helped establish the Federal National Mortgage Association (Fannie Mae), the Government National Mortgage Association (Ginnie Mae), the Federal Land Bank system, and other agencies that have played such important roles in real estate financing activities.

The Government Dilemma

In troubled economic times, government must seek a balance between intervention and waiting for natural market improvement. Often it is difficult to assess the impact of the decisions made until well after the economic crisis has abated.

As the economy seemed to spin out of control in late 2008 and early 2009, all emphasis was on saving the institutions that were perceived to be necessary for restoring economic stability and calm to the markets: the banks. Perceived as too big to be allowed to fail, the government shored up the major banks in what became known as the Bank Bailout.

Consumers who had acquired subprime financing in an effort to enjoy the American dream of home ownership found themselves initially forgotten (see the Case in Point at the end of this chapter). As foreclosures mounted, it became clear that homeowners required help if they were to remain in their homes.

The Treasury led the way with its promotion of the Recovery Act followed by the adoption of the Making Home Affordable program. Recognizing that the saving and creation of jobs was critical to consumers being able to continue mortgage payments, the American

Recovery & Reinvestment Act of 2009, later known as the Stimulus Act, was signed into law. Controversy over its effectiveness is best left to historians.

During this same period, the Treasury launched the Making Home Affordable program designed to help homeowners avoid foreclosure by promoting loan refinances and modifications. The banks were charged with administering the new programs. Amid conflicting opinions of how much assistance should be provided and to which segment of borrowers, the programs proved less than effective initially. The original rules were difficult to understand, especially when it seemed that each lender had their own interpretation of them. The program was tweaked and revised several times, and while many homeowners were eventually able to profit from the programs, many others were denied participation. The two most recognizable programs, the Home Affordable Modification Program (HAMP) and Home Affordable Refinance Program (HARP) have been extended to the current deadline of December 31, 2016.

Controversy also accompanied the stimulus portion of the government's attempts to promote economic growth. The political tug-of-war over too much or too little financial assistance to the economy was in full swing. In anticipation of providing jobs and curbing the increasing unemployment numbers, sizeable amounts of money were made available for country wide projects. The rapid infusion of funds, while leading to renewed employment, was also found to have promoted some fraud and poorly conducted projects. Advocates insisted that insufficient funds had been allotted to the stimulus package while critics complained about what they thought was wasted money.

Originally designed to assist a floundering real estate market, all of these programs have received mixed reviews regarding their success, and it is too soon to judge their effectiveness.

Much more could be said about taxing policy, deficit spending, government stimulation and intervention, and other interrelated topics, but these are better left to a course in economics. Suffice it to say that when government spending exceeds revenue from taxation, deficit spending occurs, which leads the U.S. government to borrow more, driving up interest rates, which in turn tends to fan the flames of inflation. Inflation occurs when prices for goods and services increase, usually from too much money chasing too few goods. The net result of inflation can be a mixed blessing to real estate owners and licensees. Real estate values usually keep up with—and very often exceed—the rate of inflation. However, inflation drives up the cost of housing and interest rates, which can prevent some people from acquiring homes.

1.6 COST CHARACTERISTICS OF THE MORTGAGE MARKET

From a lender's point of view, cost, interest rates, and profits are the economic factors that drive the mortgage market. This section describes the underlying cost issues that influence the California loan market.

Cost of Mortgage Money

Many economic variables affect the price of money available for California real estate loans. International factors, such as an unfavorable trade balance, can have an impact on local lending. National factors, such as actions taken by the Federal Reserve Board and the U.S. Treasury, inflation, and business cycles, are even more important. Local factors that affect the cost of mortgage money include the level of employment, population trends, and the level of development in the community. Discussions of these larger issues are better left to economists. Closer to home, the institutional factors that affect the local cost of mortgage money include the following:

1. *Deposit cost.* This is the raw cost a lender must pay to attract depositors. The higher the interest rate paid on savings accounts, the higher the rate of interest the institution must charge for lending out mortgage money.

2. *Borrowing costs.* Many lenders need to tap the bond and other markets to obtain working capital. The costs of underwriting and floating a stock or bond offering will be passed on to the real estate borrower.

3. *Sales cost.* Promotional costs to attract borrowers, including advertising, loan solicitors, and so on, will be passed on in the form of higher interest rates.

4. *Administration.* Needless to say, there are overhead and administrative expenses in any business. Rent, utilities, management, payroll, maintenance, and other operating costs must be recouped and will affect the cost of borrowing.

5. *Reserves.* As pointed out earlier, reserves are required to be set aside by commercial banks and other institutional lenders. This presents an opportunity cost, the price of money that must sit idle and unproductive.

6. *Liquidity.* With the many past problems that have plagued institutional lenders, capital requirements and the need to liquidate assets are more critical than ever. This has to be factored into the cost of money for institutional lenders. The eventual lack of

liquidity was largely viewed as the main culprit in the demise of subprime lenders.
7. *Profit.* Again, as with any enterprise, lenders are in the business of making a profit for their stockholders and for themselves.

The cost of a loan to a borrower is essentially the sum of these seven factors. An old rule of thumb that had long been followed by real estate lending institutions was that it took a spread of approximately 2 to 4 percent over the deposit interest rate paid to savers to break even before profit.

In the highly competitive California mortgage market, this spread had sometimes been squeezed down to only 2 percent or even less. Hence, if a bank was paying 4 percent interest to attract deposits, it had to receive 6 percent on its loans just to break even. Of course, there were some exceptions and variations in this rule, including the type of loan, term, points, and so on. However, it should be clear that, as in other types of businesses, the most efficient institution is likely to be the one that can make the most profit while lending at the lowest rate. Those that cannot compete because their costs exceed their income will fail. In short, it can be said that lending institutions, like retailers, try to buy money at wholesale (interest rate paid to depositors) and mark it up and sell it at retail (interest rate charged borrowers). During the housing crisis extension into 2009, the Fed reduced the cost of funds to lenders to nearly zero in an attempt to encourage home lending. At the same time, banks paid minimal interest rates on savings and CD accounts. While these actions did result in home mortgage interest rates declining, lenders were able to achieve a 4 to 5 percent margin over their cost of the funds, resulting in substantial profits for financial institutions during this period of adjustment. There were ultimate attempts to hold some of these institutions accountable via the levy of substantial institutional fines. Critics argue that they were insufficient to thwart future improprieties because institutional fines were able to be used as tax deductions reducing the ultimate impact of the punishment and coupled with the lack of individual implication provide little deterrent to similar behavior in the future. History will be the ultimate judge.

What Causes Mortgage Interest Rates to Change?

Underlying all interest rate changes for real estate loans are the market forces of supply and demand. After all, credit is a product that is bought and sold. Borrowers compete in the credit markets, just as buyers do for other goods and services. Specific forces influencing changes in mortgage interest rates include:

1. *Excessive government spending.* Government deficit spending tends to cause higher inflation and/or interest rates as the government drains away funds from the private sector or inks up the printing presses for more money.

2. *Large government borrowing amounts.* As the federal government increases its spending faster than its collection of tax revenues, it will, out of necessity (barring congressional approval of a raise in its **debt ceiling**), need to compete in the capital markets for money. Such competition invariably raises interest rates (this is the so-called crowding out effect).

    Note: Debt ceiling explained: Congress authorizes expenditures while also determining the rules governing the revenue to be collected via taxes and other sources. Congress typically determines the amount of debt beyond which the government is not expected to exceed. Often, when authorizing expenditures the revenue side is not considered. Suddenly, when the expenditures exceed income Congress is asked to increase the debt ceiling and thereby authorize the payment of bills already approved of in previous decisions. Congressional harangues in recent years regarding a reluctance to raise the debt ceiling can affect interest rates if the world's economies anticipate that the United States might potentially default on debts they have already approved.

3. *Inflation.* As a companion to excessive government spending and borrowing, inflation is an inevitable consequence that tends to cause increases in interest rates even with increases in the money supply. Monetarists hold that a rise in the supply of money may help lower interest rates, but only for a brief period. As the money supply swells, so do expectations of rapid inflation. Thus, over the long run, lenders increase interest rates to protect or maintain their real profit margins against the expected increase in inflation.

4. *Supply.* As income increases, the money stock also increases, fueling economic expansion. If demand for loans does not keep pace, interest rates trend downward.

5. *Demand.* A strong demand for credit pushes interest rates upward. Even as the money supply continues to grow, the economy becomes overheated and competing borrowers (buyers of credit) bid up prices. As prices begin to climb, lenders naturally want higher interest rates to hedge against inflation.

6. *Federal Reserve actions.* (Review the discussion of the Federal Reserve in the previous section.) Figure 1.5 illustrates how the Fed attempts to balance the problem of high interest rates against excessive inflation rates.

"Tight" versus "Easy" Money

Tight money, a frequent expression among real estate practitioners, refers to restrictive money policies of the Federal Reserve System as it attempts to combat inflation by reducing the money supply. Any action to reduce the money supply will ordinarily cause interest rates to rise, unless of course the demand for funds is correspondingly reduced. On the other hand, when demand remains the same or actually increases, competition for the restricted supply of money climbs. Money invariably is taken out of thrift institutions for greener pastures, those places where higher returns are paid for funds. This condition was referred to earlier as disintermediation.

Easy money, by contrast, is a relatively loose money policy of the Fed, which attempts to combat recession by increasing the supply of money in circulation. As money supplies increase, employment will normally increase, leading to increased income and, in theory, savings. As savings build up in the coffers of thrift institutions, interest rates move downward. With the return of funds to the thrift institutions— the major dispensers of mortgage funds— reintermediation is said to occur. Real estate activities usually pick up steam under easy money and low interest rate conditions.

The year 2009 may long be remembered as the year that these economic expectations somehow malfunctioned. In spite of massive infusions of funds to lending institutions, accompanied by historically low

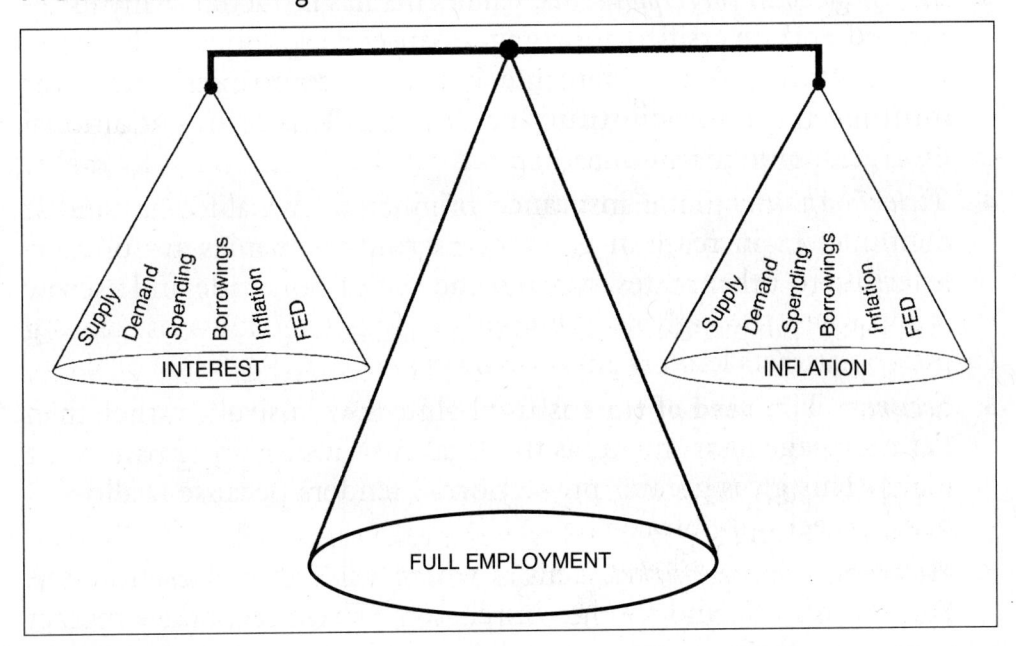

FIGURE 1.5 Balancing the interest–inflation conflict.

Source: © 2016 OnCourse Learning

home mortgage rates, home values plunged and unemployment soared. The loss of lender liquidity along with tightening home mortgage qualifying guidelines reduced home sales. The loss of home values coupled with the increasing monthly payments of the previously acquired, unwise subprime mortgages resulted in record home foreclosures. This near perfect storm of negative housing was initially felt most heavily in California, but other parts of the nation soon became victims of diminishing optimism that the housing market would recover and thrive.

The California Mortgage Market

Prior to 2008 it was widely believed that California real estate was largely immune to losing value. The recession proved that notion to be false, and we will review what happened and why as we continue this journey in real estate financing. However, California is unique in terms of the national mortgage market because of characteristics peculiar to this state.

1. *Large population and high demand.* California is the most populous state, continues to attract new residents, and has a high birth rate. State officials expect California's population to rise from nearly 37 million in 2009 to 50 million by 2040!
2. *Financial institutions.* California contains the largest number of banks and thrift institutions. Obviously, thrift institutions want to be where the greatest demand for real estate loans can be found. Californians have a greater choice of lenders than do residents of other states.
3. *Mortgage loan correspondents.* California has attracted many experienced and diversified mortgage loan correspondents (brokers) who represent out-of-state life insurance companies and other institutional and noninstitutional lenders. This brings additional mortgage money to California.
4. *Title companies.* Title insurance originated in California, and it continues to increase in volume. Escrow companies are uncharacteristic to other states, though the use of both title and escrow is spreading throughout the country. This easy, low-cost closing process attracts lenders and borrowers.
5. *Security.* The **deed of trust** is used almost exclusively, rather than the mortgage instrument, as the legal basis for securing real estate loans. This gives greater protection to lenders because it allows a quick foreclosure process.
6. *Active secondary market.* This is where existing real estate loans are sold to U.S. and foreign purchasers. These secondary market sales bring fresh capital to the California real estate market.

7. *Diversification.* California's economy is one of the most diversified worldwide and is growing with a mix of ethnic and social diversity that is expected to continue, creating new opportunities for housing and financing.

1.7 INSTRUMENTS OF REAL ESTATE FINANCE

The economic environment of the mortgage market establishes the trends for interest rates and financing terms, but the actual loan is created using a variety of financing instruments. This section introduces instruments of real estate finance, leaving specific details to later chapters.

Promissory Notes

When money is borrowed to purchase real estate, the borrower agrees to repay the loan by signing a *promissory note*, which outlines the terms of repayment and sets the due date. The promissory note is legal evidence that a debt is owed. The two most common types of promissory notes in general use are the **straight note** and the **installment note**.

The *straight note* is an *interest-only note*. Under a straight note, the borrower agrees to pay the interest periodically (usually monthly) and to pay the entire principal in a lump sum on the due date. For example, if you borrow $100,000 for five years at 8 percent interest rate, the monthly payments are $666.67 per month ($100,000 × 8% ÷ 12 months). The $666.67 payments cover just the monthly interest. Thus, five years hence, on the due date, you must pay back the entire $100,000 principal. In other words, your payments were only large enough to cover the monthly interest and did not reduce the $100,000 principal.

The second type of real estate *promissory note*, is the installment note. An installment note requires periodic payments that include both principal and interest. This reduction in principal is referred to as *amortization*. Suppose you borrowed $100,000 for 30 years at 8 percent interest, payable at $733.76 per month, including both principal and interest. At the end of 30 years you would find that the entire principal had been paid back. Each monthly payment of $733.76 not only included the monthly interest due but also reduced the $100,000 principal. An installment loan that includes both principal and interest in equal installment payments that self-liquidate the debt is called a fully **amortized loan**. Under such an amortized loan there is no **balloon payment** on the due date of the loan. The Civil Code defines a balloon payment as any payment on an amortized loan that is more than double the amount of a regular installment.

One variation of the installment note is to have monthly payments that are large enough to pay the monthly interest and reduce some of the principal, but the monthly principal portion is not sufficient to entirely liquidate the debt by the due date. Thus, on the due date the remaining unpaid principal must be paid in a balloon payment. For example, a $100,000, 30-year loan at 8 percent interest payable at $700 instead of $733.76 per month would require a balloon payment of $50,321.35 on the due date. Why? Because the $700 per month was enough to cover the monthly interest ($666.67), but not enough to cover the monthly interest plus all of the monthly principal, which would have taken $733.76 per month. Thus the unpaid balance over the 30-year life of the loan, $50,321.35, must be paid on the due date in the form of a balloon payment.

In the past, some borrowers signed negatively amortized promissory notes. Negatively amortized means that the loan payment does not cover the monthly interest. Each month this shortage is added to the principal owed, resulting in an increased loan balance, which in turn incurs additional interest. This is the magic of compound interest in reverse, as it accumulates greater debt. As mentioned previously, a $100,000 loan at 8 percent payable interest only would result in a $666.67 monthly payment ($100,000 × 8% ÷ 12 months). If a borrower only paid $600 per month, the difference between an interest-only payment of $666.67 and the $600 payment = $66.67. Each month, this $66.67 shortfall would be added to the $100,000 loan and begin to accrue interest. If this shortfall continued for 30 years, the borrower would still owe a balloon payment of $199,357.30 on top of paying $600 per month for 30 years! Total paid would be $600 × 360 payments (30 years × 12) = $216,000 + $199,357.30 balloon payment, for a grand total of $415,357.30 to pay off a $100,000 negative amortized loan during a 30-year period. In hindsight, it is unbelievable how such financing was ever perceived to be an acceptable loan option.

Variations on Fixed Interest Rate Notes

In recent years, lenders have introduced many variations of the standard promissory notes, with alphabet-soup-sounding names such as ARM, GPM, and so on. These are collectively called alternative mortgage instruments, or AMIs for short. Chapter 4 is devoted to these loans.

Deed of Trust (Trust Deed)

To give added assurance that the promissory note will be paid when due, real estate lenders require security for the obligation. The most logical security is real estate currently owned or about to be acquired by the borrower. To secure an interest in the borrower's property, most lenders in California use a deed of trust (or trust deed).

A deed of trust is a three-party instrument between a borrower, called the **trustor**; a third party, called the **trustee**; and a lender, called the **beneficiary**. Under a deed of trust, the trustor deeds bare legal title to the trustee, who keeps the title as security until the promissory note is repaid. Once the debt is repaid, the beneficiary (lender) orders the trustee to reconvey the title to the trustor (borrower) using a deed of reconveyance. If the trustor should default on the loan, the beneficiary can order the trustee to hold a trustee's sale and sell the property to obtain the cash needed to pay the loan. Figure 1.6 illustrates how title is passed between a trustor and trustee in a deed of trust.

Frequently in other states, a mortgage is used instead of a deed of trust to secure a real estate loan. But in California, mortgages are rare—most lenders insist on deeds of trust instead. Why? Because in most cases, deeds of trust favor the lender over the borrower. If the borrower should default under a deed of trust, the lender can order the trustee to sell the property without a court proceeding, and it can be accomplished in approximately four months. Once the sale takes place, the borrower loses all rights to redeem the property.

Foreclosure under a mortgage usually requires a court proceeding and can take up to one year. After this foreclosure takes place, the borrower could have a one-year right of redemption. Most California real

FIGURE 1.6 The creation of a real estate debt and its payment, using a deed of trust.

```
WHEN A REAL ESTATE DEBT IS CREATED

TRUSTOR          Deeds title              TRUSTEE
(Borrower)   ──using deed of trust──▶    (Neutral Party)


WHEN A REAL ESTATE DEBT IS PAID

TRUSTOR          Reconveys title back      TRUSTEE
(Borrower)   ◀──using a deed of reconveyance──  (Neutral Party)
```

Source: © 2016 OnCourse Learning

estate lenders therefore prefer to use deeds of trust rather than mortgages as security instruments because foreclosure is quicker, cheaper, and has no right of redemption after the sale.

Installment Sales Contracts

Another real estate financing instrument is an **installment sales contract** (agreement of sale). An installment sales contract is an agreement between the buyer and seller, where the buyer is given possession and use of the property and in exchange agrees to make regular payments to the seller. While the buyer has equitable title, legal title to the property remains with the seller until the terms of the contract are met, at which time the seller formally deeds the property to the buyer. In essence, under an installment sales contract, the seller (vendor) becomes the lender for the buyer (vendee). With the exception of Cal Vet Financing (covered in detail in Chapter 6), made using the Contract for Sale, lending institutions such as banks or thrift institutions are not needed in such a transaction.

The lack of a legal title poses some risks for the buyer. It is often several years between the time the buyer signs the installment sales contract and the time the seller delivers the deed. If the seller should die, become bankrupt, become incompetent, or encumber the title during this interim, the buyer could become involved in legal entanglements. In addition, if the seller under a contact of sale has an existing loan on the property, the use of this contract violates the lender's "due on sale" clause if one is present. During the height of the foreclosure crises from late 2008 through 2010, foreclosure-help scams surfaced using the installment sale as a device to falsely promise financially strapped homeowners that they would be able to repurchase their homes when their financial condition improved. In light of these mostly negative possibilities, except for the special area of large land developments, the advantages that an installment sales contract may have had in the past seem to fade away in favor of the use of a deed of trust.

Special Clauses

In addition to repayment terms, many real estate financing instruments contain special clauses or loan conditions that the borrower and lender agree to honor. The clauses are known by such names as acceleration clause, alienation clause, escalation clause, prepayment penalty clause, interest change clause, and so on. The clauses will be examined in detail as we progress through the textbook, and they are defined in the Glossary.

The Language of Real Estate Finance

The field of real estate finance has developed a language consisting of specific terms and concepts.. Learning the terms and concepts will assist the real estate licensee in communicating with inexperienced clients and friends who do not understand financial terms, as well as enabling conversation with real estate professionals.

1.8 THE FIVE-STEP FINANCING PROCESS

Borrowing money to purchase, exchange, refinance, construct, or make capital improvements to an existing home can be viewed as a **five-step financing process**:

1. *Application.* The loan process begins with the application filled in by the borrower, as detailed in Chapter 10. The form includes information on the applicant's financial condition, including the amount and consistency of income along with outstanding debts and expenses. The application also requests information concerning the property, including location, age, size of lot, and improvements. If the application is for a construction loan, details concerning the proposed improvements are required by lenders.

2. *Analysis/Processing.* After the completed application form is received, the lender reviews it to determine if the borrower and the property appear to meet the lender's standards. Lenders establish processing patterns in accordance with their own policies and procedures. Processing involves the collection of all required documentation from the borrower (e.g.; credit report, employment verification, available assets, etc.) and the issuing of appropriate disclosures. If the application was taken by an intermediary, such as mortgage broker, it is forwarded to the ultimate lender for approval and underwriting. If the applicant is acceptable, the lender presents the proposed financing terms to the borrower. The applicant may accept, reject, or attempt to negotiate with the lender to obtain more favorable terms. This topic is detailed in Chapters 8 and 9.

3. *Qualifying/Underwriting.* Both the borrower and the property must be qualified. After underwriter approval of the borrower, an appraisal is ordered via an Appraisal Management Company (AMC) assignment. Following the underwriter's review of any additional required conditions and signing off on the appraisal, loan documents are drawn, disclosure forms are prepared, and instructions for the escrow and title insurance companies are issued. Much more is said about this step in Chapters 7 through 10.

4. *Funding/Closing.* After final underwriter approval, the loan closing phase begins. This involves signing all loan papers and transferring the title. Practices vary within the state in the handling of the escrow. Closing is detailed in Chapter 10.
5. *Servicing.* This refers to loan collections and recordkeeping. It includes necessary follow-up to ensure that the property is maintained; that insurance, taxes, and other obligations are paid; and that delinquency is prevented in order to reduce the possibility of foreclosure. Some lenders do their own servicing, while others pay independent servicing companies fees for handling the paperwork. Chapters 10 and 11 deal with servicing and other post-closing issues.

Chapter Summary

Real estate finance is the key factor in most real estate transactions. When mortgage funds are available, real estate sales take place. If mortgage money is scarce, activity in the real estate market declines.

Money is created by the banking system using fractional reserve banking, and this money is added to the supply of money issued by the U.S. government.

Money is earned through wages, interest, profits, and rents. Some of these earnings ultimately find their way into savings in banks and thrift institutions, which account for a sizable amount of the credit extended for real estate purchases and construction. When savings are withdrawn from these banks and thrift institutions and used elsewhere for higher returns, disintermediation occurs, which can result in a decline in the real estate market.

The Federal Reserve System (the Fed) is able to increase the supply of money by decreasing reserve requirements of member banks, buying government securities in the open market, and decreasing its discount rate to borrowing banks, among other actions. The Fed is able to decrease the availability of mortgage funds by increasing reserve requirements, selling government securities, increasing the discount rates, and other means.

The U.S. Treasury, as the fiscal agent of the federal government, also greatly affects the availability of real estate funds via its spending and taxing policies. Generally speaking, when the government reduces its spending and borrowing, it is anticipated that more money will be available for real estate lending. And, conversely, when the government increases its spending and borrowing, less credit is expected to be available for real estate transactions.

The cost of mortgage money is affected by the price paid to attract deposits, lenders' borrowing costs, sales costs, administration, reserves, and profit goals. Interest rate fluctuations are largely influenced by government spending, government borrowing, inflation, and supply and demand.

Apprehension regarding new regulations including the Qualified Mortgage and the Ability to Repay rules proved unfounded. After a brief adjustment period, home loans continued unabated.

The California market is unique in terms of the national mortgage market because of characteristics peculiar to this state. Among these are its large population, high demand, large amount of big institutional lenders, existence of many diversified mortgage loan correspondents, title insurance and escrow companies, and a very active secondary market.

Just like many other professionals, real estate lenders use tools or instruments to complete a task. In California, the major instruments of real estate finance are the promissory note, the deed of trust, and, to a lesser extent, the installment sales contract.

Important Terms and Concepts

Ability to Repay (ATR)
Amortized loan
Balloon payment
Beneficiary
Consumer Financial Protection Bureau (CFPB)
Debt ceiling
Deed of trust (trust deed)
Discount rate
Disintermediation
Federal funds rate
Federal Reserve System
Fiscal policy
Five-step financing process

Fractional reserve banking
Installment note
Installment sales contract
Intermediation
Monetary policy
Open-market operations
Prime rate
Qualified Mortgage
Reintermediation
Reserve requirements
Straight note
Trustee
Trustor

Reviewing Your Understanding

Questions for Discussion

1. In addition to coins, what are the other two types of money? Do the terms *credit* and *money* mean the same thing?
2. "The source of all mortgage funds is ultimately savings." In your own words, explain this statement.
3. Explain how the Federal Reserve Board can increase or decrease the money supply using each of the following tools: reserve requirements, open-market activities, and discount rates.
4. How does an interest-only promissory note differ from an installment note?
5. Why are trust deeds used in California instead of mortgages?
6. How does an installment sales contract differ from a deed of trust as a security device for real estate financing?
7. Explain this statement: "Finance is the fuel that makes a real estate transaction run."

Multiple-Choice Questions

1. The real estate housing market can best be characterized as having
   a. a steady growth.
   ✓b. a cyclical up-and-down movement.
   c. no influence in the general economy.
   d. none of the above.

2. According to the circular flow of the economy, when people supply the land, labor, and capital to business, the people receive in return
   a. goods and services.
   b. savings.
   ✓c. income.
   d. taxes.

3. The chief requirement for acquiring most real estate is
   ✓a. sufficient financing.
   b. high initial deposit.
   c. low down payment.
   d. income tax deductions.

4. An example of disintermediation is the flow of funds from
   a. money markets to thrift institutions.
   b. bond markets to mortgage markets.
   ✓c. thrift institutions to money market funds.
   d. money markets to mortgage markets.

5. If the Federal Reserve Board wished to expand the money supply using open-market operations, it would
   a. cut federal taxes.
   b. increase government spending.
   c. sell government securities.
   ✓d. buy government securities.

6. Which of the following statements is true?
   a. The prime rate is the same as the discount rate.
   b. A decrease in reserve requirements will tend to decrease the money supply.
   c. The California mortgage market usually has an oversupply of loanable funds.
   ✓ d. The federal funds rate is the interest one bank charges another for the use of overnight funds.

7. Leverage is best defined as
   a. potential income tax write-offs.
   ✓ b. the use of other people's money.
   c. the exchange of an existing home for a higher priced home.
   d. the exchange of a higher priced home for a lower priced dwelling.

8. On a deed of trust, the borrower is called the
   ✓ a. trustor.
   b. trustee.
   c. beneficiary.
   d. mortgagee.

9. When a borrower pays off a real estate loan, the trustee issues a
   a. deed of trust.
   b. trustee's deed.
   c. deed of repayment.
   ✓ d. deed of reconveyance.

10. A $100,000 loan at 8 percent interest, amortized for 30 years, all due and payable in five years, secured by a deed of trust, will involve
    a. periodic payments.
    b. a balloon payment.
    c. a lien on the borrower's title.
    ✓ d. all of the above.

11. If savers withdraw their funds from savings banks to buy corporate bonds, this is an example of
    a. mediation.
    b. intermediation.
    ✓ c. disintermediation.
    d. reintermediation.

12. The fiscal agent of the federal government is the
    ✓ a. U.S. Treasury.
    b. Federal Reserve System.
    c. commercial banking system.
    d. Federal Housing Finance Board.

13. The 100 percent interest-only loans were designed to entice home buyers to qualify based principally on their
    a. projected income.
    ✓ b. stated income, even if untrue.
    c. net worth.
    d. negatively amortized adjustable rate mortgage.

14. Qualifying a borrower takes place at what step in the financing process?
    ✓ a. Analysis
    b. Application
    c. Servicing
    d. Closing

15. All of the following can cause mortgage interest rates to rise except
    a. rapid inflation.
    b. excessive government borrowing.
    c. a large increase in the money supply. ✓
    d. a large increase in the demand for loan funds.

16. What is sometimes called the "fourth branch" of government?
    a. U.S. Treasury
    b. Federal Reserve System ✓
    c. Resolution Trust Corporation
    d. U.S. Congress

17. So-called liar loans became commonplace from about 2000 to 2007, which were characterized by
    a. relaxed lending regulations.
    b. home buyers qualifying without sufficient resources.
    c. an explosion in appreciation of housing.
    d. all of the above. ✓

18. Loan collection and recordkeeping is referred to as loan
    a. processing.
    b. servicing. ✓
    c. analysis.
    d. closing.

19. The lender in a deed of trust is called the
    a. trustor.
    b. vendor.
    c. trustee.
    d. beneficiary. ✓

20. The party holding bare legal title under a trust deed is the
    a. beneficiary.
    b. trustor.
    c. title company.
    d. trustee. ✓

CASE & POINT

What Happened and What Is Ahead

As home values exploded in the early 2000s, homebuyers faced the fear of buy now or perhaps be priced out of the market. Subprime lending practices in which buyers encountered increasingly relaxed loan qualifying standards along with a healthy dose of greed fueled the sense that anyone could and should buy a home. It was, after all, the American dream.

Among a plethora of creative loan options, the two most egregious turned out to be the famous stated income or "liar" loan and the negatively amortized adjustable rate mortgage. While when coupled with 100 percent loan options these eventually proved toxic, buyers continued to purchase at ever-increasing values believing in the false notion that California real estate would never lose value.

These easy money years resulted in over five million foreclosures from 2008 through 2011. As home values declined, 100 percent financing trapped borrowers in their homes, unable to sell or refinance because of the lack of any equity. The short sale, wherein a borrower sold for less than the amount owed on the mortgage, became prevalent. The result was a spiraling reduction in whole neighborhood home values as homes were sold for bargain prices.

As so often occurs, an overcorrection was made to the over-easy qualifying practices—new requirements tightened, loan options reduced, and qualifying for a home loan became difficult. While the return to the saner finance practice of having to prove one's ability to afford a mortgage was necessary, in contrast to the easy money days, the standards seemed overly restrictive.

Incongruity suddenly entered the finance world. The bank bailout of billions of dollars was deemed necessary to save the economy, but no plans surfaced to save the homeowners who suddenly faced foreclosure and loss of the wealth that had heretofore accompanied home ownership. Amid the realization that economic rebound depended upon the ability of buyers to purchase homes and beleaguered homeowners to escape foreclosure and short sale, no one seemed to have a plan to re-energize the home sector. Nor did any plans emerge to rein in the banks' past behavior of speculating with consumers' funds, which had resulted in a "heads we win and tails you lose" situation for the banks.

In other words, the banks kept profits when successful and passed the losses to the consumers via the bailout.

The introduction of various versions of the Recovery Act—the plans designed to help struggling homeowners—were confusing and continually being redrafted. Left to the same banks that had created the crises to administer the new refinance plans, chaos mostly reigned. While some homeowners eventually did acquire assistance, (some only temporarily) many did not and lost their homes.

The creation of the Consumer Financial Protection Bureau (CFPB), required by the Dodd-Frank Wall Street Reform and Consumer Protection Act, continues to bring about change in the way mortgages are performed. The emphasis on the Ability to Repay and the Qualified Mortgage was expected to rein in the past excesses of mortgage lenders. (We will discuss the CFPB and its changes in greater length elsewhere in this book.)

In the past the housing segment of the economy usually was the first to rebound and lead us toward recovery. This transition and evolution of the mortgage market was slow to bring about significant strength to the housing segment. As 2014 wound down, there was at last a sense that housing might be on the cusp of recovery. In the meantime, there were some good things that had occurred:

- Home value reductions made home buying more affordable to buyers.
- Home values stabilized and began to slowly appreciate in most areas.
- The gain in equity allowed borrowers to refinance at lower rates.
- Interest rates, thanks to Federal Reserve intervention, remained historically low, encouraging buyers.
- Home purchases, rather than being done for investment, were now more motivated by the desire to own one's own home.

Looking into the crystal ball and anticipating the changes that might occur is both difficult and, some may say, foolish. The lending arena changes rapidly and without warning much of the time, but here is what might be anticipated for the future.

- While some areas have experienced accelerated values, most anticipate a more modest and sustainable appreciation factor going forward.

- As a whole, qualifying guidelines for loan options will become more flexible, accompanied by a reduction in eligible credit scores.
- Still, concerns will be resurrected regarding just how relaxed qualifying guidelines can become along with what kind of loan option flexibility can occur without risking the turmoil begun in 2006 that peaked in 2008.
- Although banks, in the anticipation of increasing the number of loan borrowers, had by late 2014 reintroduced some of the past questionable loan options, it is hoped that an expansion of loan options could occur without the return to the loan instruments that resulted in past defaults—100 percent financing, negative amortized loans, etc.
- In response to this concern, the introduction of ARM financing beginning toward the end of 2014 seemed to de-emphasize negative amortized loans in favor of fixed rate loans with options to convert to adjustable rate loans. An example is the much favored 5/5, which is a five-year fixed loan that can then be extended for another five years at the then fixed rate. Only after ten years would the loan convert to an ARM loan, thereby providing a sense of stability for at least ten years. Lenders dubbed these kinds of loans as a return to "sane subprime." The concern is always that as the housing element of the economy improves, there could be a return to the more creative type loans of the past.
- Past home buyers who were forced into foreclosure or short sale transactions will again become credit eligible for home loans, thereby promoting home purchases.
- As rents continue to climb, or should they simply peak without declining, home buying will become a better option.
- Low interest rates will continue to prevail, although modest increases are expected by early 2016. As homeowners gain equity via improving home values, refinance transactions will become popular.
- As a part of the increased oversight, the Nationwide Mortgage Licensing System (NMLS) requirements will be expanded to include bank personnel engaged in lending practices. While creating a more level playing field, the banks who had managed to escape some oversight regulations imposed on mortgage brokers will have to accommodate the new rules.

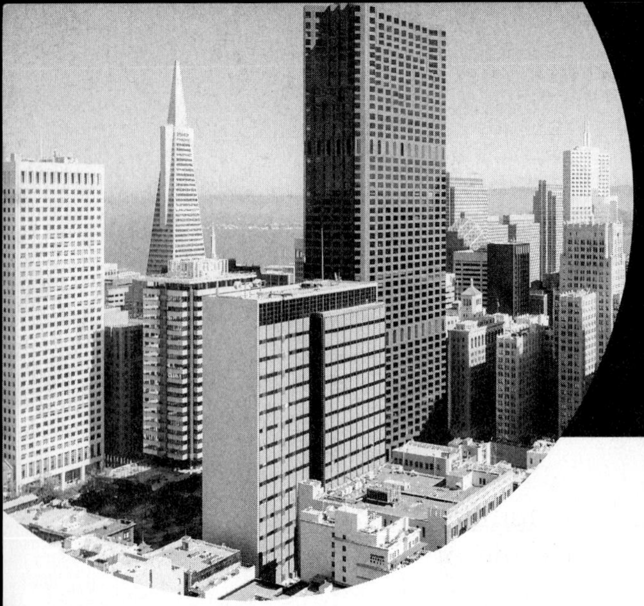

CHAPTER 2

INSTITUTIONAL LENDERS

OVERVIEW

An institutional lender, also known as a financial intermediary, is any depository that pools funds of clients and depositors and invests them in real estate loans. The lending policies of these institutions have a profound impact on the real estate market. In California, institutional lenders include savings banks (former savings and loan associations), commercial banks, credit unions, and life insurance companies. They are differentiated from non-institutional lenders, such as individual or private lenders, in the following important ways:

- Institutional lenders are highly regulated and closely supervised by federal and state agencies, whereas private lenders are relatively free of regulations.
- Private lenders invest their own funds directly, or through mortgage brokers, into real estate loans, rather than through a financial intermediary.
- Regulated institutional lenders are not subject to usury laws and may charge any rate of interest. In contrast, many private lenders make "personal" loans that are subject to **usury** laws, which place legal limits on rates of interest. (See Chapter 3 for details.)
- Many institutional lenders qualify to make Department of Veterans Affairs (VA) and Federal Housing Administration (FHA) loans.
- As described in Chapter 7, there is an active secondary market for institutional loans. The ability to sell loans to the secondary market drives prices and terms and maintains a supply of mortgage funds in the primary market.
- Institutional lenders and federal regulations, in some cases, set private mortgage insurance (PMI) requirements, discussed in Chapter 5.
- Most conforming lenders offer **rate lock-in** periods, guaranteeing an agreed-upon interest rate in advance of closing. Lock periods typically vary from 14 to 60 days; however, more recently, lenders have restricted maximum lock periods to 30, 45, or 60 days. Generally, a longer lock-in period affects the fee, rate, or both.

FIGURE 2.1 Sources of money in the mortgage market.

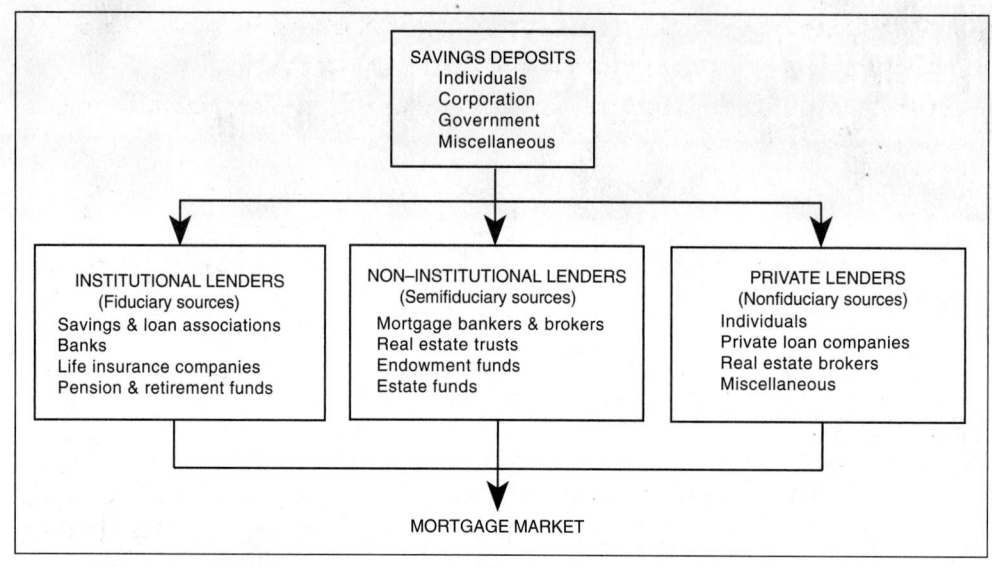

```
                    SAVINGS DEPOSITS
                       Individuals
                       Corporation
                       Government
                       Miscellaneous
         ┌────────────────┼────────────────┐
         ▼                ▼                ▼
  INSTITUTIONAL      NON–INSTITUTIONAL      PRIVATE LENDERS
     LENDERS             LENDERS          (Nonfiduciary sources)
 (Fiduciary sources) (Semifiduciary sources)     Individuals
 Savings & loan       Mortgage bankers         Private loan companies
  associations         & brokers               Real estate brokers
 Banks                Real estate trusts       Miscellaneous
 Life insurance       Endowment funds
  companies           Estate funds
 Pension & retirement
  funds
         └────────────────┼────────────────┘
                          ▼
                    MORTGAGE MARKET
```

Source: © 2016 OnCourse Learning

Figure 2.1 distinguishes three broad classifications of lenders: institutional, non-institutional, and private lenders. How these lenders fit into the mortgage market will be explained in this and upcoming chapters. In Figure 2.2, we show how savings become real estate loans.

FIGURE 2.2 How savings become real estate loans.

Source: © 2016 OnCourse Learning

After completing this chapter, you will be able to:
- Demonstrate how savings deposits become real estate loans.
- Differentiate institutional from non-institutional lenders.
- List three types of institutional lenders and briefly explain the differences between them.
- Discuss regulatory trends facing institutional lenders.
- Decide when to use one institutional lender over another.
- List five regulatory agencies that supervise the operations of institutional lenders.

THE BLURRING OF BANK IDENTITIES

The three major types of depository institutions in the United States are thrifts (which include savings and loan associations and savings banks), commercial banks, and credit unions. Their unique identities have become less distinct in recent years as they have become more like each other, but there remain some differences in real estate specialization and emphasis as well as in their regulatory and supervisory structures.

2.1 SAVINGS BANKS/THRIFTS

What Is a Savings Bank?

Referred in the past as "thrift" institutions—because they originally offered only savings accounts—or **time deposits**, the label "savings bank" has become the catch-all title that includes savings and loans, thrifts, and sometimes credit unions. A **savings bank** was defined as a **financial intermediary** that accepted savings deposits from the public and, by law, invested primarily in long term home mortgage products. Over time, however, they have acquired a much wider range of financial powers, and now offer checking accounts (demand deposits) and make business and consumer loans as well as mortgages.

While many entities use the name Savings Bank in their name, it is likely that they are hard to distinguish in any way from other banking institutions. Savings banks, as they were referred to in the past, were either mutual or capital stock institutions. As a mutual institution, depositors and borrowers were given share certificates or receipts in return for deposits of money. This is why a deposit in a mutual thrift is often referred to as a *share liability* rather than a savings deposit. A capital stock institution, on the other hand, issues shares of stock to its investors, representing fractional shares of ownership of the institution. These entities, by whatever name, still specialize in real estate lending, particularly loans for single-family homes and other residential properties.

Thrift banks of the past tended to be community-focused and smaller than retail and commercial banks. The thrift banking system was originally created in an attempt to transition mortgage loan origination away from insurance companies and into banking institutions, as early mortgages were often set up as interest-only loans that often couldn't be repaid when balloon payments came due.

Present day, to retain their charter, as well as their membership in the Federal Home Loan Bank System, savings institutions are required to retain a certain percentage of their loan portfolio in housing-related assets. Known as the "qualified thrift lender" (QTL) test, the general requirement was 65 percent of their portfolio to be in housing-related or other qualified assets to maintain their status. Liberalization over time has resulted in changes, and savings banks now compete with other banking institutions for other financial investment opportunities.

Savings banks may be chartered by either the federal Office of Thrift Supervision (OTS) or by a state government regulator, are members of the Federal Reserve System, and receive deposit insurance from the Federal Deposit Insurance Corporation (FDIC).

Lending Characteristics of Savings Banks (Thrifts)

The chief lending characteristics of savings banks include the following:

- Government regulations require that a majority of their assets must be in real estate loans. Business and consumer loans are permitted to a limited extent, but pale when compared with loans secured by real property.
- Although loan-to-value (LTV) limits vary from bank to bank and depend on the availability of money in the marketplace, the standard through 2014 was a maximum 95 percent LTV. However, Fannie Mae introduced a 97 percent loan option in January 2015. Although 97 percent LTV loans had occasionally been available, in the past this higher loan to value ratio loan would more likely have been a government loan type. Starting in 2006, down payment requirements became less flexible; by late 2014, lenders were again offering adjustable rate mortgages and introducing other riskier loan options in an effort to increase loan volume. For the most part, these early, more creative loan options

were more stable than in the past, offering mostly fixed rate loans for a period of years after which they converted to another fixed rate or ARM period. Most thrifts limit the maximum loan amount on a property to a percentage of their total assets. Hence, larger thrifts are able to accommodate large loan requests more readily than smaller savings banks and may be more flexible on LTV limits.

- Most thrifts limit their loan terms to 30- or 15-year mortgages although 10- and 20-year loans are also available. In the past, when interest rates were on the rise, some banks offered shorter-than-normal due dates. A three-, five-, or seven-year due date would still have payments amortized over 30 years, but have a "balloon" payment due at the end of the term. A "rollover" loan would ignore the principal balance due and convert it to an adjustable rate for the remainder of the term. While still available, these loan options are infrequently selected by borrowers. (These creative options will be discussed further in Chapter 13.)
- Interest rates in the past were highest among the institutional real estate lenders. This was due to the large demand for loans and to the higher risks associated with higher **loan-to-value ratios** (LTV). Currently, rates charged by commercial banks and savings banks are basically the same and most lenders have adopted "risk-based" pricing models (discussed in Chapter 9).
- Thrift banks' basic real estate lending is on single-family, owner-occupied dwellings. However, in a favorable market, but to a much more limited degree, thrifts will also finance mobile home loans, non-owner-occupied dwellings, apartments, and commercial and industrial properties.
- Combination loans may also be available. Referred to as "construction-to-permanent" loans, they combine construction (short-term financing) and **take-out loans** (long-term or permanent financing) into one loan with only one loan application and one closing. This is dealt with further in Chapter 12.
- Savings banks are permitted to make collateral loans secured by the borrower's savings accounts, savings certificates, bonds, existing secured notes, and certain other forms of readily liquid assets. These institutions started with "secured" credit cards to help restore the credit of their customers. This establishes a credit card limit that is secured with the consumer's savings account, limiting the bank's liability.

2.2 COMMERCIAL BANKS

Commercial Banks

Commercial banks are generally stock corporations whose principal obligation is to make a profit for their shareholders. Commercial banks have two different forms of deposits: demand deposits and time deposits. The bulk of their funds are in demand deposits, which are deposits in business and personal checking accounts. Referred to as transaction money or transaction accounts, the fact that they can be withdrawn on demand by the depositor makes them unreliable as funds that would be available for long-term lending.

Time deposits, on the other hand, are interest-bearing savings accounts and provide the long-term funds necessary for a variety of investments, including real estate financing. While commercial banks mostly specialize in short-term business credit, along with providing home mortgage options, they enjoy a broad range of financial powers. Their corporate charters and the powers granted to them under state and federal law determine the range of their activities.

Commercial banks operate under a license or charter from either a state or the federal government. A state-chartered bank is licensed to do business by the California Department of Financial Institutions. A nationally chartered bank is given its license by the Comptroller of the Currency and can be readily identified by the word national in its name, such as South Coast National Bank or the initials N.A. following its name such as Wells Fargo, N.A. for National Association.

Lending Characteristics of Commercial Banks

While commercial banks may make any type of loan on virtually any type of reasonable collateral, their primary function is to make short-term business loans. Commercial banks are also a primary source for short-term construction financing, discussed further in Chapter 13.

The chief characteristics of commercial bank loans are the following:

- Although active in the regular home loan market, including FHA and VA loans, shorter term loans with various forms of collateral are more the norm. Construction loans are favored and have maturity dates generally of 24 months or less, though they may extend to 60 months. Many banks require a firm take-out agreement whereby a responsible, permanent investor—such as a savings bank or other recognized lending source—will extend long-term financing upon completion of construction.

- The property offered as collateral is usually in close proximity to the bank or one of its branches.
- Commercial banks are active seekers of home improvement and home equity loans, even though they constitute a junior lien against the property.
- Commercial banks make **swing loans**, sometimes referred to as **bridge loans**, which are short-term **interim loans** used to bridge the time during which a property remains unsold. For example, if a homeowner purchases a replacement house before selling the first house, a swing loan provides the funds to fill the gap until the sale proceeds are available. The lien generally encumbers both the "old" and the "new" homes. Swing/bridge loans may have monthly payments or may be set up to be paid in a single lump sum upon sale of the old home.

Credit Unions

Unlike banks, credit unions are non-profit financial membership organizations that exist to serve their members. In order to open an account, you become a member and your deposits create a share in the credit union. As member-owned institutions, credit unions focus on savings safety and reasonable borrowing rates. In the past, credit unions tended to determine a field of membership based upon one's employment, community location, or membership in identified organizations. Credit unions have enjoyed a reputation for being more personal and focused on community, and membership today is growing as it is often open to most anyone who wishes to join.

Credit unions generally made loans from their members' savings and retained the loans in-house. More recently, credit unions have begun to resemble other banks, especially when making home loans. They often use the same underwriting guidelines and prepare their loans for possible sale in the secondary market. Federally insured credit unions are regulated by the National Credit Union Administration (NCUA) which, in turn, administers the National Credit Unions Share Insurance Fund (NCUSIF), which insures depositor share accounts. The Dodd-Frank Wall Street Reform and Consumer Protection Act of 2010 increased the share insurance coverage on all federally insured credit union accounts up to $250,000, which retains the backing of the full faith and credit of the United States government.

Lending Characteristics of Credit Unions

Membership in credit unions continues to grow as banks have come under scrutiny for what seems to be an increasing reliance upon a profit-making fee structure. A list of pros and cons of credit unions usually includes the following:

1. Credit unions, as not-for-profit membership organizations, often provide superior service. The membership aspect has been a negative in the past, but many are now using a "community" base membership open to practically everyone.

2. Their mission to provide "affordable" financial services can translate into lower interest rates on loans and higher rates on savings accounts. The gap between credit unions and banks has continued to narrow in recent years, especially as credit unions now underwrite loans to meet the same secondary market sale requirements as banks.

3. There are generally fewer strings attached to accounts such as no or very minimum balance requirements for the best rates on checking and savings accounts. Credit unions have tried to keep fees low, but regulations are causing the typical banking fees to rise and the savings gap has reduced.

Credit unions generally have less ATM availability when a member leaves the immediate area. To compensate, many credit unions will reimburse member costs if travelers are unable to conduct business at a local credit union or must use an unaffiliated ATM. The banks' advantage in this area has in most cases been eliminated because of their own fees for each ATM transaction by their own bank members.

Anticipated Future Impacts on Lending Institutions

Institutional lenders are grappling with changes, some of which could include the following in the near future.

1. While the "too big to fail" concept has been mostly ignored as banks merged and grew ever larger, there is growing concern over the fact that five or six major entities control a significantly large share of the banking activities. This concern could manifest itself in slowing and dissuading future bank mergers and growth.

2. As the reliance on Internet banking increases, greater pressure will be exerted to review the fee schedules upon which banks have been increasingly relying for revenue. The added pressure from a growing credit union presence with their reduced or non-existent fee structure will require a revenue source review from all savings and commercial bank entities.

3. As the bank customer base stabilizes or reduces due to the credit union competition, the search for more revenue sources could

result in the return to riskier mortgage loan programs as an enticement to consumers. In turn, any resurgence in what are deemed risky loans will likely trigger greater regulatory oversight for all.

4. The discussions continue around the value of revisiting the restraints imposed by Glass-Steagall in which bank activity was more clearly separated into either emphasizing the consumer savings aspects of banking or the riskier investment banking programs. Such separation, some suggest, would have prevented the excessive speculation with consumer savings that attributed to the 2008 banking meltdown. Critics claimed that the past speculation amounted to using consumer funds with the result of privatizing the profits and socializing the losses.

5. As conversations occur around the roles that banks should play, it is unlikely that those who continue to seek entry into the realms of insurance and real estate will acquire permission to do so.

6. The playing field is expected to be a bit more leveled as banks, which have managed to escape some of the oversight regulations of the CFPB already imposed on mortgage brokers, will be under greater scrutiny and will have to accommodate new rules. As a part of this increased oversight, the Nationwide Mortgage Licensing System (NMLS) requirements will be expanded to include bank personnel engaged in lending practices.

Community Reinvestment Act (CRA)

To guarantee fair lending practices, Congress passed the CRA, which requires all federally supervised financial institutions (federal thrifts, commercial banks, credit unions, etc.) to disclose lending data in their lobbies and elsewhere. Lenders are required to report data regarding the race, gender, income, and census tract of people to whom they make loans. Its stated purpose is "to assist in identifying discriminatory practices and enforcing antidiscrimination statutes." The CRA encourages lenders to offer mortgages for low- and moderately-priced housing and meet other credit needs for low- and moderate-income families. The basic idea is that if an institution accepts deposits from a certain area, it should also offer loans in that area.

CRA ratings are made public for all banks and **thrift institutions**. The government grades each institution on how well it:

- Knows the credit needs of its community
- Informs the community about its credit services
- Involves its directors in setting up and monitoring CRA programs

- Participates in government-insured, guaranteed, or subsidized loans
- Distributes credit applications, approvals, and rejections across geographic areas
- Offers a range of residential mortgages, housing rehabilitation loans, and small business loans

All of these criteria are designed to protect consumers against unlawful discrimination. A positive CRA rating is a prerequisite for institutions to open new branches and to engage in expansions, acquisitions, and mergers, since outside third parties can petition agencies to deny these activities to institutions with poor CRA grades.

Ironically, the pressure from congressional and other federal sources, including Fannie Mae and Freddie Mac, to provide loans for as many borrowers as possible is now partially blamed for the subprime loan explosion and eventual housing problems that began to surface as early as 2007. The rise of the increasingly "easy to qualify" loan instruments of the early 2000s are now criticized as the major contributor to the housing crises that resulted in record foreclosures nationally and major financial problems globally.

To be fair some institutional lenders found themselves in an untenable situation. To avoid any hint of discrimination that could affect their CRA rating, lending institutions were literally coerced into making loans to borrowers who they may well have perceived as unqualified. As inevitably occurs after a crisis, in the scramble to assess blame, lenders were then accused of having knowingly made bad loans. The point being that not all lenders bear equal responsibility as contributors to the financial crises.

Home Mortgage Disclosure Act (HMDA)

The CRA requirements include having lenders retain borrower information from which any discriminatory acts can be determined. The primary source of information for this enforcement is the information gathered via section X of the Fannie Mae/Freddie Mac loan application (known as the 1003). The Information for Government Monitoring Purposes section of the 1003 seeks information regarding a borrower's ethnicity, race, and sex. This section is considered so important that if the borrower refuses or fails to provide the information, the lender is required to "note the information on the basis of visual observation or surname." This, understandably, has resulted in some reporting errors as it is not always possible to discern this information by mere observation.

The Consumer Financial Protection Bureau (CFPB) proposed adding new data points to the current requirements as well as modifying certain existing data points. The data points that the bureau is proposing to add or modify were grouped into four broad categories:

1. Information about applicants, borrowers, and the underwriting process, such as age, credit score, debt-to-income ratio, reasons for denial if the application was denied, and the automated underwriting system results.
2. Information about the property securing the loan, such as construction method, property value, lien priority, the number of individual dwelling units in the property, and additional information about manufactured and multifamily housing.
3. Information about the features of the loan, such as additional pricing information, loan term, interest rate, introductory rate period, non-amortizing features, and the type of loan.
4. Certain unique identifiers such as property address, loan originator identifier, and a legal entity identifier for the financial industry.

All of this information is already available, but the bureau wanted it collected in a format allowing for easier evaluation. The bureau's rationale for this expansion of the data to be collected in order to assure non-discriminatory practices was heavily resisted by the lending community. Concerns immediately arose over the burden of collecting the increased information and whether the information was actually necessary for the purpose for which it was presumably intended—to assure a non-discriminatory atmosphere. As of late 2014, the issue of how to collect and report the additional information remained unresolved.

What Is a Life Insurance Company?

A **life insurance company** is a firm that specializes in the insuring of lives for specified amounts in exchange for specified premium payments. The premiums are invested until such time as funds are needed to pay claims or to establish reserves for losses. These premiums are invested in many outlets, including trust deeds and mortgage loans.

Life insurance companies are organized either as mutual companies owned by the policyholders (insureds) who share in the earnings through premium rebates, or as stock companies owned by the stockholders who, as with any other corporation, are entitled to dividends on earnings. Regardless of whether stock or mutual, insurance companies are licensed by the state in which they are incorporated and/or where they have their principal offices. Each insurance company is governed by the state where it conducts business, and each state regulates the permitted types of loans, maximum loan-to-value ratios, and other conditions.

2.3 LIFE INSURANCE COMPANIES

Life insurance companies, as a source of real estate financing, are usually most interested in commercial properties, such as shopping centers and office buildings. They are also a major source of credit for large apartment house projects, hotels and motels, industrial buildings, and regional shopping malls. Many people pay for life insurance, but not many claims are paid out at one time. So, the savings of life insurance companies can be substantial and available to lend out for added revenue. Of course, there must be a reserve account, and the investment funds have to be in a safe project.

Lending Characteristics of Life Insurance Companies

In general, life insurance companies have the broadest lending powers of the **institutional lenders**. Their investment policies are flexible and cover a wide range of financing activities. The laws governing life insurance company activities vary from state to state. Under California laws and regulations, any company not incorporated within this state, but doing business here, is subject to the same restrictions that are placed upon California-based companies.

The chief lending characteristics of life insurance companies include the following:

- Loan-to-value ratios are apt to be on the cautious side, frequently less than 80 percent.
- Payback terms are long, usually 30-year amortizations, with occasional **lock-in clauses** that prevent a loan from being paid off before a specified date. For example, there might be a 10- or 15-year lock-in clause on a 30-year loan. The borrower would not be able to pay off the loan until after the lock-in date.
- Interest rates and other fees on conventional loans have traditionally been the lowest among the institutions.
- Insurance companies prefer to grant large real estate loans (in the millions) as opposed to smaller residential home loans. Many major commercial and industrial developments have insurance company take-out loans.
- Construction loans generally are not desired. Instead, life insurance companies will make the take-out, or permanent, loan

2.3 Life Insurance Companies

after the structure has been completed according to plans and specifications.

- Loan **correspondents** are widely used as agents of insurance companies. Many life insurance companies will contract for such representation whenever they deem it profitable. In this way the insurance company is relieved of the burden of originating and processing loans, as well as some administrative and service functions. Correspondents are especially used in California, where there is a high demand for loans, but where few insurance companies are actually headquartered. Detailed information concerning lending authority for insurance companies is found in the California Insurance Code, especially in Sections 11500–11501.

Lending Practices of the Life Insurance Industry

The most often utilized forms of real estate lending practices by life insurance companies include:

1. *Equity conversion positions during inflationary periods.* Here the lender has the option to convert part of the mortgage into an equity position in the property: a shared investment. In short, the lender has the right to convert a portion of the mortgage owed into a part of the ownership of the property at a later date.

2. *Upfront participations* (piece of the action). As a condition of granting a loan, an insurance company may require an upfront share of the income produced by the property to help increase the yield on the loan. Such sharing is called **equity participation**. Participation may also take the form of an "equity kicker" such that, instead of income, the lender takes a percentage ownership in the property. Increasingly, however, insurance companies are buying whole projects as sole owners. Participations become an attractive option in periods of rapid inflation, when fixed interest rates become discouraging and investment funds become scarce.

3. *Variable and fixed annuities.* As more people purchase insurance company annuity contracts, larger supplies of funds become available for reinvestment. Real estate loans are one way insurance companies reinvest annuity contributions.

4. *Holding companies and joint ventures.* Where state law does not prohibit the practice, a number of life insurance companies are purchased or reorganized under the umbrella of holding companies. In such instances, interrelated lending activities are made possible because other firms that may be joined together under

the parent holding company include such entities as commercial banks, savings banks, and even development companies that furnish construction financing, permanent financing, and so forth.

A variation of this concept of pooling resources is through the media of joint ventures. Under such a venture, a life insurance company may provide the needed financing while a well-established developer will furnish the requisite know-how and co-develop a project.

2.4 MUTUAL SAVINGS BANKS

Mutual savings banks operate much like former savings and loan associations, but they exist chiefly in the northeastern United States. Few, if any, exist in California, but some institutions, mostly credit unions, continue to explore any advantages related to converting to a mutual savings bank designation. It is important to consider them because of the large contribution they make in furnishing capital for residential loans via the secondary marketplace. **Mutual savings banks**, also called mutual thrifts, are not commercial banks. They are organized in substantially the same way regardless of the state in which they are chartered. They are banks for savings deposits that have no stockholders and are organized to pool the interests of those of moderate means. Managed by a board of trustees, directors, or managers, mutual savings banks distribute their earnings, after payment of necessary business expenses and taxes, to the depositors in the form of dividends, or the earnings are added to the bank's surplus or reserve funds.

Depending on state law, the maximum loan-to-value ratio varies from 50 to 90 percent, exclusive of government-backed loans. When money becomes tight and the yields on other investment outlets increase, mutual savings banks pull back on their real estate lending activities and expand their lending in non-real estate areas.

2.5 DEPOSITORY INSTITUTIONS AND MONETARY CONTROL ACT

The Monetary Control Act of 1980, among other deregulations, completely phased out restrictions on interest rates that lenders can pay depositors. As a result, new systems for raising, mobilizing, and investing money were developed. All of this was intended to increase the yields offered to savers and depositors based upon the terms of their checking and savings accounts. Alas, the same deregulations resulted in interest rates in recent years declining to near zero percent even as financial institutions staged a recovery following the 2008 monetary collapse. In deregulating financial institutions, we saw the homogenization of these institutions. It had become difficult to distinguish between savings banks (thrifts) and commercial banks, so close were their respective functions. Reserves were more or less uniform, consumer lending powers of every variety were ultimately granted, territorial lending restrictions were phased out, and restrictions against junior financing were lifted; a wave of new types of deposits and classes of savings accounts continued to emerge out of the deregulation process.

Additionally, the act expanded the lending authority of federal thrift institutions to allow investment in consumer loans, commercial paper, corporate debt securities, and junior trust deeds. It authorized these institutions to make acquisitions, development and construction loans, and removed the geographical lending restrictions along with certain dollar limitations on residential real estate loans.

2.6 PENSION AND RETIREMENT FUNDS

It was anticipated in the past that the many thousands of private pension funds along with the state, local, and federal funds nationwide—all representing billions in assets—would represent a major source of real estate financing. This potential source has remained mostly unfulfilled. Investments in the ill-advised subprime mortgage market of the late 2000s resulted in large equity losses coupled with the assault on the sustainability of pension funds in many cities and states. It is unlikely that said funds will become available to the mortgage arena any time soon.

Administration and Lending Policies of Pension and Trust Funds

Administrators of **pension funds** include trust departments of commercial banks and life insurance companies; trustees of unions; boards of trustees appointed by a governor or mayor, in the case of state and local government employees; and employers. Lending policies vary considerably from fund to fund, with no uniform administrative practices followed. Prudence, market conditions, size of the fund, philosophy of the administrators, and other factors dictate how the funds might best be invested at any given time. In California, the massive PERS (Public Employees Retirement System) had a very large home loan program as did the STRS (State Teachers Retirement System). While lenders increased their down payment requirements starting in mid-2008, these programs continued to offer employees 100 percent financing by allowing them to use 5 percent of their fund contributions for a down payment accompanied by a 95 percent LTV loan. Both programs were suspended in late 2014 citing competition from other loan options having become available.

Individual Retirement Accounts (IRAs) and Keogh Plans

As private pension programs became more popular with liberalized tax-deferred contributions for individual retirement accounts for employees, and allowances under the Keogh Plan for self-employed persons, substantially more of these dollars entered the capital markets. These funds were an important source of real estate financing on all levels.

For years, most pension funds had been invested in government securities and in corporate stocks and bonds. However, the rapid increase in the assets of pension funds and the desire to diversify these investments motivated some fund managers to look at real estate loans as an additional source of investment.

But as the subprime market flourished, the mostly conservative fund managers were reluctant to invest in what they viewed as risky mortgages. Since other sources of investment money were so plentiful, these funds were hardly missed.

The Past and Present of Lending Regulation

"Too big to fail" was the phrase used to explain why the bank bailout of 2008 was necessary—it was felt that the big banks could not be allowed to collapse. In spite of expectations that regulations would be adopted to avoid a future recurrence, banks—via mergers and bank purchases of smaller institutions—have become even bigger. Just as concerning as the size of the big banks is the continued lack of meaningful regulation regarding the use of depositors' funds entrusted to them. In this practice of greater risk taking on the part of the banks, if the bank gambled and the bet paid off (often with enormous profit) the bank kept the money but when they lost, as in 2008, the public picked up the tab via the bailout. The concern is that this "heads I win, tails you lose" concept has not been corrected.

The Glass-Steagall Act of 1933 regulated bank activity for over 60 years prior to its repeal in 1999 via the Gramm-Leach Bliley Act. Glass-Steagall prohibited commercial banks from collaborating with full service brokerage firms or participating in investment banking activities. The act protected bank depositors from the risks associated with speculative investments, which are akin to gambling with depositors' money.

The excesses leading to the financial meltdown of 2008 are said to have been caused by decades of deregulation of the banking industry since 1999 coupled with the constant erosion of any oversight of the financial entities. The ultimate gambling with consumers' funds occurred with the unsound loans associated with the subprime era.

Greed proliferated through the financial system from the banks, which designed and promoted the loan instruments to the loan originators who urged borrowers to accept the unsafe and ultimately untenable loans.

While the resulting financial debacle brought about an expectation of greater oversight of the banking industry with the passage of the Consumer Financial Protection Bureau bill (the CFPB was introduced in Chapter 1), meaningful change has come slowly.

While the CFPB has tried to rein in many of the lending excesses of the past, the big banks have consolidated both in size and political influence. Many of the anticipated reforms have been delayed and/or permanently weakened by consistent resistance from the major banking institutions. The CFPB's oversight was legislatively diminished with the passage of the December 2014 legislation to fund the government. Inserted in this omnibus bill was a provision eliminating the restriction on banks from participating in their derivative speculation (noted above). This was perceived as confirmation that the bulk of the newest regulations would continue to affect mortgage brokers and appraisers while the big banks would continue to escape crucial oversight. The ability to once again return to the risky behavior that was widely viewed as the reason for the past economic crises seemed to suggest that government was unable to learn from history.

Critics' concern that there was no accountability on the part of those on Wall Street and in the big banks and that the same abuses could occur again now seemed justified. These critics also pointed to the recent resurgence of some of the loan options that were considered responsible for consumer problems of the past—the re-introduction of adjustable rate mortgages, higher loan-to-value ratio loans, and lower credit scores (all of these options will be reviewed in Chapters 9 and 13). These same critics pointed out that recognition of the potential problems without sufficient regulation of Wall Street and the big banks could result in history repeating itself.

2.7 GOVERNMENT REGULATORY AGENCIES

A variety of federal and state agencies govern activities and practices of institutional lenders. For real estate financing purposes, the most significant are briefly outlined below and discussed in greater depth in other chapters.

Massive changes in the regulatory structure at the federal level were instituted as a result of widespread failures of thrift institutions in the 1980s and early 1990s. A whole new alphabet soup of acronyms replaced many of the old, beginning with the law itself, the **Financial Institutions Reform, Recovery, and Enforcement Act (FIRREA)**. Following the perceived excesses of the subprime lending practices, in 2009 additional regulatory oversight of many of the federal agencies created by FIRREA was recommended in an attempt to further protect and reassure consumers. During the past several years we have seen the elimination and/or merging of agencies along with new entities, among them the CFPB. A short list of regulatory agencies includes:

1. *Consumer Financial Protection Bureau (CFPB)* Authorized by the Dodd-Frank Wall Street Reform and Protection Act of 2010, the CFPB was a legislative response to the financial crises of 2007–2008 and the subsequent Great Recession. With sweeping authority in all areas of financial oversight, we will hear much of this entity as we proceed with our understanding real estate financing. The re-arrangement of various oversight agencies were numerous in an attempt to gain control of the financial crises that exploded in 2008. As a part of this overhaul of agencies, three entities were eliminated upon merger into the CFPB. These included the **Office of Thrift Supervision (OTS)**, which was a federal agency under the Department of the Treasury charged with regulating all federal and state chartered savings banks and savings and loans. Like other agencies at the time, it was paid by the banks it regulated and it became lax in its oversight responsibilities. The agency ultimately failed in its supervision of non-bank entities like American International Group (AIG), Washington Mutual, and IndyMac, which all closed in the early days of the financial meltdown. As of July 2011, the other two major agencies merged along with the OTS were the **Office of the Comptroller of the Currency (OCC)** and **Federal Deposit Insurance Corporation (FDIC)**, which are now all under the purview of the Consumer Financial Protection Bureau.

    The OCC's responsibilities included regulation and supervision of national banks (and some foreign branch banks in the United States) to ensure the safety and soundness of the national banking system. While ensuring fair and equal access to financial services for all segments of the community, it also promoted competition by encouraging banks to offer new products and services. Some of those new loan programs resulted in what was known as creative financing options and were deemed a contributing cause to the banking crises. (See the Case & Point at end of Chapter 5 for more information regarding the CFPB.)

2. *Deposit Insurance Fund (DIF)* Via the enactment of the Federal Deposit Insurance Reform Act of 2005, which became effective

March 1, 2006, the DIF was created to abolish and replace both the Savings Association Insurance Fund (SAIF) and the Bank Insurance Fund (BIF). SAIF had itself replaced the Federal Savings and Loan Insurance Corporation, which became insolvent following the savings and loan collapse in the late 1980s and was later merged with BIF. Managed by FDIC, the Deposit Insurance Fund is now responsible for the collection of insurance premiums from all federally insured savings associations. The 2005 legislation also raised the federal deposit insurance level from $100,000 to $250,000 on retirement accounts.

3. *Federal Deposit Insurance Corporation (FDIC)*. Now under the guidance of the CFPB, this familiar federal agency's main task is to promote public confidence in the financial systems of commercial and savings banks and is empowered to insure deposits only (not securities, stocks, bonds, or mutual funds) up to designated amounts, presently $250,000 per depositor per bank. Originally enacted in 1933, discussions continue to occur regarding the adequacy of the level of coverage at any given time. The reasons for increases in coverage have been many but are mostly influenced by developments in the economy, and, for the most part, past congressional action has been uncontroversial. Guarding the public's deposits, the FDIC's success is measured by the fact that since its initiation, no depositor has lost a single cent of insured funds via any bank failure. The FDIC's ability to reassure the public was clearly tested in 2009 with the collapse of one of the largest entities in California, IndyMac Bank. About 95 percent of the $19 billion in deposits in the bank were insured, but $1 billion of that was not covered by FDIC guarantees. The FDIC manages the Deposit Insurance Fund (DIF).

4. *Federal Housing Finance Agency (FHFA)* This independent federal agency was created as a result of the late 2000s financial crises via the Housing and Economic Recovery Act of 2008 (HERA), replacing the Federal Housing Finance Board (FHFB). The FHFB, in turn, had been established by the Financial Institutions Reform, Recovery, and Enforcement Act of 1989 (FIRREA) in the aftermath of the savings and loan crises with a mission to support local, community-based financial institutions, facilitate access to credit, and insure that lenders carry out their housing and community development finance requirements. Most importantly, in its role as regulator, FHFA has oversight of Fannie Mae and Freddie Mac (the government sponsored entities known as GSEs, which will be discussed more fully in Chapter 5) as well as

the Federal Home Loan Banks. On September 7, 2008, FHFA placed the GSEs into conservatorship, where they currently remain. FHFA has continually tightened the reserve requirements of the entities under its purview in the interest of protecting consumers with new rules proposed as of late 2014. The agency is authorized to approve any new products that either GSE proposes to offer. And the agency has filed suit against several of the largest banking entities regarding their excesses, abusive, and fraudulent behavior with past consumer home loans during the run up to the financial crises that exploded in 2008. Although the law suits have resulted in millions of dollars in penalties, their success remains a controversial subject.

5. *Federal Reserve Bank Board (FRBB)* Comprised of a seven-member Board of Governors, the FRBB is the main governing body of the Federal Reserve System. Among its responsibilities, the Board guides monetary policy action, analyzes domestic and international economic and financial conditions, and leads committees that study current issues, such as consumer banking laws and electronic commerce. Exercising broad supervisory control over the financial services industry, the Board administers consumer protection regulations. As indicated in Chapter 1, the Board sets reserve requirements for depository institutions and approves changes in discount rates recommended by Reserve Banks. One of the more important responsibilities is participation in the Federal Open Market Committee (FOMC), which is the Fed's monetary policymaking body, responsible for formulation of a policy designed to promote stable prices and economic growth. In other words, the FOMC manages the nation's money supply. As part of its committee actions, the Board's latest focus is to guard against being caught by surprise by threats to the financial system as they suggest occurred in the 2008 crises. Committees on bank supervision, financial monitoring, and research and one entity dedicated to the identifying systemic risks regularly meet to provide stability to our financial system.

6. *Federal Home Loan Mortgage Corporation (FHLMC) and Federal National Mortgage Association (FNMA).* Known respectively as Freddie Mac and Fannie Mae, both entities function as integral parts of a "secondary mortgage market" in which loans are purchased from participating lenders. The primary purpose of both entities, referred to as government sponsored enterprises (GSEs), is to ensure stability to the mortgage market by creating liquidity, accessibility, and affordability for residential mortgage financing. By 2008 the mortgage meltdown had affected both

entities, and the Federal Housing Finance Agency was appointed conservator for FNMA when the U.S. Department of the Treasury was required to "loan" the agencies $188 billion to enable them to continue to provide liquidity to the mortgage market (discussed more fully in Chapter 7).

7. *California Department of Business Oversight (DBO)* This agency was created with the Governor's Reorganization Plans in 2012 and incorporated the **California Department of Financial Institutions (DFI)**, a department responsible for the financial regulation of California's banking system. The DBO now provides protection to consumers and services to businesses engaged in financial transactions through the regulation of a variety of financial services, products, and professionals. The department oversees the operations of state-licensed financial institutions, including banks, credit unions, and finance companies. Additionally, the department licenses and regulates a variety of financial businesses, including securities brokers and dealers, investment advisers, deferred deposit transactions (commonly known as payday loans), and certain fiduciaries and lenders. The department also regulates the offer and sale of securities, franchises, and off-exchange commodities.

Regulation and its Consequences

Congressional reaction to the financial crises was to enact stricter laws in an attempt to assure no future duplication of what was viewed as systemic greed within the financial industry. Looking around for who to blame, Congress, with the help of the big banks, settled mostly on mortgage brokers and appraisers. Forgotten was the fact that Congress had itself urged Fannie Mae and Freddie Mac to promote more flexible home financing as a way to assure more families the opportunity to acquire the American dream of homeownership. Forgotten, too, was the fact that the extremely flexible mortgage instruments had been created by the banks and heavily promoted among all sectors that were originating loans.

The Dodd-Frank Wall Street Reform and Consumer Protection Act enacted in July 2010 proposed substantial regulatory change across the entire financial landscape. Early rules put into place included the Nationwide Mortgage Licensing System or NMLS (see Case & Point at the end of this chapter), significant changes in the appraisal process (Home Valuation Code of Conduct or HVCC discussed in Chapter 8), and an attempt to limit the fees charged home buying borrowers (qualified mortgage rules discussed in Chapter 3). The large banks managed to escape or reduce the impact of most legislation while it fell mostly upon the mortgage brokers and appraisers to adapt to the new rules. Additional pending rules were attacked by the banks, and eventually many were watered down or eliminated, especially with regard to their effect upon the large financial institutions.

The signature legislation of the Dodd-Frank bill was the initiation of the CFPB proposed to oversee practically all aspects of the financial markets. As with other major financial reforms, a variety of critics attacked the law, some arguing it was not enough to prevent another financial crisis or more bailouts, and others arguing it went too far and unduly restricted financial institutions. Repeated attempts to scuttle this part of the legislation resulted in a delay until mid-2013 before many of its effects began to be felt in the financial arena.

As is often the case when restrictions are enacted, there was initially an overreaction for enforcement purposes. Loan underwriters became more conservative and required more documentation for each file. Marginal files were more routinely denied and productivity declined as fewer home loans met the stiffened requirements. The plethora of loan options shrunk, and the old standard fixed rate loan became the most desirable loan product. Tougher credit standards moved credit scores from the old minimum of 580 to 640, and any buyer with less than a 740 score was deemed a higher risk and faced increased interest rates. Available funds for real estate loans were in short supply, and the attitude had changed from one of "fog a mirror and get a loan" to "we are not sure we want to make the loan."

The housing segment of the economy has typically led us out of recession in the past, but this time, the regulations and lack of available funds stifled any quick rebound. Exacerbating the situation was the enormous number of houses suddenly in foreclosure and flooding the market, along with those offered in "short sales" (homes sold for less than owed), which in turn further reduced home values and contributed to a spiraling housing market.

By late 2013 there began an easing of credit requirements, the foreclosure inventory had been mostly disposed of, and home mortgage funds became more available, but it was still anticipated that the housing segment would not fully recover until as late as 2016–2017.

2.8 TRADE ASSOCIATIONS

In response to the proliferation of regulatory agencies, a variety of **trade associations** assumed even greater importance in their protection and promotion of the interests of individuals and member firms. Membership is strictly voluntary, but the benefits are great enough to provide broad appeal to those who join. It is a starting point where a community of interests exists, resulting in a banding together in order to protect and enhance those interests.

Several important trade associations include the following:

1. *Mortgage Bankers Association of America (MBA).* Applying their motto, "One Voice. One Vision. One Resource," the MBA is widely recognized as a very influential voice regarding all aspects of mortgage banking. Promoting fair and ethical lending practices, this trade association offers a wide range of educational programs and publications for members and the public at large. In support of its emphasis on expanding homeownership and extending access to affordable housing to all Americans, the MBA provides a platform for seeking innovative solutions to ongoing critical industry challenges via education, research, and information for those charged with making industry-wide decisions.

2. *American Bankers Association (ABA).* This voluntary organization provides a voice for the small, regional, and large banks with an emphasis on recognizing that government policies must take into account the industry's diversity. Representing the nation's $13 trillion banking industry and its two million employees, the ABA functions with the belief that banks perform a critical role in America's economic growth as well as job creation. Toward this end, the ABA supports reasoned regulation while arguing against that which will inhibit business growth. The accompanying American Institute of Banking offers a broad educational program for member banks, government agencies, economists, researchers, and the public.

3. *National Association of Mortgage Brokers (NAMB).* In existence since 1973, NAMB remains the lobbying group for loan brokers and homebuyers nationwide. Committed to promoting a high degree of professionalism, members subscribe to a code of ethics pledged to promote integrity, professionalism, and confidentiality. NAMB provides mortgage brokers with professional education opportunities, including demanding certification programs and the recognition of members with the highest levels of professional knowledge and education. The mortgage brokerage industry is regulated by federal as well as state laws and licensing boards. NAMB's active lobbying and advocacy efforts therefore focus on both national and state issues.

4. *Community Mortgage Banking Project (CMBP).* CMBP is a coalition of lenders that have come together to support legislative and regulatory reform of the mortgage market. The project's

major concern is that the consumer is at risk of losing many of the benefits attributed to access to home mortgages due to legislative and regulatory proposals promoting the consolidation of the mortgage industry into the hands of a few mega lenders. The CMBP thereby supports enhanced consumer access, consumer and investor transparency, and local competition and choice while promoting quality service and an ability to sell loans to a secondary market that will assure lower costs for borrowers.

5. *National Association of Professional Mortgage Women (NAPMW)*. While not a women's-only organization, the association focuses on members, male and female, who want to excel in what they do. Since women make up the majority of professionals in the mortgage/banking profession, the NAPMW was first organized to help them advance in business, personal, and leadership development. The association has since expanded its up-to-date education program to include any employer and/or employee who want to be able to best serve their customers and succeed in their careers.

Other entities have access to trade associations focused on their specialized endeavors. The National Association of Federal Credit Unions (NAFCU), the Consumer Bankers Association (CBA), and the National Reverse Mortgage Lenders Association (NRMLA) are but a few of the numerous organizations dedicated to improving their industries. In most instances, this is accomplished via education and lobbying efforts.

Chapter Summary

Past deregulation due to the repeal of the Glass-Steagall Act resulted in a blurring of bank identities, resulting in keen competition for many institutions to seek a share of the home mortgage business. Whereas in the past savings banks, commercial banks, and life insurance companies were more specific in their real estate financing goals, many became a part of the easing home financing environment found between 2001 and 2007, offering various home financing loan options. Credit unions emerged to capture a share of the home loan business.

In general, we can still say that savings banks favor longer term residential home loans and life insurance companies are more interested in larger loan packages. Commercial banks, while having become more active in residential lending, still prefer shorter term equity line loans and construction and auto loans. Credit unions are member organizations and have become more active in the real estate lending arena.

In the wake of the 2008 financial crises, congressional action emphasizing reform and regulation had a major impact upon the economy's housing segment. Regulatory agencies were eliminated or merged in an attempt to avoid any future repeat of the crises. New oversight measures affecting mortgage brokers and appraisers were enacted but allowing large banks to be less affected.

The increase in regulatory oversight stimulated the growth of trade associations as various segments of the financial arena sought ways to influence the changing legal environment.

Important Terms and Concepts

- Bridge loan
- California Department of Financial Institutions (DFI)
- Commercial bank
- Correspondent
- Department of Business Oversight (DBO)
- Deposit Insurance Fund (DIF)
- Equity participation
- Federal Deposit Insurance Corporation (FDIC)
- Federal Home Loan Mortgage Corporation (FHLMC)
- Federal Housing Finance Agency
- Federal National Mortgage Association (FNMA)
- Federal Reserve Bank Board (FRBB)
- Financial Institutions Reform, Recovery, and Enforcement Act (FIRREA)
- Financial intermediary
- Home Mortgage Disclosure Act
- Institutional lender
- Interim loan
- Life insurance company
- Loan-to-value ratio
- Lock-in clause
- Mutual savings bank
- Office of the Comptroller of the Currency (OCC)
- Office of Thrift Supervision (OTS)
- Pension fund
- Rate lock-in
- Savings bank
- Swing loan
- Take-out loan
- Thrift institution
- Time deposit
- Trade association
- Usury

Reviewing Your Understanding

Questions for Discussion

1. Briefly explain the difference between a commercial bank and a savings bank (thrift).
2. List three lending characteristics for each of the following lending institutions:
   a. Savings bank
   b. Commercial bank
   c. Life insurance company
3. Identify one trend affecting the lending policies for each one of the principal lending institutions operating in California.
4. What is the difference between a regulatory agency and a trade association?

Multiple-Choice Questions

1. Which of the following is not an institutional lender?
   a. Mortgage company
   b. Commercial bank
   c. Savings bank
   d. Life insurance company

2. The term "savings bank" includes
   a. thrift institutions.
   b. savings and loan associations.
   c. credit unions.
   d. all of the above.

3. Savings banks are required to have a majority of their assets in:
   a. real estate loans.
   b. savings accounts.
   c. checking accounts.
   d. the stock market.

4. The Bank Insurance Fund (BIF) merged with SAIF into a single insurance fund, the Deposit Insurance Fund (DIF), providing for up to
   a. $100,000 insurance of bank accounts.
   b. unlimited insurance for checking accounts.
   c. $250,000 insurance of bank accounts.
   d. any amount tied to inflation-indexed accounts.

5. The FDIC now insures deposits:
   a. up to $250,000 per account.
   b. up to $250,000 per depositor for each account.
   c. up to $100,000 per account.
   d. up to $250,000 per depositor per bank.

6. Easy-to-qualify loan instruments of the early 2000
   a. have had no effect on housing inventory.
   b. resulted in reducing foreclosures.
   c. made homeownership impossible for millions of potential buyers.
   d. are criticized as the major contributor to the housing crisis.

7. Loans combining construction and permanent financing are commonly referred to as
   a. dual.
   b. take-out.
   c. all-inclusive.
   d. combination.

8. Which institutional lender favors very large commercial property loans?
   a. Savings banks
   b. Credit unions
   c. Life insurance companies
   d. Savings and loan associations

9. NMLS is an acronym for:
   a. National Mortgage Loan System.
   b. Nationwide mortgage Loan Servicing.
   c. National Mortgage Licensing System.
   d. National Mortgage License Service.

10. Regarding commercial banks
    a. acquisitions and mergers became unpopular after the subprime meltdown of 2007.
    b. small banks absorbed large banks in order to stay afloat.
    c. large banks became too big to allow them to fail.
    d. regional and nationwide banks became more stable during 2007–2008.

11. In their efforts to raise money for mortgage lending, savings banks have turned to such devices as
    a. mortgage-backed bonds.
    b. disintermediation.
    c. unsecured personal loans.
    d. all of the above.

12. The bulk of funds held by commercial banks is in the form of
    a. certificates of deposit (CDs).
    b. cash.
    c. demand deposits.
    d. securities.

13. "Short sale" most nearly means:
    a. selling a house in a very short period of time.
    b. selling a house for less than what is owed to the lender.
    c. the sale of a single family residence during the recession.
    d. the selling of a house when the buyer is "short" on cash.

14. The legislation that initiated the CFPB to oversee all aspects of financial markets is
    a. Glass-Steagall Act.
    b. Dodd-Frank Bill.
    c. the Business Oversight Act.
    d. Gramm-Leach Bliley Act.

15. Freddie Mac was established to
    a. provide insurance for savings accounts.
    b. govern the operations of savings banks.
    c. create a secondary market for savings banks.
    d. regulate checking accounts for savings banks.

16. Finance companies
    a. appeal to hard-to-finance borrowers.
    b. are usually offered with no pre-payment penalty.
    c. are generally characterized by lower interest rates.
    d. make loans only if secured by personal property.

17. Insuring the deposits of commercial banks and savings banks is the
    a. Office of Thrift Supervision.
    b. Savings Association Fund.
    c. Federal Home Loan Mortgage Corporation.
    d. Federal Deposit Insurance Corporation.

18. When a lender takes an upfront share of the income produced by a property, it is called
    a. equity participation.
    b. a roll-over provision.
    c. a shared investment.
    d. intermediary subordination.

19. Which federal law tracks the lending practices of banks and thrift institutions to ensure fair borrower treatment?
    a. Borrower's Rights Act
    b. Home Fairness Act
    c. Resolution Trust Act
    d. Community Reinvestment Act

20. Since the economic debacle of 2007, down payments for the purchase of a home are expected to become
    a. more flexible.
    b. more stringent.
    c. more receptive to buyers of high-priced homes.
    d. none of the above.

CASE & POINT

The Secure and Fair Enforcement for Mortgage Licensing Act of 2009 (SAFE)

Fueled by what some believed to be overzealous action, Congress passed the Secure and Fair Enforcement for Mortgage Licensing Act of 2009, which in turn enacted the Nationwide Mortgage Licensing System (NMLS) in an attempt to create a minimum continuity and conformity regarding the licensing of mortgage originators across the country. Designed as the central repository of licensing information, state agencies (e.g., California Bureau of Real Estate, formerly called the Department of Real Estate) remain the regulatory arm of the program.

All California mortgage loan originators (MLOs) are required to take a national test after completing 20 hours of required pretest education. In every year except the initial year of registration, every MLO must meet an eight-hour continuing education (CE) and testing requirement for maintenance of their license. California DOES NOT require any state specific or additional education beyond these NMLS educational requirements. Each originator must initially provide credit information, submit fingerprints, and undergo a federal background check. California's current real estate licensing requirements are some of the most rigorous in the nation, already requiring the submission for fingerprinting background and the completion of 45 hours of continuing education study every four years.

An educational exception is made for MLOs, which function as an employee of a depository institution, a subsidiary that is owned and controlled by a depository institution and regulated by a federal banking agency, or an institution regulated by the Farm Credit Administration. These originators must register with the NMLS. It is presumed that the agency provides sufficient oversight and education that the initial test and the annual CE testing are superfluous. Initially, the ability to escape the testing requirement resulted in a flight of MLOs to seek bank employee status. There is now support, in an effort to level the playing field, to require all MLOs, regardless of with whom they are employed, to adhere to all of the licensing requirements.

The system was originated as a way to keep track of originators nationwide and to prevent MLOs who are disciplined or convicted for breaking a law in one state from merely going to another state and continuing his or her bad actions. At the same time, the new regulation has spawned a whole new industry for those offering the initial 20-hour educational course as well as the annual "crash courses" designed to help licensees pass the tests. The annual licensing process is expensive and critics wonder if the national registration process is accomplishing its goal.

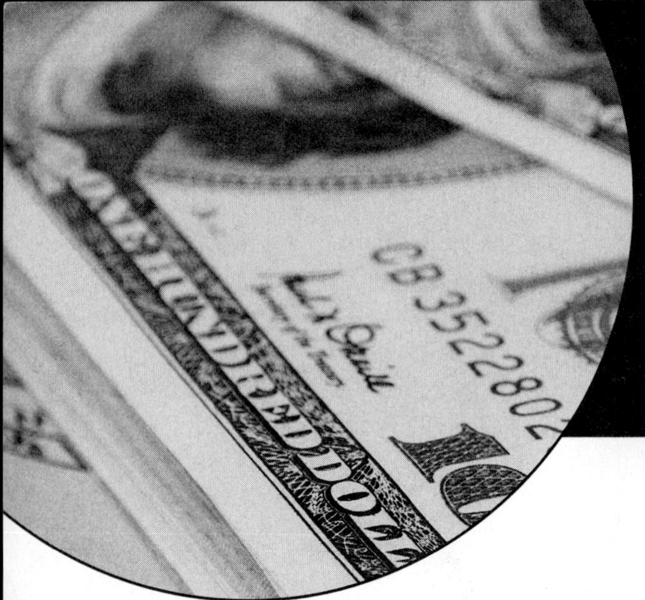

NONINSTITUTIONAL LENDERS AND THE CALIFORNIA REAL PROPERTY LOAN LAW

3

PREVIEW

In Chapter 2, institutional lenders were described as real estate lenders whose activities are highly regulated by various state and federal agencies.

In this chapter, you will study noninstitutional lenders—real estate lenders whose activities are not as strictly regulated as institutional lenders. Noninstitutional lenders include private parties, mortgage companies, syndicates, real estate investment trusts, pension and trust funds, endowment funds, and credit unions.

After completing this chapter, you will be able to:

- List at least five major noninstitutional lenders.
- Describe major provisions of the California Real Property Loan Law.
- Discuss the role that mortgage correspondents, mortgage bankers, mortgage companies, and mortgage brokers play in real estate finance.
- Discuss why pensions and trust funds are diminishing in importance while credit unions are increasing in importance in the financing process.
- Describe how and why the role of the real estate broker as a financial advisor is becoming increasingly challenging.

3.1 PRIVATE PARTY LENDERS

Although the term *private party lenders* in its broadest sense refers to virtually all nongovernment lenders, for our purpose, a **private lender** means a person who lends directly to another person. This narrow definition will help distinguish a private lender from the other forms of noninstitutional lenders discussed in this chapter.

Lack of Structure

There is no formal structure to the private lender industry. Individuals ordinarily do not operate in concert with one another. Private lenders have no association such as those found with other forms of lenders and are, at best, highly fragmented and scattered throughout California. An individual may, of course, form a partnership or a corporation, but these are mere business organizations designed to facilitate the operation of the individual's investments into real estate trust deeds or mortgage loans.

Unlike institutional lenders, private individuals had in the past fewer laws and regulations that restricted their lending activities. There were no uniform policies; practices, procedures, and policies varied considerably from one private lender to another. Usury statutes dictate the maximum interest rate that can legally be charged and was the major yardstick by which private mortgages were measured. Exemptions from the usury law are discussed later in this chapter. The benefit of using this type of loan was the possibility of more flexible standards or money available in a shorter period of time. A borrower might use this lender because he did not qualify for a more "standard" loan or did not want to undergo the more rigorous scrutiny required with an institutional loan.

New Qualified Mortgage Rules

The introduction of the Qualified Mortgage (QM) rule by the Consumer Financial Protection Bureau (CFPB) imposed rules that gave pause to private lenders, especially related to making loans on single-family residences. Broadly defined, the rule limits the cost in fees and points to 3 percent, the borrower's total debt ratio (including all housing and consumer debt) cannot exceed 43 percent of their gross income, and the loan cannot contain an interest only or balloon payment provision or exceed a thirty-year term. The new rule was coupled with its Ability to Pay (ATR) regulation requiring a lender to make a "good faith" determination of a borrower's ability to repay a mortgage.

In return for following the new criteria, the loan receives the QM safe harbor designation wherein lenders are legally protected from most law suits from consumers who might later wish to complain about their mortgage circumstances.

Types of Private Lenders

Direct Private Lenders

People invest in real estate loans for a variety of reasons, primarily because they are not satisfied with the returns paid on other forms of investments. This difficulty in finding safe investment options became particularly acute as the economy faltered in the late 2000s. The return on typical "safe" bank savings and CD accounts fell, in some cases, to near zero percent, even if deposited for a three-year term. Despite the fact that these accounts were insured by the Federal Deposit Insurance Corporation up to a designated amount, depositors were dissatisfied with this low interest rate. In more normal times, the bank or thrift institution would have turned around and re-loaned the deposit money at a much higher rate of interest. In many instances, money became very scarce for those wanting to borrow. At the same time, real estate sales slowed, reducing a potential investment opportunity for those seeking a higher return. While making direct loans on real estate, a private lender can eliminate the go-between broker. Caution must be exercised as the appraisal, loan screening, and other services provided by the intermediary are also eliminated. Thus, private lenders must perform these loan services themselves. On the plus side, however, where the risks are greater, the rewards for the private lender may also be greater in the form of higher interest rate yields, subject to usury and the new Qualified Mortgage rules.

Indirect Private Lenders

In order to obtain a higher interest rate or to overcome the loan screening burdens of direct lending, many private individuals place money through a mortgage broker. This is a cooperative relationship in which investors rely upon a mortgage broker for expertise, while the broker assists borrowers who don't necessarily meet the qualifying guidelines of institutional lenders. The private lender's lack of knowledge and sophistication can be addressed at the same time that he or she is matched with a borrower who needs private money. The key for success is that the broker recommend "suitable" transactions, protecting both the investor and the prospective borrower. In short, the broker takes a borrower and a lender and puts them together, as seen in Figure 3.1. The broker's commission is usually paid for by the borrower.

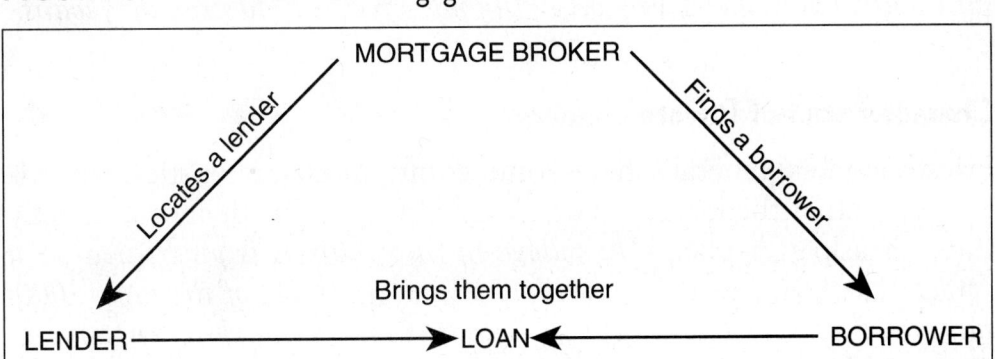

FIGURE 3.1 The role of the mortgage broker.

```
                    MORTGAGE BROKER
                    /              \
           Locates a lender    Finds a borrower
                  /                    \
                 /   Brings them together \
                ↓                          ↓
         LENDER ─────────→ LOAN ←───────── BORROWER
```

Source: © 2016 OnCourse Learning

While these transactions can be done on a non-qualified mortgage basis, both broker and lender lose the protection against subsequent lawsuits afforded by complying with the QM regulations.

Sellers as Private Lenders

In the process of selling property, a seller sometimes becomes a lender. A buyer may not have enough cash for the down payment or may choose not to tie up his or her capital in equity. Hence the seller is placed in the position of either having to turn down the offer, renegotiate more favorable terms, or "carry back a loan." This is usually the difference between the down payment plus a new loan and the sales price. The vast majority of these seller carry back loans are in the form of a junior encumbrance, typically a second trust deed. On some occasions they may be first loans, where a seller is willing to finance the entire transaction him- or herself, such as on a free and clear property (property free of any loans). In effect, sellers become lenders by financing part or all of their equity.

It should also be mentioned that seller carry back loans are exempt from usury laws; that is, sellers can charge any interest rate they wish, as noted later in this chapter.

NOTE: Logically, it was thought that seller financing would become more important as more stringent qualifying guidelines were adopted in the financing arena. For instance, it seemed to make sense that a borrower who had a 10 percent down payment with a seller willing to "carry 10 percent" as a second trust deed, allowing the institutional lender to make only an 80 percent loan-to-value ratio loan, would be acceptable to institutional lenders. But, the risk-averse lending practices in the late 2000s eliminated seller financing in such situations—resulting in a reduction of some real estate transactions—at a time when housing sales were declining. Fewer seller carry backs were also due to sellers not having enough equity in their property. By late 2014, home values had appreciated sufficiently that lenders were becoming more receptive to secondary loans.

Characteristics of Private Lenders

Private lenders generally have some common characteristics, regardless of whether the loan is made directly by the individual or indirectly through a loan broker. *The following information is predicated on a "typical" market operation. While the lending abuses of the early 2000s suspended some of the use of seller financing, the market functions in cycles and by late 2014 seller financing was reintroduced as a viable part of a few real estate financing options. It is anticipated that the trend will increase as seller equity positions grow and lender guidelines become more flexible.*

- Mortgage brokers, who represent some private lenders, are usually very sophisticated and provide guidelines and counseling for their investor clients.
- Higher interest rates are normally charged to the borrowers that present a higher risk. However, exceptions exist in seller carry back transactions. A seller may be willing to settle for the lower interest rate on the seller carry back than what an institutional lender quoted on new first loan so that buyers can complete the transaction.
- Most private lenders operate in the second trust deed market. This is created by the needs of the marketplace, when a seller carries back a second deed of trust. In some cases, these second loans are thereafter sold to investors, usually at a discount, when the seller needs cash. Today's secondary market reluctance to purchase loans that include seller carry back loans reduced, at least temporarily, the use of such second trust deeds. Part of the mortgage broker's responsibility includes "structuring" the transaction and its terms depending upon whether the seller anticipates retaining or selling the note.
- Private lenders rarely make the primary loan and almost never get involved in construction financing. Prime loans are those that involve the least risk to lenders and are usually first liens.
- Loans in the past were on single-family dwellings because this was most familiar to the typical private investor, and also because the size of the loan is relatively modest. The new QM rules may impact lenders' preference in the future.
- The term of a private loan is usually short—most commonly between two and five years—and often includes a balloon payment. When institutional lenders accept secondary financing, they usually require specific note requirements, including a minimum term and sometimes a minimum interest rate, and the note must be structured accordingly. The QM rule regarding balloon payments may limit the use of such secondary financing to non-QM first trust deeds and mortgages.
- Monthly collections may be performed through a mortgage company or financial institution, though individual lenders may in some cases collect themselves. The setup and collection fees charged by commercial and savings banks are relatively small, since these institutions are interested in obtaining the customer's account. Some offer free collection service when the customer maintains a minimum balance in a savings or checking account.

3.2 USURY LAW

Many states have passed laws establishing the maximum rate of interest that can be charged on various types of loans. Interest rates that exceed the maximum rate are considered usurious and therefore illegal. In some instances if a lender is found guilty of usury, the borrower would not have to pay any interest!

In California the maximum rate for loans secured by real property is the greater of 10 percent or 5 percent above the Federal Reserve Bank of San Francisco discount rate, unless the lender is exempt from the law. California regulations exempt from the usury law institutional lenders such as banks and their loan *correspondents*, thrift institutions, and life insurance companies. Also exempt from usury laws are noninstitutional lenders including *mortgage companies*, industrial loan companies, **credit unions**, personal property brokers, owners who carry back paper when they sell, and any transaction that uses a real estate broker. This law is almost primarily for direct private lenders. For example, real estate loans from regulated institutional lenders can be at any rate, whereas an actual direct, hard money real estate loan (not a seller carry back) from a private lender is not exempt, unless a real estate licensee is handling the transaction.

The pros and cons of usury laws have long been debated. Proponents believe that usury laws protect consumers against certain greedy lenders, while opponents believe usury laws restrict the supply of loan funds and drive some borrowers to do business with illegal loan sharks. See Figure 3.2. The emergence of payday loans (discussed next) and

FIGURE 3.2 A loan shark.

Source: © 2016 OnCourse Learning

past subprime lending abuses re-introduced the question of what is usurious in today's lending market.

Payday Loans

The **payday loan** controversy deals directly with the usury laws and their ability or inability to protect consumers. In theory, these loans were to be short term and for small amounts to tide one over to the next paycheck. Many acknowledge that there is a need for some mechanism allowing consumers to manage short-term emergencies that were not calculated in their monthly budgets. But many also believe that payday loans have become mostly predatory and their goal seems to be to keep people perpetually in debt.

Usually a payday loan requires a borrower to write a personal check payable to the lender for the amount to be borrowed plus the fee for the privilege of borrowing it. The borrower receives the amount less the fee while the company holds the check until its due date, usually two weeks or the borrower's next pay day. When due, if the borrower—who was short cash or he or she wouldn't have had to borrow—cannot pay the amount, it can be rolled over or extended for an additional fee.

Evidence suggests that the bulk of these loans are extended numerous times with the eventual fees far exceeding the initial amount borrowed. Reports conclude that it is not unusual to have interest rates on such loans, due to the numerous extensions, equal up to 300 percent or more. Essentially, many of these loans cease being short term but become long-term debt burdens that are designed to be unpayable.

The question, of course, is how do these lenders escape the usury regulations? In some states the laws are simply lax, but more recently the payday loan operators have teamed up with local banks to provide some legitimacy to the program. Remember, banks are not subject to the usury legislation. The banks became interested because payday loans represent a very lucrative fee income structure.

In fact, banks have developed their own hybrid program called "overdraft privilege" or "overdraft protection." Instead of returning a check for insufficient funds, the bank charges a fee from $15 to $35 every time the account is overdrawn. In some cases, the customer can have funds automatically transferred from a savings account to the checking account to cover the overdrawn amount. Of course, there is a fee albeit less than the above overdraft fee.

Some rules have been put into place to regulate bank practices. Federal law requires that account holders must be allowed to opt in to overdraft protection rather than be automatically enrolled. Additionally, banks are no longer able to charge for multiple "hot checks" (the practice of cashing the largest check first in order to enhance the possibility of more subsequent checks being deemed overdrawn). Plus, maximum fee schedules are now imposed. But the payday loans continue to be highly criticized, though they go mostly unregulated. A final note regarding overdraft protection: Some lenders view this use as an indication of a borrower's inability to manage credit, and multiple uses can affect how a borrower is perceived as a candidate for a home loan.

Mortgage Entities

The terms **mortgage banker** and **mortgage broker** are frequently used interchangeably, but there are significant differences. A common aspect is that both the banker and the broker generally function as an entity that matches a borrower together with a lender/investor in exchange for a fee/commission with the lender becoming the other partner in the relationship. The entities generally originate and process the loan similarly but differ in the underwriting and funding aspects of the loan procedure.

A few definitions will help clarify how it works. In the mortgage business, "originate" means to discuss the various loan options with a potential borrower and acquire the loan application. To "process" the loan refers to the acquisition of the required documentation from the borrower. "Underwriting" is the use of guidelines to determine if a loan request meets the lender's criteria for approval. This often involves adhering to the regulations imposed by secondary market entity that will eventually purchase the loan for its portfolio. The "lender/investor" is the entity that will ultimately fund the loan prior to its sale to the secondary market, which today is often Fannie Mae or Freddie Mac. Finally, the "funding" of the loan is just what it sounds like; it is the provision of the money being lent. We will hear more about each of these elements of the loan process later.

Agency Structure & Characteristics

Mortgage bankers are generally incorporated businesses that can make loans with their own funds or through a line of credit. In all but rare situations, mortgage bankers ultimately sell the loans to various investors within the secondary market.

If a mortgage banking company represents a life insurance company, bank thrift association, pension fund, or other lender, it is called a **mortgage correspondent**. It "corresponds" on behalf of its principal in dealing with prospective borrowers for which it is paid a fee.

The correspondent originates, processes, funds, closes, and possibly services the loan.

Mortgage bankers often function within exclusive territories, in which case they may be entitled to a fee even if they did not originally solicit the loan. During the height of the subprime loan era, it was not uncommon to have a mortgage banker, who was functioning as a wholesale correspondent, competing with a retail office providing loans with different rates and terms. This no longer occurs with any frequency as mortgage bankers more often represent out-of-area entities.

Mortgage brokers, on the other hand, while also arranging loans between borrowers and lender/investors, typically do not fund or service the loans they originate. After funding and closing the loan, the lending source generally sells the loan to the secondary market. The broker earns a fee or commission for his or her efforts. The word *correspondent* is also used to describe the mortgage broker, especially when originating government loans.

In California, mortgage companies are licensed by either the Department of Corporations (DOC) or the Bureau of Real Estate, and they are subject to lending and other general business regulations. There has been controversy over whether loan representatives of banks, who are generally licensed under the DOC, have an advantage in that they have functioned under less restrictive disclosure requirements than those with real estate licenses. The new Recovery Act of 2008 made some attempts to level the playing field by requiring consistent licensing laws, which is discussed more fully in the Case & Point in Chapter 2.

Mortgage entities may also engage in a number of related real estate activities including real estate brokerage, development, construction, and property management.

Bankers, Brokers, and Other Lenders

Which entity a borrower selects when seeking a home loan depends largely on personal preference or knowledge. There are advantages and disadvantages accompanying the selection including the number of loan options, closing cost differences, and processing time frames.

A mortgage banker more often has a corporate approach to home mortgage lending. While there may be a sense of stability accompanying a bank loan, the number of loan options may be limited to the few in-house programs as well as to the fee structure dictated by the bank. The loan officer is often charged with obtaining the paperwork from a would-be borrower and then passing it on to the underwriting staff.

This process can result in less scrutiny up-front of the necessary information to assure loan approval, and in some cases, the loan officer may not be as knowledgeable regarding the approval guidelines.

A mortgage broker is much like a matchmaker, pairing the borrower with the appropriate loan option. In the past, a broker might have numerous lending sources with each having varied requirements for borrower and property approval. Today, most brokers still have a few lender sources but the differences are generally related to the lender "overlays," the guidelines in excess of the secondary market general requirements but specific to the individual approving lender. These overlay differences may affect areas like the borrower's income or employment qualification and credit standards as well as property requirements. Prior to the financial crises in 2008, mortgage brokers accounted for around 70 percent of all home mortgage loans. After significant reduction, mortgage brokers are recapturing market share and in late 2014 were originating approximately 50 percent of all home mortgages.

Brokers were credited in the past with helping borrowers who had less than flawless credit. With the introduction of risk-based credit scoring (see Case & Point following Chapter 6), the playing field has been leveled among all lender types. At best a broker may devote more time to assisting in the development of more appropriate credit.

Finally, the bank representative may be salaried and not nearly as motivated as the broker, who is paid only if the loan closes. On the other hand, some believe being salaried removes any temptation to "steer" the borrower into a loan option that may pay the broker more in commission. In the past steering was not limited to only brokers, and new regulations make such action mostly unavailable.

Bottom line, a borrower generally "shops for a loan" or relies upon a recommendation from a trusted individual. Loan comparisons are more difficult in today's lending environment, and a borrower must be sure he or she understands the varying rates and fees.

We must mention a third source of loans, the **local bank** or credit union, sometimes referred to as retail or "direct" lenders. There remains a widespread belief that a regular customer of a local bank may acquire preferred treatment as a loan applicant. With nearly all loans now originated with the intent of selling the loan almost immediately to the secondary market, it is difficult for lenders to vary from the general guidelines. Preferred status might be available for other than home loans. Depending upon the entity, there may be fewer loan options available.

A final designation is the portfolio lender, usually community banks, credit unions, and savings and loans companies. Portfolio lenders use money from the customer's bank deposits to fund loans and retain them in their portfolios. Since a portfolio loan does not have to meet the specifications of a loan to be sold into the secondary market, some borrower or property approval guidelines might be more flexible. Most lenders still prefer to approve loans based on secondary market guidelines, and the number of portfolio loans has been much reduced in recent years.

3.3 REAL PROPERTY LOAN LAW

Subprime Borrowers and Predatory Lending

The collapse of the subprime lending environment led to lots of finger-pointing regarding who was to blame for the excesses and abuses committed. Questions arose such as: Was it the loan programs developed and marketed to consumers that were primarily responsible? Did the appraisers play a role in accelerating home values? Did consumers, anxious to buy a home at any price, play a part in the ultimate failure of subprime lending practices? While we continued to debate who or what to blame, the need for the Real Property Loan Law became very clear.

The original motivation for subprime loans to allow more buyers to purchase homes was credible. The constant reduction in loan qualification requirements, however, resulted in too many people buying homes that they would soon discover they could not afford. **Subprime loans** were usually granted to homeowners with low credit scores who wished to purchase or refinance a home. Subprime loans were also granted to credit-damaged or lower-income borrowers. These loans were granted at higher interest rates and fees to reflect the additional risk incurred by the lender. Many of these loans had two- or three-year terms, promoted on the basis that the short term would allow the borrower to correct any credit blemishes and then be eligible for a refinance at better rates and terms, all with the anticipation that home values would continue in their never-ending ascent. In most cases, the borrower did not improve his or her credit record over the two- or three-year term. Because of the circumstances created for these borrowers, the focus often became enticing subprime homeowners into a series of refinances in which their equity was stripped away by high fees and balloon payments that led to another larger refinance. This process was repeated until the homeowner's equity was totally depleted, often resulting in foreclosure. Then, home values not only stopped increasing, they began to decline.

Consumer advocates and various government agencies became increasingly concerned that some lenders had taken advantage of the situation by charging excessive interest and fees beyond a reasonable markup for the additional risk of granting loans to subprime borrowers. Numerous new regulations were adopted in 2009 in an effort to curb such excesses of "predatory lending."

Purpose of the Mortgage Loan Broker Law

Individuals may become indirect lenders by investing through an intermediary, called a mortgage broker. In California, this intermediary must be a licensed real estate broker, and is hence called a loan broker, and governed by Sections 10240 through 10248 of the California Business and Professions Code (B&P) (Article 7: Real Property Loans). This segment of the real estate law is popularly referred to as the "Mortgage Loan Broker Law" by real estate practitioners.

The purpose of the **Real Property Mortgage Loan Law** is to protect certain borrowers who acquire loans secured by real estate. The law requires that prospective borrowers be supplied with complete loan information. The broker must provide the applicant with a completed **Mortgage Loan Disclosure Statement** (MLDS) when the loan is initiated and prior to the borrower being obligated to proceed with the loan. The MLDS, coupled with the Loan Estimate (LE) disclosure (more fully discussed in Chapter 10) provides a borrower with the details of the prospective loan. Rules have long required that these disclosures be provided to the borrower within three days of his or her submitting a loan application. The Mortgage Disclosure Improvement Act (MDIA) imposed additional disclosure rules, as discussed in Chapter 10.

Because of the perceived abuses associated with past subprime lending, a separate non-traditional MLDS disclosure form is required with any loan other than a typical fixed rate option.

Figure 3.3 is a reproduction of the Traditional Mortgage Loan Disclosure Statement produced by the California Bureau of Real Estate. While duplicating some of the same information now contained in the new Loan Estimate form, the MLDS is still required in California. In thoroughly reviewing the MLDS, it will inform the borrower of the financial aspects of the proposed loan. In addition to information about estimated costs, expenses, and commissions to be paid by the applicant, the form addresses interest rate, monthly payment, and pre-payment options. In another attempt to ensure that borrowers are aware of their loan terms and to avoid any last minute surprises regarding loan costs, regulations require that the initial disclosure be within a certain "tolerance" of the final costs and terms. In other words, the final annual percentage rate (APR) calculation (disclosed on the LE,

FIGURE 3.3 Sample mortgage loan disclosure statement.

STATE OF CALIFORNIA
DEPARTMENT OF REAL ESTATE
Providing Service, Protecting You

MORTGAGE LOAN DISCLOSURE STATEMENT (TRADITIONAL)

RE 882 (Rev. 10/10)

Page 1 of 3

BORROWER'S NAME(S) _____

REAL PROPERTY COLLATERAL: THE INTENDED SECURITY FOR THIS PROPOSED LOAN WILL BE A DEED OF TRUST OR MORTGAGE ON (STREET ADDRESS OR LEGAL DESCRIPTION)
_____

THIS MORTGAGE LOAN DISCLOSURE STATEMENT IS BEING PROVIDED BY THE FOLLOWING CALIFORNIA REAL ESTATE BROKER ACTING AS A MORTGAGE BROKER
Humboldt Realty Corp/Humboldt Home Loans

INTENDED LENDER TO WHOM YOUR LOAN APPLICATION WILL BE DELIVERED (IF KNOWN)   ☑ Unknown

❖ For any federally related loans, HUD/RESPA laws require that a Good Faith Estimate (GFE) be provided. A RE 882 Mortgage Loan Disclosure Statement (MLDS) is required by California law and must also be provided.
❖ The information provided below reflects estimates of the charges you are likely to incur at the settlement of your loan. The fees, commissions, costs and expenses listed are estimates; the actual charges may be more or less. Your transaction may not involve a charge for every item listed and any additional items charged will be listed.

Item	Paid to Others	Paid to Broker
Items Payable in Connection with Loan		
Mortgage Broker Commission/Fee	$	$
Lender's Loan Origination Fee	$	$
Lender's Loan Discount Fee	$	$
Appraisal Fee	$	$
Credit Report	$	$
Lender's Inspection Fee	$	$
Tax Service Fee	$	$
Processing Fee	$	$
Underwriting Fee	$	$
Wire Transfer Fee	$	$
Other: _____	$	$
Items Required by Lender to be Paid in Advance		
Interest for ____ days at $_____ per day	$	$
Hazard Insurance Premiums	$	$
County Property Taxes	$	$
Mortgage Insurance Premiums	$	$
VA Funding Fee/FHA MIP/PMI	$	$
Other: _____	$	$
Reserves Deposited with Lender		
Hazard Insurance: ____ months at $_____ /mo.	$	$
Co. Property Taxes: ____ months at $_____ /mo.	$	$
Mortgage Insurance: ____ months at $_____ /mo.	$	$
Other: _____	$	$
Title Charges		
Settlement or Closing/Escrow Fee	$	$
Document Preparation Fee	$	$
Notary Fee	$	$
Title Insurance	$	$
Other: _____	$	$
Government Recording and Transfer Charges		
Recording Fees	$	$
City/County Tax/Stamps	$	$
Other: _____	$	$
Additional Settlement Charges		
Pest Inspection	$	$
Credit Life, and/or Disabilty Insurance (See Note below) *	$	$
Other: _____	$	$
Subtotals of Initial Fees, Commissions, Costs and Expenses	$	$
Total of Initial Fees, Commissions, Costs and Expenses		$

Compensation to Broker

Yield Spread Premium, Service Release Premium or Other Rebate Received from Lender $ _____
Yield Spread Premium, Service Release Premium or Other Rebate Credited to Borrower $ _____
Total Amount of Compensation Retained by Broker $ _____

* Note: The purchase of Credit Life and/or Disability Insurance is NOT required as a condition of making this proposed loan.

FIGURE 3.3 (Continued)

RE 882 -- Page 2 of 3

ADDITIONAL REQUIRED CALIFORNIA DISCLOSURES

Proposed Loan Amount $ _____
Initial Commissions, Fees, Costs and Expenses Summarized on Page 1 $ _____
Down Payment or Loan Payoffs/Creditors (List):

    Purchase / Payoff _____ $ _____
    _____ $ _____

Alterations / Land $ 0.00
Subtotal of All Deductions $ _____
Estimated Cash at Closing ☐ To You   ☐ That you must pay $ _____

GENERAL INFORMATION ABOUT LOAN

PROPOSED INTEREST RATE: _____ %

☑ FIXED RATE   ☐ INITIAL VARIABLE RATE

Proposed Monthly Loan Payments: $ _____ Principal & Interest (P&I)
If the loan is a variable interest rate loan, the payment will vary. See loan documents for details.
Total Number of Installments: _____
Loan Term: _____ Years _____ Months

BALLOON PAYMENT INFORMATION

IS THIS LOAN SUBJECT TO A BALLOON PAYMENT? ☐ Yes ☑ No

DUE DATE OF FINAL BALLOON PAYMENT (ESTIMATED MONTH/DAY/YEAR)

AMOUNT OF BALLOON PAYMENT $ _____

IF YES, THE FOLLOWING PARAGRAPH APPLIES:

NOTICE TO BORROWER: IF YOU DO NOT HAVE THE FUNDS TO PAY THE BALLOON PAYMENT WHEN IT COMES DUE, YOU MAY HAVE TO OBTAIN A NEW LOAN AGAINST YOUR PROPERTY TO MAKE THE BALLOON PAYMENT. IN THAT CASE, YOU MAY AGAIN HAVE TO PAY COMMISSIONS, FEES, AND EXPENSES FOR THE ARRANGING OF THE NEW LOAN. IN ADDITION, IF YOU ARE UNABLE TO MAKE THE MONTHLY PAYMENTS OR THE BALLOON PAYMENT, YOU MAY LOSE THE PROPERTY AND ALL OF YOUR EQUITY THROUGH FORECLOSURE. KEEP THIS IN MIND IN DECIDING UPON THE AMOUNT AND TERMS OF THIS LOAN.

PREPAYMENT INFORMATION

PREPAYMENT PENALTY? ☐ Yes ☐ No

OF YEARS THAT PREPAYMENT PENALTY IS IN EFFECT _____

MAXIMUM DOLLAR AMOUNT OF PENALTY _____

IS THERE A PREPAYMENT PENALTY FOR PAYING IN EXCESS OF 20% OF THE ORIGINAL OR UNPAID LOAN BALANCE?
☐ Yes ☑ No   If Yes, see loan documents for details.

TAXES AND INSURANCE

IMPOUND ACCOUNT? ☐ Yes ☐ No

IMPOUND ACCOUNT WILL INCLUDE

County Property Taxes	Mortgage Insurance	Hazard Insurance	Flood Insurance	Other: _____
☐ Yes ☐ No	☐ Yes ☐ No	☐ Yes ☐ No	☐ Yes ☐ No	☐ Yes ☐ No

APPROXIMATE AMOUNT THAT WILL BE COLLECTED MONTHLY
$ _____

IF NO, PLAN FOR THESE PAYMENTS ACCORDINGLY ➔

BORROWER MUST PLAN FOR PAYMENTS OF THE FOLLOWING ITEMS

County Property Taxes	Mortgage Insurance	Hazard Insurance	Flood Insurance	Other: _____
☐ Yes ☐ No	☐ Yes ☐ No	☐ Yes ☐ No	☐ Yes ☐ No	☐ Yes ☐ No

Note: In a purchase transaction, county property taxes are calculated based on the sales price of the property and may require the payment of an additional (supplemental) tax bill issued by the county tax authority. The payment of county property taxes (including supplemental bills) may be paid by your lender if an impound/escrow account has been established.

If an impound/escrow account has not been established, the payment of all tax bills including any and all supplemental tax bills will be the responsibility of the borrower(s).

OTHER LIENS

LIENS CURRENTLY ON THIS PROPERTY FOR WHICH THE BORROWER IS OBLIGATED

Lienholder's Name	Amount Owing	Priority

LIST LIENS THAT WILL REMAIN OR ARE ANTICIPATED TO REMAIN ON THIS PROPERTY AFTER THE PROPOSED LOAN FOR WHICH YOU ARE APPLYING IS MADE OR ARRANGED (INCLUDING THE PROPOSED LOAN FOR WHICH YOU ARE APPLYING):

Lienholder's Name	Amount Owing	Priority

NOTICE TO BORROWER: BE SURE THAT YOU STATE THE AMOUNT OF ALL LIENS AS ACCURATELY AS POSSIBLE. IF YOU CONTRACT WITH THE BROKER TO ARRANGE THIS LOAN, BUT IT CANNOT BE ARRANGED BECAUSE YOU DID NOT STATE THESE LIENS CORRECTLY, YOU MAY BE LIABLE TO PAY COMMISSIONS, COSTS, FEES, AND EXPENSES EVEN THOUGH YOU DO NOT OBTAIN THE LOAN.

FIGURE 3.3 (Continued)

RE 882 — Page 3 of 3

ARTICLE 7 COMPLIANCE

If this proposed loan is secured by a first deed of trust in a principal amount of less than $30,000 or secured by a junior lien in a principal amount of less than $20,000, the undersigned broker certifies that the loan will be made in compliance with Article 7 of Chapter 3 of the Real Estate Law.

WILL THIS LOAN BE MADE WHOLLY OR IN PART FROM BROKER CONTROLLED FUNDS AS DEFINED IN SECTION 10241(J) OF THE BUSINESS AND PROFESSIONS CODE?

☐ May   ☐ Will   ☐ Will Not

Note: If the broker indicates in the above statement that the loan "may" be made out of broker-controlled funds, the broker must inform the borrower prior to the close of escrow if the funds to be received by the borrower are in fact broker-controlled funds.

STATED INCOME

IS THIS LOAN IS BASED ON LIMITED OR NO DOCUMENTATION OF YOUR INCOME AND/OR ASSETS?

☐ Yes   ☑ No   If Yes, be aware that this loan may have a higher interest rate, or more points or fees than other products requiring documentation.

NOTICE TO BORROWER: THIS IS NOT A LOAN COMMITMENT

Do not sign this statement until you have read and understood all of the information in it. All parts of this form must be completed before you sign it. Borrower hereby acknowledges the receipt of a copy of this statement.

NAME OF BROKER	LICENSE ID NUMBER	BROKER'S REPRESENTATIVE	LICENSE ID NUMBER
	NMLS ID NUMBER		NMLS ID NUMBER

BROKER'S ADDRESS

BROKER'S SIGNATURE	DATE	OR SIGNATURE OF REPRESENTATIVE	DATE
BORROWER'S SIGNATURE	DATE	BORROWER'S SIGNATURE	DATE

Department of Real Estate license information telephone number: 877-373-4542, or check license status at www.dre.ca.gov

National Mortgage Licensing System:
http://mortgage.nationwidelicensingsystem.org/about/pages/nmlsconsumeraccess.aspx

The Real Estate Broker negotiating the loan shall retain on file for a period of three years a true and correct copy of this disclosure signed and dated by the borrower(s).

THE RE 885 MORTGAGE LOAN DISCLOSURE STATEMENT, NON-TRADITIONAL MORTGAGE MUST BE USED FOR NON-TRADITIONAL MORTGAGE LOANS OF RESIDENTIAL PROPERTY (1-4 UNITS).

Non-Traditional Mortgage Loans are loan products that allow the borrower to defer payments of principal or interest. If any of the payments are not full principal and interest payments, then it is considered a Non-Traditional Mortgage Loan.

Source: www.dre.ca.gov

discussed more fully in Chapter 10) must be within one-eighth percent of the original calculation or a new disclosure must be provided, signed, and returned prior to the consummation of the loan.

Exceptions to the Mortgage Loan Broker Law

It is easier to state which lenders and what transactions are not covered by the law than to list those that are covered. Exempt from the Real Property Loan Law are:

- Regulated institutional lenders.
- Purchase money transactions in which a seller, via his or her equity in the property, carries back a portion of the loan as part of the sale price. However, if a seller is in the business of carrying back loans in eight or more transactions per year, the Mortgage Loan Broker Law does apply.

- Loans secured by first trust deeds when the principal amount is $30,000 or more.
- Loans secured by junior trust deeds when the principal amount is $20,000 or more.

Maximum Commissions

The maximum commission rates mortgage loan brokers can charge on first trust deed loans under $30,000 and junior trust deeds under $20,000 (as shown in Table 3.1) have been consistently regulated for years. The difficulty of assuring that no violation of the law occurs regarding commissions or other factors on these lower loan amounts is the reason lenders impose minimum loan amounts on brokers.

As the table indicates, for loan amounts above these minimums the charges, for many years, were calculated on the basis of what the market would bear. Following the 2008 financial crises, commissions for all loans became an issue worthy of regulation. We discussed the Qualified Mortgage and the Ability to Repay rules, which limited the maximum broker income to 3 percent of the loan amount in any transaction, in Chapter 2.

Brokers must now establish a fee schedule (e.g.; 2 points per loan, calculated on the loan amount) from which they cannot deviate regardless of the loan amount and/or other circumstances. This rule is in response to past concerns that brokers determined their commission based upon the sophistication of the borrower, with a less knowledgeable borrower too often being charged a larger commission.

This inflexible rule, however, has its critics. There is no provision allowing for a reduction in the commission percentage on larger loans versus smaller loans or for allowing brokers the ability to adjust a fee in an effort to assist a cash-strapped buyer. This is another example of the fact that every decision can have an unintended consequence.

TABLE 3.1 Maximum commissions.

Type of Loan	PERCENTAGE COMMISSION			
	Less Than Two Years	Two Years but Less Than Three	Three Years and Over	Exempt Transactions
First trust deeds	5%	5%	10%	Loans of $30,000 and over
Junior trust deeds	5%	10%	15%	Loans of $20,000 and over

Source: © 2016 OnCourse Learning

Other Costs and Expenses

In another effort to avoid being labeled "predatory," lenders impose limitations on the fees that may be charged including appraisal, credit reports, escrow, title, insurance, notary, and recording. These fees may not exceed the actual costs and expenses incurred and paid. To eliminate the ability to steer a borrower to a broker-owned service provider (escrow, title, or insurance company) deemed an "affiliate," any fees paid to such related entities count as paid to the broker when calculating the 3 percent maximum income cap allowed.

For the lower loan amounts identified in Table 3.1, the total costs and expenses may not exceed 5 percent of the amount of the loan. However, if 5 percent of the loan is less than $390, the broker may charge up to that amount, provided that the charges do not exceed actual costs and expenses paid, incurred, or reasonably earned by the broker. Regardless of the size of the loan, as long as it comes under the Real Property Loan Law, the borrower cannot be charged more than $750 for miscellaneous costs and expenses.

To simplify, the foregoing costs and expenses can be translated into chart form, as shown in Table 3.2.

Balloon Payments

Under the QM rules, a balloon payment, along with interest only or negatively amortized provisions, are not allowed. These are considered to be harmful features and cannot be contained in loans wherein the lender seeks the protection against future borrower law suits afforded by a QM loan.

Loans provided to Fannie Mae, Freddie Mac, FHA, or VA (the secondary market for which most loans are destined) are all presumed to be qualified mortgages and cannot contain a balloon payment. While there is a provision in the rules for small and/or rural lenders that permit balloon payments under very specific guidelines, balloon payments are very much a thing of the past.

TABLE 3.2 Maximum charges for other costs and expenses.

LOAN AMOUNT	Under $7,801	$7,801 to $13,999	$14,000 to $29,999	First Loans of $30,000 and over and Junior Loans of $20,000 and over
MAXIMUM CHARGES	$390	5% of loan	$700	No legal limitations

—But not to exceed actual costs and expenses—

Source: © 2016 OnCourse Learning

Under the Real Property Loan Law, a balloon payment is prohibited if the term of the loan is for six years or less and the loan is secured by the dwelling place of the borrower. While these provisions do not apply to loans carried by sellers or loans made by regulated lenders, the QM protections are so coveted that the bulk of lenders forego balloon payments, especially when preparing the loan to be sold into the secondary market (noted above).

Insurance

A borrower is not required to purchase credit life or disability insurance (except in Cal Vet Loans) as a condition of obtaining the loan. However, the lender can insist, for self-protection and by the terms of the trust deed, that fire and hazard insurance be obtained on improved property until the loan has been repaid. If licensed to sell such insurance, the loan broker may also act as the insurance agent for the borrower, subject to the affiliated company rules governing total income as identified in the Qualified Mortgage guidelines. Borrowers are not obligated to purchase the coverage through the mortgage loan broker. They may purchase insurance from their own insurance agent and they are usually advised to shop around for the best rates.

3.4 SYNDICATIONS

A **syndication** is a group of two or more people who combine their financial resources for the purpose of achieving specific investment objectives. Investment capital can be pooled or combined for the purpose of financing real estate transactions or for the purchase of real property. Syndicates may take the legal form of a limited partnership (accompanied by limited liability), which is the most favored in California; a general partnership; corporation; real estate investment trust; or a joint venture.

Syndicates are formed for a variety of reasons, including these:

1. *Improved purchasing power* obtained by combining the resources of many who could not afford to purchase individually, but through the principle of leverage could acquire a relatively high-priced property.
2. *Better bargaining power* due to the application of the principle of leverage (less down payment), wherein a larger capital base can command lower prices and allow larger purchases. In purchasing larger properties, lower operating expense ratios are usually present.

3. *Diversification*, which enables investors to spread their capital into different types of investments or different properties and, thereby, limits their loss exposure in any one investment.
4. *Professional management and administration* of the real estate portfolio in order to minimize costs and maximize the benefits. Professional services may be too costly for the average investor and disproportionate to capital investment. By pooling resources with others, however, a team of specialists, such as attorneys, appraisers, real estate brokers, accountants, and investment analysts can be more affordable.

Individuals may participate in a syndication and collectively invest in a wide variety of real estate ventures. There are basically three types of syndication: (1) equity syndicates, which purchase real estate; (2) mortgage (or debt) syndicates, which grant loans to others for the purchase of real property, creating creditor/debtor relationships; and (3) a hybrid of these two, combining both equity and debt.

3.5 REAL ESTATE INVESTMENT TRUSTS AND ENDOWMENT FUNDS

The **real estate investment trust (REIT)** was created in 1960 with the goal of encouraging small investors to pool their resources with others in order to raise venture capital for real estate transactions. It has been called the mutual fund of the real estate business. Just as mutual funds invest in a diversified portfolio of corporate stocks and bonds, REITs invest in a diversified portfolio of real estate and mortgage investments, using a large number of investors who combine their funds.

Types of REITs

As with syndications, there are three types of REITs:

1. *Equity trusts*—investors buy income-producing property and obtain their return from current rents, tax benefits, and capital gains.
2. *Mortgage trusts*—investors loan money secured by real estate and obtain their income from interest and loan fees.
3. *Hybrid trusts*—a combination of these two types.

To qualify as a trust, there are many tests that must be met. Two main requirements are that there must be at least 100 different shareholders, and that at least 95 percent of its taxable income must be distributed to the investors each year. This latter requirement is to avoid the double taxation aspect of some corporations. (Note: a corporation shields the investor, but double taxation occurs as the corporate income is taxed once and then again when profits are distributed to the individuals).

The legal ramifications of REITs are beyond the scope of this book; anyone interested in forming or participating in REITs should seek legal counsel.

REITs as a Source of Financing

The favorable income tax incentives of REITs attract funds from thousands of small investors, which in turn become an important source of real estate financing. REITs concentrate on income-producing properties, most often large commercial projects. REITs generally do not limit themselves to one area or type of loan, but diversify their holdings both as to type of property and geographical location.

Lending activities of REITs center primarily around land development and take-out loans for such projects as condominiums, office buildings, shopping centers, garden and high-rise apartment complexes, hotels and motels, industrial properties, warehouses, and major single-family subdivision developments.

The Ups and Downs of REITs

During the economic crisis of the 1970s, many REITs folded under the pressures of poor management, excessive speculation, withdrawal and cancellation of take-out commitments, termination of bank lines of credit, poor credit analysis, excess building in many parts of the country (particularly in the condominium market and in recreational projects), and sagging demand.

In the 1980s, to restore confidence in the REIT, concessions worked out between REITs and the banking and securities industries slowly revived their activity. This slow revival continued until the late 1990s, when a hot stock market put a damper on REITs. People were getting better returns in their own investments. By 2001, the stock market declined and some money began to flow back into REITs. Within a few years, REITs were once again booming. REITs remain volatile, subject to the whims of the real estate market. Early in 2008, REITs gained popularity because commercial real estate was not as affected as residential property during the repositioning of the real estate market. By mid-2009, REITs became less influential as the economic slowdown grew in intensity and especially affected the speculative nature of real estate.

Pension Funds

Pension funds collect monthly contributions from workers, and occasionally from the employer, and then invest the proceeds in an attempt to create a lump sum of money upon which the worker may draw at retirement age. Examples include the California State Teachers Retirement Fund and various union funds, such as that of the United Auto Workers. The bulk of pension funds are invested in traditional securities, such as stocks, bonds, and various government instruments and are normally not used to make a direct loan in the real estate market.

However, with the advent of mortgage-backed securities, pension funds did become a significant player in the real estate market through the purchase of existing real estate loans in the secondary market.

It was anticipated that the many thousands of private pension funds, along with the state, local, and federal funds nationwide—all representing billions in assets—would represent a major source of real estate financing. This potential source has remained mostly unfulfilled. Investments in the ill-advised subprime mortgage market of the late 2000s, in expectation of promised high yields, resulted in large equity losses. Coupled with the assault on the sustainability of pension funds in many cities and states, it is unlikely that said funds will become available to the mortgage arena any time soon. Plus, when the subprime meltdown and its accompanying collapse of the derivative market occurred, huge losses were absorbed by some funds.

The heavy losses of these funds resulted in a significant withdrawal from the real estate investment arena. The California Public Employees' Retirement System (CalPERS) and the California State Teachers' Retirement System (CalSTRS) were two of the largest pension funds very involved in real estate investing, including programs that assisted their members in the acquisition of a home. In some cases, members could borrow against their account for the low down payment required and in other circumstances, actual loans were provided by the funds. The programs were discontinued and have yet to be resurrected, perhaps because new loan options now offer low down payments with which it would be difficult for the funds to compete. Bottom line, both CalPERS and CalSTRS were victims, along with many other pension funds, of the financial crises from which they never truly recovered and their members lost a valuable loan option.

Endowment Funds

Endowment funds of colleges and universities, hospitals, cemeteries, charitable foundations, and other endowed institutions operate like pension funds. They receive their funds in the form of gifts and attempt to invest in "safe" mortgages that will offer high returns. Accordingly, they have been perceived as a large potential source of financing for commercial and industrial properties, and in sale-leaseback arrangements. But, to a large extent, this has never materialized. Many commercial banks and mortgage companies handling investments for endowment funds were also hard hit by the collapse of the real estate derivative market noted above. Such funds, in large part (as of 2015), have yet to be recaptured in real estate investments.

3.6 FINANCE COMPANIES

Although involved chiefly in personal and consumer loans, **finance companies** (also known as credit companies or industrial banks) increased their participation in real estate lending as a precursor to subprime loans. These high-risk loans with high rates and short-term duration were typically less than seven years, and were often secured by a combination of real and personal property.

Many of these loans were junior trust deeds. The typical borrower was one who did not qualify for a prime loan from a thrift institution or bank. But as the explosion of subprime loans expanded to a new group of "niche" lenders who made riskier loans with constantly diminishing qualifying guidelines, the influence of finance companies diminished. While continuing to provide financing to the riskiest of borrowers, even this group of borrowers was reduced as payday loans (loans to be paid from a future pay check) grew in popularity. (See earlier payday loans comments.)

3.7 FINANCIAL ADVISORY ROLE OF THE REAL ESTATE BROKER

The idea of a "one-stop shop" has been discussed for years. It has always been enticing to think that real estate agents could assist buyers, to whom they have just sold a home, to acquire both home insurance and home financing through related entities and collect additional compensation for their efforts. Plus, agents would retain control of the transaction and thereby assist their buyers through the entire process. The introduction of computerized loan origination programs re-fueled the discussion with many believing that real estate agents were in a prime position to fulfill the mortgage needs of their clients. The QM rules around fees acquired from "affiliated" companies generally dampened enthusiasm for pursuing these additional revenue sources.

The temptation to seek a referral fee for assisting the borrower with the acquisition of financing should be approached with caution. A person who performs only real estate brokerage services is not a loan originator or "an arranger of credit." So, while with full disclosure, real estate agents may collect a fee for this service, there is a slippery slope to watch out for here—if the real estate broker assists the consumer by arranging financing in return for compensation, then he or she is a loan originator for purposes of Section 226.36. In addition, along with the court's affirmation that personal liability for providing accurate loan information accompanies the agent's involvement, regulations also mandate that the agent must perform actual services (often difficult to demonstrate or prove) to legally collect such fees.

Many real estate brokers do not want to take the chance that agents would get into areas beyond their expertise and that an inadvertent violation would occur.

Computerized Loan Origination

The advances in automated lending services by institutional lenders have had a dual effect on loan originations. While it made the preparation and submission process faster and easier, it also caused some mortgage originators to become less educated about loan requirements. It became easy to submit the loan to the automated program and let it determine if the borrower was qualified. The result was a substantial increase in what turned out to be less than qualified mortgage originators.

While a loan could be inserted into a desktop underwriting (DU) process, and the loan originator could acquire a loan approval, the loan still had to be submitted to an underwriter whose job it was to confirm all of the documentation. The old adage of "garbage in, garbage out" became prevalent as some computer approvals were obtained without obtaining the necessary documentation. When the final loan was submitted, too often underwriters required additional documentation or, in the worst cases, denied the loan.

As the subprime market faltered, qualifying guidelines tightened, and available sources of loan funds were reduced, the computerized models were best accompanied by well-informed loan originators who could counsel potential borrowers and acquire the necessary documentation for the loan process. In an effort to avoid the subprime abuses of the past, new regulations proliferated and loan originations once more became an arena requiring considerable expertise.

Buyer-Borrowers Going Directly Online to Obtain a Real Estate Loan

As the market boomed in the early 2000s, a surge of Internet use, coupled with heavy website advertising by lenders (like Lending Tree, Ditech, and Quicken Loans) encouraged many consumers to obtain real estate loans online. As the subprime market grew, these Web lenders depended upon the fact that borrowers required little documentation and could qualify with very low credit scores. It was easy to put everyone into a subprime loan, whether or not it was the best loan option for them or if they qualified for a less risky loan program.

When the market collapse occurred, most of the online purveyors were at least temporarily out of the market due to heavy losses. It took a number of years (Ditech didn't re-enter the market in any significant way until mid-2014) before the familiar names began to again appear, again promoting themselves heavily on television. As they re-emerged, the emphasis was on the well-qualified, "A type" borrowers. Internet lenders have neither the inclination nor the methods in place to perform a consulting function around credit correction or working through the "sticky" details related to employment, sourcing of funds, etc. Only local lenders generally provide this "service" on an everyday basis.

While Internet lenders are again promoting themselves, many borrowers recognize that local lenders are more often able to walk them through the maze of new qualifying requirements. But lending is cyclical and we could again see the emergence of the Internet lenders, especially if loan requirements become more flexible.

A more concerning development of the Internet world is the inaccurate information that proliferates and the number of potential borrowers who consequently become misinformed. While an informed borrower is welcome, the total reliance upon information obtained via the Internet and/or social media communications can too often result in borrowers either inappropriately opting themselves out of the loan arena or erroneously anticipating a higher than possible purchasing capacity. In either case, reliance upon the Internet for information does not necessarily serve potential borrowers very well.

Chapter Summary

Noninstitutional lenders include private parties, mortgage companies, syndicates, a variety of funds, and credit unions. Compared with institutional lenders, and in spite of the recent more limiting rules, there are comparatively fewer restrictions placed upon their lending activities.

Private lenders include direct private lenders, indirect private lenders, and sellers who carry back purchase money trust deeds. Junior loans were a major part of their past participation and catered to the borrower wishing to avoid the rigors of qualifying for an institutional loan. Their popularity typically grew as general lending qualifying guidelines tightened. Newly enacted Qualified Mortgage (QM) and Ability to Repay (ATR) rules have caused adjustments in this form of financing.

Mortgage bankers and mortgage companies are usually incorporated businesses that act as agents, or loan correspondents, for institutional lenders. As such, they are generally subject to the same laws and regulations as their principals. Many mortgage bankers also lend out their own funds, while mortgage brokers do not.

Under the Real Property Loan Law, mortgage loan brokers are limited as to the amount of costs, expenses, and commissions they may charge borrowers. These restrictions apply only to first loans of less than $30,000 and junior loans of less than $20,000.

Syndicates and real estate investment trusts each pool the funds of many people to invest in real estate and mortgages. In theory, they should be able to offer improved purchasing power, stronger bargaining positions, diversification, and professional management of their portfolios. But, to date, their success has been mixed.

Pension funds, trust funds, endowment funds, and credit unions are playing ever-expanding roles in financing real estate transactions, particularly where the traditional sources of financing are unwilling or unable to lend.

Computerization and rapidly expanding Internet use retain the potential to change the way real estate loans are analyzed and granted.

Important Terms and Concepts

Credit union
Endowment fund
Finance company
Local bank
Mortgage banker
Mortgage broker
Mortgage correspondent
Mortgage Loan Disclosure Statement
Payday loans
Private lender
Real Estate Investment Trust (REIT)
Real Property Mortgage Loan Law
Subprime loan
Syndication

Reviewing Your Understanding

Questions for Discussion

1. Differentiate between institutional and noninstitutional lenders.
2. How do the Qualified Mortgage and Ability to Repay rules impact lending?
3. How do sellers of real estate help finance the sale? To what extent are they governed by the usury law?
4. Who is exempt from the California Usury Law?
5. Distinguish among the following:
   a. mortgage banker
   b. mortgage company
   c. mortgage broker
   d. mortgage loan correspondent
6. What is a syndicate? How does it differ from a real estate investment trust?
7. What information does the Mortgage Loan Disclosure Statement (MLDS) convey to prospective borrowers?

Multiple-Choice Questions

1. The law specifically governing the amount of commissions loan brokers may earn is called the
   a. Real Estate Law.
   b. Real Property Loan Law. ✓
   c. Mortgage Loan Disclosure Law.
   d. Real Property Securities Act.

2. The Real Property Loan Law is embodied in the
   a. Civil Code.
   b. Code of Civil Procedures.
   c. Real Estate Code.
   d. Business and Professions Code. ✓

3. Exempt under the Real Property Loan Law are
   a. first trust deeds of under $30,000.
   b. second trust deeds of under $20,000.
   c. purchase money loans carried back by sellers. ✓
   d. loans maturing in more than six years.

4. Regarding computerized loan originations, the advances in automated lending services by institutional lenders has had a profound effect by
   a. making the preparation and submission process slower and more complicated.
   b. causing some mortgage originators to become less educated about loan requirements. ✓
   c. easing the qualifying of loan applicants.
   d. leading to more denials of loans even for well-qualified applicants.

5. Private lenders possess the following characteristic:
   a. they make highly subjective loan decisions.
   b. they charge lower interest rates on higher priced homes.
   c. they usually sell junior trust deed loans to financial institutions.
   d. they make loans usually secured by free and clear properties. ✓

6. The term of a private loan is usually:
   a. 30 years.
   b. 15 years.
   c. 10 years.
   d. 25 years.

7. The original motivation for subprime loans was to
   a. allow more buyers to purchase homes.
   b. meet the requirements of the Federal Housing and Recovery Act.
   c. upgrade lending standards.
   d. assist the home building industry to improve their profit margins.

8. The most popular organizational form of real estate syndication in California is
   a. general partnership.
   b. living trust.
   c. limited partnership.
   d. real estate investment trust.

9. An organized group of people who agree to save their money and to make loans to one another is called a
   a. syndication.
   b. credit union.
   c. pension fund.
   d. trust fund.

10. As a rule, credit unions most often deal with which of the following types of loans?
    a. Apartment property loans
    b. Short-term consumer loans
    c. Industrial property loans
    d. Commercial property loans

11. What is popularly called the "mutual fund" of the real estate business?
    a. Pension fund
    b. Credit union
    c. Syndication
    d. Real estate investment trust

12. Under the Real Property Loan Law, before a loan can be made, a loan broker must provide the applicant with
    a. an escrow closing statement.
    b. a Mortgage Loan Disclosure Statement.
    c. a RESPA Disclosure Statement.
    d. a deposit receipt.

13. A balloon payment is
    a. the same as a lump sum payment due on a straight note at maturity.
    b. a term used to describe a prepayment penalty.
    c. any payment made on a loan when the sales price has been inflated.
    d. any payment on a loan that is more than double the amount of the regular payment.

14. The Mortgage Loan Disclosure Statement (MLDS), coupled with the Loan Estimate Disclosure, provides a borrower with details of a prospective loan within how many business days of submitting a loan application?
    a. 3
    b. 5
    c. 7
    d. 10

15. California law sets the usury maximum for certain limited types of loans secured by real property at
    a. 10 percent.
    b. the discount rate charged by the Fed.
    c. 10 percent, or 5 points above the current Fed discount rate, whichever is higher. ✓
    d. 5 points above the prime rate.

16. Who is not exempt from California's usury law?
    a. Private hard money lenders who make direct loans ✓
    b. Commercial banks
    c. Transactions involving a real estate broker
    d. A seller who carries back a loan on behalf of the buyer of an owner-occupied home

17. The chief characteristic of private lenders is that they invest
    a. their own funds. ✓
    b. in prime real estate loans.
    c. large sums of money in any one loan.
    d. primarily in commercial real estate properties.

18. The traditional Mortgage Loan Disclosure produced by the California Bureau of Real Estate requires that the annual percentage rate (APR) calculation must be within what percentage of the original calculation or a new disclosure must be provided before the loan can be consummated?
    a. One-eighth percent ✓
    b. One-quarter percent
    c. One-half percent
    d. None of these

19. To prevent from being taxed on its income, an REIT must distribute annually at least what percent of its ordinary income to its shareholders?
    a. 100 percent
    b. 95 percent ✓
    c. 90 percent
    d. 85 percent

20. Which of the following, using a line of credit, lends its "own" money?
    a. Mortgage broker
    b. Mortgage banker ✓
    c. Loan agent
    d. Real estate agent

CASE & POINT

Yield-Spread Premiums: Good or Bad?

Mortgage brokers/lenders are usually paid for their efforts via an origination fee. This fee is disclosed on the HUD-1 Form along with identifying all of the costs associated with the acquisition of the loan. A yield spread premium (YSP) is a form of compensation received from a source lender/investor when the interest rate on the loan exceeds a lower rate for which the borrower qualifies, usually called the lender's par rate. It can also be used as an incentive for a broker to use a specific product or program. The YSP is not always disclosed on the HUD-1, as it is not a cost to the buyer. While YSP, often referred to as "rebate pricing," has been a part of lending for many years, it became an issue with the pricing of loans during the subprime lending explosion.

In a more normal lending environment, those who refinance home loans are sometimes encouraged to use YSP to pay their loan fee because of tax circumstances. But for most home buyers, paying an origination fee makes sense since it qualifies for a tax deduction in the year that it is paid on a purchase loan.

The complaint in recent years is that borrowers were enticed by offers of a "no-cost" mortgage, only to discover that they had agreed to pay an interest rate above the current market rate. In other words, there is no such loan as a no-cost option. A borrower paid the lender for his or her efforts in obtaining the loan funds either with an origination fee or a higher interest rate, which produces a yield spread premium, which was then paid to the originating lender.

Paying an interest rate above market rates to compensate a mortgage broker/lender is not necessarily a bad thing for the borrower, as it can reduce the upfront costs of the mortgage. Depending upon how long a borrower anticipates holding the mortgage, paying a higher interest rate could be more economical than paying high up-front fees.

Advocates insist that YSP, when used responsibly, can be a tool to assist borrowers, especially those short of cash. Critics, on the other hand, point to the fact that too often, borrowers can still be "sold" a higher rate loan for which the lender collects both an origination fee plus the YSP, which an unscrupulous lender can still keep largely undisclosed.

Disclosure requirements have been updated and, in response to this past abuse, many lenders now limit the amount of service release that can be charged. The rationale of the past, in which brokers defended the payment of YSP on the grounds that they helped a person who would otherwise not been able to obtain financing acquire a loan, is no longer viable.

The motivation for the original Good Faith Estimate (GFE) form (see the Case & Point in Chapter 9) introduced in January 2010 was primarily to eliminate the ability of loan originators to obtain undisclosed YSP income. YSP must now be disclosed only as a credit to buyer costs and the GFE attempted to more clearly alert borrowers to the relationship of YSP to the acceptance of a higher interest rate. Whether the form accomplished its goals continues to be debated by various industry participants. The Loan Estimate and Closing Statement are the newest forms introduced in October 2015 to provide this disclosure.

It was anticipated that with the return to less exotic loan options accompanied by the new disclosure rules, the use of YSP would be used less frequently. That has proven not to be the case as YSP is often used with all types of loans. But the question is still viable regarding whether YSP is good or bad, ethical or not, promotes unscrupulous pricing or is a real help to cash-strapped borrowers. It is important to determine for oneself the answers to the following:

1. Do the opportunities for YSP to assist borrowers outweigh the potential for abuse?
2. Are the new disclosure requirements sufficient to curb the potential abuses of YSP use?
3. Can you think of an alternative that could provide help to borrowers while avoiding the potential for abuse that YSP affords?
4. Would the loan industry be better served with the elimination of the use of YSP?

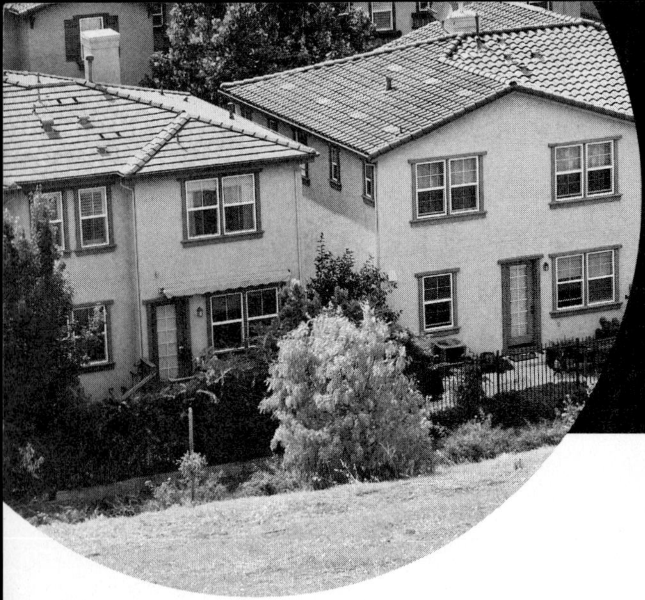

© Shutterstock / pbk-pg

CHAPTER 4

ADJUSTABLE RATE AND OTHER ALTERNATIVE MORTGAGE INSTRUMENTS

OVERVIEW

The term *alternative mortgage instruments* refers to financing options other than the standard fixed rate, fully amortized loan. In the early part of 2000, the adjustable rate mortgage (ARM) presented an overabundance of variations and combinations of loans that became widely used in an effort to presumably create more purchasing opportunities for home buyers.

In retrospect, as the number of loan programs grew, so did the opportunities for unscrupulous lenders to sell loan options that resulted in the subprime meltdown of 2007–2009.

After completing this chapter, you will be able to:

- Discuss why, under certain market conditions, the fixed rate mortgage is again popular with many lenders.
- List and briefly describe the circumstances under which an adjustable rate mortgage might benefit the borrower.
- Explain how negative amortization works.
- Give reasons why balloon mortgages are not favored by consumers.
- Demonstrate how a reverse annuity mortgage may be helpful for some older homeowners.
- Compare the differences between 15-year loans and biweekly loan payments, and the payments on a standard 30-year loan.

4.1 OBJECTIVES AND RATIONALE

The principal objective of ARMs and other alternatives was initially to transfer some of the risk of continually rising inflation from the lender to the borrower, while at the same time tailoring loans more closely

---

Note: You'll encounter some math in this chapter, but all problems have been completed for you. Chapter 14 will introduce the Calculated Industries Qualifier Plus IIIx calculator and demonstrate its use in solving various Real Estate math problems.

to the borrower's financial circumstances. In an effort to broaden the number of borrowers, the loan options became more and more flexible. To remain competitive, many lenders who traditionally granted only standard fixed interest rate loans felt compelled to participate. The result was that ARM options literally exploded into use. The darling of the industry became the option ARM, sometimes referred to as the pick-a-pay loan, which was negatively amortized. The interest only and stated income qualifying options also expanded the use, or abuse, in the loan arena. In many cases, borrowers erroneously relied upon expected appreciation to bail them out of the accruing negative amortization and resulting increasing principal balance. What was the driving force behind this change to ever more flexible loan programs? There was no single cause, but the most notable was a desire to expand homeownership to more borrowers, which the advent of mortgage-backed securities helped promote.

There was a concern that the continued appreciation of home values would prohibit borrowers from ownership. There was also a false sense that these same appreciating home values would continue into the foreseeable future, accompanied by the failure to accept the reality that markets always adjust.

Purpose of Adjustable Rate and Other Alternative Loans

Adjustable rate financing has been available for years. The virtue of ARM loans varies depending upon whether they are viewed from the lender's or the borrower's perspective.

For many years, banks promoted mostly ARM loans. The ARM shields the bank from interest rate increases or decreases as borrowers shared in the risk of rate fluctuations, especially in a rising market. When the bank has to pay more, the borrower has to pay more. The inability of the banks to sell ARM loans to the secondary market (Fannie Mae and Freddie Mac, discussed in Chapter 7) prompted them to eventually offer fixed rate products.

ARM loans had a resurgence during the heyday of the subprime lending frenzy. But, following the 2008–2009 recession, ARM financing rapidly lost popularity and was mostly unavailable for a number of years. By late 2014, ARMs were again available but not vigorously promoted or obtained by consumers. The product line is much reduced and conservative in comparison to the array of past options. Negatively amortized loans were not made an available option, likely due to the slower appreciation of home values, which caused them to be perceived as too risky.

Emphasis today is on loans with an initial fixed term of 5, 7, or 10 years, which can then convert to a one-year ARM with annual adjustments to both rate and payment. This change has largely eliminated what used to be perceived as major benefits accruing to adjustable rate financing. (Financing is cyclical, and while not currently used extensively, we may see additional ARM financing reintroduced more in the future.) Thus, the Case & Point at the end of this chapter addresses features of past ARM loans and their perceived benefits to past borrowers.

We should remember that this form of financing has a long history, and continues to be used more extensively in Europe and other places. In California, the Cal-Vet loan program has been using adjustable rates since the program was initiated over 90 years ago. We will review Cal-Vet loans in Chapter 6, but it should be noted here that this program has had a very stable experience with adjustable rates.

4.2 ADJUSTABLE RATE MORTGAGES (ARMS)

What Is an Adjustable Rate Mortgage?

The **adjustable rate mortgage (ARM)** is a flexible loan instrument, in which the interest rate and the monthly payments may be adjusted periodically to correspond with changes in a selected index. While ARM financing has, temporarily, lost some of its luster, these loans remain available and, as financing, are likely to make a comeback sometime in the future.

Historically, adjustable rate mortgages have been made by mortgage companies, thrift institutions, and banks. The earliest adjustable terms were labeled variable rate mortgages, variable interest rate loans, and adjustable mortgage loans. Although there may be some minor differences between these and today's ARMs, they basically work in the same way. For our purposes, ARM means any loan without a fixed interest rate during its term.

Some Things to Know About Adjustable Rate Mortgages

Although the terms of any loan may vary considerably from another, there are several common characteristics of practically any adjustable rate financing. The following is an attempt to help you understand the language of ARMs.

INTEREST RATE ADJUSTMENTS: Adjustments to the interest rate must reflect the movement of a single, specific, neutral index, subject to rate adjustment limitations contained in the loan contract.

INDEX: The LIBOR (London Interbank Offered Rate) is currently the most frequently selected index. Other common indexes in the past included Treasury bills, Treasury securities, and the 11th District Cost of Funds. The index, while beyond the control of the lender, is an indicator of current economic conditions that guides lenders in their interest rate adjustments. With the LIBOR being the most often preferred index, opinions regarding which index is the most stable under various conditions are moot. All indexes have a public history and daily values that are easy to find in any Internet search engine.

MARGIN: The margin is the percentage amount added to the index at each adjustment period to determine the new interest rate to be paid by the borrower. Sometimes referred to as the lender's profit, but more commonly known as the differential or spread, the margin is established by individual lenders based on their estimated expenses and profit goals. While the margin in any given loan remains constant, in relation to the index, for the life of the loan, margins between lenders can and do vary.

PAYMENT ADJUSTMENTS: Another flexible feature of an ARM is that the monthly payment amount may be increased or decreased by the lender to reflect changes in the interest rate. The frequency with which such adjustments can occur is determined by the specific terms of the ARM loan acquired by the borrower. While in the past such adjustments could be monthly, quarterly, or biannually, today's adjustments are more typically on an annual basis.

THE CEILING RATE: Loans have two **cap** rates: a limitation on the amount by which the interest rate can change at any single adjustment and a life time cap. While in the past there were varying cap rates, the most frequently used today is a maximum 2 percent per year interest rate adjustment with a 5 percent maximum ceiling hike over the life of the loan.

Borrowers are cautioned against an overemphasis on these maximum adjustments since, in most instances, they depend on the stability of the index and market adjustments.

NOTICE OF PAYMENT ADJUSTMENTS: The lender must usually send a notice of an adjustment to the payment amount within 30 days but not more than 45 days before it becomes effective. This notice will contain at least the date and amount of payment adjustment, change in index and interest rate, change in principal loan balance, and who to contact for further information and clarification.

PREPAYMENT PRIVILEGE: Most ARMS may be prepaid in whole or in part without penalty at any time during the term of the loan. Today's ARM offerings are more standardized than in the past when the terms more often differed between lenders.

ASSUMABILITY: Most ARM loans are assumable by a qualified borrower acceptable to the lender only after the fixed period has elapsed.

Even though ARM financing is less complicated than in the past, the borrower needs to fully understand the loan characteristics of the selected loan.

A comprehensive list of questions that borrowers should ask when considering any ARM loan is located at the end of this section.

What Does Today's ARM Loan Look Like?

Depending upon the term for which it is fixed, the fixed to ARM rate is generally lower than a comparable conventional fixed rate. The shorter the fixed period, the greater the differential between comparable initial rates. For instance, the borrower who risks the adjustment to annual rate changes after five years will have an initial rate lower than the 10-year fixed option. For instance, the 7-year fixed ARM may have an initial rate a full percentage point lower than the current 30-year conventional fixed rate. (The 5-year term is often little better than the 7-year rate, while the 10-year rate is more likely to be only three-eighths of a percent less than the comparable 30-year conventional fixed. Clearly, lenders are promoting the 7-year fixed to ARM loan as possessing the most competitive initial start rate differential.)

In each case, the adjustments upon roll over to an ARM are as follows:

Maximum First and Subsequent Adjustment:	2%
Lifetime Cap:	5%
Margin:	2.25%
Floor:	2.25%

Let's explain how this works in practice. Using the 7-year fixed adjustable rate mortgage as an example, assume the starting fixed rate is 3 percent with the comparable conventional fixed at 4 percent. The lowest rate adjustment or floor rate would be 2.25 percent, the margin amount. The maximum life rate would be 8 percent (3 percent start rate plus 5 percent lifetime cap). The rate at the first adjustment at the end of seven years fixed rate portion could not exceed 5 percent (3 percent start rate plus 2 percent). This adjustment and all subsequent adjustments would depend upon the index at the time of the roll over plus 2.25 percent. For purposes of our sample, assume the one-year LIBOR rate was 1.25 percent at the first adjustment time. The maximum first adjustment would be to 3.5 percent. This gets a little tricky—the adjustment rate is calculated by adding the LIBOR rate of 1.25 plus the margin of adjustment 2.25 percent. This must then be compared with the maximum allowable adjustment of 2 percent over the start rate, which would be 5 percent. Comparing the two rates, the borrower gets the lower of the two or the 3.5 percent—only a half percent more than the initial loan rate. This calculation and comparison exercise will be done annually to determine the rate for the next year.

While this scenario appears benign, recognize that had the LIBOR index been 2.75 percent plus the 2.25 percent margin, the first-year adjusted rate would have jumped to the fully allowable 5 percent. Borrowers must be willing and prepared to accept significant rate changes depending upon market conditions.

Why Use an Adjustable in a Fixed Rate World?

Given the unpredictability of ARM loan adjustments, why do some borrowers select them as their preferred loan option? ARM loan popularity can most often be traced to the fact that it is usually offered at a lower initial interest rate than a traditional fixed rate.

Presumably this allows borrowers to qualify for a larger loan amount. This was certainly true in the past when borrowers actually qualified at low "teaser" start rates, which resulted in their being able to borrow considerably more money and purchase a more expensive home. The current fixed-for-years ARM options with at best around a 1 percent better qualifying rate might represent between $50,000 to $60,000 of additional loan amount. In some markets, that increased purchasing power might make the acceptance of an ARM loan more palatable.

Another reason to use an ARM in the past was the ability to make substantial principal reduction payments which, in turn resulted in a reduction in the monthly payment. An example would be the borrower who purchases a new home prior to selling a current residence. Because borrowers expected to have a significant principal reduction payment on their newly acquired loan, the ARM made sense as it would reduce the monthly payment based on the reduced loan amount. Again, with the fixed-for-years ARM today, this option could not be exercised until after the loan converted to its ARM portion in year 5, 7, or 10, making it a less desirable reason for selecting an ARM loan.

Finally, the current ARM options represent a lower initial monthly payment. This might be important to borrowers who are starting a career with the expectation that their future income will enable them to afford any future ARM adjustments and/or increases to their monthly payment.

So although used more sparingly now, adjustable rate mortgages may make perfect sense in some situations. When acquiring such financing, a borrower must be certain to understand all of the characteristics of the selected loan. It is important to avoid surprises after the loan process has been completed and it is too late to make adjustments to the loan terms.

Disclosure Requirements for ARMs

Even though ARM loan options are fewer, their technical aspects and features can still be confusing to borrowers. Therefore, lenders who issue ARMs must comply with Regulation Z of the Federal Truth-in-Lending Law. Regulation Z requires lenders who offer ARMs to give each potential borrower certain specific information about ARM loans. The major disclosure items are

1. The index used, where the index is found, and a five-year history of the index.
2. How interest rates and margins interact to determine payments and what the current rates are.
3. The interest and payment adjustment periods and how many days' warning *will be provided* before a change occurs.
4. Negative amortization features, if any.
5. Maximum caps on (1) the annual interest rate increase and (2) the total rate increase over the life of the loan.

The lender may comply with Regulation Z by giving the potential borrower the ARM edition of Know Before You Owe brochure authorized by the CFPB. A "non-traditional" Mortgage Loan Disclosure Statement (MLDS) has been developed to assure the full disclosure of any ARM loan. Finally, California lenders are required to have the borrower sign an adjustable rate loan rider to the promissory note (see Figure 4.1).

Advantages of an Adjustable Rate Mortgage to the Borrower

The advantages as previously espoused have diminished with the current adoption of an early fixed rate term prior to the loan rolling over to its ARM term. A major current benefit would depend upon the length of ownership. Accepting a seven-year fixed-to-ARM term loan at a 1 percent lower rate than that available on a conventional loan would result in considerable overall interest savings for the first seven years. Depending upon the adjustments when the loan rolls over to the ARM and the subsequent interest rates, a borrower could save on interest payments during his or her ownership. This would be particularly true should the borrower relinquish the property during the first seven years. Given that the average life of a loan is only seven to eight years, this could easily occur. If the property is retained for a longer term there will be the risk of adjustments to the ARM roll over that could erode some of the initial interest savings.

FIGURE 4.1 Sample adjustable rate loan rider.

ADJUSTABLE RATE RIDER
(1 Year Treasury Index--Rate Caps)

THIS ADJUSTABLE RATE RIDER is made this _____ day of _____, _____, and is incorporated into and shall be deemed to amend and supplement the Mortgage, Deed of Trust, or Security Deed (the "Security Instrument") of the same date given by the undersigned (the "Borrower") to secure Borrower's Adjustable Rate Note (the "Note") to _____ (the "Lender") of the same date and covering the property described in the Security Instrument and located at:

_____
[Property Address]

THE NOTE CONTAINS PROVISIONS ALLOWING FOR CHANGES IN THE INTEREST RATE AND THE MONTHLY PAYMENT. THE NOTE LIMITS THE AMOUNT THE BORROWER'S INTEREST RATE CAN CHANGE AT ANY ONE TIME AND THE MAXIMUM RATE THE BORROWER MUST PAY.

ADDITIONAL COVENANTS. In addition to the covenants and agreements made in the Security Instrument, Borrower and Lender further covenant and agree as follows:

A. INTEREST RATE AND MONTHLY PAYMENT CHANGES

The Note provides for an initial interest rate of _____ %. The Note provides for changes in the interest rate and the monthly payments as follows:

4. INTEREST RATE AND MONTHLY PAYMENT CHANGES

(A) Change Dates

The interest rate I will pay may change on the first day of _____, _____, and on that day every 12th month thereafter. Each date on which my interest rate could change is called a "Change Date."

(B) The Index

Beginning with the first Change Date, my interest rate will be based on an Index. The "Index" is the weekly average yield on United States Treasury securities adjusted to a constant maturity of one year, as made available by the Federal Reserve Board. The most recent Index figure available as of the date 45 days before each Change Date is called the "Current Index."

If the Index is no longer available, the Note Holder will choose a new index which is based upon comparable information. The Note Holder will give me notice of this choice.

(C) Calculation of Changes

Before each Change Date, the Note Holder will calculate my new interest rate by adding _____ percentage points (_____ %) to the Current Index. The Note Holder will then round the result of this addition to the nearest one-eighth of one percentage point (0.125%). Subject to the limits stated in Section 4(D) below, this rounded amount will be my new interest rate until the next Change Date.

The Note Holder will then determine the amount of the monthly payment that would be sufficient to repay the unpaid principal that I am expected to owe at the Change Date in full on the maturity date at my new interest rate in substantially equal payments. The result of this calculation will be the new amount of my monthly payment.

(D) Limits on Interest Rate Changes

The interest rate I am required to pay at the first Change Date will not be greater than _____ % or less than _____ %. Thereafter, my interest rate will never be increased or decreased on any single Change Date by more than one percentage point (1.0%) from the rate of interest I have been paying for the preceding 12 months. My interest rate will never be greater than _____ %.

(E) Effective Date of Changes

My new interest rate will become effective on each Change Date. I will pay the amount of my new monthly payment beginning on the first monthly payment date after the Change Date until the amount of my monthly payment changes again.

(F) Notice of Changes

The Note Holder will deliver or mail to me a notice of any changes in my interest rate and the amount

MULTISTATE ADJUSTABLE RATE RIDER--ARM 5-1--Single Family--Fannie Mae/Freddie Mac UNIFORM INSTRUMENT   Form 3108 1/01 *(Page 1 of 2 pages)*

FIGURE 4.1 (Continued)

of my monthly payment before the effective date of any change. The notice will include information required by law to be given to me and also the title and telephone number of a person who will answer any question I may have regarding the notice.

B. TRANSFER OF THE PROPERTY OR A BENEFICIAL INTEREST IN BORROWER

Section 18 of the Security Instrument is amended to read as follows:

Transfer of the Property or a Beneficial Interest in Borrower. As used in this Section 18, "Interest in the Property" means any legal or beneficial interest in the Property, including, but not limited to, those beneficial interests transferred in a bond for deed, contract for deed, installment sales contract or escrow agreement, the intent of which is the transfer of title by Borrower at a future date to a purchaser.

If all or any part of the Property or any Interest in the Property is sold or transferred (or if Borrower is not a natural person and a beneficial interest in Borrower is sold or transferred) without Lender's prior written consent, Lender may require immediate payment in full of all sums secured by this Security Instrument. However, this option shall not be exercised by Lender if such exercise is prohibited by Applicable Law. Lender also shall not exercise this option if: (a) Borrower causes to be submitted to Lender information required by Lender to evaluate the intended transferee as if a new loan were being made to the transferee; and (b) Lender reasonably determines that Lender's security will not be impaired by the loan assumption and that the risk of a breach of any covenant or agreement in this Security Instrument is acceptable to Lender.

To the extent permitted by Applicable Law, Lender may charge a reasonable fee as a condition to Lender's consent to the loan assumption. Lender may also require the transferee to sign an assumption agreement that is acceptable to Lender and that obligates the transferee to keep all the promises and agreements made in the Note and in this Security Instrument. Borrower will continue to be obligated under the Note and this Security Instrument unless Lender releases Borrower in writing.

If Lender exercises the option to require immediate payment in full, Lender shall give Borrower notice of acceleration. The notice shall provide a period of not less than 30 days from the date the notice is given in accordance with Section 15 within which Borrower must pay all sums secured by this Security Instrument. If Borrower fails to pay these sums prior to the expiration of this period, Lender may invoke any remedies permitted by this Security Instrument without further notice or demand on Borrower.

BY SIGNING BELOW, Borrower accepts and agrees to the terms and covenants contained in this Adjustable Rate Rider.

_____(Seal)
-Borrower

_____(Seal)
-Borrower

Source: © 2016 OnCourse Learning

The following list identifies this and other potential advantages:

- Lower initial rates when compared with conventional fixed rates (although the difference could be slight depending upon the initial fixed term selected).
- Ability to qualify for a larger loan at the lower interest rate in some situations.
- Potential for lower payments as the index comes down (possible but unlikely).
- Generally easier assumability upon resale if the loan has rolled over to its ARM term.
- Ability to make principal reduction payments following the roll over to ARM term. The ARM allows for principal payments that affect the monthly payment, whereas principal reduction payments with a fixed rate merely affect the term of the loan.

- A better investment may be made with an ARM. For every month your rate is lower than the fixed rate, you are saving money. If you save money for 84 months on the fixed term and pay a comparative rate no higher than what the original fixed rate would have been for a remaining period less than 84 months, your overall loan payments would still be less over the total period.

Disadvantages of an Adjustable Rate Mortgage to the Borrower

These would apply in today's loan option only after the roll over provision has occurred.

- Income may not increase proportionately with increases in payments.
- In a slow real estate market, the rate of appreciation may be less than the rate of increase in the interest rates; that is, the spread between the value of the property and the outstanding loan balance could shrink each year, rather than increase.
- The risk of rising interest rates is borne partly by the borrower, since the risk of change in the cost of funds can be shifted entirely to the borrower, within maximum caps allowed over the life of the loan.

4.3 HYBRID LOAN OPTIONS

Following the recession, several loan options that had existed for years disappeared. Known as "hybrid" loan options, they consisted of some form of fixed and adjustable combination. The adjustable loan highlighted in this chapter with its 5-, 7-, or 10-year fixed term prior to rolling over to a one-year ARM was considered a hybrid in the past.

The other past hybrid that was somewhat popular at the time was the ARM to fixed rate loan. This option to convert to a fixed rate had fairly complicated rules governing its conversion. The time frame during which a conversion was allowed is called the window period. The conversion terms are identified at the time the loan was created, but the most likely option allowed an election on the loan's annual anniversary starting the thirteenth month through the sixtieth month or the second, third, fourth, and fifth years of the loan. Since the conversion was limited to taking place only on the anniversary date each year, the timing could result in missing a lower rate that may have occurred outside the allowed time frame.

The usual reason for exercising a conversion option is the borrower's fear that the existing ARM rate is likely to exceed any converted fixed rate. The conversion privilege, when exercised, will be to a fixed rate anywhere from 0.375 percent to 0.5 percent above the 60-day

Freddie Mac rate at the time. The amortization period will be for the remaining term of the loan. The converted rate will likely be slightly above the prevailing fixed rate. There may also be a cost for exercising the conversion.

The willingness to provide any type of creative loans vanished with the start of the recession. So, while there are not many current options to the one highlighted here, the loan industry is cyclical and a re-emergence of creative loans may happen in the future.

4.4 BALLOON PAYMENT FIXED RATE LOANS

In a mortgage with a **balloon payment**, the amortization period might be 30 years, but the entire unpaid balance becomes due sooner, most often at the end of the fifth or seventh year. A payment that is more than double the amount of a regular installment is, by Civil Code definition, a balloon payment.

The balloon payment mortgage, although still used in financing commercial property, was not frequently used in single home financing. The new QM rules and balloon payments were detailed in Chapter 3. These rules makes it even less likely that a balloon option will now be used. Remember, the QM rules consider the inclusion of a balloon payment in a mortgage a "risky feature" that is prohibited if the lender is to be protected under said rules.

Balloon payments are more likely to occur in seller carry financing, particularly used during tight or high-interest rate markets.

The major concern with balloon payments is the potential inability to meet the balloon payment requirements at maturity. Unless the original mortgage contains a rollover provision or identifies terms under which the mortgage may remain in force, the borrower faces the risk of not being able to either pay the balloon amount or being able to refinance appropriately.

4.5 REVERSE ANNUITY MORTGAGE (RAM)

General Provisions

A **reverse annuity mortgage (RAM)** is a loan enabling homeowners 62 years of age or older to convert their home equity into various forms of financial assistance. This loan is designed to help retirees, who are often found to be "equity rich but cash poor," subsidize their monthly living condition. While the use of reverse mortgage funds is not restricted, they are most often used to assist seniors with limited income who are struggling to make ends meet.

The concept is the reverse of the traditional mortgage loan as seniors receive payments rather than having to pay a monthly mortgage amount. The homeowner is not required to pay back the loan nor make any monthly payments as long as they occupy the home. The mortgage will require payment when the home is vacated or sold. The occupant is obligated to pay the property tax, homeowners insurance, and condo fees if the property is a condominium.

There are three plans under which a reverse mortgage may be acquired. While each has similar characteristics, there are some differences about which seniors need be aware. The similarities are those noted above regarding no mortgage payments during continued occupancy and no restrictions on the use of funds. The amount of funds available are determined by the age of the recipients, the value of the property (determined via an appraisal), current interest rate, and lender program restrictions regarding maximum loan limits. Payments may be obtained in one or a combination of three ways: a lump sum payment, fixed payments—usually on a monthly basis for life—or a line of credit to be drawn upon as needed.

The most popular program is the FHA Home Equity Conversion Mortgage (HECM) but there is also a Fannie Mae Home Keeper Loan and conventional sources, known as proprietary plans. The downside of any option is that the up-front fees are considerable, typically much more costly than a more conventional type loan. This is understandable in as much as the RAM lender is guaranteeing the owner the right to remain in the property without a monthly payment for life. This can result in the lender losing money should the owner outlive the value of the equity in the home. In other words, the lender bets that the owner will vacate the home before using the equity and loses that bet if the owner lives beyond the anticipated years, as the total amount due cannot exceed the value of the home when the RAM comes due. Note that all programs allow the heirs to inherit any remaining equity, but they must either sell the home and pay off the accumulated amount of the reverse mortgage or pay off the reverse mortgage via cash or a refinance loan. In either case, they retain any remaining equity.

These loans have been available for decades but few had taken advantage of them until recently. The popularity is consistently growing as the population ages and the loans are heavily promoted on TV and in print media. As millions become eligible and lender profitability is recognized, the concern is that more lenders will be drawn to the program for profit motives rather than service to seniors. All programs require that counseling occur to educate potential recipients of the pros and cons. Family members are usually encouraged to participate in the counseling sessions, especially with older homeowners.

Program Concerns

Families need to consider:

- With the significantly higher fees attached to a reverse mortgage, are there alternatives that should be considered?
- What is the general health of the occupants? Is it likely they will vacate the home in need of special care? The loan will come due within a year of when the home is vacated, and the high upfront fees may not be recouped.
- What is the condition of the home? The appraisal may require some repairs prior to the loan being consummated, but how will normal repairs be accommodated financially?
- The required counseling session will focus on making sure the recipients understand the program but will not advise as to its appropriateness. That will be for the family to determine after fully comprehending the loan terms and conditions.
- While these programs sound terrific—stay in the home, no monthly payments, maybe even a monthly stipend received—the program is not for everyone. Carefully weigh the costs versus the anticipated time to remain in the home.

RAM recipients are responsible for paying their own annual taxes and insurance obligations. A mounting number of tax sales, foreclosures, and evictions of borrowers because these obligations have gone unpaid have resulted in new financial assessment requirements beginning April 27, 2015.

In addition to increased origination and servicing costs, borrowers will now undergo credit checks. Lenders will have to look at all of the borrower's income streams, such as Social Security and pensions, plus any additional resources, such as investments. Borrowers will have to provide documents such as tax returns and bank account statements.

The financial assessment includes a residual calculation (similar to that used in VA loans) to determine if funds must be set aside with which to pay insurance and tax expenses over the life of the loan. If so, available loan proceeds to the borrower will be reduced.

Depending upon the assessment, a borrower may be required to set aside an amount in a separate account sufficient to fully fund or partially fund the future payments of taxes and insurance premiums as they come due. Many borrowers are expected to be unaffected by the new rules, but critics worry that the most needy of seniors will be denied RAM loans. While the claim is that borrowers with large equity positions will be minimally affected, seniors with smaller homes and equity may find the rules prohibitive.

There is loud criticism, and many believe that there will be modifications to the rules in the future. For some, this is another example of FHA abandoning their mission of serving the most vulnerable and needy borrowers.

Although seldom used in the past, to compensate for the expectation of fewer future RAM users, we might expect more promotion of the RAM as a loan with which to purchase another home. Again, this is most likely to be used by those with large equity positions as seniors must have the means to pay in cash the difference between the sales price and the maximum available to be drawn from their HECM loan.

The three main programs are:

1. *Home Equity Conversion Mortgage.* FHA loan limits apply; this is an ARM loan, usually adjusted annually. In spite of the fact that the loan amount with this option may be lower because FHA establishes maximum loan amounts on a county-by-county basis, this is the most frequently used program and is often perceived to offer the borrower the most protection. In addition to the guarantee of payments, the interest rates and the ARM adjustments tend to be lowest among available RAM options.

2. *Home Keeper Program.* Fannie Mae loan limits apply; this is an ARM loan, adjusted on a monthly basis. Because Home Keeper's maximum lending limit is usually higher than the HECM, it might better serve homeowners with higher property values. Interest rates are significantly higher, and absent mortgage insurance, there is not the same guarantee as with the HECM. A home purchase option is available, but the details are beyond the scope of this text.

3. *Conventional or Proprietary Programs.* Lenders offering RAM loans not backed by FHA insurance or Fannie Mae secondary mortgage requirements can establish their own loan limits and other requirements. The result is that larger loan amounts are often available but are accompanied by higher fees and interest rates and without guarantee of payment should the lender for any reason fail to perform.

Under all programs, the maximum LTV ratio is determined by a formula based on the borrower's age, interest rates, and appraisal and/or maximum loan limits. In all cases, the funds received are tax free because they represent a loan that must ultimately be repaid. Payment options for the borrower usually include:

1. *Term option.* Equal monthly payments for a fixed number of years.
2. *Tenure option.* Equal monthly payments for as long as the borrower occupies the home. The borrower may be absent up to one

year—often due to health or entry to a care facility—without triggering the payoff requirements.
3. *Line of credit option.* Funds drawn as needed (including a lump sum) up to the maximum loan amount. Caution must be exercised with this option, as the funds could be exhausted requiring a refinance (if the home value has appreciated) and bring another round of steep fees. If the home has not appreciated, disallowing any future funds and thereby eliminating the owner's ability to retain their home, a sale may have to occur and the owner could lose his or her property.

4.6 MISCELLANEOUS ALTERNATIVE PLANS

There are two other alternative mortgage programs that are frequently used. Because lending practices are continually changing, perhaps there will be other options proposed in the future.

Fifteen-Year and Twenty-Year Mortgages

In an effort to build equity faster, to have a free and clear home sooner, and to obtain lower interest rates, borrowers can opt for a 15-year, as opposed to a 30-year, loan. Depending upon the market conditions, a borrower may acquire a lower interest rate, usually between one-quarter and one-half percent less than the 30-year loan. (See the Example for interest rate comparisons.) Twenty-year term loans are available, which also represent a lower interest rate, but they are not as readily sold to the secondary market and thus rarely used except in refinance transactions. Refinancing borrowers may wish to avoid returning to a 30-year term but opt for the lesser increase in the payment in comparison to the 15-year mortgage.

Biweekly Loan Payments

You can reduce your 30-year loan term without having to make the higher monthly payments associated with the 15- or 20-year mortgage. Some lenders offer borrowers the option of a biweekly payment schedule instead of traditional monthly payments.

A **biweekly loan payment** is made every two weeks, resulting in 26 biweekly payments per year. This is the equivalent of making 13 monthly payments. A biweekly payment is merely one-half of a monthly payment paid every 14 days. The extra payments apply more money against the principal loan amount, thereby greatly reducing the time it takes to pay off the loan. More important to some borrowers may be the fact that they are paid on an every two-week basis and paying half the loan payment each pay period may be easier for personal budgeting purposes.

If you get paid monthly, you can also acquire the savings by paying a little extra with each monthly payment. This can be done by taking your normal monthly payment and dividing it by twelve. Add this one-twelfth payment to your monthly payment to lower your principle balance faster.

How much faster is a loan paid off using biweekly instead of monthly payments? Depending upon the size of the loan and its terms, a rule of thumb is that it is approximately one-third faster, with a traditional 30-year monthly amortized loan being paid off in about 21 years using biweekly payments.

Lenders will make these loans as long as they can sell them in the secondary market. Sometimes these loans are not popular to investors as servicing them is more time consuming and costly. Homeowners often receive notices from companies that will arrange such a payment plan. Caution! In most cases, the lender and/or the company will charge $350 to $750 as a one-time fee to initiate the service. Plus, there is usually a monthly charge for maintaining the service. The process involves simply collecting the biweekly payments via an automatic deduction process from your checking account and then making the one extra payment for the borrower at the end of each year. With a bit of self-discipline, homeowners can do it themselves.

Here is one way to do it: Deposit one-twelfth of the monthly payment into a savings account each month. In November, write a separate check for the one extra payment amount and send it to the lender with a note indicating that the payment is for principal pay down only. This will enable a borrower to identify within 60 days of when the lender provides a year-end statement regarding loan balance, interest paid, etc. that the lender has credited the account accurately. Some feel that this one payment method is better than a small additional monthly payment made to principal pay down because accurate accounting with the lender is easier to track.

Example: A $100,000 fixed rate loan at 6 percent, amortized for 30 years, requires a monthly principal and interest payment of $599.55. The same $100,000 loan at 5 3/4 percent, amortized for 15 years, requires a monthly payment of $830.41.

$830.41	per month for 15 years at 5 3/4 percent
$599.55	per month for 30 years at 6 percent
$230.86	per month more for a 15-year than for a 30-year loan program

This 15-year loan is especially attractive to high-income borrowers who wish to have their homes paid off prior to retirement. For the interest-rate conscious borrower, the amount of interest that is saved can be substantial. Using the above data:

$115,838	interest payable over 30 years at 6 percent ($599.55/mo. × 360 pmts., less $100,000 loan amount)
$ 49,474	interest payable over 15 years at 5 3/4 percent ($830.41/mo. × 180 pmts., less $100,000 loan amount)
$ 66,364	interest saved

(Mortgage amounts differ. To determine the savings obtained with a $300,000 loan, for instance, merely multiply the above numbers by three.)

Of course, no analysis of interest costs can be complete without comparing income tax consequences of one structure over another, nor should the time value of money be ignored, but these aspects are well beyond the scope of this text.

(Biweekly loan payments are computed in Chapter 15.)

For many borrowers, this is a way to have a 30-year loan—with its smaller monthly payment and with just one voluntary extra principal and interest payment every year or more often if it is affordable—save on interest paid and shorten the loan term. And it's possible to do without being locked into the larger required payments, should they become burdensome. Of course, these prepayments can be accomplished only if they are not prohibited under the terms of the promissory note. If the borrower makes the thirteenth monthly payment, he or she must make sure the lender is aware of its purpose: principal reduction only.

Typical Questions

1. WILL IT WORK ON ANY LOAN OPTION? Absolutely! FHA, VA, and conventional loans, both fixed and adjustable rate mortgages, 30- or 15-year terms. This can benefit you by paying less interest over the life of the loan, regardless of the type of loan.
2. WHEN CAN ONE START? The sooner the better! Whether one has a brand new loan or has been making payments for months or years, money can be saved in the form of unpaid interest. It works for both new and existing loans.
3. HOW LONG DOES ONE HAVE TO PARTICIPATE TO MAKE IT WORTHWHILE? Money is saved the very first payment, but the longer one participates, the greater the savings in unpaid interest and the shorter the payoff term. It is advised that one retain his or her own record of extra payments and an analysis

of the benefit via year-by-year savings. Here's an example of the possible savings on a $100,000 loan at 8 percent interest:

Mortgage paid off:	30 years versus 21 years
Total interest paid:	$164,155 versus $106,748
Total interest saved:	$57,407

4. IF I DON'T PLAN TO STAY IN THE HOME FOR 30 YEARS, IS IT STILL A GOOD THING TO DO? An analysis of the current loan situation can identify the possible savings over the next several years and assist in the decision making. Generally, it is a good plan for practically everyone simply because it initiates a habit that saves money immediately and that hopefully would continue with any new mortgages acquired.

5. SHOULD THE PLAN ONLY BE USED WITH A PERSONAL RESIDENCE? The same kind of savings will occur with any mortgage, including mortgages on rental or commercial properties. It is best to analyze each mortgage separately to determine the savings that could occur. This plan could be particularly good for people hoping to retain and use rental property for future income purposes by paying off the mortgage early.

4.7 EPILOGUE

In this chapter just a sampling of mortgage alternatives has been discussed. The financial market's climate at any given time determines its acceptance of creative loan options. Following the 2007–2009 recession, there was a return to more standard loan products. This was a reaction to the extremely flexible loan options that characterized the subprime loan market. Under all market conditions, licensees must be cautious in recommending loan plans that may not be suitable for the client. As the foreclosure crises beginning in 2006 grew, buyers blamed everyone, including real estate licensees, for promoting loan options that proved unsustainable.

The financing smorgasbord offered in the mortgage cafeteria should provide alternatives paired with individual needs and abilities to repay. The real estate broker today is expected to be knowledgeable about financing alternatives, which means continuous exposure to and understanding of new financing vehicles, techniques, and choices. But the real estate licensee is well advised to depend upon knowledgeable mortgage representatives to help their borrowers make final loan decisions.

Chapter Summary

Beginning in 2002, financing of real estate underwent a revolution, as a host of innovative mortgages were created so that, in theory, loans could be matched to the borrower instead of tying all borrowers to just one loan type.

In the past, loan applicants were concerned about how much they could borrow, at what interest rate and fees, and how much the monthly payments would be. The more savvy applicants might ask about prepayment penalties and loan assumability. As housing appreciation grew to double digits, the focus shifted to "how can potential future borrowers afford to purchase with such an increase in appreciation?" Thus, more and more flexible loan options emerged in an effort to assure that practically everyone could enjoy the American dream of homeownership. Adjustable rate mortgages are loans whose interest rate moves up and down based upon a neutral index. These loans became increasingly popular from 2004–2006. Elements of the ARM include a neutral index that regularly adjusts and a margin that adds to that index adjustment. Adding these two elements together totals the borrower's interest rate. The maximum rate allowed over the term of the loan is the life cap or ceiling, and there is an additional limitation, the payment cap, exercised at each loan adjustment period. Understanding the language of ARMs allows a borrower to recognize if the loan will be a negatively amortized or a no-neg loan.

A balloon-type loan that is amortized for 30 years, with the entire unpaid balance due at the end of the fifth or seventh year, is most often used in seller-carry financing. A payment that is more than double the amount of a regular installment is, by Civil Code definition, a balloon payment.

A reverse annuity mortgage allows homeowners aged 62 or older to tap their owner-occupied home equity with no monthly repayments. In essence, the homeowner receives a monthly payment from the lender and does not need to pay the loan back until he or she moves out, sells, or dies. The home must be owned free and clear, or have a low-balance existing loan. Neither Fannie Mae nor FHA makes direct reverse loans. Instead, approved lenders make the loans with Fannie Mae and FHA approval.

Other alternative loan packages include 15- or 20-year loans and biweekly payment plans. Since real estate and its financing are cyclical, it is likely that we will see the emergence of other creative loan options again in the future. Each of the alternative mortgage instruments discussed in this chapter is intended to answer borrowers' questions and to provide potential solutions to various borrowing needs. While there may not be a solution to every buyer's loan needs, these options do offer some alternatives to financing, without which the purchase of real estate could be severely limited.

Important Terms and Concepts

Adjustable rate mortgage (ARM)
Balloon payment
Biweekly loan payment
Cap
Negative amortization
Not called out
Reverse annuity mortgage (RAM)

Reviewing Your Understanding

Questions for Discussion

1. What are the key characteristics of ARM loans?
2. What is the main lender risk in granting loans amortized in 30 years, but due in 7 years?
3. List the main elements of a reverse annuity mortgage loan.

Multiple-Choice Questions

1. The principal objective of an adjustable rate mortgage (ARM) loan is to
   a. reduce the risk of foreclosure.
   b. limit mortgage choices during periods of tight money.
   c. establish predictable cash flow during erratic real estate markets.
   d. share the risks of rising interest rates between lender and borrower.

2. Under an ARM loan, the distance between the actual rate paid by the borrower and the index is called the
   a. adjustment.
   b. cap.
   c. term.
   d. margin.

3. The maximum interest rate that a lender can charge under an ARM is called the
   a. cap.
   b. margin.
   c. term.
   d. adjustment.

4. In an ARM loan, when the initial interest rate is abnormally low it is known as the ___ rate.
   a. index
   b. teaser ✓
   c. capped
   d. basement

5. Reverse annuity mortgages are growing more popular with an aging population. Those who qualify
   a. must be over age 59.
   b. usually have very little equity in their homes.
   c. can borrow either in lump sum or in monthly payments. ✓
   d. must remain in their home until sold.

6. The first month's interest on a $200,000 loan at 9 percent payable at $1,800 per month is
   a. $1,800.
   b. $1,600.
   c. $1,500. ✓
   d. $1,300.

7. The first month's negative amortization amount on a $200,000 loan at 9 percent payable at $1,300 per month is
   a. $600.
   b. $500.
   c. $300.
   d. $200. ✓

8. The reverse annuity mortgage is especially designed for
   a. poor families.
   b. younger borrowers.
   c. older borrowers. ✓
   d. those unable to meet balloon payments.

9. The loan plan that offers borrowers an adjustable interest rate with the right to switch to a fixed rate at a later date is the
   a. dual rate, variable rate mortgage.
   b. rollover mortgage. ✓
   c. reverse annuity mortgage.
   d. pledged account mortgage.

10. Under a convertible loan, the time period when the borrower is allowed to switch from an ARM to fixed rate or vice versa is called the ___ period.
    a. shift
    b. crossover
    c. section
    d. window ✓

11. An advantage of a 15-year mortgage over a 30-year loan is that
    a. borrowers can qualify with a smaller down payment.
    b. monthly payments are always lower than in the traditional 30-year loan.
    c. borrowers can usually secure a lower interest rate. ✓
    d. borrowers build up equity faster, even with a much higher interest rate.

12. If a borrower is unable to meet a balloon payment, the borrower might arrange to
    a. obtain an extension of the loan with the existing lender.
    b. refinance the property.
    c. sell the property.
    d. all of the above. ✓

13. One option under a reverse annuity mortgage program, where the borrower is scheduled to receive monthly payments for a fixed number of years, is called the
    a. tenure option.
    b. set option.
    c. term option.
    d. line of credit option.

14. Which of the following will trigger a demand for payoff for a borrower under a reverse annuity mortgage loan?
    a. Moving to a second home for six months
    b. Staying in a rest home for more than one year
    c. Taking in a roommate
    d. Receiving a cash inheritance of more than $250,000

15. Adjustable rate mortgages
    a. represent alternatives to standard fixed rate, fully amortized mortgages.
    b. are available only for owner-occupied dwellings.
    c. are the preferred choice by most borrowers.
    d. transfer some of the risk of rising inflation from borrower to lender.

16. The reason why a home buyer may opt for an adjustable rate mortgage over a fixed rate mortgage containing a teaser rate is to
    a. reduce initial monthly payments.
    b. avoid late charges commonly associated with fixed rate loans.
    c. avoid negative amortization.
    d. avoid prepayment penalties.

17. A 15-year loan, as opposed to a 30-year loan, will
    a. have no impact on annual interest deductions for income tax purposes.
    b. result in slower equity buildup.
    c. create a faster equity in the property, all other things being equal.
    d. initially generate lower monthly payments.

18. A biweekly payment program requires the borrower to make _____ payments per year.
    a. 12
    b. 13
    c. 24
    d. 26

19. When compared with a 30-year loan, the 15-year loan is especially attractive for borrowers who desire to reduce their
    a. monthly installment.
    b. total interest payments.
    c. principal payments.
    d. mortgage insurance premiums.

20. ARM loans pose difficulties for prospective borrowers to understand due to each of the following, except
    a. its simplicity compared to fixed rate instruments.
    b. the relationship of an index to U.S. Treasury securities.
    c. the relationship of the index to the margin.
    d. how interest rates are adjusted to reflect a particular index.

CASE & POINT

Are Negatively Amortized Loans a Thing of the Past?

Widely blamed as a major contributor to the 2008 financial crises, negatively amortized loans disappeared. More stable ARM options re-entered the market and are explained in this chapter. But with financial markets being cyclical, is it possible that negatively amortized loans will be resurrected in the future? Loan products are usually introduced when lenders wish to increase the borrowing habits of the public. For these reasons, the following is a synopsis of the negatively amortized loan as it existed prior to its demise, just in case it is re-introduced in the future.

Negatively amortized loans become more popular during periods of high inflation, usually accompanied by rapid appreciation of home values. This was the exact economic atmosphere we experienced during the early 2000s. Rapid inflation can create a need to qualify a borrower at a low entry-level rate of interest, even though the payments may later increase via regular rate adjustments. The loan, particularly if negatively amortized, will require re-amortization over a shorter term of years.

By definition, with a negatively amortized loan, the initial monthly payments are inadequate to pay the interest, let alone provide for any principal reduction. Whatever the amount of the interest shortfall, it is added to the existing principal balance of the loan, and the following month, the process is repeated. Since the interest shortfall is always added to the principal balance existing at the time, the borrower ends up paying interest on interest, and the principal balance grows with compounding effect. Every month, the amount owed gets larger!

In concept the negatively amortized loan possessed some features that made sense for some borrowers. But abuses occurred, especially when it was used in connection with a minimal or no down payment resulting in little or no equity in the property from very beginning of the loan. Two most egregious loan options were the Pick-A-Pay or option ARM and a loan that capped the payment adjustments to 7.5 percent per year. With the option ARM the borrower was provided a choice of three payment options, the lowest being the most often selected and the one resulting in negative amortization. Everyone wanted to believe that ever-appreciating home values would always protect the borrower in case they needed to sell. When real estate values instead adjusted downward, coupled with the pending higher adjustment of the ARM interest rate and the accompanying increased payment, borrowers found themselves with insufficient equity to either refinance or sell. Foreclosures and short sales were the inevitable result as borrowers found they had merely rented their homes for a few years.

The second option capped any annual payment increase to no more than 7.5 percent of the current payment. Appealing to those who wanted a low monthly payment and knowing the exact amount of each year's increase, it was commonly thought that anticipated increases in income would compensate for the payment increases. The fact that even greater amounts of negative amortization could mount were ignored. These loans are more likely to have prepayment penalties assessed during the first three years of the loan, further impacting those who might want to sell to relieve themselves of mounting home debt. Even though this loan typically required a 5 or 10 percent down payment, that initial equity position was soon eroded and homes were lost to short sale and foreclosure.

There was one additional provision that added to borrower woes as the crises unfolded. All negatively amortized loans contained a provision limiting the amount of deferred interest that could be added to the loan balance before requiring the loan to be recast, amortizing the new balance over the remaining term of the loan. Most lenders adopted the guideline requiring recasting when the deferred interest reached 20 percent of the original loan balance. It was anticipated that this threshold would be reached between four and five years. The recast was generally to a fixed rate, higher than the current ARM rate, again burdening the borrower with an increase in the monthly payment that they often could not accommodate.

During the early negatively amortized loan era, initial low start rates, known as "teaser rates," were kept abnormally low to attract borrowers. Once the loan was granted, the low teaser rate soon disappeared and the usually higher ARM rate took effect. While the low teaser rates allowed some buyers to qualify for a loan that they would not have otherwise been able to obtain, some borrowers did experience difficulty with the increasing monthly payments. Lenders made changes. While still offering teaser rates in their advertising, lenders required borrowers to qualify at the more normal fully indexed rate (i.e., the index plus the margin).

The fully indexed rate was usually slightly lower than a comparable fixed rate but hardly allowed a borrower to qualify for much additional loan amount. Thus, this ARM option was not the more popular variety, and borrowers began to opt for fixed rate financing.

Negative amortization features are not part of the recent ARM products. Given that financing is cyclical and that lenders are always seeking ways to increase borrowing, it may not be farfetched to find some form of negatively amortized loans being promoted again in the future, especially among lenders offering non-Qualified Mortgage loan options.

History has a way of repeating itself, and knowledge of these past loans may help future borrowers determine their use.

© Shutterstock / welcomia

CONVENTIONAL LOANS

OVERVIEW

This chapter covers conventional loans, their advantages and disadvantages, and how to compare one lender with another. Buy-down loans are explained and several examples are given. The California Fair Lending Regulations are outlined and analyzed. This chapter concludes with a discussion of private mortgage insurance (PMI) companies.

After completing this chapter, you will be able to:

- Define a conventional loan.
- List several advantages and disadvantages of a conventional loan.
- Describe what to look for when choosing a lender.
- Give an example of a buy-down loan.
- Outline the basic features of the California Financial Discrimination Act.
- Explain how private mortgage insurance (PMI) works.

5.1 WHAT IS A CONVENTIONAL LOAN?

There are two major categories of loans. One is **government-backed loans**, which include the Federal Housing Administration (FHA), the U.S. Department of Veterans Affairs (VA), the California Department of Veterans Affairs (Cal-Vet), the U.S. Department of Agriculture (USDA), and various other state, county, and city-backed subsidized home loan options, usually funded via bond issued programs. Any loan that is not a government-backed loan is called a **conventional loan**. Although government loan programs have remained mostly stable, conventional loan options have undergone considerable transformation.

Conventional versus Government-Backed Loans

Today's borrowers are encouraged to become pre-qualified or pre-approved for a loan prior to initiating their search for a home to purchase. They are challenged to determine what loan will best serve their home-buying need from a shrinking list of available options. Potential buyers will profit from competent guidance when comparing loan types as well as identifying the option(s) for which they can actually qualify. The advantages and disadvantages of conventional loans versus government-backed loans are outlined below. Recognize that the differences between the two types of loans have diminished following the return to the less-flexible underwriting guidelines of conventional loans.

Advantages of Conventional over Government-Backed Loans

1. *Time Frames.* Conventional loans were generally able to be processed in less time. Automated underwriting revolutionized the industry by reducing processing time frames for conventional loans. The government agencies also streamlined their processing via direct endorsement and VA automatic underwriting, covered in Chapter 6, but the time frame for loan approvals still lagged compared to the conventional procedure. Recent regulations, coupled with less flexible qualifying guidelines, have extended the time periods, making any difference between the processing time frames for conventional versus government loans much less obvious today. Whereas 30-day—and sometimes much shorter—loan approvals used to be fairly commonplace, borrowers must be more patient today with all loan options.

2. *Documentation.* Processing a conventional loan generally involves less paperwork. There may be fewer forms to complete, and the routine of processing can be more flexible. The subprime loan explosion resulted in a dramatic reduction in documentation, particularly with the limited or no doc loans. It was clear, following the collapse of the subprime programs, that lenders needed more borrower data with which to make informed decisions. Critics, however, believe that the pendulum swung from requiring virtually no documentation to asking for way too much information. Advocates, on the other hand, insist that this documentation is necessary to ensure an acceptable, quality loan. We will review today's somewhat more relaxed documentation requirements in Chapter 9.

3. *Loan amounts.* In theory, there is no legal limitation on conventional loan amounts when the loan-to-value (LTV) ratio is 80 percent or less. The majority of loans originated are sold into the secondary market (discussed in Chapter 7) where guidelines are well established. The FHA sets maximum loan amounts on a

home loan depending on geographical location. The VA has no dollar loan maximum, but individual lenders do limit veterans' loan amounts because the VA guarantees only part of the loan. Cal-Vet's maximum loan on a single-family dwelling is limited and can vary from year to year. While not directly establishing loan amount limits, the USDA's maximum borrower income levels, based upon family size, effectively limit purchase prices. Government-backed loans will be covered in detail in Chapter 6.

4. *Number of lenders.* If you apply for a VA-guaranteed loan and the loan is rejected by the VA, you have no alternative lender. There is only one U.S. Department of Veterans Affairs, just as there is only one FHA and one California Department of Veterans Affairs. In the past, if a loan was turned down by one conventional lender, there may have been another who could approve the loan due to differences in underwriting guidelines, providing a distinct advantage over government-type loans. Those options have mostly disappeared as qualifying requirements have become less flexible and more uniform along with fewer loan programs being available. When a loan is denied by one lender, the likelihood of approval elsewhere is now slim.

5. *Flexibility of portfolio lenders.* When a lender keeps a loan in-house, instead of reselling it in the secondary market, it is called a **portfolio loan**. These loans became enormously popular during the subprime frenzy, requiring only minimum paperwork or documentation, as evidenced by their names: No Income/No Asset (NINA) documentation or a Stated Income/Stated Assets (SISA) loan.

Initially requiring larger down payments, high credit scores and appraisal value, these loans eventually relaxed their guidelines and relied almost exclusively on the borrowers' credit scores. Mostly ARM loans and finally allowing 100 percent financing (often using both a first and second loan), the loans were characterized as mirror loans—if one could prove they were alive by fogging a mirror, a loan could usually be acquired. These were ultimately referred to as liar loans as borrowers increasingly exaggerated their income for qualification purposes.

In the beginning, portfolio loans were sold more directly to Wall Street, rather than via Fannie Mae or Freddie Mac. As this market segment grew, both Fannie and Freddie began purchasing the loans resulting in eventual major losses, a major government bail-out, and being currently in receivership. Wall Street acquired the loans, conspired with bond rating companies to highly rate the paper, and then packaged and sold them around the globe. The financial crisis was the ultimate outcome.

While major banks and credit unions have the capacity to portfolio (retain the loan in-house versus selling it to the secondary market) a loan today, it is seldom done, and banks prefer instead to qualify the loan for secondary sale to either Fannie Mae or Freddie Mac. These entities will still provide land and commercial financing and some residential type properties for special customers and portfolio them but the bulk of financing is done in preparation for sale to the secondary market.

Disadvantages of Conventional over Government-Backed Loans

1. *Higher down payments.* In certain price ranges, especially among first time homebuyers, many choose government-backed financing because they often require smaller down payments. In appropriate price ranges, VA and USDA loans require no down payment, and FHA and Cal-Vet programs usually require comparatively small down payments.

    While government loans were still acquired during the subprime era, the no to low down payments accompanied by virtually no documented qualifying requirements were the predominant choice of the time. For today's borrowers who fall outside the government loan guidelines there are conventional loans with as little as 5 percent required down payment, and in early 2015, a 3 percent down payment conventional loan became available.

2. *Credit scores.* Today's home buyers are more likely to select a government loan versus a conventional loan because of credit score rather than down payment difference. Conventional loans generally require a higher credit score unless the borrower is prepared to pay a penalty by way of a higher interest rate and/or cost in fees. Required credit scores had mostly increased across all loans as the industry tried to rebound. Currently scores have declined and government loan borrowers can qualify with scores under 600. Conventional borrowers require, with rare exception, a 620 or higher score, although scores as low as 580 are being considered.

3. *Prepayment penalties.* Government loans have long been without prepayment penalties. Most of the ARMs of the subprime days included prepayment penalties, especially during the first three years of the loan. Fannie Mae and Freddie Mac loans usually did not contain prepayment penalties and with the advent of the QM rules, such clauses are not currently allowed. Interestingly, equity loans (usually a second loan allowing for consumers to draw upon the loan when funds are needed) have skirted the pre-payment ban by simply referring to the payoff as an early closure fee if the equity or line of credit is closed within usually three to five years.

Sources of Conventional Money

Determining where to acquire a loan can be confusing. The main sources of conventional money are mortgage bankers and mortgage companies, commercial banks, credit unions, and savings banks.

Lenders who retain their loans, rather than selling them to Fannie Mae or Freddie Mac, can establish their own criteria for loan submissions. Other than having to adhere to basic state and federal regulations, these lenders have relative freedom in making loans. Often these are local lenders who are able to somewhat customize a loan to meet the specific needs of a local borrower. However, most lenders wish to resell their loans in the secondary market, and the number of portfolio loan options has comparatively diminished.

Two of the main players in the secondary market are the **Federal National Mortgage Association (Fannie Mae)** and the **Federal Home Loan Mortgage Corporation (Freddie Mac)**. For a bank to sell to them, they must adhere to standards established by these major loan purchasers. In order to compare lenders, you have to know what items to evaluate. While there can be minor differences, here are the basic loan guidelines.

1. *Loan-to-value ratios.* Conventional lenders have retreated from those overly flexible loan options (e.g., 100 percent) and now limit loans to the 93 percent loan-to-value level. As a matter of evaluating risk, conventional lenders often reduce their LTV ratios on two- to four-unit residential properties, condos, non-owner-occupied, raw land, and cash out refinance loans.

2. *Type of property.* It can be said that there has been a flight to quality regarding property that lenders will finance. Appraisers have become increasingly cautious, and new rules have been introduced (to be detailed in Chapter 8) in an effort to reassure investors' reliance upon home values. Lenders also make decisions regarding the type of property they will accept as security for a loan. Property condition, minimum size requirements, zoning restrictions, multiple unit, and/ or condo limitations are a few of the lenders' considerations. There is less variation between lender requirements following the excesses of a few years ago.

3. *Maximum loan amounts.* As the number of portfolio lenders continues to dwindle, most lenders have adopted the Fannie Mae/ Freddie Mac loan maximums discussed in Chapter 7. These are called conforming loans and allow participating lenders to sell their loans in the secondary market. These loan limits can change each year based upon government guidelines but have remained stable in recent years. A new category of loan limits, called conforming high balance loans, sometimes referred to as jumbo loans,

are available in some areas. These high balance loans are not available in all communities and are accompanied by higher interest rates and varying terms.

4. *Interest rates.* Perhaps the one item most shopped by consumers is the interest rate. Interest rates reflect the risk level accompanying each loan, for instance, a higher loan-to-value ratio loan likely requiring a higher interest rate. With a greater desire to resell their loans to Fannie Mae, Freddie Mac, and the government entities (e.g., FHA, VA), interest rates have become much more competitive and there is often little, if any, difference between lender quoted rates. Rates do frequently adjust, mostly as investors perceive market risk changes. When a rate change occurs, the adjustment is reflected simultaneously in all lenders' quotes. Lenders have adopted risk based pricing wherein there is a rate adjustment depending upon LTV, credit scores, and property type. It is not easy for a consumer to compare rates between lenders if the lender does not have an accurate profile of the borrower. This makes the consumers' opportunity to shop rates less advantageous.

5. *Loan fees.* The loan fee is how the lender gets paid, and the amount is determined by each lender. For the most part, these have also become more competitive as the source lenders (those ultimately funding the loan) have limited the amount a loan originator can earn on any given loan. These rules were enacted in response to perceived past abuses in subprime loan charges. That said, consumers who mostly concentrate on interest rates (noted above) need to pay more attention to how loan fees are identified. Tiered pricing has become the norm, with loan fees decreasing as the interest rate accepted by the borrower increases. In essence, the ultimate investor is willing to provide the lender with a rebate or fee for providing a higher yielding interest rate. Called rebate pricing or the use of yield spread premium, this will be discussed in greater detail in Chapter 7. Suffice it to say here that the enticing no points loan is a good example of the use of rebate pricing, wherein the borrower trades a higher interest rate in exchange for a rebate, which can be used to pay for the loan fee and other closing costs. This is an acceptable strategy in some situations, but the borrower must recognize that the no points offer is not a lender giveaway, but is being compensated via a higher interest rate.

6. *Prepayment penalties.* As discussed previously, most loans today are unlikely to include a prepayment penalty. True portfolio loans

and non-QM loans are much more likely to contain such payoff penalty clauses. As mentioned earlier, equity line loans now often charge an early closure fee of between $300 and $500.

7. *Borrower qualifications.* There is now greater standardization among lenders in regards to how they qualify borrowers. Local lenders retain some flexibility in qualifying guidelines for loans they choose not to sell. Most conventional lenders adhere to the Fannie Mae/Freddie Mac guidelines outlined in Chapter 9. The emphasis on tougher and ever-changing qualifying guidelines, and the need to fully understand them, are reasons enough to seek out professional lender representation when seeking a loan.

8. *Types of loans.* During the height of the subprime frenzy, lenders seemed to be competing with each other in designing loan options to meet every borrower's situation. The number of new loan instruments seemed to expand daily. After the collapse of what turned out to be mostly unsafe loans, the number of loan options reduced significantly. Whereas different lenders used to emphasize different loan types, most lenders now offer the same fixed rate, ARM, and other loans. One difference may be those lenders' ability to offer FHA loans. Government financing and what is required to be an authorized FHA lender will be addressed in Chapter 6.

Lenders regularly review their loan portfolios and revise lending policies based on economic changes, lending goals, and available funds. The examination of default ratios for various loans determines if a particular loan type will be continued or eliminated. For instance, it was easy to predict that the option ARM would be modified or eliminated when home appreciation rates began to decline and many of the loans went into default.

The point is that policies and standards set by conventional lenders are not static. Conventional lenders change their property and borrower standards in order to accomplish certain goals. In the past if a lender had a surplus of money, it might lower its property or borrower standards, lower the interest rate or change some other policy to enable it to make more loans. On the other hand, preferring to reduce loan demand, it could tighten up on its standards and increase the interest rate and loan fees—only, however, as long as its policies and standards were not discriminatory under fair housing laws. It is much more difficult to make such adjustments today and retain loan quality that is acceptable for sale to the secondary market.

5.2 KEEPING UP WITH LENDER POLICIES

Since conventional lender and market policies are subject to frequent changes, it can be a challenge to stay up-to-date. Professional real estate salespeople recognize the importance of financing to their success: if a property cannot be financed, it is less likely to be sold. As we have seen, the world of real estate financing has become increasingly complicated. So, what kind and how much information does a real estate licensee need to best represent his or her sellers and buyers? The most obvious information sought is the current interest rate. With each borrower and each property representing a unique situation, real estate licensees may find it advantageous to convey only basic finance information to clients and depend upon competent mortgage representatives to identify appropriate financing. This said, let's look at some of the ways to acquire information.

1. *Communication with lenders.* Recognizing that there may be less difference between lenders and their financing capacity, most salespeople determine a lender or two who they can call for up-to-date interest rate quotes. Since this is usually done when the licensee has a specific property in mind, they can discuss any potential property issues (e.g., condition of the home, excess land, well-water requirements). Some real estate offices survey lenders periodically, especially regarding interest rates, and this information is then distributed to all the salespeople within an office. With rate changes occurring so frequently, caution should be exercised before relying upon such surveys.

2. *Representatives* from lending institutions visit real estate offices and builders to solicit business and to inform them of their companies' current lending practices. Any changes in interest rate, loan programs, and so on can immediately be brought to the attention of the real estate agents and builders. Some offices, however, now restrict what they consider interruptions to real estate staff, and this option for obtaining information is not always available. With the increased use of e-mail marketing, many lenders use this avenue to push information out to agents. The result may be for agents to depend upon this information without doing their own searching for or verification of the information.

3. *Other salespeople* who have recently secured a loan are a good source of loan information. Since they have recently secured a loan, they know which lenders offered appropriate financing. Again, be cautious as each transaction can be unique; the loan that worked for one situation may not work for another and/or may not be the best option for the new transaction.

4. *Internet services.* A wide variety of Internet services are available for those seeking up to the minute (or at least daily) rate quotes and other pertinent data for loans of all types. The difficulty with Web sources is that the information may be outdated or, worse, may be too good to be true. Additionally, comparisons with local rates can be difficult. Check with your favorite local lender to see if it has a website that you can consult.

    Caution: There are fees accompanying any loan acquisition. The lender portion of the fees is often quoted in points, one point representing one percent of the loan amount. Zero-point or no cost loan offers can be deceptive as the borrower pays for said costs via an increase in the interest rate. As indicated in past chapters, these fees can be mitigated via seller assistance or rebate pricing, but they must be paid.

5. *Newsletters and flyers* distributed by lenders show the current policy and rates. Other organizations such as title and escrow companies occasionally distribute reports on current financing. E-mail has become more popular for this purpose.

6. *MLS meetings.* Almost every area in California has periodic Multiple Listing Service (MLS) meetings, during which lenders are permitted to quote their current programs and rates and may offer handouts and flyers.

Note of Interest—Risk Based Pricing

Interest rates are the one element of the lending process most understood by borrowers. After all, everyone knows that 4.5 percent is higher than 4.25 percent and thus is a more desired interest rate when borrowing. Hence, the first question typically asked when shopping for a loan is, "What is your interest rate?" The truthful answer is to quote the base rate at the time but to further inform the caller that "I cannot quote what your interest rate might be until I can assess your loan profile."

Loans have always been priced according the perceived risk for the lender. For the past few years, credit scores were a major determiner of loan terms and pricing. With high credit scores, borrowers could often obtain financing on a stated or no doc basis.

Lenders now consider borrowers' credit scores as well as the LTV of the new loan in what is being called risk based pricing. Mortgage lenders must consult a grid to determine the pricing. As credit scores reduce and LTV levels increase, the lender's perceived risk increases and is accommodated via an increase in the pricing. *The additional risk cost is added to the cost and not to the rate for the loan.*

The amount of down payment available will further identify the potential loan available to the borrower. There may be reserve requirements (an amount remaining as cash reserves following the close of escrow), borrower income limitations, or the need for rebate pricing (the Case & Point in Chapter 3) to assist with paying closing costs. These all factor into the interest rate that will be available to and/or ultimately selected by a specific borrower.

The emphasis on interest rates, per se, is misplaced. While providing a guide to the general condition of the economy, they should not be quoted to a potential borrower without attention to the other aspects related to loan pricing.

Which Lender to Use?

Experienced real estate licensees usually put together a team that includes various consultants, and certainly includes several favorite lenders. When you are ready to obtain financing for or have questions about a specific property, you depend upon your team members for accurate answers. In many cases, the more savvy licensees will shop service and expertise rather than simply looking for the lowest interest rate. Since, as we've noted, many lenders offer the same loan programs, rates, and terms (i.e., so that the loan can be sold to Fannie Mae or Freddie Mac), competency, reliability, and quality of service become more important than just the rate.

While everyone talks about service, what does it really mean? Does a lender communicate with everyone in the transaction, regularly and honestly? Are the processing times promised reliable? Is the lender organized and detail oriented and capable of meeting the various timelines required in every loan transaction? Will the lender take time to help a potential buyer know what he or she must do to prepare for acquiring a loan? Finally, if the lender can't offer the best loan option for your borrower, does he or she help find an appropriate lending source?

5.3 BUY-DOWN LOANS

The goal of every real estate transaction should be to create a win–win situation for both buyer and seller. At the same time, it seems that everyone wants a good deal, too. An interest rate buy-down can often be the vehicle to accomplish this win–win arrangement.

On a **buy-down loan**, the interest rate reduction is financed upfront by placing funds into an account from which the lender subsidizes the monthly payments.

Sellers generally compensate the lender, but it can also be the borrower who pays the lender to reduce the rate.

Why the Seller Participates

There are typically three primary ways that a seller can profit by offering a buy-down to a buyer. It will differentiate the seller's property within the marketplace and thereby create an interest to attract buyers. The buy-down can also increase the buyer's ability to qualify for a loan by qualifying at the lower bought down interest rate. Finally, a buy-down offer can often be less than a price reduction, the latter being too often the only method used to stimulate interest in the seller's property. The buy-down can actually maximize the seller's profit by eliminating the need for any price reductions.

Temporary Buy-Down Plans

From the buyer's perspective, a buy-down will assist in his or her qualifying to purchase and is usually of greater benefit than a price reduction. Buy-downs can be either temporary or permanent. The most common form of a temporary buy-down is known as the 2/1 buy-down. The buyer's initial interest rate is reduced 2 percent below the normal start rate. For instance, if the current fixed rate is 6.5 percent, payments for the first year of the mortgage would be calculated at 4.5 percent, the second year payments at 5.5 percent, and the third and subsequent years would be at the full 6.5 percent rate. The buyer qualifies at the second year buy-down rate of 5.5 percent and, thus, qualifies for a larger loan amount and a higher purchase price. Qualifying at the second year buy-down rate is a more recent program adjustment due to modifying the risk willingness of today's lenders.

Using the abovementioned scenario, if the loan is bought down from 6.5 percent to 4.5 percent for the first year and to 5.5 percent for the second year, let's calculate the amount necessary to affect the buy-down on a $100,000 loan. We must calculate the difference in the payments between the 6.5 percent loan and the payments at 4.5 percent and then at 5.5 percent. This difference is the amount that must be deposited in an account at the close of escrow. In our example, the total amount would be approximately $2,276. In most cases, this is paid by the seller as an incentive for the buyer to purchase. For an example, see the chart below.

A temporary buy-down can benefit the buyer whose current income is a bit low, but who anticipates that it will increase during the next two years. The lower payments during the first two-year period can help the buyer qualify and be able to comfortably make the increased payments as his or her income grows.

BUY-DOWN ON A $100,000 LOAN AT 6.5 PERCENT INTEREST

Months	Interest Rate	Monthly Payment @6.5%	Borrower's Payments	Monthly Buy-Down Amount	Total Buy-Down Amount
1–12	4.5%	$632.06 −	$506.69 =	$125.38 × 12	= $1,504.56
13–24	5.5%	$632.06 −	$567.79 =	$ 64.28 × 12	= $ 771.36
25–360	6.5%	$632.06 −	$632.06 =	0 × 12	= 0
				Total	= $2,275.92

Depending upon the economic climate at the time, the seller may want to add this subsidy to the price of the house, which then must reflect the added cost in the appraised value. As the buy-down subsidy increases, trying to recapture it in the sales price can become problematic.

Permanent Buy-Down Plans

Another alternative is the permanent buy-down, in which the interest rate is reduced for the entire life of the loan; for instance, if the current rate is 6.5 percent, the rate might be reduced to 5.5 percent for the full 30-year period. While the seller's cost for each of these options is nearly the same, many buyers prefer the temporary buy-down. Under most circumstances, the buyer is unlikely to remain in the home for a 30-year period. Thus, the temporary buy-down is typically a better arrangement.

Obviously, in a brisk real estate market, sellers are not enthusiastic about providing this kind of incentive. With a more difficult-to-sell property, or during slower market conditions, buy-downs become more popular. Lenders and buyers may also pay the fee for a buy-down. The lender buy-down is infrequently used and, in many cases, the buyer does not have sufficient cash available to contemplate a buy-down.

5.4 LOW DOWN PAYMENT CONVENTIONAL LOANS

Both the Federal National Mortgage Association and the Federal Home Loan Mortgage Corporation recognize that accumulating a down payment, and the required closing costs, keeps many people from buying a home. To help this situation, both have created a

low down payment program. Freddie Mac's Home Possible and Fannie Mae's My Community loans have similar requirements (broadly presented here as they tend to change).

- A low down payment – often 3 percent or less.
- The down payment can be a gift.
- Income qualifying ratios are easier.
- Borrowers can have a less than perfect credit history and lower scores are usually acceptable. Borrowers must participate in a home buyer educational seminar usually conducted via the Internet.
- In some cases, there may be a maximum income level requirement for the borrower based on the income of all family occupants.
- The loan can be used to buy only principal residences, including single-family residences, condos, planned unit developments, one- to four-unit residential income property, and manufactured homes attached to a permanent foundation.

Another popular Fannie Mae/Freddie Mac offering called the Community Home Buyer's Program was discontinued in late 2008 and as of mid-2015 had not yet been re-instated.

NOTE: Most low down payment programs were temporarily phased out by many lenders during 2009 when the PMI companies scaled back coverage to 90 percent loan-to-value ratio loans. Despite criticism from the lending industry indicating that the PMI companies' reactions were counterproductive in an environment where housing required help, not impediments, these loans continued, only at a much reduced level. The action, at the time, resulted in a flight to government-backed loan options, especially FHA (to be discussed in Chapter 6). These programs now face competition from other loan programs including the conventional Lender Paid Mortgage Insurance (LPMI) loan (discussed under New Rules later in this chapter) and the government USDA loan (discussed in Chapter 6).

97 Percent Financing Returns

In mid-December 2014, Fannie Mae announced the introduction of a 3 percent down payment loan option. The goal, announced by Fannie Mae, "is to help additional qualified borrowers who may not have the ability to acquire large down payment amounts gain access to mortgages." The introduction of this higher LTV loan followed a review that identified that other low down payment type mortgages have performed as well or better than other loans in regards to foreclosures.

At least one of the borrower-occupants must be a first-time buyer (e.g., not having owned a home in the previous three years).

No income limits or educational/counseling requirements apply as they do in the My Community Mortgage. Fixed rate mortgages up to 30 years are available up to the current conforming limit of $417,000. Only single family residences are allowed with no second units of any kind permitted. The 3 percent down payment may be gift funds but then the required credit score is a minimum 740. If the down payment money is the borrower's own verified funds, the minimum credit score reduces to 680. The debt-to-income also varies depending upon whether the down payment is gift funds. If the funds are the borrower's own, the ratio may not exceed 45 percent. If the down payment is a gift, the ratio reduces to 41 percent. In all cases, the required reserve amount may be gifted without penalty of any kind. These loans must meet Fannie Mae's usual eligibility requirements—including underwriting, income documentation, and risk management standards—and require private mortgage insurance consistent with general loans over 80 percent LTV.

Special Interest Topic

Lack of oversight = Bank failure = Loan changes

The loss of integrity accompanied by a substantial dose of greed among all participants, (congressional leaders, banks and lenders, mortgage originators, and regulators) culminating in the recession begun in 2008 followed by the bank failures, foreclosure scandals, and ultimate reduction in available loan programs, began way back in 1996. The passing of the National Homeownership Strategy bill seemed innocuous and well intentioned at the time but promoted events from which we have yet to fully emerge by mid-2015.

The bill was meant to extend the American dream of home ownership to a widening group of potential buyers. By 1998, fueled by double digit home appreciation rates, the housing bubble was initiated. Wall Street introduced credit default swaps (CDS), which were hardly understood but adopted by investors, creating $47 trillion in CDS contracts by 2008 in an unregulated and non-transparent process.

Late 1999 saw two major events occur: (1) Fannie Mae eased credit requirements to encourage banks to make loans to borrowers whose credit was insufficient to qualify for conventional financing and (2) Congress passed the Gramm-Leach-Bliley Act which repealed the Glass-Steagall Act that had controlled banking practices since 1933.

To a large degree, all financial oversight vanished, promoting the speculation in investment purchases (85 percent of the condo purchases in Miami were for investment purposes) while subprime lending reached 600 billion in 2006. From 2004 to 2007 more and more financial institutions invested large amounts in mortgage-backed securities (MBS), all on the belief that home prices would continue rising unabated. By 2004 the home ownership rate was at an all-time high of 69.2 percent.

Countrywide Financial, referred to as the largest provider of subprime loans in the nation, introduced automated loan approvals. Quickly followed by most other lending institutions, critics argued that loans were subjected to inappropriate review and the minimum documentation did not meet quality underwriting standards. But by late 2006 banks began to see looming problems. While divesting their own portfolios of what they began to view as crumbling investments, the big banks continued to sell subprime to consumers and to the global market but in significantly reduced amounts from the high of 2006.

While only 25 bank failures occurred in 2008 (after only 3 in 2007) the number ballooned to 140 in 2009 and 157 in 2010. IndyMack Bank, one of the largest California subprime lenders, was seized in 2008 with a 10.7 billion FDIC loss, the fourth largest bank failure in U.S. history. This was later dwarfed by the 307 billion dollar failure of Washington Mutual which was then absorbed by JPMorgan Chase. As the economic crises unfolded, the term "too big to fail" was coined, referring to the huge institutions. The following mergers seem to have exacerbated the situation as many feel that the banks are even larger today.

After 92 failures in 2011 and 51 in 2012, the numbers reduced to 24 in 2013 and 15 in 2014. In spite of these record bank closures, consumer deposits were protected as the insured amount had increased in 2009 to $250,000 from $100,000. But the ensuing foreclosure crises getting up to full steam by 2010 eroded consumer confidence, especially in view of the fact that no major financial corporation executive suffered any penalty. The public disgust was amplified by the Wall Street bonuses of 2010 and 2011 while homeowners were losing their homes in record numbers. (See the Case & Point in Chapter 11 for more information on foreclosures and short sales.)

The findings of the U.S. Financial Crisis Inquiry Commission in 2010 concluded that "the crisis was avoidable and was caused by: Widespread failures in financial regulation, including the Federal Reserve's failure to stem the tide of toxic mortgages; Dramatic breakdowns in corporate governance including too many financial firms acting recklessly and taking on too much risk." The term "greed" was not mentioned but was clearly an initial and driving aspect by everyone including banking institutions, borrowers, mortgage originators, and investors.

The new lending regulations and guidelines noted in this book are the direct result of this greed-spawned economic failure.

5.5 CALIFORNIA FAIR LENDING REGULATIONS

The Housing Financial Discrimination Act (Redlining Law) applies to owner-occupied residential properties of one to four units. The act also includes non-owner-occupied loans up to four units if 50 percent or more of the loan proceeds are to be used to improve the property.

The act states that financial institutions cannot deny or discriminate in fixing the amount, interest rate, or length of the loan based upon:

1. Neighborhood considerations as listed below, unless the institution can prove that such considerations are necessary to avoid unsafe and unsound business practices.
   a. Age of other properties in the neighborhood.
   b. Location of the property in the neighborhood.
   c. Location of the property on or near land zoned industrial or commercial.
   d. Other conditions, characteristics, or trends in the neighborhood.
2. Race, color, religion, sex, marital status or registered domestic partnership, sexual orientation, national origin, handicap, ancestry, family size, or other characteristics of the borrower.
3. Racial, ethnic, religious, national origin, or income-level composition of a neighborhood or whether that composition is expected to change.

The act also prohibits **discrimination by effect**. That means that the institution cannot engage in a lending practice that has a discriminatory effect against a protected group, unless that practice is required to achieve a legitimate business purpose. If it is clear that a practice could have a discriminatory effect, then the burden is on the institution to show that the practice is required. Called the Effects Test, it is difficult to adequately define and confusing when attempting to implement it.

To avoid accusations of discrimination by effect, the lending industry has adopted practices like credit scoring models and qualification guidelines that presumably apply to all borrowers. The debate continues regarding whether high credit score requirements, for instance, discriminate against the minority and lower-income groups, or whether this same group is disadvantaged when the rule for counting part-time income requires the part-time employment to be in the same field over a minimum two-year period.

The act has spelled out additional regulations in its attempt to clarify what loan terms an institution can enforce in its efforts to avoid *unsafe and unsound* business practices.

1. If the institution can document the factors in the neighborhood that are likely to cause the value of the property to decrease during the first five years, then it may make adjustments to the loan (reduce the loan amount, for example). As an example, during the economic housing downturn of 2006–2009, appraisers were required to address a neighborhood's declining values in determining the appraised value of the subject property.

2. The institution may consider natural or other hazardous conditions surrounding the property. A steep, unstable site would be an example of a hazardous condition and reason for rejection of the property. Requiring flood insurance for a property located near a potentially flooding water source is another acceptable way to mitigate a lender's risk.

3. A loan does not have to be made if it is clearly evident that the physical condition of the property would create an imminent threat to the health or safety of the occupant. Again, appraisers are relied upon to serve as the eyes for the lender and report any such threats.

4. Decisions on the loan security must be based solely on the value of the individual property, unless the institution can document specific neighborhood conditions that affect its present or short range value (three to five years). Such conditions may include market trends based upon actual transactions involving comparable property and trends indicating increasing numbers of abandoned, vandalized, or foreclosed properties in the immediate vicinity of the property. A statement that there are abandoned, vandalized, or foreclosed properties in the neighborhood will not, by itself, support a conclusion that a neighborhood is declining. The evidence necessary to document a probable decline must be specific.

5. If pending or recent zoning would affect the short-term value of the property, the loan may be denied or the terms may be altered. However, the fact that a property is located on or near land zoned industrial or commercial will not, in itself, be an adequate basis for denying the loan. On the other hand, a trend of converting many homes in the area to commercial use could present a reason for a reduction in the loan amount or even for a loan denial, based on the changing use in the community. If the lender is reasonably

sure that a building permit would not be issued in the event of casualty loss due to zoning, the lender may be justified in denying the loan.

6. Supplemental income such as overtime, bonuses, and part-time employment must be considered, *if stable*. Lenders consider such income stable when it can be verified as having occurred within the same employment field for a minimum of two years. Not to consider stable supplemental income could be discriminatory because minority and low- and moderate-income families often rely on this type of income.
7. The combined income of husband and wife must be considered.
8. The lender cannot favor applicants who have previously owned homes.
9. Payment-to-income ratios should be flexible. Inflexible ratios could discriminate against low- or moderate-income persons who often devote a greater percentage of their income to housing.
10. A lender may not deny a loan or require corrective work because of code violations or conditions of the property unless the cost of corrective work is more than 10 percent of the value before repairs or it is necessary to correct conditions that are a threat to the health and safety of the occupants. An example of this is the house having no heater or a lack of gas, broken glass, chipped or peeling paint that may contain lead, etc.
11. A lender cannot use a rigid list of onsite characteristics as an automatic basis for rejecting a loan, such as a minimum square footage requirement.
12. Each lender must have written loan standards available to the public.
13. Upon submission of a written loan application, the applicant must be given a fair lending notice (see Figure 5.1). The Federal Fair Lending Regulations, which also apply, can be found in Chapter 10.

5.6 PRIVATE MORTGAGE INSURANCE (PMI)

Private mortgage insurance (PMI) is designed to protect a lender in the case of a loan default in the higher loan-to-value ratio loans. Typically required for any loan exceeding a loan-to-value ratio of 80 percent, PMI guarantees the payment of the upper portion of a conventional loan in case the lender forecloses and suffers a loss.

A bit of history will help us understand the evolution of private mortgage insurance and the role it plays in allowing borrowers to acquire low down payment mortgages. The insurance for conventional

FIGURE 5.1 Fair lending notice.

THE HOUSING FINANCIAL DISCRIMINATION ACT OF 1977

FAIR LENDING NOTICE

DATE: COMPANY:

APPLICATION NO:

PROPERTY ADDRESS:

It is illegal to discriminate in the provisions of or in the availability of financial assistance because of the consideration of:

1. Trends, characteristics or conditions in the neighborhood or geographic area surrounding a housing accommodation, unless the financial institution can demonstrate in the particular case that such consideration is required to avoid an unsafe and unsound business practice; or

2. Race, color, religion, sex, marital status, national origin or ancestry.

It is illegal to consider the racial, ethnic, religious or national origin composition of a neighborhood or geographic area surrounding a housing accommodation or whether or not such composition is undergoing change, or is expected to undergo change, in appraising a housing accommodation or in determining whether or not, or under what terms and conditions, to provide financial assistance.

These provisions govern financial assistance for the purpose of the purchase, construction, rehabilitation or refinancing of a one-to-four unit family residence occupied by the owner and for the purpose of the home improvement of any one-to-four unit family residence.

If you have any questions about your rights, or if you wish to file a complaint, contact the management of this financial institution or the agency noted below:

I/we received a copy of this notice.

_____   _____
                        Date   Date

Calyx Form - fln.hp (2/99)

Source: © 2016 OnCourse Learning

loan coverage is sold by PMI companies. FHA's Mortgage Insurance Premium (MIP) and Mutual Mortgage Insurance (MMI) and the VA's funding fee are discussed in Chapter 6. Before the depression of 1929–1934, there were a number of PMI companies in operation. Most of them went into bankruptcy during the depression due to poor policies and inadequate regulations. The industry was dormant until the Mortgage Guarantee Insurance Corporation (MGIC) in Milwaukee began operations in 1957. Figure 5.2 shows the relationship between borrower, lender, and insurer.

FIGURE 5.2 Mortgage insurance.

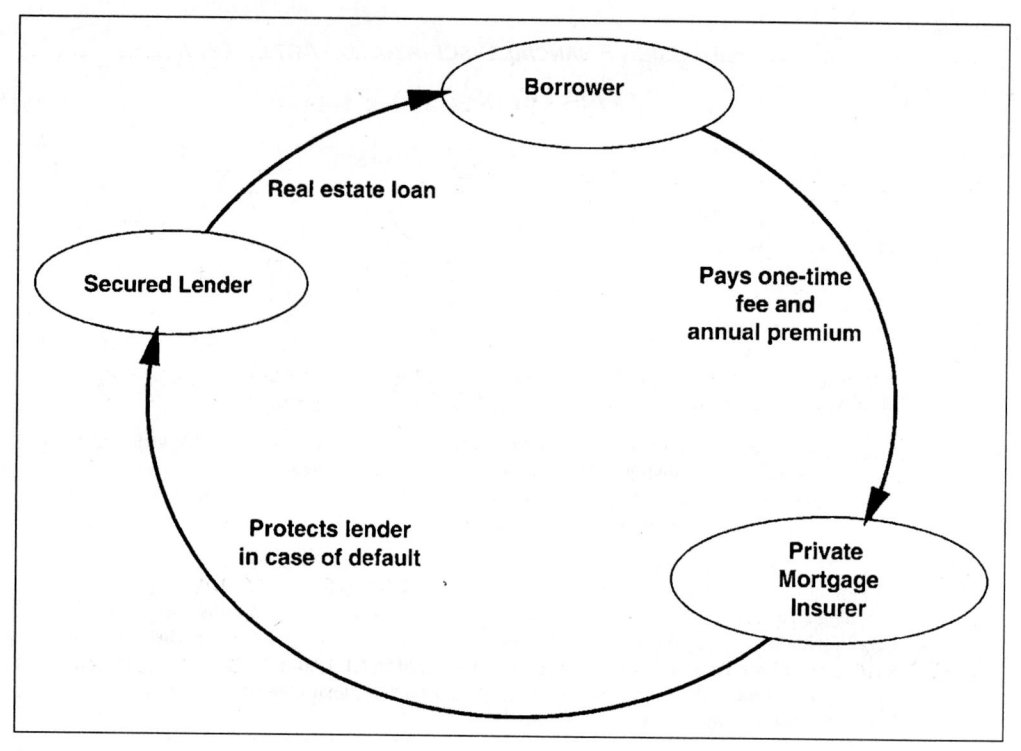

```
                    Borrower
       Real estate loan        Pays one-time
                               fee and
   Secured Lender              annual premium

       Protects lender
       in case of default      Private
                               Mortgage
                               Insurer
```

Source: © 2016 OnCourse Learning

The major growth of the PMI industry took place after 1970. One reason was that lenders and builders had become disenchanted with the FHA because of the red tape and the artificially low interest rate set by the government. Due to the low FHA interest rate, builders in those days had to pay high discounts (points) to sell their houses. To avoid these problems, builders and lenders turned to conventional mortgages insured by private mortgage insurance companies. As a result, they were able to eliminate high discounts and costly red tape. In addition, the mortgage insurance allowed lenders to continue making loans with low down payments.

Private mortgage insurance companies began to skyrocket in 1971 when lending institutions were given the authority to make 95 percent loan-to-value loans. In the same year, the Freddie Mac and Fannie Mae were given the authority to purchase high-ratio conventional loans. However, one of their requirements was that all loans above 80 percent must have mortgage insurance. When Freddie Mac and Fannie Mae began buying high-ratio conventional loans, they sparked the secondary market for conventional loans. Since these loans required mortgage insurance, this accelerated the growth of private mortgage insurance companies.

FIGURE 5.3 The difference between private mortgage insurance and credit life insurance.

PMI = If foreclosure occurs, the lender is reimbursed for any loss up to the maximum dollar coverage.

Credit Life Insurance = If borrower dies, the remaining loan balance is paid off by the insurance company.

Source: © 2016 OnCourse Learning

It should be noted that private mortgage insurance is not the same as **credit life insurance**. These two types of insurance are contrasted in Figure 5.3.

New Rules Emerge

Loan options up until the 2008 financial crises made it possible for buyers to purchase with as little as three percent down or even with no down payment (100 percent financing). To avoid the mortgage insurance rule that any home loan with less than 20 percent down payment required PMI coverage, much of the 100 percent financing was creatively completed via two loans: a first trust deed for 80 percent of the purchase price, thereby eliminating the need for PMI, and a second trust deed for the remaining 20 percent of the purchase price. As loan options became increasingly risky, the rules were revised; today's lenders are required to provide better disclosure regarding PMI coverage and how it might be eliminated in the future.

The most recent rules, while continually revised, are contained in the Homeowner's Protection Act of 1998, which became effective July 29, 1999. The act provides borrowers with certain rights when private mortgage insurance is required as a condition for obtaining certain residential mortgages. The current rules for conventional loans only include:

- PMI must be canceled upon the borrower's request under certain circumstances.
- PMI must be terminated automatically under certain circumstances.
- A borrower is entitled to receive notice of the right to cancel PMI, both at the consummation of the loan transaction and annually thereafter.
- Borrowers opting for *lender-paid mortgage insurance* programs must be provided with sufficient disclosures.

The general rule remains that PMI must continue for a minimum of two years, after which the equity in the home must have reached a minimum of 20 percent either via mortgage principal pay down, increased value due to home improvements, substantiated via a new appraisal, home appreciation, or a combination of these factors. Again, depending upon the investor, the combination of factors required to allow expunging the PMI could vary. In some cases, a borrower may be required to retain the PMI coverage for as long as five years, especially if the borrower is considered a high risk at the inception of the loan (see additional information below). Typically, a borrower signs a disclosure when signing loan documents that identifies the rules governing PMI coverage and its eventual elimination.

The rules indicate that a homeowner may cancel PMI when 20 percent equity is achieved. Automatic cancellation would occur when a 22 percent equity position is achieved. The only way a lender would know that the 22 percent equity position has been reached is via principal pay down, which could take many years. Thus, borrowers are advised to be aware of their equity position and petition their lender to have their PMI eliminated.

With lower annual appreciation rates accompanied by longer periods of ownership (past estimates indicated that many homeowners liquidated within seven years or less), a lender-paid mortgage insurance (LPMI) option has become popular. Applied to up to 93 percent loan-to-value ratio loans, LPMI incorporates the private mortgage premium in the interest rate. The advantage is that there can be substantial savings in monthly payment versus the traditional monthly mortgage insurance premium method. The disadvantage is that the slight increase in the original interest rate will persist for as long as the loan is retained.

PMI as a separate payment that can eventually be expunged might represent a better option for those borrowers anticipating long-term ownership. Mortgage insurance as it applies to government loans will be discussed in Chapter 6.

When the time comes to seek elimination of the PMI coverage, homeowners have to be current on their payments and have no subordinate liens against the property. Requests to cancel mortgage insurance must be in writing. Past jumbo loans (those loans that exceed the Fannie Mae/Freddie Mac conforming loan amount of $417,000) will be eligible for PMI cancellation at the 77 percent equity position. The availability in some high cost areas, where a high balance conforming loan limit exceeds the $417,000 loan amount, raises questions that can only be answered by contacting the lender.

As mentioned above, with the advent of credit scoring, borrowers are risk rated in relation to both their ability and willingness to pay back a mortgage. The lower the credit score, the higher the risk for the lender in making the loan. High risk mortgages, those made to borrowers with lower credit scores, may have additional conditions imposed for the elimination of mortgage insurance. Fannie Mae and Freddie Mac continually redefine industry guidelines that identify a risky borrower. For instance, in 2009, PMI companies reduced their risk exposure by refusing to cover loans in excess of 90 percent loan-to-value. The reason provided for the change was the concern over declining values in many housing areas, increasing the risk of exposure when there was less than 10 percent equity available. The conventional loan landscape was dramatically altered and the result was a flight to government-backed loans (discussed in Chapter 6) for any borrowers requiring a low down payment loan option.

How Is Mortgage Insurance Obtained?

Each PMI company sets its own policy regarding property and borrower standards. Generally, it follows the typical conventional lender standards set forth by FNMA/FHLMC. To obtain the insurance, an approved lender submits a loan package to the PMI company. After the package is received, the PMI company acts very quickly. The lender receives an answer by fax, e-mail, or telephone, usually the same day, and a written commitment follows later. This fast service is one of the main advantages of dealing with a PMI company. Some lenders are allowed to do in-house underwriting for PMI.

How Are Claims Handled?

If a foreclosure occurs on a property that is insured, the PMI company either:

1. Pays off the lender in full and takes title to the property, or
2. Pays the lender in accordance with the insurance, usually 20 to 25 percent of the principal balance plus certain expenses. The lender then keeps the property and is responsible for reselling it after foreclosure.

Chapter Summary

Any loan that is not a government-backed loan is called a conventional loan. Some of the perceived advantages of a conventional loan are faster processing, higher loan amounts, and perhaps less red tape. In some cases, the disadvantages include higher down payments and loan amounts.

There are many sources of conventional loans. The main sources are thrift institutions, commercial banks, credit unions, and mortgage companies. Each lender that keeps its paper (called portfolio loans) sets its own policy regarding loan-to-value ratio, type of property, interest rates, loan fees, and borrower qualifications, as long as it is not discriminatory.

However, most lenders plan on reselling the loan in the secondary market to Fannie Mae or Freddie Mac. In doing so, the lender originating the loan loses flexibility and must abide by the Fannie Mae or Freddie Mac guidelines.

On a buy-down loan, the interest rate is reduced by paying the lender an up-front fee or discount. A standard buy-down loan allows the rate to be reduced no more than 2 percent. The California Housing Financial Discrimination Act forbids discrimination in residential loans based on neighborhood considerations or on race, color, religion, sex, marital status or registered domestic partnership, sexual orientation, handicap, national origin, family size, or ancestry of the borrower.

Mortgage insurance is used to guarantee the upper portion of conventional loans and is used primarily on loans whose loan-to-value ratio exceeds 80 percent.

Important Terms and Concepts

Buy-down loan
Community Home Buyer's Program
Conventional loan
Credit life insurance
Discrimination by effect (Effects Test)
Federal Home Loan Mortgage Corporation (Freddie Mac)
Federal National Mortgage Association (Fannie Mae)
Government-backed loans
Low down payment program
Portfolio loan
Private Mortgage Insurance (PMI)

Reviewing Your Understanding

Questions for Discussion

1. List five items of comparison when shopping with conventional lenders for a real estate loan.
2. Identify the "win–win" features of a buy-down mortgage.
3. Describe how private mortgage insurance (PMI) works, including coverage and costs and the occasional advantage of the LPMI option.
4. The Housing Financial Discrimination Act (Redlining Law) prohibits discrimination based upon a variety of considerations. List at least five of these.

Multiple-Choice Questions

1. A nongovernment-backed loan is best known as a
   a. portfolio loan.
   b. standard loan.
   c. conventional loan.
   d. normal loan.

2. Assume an application for a $450,000 loan is made and that the lender charges 1.5 points as a condition for granting the loan. The loan fee will be
   a. $6,750.
   b. $4,500.
   c. $67,500.
   d. none of the above.

3. Private mortgage insurance covers the
   a. upper portion of the loan amount.
   b. middle portion of the loan amount.
   c. lower portion of the loan amount.
   d. entire loan.

4. The most flexible loan terms, not necessarily the lowest interest rate, are usually obtainable on what type of loan?
   a. Portfolio
   b. Standard
   c. Conforming
   d. FHA

5. Subsidized loans issued by the state of California and its counties and cities are usually funded by
   a. conventional sources.
   b. bond issues. ✓
   c. stock issues.
   d. the Federal Reserve Bank.

6. In the event of foreclosure of a PMI-backed conventional loan, the insurer may
   a. pay off the lender in full and take back the property.
   b. pay the lender up to the amount of insurance.
   c. do either (a) or (b). ✓
   d. do neither (a) nor (b).

7. When a seller or builder buys down the borrower's interest rate for the life of the loan, it is called
   a. a 3/2/1 buy-down.
   b. an adjustable buy-down.
   c. a fixed buy-down.
   d. a permanent buy-down. ✓

8. Private mortgage insurance
   a. protects lenders in case of loan default. ✓
   b. protects homebuyers in case they default on their loans.
   c. is required for any loan in excess of 20 percent loan-to-value.
   d. is required of all government-backed loans.

9. One might expect to find the shortest processing time in the case of
   a. government-backed loans.
   b. portfolio loans. ✓
   c. loans that are to be sold in the secondary market.
   d. loans on which discount fees are charged.

10. Which of the following is often required for a Fannie Mae/Freddie Mac low down payment first-time home buyer loan?
    a. An educational seminar ✓
    b. Sufficient rental income
    c. A five-year work history
    d. Tougher income qualifying ratio

11. Regulations affecting a lender's policy on qualifying borrowers would include
    a. supplemental income, such as overtime pay.
    b. part-time employment.
    c. combined income of both spouses.
    d. all of the above. ✓

12. When might a buyer want to pay down the interest rate on a loan?
    a. When the seller needs to net more profit
    b. When the buyer plans to move within two years of the purchase
    c. When the buyer plans to own the property for a long time ✓
    d. When the bank requires it

13. When lenders regularly review their loan portfolios and revise lending policies, they do not base their decisions on
    a. economic changes.
    b. available funds.
    c. racial considerations. ✓
    d. lending goals.

14. Qualifying standards for borrowers using conventional loans that are to be sold to Fannie Mae/Freddie Mac
    a. differ widely, depending upon the particular lender.
    ✓ b. are usually the same throughout the range of lenders.
    c. are set by various government bodies.
    d. differ greatly, depending upon whether the lender is state or federally chartered.

15. An interest rate that is tied to an index that is subject to change is most commonly called
    a. fluctuating.
    ✓ b. adjustable.
    c. changeable.
    d. irregular.

16. California's Housing Financial Discrimination Act allows lenders to discriminate in residential lending only in the case of
    a. the loan applicant's low ratio of payment to income.
    b. the location of the property near industrial property.
    ✓ c. a situation that would lead to unsafe and unsound business practices.
    d. ethnic or racial mix.

17. Buy-down loans offer sellers an opportunity to
    a. profit at the buyer's expense.
    ✓ b. help a buyer qualify for a loan.
    c. attract primarily buyers of lower-priced homes.
    d. increase the asking price in exchange for the buy-down.

18. The erosion in the purchasing power of money, and for which lenders may adjust interest rates under ARM loans, is labeled
    a. deflation.
    ✓ b. inflation.
    c. devaluation.
    d. stagflation.

19. The type of insurance that pays off the mortgage balance in the event of the borrower's death is called
    a. private mortgage insurance.
    b. standard life insurance.
    ✓ c. credit life insurance.
    d. disability insurance.

20. Of the buy-down loan plans, the type that's usually best for the buyer is the
    a. temporary buy-down for two years.
    b. temporary buy-down for five years.
    ✓ c. permanent buy-down plan.
    d. plan with full amortization.

CASE & POINT

Consumer Financial Protection Bureau (CFPB)

The new rules defined

Authorized by the Dodd-Frank Wall Street Reform and Protection Act of 2010, the CFPB was a legislative response to the financial crises of 2007–2008 and the subsequent Great Recession. With jurisdiction over nearly all activities originating from numerous entities (i.e., banks, credit unions, security firms, payday lenders, debt collectors, student loan providers), the CFPB focused largely on perceived past home mortgage excesses and abuses.

The act's rules were largely based on the belief that a more informed consumer awareness of the cost of credit would both protect against future lending abuses and create an economic stability among credit providers. The Truth in Lending Act (TILA) of 1968 established a standardized form of disclosure of costs and charges in an effort to provide a means with which borrowers could shop for their best loan. CFPB rules now regulated the actual charges that could be imposed for consumer credit.

Thus was spawned the QM, the ATR rules, and a host of disclosures that some critics say are more confusing than helpful to consumers attempting to understand their proposed home mortgage.

Qualified Mortgages may not contain certain features that are deemed to increase lending risks to consumers. The main focus, however, was to limit the points and fees accompanying any new home loan. A limit of 3 percent on the mortgage provider's compensation per loan was to combat what was perceived as past steering of consumers to more expensive loan options. The attempt was to provide a more transparent understanding of the costs associated with home financing. Perhaps the greater limiting factor for a Qualified Mortgage is that the borrower's overall debt ratio cannot exceed 43 percent.

The Ability to Repay rules indicate that the mortgage originator make a reasonable and good faith determination, based on verified and documented information, that the consumer has reasonable ability to repay the loan with its terms, including taxes, insurance, and other identified assessments. This meant no change for lenders who had adhered to what was referred to as a fully documented loan in which they always obtained appropriate documentation to support the borrower's ability to repay the loan.

There was another provision referring to the lack of risky features that mostly suggested no prepayment penalties and a caution regarding the promotion of adjustable rate financing. By mid-2014 most lenders had adjusted to the rules, fixed rate mortgages had become the prime loan option, and the initial apprehension accompanying the new regulations had been dispelled. October 2015 saw the introduction of the new Loan Estimate (LE) and Closing Disclosure (CD) forms that were more than a year in development. The LE replaced the GFE and TIL and the CD replaced the long time used HUD 1 final disclosure. In spite of an aggressive lobbying from lending institutions, use of the forms was initiated with seemingly few problems. As with most new procedures, time will determine if the initial concerns were justified.

As with many well-meaning government regulations, unintended consequences occur, requiring nearly constant revision and re-interpretation. Toward the end of 2014, the large banking institutions (the same "too big to fail" banks) were again promoting adjustable rate mortgages along with what would be a slow return to loan procedures that had precipitated all of the regulations in the first place. Among more responsible lenders there was a concern that the old adage that if we don't pay attention to our history we are bound to repeat it was about to be demonstrated again.

As if right on cue, in December 2014, the omnibus bill to fund the government for the year ahead had buried in its 1582 page legislation removing the provision wherein the CFPB could restrict banks from participating in the derivative market. It was these swaps related to the selling of derivatives globally that most experts concur greatly contributed to the economic disaster in 2008. While too much regulation was causing banks to restrict lending, this buried piece of legislation re-allowed the gambling appetite of the big banks to continue unrestricted by the CFPB's oversight. The banks have resisted regulation and control since the inception of the CFPB, and we will have to see if this latest success is the precursor to the unraveling of oversight.

The lack of clear guidelines accompanying the programs developed to assist borrowers in dealing with a loss of equity and the inability of borrowers to now qualify for refinanced or modified loans too often fell short of anticipated results.

Programs wherein refinancers had to document their income (remember the exaggeration of incomes with all of the liar loans) eliminated many struggling borrowers who found themselves waiting months only to find that their application for refinancing and/or loan modification had been denied. Foreclosure or a short sale (see the Case & Point following Chapter 11) soon followed.

During this same period of time, the FHA was being promoted as the agency that would allow many borrowers to refinance loans with more affordable rates and terms. The FHA's response was a reluctance to be the depositor of what it sensed was a lot of bad debt. By March of 2010, FHA announced that nearly 30 percent of the streamline refinances that they had funded during the past two years were underwater (had lost value) and were possible foreclosures.

The resulting FHA guidelines became so restrictive that far fewer borrowers could acquire relief than originally anticipated. After several years of increasing Mortgage Insurance Premiums MIP), in early 2015, FHA made a few adjustments, including lowering their up-front MIP premium. This attempt to make FHA a more competitive loan option may have been prompted by the introduction of the 97% conventional loan which was touted as an FHA "look alike" loan.

While some borrowers did find relief, the well-meaning efforts of all the legislation may be deemed mostly ineffective in staving off an increasing number of foreclosures during 2009 and 2010. In its final analysis, the lack of a clear concept of how to really solve the needs of distressed borrowers accompanied by the desire to protect both borrowers and lenders resulted in mostly ineffective legislation.

© Shuttertock / David Evison

GOVERNMENT-BACKED FINANCING

OVERVIEW

This chapter covers five major sources of government-backed loans: the Federal Housing Administration (FHA), U.S. Department of Veterans Affairs (VA), California Department of Veteran Affairs (Cal-Vet), U.S. Department of Agriculture (USDA), and the California Housing Finance Agency (CalHFA).

After completing this chapter, you will be able to:

- List the main advantages and disadvantages of FHA-insured loans.
- Identify the guidelines governing FHA loans.
- Explain the key features of VA-guaranteed loans.
- List the main characteristics of the Cal-Vet loan system.
- Understand the benefits of the USDA loan.
- Outline the CalHFA first-time home buyer program.

6.1 FEDERAL HOUSING ADMINISTRATION

In this section, we discuss what the Federal Housing Administration (FHA) does and some of the advantages and disadvantages of an **FHA-insured loan**. Commonly used FHA programs are explained here, with examples. Full details regarding the FHA can be found at www.hud.gov.

What Is the FHA?

The FHA, part of the Department of Housing and Urban Development, was established in 1934 to improve the construction and financing of housing. Since its creation, it has had a major influence on real estate financing. Some of today's loan features that are taken for granted were initiated by the FHA. For example, before the FHA, it was common practice to make real estate loans for short periods of time (usually for a period of one to five years). These loans were not fully amortized and every few years, borrowers had to renegotiate loans with their lender. This created problems, particularly during the Great Depression of the 1930s, during which time, when loans were due, many lenders were not willing or able to renew the loans and as a result there were massive foreclosures.

The need for reform created the FHA and its three major goals:

1. Provide affordable financing
2. Create increased homeownership
3. Upgrade property standards

To accomplish the stated goals, the following were introduced:

- Fully amortized loans
- Low down payment loans
- Low interest rates
- Mandatory collection of taxes and fire insurance premiums via the establishment of impound accounts
- Minimum property standards to promote an improved quality of construction and create some uniformity via a new appraisal process
- Standards for qualifying owner-occupant borrowers

The FHA is not a lender—it insures authorized lenders, who do make the loans, against loss in the event of foreclosure. Among the qualified lenders are typically mortgage companies, savings banks, and commercial banks. Referred to as correspondents, authorized lenders use FHA guidelines for approving the borrower and the property. After the loan is funded and has closed escrow, the loan is insured by the FHA.

FHA: Its Role in the Recovery

The main thrust of the Economic Recovery Act of 2008 was to help homeowners in immediate risk of losing their homes to foreclosure. The FHA was perceived as the agency that would do much of the refinancing and was thus compelled to offer to refinance many of these on-the-verge-of defaulting loans.

The FHA's reluctance to become the depositor of what it sensed was a lot of bad debt led to an attempt to design affordable guidelines that would create payment stability. These new rules included a maximum 90 percent LTV ratio based on the current market value of the home and a 3 percent insurance fee to compensate for the risk. Determining eligibility proved confusing in that borrowers were required to demonstrate a lack of capacity to pay their current mortgages but had to show sufficient income to qualify for the new, presumably smaller, fixed rate FHA loan. An equity sharing component related to the future sale of the home was, for many, the deal breaker. It was not surprising that the anticipated FHA refinance program to save homeowners was not very successful. FHA's response to criticism was that they were merely attempting to design appropriate guidelines that would create payment stability while avoiding accumulating untold numbers of bad loans.

In spite of these efforts, the result for FHA was an increased number of defaulted loans negatively impacting the agency's reserve fund from which mortgage insurance premiums are paid. Since legislatively, FHA's mortgage insurance reserve fund must be maintained at a required level, a way had to be found to replenish the dwindling fund. Over the next few years, the mortgage insurance premiums were raised five times until the premiums reached an all-time high.

In 2006 two mortgage insurance premiums were introduced, the first identified as the Upfront Mortgage Insurance Premium (UFMIP) as well as a monthly MIP. By late 2014 the UFMIP was 1.75 percent and the annual MIP had recently been reduced from 1.35 percent to 0.85 percent. A little math will put these fees into perspective. Assuming a purchase price of $300,000, the 3.5 percent required down payment equals $10,500 with a base loan amount of $289,500. Now add to the base loan amount 1.75 percent of UFMIP or $5,066.25. The total loan amount is then $294,566 upon which the monthly mortgage insurance fee of 0.85 percent (reduced from 1.35 percent in late 2014) is calculated: $2,503.81 divided by 12 equals the monthly MIP of $208.65.

These two insurance premiums were viewed as cost prohibitive, and an FHA loan became uncompetitive with other loan options. The FHA's loan volume declined significantly and in an effort to make the loans more accessible and desirable, the FHA HAWK program was proposed in late 2014.

Late legislation designed to fund the government through 2015 was passed in December 2014, but it did not fund the newly designed HAWK program. In the meantime, in response to the complaints about excessive mortgage insurance fees (noted above) and with the HAWK program temporarily delayed, FHA unexpectedly announced a reduction of 50 basis points (0.50 percent) to the annual MIP premium (noted above) for the 30 year loans beginning January 26, 2015. It is anticipated that the reduction from 1.35 percent to 0.85 percent will result in qualifying more borrowers and keep FHA financing competitive with the 97 percent conventional loan options.

New Hawk Program Introduced

While delayed, FHA is committed to its Blueprint for Access. The HAWK program is expected to eventually be rolled out as a pilot program in 2015 and is anticipated to provide another assist to FHA's attempt to recapture some of its lost loan participation. "HAWK" is an acronym standing for Homeowners Armed with Knowledge. The anticipation is that home buyers who acquire counseling and education will be less likely to default on their loans.

The incentive to participate is that HAWK homeowners will be eligible for reduced Upfront MIP, reduced monthly premiums, and with an 18 month consistent payments history, another reduction in the monthly MIP would be available. A summary of the planned reductions is as follows:

1. 0.50 percentage point reduction in upfront MIP.
2. 0.10 percentage point reduction in annual MIP (this will presumably be on top of the recent 0.50 percent reduction noted above).
3. If there is no 90-day delinquency within the first 18 months, beginning with the start of the loan's third year (i.e. 25th month), annual MIP will be reduced an additional 0.15 percentage points.

The program is available to only first-time buyers (defined as not having owned a home in the past 36 months) and will not apply to borrowers wishing to refinance. Participating borrowers are required to commit themselves to a series of counseling and educational practices and time frames, including:

Prior to Going to Contract: Borrowers must have six hours of housing education and counseling via an approved counseling agency. It is anticipated that this may be acquired via the Internet but was not yet determined at publication time. The time frame requires that this process be completed at least 10 days prior to entering into any purchase contract. If a sales contract is signed before the 10-day period has elapsed, one is ineligible for a HAWK loan.

Prior to Closing Your Loan: A one-hour pre-closing counseling session must occur between the time of the completed loan application and three days prior to the actual loan closing.

After Loan Closing: Another one hour of counseling no sooner than 30 days or later than one-year post closing. This coupled with the good payments record (noted above) will further reduce the monthly MIP another 0.15 percentage points.

Critics claim that the process is too cumbersome and the incentives too little to entice borrowers and/or lenders to participate in this four year pilot program. Complicating matters for the FHA is the competition from the U.S. Department of Agriculture (USDA) loan described later in this chapter and the introduction of 3 percent down payment conventional loans. As with any new program, time will tell if the HAWK loan will restore the FHA loan program to competitiveness.

Why Use FHA Loan?

Although FHA loans have declined somewhat in popularity, there are advantages that still make the program viable. The two largest detractions are the mortgage insurance costs noted above (in spite of the recent reduction in the monthly MIP) and the purchase price caps (by county) that are generally less than competing loan programs. Financing programs are cyclical, depending upon economic conditions, and the following FHA loan advantages will likely result in the program's continued use.

1. The low down payment, generally 3.5 percent, remains attractive. This required cash investment may be acquired via gift funds from appropriate sources. The gifting party (family, government agency, etc.) is not required to be on the loan. A friend may provide a gift but the relationship must be well documented or the gift will be considered merely a disguised loan. Gifts cannot come from a seller, builder, or outside private source. The seller can provide an incentive whereby some of closing costs can be paid (see #12 below). The down payment may also be borrowed in some instances via the CalHFA program, discussed later. It remains to be seen if the conventional 97% loan, discussed in Chapter 5, becomes a competitive option to the FHA loan.

2. The new compensation rules mandated by the CFPB eliminated the old 1 percent maximum loan fee, but loan compensation limits remain competitive with other loan options.

3. Interest rates and discount points are negotiable between lender and borrower, consistent with competitive loan options.

4. The maximum loan amount limits (noted above) are little impediment to the lower income borrowers most likely to use FHA financing. The buyer can pay more than the FHA appraisal value; the loan amount remains, as with all loan options, based upon the appraised value or the purchase price, whichever is lower.

5. FHA appraisals (called **"conditional commitments"**) are good for six months on existing property or one year on new construction. The appraisal process changed in 2010 when FHA adopted a process similar to the Home Valuation Code of Conduct (HVCC)

that is used in conventional financing. A full discussion of the HVCC can be found in Chapter 8.

6. Pest control reports are no longer automatically required. Instead, HVCC assigned appraisers are charged with determining if a pest control and/or other inspections (e.g., roof, electrical, etc.) are to be required.

7. An impound account in which the tax, homeowner's insurance, and monthly mortgage insurance (MMI) costs paid as part of the monthly mortgage payment is deposited in a separate account, sometimes called an escrow account. An impound account generally assists FHA buyers who are relieved of the concern to save during the year in order to pay these expenses when they come due.

8. FHA loans may be paid off at any time without prepayment penalty.

9. The more credit challenged borrowers with lower credit scores or with less than typical credit history may purchase with a score as low as 580 (as of mid-2015). A non-traditional credit history may be assembled by reviewing the borrower's payment record on monthly bills, rent, and other references, which can build an acceptable credit history.

10. Non-occupant co-borrowers may be used to strengthen the loan file for qualifying purposes. The co-borrower will be accountable for the payments, and his or her credit will be affected if monthly payments are late or unpaid.

11. The maximum loan term is 30 years or 75 percent of the remaining economic life of the property, whichever is less. The remaining economic life, identified in the appraisal, must be at least 40 years to meet these criteria.

12. **Direct endorsement (DE),** in which lenders have the authority to process, underwrite, and fund an FHA loan prior to delivery to FHA for insuring purposes, has eliminated a major disadvantage as loans can now be completed within the same times frames as competing loan options.

13. Sellers may pay up to 3 percent of the buyer's "customary and reasonable" closing costs (figure reduced from 6 percent allowed until early 2010). Rebate pricing (lender-paid fees via acceptance of a higher interest rate), coupled with seller concession up to 3 percent, can now accommodate most, if not all, of the buyer's expected closing costs.

14. FHA loans may be assumed on a "subject to" basis, wherein a credit worthy owner-occupant buyer may take over the loan

without change to the interest rate. While low interest rates of the past few years have blunted this advantage, during high-interest rate times, being able to allow someone to take over one's lower interest rate loan might benefit a seller.

15. While seldom used, secondary financing is allowed with a new FHA loan provided the combined FHA first and second loans do not exceed the FHA maximum.

Calculating FHA Loan Amounts

The low down payment of only 3.5 percent is a major attraction of the FHA loan. As with conventional lenders, FHA-insured base loan amounts are calculated using the lower of the property's sales price or appraisal value. This base loan amount cannot exceed the annually determined statutory limit for the county in which the property is located. These county limits vary, with some areas now designated as high-cost areas.

The high balance amount up to $729,750 represented a temporary increase in FHA's loan limits in an effort to accommodate borrowers who found themselves in difficulty during the 2008 financial crises. On January 1, 2014, the maximum loan amount was reduced to the current $625,500 to create congruency with conventional loan limits. (There are four locations for which the FHA high balance amount exceeds this current limit: Alaska, Guam, Hawaii, and the Virgin Islands.) While these high balances were to be temporary, set to expire in 2010, there is no indication that they will not remain permanent. With few exceptions where loan limits were raised, they remained the same for most locations.

The 3.5 percent cash investment cannot come from loans from sources such as the seller, the builder, or an outside private source. If the seller or builder attempts to circumvent this rule by offering a decorating allowance or any other inducements, the maximum FHA-insured loan is decreased by said amounts.

Calculating the final loan amount can be complicated and is best left to mortgage lenders. The Upfront Mortgage Insurance Premium must be added to the base loan amount to determine the total amount to be financed.

FHA Programs

The National Housing Act of 1934 created the FHA. The act has 11 titles, or subdivisions, with further subdivisions called sections.

This chapter deals with only some of the sections under Title II of the act, since these are the most important to the average consumer or real estate agent. Title II authorizes the FHA to insure the financing on proposed or existing dwellings for one- to four-family residences. The main sections are 203(b) and 245(a). Each of these programs is discussed below.

Section 203(b)

This is the loan to which most refer when discussing FHA financing. Under the 203(b) program:

1. Anyone 18 and over is eligible.
2. Loans are available on owner-occupied properties of from one to four units.
3. U.S. citizenship is not required; resident aliens are eligible.
4. As indicated before, the FHA establishes a range of maximum loan amounts for one- to four-unit dwellings that vary according to state and county.

Occupancy required

The FHA requires the borrower to occupy the property. The only exception is if an investor purchases a HUD repossession and provides a 25 percent down payment. A non-occupant co-borrower (e.g.; parents borrowing with a son or daughter) is allowed.

Houses less than one year old

You cannot obtain a standard maximum FHA loan on a house that is less than one year old that was not built under FHA or VA inspections. This restriction also applies to houses that were moved onto the site less than one year earlier. The underlying reason for this requirement is that the FHA wants a property to have endured all four seasons. The FHA's maximum loan on these properties is reduced to 90 percent LTV of the sales price or appraised value, whichever is lower.

Section 245(a) and 251 FHA Adjustable Rate Loans

Although considered relatively stable in regards to adjustable rate mortgages, the FHA ARM programs have lost some of their past appeal. The section 245 loans were Graduated Payment Mortgages (GPM) made to low or moderate income borrowers anticipating increasing incomes over the loan terms. Of the five plans, number III was the most popular, wherein the 7.5 percent annual increases to the annual payments were the steepest of the options but were predictable, allowing borrowers to adequately plan for the increases. Limiting the payment increases could result in negative amortization over the first five years depending upon market conditions and rate increases. The down payment was generally 10 percent versus the more normal 3.5 percent to allow for any loss of equity via negative amortization. As home values declined in the past, negatively amortized loans lost popularity with both lenders and borrowers.

More recently, the FHA Adjustable loans mirror the conventional loan options. Loans are issued for 1, 3, 5, 7, or 10 year fixed periods followed by the balance of the term as one-year adjustable loans. (these types of loans were discussed in Chapter 4) The anticipation with these fixed to adjustable loans is that the borrower may liquidate the home prior to any ARM conversion, depending, of course, on the initial fixed period. The one-year Treasury Constant Maturities Index is used for determining the interest rate changes. The interest rate for one-year and three-year insured ARMs may not be increased or decreased by more than one percentage point per year after the fixed-payment period is over, with a maximum change of 5 percentage points over the life of the loan. For 5-year, 7-year, and 10-year ARMs, the interest rate may change a maximum of 2 percentage points annually and 6 percentage points over the life of the loan. A 5/5 ARM loan has become the more popular loan option wherein the loan is fixed for the first five years and then adjusted and fixed for a second five year period. Lenders refer to this product as "sane" adjustable as it provides relative stability for a ten year period.

Section 203k Rehabilitation Mortgage

Used primarily for the acquisition of properties that need repairs or rehabilitation, the 203k is much like a construction/take-out type loan. The loan is sufficient to acquire the property, with the money for rehabilitation placed into an escrow account. The work is to be performed by a licenses contractor to whom the funds will be dispersed in increments as the renovation occurs. The loan amount is determined by taking the "as is" appraised value or purchase price, whichever is less, plus the rehabilitation cost (identified via submitted plans) plus a minimum 10 percent reserve. Qualifying homes can include even a one- to four-family home that has been torn down, provided that some of the existing foundation is still in place.

Unlike most construction loans, the 203k loan is completely funded when the escrow closes. While the rehabilitation funds are held in an escrow account (noted above), the borrower begins payments on the entire loan amount at the close of escrow. If the home is uninhabitable, the borrower can finance up to six months PITI for living expenses while rehabilitation work is completed.

While major repairs can be accomplished via this 203k loan, there is a streamline version available for more minor updating of purchased property. Limited to $35,000, the loan is designed for fixer-upper type properties. The streamline allows for simple repairs that can easily be estimated and completed within a short time span. The rules and guidelines regarding appropriate expenditures are quite specific and need to be thoroughly understood prior to initiating such a loan.

What Is Ahead for the FHA?

As conventional lenders became more conservative in their loan options, low down payment FHA loans, in spite of many qualifying restrictions, continued to appeal to large numbers of potential home buyers. Real estate financing, however, remains an evolving process, and as the FHA continues to adjust to the changing lending environment, the following have already been adopted and are likely to impact how FHA conducts business in the future.

- Emphasis on Controlling Risk: The aforementioned HAWK program is one way that FHA is trying to improve the quality of their loan portfolio and limit the risk of foreclosure. The adoption of risk management grids, much like conventional lenders, requires higher interest and/or costs for borrowers deemed of greater risk. The agency has introduced practices for their lending partners that target a better loan review process for earlier discovery of poor product performance and/or policy problems. Critics suggest that the continuing emphasis on risk management is interfering in FHA's original mission of providing loans to borrowers otherwise unable to acquire financing.
- Oversight of Lenders: Accompanying risk management practices is the monitoring of early default rates and lenders who do not meet agency standards. Poor performing lenders will be precluded from continuing to offer FHA loans. Higher net worth requirements for approved direct endorsement lenders to $1 million was imposed by 2011. These lenders, in turn, now determine the mortgage brokers/originators from whom they will accept FHA- originated loans. In other words, loan correspondents will no longer receive independent FHA approval for origination eligibility. The direct endorsement lenders will be responsible for the origination and oversight process of these lenders and loans, much like retail loans are currently treated in the conventional loan arena.

Underwriting Changes: The fear that tightening underwriting standards would accompany the development of the FHA's own automated underwriting system has not occurred. With the introduction of their automated loan approval system, FHA underwriters now function more like their conventional loan counterparts, responsible for making sure that accurate documentation accompanies every automatically approved loan application. As part of the lender oversight measures noted above, DE lender underwriter guidelines were revised requiring an authorized FHA underwriter to possess increased experience and credentials.

Introduction of a New Handbook in June 2015: In October 2014 the Federal Housing Administration (FHA) announced the publication of its new Single Family Housing Policy Handbook. Covering all aspects of FHA lending from origination through post-closing and endorsement, the publication's intent is to provide a comprehensive, single source for assessing policy and procedures. Lenders had adopted overlays (e.g., individual lender/investor qualifying requirements, usually in excess of FHA actual guidelines) as a way to protect themselves from oft times confusing regulations and guidelines. The handbook, it is hoped, will provide increased clarity. Toward that end, there is greater concentration on the post-closing and endorsement policies as these most affect the lenders making FHA loans. Mortgagee letters are being consolidated and updated to reflect the updated and hopefully clearer guidelines. The handbook will likely be a work in progress but became effective after September 14, 2015. It will hopefully increase lender interest in marketing FHA loans. More info can be found at www.hud.gov.

Relaxation of Loan Correspondent Eligibility: The elimination of loan correspondent approval was perhaps the most significant change in 2011. Permitting FHA direct endorsement lenders to accept applications from any source that meets state and federal guidelines (e.g., RESPA) eliminates current lender approval requirements. Mortgage brokers, for instance, will no longer undergo even a cursory review and will not have to demonstrate a minimal net worth. Seemingly incongruent with the risk aversion guidelines implemented above, this rule alone will change the FHA landscape over time. FHA transferred the oversight responsibility for new FHA representatives to the DE lenders. The results of the approval relaxation rules are still being evaluated but could be mixed. The number of lenders offering FHA loans clearly increased, but the knowledge and expertise of many of the new lenders has, at times, been called into question.

Appraisal Change: After indicating that FHA would not change its appraisal process, by mid-2010, it was announced that its own HVCC system would be created. Loan originators are no longer allowed to order appraisals nor have any contact with the appraisers. Interestingly, the conventional market had early on been so negatively impacted by the HVCC appraisal process that during this same period in 2010 consideration was still being given to its elimination. (More information on HVCC can be found in the Case & Point at the end of Chapter 8.) Everyone since has adjusted to the appraisal process and in spite of continued criticism, the process prevails.

Streamline Refinances: HUD now requires income, asset, and employment documentation as well as limits the amount of closing costs that can be rolled into a streamline refinance loan. In the past, the streamline loan was easy to acquire, requiring only that the borrower had made previous payments on time and verification that the new payment would be lower than the one being refinanced. This move toward documentation in the name of controlling risk substantially reduced the number of such refinances.

Higher Down Payments: Critics have for a long time indicated that the current 3.5 percent down payment is too small an amount of "skin in the game." Some have suggested raising the required down payment to 10 percent, but critics argue that this fails to support the FHA's purpose of serving consumers of modest means. As conventional lenders have adopted both a 3percent and a 5 percent down payment option, FHA could decide to follow suit by modifying current down payment requirements. On the other hand, FHA moves slowly in such matters and as the economy has improved and conventional lender guidelines have become more flexible, most think the current down payment requirement is unlikely to change.

Higher Mortgage Insurance Premiums: Adjustments to both the Upfront and Monthly Mortgage Insurance Premiums have already been discussed. The reduction in late 2014 in the annual premium from 1.35 percent to 0.85 percent was the result of pressure to make FHA loans more competitive. Critics suggest that additional downward adjustment should occur, but as of late 2015 there remained resistance to this at the agency level.

Credit Standards: Sensing that credit is difficult to acquire today for many borrowers, FHA continues to seek ways to make the program more competitive. Unfortunately, that has not included addressing the very high mortgage insurance premiums noted above. The focus instead is on urging borrowers to undergo education in exchange for a reduction in the mortgage interest rate, as proposed in the aforementioned HAWK program. After resisting for some time, FHA had finally raised minimum qualifying credit scores to 640 (from a low of 580) several years ago. In so doing, FHA was following conventional lending guidelines whose minimum scores went dramatically higher. Not until late 2014 did credit score requirements decline, back to 580 for most FHA lenders. In so doing, FHA was re-establishing its long cherished position as being a more lenient and flexible home lender in regards to evaluating credit worthiness.

Reducing Home-Seller Concessions: In 2010 the home seller's ability to provide credit toward the buyer's closing costs was reduced from 6 percent to a maximum 3 percent of the loan amount. This was mostly the result of long time critics claiming that borrowers needed to have some skin in the game and that 6 percent was excessive and contributed to financially marginal buyers being encouraged to purchase homes beyond their qualifying capacity.

Look Back Period Eliminated: One excellent change, in response to the CFPB, the look-back period for charging interest has been brought current with how all other loans charge interest on the loan being paid off. In the past, FHA required that a full month interest be paid regardless of the day in the month the transaction closed escrow. Interest now will be charged, as in all loan transactions, to the day of closing. The new rule became effective January 2015.

6.2 U.S. DEPARTMENT OF AGRICULTURE (USDA) LOANS

Known also as Guaranteed Rural Housing (GRH), the USDA loan features 100 percent LTV financing accompanied by competitive interest rates and mortgage insurance premiums. The program is designed to meet the needs of home buyers who have the ability to qualify income- and credit-wise but do not possess down payment.

The program possesses two major restrictions: borrower income limits apply and property location is critical. Rural is the operative word in the program as property usually must be located outside city limits but may be considered rural if the population is between 10,000 and 35,000, is rural in character, and has a serious lack of mortgage credit. But borrowers are cautioned to never assume that a particular property is not eligible. Many properties located near some major metropolitan areas do qualify. An address can be easily checked for eligibility on the USDA website. Much like FHA, income limits are according to counties and can also be checked on site.

Highlights of the program include:

1. Borrowers do not have to be first-time homebuyers; however, they cannot currently own property.
2. If the appraisal value exceeds the purchase price, closing costs and possible improvements may be included.
3. No limit on purchase price, no prepayment penalty, no cash reserves required and low credit scores eligible (these change regularly and need to be checked with a loan officer).
4. Seller credit and/or rebate pricing is allowed to pay closing costs.

There are a few limitations:

1. Single family homes ONLY—no units; must be owner–occupied.
2. Qualifying ratios can be a bit lower than conventional loans.
3. The lot cannot be dividable. This is critical; for instance, a large lot that might be able to be split or allow a second unit to be constructed would be ineligible.
4. Fully documented, 30-year fixed rate loans only.

Confusion sometimes occurs around whether the agency runs out of funds. This has not been a major concern in recent years. Mortgage representatives who report the scarcity of funds are sometimes those who prefer not to do the loans, instead funneling borrowers into the more often used FHA option.

6.3 DEPARTMENT OF VETERANS AFFAIRS

What Is the Department of Veterans Affairs (VA)?

The U.S. Veterans Bureau was founded in 1916 to assist needy veterans of the Civil War and Spanish American War. Its name changed to the Veterans Administration in 1930, then again in 1989, when it was elevated to cabinet level with the designation Department of Veterans Affairs. Full details regarding VA-guaranteed loans can be found at www.VA.gov. Note: The VA does not make loans but guarantees those made by authorized mortgage lenders.

Administration of VA Home Loan Program

The Loan Guarantee Division of the VA is responsible for the administration of its home program. Like the FHA, the VA is a government program; however, there are some major differences.

1. The VA guarantees a loan, whereas the FHA insures a loan.
2. The VA guarantees only a part of the loan, whereas the FHA insures the entire loan.

The **VA-guaranteed loan** amount that will be paid to a lender in case of foreclosure, for most loans, is calculated as 25 percent of the current Freddie Mac conforming loan amount. For example, since December 2009, the maximum Freddie Mac conforming loan has been $417,000, thus 25% × 417,000 = $104,250 maximum VA lender guarantee.

The current $104,250 guarantee applies to most counties except that a high-balance loan amount is allowed for some identified counties with high-cost home values.

Whether a loan is insured or guaranteed is important only if a foreclosure occurs. If a foreclosure occurs, the VA has two options:

1. It can pay the lender the principle balance and take back the property.
2. It can give the lender the property and pay it the amount of any deficiency, up to the maximum amount of the VA guarantee.

VA Loans

What You Need to Know

1. *No down payment.* It is often believed that a veteran needs absolutely no money to purchase a home. While a qualified veteran may purchase a home with 100 percent financing (i.e., no down payment) there are other costs that must be accommodated. Closing costs can, however, be paid for the veteran (see #2 below). In some situations, a veteran may be required to have two months of principal, interest, taxes, and insurance payments in the bank as reserves at the close of escrow, but these funds can be gift funds. So, in essence, a veteran can purchase without any cash of his or her own.
2. *Other costs.* While there are typical closing costs required, in some situations a seller may be willing to pay these fees on behalf of the veteran in what is called a "no-no" loan, meaning that the veteran has no down payment and no closing costs. A gift could also come from a relative or friend (with sufficient documentation of the relationship), similar to the allowances of the FHA. Finally, as in other loan options, rebate pricing (discussed in the Case & Point following Chapter 3) can be used to defray closing costs.
3. *Qualification requirements.* A VA loan is unusual in that a buyer qualifies via both a ratio calculation and a residual requirement.

—Ratio: the total amount of monthly housing debt, which includes principal, interest, taxes, and homeowner's insurance, plus total monthly consumer debt should not exceed 41 percent of the buyer's gross monthly income. Compensating factors allow exceeding this ratio.

—Residual: a required amount left over after subtracting from a buyer's gross monthly income all his or her estimated taxes, monthly consumer debt, as well as monthly housing debt. The amount of residual required is dependent upon the size of the family.

4. *Funding fee.* This fee is much like the private mortgage insurance premium assessed in conventional financing. Rather than requiring the fee to be paid in cash, VA allows the fee to be added to the loan amount, as long as the maximum loan limits are not exceeded. A funding fee schedule can be found ahead under General Guidelines #3.

5. *Rating factor worksheet.* The VA qualification process requires this worksheet to be completed, with satisfactory ratings on the following:

   - Job stability
   - Credit history
   - Debt ratio
   - Balance available for support (residual)
   - Liquid assets (reserves)

6. *Possible assumability.* VA loans recorded after February 29, 1988, can be assumed only if the new buyer meets VA qualifications. However, the veteran who obtained the original loan remains personally liable to the VA. If there is a foreclosure and subsequent loss to the VA, the veteran can be charged for the amount of the loss. A veteran can be released from liability by obtaining a Release of Liability from the VA. The new owner must be an owner-occupant and complete the specific procedure set up by the VA to obtain the release.

7. *Certificate of Reasonable Value (CRV).* VA appraisals are made by independent licensed fee appraisers. The VA then issues the CRV to the veteran buyer, identifying what it believes to be the reasonable value of the property. The buyer is allowed to pay more than that value but must do so by increasing down payment funds.

Dispelling Some Myths

As with all elements of home financing, the VA continues to make changes, sometimes slowly. Recent years have seen the VA streamline many of its processes and many of the old criticisms have been resolved.

1. *Red tape and processing time.* The increase in local lenders' authorization to process VA loans on an automatic basis has eliminated much of the frustration that used to accompany long time frames in closing a VA loan. Much like the FHA, the loan is completed by the local lender, according to VA requirements, and then sent for the guarantee.

2. *Excessive repairs.* This concern is a holdover from the past days when sellers were sometimes required to perform all kinds of repair work. The VA has adopted a habitability standard, and only items identified by the appraiser as health and safety factors need be done. Cosmetic repairs are no longer required.

3. *Accepting a VA loan offer costs the seller too much.* While this may have been true several years ago, the additional costs for accepting a VA offer are fairly minimal today. The additional seller paid fees include the entire escrow fee including the portion normally paid by the buyer. VA prohibits a veteran from paying an escrow fee. There are items like tax service, flood certification, and document preparation that must be paid by the seller on behalf of the veteran. The additional cost to the seller on a conforming $417,000 VA loan is likely to be about $1,200 to $1,500. This does not include a lender's processing fee that could be another $500 plus. Many VA lenders waive this fee in order to reduce the total seller costs. This relatively minor amount of extra cost can often be accommodated in the negotiated sales price. The increased ability for buyers to be qualified via the VA's more flexible guidelines often far outweighs any adverse consequences of the additional seller costs.

4. *Discount points.* Many sellers still remember the days when the VA required sellers to pay discount points on behalf of the veteran buyer to allow a lower market interest rate. This is no longer the case.

Who Is Eligible for a VA-Guaranteed Loan?

General Rules for Eligibility

Long unchanged, the general rules of eligibility state that a veteran is eligible for VA home loan benefits if he or she is currently serving or has served duty in the U.S. Army, Air Force, Marine Corps, or Coast Guard. If he or she has served in the past, the discharge must be for other than dishonorable reasons.

Specific time frames for having served during wartime and/or peacetime are available on the VA website. Questions about eligibility for a VA loan can be addressed with the agency directly.

Under all service time frames, if the veteran was discharged for a service-connected disability before meeting the service time requirement, he or she may still be eligible for a VA-guaranteed home loan. There are other special rules for unmarried spouses of veterans who died in the service because of war or a service-connected accident, for spouses of veterans missing in action or prisoner of war, and for those who have served as a U.S. public health officer, as cadet in the U.S. military academies, and so on.

Certificate of Eligibility

To establish eligibility for a VA loan, a veteran must obtain a **Certificate of Eligibility**, which indicates the amount of the veteran's entitlement. The entitlement is the maximum number of dollars that the VA will pay, up to the VA's maximum guarantee amount (currently $104,250 in non-high-balance loan areas), if the lender suffers a loss.

Reinstatement of Full Entitlement

In the past, a veteran could have full entitlement restored only if an originally VA financed property was sold and the original loan paid in full. New rules allow full entitlement reinstatement and the veteran to purchase another home if the original property has been refinanced. This can be done only once. Entitlement may continue to be restored if an eligible veteran agrees to assume the loan and substitute his or her entitlement for that of the original veteran. The new veteran must also qualify for the loan.

If a veteran sells a home with the new buyer assuming the loan, the veteran may be released from liability by the VA if the new buyer is qualified. The veteran remains personally liable for any deficiency if the release is not obtained. The veteran must obtain both the Reinstatement of Entitlement and Release of Liability.

Partial Entitlements

The entitlement amount has been increased several times since the VA program began, so veterans who have previously used their entitlement may have an unused partial entitlement. A veteran may purchase another home with a partial entitlement even if the previous VA loan has not been paid off. The veteran can keep the first home and purchase another using VA financing. This is the only way in which a veteran can technically have two or more VA loans at the same time.

To determine partial entitlements and their maximum loan amounts, veterans should contact their nearest VA regional office.

General Guidelines

In contrast to FHA loans, the VA has only one program. It offers either fixed or adjustable interest rates and one set of guidelines that generally apply to all its loans. Note: The ARM loan is classified as a hybrid wherein the loan is fixed for a three- or five-year period before converting to its adjustable portion. As in other adjustable loans discussed, the VA ARM has clearly defined guidelines regarding maximum interest rate adjustments, time periods, etc.

1. *Type of property.* The VA guarantees loans on properties from one to four units and units in approved planned unit developments and condominiums projects. The VA approves new properties only if they were built under FHA or VA inspections. If a property was not built with FHA or VA inspections, one year must elapse after the house has been completed before ordering the appraisal. While some exceptions to this one-year rule are identified in the guidelines, they are not easily obtained. The two more common exceptions are (a) property located in a remote area where obtaining FHA or VA inspections would be inconvenient; and (b) property built by a small builder who does not normally use VA loans to finance the sale of houses.

2. *Interest rate.* The interest rate and discount points are negotiable between the lender and veteran-borrower. Contrary to past practices, when the seller was required to pay all discount points, the seller or the buyer may pay the discount points, the buyer and seller may split the payment, or these points can be paid by a third party or rebate pricing.

3. *Loan origination and funding fees.* The old rule that the loan fee could not exceed 1 percent of the loan amount is no longer enforced. This loan fee goes to the lender based upon the agreed upon loan structure. The veteran is charged a funding fee, originally designed as a way to reduce the cost of 100 percent VA loans to tax-payers. The funding fee, in actuality, is used primarily for lender reimbursement up to the VA guarantee amounts in case of loan defaults. Veterans who receive disability compensation for service-related medical issues, or who are entitled to get compensation while not drawing retirement pay, are exempt from the VA funding fee. The funding fee is calculated as a percentage of the loan amount, and the veteran has the option of paying the fee up

front or financing it as part of the VA-guaranteed loan as long as the amount to be financed does not exceed the maximum allowed loan amount. The current funding fee schedule for a home purchase is given below:

Type of Veteran	Down Payment	First Time Use	Subsequent Use
Regular Military	None	2.15%	3.30%
	5%–9.99%	1.50%	1.50%
	10% or more	1.25%	1.25%
Reserves/National Guard	None	2.4%	3.30%
	5–9.99%	1.75%	1.75%
	10% or more	1.50%	1.50%

Note: There are different funding fees for a VA-guaranteed refinance and for manufactured home loans and loan assumptions.

4. *Term of loan.* The term cannot exceed the remaining economic life of the property, with a maximum term of 30 years.
5. *Down payment.* The VA does not require a down payment— the veteran is allowed to borrow the full amount of the purchase price up to the maximum allowed by the VA-approved lender. While the veteran, for many years, was prohibited from paying more than the appraised value for a home, the VA will now allow a veteran to pay more than the appraisal, but the loan amount cannot exceed the appraisal. The difference between the purchase price and the appraisal has to be in cash.
6. *Maximum loan.* There is no maximum loan amount under VA rules. This can be confusing because since the VA guarantees only a portion of the loan, lenders do limit the amount they will lend on VA loans.
7. The main point to remember is that the VA does not set the maximum loan amount; it is the lender that determines the amount. And that maximum loan amount is based upon the VA's requirement to reimburse the lender only for the amount of entitlement, regardless of what the lender's loss may be upon foreclosure. The current maximum loan amount for most counties remains at $417,000. VA has adopted a higher loan amount for those counties deemed a high-cost area with only a few counties exceeding the $625,500 loan amount. Each county's loan limit can be checked at the va.gov website. The VA guarantee is 25 percent of

maximum loan amounts identified for each county. VA borrowers may exceed the loan limits but are required to pay 25 percent of the amount borrowed that exceeds the loan limit in cash. *Occupying the property.* The veteran must occupy the property. The VA does not have a program for veterans who do not intend to occupy the property.

8. *Monthly installments.* Technically, the VA requires only monthly principal and interest payments. It does not require property taxes and insurance to be included. However, the VA recommends that these be included, and the deed of trust provides lender authority to collect them. As a practical matter, all lenders establish an impound account and collect the taxes and insurance in the monthly payment.

9. *Appraisal and* **Certificate of Reasonable Value (CRV)**. We have discussed previously that the issued CRV represents the VA's opinion of reasonable or current market value.

    It is no coincidence that the CRV never exceeds the purchase price. In practice, the VA never issues a certificate showing a value greater than the sales price. If a home sells for $400,000, but the appraisal comes in at $425,000, the CRV will be for the $400,000 sales price, not the $425,000 appraised value. However, if the sales price is $400,000, but the appraisal comes in a $375,000, the CRV will be for the $375,000 appraised value.

10. *Secondary financing.* It is commonly believed that a second loan on a VA transaction is prohibited. This is not technically correct. Seconds are allowed but rarely used because they are not practical or not understood.

    Secondary financing can be approved on a case-by-case basis. The VA Regional Office will determine on what basis it is acceptable. Generally, it is desirable that the second carry the same interest rate and terms as the first loan. The first and second loans added together cannot under any circumstances be more than the CRV. An example where a second can be used is as follows:

Sales price/CRV	$450,000
Maximum loan available from lender	−417,000
Down payment from buyer	−20,000
Second mortgage	$13,000

In this example, we need an additional $13,000 to complete the transaction. If the seller is willing to carry back a second loan at the same rate and terms as the first, the sale can be made.

11. *Pest inspections, reports, and clearances.* The VA requires that a structural pest control report be obtained from a recognized inspection company. Required repairs indicated under both sections 1 and 2 (active infestation and that which might lead to infestation) of the report must be completed, and both the veteran and an inspector must certify that the work is done satisfactorily.
12. The VA requires inspection of all detached buildings (e.g., detached garages, cottages, potting sheds, or green houses). The veteran cannot waive this requirement. The veteran is prohibited from paying for the report but may pay for repairs.

    On older properties this can be a problem. A detached garage may cost more to repair than it is worth. If it is not economical to repair the garage, then it may be torn down and the value of the property adjusted accordingly. For example, assume that it costs $25,000 to repair a garage and the VA has appraised it at only $23,000. You would be better off removing the garage and reducing the value by $23,000. Always consult with the VA first in such situations.
13. *Closing costs.* As previously discussed, the VA will not allow the veteran to pay for nonrecurring (one time) closing costs, such as termite reports, escrow fees, tax service fees, document preparation fees, notary fees, or a certificate of reasonable value that was ordered before the veteran agreed to purchase the property. While these may be considered additional seller expenses, it may be worth paying the costs, depending upon the purchase price offer.

    The VA allows the seller to pay all of the closing costs (not to exceed 4% of the appraised value), including prepaid expenses and **recurring closing costs** such as tax impounds, fire insurance, and so on. Most lenders require buyers to pay for prepaid items. A seller pay all is often referred to as a "VA no-no"—no down, no closing costs.
14. *Internet underwriting.* Today's lenders are referred to as LAPP (Lender Appraisal Processing Program) approved, and the processing time for approval is greatly reduced via this Web-based direct underwriting (DU) capacity.

Choosing a Lender for FHA and VA Loans

Many lenders, such as commercial banks, savings banks, and mortgage companies, are authorized to process FHA and VA loans. Because they have authorization does not automatically mean they are familiar with the increased paperwork requirements and stay current regarding program changes. Processing FHA and VA loans can be very complex, technical, and time consuming. Certain lenders specialize in processing government loans. They are experienced, they know what to do, and they keep up to date. Choose a lender that has this type of experience; otherwise, it can be very frustrating and costly.

6.4 CAL-VET LOANS

The **Cal-Vet loan** program is administered by the California Department of Veterans Affairs, Division of Farm and Home Purchases. Applicants can apply directly to Cal-Vet or apply through a Cal-Vet certified mortgage broker. In as much as the 1 percent maximum loan fee remains the same whether the borrower goes to Cal-Vet or uses a mortgage lender, borrowers may find it convenient to use professional representation. The money that funds Cal-Vet loans is obtained from the sale of general obligation bonds and revenue bonds. There are three sources of Cal-Vet funds with the most attractive interest rate available to qualified veterans with wartime service, which uses designated unrestricted funds. This can be used only as funds are available. Full details regarding Cal-Vet loans can be found at www.cdva.ca.gov.

Who Is Eligible for Cal-Vet Loans?

Cal-Vet eligibility rules are more liberal than the federal VA rules. A veteran is eligible with the required income and credit rating and the following service: currently on active duty, received an honorable discharge, and served for a minimum of 90 days, not counting basic training. It makes no difference if the service was during war or peacetime.

Veterans who served for fewer than 90 days may still be eligible under certain circumstances. Details can be found at the Cal-Vet Web page.

Current members of the U.S. Military Reserves and the California National Guard—who do not otherwise qualify under the aforementioned rules—become eligible after they serve a minimum of one year of a six-year obligation, provided they qualify as a first-time home buyer or purchase a home in certain targeted areas.

It should be noted that if the veteran is currently in the military, Cal-Vet requires that the veteran, or a member of the immediate family, must occupy the home until the Cal-Vet loan is paid off. Therefore, a change in active duty station would require a payoff of the Cal-Vet loan unless the veteran's family remains in the home. This required resale could result in a loss if a veteran is transferred after a short period of time, since any short-term appreciation may be insufficient to cover closing costs and the remaining loan balance.

General Information about Cal-Vet Loans

1. *Property.* Cal-Vet has the same property standards as the FHA and VA. The property must be an owner-occupied, single-family dwelling or a unit in an approved condominium or planned unit development complex. Owner-occupied farms and mobile homes are also acceptable.

2. *Maximum loan.* While the maximum Cal-Vet loan amounts can vary each year, the maximum single-family home loan has remained the same for some time at $521,250. There are separate maximums for single-family dwellings, farms, and mobile homes. To find the current maximum for other loan options go to the Cal-Vet website, www.cdva.ca.gov. The Cal-Vet loan maximum is higher than the typical VA loan amount limit of $417,000, but there are no high-cost area loan adjustments.

3. *Down payment and loan fees.* A Cal-Vet loan can be submitted one of two ways—by adhering to regular VA guidelines or to Cal-Vet guidelines. Cal-Vet/VA loans are available for no money down up to the current maximum VA-guaranteed loan amount. On straight Cal-Vet loans, without a VA guarantee, the loan amount available is greater, as noted above, but requires a down payment of 3 percent of the purchase price or appraised value, whichever is the lesser value.

   Cal-Vet charges a 1 percent loan origination fee, plus a loan guarantee fee that ranges from 1.25 percent to 3.3 percent of the loan amount. Under certain circumstances, the loan guarantee fee may be financed, but the 1 percent loan origination fee is treated as a closing cost and must be paid in escrow. If a veteran puts 20 percent or more down, only the 1 percent loan-origination fee applies and the loan guarantee fee is waived.

4. *Term of loan.* Cal-Vet loans are set up as 30-year loans. A veteran is allowed to make additional principal payments to shorten the length of the loan, and there is no prepayment penalty for paying off the loan early.

5. *Interest rate.* All Cal-Vet loans have a variable interest rate. The initial interest rate is set at the time of the loan based on the cost of bond funds and market conditions. Once set, the interest rate has a lifetime cap of only a half percent over the start rate.

6. *Secondary financing.* At the time of purchase, secondary financing is permitted. However, the two loans together cannot exceed 98 percent of the Cal-Vet appraisal. Some lenders are unwilling to make a loan behind a land contract of sale.

7. *Occupancy.* The veteran or an immediate member of the family who qualifies as a dependent must occupy the property for the life of the loan.

8. *Insurance.* All properties are covered by Cal-Vet's Disaster Indemnity program, which provides protection against loss from floods and earthquakes (with limitations). All Cal-Vet contract holders under age 62 must carry basic life insurance. Based on health status at time of application, coverage provides payments of principal and interest for up to five years following the death of the insured. Buyers with substandard health risks will have payments made for only 36 months; those with highly substandard health risks for only 12 months. Under certain circumstances, optional life insurance, spouse life insurance, and disability insurance may be obtainable. Disability insurance terminates at age 62 and all life insurance coverage terminates at age 70.

9. *Monthly payments.* In addition to monthly mortgage payments of principal and interest, property taxes, fire, disability, and life insurance premiums are also collected and placed into an impound account.

10. *Title to property.* When a property is being financed with a Cal-Vet loan, the title is first conveyed to the Department of Veterans Affairs of the State of California by the seller. The department then sells the property to the veteran under a **land contract of sale**. The department continues to hold the legal title, while the veteran holds what is called equitable title. Only after the veteran has paid the loan in full does he receive a grant deed. The department uses a standard CLTA joint protection title policy, rather than a lender's ALTA policy.

11. *Application fee.* A small application fee and an appraisal fee are paid by the applicant.

12. *Construction loan.* All other qualifications remain the same. Cal-Vet usually uses a five-draw system, with the construction period ordinarily nine months, followed by 29-year/3-month amortization.

13. *Refinancing.* For the most part, no refinancing is available. However, if your old loan is paid off, a new Cal-Vet loan is available. Cal-Vet loans may be paid off without penalty and may be obtained multiple times.

14. *Source of Funds.* Cal-Vet home loan rates are linked to voter approved bonds with the actual rates determined by the bond market at the time of sale. The three sources of funds bear different interest rates and vary also based upon the eligibility of the veteran applicant. The Qualified Veterans Mortgage Bond (QVMB) is usually the most attractive rate.

For additional information about your area and qualifications, refer to the California Department of Veterans Affairs website at www.calvet.ca.gov.

Advantages and Disadvantages of Cal-Vet Loans

The main advantages of the Cal-Vet loan are:

1. Its relatively low interest rate via the use of very stable ARM loans
2. Inexpensive life, fire, and disaster insurance (flood and quake)
3. Origination fee
4. A veteran must apply within 25 years of discharge

Disadvantages include:

1. Lack of refinancing opportunity
2. Occasional shortage of available funds for the program
3. Life of loan occupancy requirement
4. Use of land contract form of ownership (which can restrict secondary financing options)

For unmarried couples who are not registered as domestic partners, another disadvantage might be that Cal-Vet can refuse to allow assignment of the veteran's contract of sale to the couple as joint tenants.

6.5 CALIFORNIA HOUSING FINANCE AGENCY PROGRAM (CALHFA)

A major hurdle for many first time borrowers is accumulating the necessary down payment. The **CalHFA** program, established in 1975, was founded to provide down payment and closing cost assistance to mostly low- and moderate-income families. As of September 2010, following the financial crises, two first mortgage loans became available to first time homebuyers. Income limits apply and vary by county and type of loan. Information can be obtained at the CalHFA website. This state agency sells mortgage revenue bonds to investors, and then uses the funds to buy loans from approved lenders who make loans under CalHFA guidelines. Thus, like the FHA, VA, Fannie Mae, and Freddie Mac, CalHFA does not make loans directly to borrowers. Instead, this state agency purchases the loans made by approved lenders. CalHFA prides itself on not using state funds and taxpayer dollars to operate its program. Full details regarding CalHFA can be found at www.calhfa.ca.gov.

Two Main Programs

CalHFA offers both a 30-year fixed rate conventional loan (CalPlus) and an FHA-insured mortgage (CalPLUS FHA). These down payment and closing cost assistance programs were the more popular loan options using subordinated trust deeds as silent second loans requiring no payments until the home was sold, refinanced, or paid in full. The goal was to keep monthly mortgage payments affordable.

Various Programs Available

The programs varied depending upon the borrower's needs and qualifying capacity. The assistance programs complemented CalHFA, FHA and conventional loan options. Unfortunately, the popular Cal Plus, CHDAP and Zero Interest Program (ZIP) were, at least temporarily, canceled in late 2015. Because of the program benefits, there is expectation that the programs will be resurrected and it is in that interest that the common elements of the programs are identified below.

1. First-time home buyers only (defined as not having owned a home in the past three years)
2. Single family, one unit properties and FHA approved condo units
3. All borrowers must intend to live in the home (no non-occupant co-borrowers)
4. Minimum 640 credit score required (this could change depending upon continued flexibility in credit score eligibility for FHA and conventional loans)
5. Borrower income limits apply; current FHA and conventional county guidelines usually prevail
6. Sales price limits apply in some cases per county
7. Borrower's overall debt to income ratio cannot exceed 43 percent
8. Completion of a homebuyer education counseling program is required

A minimum borrower investment between $1,000 and $1,500 based upon credit score can apply to some programs.

TABLE 6.1 Comparison of government-backed loans (January 2015).

Feature	Federal Housing Administration	U.S. Department of Veterans Affairs (VA)	Cal-Vet
Purpose of loan	1–4 units	1–4 units	Single dwellings, condominiums
Eligibility	Any U.S. resident	U.S. veteran	Qualified veterans
Expiration of eligibility	Indefinite	Indefinite	Must apply within 25 years from date of discharge
Maximum purchase price	None	None	None
Maximum loan	Varies by counties	None by VA; lenders limit loan amount	Varies for homes, farms, and mobile homes
Down payment	Section 203(b) Minimum 3.5%	None, but loan limited to CRV	0–3%
Maximum term	30 years	30 years	30 years
Secondary financing	Allowed with limitations	Allowed with limitations	Allowed with limitations
Interest rate	Fixed	Fixed	Floating (variable) rate
Prepayment penalty	None	None	None

Source: © 2016 OnCourse Learning

Chapter Summary

The FHA, VA, USDA, and CalHFA are government agencies that do not make loans; they insure, guarantee, or purchase loans made by approved lenders using their agency's guidelines. FHA-insured loans are made to any qualified borrower, whereas VA-guaranteed loans are made to qualified veterans. USDA loans have location and income limitations while CalHFA-backed loans focus on California first-time home buyers. Contrary to the FHA, VA, USDA, and CalHFA programs, the Cal-Vet program is a direct loan made to qualified veterans. Table 6.1 compares the major features of the FHA, VA, and Cal-Vet programs.

Important Terms and Concepts

CalHFA
Cal-Vet loan
Certificate of Eligibility
Certificate of Reasonable Value (CRV)
Conditional commitment
Direct endorsement

FHA-insured loan
Land contract of sale
Nonrecurring closing costs
Recurring closing costs
VA-guaranteed loan

Reviewing Your Understanding

Questions for Discussion

1. List three advantages and three disadvantages of an FHA-insured loan.
2. Compare the borrower requirements for an FHA, VA, Cal-Vet, USDA and CalHFA loan. What are the down payment requirements for each?
3. What are the maximum loan fees a lender can charge for FHA, VA, Cal-Vet, USDA and CalHFA loans?
4. In your area, which of the five programs listed in Question #3 will allow the greatest loan amount?

Multiple-Choice Questions

1. The major goals of the Federal Housing Administration include
   a. upgrading property standards.
   b. financing homes priced over $417,000.
   c. promoting rental housing.
   d. all of the above.

2. The maximum entitlement under the VA non-high-cost loan program can be as high as 50 percent of the loan balance, but not to exceed
   a. $22,500.
   b. $36,000.
   c. $60,000.
   d. $104,250.

3. A veteran purchased a home for $200,000 five years ago with VA 100 percent financing. Three months ago the property went into foreclosure and there was a balance of $195,000 owing on the loan. The sale price at the time of foreclosure is $178,000. The maximum amount of liability, excluding costs of sale, is
   a. $50,750.
   b. $46,000.
   c. $17,000.
   d. None of these.

4. Cal-Vet financing
   a. requires no down payment.
   b. has no prepayment penalties.
   c. cannot be used for construction.
   d. uses a mortgage as security for the loan.

5. Which program is specifically designed for first-time home buyers?
   a. FHA
   b. VA
   c. Cal-Vet
   d. CalHFA ✓

6. To accomplish its goals, the FHA introduced
   a. partially amortized loans.
   b. high down payment loans.
   c. impound or escrow accounts. ✓
   d. high interest rates.

7. The VA differs from the FHA in that the
   a. VA insures loans, while the FHA guarantees loans.
   b. VA guarantees only part of the loan, whereas the FHA insures the entire loan. ✓
   c. VA loan limits exceed maximum FHA loan limits.
   d. down payments increase with higher loan amounts for both FHA and VA loans.

8. Cal-Vet loans
   a. require a land contract of sale.
   b. are available only for owner-occupied properties.
   c. are subject to a 1 percent loan origination fee plus a loan guarantee fee.
   d. each of the foregoing is true. ✓

9. The FHA
   a. makes most of the nation's single-family dwelling loans.
   b. insures loans made by approved lenders. ✓
   c. does not require a down payment on approved loans.
   d. all of the above are correct.

10. Which statement regarding the FHA is correct?
    a. The down payment is generally 25 percent or more.
    b. The buyer normally pays the loan fee. ✓
    c. The maximum loan fee is 10 percent of the loan amount.
    d. Secondary financing is not permitted.

11. Eligible for FHA loans are
    a. any U.S. residents. ✓
    b. only naturalized citizens.
    c. qualified veterans.
    d. those meeting the 10 percent required down payment.

12. The Lender Appraisal Processing Program is associated with
    a. automatic underwriting standards.
    b. conventional appraisals.
    c. loan processing of VA loans via the Internet. ✓
    d. in-house appraisals.

13. The FHA requires a 3.5 percent cash investment that must come from the borrower's own funds, or from
    a. a bona fide gift.
    b. a loan from a family member.
    c. a governmental agency or instrumentality.
    d. any of the above sources. ✓

14. The U.S. Department of Veterans Affairs
    a. guarantees loans made to qualified veterans by approved lenders.
    b. permits interest rates to be set by mutual agreement with the lender.
    c. operates its real estate loan program under the GI Bill of Rights, passed by Congress in 1944.
    d. does all of the above. ✓

15. Another name for local FHA lenders is
    - ✓ a. correspondents.
    - b. model lenders.
    - c. guideline lenders.
    - d. risk-based lenders.

16. Which of the following is a recurring closing cost?
    - ✓ a. Cal-Vet hazard insurance policy
    - b. FHA loan origination fee
    - c. VA funding fee
    - d. CalHFA credit report

17. The initials CRV refer to
    - a. certified regional valuations.
    - ✓ b. a VA appraisal.
    - c. a loan guaranteed by the Department of Veterans Affairs.
    - d. a real estate agent who specializes in GI loans.

18. The following is used as the security instrument to finance a Cal-Vet loan:
    - a. deferred deed.
    - b. land contract.
    - c. mortgage.
    - ✓ d. trust deed.

19. FHA-insured loans insure lenders against
    - a. decline in real estate values.
    - ✓ b. loss due to foreclosure.
    - c. loss due to borrowers losing their jobs.
    - d. late payments by borrowers.

20. The stated goal of all government home loan programs is to
    - a. encourage speculation in housing.
    - b. assist struggling real estate agents during down markets.
    - c. offer subsidized interest rates to minority groups.
    - ✓ d. foster homeownership.

CASE & POINT
Risk Based Pricing and What It Means

When borrowers initiate their search for financing, they most often seek interest rate information. It is the one item most easily understood. But the interest rate is but one aspect in reviewing a potential buyer's qualifying capacity. In fact, the specific rate that any buyer can obtain is determined by these other items in assessing the lender's risk.

Loans have always been priced according the perceived risk for the lender. During the early 2000s, credit scores were the major determiner of loan terms and pricing. With high credit scores, borrowers could often obtain financing with the "best" loan rates and, during the subprime loan era, even on a stated or no-doc basis.

Lenders now consider borrowers' credit scores as well as the loan-to-value (the loan amount divided by the purchase or appraised value, whichever is less) of the new loan in what is being called risk based pricing. Mortgage lenders must consult several grids to determine the pricing. As credit scores reduce and/or LTV levels increase, the lender's perceived risk increases and is accommodated via an increase in the pricing/interest rate. Other risks that can impact the final interest rate include the length of time for locking in the rate (guaranteeing the rate for a longer period of time, particularly over 30 days, requires an additional cost), a borrower deciding to forego establishing an impound account, available reserves (funds available after down payment and closing costs have been accommodated), or if multiple units are involved.

FHA, for a long time, resisted adopting a risk-based formula for borrower loan approval. Beginning in 2010, FHA concluded that they had to also initiate risk based approval practices in an attempt to improve the quality of their loan portfolio. While VA has not yet adopted any such procedures, they have increased, as have all lenders, an acceptable minimum credit score. Risk-based pricing in some form impacts nearly all loan options today.

The danger for a would-be borrower shopping only interest rates is that they will receive an interest rate quote based upon the optimum conditions and be disappointed when their profile requires what are called "pricing hits," resulting in an interest rate increase.

The danger is equally present for real estate professionals who quote the best rates only to discover that their borrower is ineligible for the rate due to credit or other conditions.

The more experienced loan officers are reluctant to quote a rate until the borrower's loan profile is clearly identified. While frustrating to borrowers shopping for the best rate, unless the lender has all of the supporting documentation prior to quoting a potential interest rate, one cannot depend upon the information. For the borrower, interest rate alone no longer identifies the best loan option to meet their specific needs.

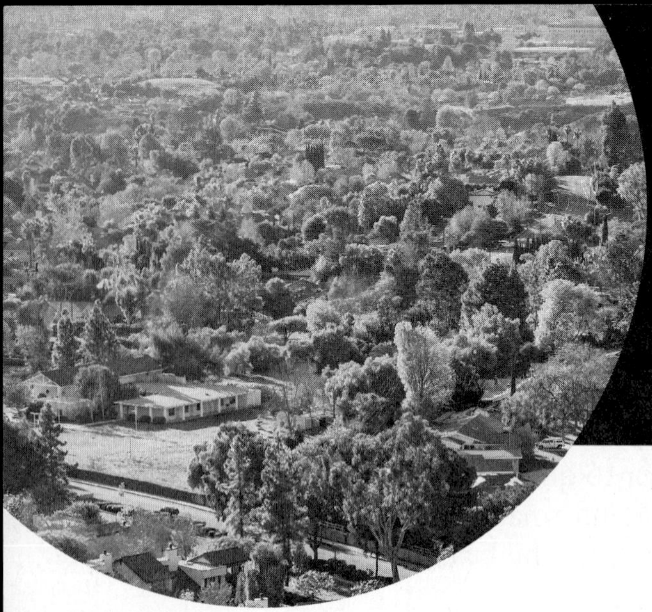

POINTS, DISCOUNTS, AND THE SECONDARY MORTGAGE MARKET

7

OVERVIEW

This chapter explains points and discounts along with the terms price and yield. These terms apply in this chapter to how they impact the sale and purchase of real estate loans in what is known as the **secondary mortgage market**. Not to be confused with secondary financing, when using the term secondary mortgage market in relationship to home lending, the term refers to how real estate loans made to individual borrowers are transferred or sold to replenish the lender's funds. The difference between a secondary mortgage market and secondary financing is illustrated in Figure 7.1.

After completing this chapter, you will be able to:

- Explain the difference between the terms, points and discounts.
- Define the term premium and contrast premium to discount.
- Differentiate between secondary financing and secondary mortgage market.
- Describe the purpose of Fannie Mae and Freddie Mac.
- Explain how a Ginnie Mae mortgage-backed security works.
- Discuss the role of investment bankers in mortgage-backed securities and the secondary market.

7.1 SECONDARY MORTGAGE MARKET

The secondary market is where the primary loan, after being made with the lender's funds, is sold and the lender's funds are replenished so that another new loan can be made to an individual. This is known as maintaining liquidity for lending purposes.

Decades ago, depository institutions retained most of the loans they originated. Depositors' savings provided sufficient funds with which to meet the demand for real estate loans. Long before savings rates dipped, as they are today, to below 1 percent on a nationwide

FIGURE 7.1 The difference between secondary financing and secondary mortgage market.

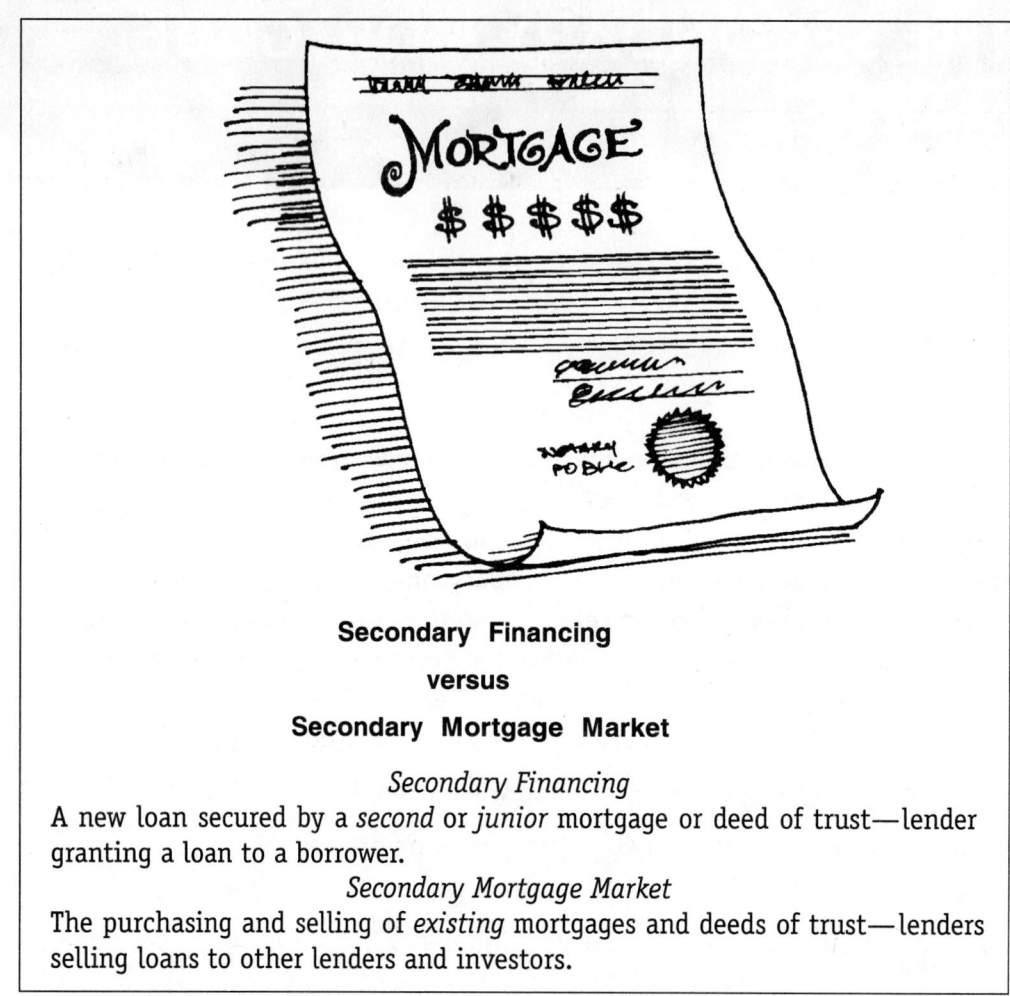

Secondary Financing

versus

Secondary Mortgage Market

Secondary Financing
A new loan secured by a *second* or *junior* mortgage or deed of trust—lender granting a loan to a borrower.

Secondary Mortgage Market
The purchasing and selling of *existing* mortgages and deeds of trust—lenders selling loans to other lenders and investors.

Source: © 2016 OnCourse Learning

basis, the demand for loan funds outstripped the funds provided by consumer savings.

Purpose of the Secondary Market

In the early 1970s, depository institutions sold only a small portion of the loans they originated. They were able to rely on their savings inflow to finance the loans they made. During this time, interest rates and the flow of deposits were relatively stable. As the 1970s progressed, the institutions were forced to sell more loans in the secondary market because loan volume had increased greatly. A slow rate of new deposits, typically referred to as rate of savings inflow, was not sufficient to take care of the higher demand for loans.

In the 1980s, institutions found their cost of acquiring deposits increasing dramatically. They also experienced a major outflow of deposits due to higher rates offered by competing investments, such as mutual funds and certain bonds. Recall from Chapter 1 that this is labeled disintermediation. With less money to support the demand for loans, the institutions have increasingly turned to the secondary market for funds.

The secondary market has three main functions: provide a continuing source of funds, manage the flow of money in the mortgage market, and provide mortgage funds in a tight money market. It is said, then, that the secondary market's prime purpose is to provide mortgage liquidity. Imagine if every home loan made by a lending institution was funded and the mortgage, representing the debt owed, was merely placed in that lender's vault. The lender, in turn, would collect the monthly payments due on the mortgage but, having to depend upon additional consumer deposits before new loans could be funded, would not be able to make many loans before depleting available loan funds. This would only work if the lender had a perfect balance between demand for loans and a supply of money via deposits.

The major entities that purchase conventional real estate loans are the Federal National Mortgage Association (Fannie Mae) and the Federal Home Loan Mortgage Corporation (Freddie Mac), known as Government Sponsored Enterprises (GSEs). The Government National Mortgage Association (Ginnie Mae) serves this same secondary market task for government loans. While private investors, pension funds, insurance companies, and other agencies may participate in some way in the purchase and sale of loans in the secondary market, the government enterprises are the major sources of recirculated funds and upon which most lending institutions depend to provide liquidity to the lending market. It is within these transactions that both discounts and yields are calculated.

The GSEs Importance

Fannie Mae was founded in 1938 with a primary purpose of providing a vehicle for shifting money from areas where there was a surplus to areas where there was a shortage and thereby maintain a steady supply of available loan funds.

Fannie Mae and Freddie Mac began functioning as GSEs in 1968. In the 1980s, the cost of acquiring deposits increased dramatically as the competition with mutual funds and certain bond issues created an outflow of deposits. (Remember from Chapter 1 this is called disintermediation.) The ever increasing demand for funds prompted the expansion of the secondary market entities to the point of nearly all home mortgage loans were, and continue to be, sold to them.

In the early 2000s efforts devoted to making home ownership available to the maximum number of people resulted in runaway appreciation rates and ultimately to the introduction of subprime lending practices. As the euphoria of ever-increasing home values coupled with a more relaxed lending environment exploded, the GSEs succumbed to the temptation of purchasing subprime mortgages, which eventually imploded and resulted in the 2008 recession.

Why and How Are Mortgage Funds Shifted?

Banking institutions are obligated by law to maintain certain levels of reserves, either as reserves with the Federal Reserve (Fed) or within their vault as cash. While we need not understand the calculations that determine the amount of required reserves, banks must attend to having sufficient reserves on a daily basis.

The needed funds to assure liquidity requirements can be acquired in several ways. Interbank borrowing occurs frequently in which banks borrow from each other. An institution in one location may have excess funds beyond what they can lend while another bank has the opposite situation. The actual mechanism generally occurs via the Federal Reserve where the institutions maintain accounts and the funds can simply be a paper transaction between the bank with excess funds in its account to the bank needing to augment its account. The interest rate paid by the borrowing bank to the lending bank is negotiated between the two banks with the result labeled the federal funds rate.

Banks can borrower directly from the FED via the discount window, but this discount interest rate is generally higher than when borrowing on an interbank basis. The difference between this discount rate and the federal funds rates can be confusing. The important thing to know is that the Fed, via its Federal Open Market Committee (FOMC), establishes the federal funds target rate by which it can control the flow of lendable money. For instance, a higher discount rate discourages bank borrowing while a lower rate tends to encourage lending.

A final method for banks to obtain funds for meeting liquidity requirements is called **participation.** When a borrower is informed that his or her loan has been sold, it is usually via the sale of the servicing rights to the loan to another entity. In some cases, the selling bank may sell only a portion or percentage of the loan package and retain the right to service (e.g., send the monthly mortgage statements, retain the impound accounts) the loan package and then send only the appropriate percentage of the collected mortgage payments to the selling bank each month. More frequently, the whole loan or group of loans is released and a new servicer assumes the responsibility for collecting payments, etc.

The Federal Government's Involvement

We've seen above how the Federal Funds Rate can be manipulated by the Fed to influence the flow of funds and the amount available for lending purposes. As noted, raising the federal funds rate will dissuade banks from taking out such interbank loans, which in turn will make cash that much harder to procure. Conversely, dropping the interest rates will encourage banks to borrow money and therefore invest more freely. The Federal Reserve decided in 2009 to reduce the federal funds rate to near zero, which continued and by late 2015 remained between 0 to 0.25 percent. This meant that lenders could borrow funds at a quarter percent or less and loan it to home buyers at current rates. Designed to stimulate the economy, especially the housing sector, the low interest rates have, to some degree, been offset by less flexible home buyer qualifying guidelines (discussed in Chapter 9).

7.2 POINTS AND DISCOUNTS

Focusing primarily on loans sold to the secondary market, points and discounts are a way of calculating yield to the purchasing entity. To the home loan borrower, the terms also indicate cost or rebate related to an individual loan.

The term **"points"** or discount points represents a form of pre-paid interest and is calculated as 1 point representing 1 percent of the loan amount (not the sales price). A lender's yield is increased when discount points are collected on a loan. Generally, known as buying down the rate, a borrower may reduce his or her interest rate by one-eighth to one-quarter percent (depending upon the economic climate at the time) for every 1 point paid in discount and, in turn, reduce the monthly payment. Buy-down transactions were covered in detail in Chapter 5.

A **discount** is the amount of money a lender deducts from the loan amount when loan proceeds are funded. In its simplest form, the discount in a loan would be calculated as in the example below.

Example:
Loan amount	$150 000
Less 2-point discount	3 000
Net funds	$147 000 excluding appraisal and other fees

The lender net funds a loan amount after having deducted the discount points.

A **premium**, on the other hand, involves a loan sold for more than the face amount or balance of the loan. A $100,000 loan sold at a premium of 2 percent is sold for $102,000. Regarding home loans, a premium is the result of a borrower accepting a higher than market interest rate, thereby increasing the lender's yield.

Referred to as a "service release premium" (SRP), yield spread premium (YSP), or "rebate pricing," this use of points to help pay for closing costs has become more popular of late. While abused by some lenders in the past, resulting in limitations to brokerage earnings, when used appropriately, rebate pricing can be beneficial to borrowers. (YSP: Good or Bad is covered in the Case & Point following Chapter 3.)

Buyers who are short of cash use the rebate to defray some or all of their closing costs. This same method of calculating rebate is how lenders offer zero point loans—a higher interest rate accepted by the borrower can lure them into thinking that they are acquiring a no-cost loan. There is no such thing, and the borrower will either pay in fees or via a higher interest rate. The key is whether the transaction is appropriately disclosed. The controversy over appropriate disclosure and the borrowers' understanding resulted in the three-page Good Faith Estimate and replaced in late 2015 by the Loan Estimate, both discussed fully in the Case & Point following Chapter 9.

The term discount points should not be confused with origination fees or broker fees, also referred to as points, paid for the acquisition of the loan. These fees will be discussed in Chapter 10.

Lenders' Use of Discounts

This use of discount points in the calculation of a lender's yield is the same calculation used to determine the annual percentage rate (APR) or the effective interest rate for a loan. The APR is discussed in detail in Chapter 10 and 15.

Example: Assume you borrowed $100,000 for one year at a 10 percent interest rate. At the end of the year, you would repay the lender the $100,000 plus $10,000 in interest. The lender's yield would be calculated as follows:

$$\frac{\text{Interest}}{\text{Money Borrowed}} = \frac{\$10,000}{\$100,000} = 10\%$$

If the lender charged you a loan fee, the result would be different. If the fee were five points, or $5,000, you would receive only $95,000, because the lender subtracts the points from the loan amount and remits the difference. At the end of the year, you would pay the lender the $100,000 principal balance plus $10,000 in interest.

In addition to the interest, the lender also collects the $5,000 in points. The **effective interest rate** that the lender has achieved is 15.8 percent, calculated as follows:

$$\frac{\text{Interest} + \text{Discount}}{\text{Money Disbursed}} = \frac{\$15,000}{\$95,000} = 15.8\%$$

To determine yields at various discounts, lenders can use a table such as the one shown in the following pages. The yield representations in Tables 7.1, 7.2, and 7.3 are more likely yield calculations used in what is called the "hard money lending" arena where loans are made to riskier borrowers.

Table 7.1 shows yields on 11 percent, 30-year loans at fees ranging from 1 to 10 points. Yields are also determined by the date the loan is paid off. Even though the term is 30 years, the average life of a loan is considerably less. While past industry studies identified the average home ownership period to be seven to eight years, it is expected to lengthen in the future. The **yield**, and the discounts required on any given loan, however, is also dependent upon the initial interest rate, the term of the loan, and the payback rate.

Table 7.1 and the two that follow, 7.2 and 7.3, are for demonstration purposes only, to show that such tools exist. Real estate calculators have made yield and discount calculations much easier. The formulas and the calculator operations required for performing the computations are beyond the scope of this text, but readers may find the topic to be of at least marginal interest.

TABLE 7.1 Yields on an 11 percent, 30-year loan at various discounts prepaid in 12 years.

Discount (# of points)	Effective Yield (%)
0	11.00
1	11.16
2	11.31
3	11.48
4	11.64
5	11.81
6	11.97
7	12.14
8	12.00
9	12.49
10	12.67

Source: © 2016 OnCourse Learning

Price and Yield

When real estate salespeople and borrowers deal with lenders, the terms used are typically points and loan fees. When lenders sell loans to other lenders or investors, they deal in terms of price and discount. Price + Discount = Face Value, or par.

Price is another way of quoting the discount. A lender selling a loan at a five-point discount would quote a price of 95. The lender is saying that it will sell the loan for 95 percent of the loan amount.

Therefore, an existing $100,000 loan would be sold to another lender for $95,000 (95 percent × $100,000). Price and discount added together always equal 100, which is called par (face value). To determine price, you deduct the discount from 100. For example, if the discount is three points, what is the price?

Par	100
Discount	3
Price	97

If you know the price and you want to determine the discount, you reverse the process. If the price is 97, what is the discount?

Par	100
Price	3
Discount	97

If you know the price, it is simple to determine the effective return, which lenders call yield. When a loan is sold with no discount, at par, the return on the loan and the yield are the same. With a discount, the yield will be higher than the interest rate on the loan.

At a price of 97, based on a 12-year payoff, the yield is 10.46 percent. Investors who purchase existing loans use such tables or financial calculators to determine the price they can pay to achieve a certain yield. They are usually comparing mortgage loans with other competing investments, such as corporate bonds; these are compared on the basis of yield. For example, if an investor wants to achieve a yield of 11.10 percent on the purchase of an existing $100,000 mortgage, what price should the investor pay? Looking at Table 7.2 and assuming the loan will be prepaid in 12 years, the investor would pay a price of 93, or $93,000 (93 percent of $100,000).

All lenders use computerized pricing modules to price their loan options on a daily basis. As previously indicated, for those skilled with the use of financial calculators, tables such as these can be constructed

TABLE 7.2 Desired yield on a 10 percent, 30-year loan at various prices prepaid in 12 years.

Price	Effective Yield (percent)
90	11.61
91	11.43
92	11.26
93	11.10
94	10.93
95	10.77
96	10.61
97	10.46
98	10.30
99	10.15
100	10.00

Source: © 2016 OnCourse Learning

for virtually any interest rate, term, and prepayment period. Chapter 15 examines some calculator applications to real estate problems.

Where Are Discounts Used?

A mortgage or deed of trust recorded after the first mortgage is called a **junior mortgage**. If the junior mortgage is recorded after the first mortgage, it is called a second mortgage, not to be confused with the secondary market. A mortgage recorded after the first and second mortgages is called a third mortgage. While there is no limit on how many liens can be placed on a property, the risk for the lien holder can increase depending upon its position. A detailed discussion of junior mortgages and deeds of trust is presented in Chapter 14.

Junior loans are also bought and sold by investors. For example, sellers of a property may need to carry back a second deed of trust to sell their house. After the sale, the sellers may want to sell the second to obtain cash. To sell, they probably have to offer the second deed of trust at a discount. Discounts on junior loans vary widely—sometimes from 10 to 50 percent depending on note rate, size of monthly payments (rate of payoff), due date, borrower payment history, amount of equity in the property, and prevailing yields in the marketplace. As the risk increases, the discount increases, resulting in a higher yield.

Yields at various discounts can be determined from published tables, as shown in Table 7.3, or by a financial calculator like those reviewed in Chapter 15.

Assume that in the real estate market, as interest rates increase, seller-carried seconds will increase proportionately.

When first mortgages were charging 18 percent and more in 1980 to 1982, junior liens commanded more than 15 percent! While 15 percent seems high in the current low interest rate market, interest

TABLE 7.3 Discount required for various yields on a loan with a 15 percent interest rate with the balance due in five years.

| | Monthly Payoff Rate | | |
Desired Yield (%)	1.25%	1.5%	2%
15	0.0	0.0	0.0
17	6.7	6.2	5.1
19	12.9	11.8	9.8
21	18.5	17.1	14.2
23	23.7	21.9	18.3
25	28.4	26.3	22.1
27	32.8	30.4	25.7

Source: © 2016 OnCourse Learning

rates are a reflection of risk and the desire of a borrower to acquire financing that may be unavailable via other sources. Table 7.3 is merely an example of yields and discounts for mortgages at a 15 percent interest rate, with the entire remaining balance due in five years. Note that the rate of monthly payoff has an effect on the discount. To obtain a 21 percent yield, with a 1.25 percent per month payoff rate, you would need an 18.5 percent discount. If the loan pays off at a rate of 1.5 percent per month, the discount to obtain the same 21 percent yield reduces to 17.1 percent. At a payoff rate of 2 percent per month, only a 14.2 percent discount is required to obtain the 21 percent yield.

The monthly payoff rates are derived by dividing monthly payment by the principal balance. For example:

$$\text{Monthly payment} \div \text{Principal balance} = \text{Rate of payoff}$$
$$\$200 \div \$10\,000 = 2\% \text{ per month}$$

Example: If a 15 percent second loan due in five years has a balance of $50,000, and monthly payments of $1,000, how much of a discount would be required to yield 25 percent?

Solution:

$$\frac{\text{Monthly payment}}{\text{Principal balance}} = \frac{\$1,000}{\$50,000} = 2\% \text{ rate of payoff}$$

To achieve a 25 percent yield, the last column in the table shows that a discount of 22.1 percent will be required. The purchase price of the junior lien is calculated as follows:

Principal balance	$50,000
Less : 22.1% of 50,000	−11,050
Purchase price	$38,950

Mortgage-Backed Securities

Today, the most common method used to move funds is the use of mortgage-backed securities, which are backed by a pool of mortgages. Mortgage-backed securities were created to make investing in mortgages as simple as buying stocks or bonds. Before these securities, lending institutions sold and purchased loans among themselves. This was not an efficient method—it was time consuming and involved a lot of paperwork. In addition, each lender had its own property and borrower standards, which further complicated transactions. More importantly, there was no system to obtain money from the capital markets. Lenders had to depend on deposits, which had proven to be volatile. The invention of the mortgage-backed security revolutionized the operation of the secondary market.

As the number of home mortgages grew, fueled by the subprime, these securitized instruments morphed into what became known as mortgage swaps. In retrospect, the swap was a created mortgage instrument and was so complicated that no one truly understood how it functioned. These swaps were sold worldwide with the anticipation that the Wall Street companies that sold them also insured and guaranteed them. When the mortgage collapse occurred, it was quickly discovered that these Wall Street sellers did not have the reserves to cover the mounting losses from the increasing number of mortgage defaults and that they were only presumed to have been guaranteed by the U.S. government. The ensuing monetary crises, the lack of liquidity, and the government's intervention to prop up not only the nation's economy but the world's is now well documented. We discuss the continuing impacts upon our real estate financial options in various sections of this book.

Three agencies play an important role in the secondary market: the **Government National Mortgage Association (GNMA)**, the **Federal Home Loan Mortgage Corporation (FHLMC)**, and the **Federal National Mortgage Association (FNMA)**. The GNMA is a government agency; the FHLMC was a quasi-government agency until 1989; and the FNMA was a former government agency turned private corporation in 1968 but has now, along with the FHLMC, been placed under conservatorship and is literally owned by consumers through this latest government intervention (see the Case & Point at the end of this chapter for further explanation). The function of these agencies, known as **government-sponsored enterprises (GSEs)**, is to support the secondary market through the purchase of loans or the guarantee of **mortgage-backed securities** issued by lenders. The contribution of these three agencies to the secondary market is illustrated in Figure 7.2.

CHAPTER 7 Points, Discounts, and the Secondary Mortgage Market

FIGURE 7.2 Contribution of secondary markets to home loans.

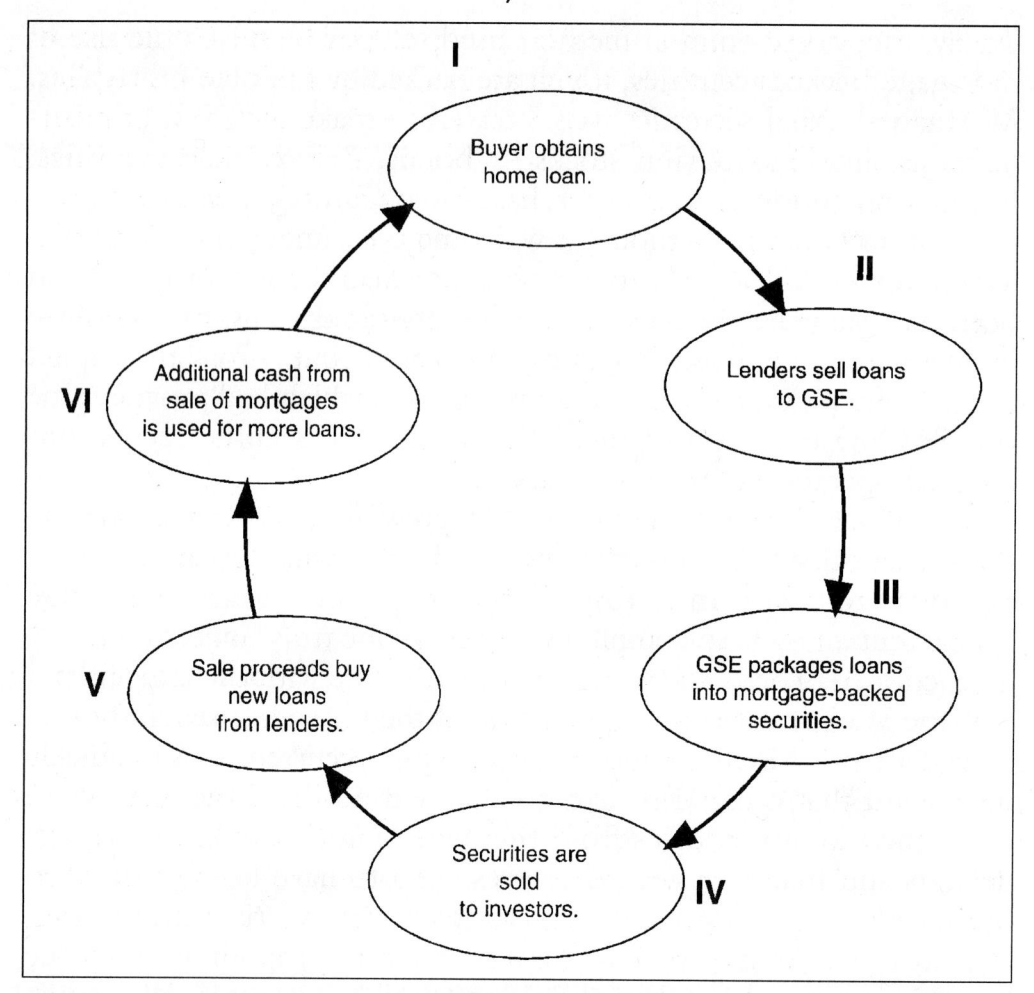

I. Buyer obtains home loan.
II. Lenders sell loans to GSE.
III. GSE packages loans into mortgage-backed securities.
IV. Securities are sold to investors.
V. Sale proceeds buy new loans from lenders.
VI. Additional cash from sale of mortgages is used for more loans.

	Ginnie Mae	Freddie Mac	Fannie Mae	Bonds
Who Owns	Government agency	Government chartered Stockholder owned	Started as gov't now private corp.	State/local gov't issued
Buy What	FHA & DVA loans	Conventional	Conventional	Low income loans
How	Backed by U.S. gov't; Pool loans into package; Sell stock for funds; Guarantee P/I for fee	Pool loans into package; Sell stock for funds; Guarantee P/I for fee	Pool loans into package; Sell stock for funds; Guarantee P/I for fee; Can tap U.S. Treasury	Offers tax-exempt returns; Offers less return to investor; Offers less APR to buyers
When Pay	Through stock/bond returns	Tiered at buyer payoff	In "classes" of CMO	Over long term/fixed amount
More Info	www.ginniemae.gov	www.freddiemac.com	www.fanniemae.com	www.treasurydirect.gov www.investinbonds.com

Source: © 2016 OnCourse Learning

Government National Mortgage Association (GNMA)

The first mortgage-backed security was developed by the Government National Mortgage Association, commonly called Ginnie Mae. Ginnie Mae was established in 1968 as a government agency within the Department of Housing and Urban Development (HUD). Its basic mission was to create and operate a mortgage-backed security program for FHA and VA mortgages. It took over the duties formerly performed by FNMA after it was given private status.

In 1970, Ginnie Mae issued the first security backed by a pool of FHA and VA mortgages. It was called a **pass-through security** because the monthly principal and interest payments collected from the borrowers were passed through to the investor. Ginnie Mae does not purchase mortgages. Its function is to guarantee that principal and interest will be paid every month. Since it is a government agency, the guarantee is backed by the full faith and credit of the government. For this guarantee, Ginnie Mae receives a small fee from the lender, which is collected monthly. The minimum amount that can be placed in a pool is $1,000,000. The mortgages cannot be more than one year old and must have met predetermined average yields for the pool of loans. The pool can contain any combination of FHA and VA mortgages. The lender can apply to Ginnie Mae for a commitment to issue a certificate at any time. When applying, it must indicate the size of the pool and the rate of interest on the mortgages. If Ginnie Mae approves the request, it issues a commitment that is good for one year.

Before the certificate is sold, Ginnie Mae requires that the mortgages be in the hands of a third party. This party acts as a trustee for Ginnie Mae and is called the custodian. The custodian is usually a bank, but it could be any federal or state financial institution acceptable to Ginnie Mae. The lender delivers the mortgage documents to the custodian, who checks the information carefully. Once the custodian is satisfied that it has all the documents, it notifies Ginnie Mae. The certificate is then issued to the lender.

With the certificate in hand, the lender is able to sell the mortgages to an investor. When the investor buys the mortgages, it receives the certificate. Typically, the securities are purchased by securities dealers who trade in Ginnie Mae securities. They in turn sell the securities to other investors, such as insurance companies, pension funds, other lenders who need mortgages, and individuals. The securities can be broken down into smaller denominations to satisfy the demands of the various investors (the smallest denomination is $25,000). The securities are traded on Wall Street just like stocks and bonds. There is an active market for the securities, which makes them a liquid investment.

Readers wishing more information on the GNMA can access its website at www.ginniemae.gov.

Federal Home Loan Mortgage Corporation (FHLMC)

Because Ginnie Mae included only FHA and VA mortgages in its securities, there was a great need to develop a mortgage-backed security for conventional loans. In 1971, the Federal Home Loan Mortgage Corporation, also known as Freddie Mac, introduced the first security backed by conventional loans. Freddie Mac was a subsidiary of the Office of Thrift Supervision, which supervised the federally chartered thrifts. As a government-chartered, stockholder- owned corporation, FHLMC bought mortgages and sold them in the secondary market.

Freddie Mac bought conventional loans from lenders such as savings banks, commercial banks, and mortgage companies. It then assembled a pool of mortgages and issued a security backed by the mortgages. The security is called a *Participating Certificate* or Guaranteed Mortgage Certificate. The agency guarantees the full payment of principal and the timely payment of interest. The security is later sold to investors in the capital markets. For the guarantee, Freddie Mac receives a monthly fee paid by the investors.

For more information on FHLMC, access its website through a link at www.freddiemac.com.

Federal National Mortgage Association (FNMA)

The Federal National Mortgage Association, known as Fannie Mae, was established by Congress in 1938 to provide a secondary market for mortgages. It remained a part of the federal government until 1968, when it became a private corporation. Even though it was private, the corporation had a public purpose and maintained strong government ties. It was subject to some regulations by the Department of Housing and Urban Development (HUD). It also had the ability to tap the U.S. Treasury if necessary.

Fannie Mae issues a security backed by conventional loans and operates the issuance of its securities much like Freddie Mac. It buys mortgages from lenders, places them in a pool, and issues a security.

The security is sold to investors, who *receive a guarantee that principal and interest will be paid monthly, whether or not payments have been collected from the borrowers.* Fannie Mae charges a monthly fee for the guarantee.

Note: The italicized statements regarding guarantees led to problems in 2008 that could no longer be ignored. See the Case & Point at the end of the chapter.

Collateralized Mortgage Obligations

Fannie Mae issues mortgage-backed securities called **collateralized mortgage obligations (CMOs)**. They were designed to limit prepayment risk to investors. Prior to this time, mortgage-backed securities were a pass through, which means that all the principal and interest collected were passed on to the investor. The investor had no protection from the early prepayment of principal. If borrowers in the pool decided to pay their mortgages in full, the proceeds were passed on to the investors.

When investors calculate yield, they make assumptions regarding the repayment of principal. When mortgages are paid early, the investors' yield is reduced, since they collect less total interest. Therefore, investors are looking for a security that can provide some protection against early prepayment and loss of return on investment.

A CMO is divided into classes. For example, the first CMO had three classes. Each class paid interest on the outstanding balance. However, all collections of principal from the pool were first applied to class one. After that class had been paid in full, all principal collections went to class two. After class two had been paid in full, the remaining principal payments went to class three. The CMO gives investors opportunities to choose classes that offer different rates and maturities. The creation of the CMO attracted investors that were not normally mortgage investors and, in the end, not savvy enough to understand the process. Those notorious swap instruments created by Wall Street were not far behind in attractiveness for investors and equally misunderstood.

For readers wishing more information on the FNMA and on Fannie Mae Foundation, which offers information on finding and financing homes, access their websites through links at www.fanniemae.com.

Nonconforming Loans

The U.S. Congress sets the maximum loan amount on conventional loans purchased by Freddie Mac and Fannie Mae. Since 2006 the maximum for single-family loans in most areas has remained $417,000. The maximum loan amount can change based on economic conditions and can be adjusted each year by FNMA and Freddie Mac—who bundle these loans to resell to investors—to reflect local price trends. Resistance to discussions around possibly lowering the $417,000 amount during the recession resulted in it being retained.

In early 2009, a new category of **conforming loan** was introduced called the high balance conforming loan, with loan amounts up to

$729,750, but since October 2011 reduced to $625,500. Up until 2009, the name **jumbo loan** applied to any loan amount above the conforming loan amount. The introduction of the high-balance loan caused some confusion. It was unclear if the high-balance loan was replacing the jumbo loan or was a category between conforming and a new to-be-created jumbo loan amount. For many, the terms *high-balance* and *jumbo* loan seemed synonymous.

Jumbo loans had all but disappeared soon after the recession began. These higher loan amounts were created to provide affordable financing for those areas that had experienced substantial home value appreciation. This led to some confusion, as some areas remained at the $417,000 conforming loan limit while other areas were eligible for the higher loan amount. For loans that exceeded the conforming or high-balance loan amounts, a new jumbo option was available on a very limited basis.

Whereas in the past, jumbo loan interest rates were priced at approximately one-quarter percent higher than the normal conforming loan, by early 2009, jumbo financing had become not only largely unavailable but nearly unaffordable. To add to the confusion, in those areas designated as lower cost, a jumbo loan meant any loan over $417,000. In the higher cost areas, jumbo financing was above the new high-balance amount of $729,750, since changed to $625,500. Jumbo loan financing during this time dried up, leaving many homeowners little recourse for new purchases or refinances.

The private corporations, often subsidiaries of large financial institutions, that had formed to issue mortgage-backed securities backed by jumbo loans, had become cautious and found little market for their securities. Their parent organizations were facing difficult times with bank failures and mergers seemingly occurring daily. This withdrawal from the market led to a lack of lending for the purchase of expensive homes resulting in further downward pressure on home prices. Not until early 2010 did jumbo loans begin to slowly reappear as available financing.

Investment Bankers

Investment bankers made a market for both new and seasoned mortgage-backed securities. These Wall Street firms, called *securities dealers*, bought and sold securities from lenders and investors.

Defining themselves as bankers, these investment firms were perceived by the public to function like a bank with required reserves, insurance for protection of clients' investments, and a relative safety for investment purposes. These companies developed the instrument now known as a swap, a complicated and little understood method of reducing a subprime loan into pieces for sale, mostly abroad. Purchasers were led to believe that these swaps had not only the safety of a bank investment but enjoyed the full backing of the U.S. government, and these investments were sold at what turned out to be exorbitant prices.

Morgan Stanley, Lehman Brothers, and Merrill Lynch are three of the well-known entities that were exposed in 2008 as being a virtual house of cards. When the subprime market totally collapsed in 2008, the investment banks were found to have no reserves or insurance and were unable to cover the mounting losses. They turned instead to the government to pay their investors. (See note below.)

Mergers were encouraged with Merrill Lynch merging with Bank of America Corporation and Morgan Stanley with Goldman Sachs. The latter merger redefined Goldman Sachs as a traditional bank holding company rather than an investment firm. This brought an end, at least for the present, to the era of investment banking on Wall Street.

Note: Representing themselves as bankers implied to the world that their activities were backed by the full force and credit of the United States government. When this proved untrue and the investment firms were on the verge of total collapse, they were designated as "too big to fail" and the government bailout occurred.

As the troubles mounted, it was discovered that the investment bankers had enlisted the bond rating entities in the scheme of highly endorsing their packages of swaps (which no one understood) so that they could be sold at high cost to the world, clamoring to buy what they had been duped into believing were great investments. The investment bankers had gambled on the subprime loan instruments—often knowing that they were bad bets—and after making lots of money, turned to the government to save them. In other words, the bankers gambled on what turned out to be a situation in which "if we win we keep the money and if we lose, the American consumer gets the bill." Critics continue to complain that the bankers were saved and the homeowners were abandoned.

As the failures mounted, IndyMac, one of the first to embrace subprime loans, collapsed. Among the other mergers at the time, Bank of America absorbed Countrywide Home Loans and JPMorgan Chase absorbed Washington Mutual Savings Bank. Countrywide was notorious for its subprime loan excesses and Washington Mutual was the largest institutional failure in our history.

The excesses resulted in the legislation that empowered the Consumer Financial Protection Bureau (CFPB discussed earlier) and an array of new rules and guidelines around home mortgages. By the end of 2014, Congress was divided in how to continue its struggle to rein in Wall Street's bad practices and provide for more safety in the investment arena. Some in Congress, citing that too much regulation stifled the banking industry, wanted to weaken the oversight of the CFPB. Critics charged that loosening guidelines would again give banks permission to gamble with consumer funds and promote a replay of the past financial crises. Home loan financing is likely to be impacted by how this tug of war plays out in Congress.

Standardization

One major benefit brought about by the creation of mortgage-backed securities by Freddie Mac and Fannie Mae is the standardization of conventional loan forms and property and borrower standards. FHA and VA loans have been readily sold in the secondary market for years. One of the reasons is that their forms are standardized. As an investor, you could buy an FHA or VA loan anywhere in the United States and know the exact loan provisions. Previously this could not be done with a conventional loan.

To have a functional secondary market for conventional loans, you must also have *standardization*. Freddie Mac and Fannie Mae have accomplished this by using the same forms and by having basically the same property and borrower standards. Almost all lenders today use the standard forms, and many adhere to the property and borrower standards set forth by the agencies. This gives the lenders great flexibility in ensuring that their loans can be sold in the secondary market.

Mortgage Revenue Bonds

The State of California and local governments—cities and counties—have the authority to issue bonds. Interest paid on the bonds is tax exempt to the investors. Bonds sold by state and local governments and used to finance mortgages are called **mortgage revenue bonds**. Because the bonds are tax exempt, the interest rate is less than on a standard bond and, as a result, mortgage loans can be made at below-market rates. The government agencies do not guarantee the bonds. The bonds are backed by the mortgages created by the bond funds. The issuer of the bond merely acts as a conduit; local lenders process, close, and then service the loans for the government. These bond issues generally work the same way as other mortgage-backed securities, but the paperwork is much more complex. Local bond issues typically are used to promote lower-income or affordable housing ventures. Borrower requirements usually include income and/or price limits, length of time ownership requirements, and limitations on the amount of equity to be retained upon resale. (See Figure 7.2 where the contribution of bonds to the secondary market is shown along with the GSEs)

Chapter Summary

A point, by definition, is 1 percent of the loan amount. Points are used to measure discounts, loan origination fees, and premiums. Lenders charge discounts to increase the effective yield they receive on a loan. When lenders sell loans to investors, they sell on the basis of price. Price is another way of quoting discount. A loan with a discount of three points would have a price of 97; price and discount added together equal 100, or **par**. When lenders buy or sell loans, they look at the yield, or effective interest rate. Yield on a loan can be adjusted by varying the discount. Lenders use discounts to increase their yield on any given loan. As the discount increases the yield increases. Discounts are also used on conventional loans, government loans, and junior mortgages and in the secondary mortgage market. Discount and yield calculations, as used with home financing, contribute to yield spread premiums (YSP) widely used by borrowers to defray closing costs. Existing loans are bought or sold in the secondary market. The primary purpose of the secondary market is to provide liquidity to the market. One of the ways to accomplish this is to shift funds from capital surplus areas to capital short areas. Mortgage-backed securities are another tool used to obtain money from the capital market. There are securities backed by FHA and VA loans and others backed by conventional loans. Since 1978, tax-exempt bonds have been widely used by state and local governments to finance housing, especially providing for lower-income borrowers.

Important Terms and Concepts

Collateralized Mortgage Obligation (CMO)
Conforming loan
Discount
Effective interest rate
Federal Home Loan Mortgage Corporation (FHLMC)
Federal National Mortgage Association (FNMA)
Government National Mortgage Association (GNMA)
Government-Sponsored Enterprises (GSE)
Jumbo loan

Junior mortgage
Mortgage revenue bonds
Mortgage-backed securities
Nonconforming loan
Par
Participation

Pass-through security
Points
Premium
Price
Secondary mortgage market
Yield

Reviewing Your Understanding

Questions for Discussion

1. Describe what price means when one lender sells existing real estate loans to another lender. How is yield computed?
2. Explain why borrowers pay loan origination fees when obtaining a loan.
3. What is the difference between secondary financing and the secondary mortgage market?
4. What are the main functions of the secondary market?
5. Why is liquidity so important to the lending environment?
6. What is a mortgage-backed security?

Multiple-Choice Questions

1. Securities that are usually exempt from federal and state income taxation are popularly labeled
   a. conventional mortgage-backed securities.
   b. mortgage revenue bonds.
   c. private mortgage-backed certificates.
   d. participation loans.

2. Interest rates on FHA and VA loans are set by
   a. HUD.
   b. the Department of Veterans Affairs.
   c. an agreement between the borrower and lender.
   d. the lender solely.

3. A lender selling a loan at a six-point discount would quote a price of
   a. 106.
   b. 94.
   c. 100.
   d. none of the above.

4. Which of the following parties would likely not sell mortgage loans to Freddie Mac?
   a. Mortgage companies
   b. Commercial banks
   c. Individuals
   d. Savings banks

5. The chief purpose of the secondary mortgage market is to
   a. shift funds from the capital shortage areas to capital surplus area.
   ✓b. shift funds from the capital surplus areas to capital shortage areas.
   c. guarantee a market so money can be recirculated.
   d. both (a) and (c) are correct.

6. Regarding points charged for a home loan
   a. one point is equal to 1 percent of the sales price.
   ✓b. one point is equal to 1 percent of the loan amount.
   c. points are always paid by the buyer-borrower.
   d. points are always paid by the seller.

7. Which of the following is a major buyer and seller in the secondary mortgage market?
   a. FHA
   ✓b. FNMA
   c. VA
   d. Cal-Vet

8. Which of the following is also significantly involved in the secondary mortgage market?
   a. Federal Reserve Board
   b. Federal Housing Administration
   c. California Housing Finance Agency
   ✓d. Federal Home Loan Mortgage Corporation

9. Fannie Mae is the popular name for
   ✓a. Federal National Mortgage Association.
   b. Federal National Marketing Association.
   c. Federal Home Loan Mortgage Corporation.
   d. Federal Housing Administration.

10. The federal government is intimately involved in the transfer of mortgage funds through its federal funds rate, which
    a. determines what banks charge each other for overnight loans.
    b. influences the available supply of money.
    c. can drop to near zero in order to increase liquidity and encourage lending.
    ✓d. all of the above.

11. When forwarding loan proceeds to the escrow holder, lenders generally
    a. forward the loan amount, and look to the escrow holder to disburse the discount and lender's fees.
    ✓b. deduct the amount of the discount and its fees.
    c. insist on having a check for the amount of any discount or fee.
    d. none of the above.

12. When dealing in the secondary market, price and discount
    a. are synonymous with points and discounts.
    ✓b. when added together, equal 100 percent, or par.
    c. actually describe sales price and effective yield.
    d. none of the above.

13. Conforming loans are periodically adjusted by the
    a. U.S. Treasury.
    b. Federal Reserve Board.
    c. Real Estate Commissioner.
    ✓d. government-sponsored enterprises.

14. The term secondary market
    a. describes any junior lien, whether second or lower in priority.
    b. is where loans are actually made to the borrower.
    c. describes a market where existing loans are bought and sold. ✓
    d. involves FNMA, GNMA, and FHLMC as the only participants.

15. Mortgage swaps
    a. grew out of the subprime easy money mortgage market.
    b. were sold worldwide with the anticipation that the Wall Street firms selling them also insured and guaranteed them.
    c. led to the mortgage collapse of the mid-2000s.
    d. each of the above is connected to mortgage swaps. ✓

16. Investment bankers
    a. make a market for both new and seasoned securities.
    b. buy and sell securities from lenders and investors.
    c. are very active in the secondary market.
    d. are involved in each of the foregoing activities. ✓

17. If you were selling a loan at a two-point premium, you would quote a price of
    a. 2.
    b. 102. ✓
    c. 98.
    d. 100.

18. The objectives and mechanics of the secondary mortgage market are many and varied, including
    a. making below-market interest rate loans to home buyers.
    b. buying and selling existing mortgages. ✓
    c. providing funds for needy sellers.
    d. insuring loans for home buyers.

19. Which of the following is the popular name for the Federal Home Loan Mortgage Corporation?
    a. Fannie Mae
    b. Freddie Mac ✓
    c. Ginnie Mae
    d. Fed Mae

20. You list a home for $220,000, and then the real estate market begins to decline. A young couple offers to purchase the home for $175,000, and after a series of counteroffers it sells for $180,000. The couple applies for a $150,000 loan, and the lender commits to a two-point fee. Ignoring other charges, the amount of proceeds to be disbursed will be
    a. $147,000. ✓
    b. $176,000.
    c. $196,000.
    d. $150,000.

CASE & POINT

Fannie/Freddie ... Now and In the Future!

The charters of both Fannie Mae and Freddie Mac guaranteed the payment of principal and interest for the securitized loans, known as mortgage-backed securities (MBS), that were sold to investors. When Wall Street divided these securities into what would come to be known as swaps and sold them globally, ambiguity with the word *guarantee* allowed investors to claim that the government guaranteed their investment and that they believed their investments to have been risk-free. As mortgage defaults ballooned, it became clear that the GSEs did not have sufficient insurance and/or reserves to cover the mounting losses. Because the U.S. government created the ambiguities, the U. S. Treasury determined that it had the responsibility to avert the global panic being created by the failure of the GSEs. The result was the government's decision to place Fannie and Freddie under conservatorship in an effort to avoid a complete collapse of the mortgage market. The initial infusion of funds was promoted to the public as a temporary measure to provide liquidity and to quiet the concerns of the investment community. The federal government ultimately became the major shareholder of both GSEs. By late 2014, the GSEs had paid their debt to the government and, while still a bit tenuous, were viewed as having been restored to stability but remained in conservatorship.

In the meantime, borrower qualification guidelines tightened, new lender oversight rules emerged, and there was a period during which lenders and borrowers alike viewed the process of acquiring a home loan as difficult. The financial crises urged long-time critics to increase their questioning regarding the GSEs soundness, structure, and even their continuation, and the long held desire by some legislators to encourage private investment in the lucrative mortgage market gained some momentum.

Looking ahead, Congress has found it difficult to agree to legislation that would both wind down Fannie Mae and Freddie Mac while engaging the private sector to shoulder at least some of the risk of providing liquidity to the mortgage market. The elimination of the incentive provided by the mortgage "guarantee" was seen as critical to avoiding any encouragement to the taking of excessive risk resulting in the making of risky loans in the future.

While many anticipate that a future reduction in the portfolio holdings of both Fannie Mae and Freddie Mac is inevitable, most agree that the change should not totally eliminate government guarantees. Many believe that any plan going forward must ensure that the 30-year mortgage will remain accessible and affordable. Another piece of any proposed reform is to adopt a market discipline that requires shareholders to bear both the risk and the reward of their investments. In other words, eliminate the ability of investors to gamble with the ability to privatize profits and socialize losses.

Late 2013 saw the Protecting American Taxpayers and Homeowners (PATH) Act introduced in Congress. Believing that any reform of the mortgage market guarantee process must also include FHA reform, the act purported to (a) end the bailout, (b) right size and more clearly define the mission of FHA, (c) implement reforms to increase market competition and maximize consumer loan choice, and (d) break down the barriers for the entry of private investment capital. More specifically, the proposal would shrink the GSEs' current near 6 billion dollar portfolios over a five year period while reducing the high-balance loan amount (currently $625,500) over the same period. More troubling to some is the elimination of the 30-year mortgage, viewed by some as the loan vehicle that has allowed continuing home ownership over the decades. The loss of the 30-year mortgage coupled with the intent to repeal the affordable housing goals mandate and the restriction that the GSEs be limited to the purchase of only Qualified Mortgage (QM) loans (the QM requirements are discussed in the Case & Point in Chapter 5) has resulted in many viewing the PATH Act as too draconian, and it has not found sufficient support for passage.

While reform may create some anxiety and be inevitable, Fannie and Freddie continue as the main conduits for conventional financing. The sale of loans to the GSEs ensures a steady supply of financing for residential mortgages while also continuing programs to assist low and moderate income families to purchase homes.

Private capital may have to eventually assume more risk in the mortgage market along with the existing GSEs. What a transition might look like has to accommodate the continuing role of the GSEs, structuring and regulating the secondary market to continue its support of affordable housing, and deal with regulating the incentives to control risk taking. Finally, how will the existing portfolios and guarantee obligations be managed during any transition without unduly disrupting the house buying market? A fear is that the uncontrolled inclusion of private capital could result in a more for-profit climate with accompanying restrictions on loan amounts, higher interest rates, and the diminishing capability of middle class borrowers to purchase homes. The idea that private capital will increase competition and give consumers more opportunity to select loan options that better suit their needs has skeptics worried.

So, while the housing finance system may need reform, that reform depends upon striking the appropriate balance between any benefits of a private market with the strength and support of a government program. Striking the right balance may be tricky but necessary to strengthen the housing market, stabilize the financial system, and create a healthier economy.

On the positive side, Fannie Mae has reintroduced a 3 percent down payment loan option and seems poised to continue creating flexibility in borrower qualification guidelines. Credit issues are being addressed with the anticipation of borrowers with lower scores being able to purchase without severe rate penalties now imposed by the risk-based approval models. Perhaps we can anticipate the return of stated income loans for self-employed borrowers and other qualification relaxation efforts to encourage home ownership.

The one thing that we may know for certain is that change will occur.

© Shutterstock / Galina Barskaya

QUALIFYING THE PROPERTY

OVERVIEW

This chapter describes the procedures lenders use in qualifying or appraising a property for loan purposes: The neighborhood is analyzed, the property is inspected, and a value is determined based upon market variables. This chapter also reviews the use of an appraisal form in depth and lists special considerations by lenders on planned unit developments and condominiums.

After completing this chapter, you will be able to:

- Discuss the influence of Freddie Mac and Fannie Mae and the new Home Valuation Code of Conduct (HVCC) on a lender's property qualifying standards.
- Describe what an appraiser looks for when analyzing a neighborhood.
- Outline the steps used in the market data approach to estimating loan value.
- Demonstrate why sales price is not the same as fair market value.
- Differentiate the formal classifications of real estate appraisers in California.
- Suggest possible ways to communicate with an appraiser within the rules of the new Home Valuation Code of Conduct.

8.1 WHAT DOES QUALIFYING THE PROPERTY MEAN?

The expression "qualifying the property" often is used interchangeably with the term "appraising the property." When making a loan, one of the lender's early actions is to obtain an appraisal to determine whether the property is sufficient collateral for the requested loan amount.

Although state and federal laws prohibit a lender from redlining an area based on neighborhood, ethnic, racial, or other illegal reasons, a lender is allowed to require that the value of the property be high enough to justify the loan. A lender will base the loan amount on the market value of the property or the purchase price, *whichever is the lesser*. This, coupled with the borrower's income and credit profile, determines the maximum loan-to-value ratio the lender will allow as a condition for making the loan.

Note: Appraisers' prime responsibility is not necessarily to determine market value. Their major objective is to determine if the value is sufficient to serve as security (enough collateral) for the lender's projected loan amount which, in turn, we refer to as the market value.

Lenders' Property Standards

While Fannie Mae and Freddie Mac guidelines are widely accepted as property standards, lenders who do not intend to sell their loans to Fannie Mae or Freddie Mac can establish their own guidelines. Depending upon the economic climate, the availability of funds, and the strength of the borrower, some flexibility among lenders can exist. When exceptions to a lender's basic policy occur, the possibility of being accused of illegal discrimination must be addressed.

Changes in lenders' basic property standards are generally related to fluctuations in the availability of funds to loan out and/or market conditions. When funds are plentiful, the lender will be more likely to loosen its standards. Conversely, when there is less money available for the loans being requested, the lender will stiffen property standards. Market conditions also affect lenders' flexibility. When property values are increasing—much like the run-up in home values from 2000 to early 2006—appraised values and property standards became secondary to a borrower's credit score and creating easy-to-purchase guidelines. On the other hand, when home values adjust downward, property standards toughen and reliance upon appraised values increases. As noted in the next section, a lender's attitude will also be influenced by whether the loan will be sold in the secondary market or kept in its own portfolio.

Influence of Freddie Mac and Fannie Mae

Freddie Mac and Fannie Mae influence a conventional lender's property standards. A lender that intends to sell its loans to either agency must follow the particular agency's standards. Thus a mortgage company will not approve a loan on a property unless the property is acceptable to the intended secondary market purchaser. If the property were not acceptable, the mortgage company would be stuck with the loan. There are other lenders, such as savings banks, that retain loans in their own portfolio. They may still want to use Freddie Mac or Fannie

Mae property standards for all of their loans to ensure that their loans are saleable to these agencies; this gives the lender more flexibility in managing its funds. Therefore, most lenders adhere to the property requirements of both Fannie Mae and Freddie Mac.

FHA and VA Property Standards

The Federal Housing Administration and the Department of Veterans Affairs do not operate like conventional lenders; they *insure* or *guarantee loans*. In the past, government loans often required extensive repairs and improvements to property prior to issuing a loan. More recently, they have adopted more flexible guidelines, known as habitability standards. Some of these standards include a working heater, water, and electricity and include any health and safety issues, such as broken glass, peeling paint, etc. Both the FHA and the VA rely heavily upon appraisers to determine if a home meets specific property requirements. They do not adjust the loan-to-value ratio because of the property—if the property meets the minimum standards, it will be entitled to the maximum loan amount under existing FHA and VA guidelines. Likewise, the interest rate is not affected by the property.

Procedure for Qualifying a Property

How do lenders qualify or appraise a property? FHA and VA requirements differ from most requirements for conventional loans. First let's discuss how the FHA and the VA qualify property.

Qualifying for FHA and VA

The primary responsibility of the FHA and the VA is to ensure that a property meets their minimum property standards. The appraiser serves as the eyes of the lender. In addition, he or she must establish a market value for the property. An FHA appraisal must be ordered through an approved FHA lender (commercial banks, savings banks, and most mortgage companies can be approved lenders).

When FHA abandoned their process whereby they assigned appraisers, a web-based program called FHA Connection became the way appraisers were requested and assigned. To be approved and eligible for assignment from the Connection, appraisers were required to be state certified and had to undergo annual FHA recertification.

Prior to 2010, local mortgage companies and banks met stringent requirements, including minimum cash reserves, and were FHA approved to originate FHA mortgages. As requirements increased, especially for required financial reserves, small local lending entities were slowly priced out and eliminated. Most of these local mortgage originators now function as a correspondent sponsored by an FHA approved lending source, which in turn, acquires the appraisal assignment via their FHA Portal connection. After the FHA indicated that they did not intend to follow conventional lenders' 2009 adoption of the Home Valuation Code of Conduct (HVCC), a similar process was created by mid-2010. The Case & Point at the end of this chapter explains more about the HVCC process.

After the appraiser has inspected and appraised the property, a **conditional commitment** is issued. The conditional commitment includes any other conditions that the FHA is requiring, such as termite work and repairs. A copy of the conditional commitment is sent back to the sponsoring lender who ordered the appraisal. Whereas in the past, pest control reports were always required, FHA appraisers are now responsible for determining if a report should be acquired. Along with all other appraisal conditions, any pest work or repairs identified in a required report must be completed and a clearance provided before FHA insurance will be issued.

The VA operates in much the same way as the FHA. A VA appraisal is ordered by a VA-qualified lender, usually a sponsoring entity of a local lender. The appraisal is sent by the VA to a licensed independent fee appraiser who is VA qualified. The VA uses fee appraisers for all of its field work. It does have full-time staff appraisers, but their function is to act as reviewers and supervisors. Once the fee appraiser has completed the appraisal, it is sent to the VA office for review. If approved, a **Certificate of Reasonable Value (CRV)** is issued, which includes other conditions and repairs that the VA requires on the property. A pest control report and clearance are still required on all VA loans. A copy of the CRV is mailed to the person who ordered it and to the veteran-buyer.

Conventional Lenders and the Appraisal Process

Conventional lenders had generally used a less complicated process than FHA or VA in appraising the property. Typically, the borrower completed a loan application, which was reviewed by the lender or its loan correspondent. If the application and the accompanying required documentation was sufficient to proceed with a borrower's loan request, a credit report and appraisal was ordered.

Since the appraisal process can take some time, ordering it as soon as possible is usually advised. With the escalating costs of the appraisal pursuant to the introduction of the HVCC process, ordering it may now be delayed, at the borrower's request, while inspections (e.g.;

home inspection, pest inspection, etc.) are conducted. (See the loan processing time chart in the Case & Point in Chapter 10.) Obtaining recommended inspections safeguards the potential buyer and may identify issues that impact the buyer's intentions to proceed. Holding off on ordering the appraisal until all inspections and issues have been reconciled guarantees that the buyer will not have an expense for an unused appraisal. Of course, the appraiser may uncover issues undetected in the inspections.

In the past, local licensed staff or fee appraisers were contacted directly by the local lending entity to conduct the appraisal. The current HVCC establishes a more complicated system whereby appraisals must be ordered via Appraisal Management Companies. The process can impact both the timeliness and the quality of the appraisal (see the Case & Point at the end of the chapter for details).

The process remains the same in that after an appraisal is completed, the lender reviews it for completeness as well as to determine whether the value of the property is sufficient for the loan request. While the appraisal is being done, the lender uses this time to acquire any additional information or lender conditions required to qualify the borrower.

The final loan amount is always based on the lesser of the purchase price or the appraised value. For instance, with a sales price of $300,000 and an appraised value of only $280,000, the lender will base the maximum loan on the lower $280,000 figure. If the appraisal were at a value of $320,000, then the lender would base the maximum loan on the lower sales price of $300,000.

Assuming that the appraisal issue is settled and the borrower is qualified, the entire loan package is submitted to a loan committee, or underwriter, who reviews the package and makes the final approval or rejection. If the loan committee or underwriter needs additional information prior to making a final decision, the request for additional information is sent back down the chain to the loan officer or correspondent.

New Rules Impact Appraisal Time Frames

The new regulations, adopted in 2009, (discussed in this chapter's Case & Point) continue to influence the appraisal process. Another new rule at the time, the Mortgage Disclosure Improvement Act (MDIA) coupled with the HVCC rules, can seriously increase the time in which appraisals can be completed. Beginning July 30, 2009, the MDIA reemphasized that disclosures must be delivered to the customer within three days of receipt of an application. While several other mandates are included in this legislation, the one affecting appraisals is that "no fee (except for a credit report fee) can be collected from the customer until delivery of the disclosures has occurred."

The other regulations contained in the MDIA legislation are beyond the scope of this book at this time.

The time frame may be made more clear if ordering the appraisal is identified in the purchase contract as subject to approval of the inspections (as noted above). There is then time to acquire any additional information after which the appropriate disclosures can be issued. If the purchase contract time frame is shortened, waiting three days or more before even ordering the appraisal can impact the ability to complete the transaction on time.

Although the appraisal is a critical aspect of the loan process, there are numerous other time sensitive considerations that occur during the processing period. Current practices regarding inspections and appraisals have implications for real estate licensees when determining time frames in their purchase contracts. Rate lock times can also be impacted wherein 45 days may be a more reasonable time period than the 30-day contracts of the past.

See the Case & Point after Chapter 10 for a more complete list of the steps to be managed in the acquisition of a loan.

8.2 APPRAISING A PROPERTY

Qualifying a property with an appraisal report is one of the most critical phases of the lending process. (Qualifying the borrower is another; that is covered in the next chapter.) The lender relies on the appraisal report to determine the acceptability of the property as collateral. The main purpose of an appraisal is to estimate **fair market value (FMV)**, defined as "the most probable price in terms of money that a property should bring in a competitive and open market under all conditions requisite to a fair sale, the buyer and seller acting prudently, knowledgeably and assuming the price is not affected by undue stimulus."

The number of foreclosures and short sales in recent years placed downward pressure on home values. There are many reasons for appraisals—lending, insurance, income taxes, property taxation, probates, divorce, bankruptcy, and other legal concerns. The reason for the appraisal will affect the appraiser's approach to the task. For example, insurance appraisals are done to estimate replacement value of the improvements and therefore are not concerned with land value.

In this chapter, we're concerned with appraisals only for loan purposes. An appraisal for loan purposes is to determine that the current value is sufficient in relation to the purchase price and the accompanying loan-to-value represented by the loan amount. The appraisal may not, in this instance, represent its highest value, as the lender is interested only in assurance that the property is worth at least an amount required to serve as collateral protection for the lender.

Unfortunately, in rare cases and in an effort to not create conflict should there be a large variation in values between the appraised value and the purchase price, the appraisal may not represent the maximum highest value but reflect a more modest value over purchase price. There is no incentive for the borrower to be purchasing with loads of built-in equity, but a seller made aware that he may have sold well below value could be incentivized to squelch the transaction in hopes of selling for a higher price.

In spite of newer regulations affecting the appraisal process, the elements influencing value remain the same. It is important, that we know how the value of properties is determined.

Location

We've heard it said that "location, location, location" is essential in determining property value. In analyzing the location, both city and neighborhood influences must be considered. But appraisers must not be influenced by lenders who may attempt to systematically exclude certain neighborhoods under a prohibited, discriminatory practice called **redlining**, discussed in Chapter 11.

Neighborhood Influence

Within a given city, there are many neighborhoods, each of which can vary greatly in quality and desirability. In most cases, an appraiser evaluates a neighborhood much the same way a cautious buyer might evaluate it. The main items that buyers and appraisers check when considering a neighborhood's influence include the following:

1. *Approach to the property.* This is the first thing of which a prospective buyer will be aware. To get to the property, do you drive through a pleasant neighborhood, or do you have to drive through a run-down area?
2. *Appeal of neighborhood.* Does the neighborhood have sales appeal? For example: Is it attractive? Does it have tree-lined streets? Is it laid out in a grid pattern, or does it have winding streets with cul-de-sacs? Does it have overall curb appeal?
3. *Neighborhood homogeneity.* Are the properties all single-family dwellings, or is there a mixture of apartment houses and

commercial buildings? Are the properties of about the same age and same price range? Homogeneous neighborhoods are considered more desirable by most buyers and therefore more desirable to lenders.

4. *Neighborhood condition.* Do the neighbors take care of their homes, exhibiting what is called pride of ownership, evidenced by the care given to the landscaping and the exterior of the homes? Homes in well-maintained neighborhoods have greater value and marketability.

5. *Neighborhood trend.* Is it stable, improving, or declining? Since the lender is concerned about the future of the property, this determination is very important. A neighborhood may be in a state of transition where single-family homes are being replaced by apartment houses. Have a lot of the homes been turned into rentals? These kinds of trends have an effect on the desirability of the neighborhood. Again, appraisers and lenders must guard against redlining.

6. *Adverse influences.* Examples of adverse influences include property located next to a noisy freeway, airport flight patterns, slide and flood areas, climate (too foggy or windy), and obnoxious odors.

7. *Proximity to Neighborhood Amenities.* Proximity to schools can be a concern, especially to families with young children. Availability of local transportation, close-by shopping opportunities, and proximity to employment or hospital, fire, and police locations may be important depending upon personal circumstances.

Appraisers also look for such items as curbs and gutters, street maintenance, garages versus carports, and general appearance.

An experienced appraiser is likely to already know the quality of the neighborhood since he or she usually performs most appraisals within a designated area. An appraiser who is unfamiliar with the immediate neighborhood develops an opinion of the area while approaching the property. The greater challenge in an unfamiliar area is determining the condition of surrounding neighborhoods, which may have an effect on value.

There are other location features that the appraiser must check—see the sample appraisal form (Figure 8.1). Many appraisal forms are used, based upon the type of property to be evaluated (e.g., investment, commercial, units), but they all contain the same basic information.

FIGURE 8.1 Residential appraisal report.

Uniform Residential Appraisal Report

File #

The purpose of this summary appraisal report is to provide the lender/client with an accurate, and adequately supported, opinion of the market value of the subject property.

SUBJECT

Property Address City State Zip Code
Borrower Owner of Public Record County
Legal Description
Assessor's Parcel # Tax Year R.E. Taxes $
Neighborhood Name Map Reference Census Tract
Occupant ☐ Owner ☐ Tenant ☐ Vacant Special Assessments $ ☐ PUD HOA $ ☐ per year ☐ per month
Property Rights Appraised ☐ Fee Simple ☐ Leasehold ☐ Other (describe)
Assignment Type ☐ Purchase Transaction ☐ Refinance Transaction ☐ Other (describe)
Lender/Client Address
Is the subject property currently offered for sale or has it been offered for sale in the twelve months prior to the effective date of this appraisal? ☐ Yes ☐ No
Report data source(s) used, offering price(s), and date(s).

CONTRACT

I ☐ did ☐ did not analyze the contract for sale for the subject purchase transaction. Explain the results of the analysis of the contract for sale or why the analysis was not performed.

Contract Price $ Date of Contract Is the property seller the owner of public record? ☐Yes ☐No Data Source(s)
Is there any financial assistance (loan charges, sale concessions, gift or downpayment assistance, etc.) to be paid by any party on behalf of the borrower? ☐ Yes ☐ No
If Yes, report the total dollar amount and describe the items to be paid.

NEIGHBORHOOD

Note: Race and the racial composition of the neighborhood are not appraisal factors.

Neighborhood Characteristics	One-Unit Housing Trends	One-Unit Housing		Present Land Use %	
Location ☐ Urban ☐ Suburban ☐ Rural	Property Values ☐ Increasing ☐ Stable ☐ Declining	PRICE	AGE	One-Unit	%
Built-Up ☐ Over 75% ☐ 25–75% ☐ Under 25%	Demand/Supply ☐ Shortage ☐ In Balance ☐ Over Supply	$ (000)	(yrs)	2-4 Unit	%
Growth ☐ Rapid ☐ Stable ☐ Slow	Marketing Time ☐ Under 3 mths ☐ 3–6 mths ☐ Over 6 mths	Low		Multi-Family	%
Neighborhood Boundaries		High		Commercial	%
		Pred.		Other	%

Neighborhood Description

Market Conditions (including support for the above conclusions)

SITE

Dimensions Area Shape View
Specific Zoning Classification Zoning Description
Zoning Compliance ☐ Legal ☐ Legal Nonconforming (Grandfathered Use) ☐ No Zoning ☐ Illegal (describe)
Is the highest and best use of the subject property as improved (or as proposed per plans and specifications) the present use? ☐ Yes ☐ No If No, describe

Utilities	Public	Other (describe)		Public	Other (describe)	Off-site Improvements—Type	Public	Private
Electricity	☐	☐	Water	☐	☐	Street	☐	☐
Gas	☐	☐	Sanitary Sewer	☐	☐	Alley	☐	☐

FEMA Special Flood Hazard Area ☐ Yes ☐ No FEMA Flood Zone FEMA Map # FEMA Map Date
Are the utilities and off-site improvements typical for the market area? ☐ Yes ☐ No If No, describe
Are there any adverse site conditions or external factors (easements, encroachments, environmental conditions, land uses, etc.)? ☐ Yes ☐ No If Yes, describe

IMPROVEMENTS

General Description		Foundation		Exterior Description materials/condition		Interior materials/condition	
Units ☐ One ☐ One with Accessory Unit		☐ Concrete Slab ☐ Crawl Space		Foundation Walls		Floors	
# of Stories		☐ Full Basement ☐ Partial Basement		Exterior Walls		Walls	
Type ☐ Det. ☐ Att. ☐ S-Det./End Unit		Basement Area	sq. ft.	Roof Surface		Trim/Finish	
☐ Existing ☐ Proposed ☐ Under Const.		Basement Finish	%	Gutters & Downspouts		Bath Floor	
Design (Style)		☐ Outside Entry/Exit ☐ Sump Pump		Window Type		Bath Wainscot	
Year Built		Evidence of ☐ Infestation		Storm Sash/Insulated		Car Storage	☐ None
Effective Age (Yrs)		☐ Dampness ☐ Settlement		Screens		☐ Driveway	# of Cars
Attic	☐ None	Heating ☐ FWA ☐ HWBB ☐ Radiant		Amenities	☐ Woodstove(s) #	Driveway Surface	
☐ Drop Stair	☐ Stairs	☐ Other	Fuel	☐ Fireplace(s) #	☐ Fence	☐ Garage	# of Cars
☐ Floor	☐ Scuttle	Cooling ☐ Central Air Conditioning		☐ Patio/Deck	☐ Porch	☐ Carport	# of Cars
☐ Finished	☐ Heated	☐ Individual	☐ Other	☐ Pool	☐ Other	☐ Att. ☐ Det.	☐ Built-in

Appliances ☐Refrigerator ☐Range/Oven ☐Dishwasher ☐Disposal ☐Microwave ☐Washer/Dryer ☐Other (describe)
Finished area **above** grade contains: Rooms Bedrooms Bath(s) Square Feet of Gross Living Area Above Grade
Additional features (special energy efficient items, etc.)

Describe the condition of the property (including needed repairs, deterioration, renovations, remodeling, etc.).

Are there any physical deficiencies or adverse conditions that affect the livability, soundness, or structural integrity of the property? ☐ Yes ☐ No If Yes, describe

Does the property generally conform to the neighborhood (functional utility, style, condition, use, construction, etc.)? ☐ Yes ☐ No If No, describe

Freddie Mac Form 70 March 2005 Page 1 of 6 Fannie Mae Form 1004 March 2005

CHAPTER 8 Qualifying the Property

FIGURE 8.1 (Continued)

		Uniform Residential Appraisal Report				File #	
There are ___ comparable properties currently offered for sale in the subject neighborhood ranging in price from $ ___ to $ ___							
There are ___ comparable sales in the subject neighborhood within the past twelve months ranging in sale price from $ ___ to $ ___							
FEATURE	SUBJECT	COMPARABLE SALE # 1		COMPARABLE SALE # 2		COMPARABLE SALE # 3	
Address							
Proximity to Subject							
Sale Price	$		$		$		$
Sale Price/Gross Liv. Area	$ sq. ft.	$ sq. ft.		$ sq. ft.		$ sq. ft.	
Data Source(s)							
Verification Source(s)							
VALUE ADJUSTMENTS	DESCRIPTION	DESCRIPTION	+(-) $ Adjustment	DESCRIPTION	+(-) $ Adjustment	DESCRIPTION	+(-) $ Adjustment
Sale or Financing Concessions							
Date of Sale/Time							
Location							
Leasehold/Fee Simple							
Site							
View							
Design (Style)							
Quality of Construction							
Actual Age							
Condition							
Above Grade	Total Bdrms. Baths	Total Bdrms. Baths		Total Bdrms. Baths		Total Bdrms. Baths	
Room Count							
Gross Living Area	sq. ft.	sq. ft.		sq. ft.		sq. ft.	
Basement & Finished Rooms Below Grade							
Functional Utility							
Heating/Cooling							
Energy Efficient Items							
Garage/Carport							
Porch/Patio/Deck							
Net Adjustment (Total)		☐ + ☐ -	$	☐ + ☐ -	$	☐ + ☐ -	$
Adjusted Sale Price of Comparables		Net Adj. ___ % Gross Adj. ___ %	$	Net Adj. ___ % Gross Adj. ___ %	$	Net Adj. ___ % Gross Adj. ___ %	$

I ☐ did ☐ did not research the sale or transfer history of the subject property and comparable sales. If not, explain

My research ☐ did ☐ did not reveal any prior sales or transfers of the subject property for the three years prior to the effective date of this appraisal.
Data source(s)
My research ☐ did ☐ did not reveal any prior sales or transfers of the comparable sales for the year prior to the date of sale of the comparable sale.
Data source(s)
Report the results of the research and analysis of the prior sale or transfer history of the subject property and comparable sales (report additional prior sales on page 3).

ITEM	SUBJECT	COMPARABLE SALE # 1	COMPARABLE SALE # 2	COMPARABLE SALE # 3
Date of Prior Sale/Transfer				
Price of Prior Sale/Transfer				
Data Source(s)				
Effective Date of Data Source(s)				

Analysis of prior sale or transfer history of the subject property and comparable sales

Summary of Sales Comparison Approach

Indicated Value by Sales Comparison Approach $
Indicated Value by: Sales Comparison Approach $ ___ Cost Approach (if developed) $ ___ Income Approach (if developed) $

This appraisal is made ☐ "as is", ☐ subject to completion per plans and specifications on the basis of a hypothetical condition that the improvements have been completed, ☐ subject to the following repairs or alterations on the basis of a hypothetical condition that the repairs or alterations have been completed, or ☐ subject to the following required inspection based on the extraordinary assumption that the condition or deficiency does not require alteration or repair:

Based on a complete visual inspection of the interior and exterior areas of the subject property, defined scope of work, statement of assumptions and limiting conditions, and appraiser's certification, my (our) opinion of the market value, as defined, of the real property that is the subject of this report is $ ___ , as of ___ , which is the date of inspection and the effective date of this appraisal.

Freddie Mac Form 70 March 2005   Page 2 of 6   Fannie Mae Form 1004 March 2005

FIGURE 8.1 (Continued)

Uniform Residential Appraisal Report File #

ADDITIONAL COMMENTS

COST APPROACH TO VALUE (not required by Fannie Mae)

Provide adequate information for the lender/client to replicate the below cost figures and calculations.
Support for the opinion of site value (summary of comparable land sales or other methods for estimating site value)

COST APPROACH	
ESTIMATED ☐ REPRODUCTION OR ☐ REPLACEMENT COST NEW	OPINION OF SITE VALUE ....= $
Source of cost data	Dwelling Sq. Ft. @ $ =$
Quality rating from cost service Effective date of cost data	Sq. Ft. @ $ =$
Comments on Cost Approach (gross living area calculations, depreciation, etc.)	Garage/Carport Sq. Ft. @ $ =$
	Total Estimate of Cost-New = $
	Less Physical Functional External
	Depreciation =$( )
	Depreciated Cost of Improvements..................=$
	"As-is" Value of Site Improvements..................=$
Estimated Remaining Economic Life (HUD and VA only) Years	Indicated Value By Cost Approach ....=$

INCOME APPROACH TO VALUE (not required by Fannie Mae)

Estimated Monthly Market Rent $ X Gross Rent Multiplier   = $ Indicated Value by Income Approach
Summary of Income Approach (including support for market rent and GRM)

PROJECT INFORMATION FOR PUDs (if applicable)

Is the developer/builder in control of the Homeowners' Association (HOA)? ☐ Yes ☐ No   Unit type(s) ☐ Detached ☐ Attached
Provide the following information for PUDs ONLY if the developer/builder is in control of the HOA and the subject property is an attached dwelling unit.
Legal name of project
Total number of phases   Total number of units   Total number of units sold
Total number of units rented   Total number of units for sale   Data source(s)
Was the project created by the conversion of an existing building(s) into a PUD? ☐ Yes ☐ No If Yes, date of conversion
Does the project contain any multi-dwelling units? ☐ Yes ☐ No Data source(s)
Are the units, common elements, and recreation facilities complete? ☐ Yes ☐ No If No, describe the status of completion.

Are the common elements leased to or by the Homeowners' Association? ☐ Yes ☐ No If Yes, describe the rental terms and options.

Describe common elements and recreational facilities

Freddie Mac Form 70 March 2005   Page 3 of 6   Fannie Mae Form 1004 March 2005

FIGURE 8.1 (Continued)

Uniform Residential Appraisal Report File

This report form is designed to report an appraisal of a one-unit property or a one-unit property with an accessory unit; including a unit in a planned unit development (PUD). This report form is not designed to report an appraisal of a manufactured home or a unit in a condominium or cooperative project.

This appraisal report is subject to the following scope of work, intended use, intended user, definition of market value, statement of assumptions and limiting conditions, and certifications. Modifications, additions, or deletions to the intended use, intended user, definition of market value, or assumptions and limiting conditions are not permitted. The appraiser may expand the scope of work to include any additional research or analysis necessary based on the complexity of this appraisal assignment. Modifications or deletions to the certifications are also not permitted. However, additional certifications that do not constitute material alterations to this appraisal report, such as those required by law or those related to the appraiser's continuing education or membership in an appraisal organization, are permitted.

SCOPE OF WORK: The scope of work for this appraisal is defined by the complexity of this appraisal assignment and the reporting requirements of this appraisal report form, including the following definition of market value, statement of assumptions and limiting conditions, and certifications. The appraiser must, at a minimum: (1) perform a complete visual inspection of the interior and exterior areas of the subject property, (2) inspect the neighborhood, (3) inspect each of the comparable sales from at least the street, (4) research, verify, and analyze data from reliable public and/or private sources, and (5) report his or her analysis, opinions, and conclusions in this appraisal report.

INTENDED USE: The intended use of this appraisal report is for the lender/client to evaluate the property that is the subject of this appraisal for a mortgage finance transaction.

INTENDED USER: The intended user of this appraisal report is the lender/client.

DEFINITION OF MARKET VALUE: The most probable price which a property should bring in a competitive and open market under all conditions requisite to a fair sale, the buyer and seller, each acting prudently, knowledgeably and assuming the price is not affected by undue stimulus. Implicit in this definition is the consummation of a sale as of a specified date and the passing of title from seller to buyer under conditions whereby: (1) buyer and seller are typically motivated; (2) both parties are well informed or well advised, and each acting in what he or she considers his or her own best interest; (3) a reasonable time is allowed for exposure in the open market; (4) payment is made in terms of cash in U. S. dollars or in terms of financial arrangements comparable thereto; and (5) the price represents the normal consideration for the property sold unaffected by special or creative financing or sales concessions* granted by anyone associated with the sale.

*Adjustments to the comparables must be made for special or creative financing or sales concessions. No adjustments are necessary for those costs which are normally paid by sellers as a result of tradition or law in a market area; these costs are readily identifiable since the seller pays these costs in virtually all sales transactions. Special or creative financing adjustments can be made to the comparable property by comparisons to financing terms offered by a third party institutional lender that is not already involved in the property or transaction. Any adjustment should not be calculated on a mechanical dollar for dollar cost of the financing or concession but the dollar amount of any adjustment should approximate the market's reaction to the financing or concessions based on the appraiser's judgment.

STATEMENT OF ASSUMPTIONS AND LIMITING CONDITIONS: The appraiser's certification in this report is subject to the following assumptions and limiting conditions:

1. The appraiser will not be responsible for matters of a legal nature that affect either the property being appraised or the title to it, except for information that he or she became aware of during the research involved in performing this appraisal. The appraiser assumes that the title is good and marketable and will not render any opinions about the title.

2. The appraiser has provided a sketch in this appraisal report to show the approximate dimensions of the improvements. The sketch is included only to assist the reader in visualizing the property and understanding the appraiser's determination of its size.

3. The appraiser has examined the available flood maps that are provided by the Federal Emergency Management Agency (or other data sources) and has noted in this appraisal report whether any portion of the subject site is located in an identified Special Flood Hazard Area. Because the appraiser is not a surveyor, he or she makes no guarantees, express or implied, regarding this determination.

4. The appraiser will not give testimony or appear in court because he or she made an appraisal of the property in question, unless specific arrangements to do so have been made beforehand, or as otherwise required by law.

5. The appraiser has noted in this appraisal report any adverse conditions (such as needed repairs, deterioration, the presence of hazardous wastes, toxic substances, etc.) observed during the inspection of the subject property or that he or she became aware of during the research involved in performing this appraisal. Unless otherwise stated in this appraisal report, the appraiser has no knowledge of any hidden or unapparent physical deficiencies or adverse conditions of the property (such as, but not limited to, needed repairs, deterioration, the presence of hazardous wastes, toxic substances, adverse environmental conditions, etc.) that would make the property less valuable, and has assumed that there are no such conditions and makes no guarantees or warranties, express or implied. The appraiser will not be responsible for any such conditions that do exist or for any engineering or testing that might be required to discover whether such conditions exist. Because the appraiser is not an expert in the field of environmental hazards, this appraisal report must not be considered as an environmental assessment of the property.

6. The appraiser has based his or her appraisal report and valuation conclusion for an appraisal that is subject to satisfactory completion, repairs, or alterations on the assumption that the completion, repairs, or alterations of the subject property will be performed in a professional manner.

Freddie Mac Form 70 March 2005   Fannie Mae Form 1004 March 2005

FIGURE 8.1 (Continued)

Uniform Residential Appraisal Report   File #

APPRAISER'S CERTIFICATION: The Appraiser certifies and agrees that:

1. I have, at a minimum, developed and reported this appraisal in accordance with the scope of work requirements stated in this appraisal report.

2. I performed a complete visual inspection of the interior and exterior areas of the subject property. I reported the condition of the improvements in factual, specific terms. I identified and reported the physical deficiencies that could affect the livability, soundness, or structural integrity of the property.

3. I performed this appraisal in accordance with the requirements of the Uniform Standards of Professional Appraisal Practice that were adopted and promulgated by the Appraisal Standards Board of The Appraisal Foundation and that were in place at the time this appraisal report was prepared.

4. I developed my opinion of the market value of the real property that is the subject of this report based on the sales comparison approach to value. I have adequate comparable market data to develop a reliable sales comparison approach for this appraisal assignment. I further certify that I considered the cost and income approaches to value but did not develop them, unless otherwise indicated in this report.

5. I researched, verified, analyzed, and reported on any current agreement for sale for the subject property, any offering for sale of the subject property in the twelve months prior to the effective date of this appraisal, and the prior sales of the subject property for a minimum of three years prior to the effective date of this appraisal, unless otherwise indicated in this report.

6. I researched, verified, analyzed, and reported on the prior sales of the comparable sales for a minimum of one year prior to the date of sale of the comparable sale, unless otherwise indicated in this report.

7. I selected and used comparable sales that are locationally, physically, and functionally the most similar to the subject property.

8. I have not used comparable sales that were the result of combining a land sale with the contract purchase price of a home that has been built or will be built on the land.

9. I have reported adjustments to the comparable sales that reflect the market's reaction to the differences between the subject property and the comparable sales.

10. I verified, from a disinterested source, all information in this report that was provided by parties who have a financial interest in the sale or financing of the subject property.

11. I have knowledge and experience in appraising this type of property in this market area.

12. I am aware of, and have access to, the necessary and appropriate public and private data sources, such as multiple listing services, tax assessment records, public land records and other such data sources for the area in which the property is located.

13. I obtained the information, estimates, and opinions furnished by other parties and expressed in this appraisal report from reliable sources that I believe to be true and correct.

14. I have taken into consideration the factors that have an impact on value with respect to the subject neighborhood, subject property, and the proximity of the subject property to adverse influences in the development of my opinion of market value. I have noted in this appraisal report any adverse conditions (such as, but not limited to, needed repairs, deterioration, the presence of hazardous wastes, toxic substances, adverse environmental conditions, etc.) observed during the inspection of the subject property or that I became aware of during the research involved in performing this appraisal. I have considered these adverse conditions in my analysis of the property value, and have reported on the effect of the conditions on the value and marketability of the subject property.

15. I have not knowingly withheld any significant information from this appraisal report and, to the best of my knowledge, all statements and information in this appraisal report are true and correct.

16. I stated in this appraisal report my own personal, unbiased, and professional analysis, opinions, and conclusions, which are subject only to the assumptions and limiting conditions in this appraisal report.

17. I have no present or prospective interest in the property that is the subject of this report, and I have no present or prospective personal interest or bias with respect to the participants in the transaction. I did not base, either partially or completely, my analysis and/or opinion of market value in this appraisal report on the race, color, religion, sex, age, marital status, handicap, familial status, or national origin of either the prospective owners or occupants of the subject property or of the present owners or occupants of the properties in the vicinity of the subject property or on any other basis prohibited by law.

18. My employment and/or compensation for performing this appraisal or any future or anticipated appraisals was not conditioned on any agreement or understanding, written or otherwise, that I would report (or present analysis supporting) a predetermined specific value, a predetermined minimum value, a range or direction in value, a value that favors the cause of any party, or the attainment of a specific result or occurrence of a specific subsequent event (such as approval of a pending mortgage loan application).

19. I personally prepared all conclusions and opinions about the real estate that were set forth in this appraisal report. If I relied on significant real property appraisal assistance from any individual or individuals in the performance of this appraisal or the preparation of this appraisal report, I have named such individual(s) and disclosed the specific tasks performed in this appraisal report. I certify that any individual so named is qualified to perform the tasks. I have not authorized anyone to make a change to any item in this appraisal report; therefore, any change made to this appraisal is unauthorized and I will take no responsibility for it.

20. I identified the lender/client in this appraisal report who is the individual, organization, or agent for the organization that ordered and will receive this appraisal report.

Freddie Mac Form 70   March 2005   Page 5 of 6   Fannie Mae Form 1004   March 2005

FIGURE 8.1 (Continued)

Uniform Residential Appraisal Report   File #

21. The lender/client may disclose or distribute this appraisal report to: the borrower; another lender at the request of the borrower; the mortgagee or its successors and assigns; mortgage insurers; government sponsored enterprises; other secondary market participants; data collection or reporting services; professional appraisal organizations; any department, agency, or instrumentality of the United States; and any state, the District of Columbia, or other jurisdictions; without having to obtain the appraiser's or supervisory appraiser's (if applicable) consent. Such consent must be obtained before this appraisal report may be disclosed or distributed to any other party (including, but not limited to, the public through advertising, public relations, news, sales, or other media).

22. I am aware that any disclosure or distribution of this appraisal report by me or the lender/client may be subject to certain laws and regulations. Further, I am also subject to the provisions of the Uniform Standards of Professional Appraisal Practice that pertain to disclosure or distribution by me.

23. The borrower, another lender at the request of the borrower, the mortgagee or its successors and assigns, mortgage insurers, government sponsored enterprises, and other secondary market participants may rely on this appraisal report as part of any mortgage finance transaction that involves any one or more of these parties.

24. If this appraisal report was transmitted as an "electronic record" containing my "electronic signature," as those terms are defined in applicable federal and/or state laws (excluding audio and video recordings), or a facsimile transmission of this appraisal report containing a copy or representation of my signature, the appraisal report shall be as effective, enforceable and valid as if a paper version of this appraisal report were delivered containing my original hand written signature.

25. Any intentional or negligent misrepresentation(s) contained in this appraisal report may result in civil liability and/or criminal penalties including, but not limited to, fine or imprisonment or both under the provisions of Title 18, United States Code, Section 1001, et seq., or similar state laws.

SUPERVISORY APPRAISER'S CERTIFICATION: The Supervisory Appraiser certifies and agrees that:

1. I directly supervised the appraiser for this appraisal assignment, have read the appraisal report, and agree with the appraiser's analysis, opinions, statements, conclusions, and the appraiser's certification.

2. I accept full responsibility for the contents of this appraisal report including, but not limited to, the appraiser's analysis, opinions, statements, conclusions, and the appraiser's certification.

3. The appraiser identified in this appraisal report is either a sub-contractor or an employee of the supervisory appraiser (or the appraisal firm), is qualified to perform this appraisal, and is acceptable to perform this appraisal under the applicable state law.

4. This appraisal report complies with the Uniform Standards of Professional Appraisal Practice that were adopted and promulgated by the Appraisal Standards Board of The Appraisal Foundation and that were in place at the time this appraisal report was prepared.

5. If this appraisal report was transmitted as an "electronic record" containing my "electronic signature," as those terms are defined in applicable federal and/or state laws (excluding audio and video recordings), or a facsimile transmission of this appraisal report containing a copy or representation of my signature, the appraisal report shall be as effective, enforceable and valid as if a paper version of this appraisal report were delivered containing my original hand written signature.

APPRAISER

Signature _____
Name _____
Company Name _____
Company Address _____

Telephone Number _____
Email Address _____
Date of Signature and Report _____
Effective Date of Appraisal _____
State Certification # _____
or State License # _____
or Other (describe) _____ State # _____
State _____
Expiration Date of Certification or License _____

ADDRESS OF PROPERTY APPRAISED
_____
_____

APPRAISED VALUE OF SUBJECT PROPERTY $ _____
LENDER/CLIENT
Name _____
Company Name _____
Company Address _____
_____
Email Address _____

SUPERVISORY APPRAISER (ONLY IF REQUIRED)

Signature _____
Name _____
Company Name _____
Company Address _____

Telephone Number _____
Email Address _____
Date of Signature _____
State Certification # _____
or State License # _____
State _____
Expiration Date of Certification or License _____

SUBJECT PROPERTY

☐ Did not inspect subject property
☐ Did inspect exterior of subject property from street
   Date of Inspection _____
☐ Did inspect interior and exterior of subject property
   Date of Inspection _____

COMPARABLE SALES

☐ Did not inspect exterior of comparable sales from street
☐ Did inspect exterior of comparable sales from street
   Date of Inspection _____

Freddie Mac Form 70   March 2005   Fannie Mae Form 1004   March 2005

FIGURE 8.1 (Continued)

Instructions

Uniform Residential Appraisal Report
This report form is designed to report an appraisal of a one-unit property or a one-unit property with an accessory unit; including a unit in a planned unit development (PUD), based on an interior and exterior inspection of the subject property. This report form is not designed to report an appraisal of a manufactured home or a unit in a condominium or cooperative project.

Use
This report form is designed to report an appraisal of a one-unit property or a one-unit property with an accessory unit; including a unit in a planned unit development (PUD), based on an interior and exterior inspection of the subject property. This report form is not designed to report an appraisal of a manufactured home or a unit in a condominium or cooperative project.

Modifications, Additions, or Deletions
This appraisal report is subject to the scope of work, intended use, intended user, definition of market value, statement of assumptions and limiting conditions, and certifications contained in the report form. Modifications, additions, or deletions to the intended use, intended user, definition of market value, or assumptions and limiting conditions are not permitted. The appraiser may expand the scope of work to include any additional research or analysis necessary based on the complexity of this appraisal assignment. Modifications or deletions to the certifications are also not permitted. However, additional certifications that do not constitute material alterations to this appraisal report, such as those required by law or those related to the appraiser's continuing education or membership in an appraisal organization are permitted.

Scope of Work
The scope of work for this appraisal is defined by the complexity of this appraisal assignment and the reporting requirements of this appraisal report form, including the following definition of market value, statement of assumptions and limiting conditions, and certifications. The appraiser must, at a minimum: (1) perform a complete visual inspection of the interior and exterior areas of the subject property, (2) inspect the neighborhood, (3) inspect each of the comparable sales from at least the street, (4) research, verify, and analyze data from reliable public and/or private sources, and (5) report his or her analysis, opinions, and conclusions in this appraisal report.

Required Exhibits
- A street map that shows the location of the subject property and of all comparables that the appraiser used;

- An exterior building sketch of the improvements that indicates the dimensions. The appraiser must also include calculations to show how he or she arrived at the estimate for gross living area. A floor plan sketch that indicates the dimensions is required instead of the exterior building or unit sketch if the floor plan is atypical or functionally obsolete, thus limiting the market appeal for the property in comparison to competitive properties in the neighborhood;

- Clear, descriptive photographs (either in black and white or color) that show the front, back, and a street scene of the subject property, and that are appropriately identified. (Photographs must be originals that are produced either by photography or electronic imaging.);

- Clear, descriptive photographs (either in black and white or color) that show the front of each comparable sale and that are appropriately identified. Generally, photographs should be originals that are produced by photography or electronic imaging; however, copies of photographs from a multiple listing service or from the appraiser's files are acceptable if they are clear and descriptive;

- Any other data--as an attachment or addendum to the appraisal report form--that are necessary to provide an adequately supported opinion of market value.

Instructions Page

Source: www.efanniemae.com

At the Property

Before entering the property, the appraiser visually identifies if the subject house is congruent with the rest of the neighborhood. Is it in about the same price range or is it over improved or under improved? What is the sales appeal of the house? Are the exterior and landscaping well maintained and consistent with its neighbors? The answers to these questions have a significant bearing on the value of the property and will be included in the appraiser's remarks in the neighborhood section of the appraisal form.

8.3 USING A STANDARD APPRAISAL FORM

A lender carefully reviews a completed appraisal to determine the acceptability of the property as security to satisfy the amount of the loan. The form shown in Figure 8.1 is the standard used by Fannie Mae and Freddie Mac. Since its adoption by the agencies, most lenders have come to use it as well. The following is a discussion of the three basic sections of the appraisal form (Figure 8.1), which include neighborhood characteristics and trends, property description and information, and valuation.

Neighborhood

Following the identification of the property at the top of the appraisal form is the neighborhood section. A **neighborhood** is a group of properties relatively similar in land use and value. It can be large or as small as a single block or street. Some of the items that are important when analyzing a neighborhood are listed on the appraisal form and are discussed below.

Supply and Demand

If supply and demand is not in balance, it can affect prices in the neighborhood. A buyers' market exists when available home inventory is greater than the demand to purchase. The opposite or a sellers' market is when there are more buyers than homes available to buy. The foreclosure and short sales for a number of years following the initial crises in 2008 affected home values in two ways. By providing excess homes to the market while also selling at depressed prices, home values, especially in some areas, plummeted.

Price Range

The price range of properties in a neighborhood is important for determining if the subject property is over or under improved. If the sales price of the property exceeded the upper price level in the area, it could be because of over improvement. Over improvements have less marketability, because they can too often be classified as one-of-a-kind for the neighborhood and be less acceptable to the average buyer. A property with a sales price below the lower price level (under improvement) generally has good marketability because it provides buyers an opportunity to live in a neighborhood they want but could not otherwise afford. It also provides the new buyer an opportunity to improve the property and enjoy the ensuing increase in value.

Neighborhood Description

The appraiser will summarize the items in a neighborhood that buyers most frequently consider to be of importance. These are a few of the main items:

1. *Employment stability.* An area where employment is provided primarily by just one industry would not have good employment stability. Small towns built around a lumber mill or auto manufacturing plant or a community that depends primarily on the computer and software industry are all good examples. A severe depression of any one such industry can caused widespread unemployment.

2. *Convenience to employment, shopping, and schools.* Buyers care about these convenience factors, in terms of both time and mileage. As the cost of operating an automobile increases, these factors become more important.

3. *Protection from detrimental conditions.* A detrimental condition in a neighborhood affects the marketability and, therefore, the value of the property. Examples of detrimental conditions are high vacancy rate, poorly maintained properties, abandoned properties (e.g., caused in the recent past by increased foreclosures), obnoxious odors, poor climate, and annoying airport flight patterns.

Property

After the neighborhood has been analyzed, the appraiser inspects the site and the physical property. This portion of the report is divided into various sections: site, improvements, room list, interior finish and equipment, and a property rating.

Site

As the appraiser checks the site, these are some of the items that are carefully analyzed:

1. It is important to know if the improvements conform to the current zoning of the site. If they do not, there may be a problem, since nonconforming properties generally cannot be reconstructed if destroyed. If the lender is positive that a new building permit would not be issued, it may deny the loan entirely. Note: Older properties may be grandfathered in regarding their zoning. The city or county may provide what is called a burn-down letter,

indicating that the property, in its current state, could be rebuilt if it were, for any reason, destroyed.

2. *The lot.* The topography and drainage on a lot could be very important. A home built on a steep hillside could be subject to earth slides, particularly if there are drainage problems. The appraiser may reduce the value of a large parcel as excess land or mostly unusable property. A lender, in turn, may allow value for only 10 acres of a 20-acre parcel.

3. *Flood area.* If the property is located in a HUD-identified flood area, the property must carry flood insurance if a loan is made. It is the responsibility of the lender to make sure flood insurance is obtained, if required. The Federal Emergency Management Agency (FEMA) maintains flood maps. Designations do change and any property located in a low-lying area or near a stream, lake, or other body of water should be checked against the appropriate map. Most sales also include a Natural Hazards Report, which also shows this possible issue.

Improvements, Room List, Interior Finish and Equipment, Property Rating

These sections of the report serve as a good checklist while the appraiser is inspecting the property. The appraiser starts by checking the exterior of the improvements. The number and type of rooms and the floor plan are the next items noted.

The appraiser carefully checks for poor structural designs or unusual floor plans that could affect marketability of the property. This is referred to as **functional obsolescence**, a loss in value from sources within the property that affect its usability. In contrast, **economic obsolescence** is a loss in value from forces outside of the property that cannot be changed, such as adverse zoning or a freeway behind the property.

Examples of functional obsolescence include houses with unusual floor plans, such as five bedrooms with one bath; access to the bath through another bedroom; and a bathroom opening into the kitchen, as was common for homes built in the 1920s. If there is evidence of improvements or additions, permits may be an issue and may require checking with the local building department.

Continuing to the inspection of the interior, the appraiser notes the condition of the paint, floor, kitchen equipment, and garage. The appraiser looks for signs of problems; water stains or moisture could be evidence of a roof or plumbing leak. Structural problems might be evidenced by sagging floors, sticky doors, and large cracks which could have been caused by a settling foundation or a shifting of the structure—all forms of **physical depreciation**. Among health and safety issues are cracked or broken windows, evidence of mold or mildew, or lack of a stair railing. Characterizing a condition as structural or cosmetic can make a big difference to value and to how the lender will view the situation. Common sense has to prevail.

Photographs and Square Footage Measurement

Among the required photographs are the front of the property, a street view, and the side and back yards. In the past, these were sufficient. Now, the appraisal must contain pictures of every room, identify that the water heater is double strapped and that smoke and carbon monoxide detectors are in place, and include pictures with special emphasis on any non-cosmetic condition (e.g., holes in the wall, plumbing leaks, etc.).

Appraisers are not allowed to submit photos of the property with people visible. Banks have to be careful not to discriminate, as mentioned above, and this is one way they avoid it. The appraiser must also obtain the square footage of the house, since this information is used in calculating the value.

To obtain the square footage, the appraiser measures the house from the outside and draws a sketch as shown in Figure 8.2. The photographs and the sketch are attached to the report when it is completed.

Valuation

The valuation section outlines market data, cost, and income approaches that will aid in determining market value.

Sales Comparison Approach

The basis of the **sales comparison approach** to value, also popularly called **market data approach**, is that a buyer will not pay more for a property than the cost of acquiring an equally desirable substitute property. This is what economists refer to as the principle of substitution. Although exceptions occur, buyers are often guided by another principle, that of not purchasing the most expensive home in the neighborhood.

Real estate salespeople, when asked by buyers to evaluate a home's value, use a simplified market data approach to provide what are referred to as a list of comparable sales. To estimate a value of a property, licensees search for close-by properties that have sold recently and are similar to the subject property. After subtracting or adding a dollar amount, referred to as an **adjustment**, to any differences between the

FIGURE 8.2 Computing square footage.

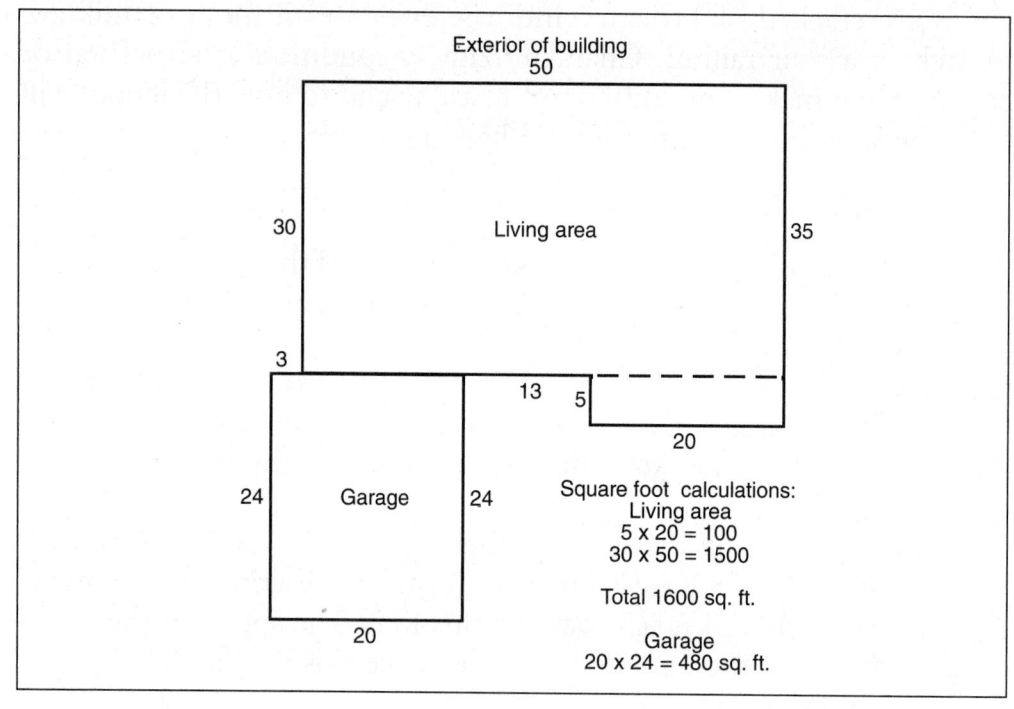

```
                    Exterior of building
                            50
         ┌──────────────────────────────────┐
         │                                  │
      30 │          Living area             │ 35
         │                                  │
         │                                  │
       3 └──────┬───────────┐               │
              13│         5 │               │
       ┌────────┤           └───────────────┘
       │        │                20
    24 │ Garage │ 24      Square foot calculations:
       │        │              Living area
       │        │              5 x 20 = 100
       │        │              30 x 50 = 1500
       └────────┘
            20              Total 1600 sq. ft.
                                Garage
                           20 x 24 = 480 sq. ft.
```

Source: © 2016 OnCourse Learning

comparable and the potential home purchase, they arrive at a comparable value for the subject property. Appraisers use the same procedure; however, they do it in a more systematic and precise manner, utilizing such specialized types of appraisal resources as Marshall & Swift to identify home component cost values.

Determining value through the sales comparison approach involves a four-step procedure:

1. Obtain recent sales of properties that are comparable to the subject property within the closest proximity as possible.
2. Analyze these sales in relationship to the subject property.
3. Determine dollar adjustments for differences between these sales and the subject property.
4. Arrive at an estimate of market value.

In the market data analysis section of the appraisal report, the subject property is listed in the first column and comparable sales in the next three columns. Note that the properties are rated on various items such as location, design and appeal, condition, and so on. A time adjustment based upon the sale dates of the comparables becomes increasingly important in a rapidly increasing or declining market. Appraisers use guidelines when assessing a dollar adjustment value to a difference between the properties (e.g., the dollar value per square foot adjustment). **Comparables** chosen by the appraiser should be as similar to the subject property as possible, because this minimizes the need for and size of dollar adjustments, which ordinarily should not exceed 15 percent. The appraiser attempts to obtain comparables that have sold recently and are in the same neighborhood. This reduces the need for time and location differences. Dollar adjustments should reflect the market reaction to the differences, not necessarily the cost of the differences. For example, swimming pools, intercom systems, and elaborate landscaping may not increase market value to the full extent of their cost. Any adjustment that exceeds what is considered typical must be fully explained by the appraiser (e.g., the use of a comparable sale outside the immediate neighborhood).

Appraisers must pay particular attention to the "Sales or Financing Concessions" item including adjustments for different types of financing. For instance, a seller agreeing to pay at least a portion of the buyer's closing costs is a more frequent contract condition than in past years. Other examples might include a seller carrying a second loan at a lower than market interest rate or participating in paying a fee for the buyer to obtain a buy-down of the interest rate. Of particular concern to the lender are concessions made for roof repairs, a carpet, or painting allowance or the inclusion of personal property (e.g., refrigerator, washer, or dryer) in the contract. While the appraiser can comment that personal property has no value and does not affect the appraised value, projected repairs or replacement (carpeting, a new door, or painting if a dollar concession has been made) must usually be completed before close of escrow. These are all reasons why the appraiser must indicate whether the purchase contract has been reviewed and all such concessions have been accommodated.

Because choosing good comparables is so important, appraisers use many sources in obtaining information on comparable sales:

1. The appraiser's own files.
2. Multiple listing service of real estate boards.
3. Real estate agents.
4. Public records (county assessor and recorder via documentary transfer tax shown on deeds).
5. Web-based sites. These have proliferated in recent years; however, the data contained on them is viewed cautiously as they are often inaccurate and outdated.

Note how the adjustments are handled: If the item on the comparable property is *superior* to the subject property, a *minus* (−) adjustment is made. If *inferior*, a plus (+) adjustment is made. After the adjustments have been made for each comparable, they are totaled at the bottom of the column. This plus or minus total is applied to the sales price of the comparable to arrive at an indicated value of the subject property.

The appraiser's next task is to arrive at one figure, which represents the indicated value by sales comparison approach. There is no formula that the appraiser can use. You cannot average the three results and come up with a figure. This reconciliation of value requires exercising good judgment and typically, the appraiser giving the greatest weight to the comparable sale that required the least adjustments.

Declining Values Affected the Use of Comparables

The economic downturn in housing was pronounced and declining home values were commonplace. For some time, appraisals contained the phrase "the property is in an area of declining value," thereby significantly impacting home values. Appraisers are still required to include additional information to satisfy lenders that a given property is indeed sufficient collateral for the requested loan amount. The comparable section of the appraisal has to reflect several current listings as well as the most recent sales. Appraisers must now provide a market conditions report which identifies the number of properties currently on the market within the property's price range and the rate of sales (called the absorption rate). Even though short sales and foreclosure transactions have declined, they have to be included if they are within the neighborhood. In spite of the fact that these sales are accompanied by the appraisers' comment that "as a distress sale, the value does not reflect a typical sale between a willing buyer and a willing seller," lenders sometimes allow these lower sales to affect their value decisions.

Additional Conditions

We mentioned that appraisers now must supply more pictures with their appraisals. The Uniform Appraisal Dataset (UAD) Definitions Addendum is the newest appraisal requirement. Condition (C1 to C6) and Quality (Q1 to Q6) ratings are now a part of the appraisal process. The rating scales are well defined but beyond the scope of this text. Suffice it to say that any assessment above a C4 or a Q4 will result in the property being deemed insufficient collateral for any loan. It is yet one more part of the appraisal, along with the comparables, the pictures, and the appraiser comments, that affect value.

Cost Approach

Cost approach is based on the principle that property is worth what it would cost to duplicate. Adjustments to cost are made to allow for any loss in value due to economic age, condition, and other factors that reduce marketability.

Determining value through the cost approach involves a three-step procedure:

1. Estimate the total cost to reproduce the structure at current prices.
2. Subtract the estimated depreciation from all sources.
3. Add the estimated value of the land, based on the comparison or market data approach.

Note: The cost approach is the most reliable method of establishing value for a unique property (e.g., church, school).

Income Approach

The principle of the **income approach** is that there is relationship between the income the property can earn and the property's value. On owner-occupied homes, an appraiser may omit the income approach on the theory that an owner-occupied home will not be rented. But if an income approach is used on a home, the appraiser will usually use a **gross rent multiplier (GRM)**, instead of standard income approach to value.

Gross rent multipliers are ratios that state the relationship between gross rental income and sales price. They are typically used on an annual basis. GRMs provide a ballpark amount and not a precise figure of value.

The formula for the gross rent multiplier is:

$$\frac{\text{Sales Price}}{\text{Gross Annual Rent}} = \frac{\text{Gross Rent Multiplier}}{\text{GRM on an annual basis}}$$

Example: A single family home sold for $500,000. The property could be rented for $2,500 per month. What is the GRM?

Solution:

$$\text{Annual basis}: \frac{\$500,000}{\$30,000\ (\$2,500\ \text{month} \times 12\ \text{months})} = 16.67 = \text{GRM}$$

To establish a valid market GRM, the appraiser must locate similar properties in comparable neighborhoods that were recently sold or rented at the time of the appraisal. Sometimes it may be difficult to establish a market GRM because of the lack of recent information. However, once a valid market GRM is established, the appraiser uses the following formula to arrive at indicated value.

Subject Property's Annual Rent × Market GRM = Indicated Value

---

Example: On another property, an appraiser determines that the market rent should be $2,000 per month. What is the indicated value?

Solution: $24,000 annual rent ($2,000 × 12) × 16.67 GRM = $400,080 Indicated Value

---

On larger-income properties such as apartment buildings, office buildings, and shopping centers, the standard income approach—often called the **capitalization** method—is used. This approach determines the present value of a property based on the net operating income of the property (or property income less property expenses; this does *not* include any loan payments).

The standard income approach uses this procedure:

1. Calculate the annual gross scheduled income (GSI), which is income from all sources (including any parking or laundry income), assuming 100 percent occupancy.
2. From the GSI, deduct reasonable vacancy and collection losses to arrive at the **gross operating income**.
3. Estimate all expenses such as taxes, wages, utilities, insurance, repairs, and management, and deduct them from the gross operating income to determine the **net operating income (NOI)**. It is important to note that mortgage payments, called debt service, are not considered an operating expense.
4. The **capitalization rate** is the rate of return that an investor would seek as a reasonable return on an investment as if he was paying all cash for the property. Again, the cap rate does not include any debt service.
5. Divide the market capitalization rate into the subject property's net operating income.

$$\frac{\text{Subject Property's Net Operating Income}}{\text{Market Capitalization Rate}} = \text{Indicated value}$$

Example: Small Rental Property:

Annual Gross Scheduled Income	$100,000
Less : Vacancy and Collection Losses	−5,000
Equals : Gross Operating Income	$95,000
Less : Annual Operating Expenses	−35,000
Equals : Net Operating Income	$60,000

Assume Market Capitalization Rate (Cap Rate) @ 8 percent

$$\frac{\$60{,}000 \text{ Net Operating Income}}{8 \text{ percent Market Capitalization Rate}} = 750{,}000 \text{ Indicated Value}$$

Final Market Value

The appraiser's approach to determine value, called a final reconciliation, depends on the type of property being appraised. In the appraisal of single-family properties, more weight is given to the sales comparison or market approach because it is the most reliable. The cost approach is not as reliable, because it is difficult to estimate depreciation and to determine the value of land in a built-up neighborhood. The cost approach is best used for special-purpose properties such as churches, schools, government buildings, and anything unusual that does not sell routinely in the marketplace. The use of a gross rent multiplier may not be used in appraising a single-family owner-occupied property, because the majority of buyers do not buy them for income purposes.

Next, the appraiser analyzes the data used in the report for completeness and reliability. The final step is to arrive at market value. Again, this is not an averaging process, but one in which the appraiser evaluates each approach, and then selects a single estimate of value.

Sales Price versus Fair Market Value

The typical definition of fair market value (FMV) is "the price at which the property would change hands between a willing buyer and a willing seller, neither being under any compulsion to buy or sell and both having reasonable knowledge of relevant facts." The difference between the FMV and the sales price may be an unknowledgeable buyer or seller—one who pays too much, the other who sells for less than the actual value. Or the buyer may consider the home perfect regardless of the price, or the seller may be under pressure or anxious to sell, perhaps facing foreclosure or other personal situations.

Appraisers realize that appraising is not an exact science and that a lot of judgment is involved. Although the value of a property cannot be pinpointed, appraisers know that the sales price is one of the best indications of value. If the data in the appraisal report support the sales price, then the lender should have no problem accepting the sales price as market value for the purposes of the intended transaction. If the figures are different, the lender bases the loan on the sales price or the appraised value, whichever is lower.

8.4 UNDERWRITING THE APPRAISAL

After the appraisal has been completed, it may also undergo a review process, either by an in-house appraiser or a review appraiser. Then, the appraisal is ready for underwriting by the lender. The purpose of underwriting is to determine if the property is acceptable by lender standards and if the market value supports the loan requested and meets the lender's requirements in other ways. The lender may alter the terms or conditions of a borrower's loan request based on the appraisal findings. For example, if the appraisal indicates that the roof leaks, the lender may add a condition to the loan approval that the roof be repaired.

Underwriting the appraisal is only one portion of the whole loan underwriting process wherein the borrower must also be approved as eligible for the requested loan. In an unpredictable economic market (as evidenced beginning in late 2007 and continuing through 2014) the appraisal can take on additional importance. The reviewer is useful, for instance, in helping the lender evaluate the future value of the property because, in case of foreclosure, there must be sufficient value to cover the loan. Lenders are very concerned about the early years of the mortgage. If the underwriter is certain, and able to document, that value will likely decrease during the first one to five years, then the terms of the loan may be adjusted, such as reducing the loan amount. In most cases, unless there is a glaring irregularity in the appraisal, the underwriter relies upon the appraiser's determined value.

8.5 PLANNED UNIT DEVELOPMENTS AND CONDOMINIUMS

Many **planned unit developments (PUDs)** and **condominiums** have been built in the United States, and it is important that you know what they are and how they are appraised. It is important because some lenders have different loan policies on PUDs and condominiums as opposed to single-family homes.

A PUD or condominium can be defined as a type of development, usually accompanied by a specific management process. A PUD refers to separate, individual fee ownership of a lot and dwelling. In addition, you own a proportionately undivided interest jointly with others in the development of the common areas and any recreational facilities. A typical PUD is illustrated in Figure 8.3. While sometimes called a townhouse development, the term townhouse refers to a type of architecture and not the type of ownership. A PUD could be a group of single-family homes if there were joint ownership of a common area. In a PUD, there is no one living in the airspace above anyone else. A PUD, a common development in California, is one in which the common areas are limited (e.g., greenbelts, parking areas, playground) and have minimal effect on value.

A condominium (see Figure 8.3) is a type of development in which a person owns a specified residential unit, together with an undivided interest in all the land including recreational facilities. A condominium may be part of a high rise, attached row house, or even a single-family detached development. In a legal sense, a condominium owner acquires a fee title interest in the airspace of the particular unit and an undivided interest, with the other condominium owners, in the land plus all other common areas such as hallways, elevators, utility rooms, carports, and recreational facilities.

Both PUDs and condominiums have homeowner association (HOA) groups that are responsible for the management of the development. These groups meet regularly and are governed by specific regulations. It is the association's responsibility to maintain the common areas. It also sets the dues that each owner must pay in order to maintain the common areas and the exteriors of the individual structures. To be eligible for loans, occupancy ratios are reviewed, with lenders usually requiring a high owner-occupancy ratio compared to the number of rental units within the project. A review of the budget will reveal if owners are current on dues and if sufficient reserves are in place for anticipated future repairs. Finally, the officers will most likely have to be covered by errors and omissions insurance. As a side note, FHA loans require a condo complex to be approved, which fulfills the FHA's concerns above. PUDs, however, are not required to complete this process.

A lender appraising a PUD or condominium unit is interested in more than just that particular unit. The lender is interested in the overall project, because the value of one unit is affected by the quality

FIGURE 8.3 (a) A typical PUD (b) A typical condominium.

Source: (a) Planned Unit Development: © Shutterstock /jessicakirsh
(b) Condo: © Shutterstock / Chuck Wagner

and the operation of the entire project. For this reason, the lender will review, in addition to the budget mentioned above, the Articles of Incorporation, the Covenants, Conditions & Restrictions (CC&Rs), and the bylaws. When an appraiser appraises a PUD or condominium, these are some of the items checked:

1. General appearance of the project.
2. Recreational and other amenities that are adequate and well maintained.

3. Adequate parking for owners and guests.
4. Maintenance of common areas.

A unit in a PUD or condominium is appraised basically the same way as a single-family dwelling. The appraiser uses the three approaches to value and relies primarily on the market data approach in arriving at a final value.

Figure 8.4 is the uniform FNMA/FHLMC rider attached to condominium loans.

Figure 8.5 is the FNMA/FHLMC rider for PUD loans.

8.6 THE LICENSING OF REAL ESTATE APPRAISERS

Federal law has created the requirement that real estate appraisers must be licensed if the property transaction requires financing by a lender that is insured or backed by a federal agency, such as the Federal Deposit Insurance Corporation and similar such agencies. Under federal law, each state is charged with enforcing the law within their borders. In California, the Office of Real Estate Appraisers (OREA) is the enforcement agency.

There are four levels of real estate appraiser licensing. The levels define an appraiser's experience and the kind of eligible property and under what conditions he or she may perform appraisals

They are:

1. *Trainee License.* A trainee cannot do an appraisal on his/her own. He/she can only work under the technical supervision of a licensed appraiser.
2. *Residential License.* This license allows a person to appraise non-complex, one- to four-unit residential property up to a transaction value of $1 million, and nonresidential property up to a transaction value of $250,000.
3. *Certified Residential License.* This license allows a person to appraise all one- to four-unit residential property without regard to complexity or value, and nonresidential property up to a transaction value of $250,000.
4. *Certified General License.* This license allows a person to appraise all types of property without any value or complexity restrictions. Certified General is currently the highest level of licensed appraiser.

There are various educational and experience requirements for each license level. New requirements were adopted as of January 1, 2015, that affect not only the time frames in which education must be completed, but also the amount of course work and degrees required to

FIGURE 8.4 FNMA/FHLMC condominium rider.

CONDOMINIUM RIDER

THIS CONDOMINIUM RIDER is made this _____ day of _____, _____ and is incorporated into and shall be deemed to amend and supplement the Mortgage, Deed of Trust or Security Deed (the "Security Instrument") of the same date given by the undersigned (the "Borrower") to secure Borrower's Note to

_____ (the "Lender")

of the same date and covering the Property described in the Security Instrument and located at:

_____
[Property Address]

The Property includes a unit in, together with an undivided interest in the common elements of, a condominium project known as:

_____
[Name of Condominium Project]

(the "Condominium Project"). If the owners association or other entity which acts for the Condominium Project (the "Owners Association") holds title to property for the benefit or use of its members or shareholders, the Property also includes Borrower's interest in the Owners Association and the uses, proceeds and benefits of Borrower's interest.

CONDOMINIUM COVENANTS. In addition to the covenants and agreements made in the Security Instrument, Borrower and Lender further covenant and agree as follows:

A. Condominium Obligations. Borrower shall perform all of Borrower's obligations under the Condominium Project's Constituent Documents. The "Constituent Documents" are the: (i) Declaration or any other document which creates the Condominium Project; (ii) by-laws; (iii) code of regulations; and (iv) other equivalent documents. Borrower shall promptly pay, when due, all dues and assessments imposed pursuant to the Constituent Documents.

B. Hazard Insurance. So long as the Owners Association maintains, with a generally accepted insurance carrier, a "master" or "blanket" policy on the Condominium Project which is satisfactory to Lender and which provides insurance coverage in the amounts, for the periods, and against the hazards Lender requires, including fire and hazards included within the term "extended coverage," then:

(i) Lender waives the provision in Uniform Covenant 2 for the monthly payment to Lender of one-twelfth of the yearly premium installments for hazard insurance on the Property; and

(ii) Borrower's obligation under Uniform Covenant 5 to maintain hazard insurance coverage on the Property is deemed satisfied to the extent that the required coverage is provided by the Owners Association policy.

Borrower shall give Lender prompt notice of any lapse in required hazard insurance coverage.

In the event of a distribution of hazard insurance proceeds in lieu of restoration or repair following a loss to the Property, whether to the unit or to common elements, any proceeds payable to Borrower are hereby assigned and shall be paid to Lender for application to the sums secured by the Security Instrument, with any excess paid to Borrower.

C. Public Liability Insurance. Borrower shall take such actions as may be reasonable to insure that the Owners Association maintains a public liability insurance policy acceptable in form, amount, and extent of coverage to Lender.

D. Condemnation. The proceeds of any award or claim for damages, direct or consequential, payable to Borrower in connection with any condemnation or other taking of all or any part of the Property, whether of the unit or of the common elements, or for any conveyance in lieu of condemnation, are hereby assigned and shall be paid to Lender. Such proceeds shall be applied by Lender to the sums secured by the Security Instrument as provided in Uniform Covenant 10.

E. Lender's Prior Consent. Borrower shall not, except after notice to Lender and with Lender's prior written consent, either partition or subdivide the Property or consent to:

(i) The abandonment or termination of the Condominium Project, except for abandonment or termination required by law in the case of substantial destruction by fire or other casualty or in the case of a taking by condemnation or eminent domain;

(ii) any amendment to any provision of the Constituent Documents if the provision is for the express benefit of Lender;

(iii) termination of professional management and assumption of self-management of the Owners Association; or

(iv) any action which would have the effect of rendering the public liability insurance coverage maintained by the Owners Association unacceptable to Lender.

F. Remedies. If Borrower does not pay condominium dues and assessments when due, then Lender may pay them. Any amounts disbursed by Lender under this paragraph F shall become additional debt of Borrower secured by the Security Instrument. Unless Borrower and Lender agree to other terms of payment, these amounts shall bear interest from the date of disbursement at the Note rate and shall be payable, with interest, upon notice from Lender to Borrower requesting payment.

BY SIGNING BELOW, Borrower accepts and agrees to the terms and provisions contained in this Condominium Rider.

_____ (Seal)   _____ (Seal)
            -Borrower   -Borrower

_____ (Seal)   _____ (Seal)
            -Borrower   -Borrower

MULTISTATE CONDOMINIUM RIDER -- Single Family -- **Fannie Mae/Freddie Mac UNIFORM INSTRUMENT**   **Form 3140 9/90**
ITEM 1623L0 (9102)   Great Lakes Business Forms, Inc. ■ To Order Call: 1-800-530-9393 □ FAX 616-791-1131

Source: © 2016 OnCourse Learning

FIGURE 8.5 FNMA/FHLMC planned unit development rider.

```
                    PLANNED UNIT DEVELOPMENT RIDER

    THIS PLANNED UNIT DEVELOPMENT ("PUD") RIDER is made this..........................day of
..............................,  ...., and is incorporated into and shall be deemed to amend and supplement
a Mortgage, Deed of Trust or Deed to Secure Debt (herein "security instrument") dated of even date herewith, given by
the undersigned (herein "Borrower") to secure Borrower's Note to.........................................
...................................(herein "Lender") and covering the Property described in the
security instrument and located at..........................................................
                                        (Property Address)
..................... The Property comprises a parcel of land improved with a dwelling, which, together with
other such parcels and certain common areas and facilities, all as described in...........................
................................................................................
(herein "Declaration"), forms a planned unit development known as.................................
................................................................................
                              (Name of Planned Unit Development)
(herein "PUD").

    PLANNED UNIT DEVELOPMENT COVENANTS. In addition to the covenants and agreements made in the security
instrument, Borrower and Lender further covenant and agree as follows:
    A. PUD Obligations. Borrower shall perform all of Borrower's obligations under the: (i) Declaration; (ii)
articles of incorporation, trust instrument or any equivalent document required to establish the homeowners
association or equivalent entity managing the common areas and facilities of the PUD (herein "Owners Association");
and (iii) by-laws, if any, or other rules or regulations of the Owners Association. Borrower shall promptly pay, when
due, all assessments imposed by the Owners Association.
    B. Hazard Insurance. In the event of a distribution of hazard insurance proceeds in lieu of restoration or repair
following a loss to the common areas and facilities of the PUD, any such proceeds payable to Borrower are hereby
assigned and shall be paid to Lender for application to the sums secured by the security instrument, with the excess,
if any, paid to Borrower.
    C. Condemnation. The proceeds of any award or claim for damages, direct or consequential, payable to
Borrower in connection with any condemnation or other taking of all or any part of the common areas and facilities
of the PUD, or for any conveyance in lieu of condemnation, are hereby assigned and shall be paid to Lender. Such
proceeds shall be applied by Lender to the sums secured by the security instrument in the manner provided under
Uniform Covenant 9.
    D. Lender's Prior Consent. Borrower shall not, except after notice to Lender and with Lender's prior written
consent, consent to:
        (i) the abandonment or termination of the PUD;
        (ii) any material amendment to the Declaration, trust instrument, articles of incorporation, by-laws of the
Owners Association, or any equivalent constituent document of the PUD, including, but not limited to, any
amendment which would change the percentage interests of the unit owners in the common areas and facilities of
the PUD;
        (iii) the effectuation of any decision by the Owners Association to terminate professional management and
assume self-management of the PUD; or
        (iv) the transfer, release, encumbrance, partition or subdivision of all or any part of the PUD's common areas
and facilities, except as to the Owners Association's right to grant easements for utilities and similar or related purposes.
    E. Remedies. If Borrower breaches Borrower's covenants and agreements hereunder, including the covenant
to pay when due planned unit development assessments, then Lender may invoke any remedies provided under the
security instrument, including, but not limited to, those provided under Uniform Covenant 7.

    IN WITNESS WHEREOF, Borrower has executed this PUD Rider.
```

Source: © 2016 OnCourse Learning

advance through the appraiser designated levels. For the latest requirements, contact the Office of Real Estate Appraisers website at www.orea.ca.gov.

It is important to note that a real estate licensee may provide what is called a **comparative market analysis (CMA)** outlining what other similar properties have sold for, but under no circumstance can the real estate licensee call this a certified appraisal, unless the real estate licensee also holds an appropriate, separate appraisal license.

A **certified appraisal report** is any written communication of an analysis, opinion, or conclusion relating to the value that is termed certified. For property containing one to four residential units, almost all appraisers use the standard FNMA/FHLMC appraisal form, illustrated in Figure 8.1. The details go beyond the scope of this text but are thoroughly covered in any appraisal course.

8.7 WORKING WITH APPRAISERS: THE DO'S AND DON'TS

People in the real estate business who are involved in buying or selling will come into contact with appraisers. The new rules have redefined how we can relate to appraisers. In an attempt to avoid undue influence or coercion of an appraiser, real estate licensees and mortgage lenders are now prohibited from contacting an appraiser directly. All contact is to be made from the mortgage originator to the lender to the **appraisal management company (AMC)** and to the appraiser, and all via e-mail or the AMC's electronic system. The process can be lengthy and unsatisfactory, especially when trying to resolve a problem and/or error in an appraisal. In reality, real estate licensees will likely have some contact with the appraiser during scheduling and inspections. It pays to know the current do's and don'ts in dealing with appraisers.

1. *Access to property.* Upon ordering the appraisal, instructions about whom to contact and how to access the property are conveyed. The real estate licensee is often identified as the contact person and is the one with whom the appraiser makes arrangements for access. This appraiser relationship has not changed: Make it easy for the appraiser to see the property. Be on time for the appointment. If the appraiser is to meet the owner, be certain that the owner will be there. Nothing irritates an appraiser more than to be told to go directly to the property because "the owner is always home." Then, when the appraiser arrives, no one is there. Be considerate of his or her time, and make it convenient to see the property.

2. *At the property.* Whether the owner or salesperson is at the property when the appraiser arrives, do not follow the appraiser around the property. Some people do this while talking constantly about all the good features of the property. Do not distract the appraiser; however, most appraisers welcome any information on the property that would be helpful to them (e.g., the licensee's comparables used to determine the sales price). Be available, but not pushy. It might be helpful, for instance, to give the appraiser a printed list of those special amenities that may not be obvious

in an initial observation. Prepare the owner in advance regarding what to expect. Homeowners are often concerned because the appraiser seemed to be in and out so quickly.

3. *Comparable sales.* If you have information on comparable houses that have sold, ask the appraiser if he or she would like to have it. Most appraisers still appreciate any data that will help them in their appraisal. If you prepare such information, make it as complete as possible. On comparable sales the appraiser needs to know such things as the date of sale, number of bedrooms and baths, square footage, age of property, sale price, and so on. Most likely, the appraiser has this information, so use it to be helpful and never assume your information will affect their valuation.

4. *Influencing the appraiser.* Don't try to influence appraisers by giving them a sales talk. Most appraisers are experienced and knowledgeable. They are not influenced by a sales pitch—in fact, it may backfire on you. Appraisers try to be objective; however, if they are irritated while at the property by an overaggressive individual, it may affect their outlook on the property. And finally, it can be tempting to ask an appraiser to overlook or minimize a condition in the property (e.g. uncompleted repair work). To do so could be viewed as a request for an appraiser to violate his or her standards of practice or ethics.

Chapter Summary

It is the future, not the past that will determine whether a loan is good or bad. That is why conventional lenders emphasize the future resale potential of a property. Lenders want to make sure that if they must foreclose, they can resell the property quickly and recover the loan amount. Conventional lenders set up specific property standard policies. These standards vary with each lender, are flexible, and vary with market conditions. But, if the loan is to be resold to Fannie Mae or Freddie Mac, the lender must follow their appraisal standards and forms.

The ordering and monitoring of the appraisal process changed with the introduction of new rules under the HVCC. Although improved since early implementation, transaction time frames continue to be sometimes impacted by the new appraisal process. With a still fragile housing component in the economy, market conditions have taken on greater importance, and appraisers are required to provide additional information and comment accordingly.

Real estate appraisers evaluate a neighborhood with great care because location has a great influence on the value of a property. Appraisers also pay particular attention to the condition and quality of the property. It is important to note, however, that redlining is illegal.

In determining market value, the appraiser can use three approaches: the cost, sales comparison, and income approaches. On one- to four-unit properties, the sales comparison approach is the most reliable. Even when using the income approach, comparable properties must be used for the evaluation.

PUDs and condominiums present special appraising and lending problems. Lenders are concerned about the entire project as well as the value of a single unit within the project.

Important Terms and Concepts

Adjustments
Appraisal Management Company (AMC)
Capitalization
Capitalization rate
Certificate of Reasonable Value (CRV)
Certified appraisal report
Comparables
Comparative Market Analysis (CMA)
Conditional commitment
Condominiums
Cost approach
Economic obsolescence

Fair Market Value (FMV)
Functional obsolescence
Gross Rent Multiplier (GRM)
Gross operating income
Income approach
Market data approach
Neighborhood
Net Operating Income (NOI)
Physical depreciation
Planned Unit Development (PUD)
Redlining
Sales comparison approach

Reviewing Your Understanding

Questions for Discussion

1. "The sales price and the fair market value of a property are not always the same." Explain this statement.
2. Discuss how property standards for local lenders are influenced by Freddie Mac and Fannie Mae.
3. List five characteristics an appraiser looks for when checking a neighborhood.
4. What are the basic steps in the cost approach to value?
5. Explain the sales comparison (market data) approach to value.
6. When appraising single-family homes and large apartments, do appraisers use the same income approach techniques? Explain the techniques used.
7. How does a planned unit development (PUD) differ from a condominium?
8. List some dos and don'ts for establishing a good working relationship with a real estate appraiser.

Multiple-Choice Questions

1. Adverse influences that tend to reduce property values include
   a. gentle curving in street pattern.
   b. noisy freeways.
   c. acceptable school system.
   d. presence of recreational facilities.

2. The loss in value due to negative neighborhood influences is called
   a. physical deterioration.
   b. economic obsolescence.
   c. functional obsolescence.
   d. structural obsolescence.

3. To arrive at total square footage of a structure, appraisers measure the
   a. exterior of the structure.
   b. interior dimensions of the house, plus the garage.
   c. interior dimensions of the house, excluding the garage.
   d. length, width, and height of the building.

4. Loss in value from poor structural design is referred to by appraisers as
   a. physical deterioration.
   b. economic obsolescence.
   c. functional obsolescence.
   d. structural obsolescence.

5. Buyers will not pay more for a property than the cost of acquiring an equally desirable substitute property. Economists refer to this as the principle of
   a. conformity.
   b. desirability.
   c. acquisition.
   d. substitution.

6. The cost per square foot would usually be the least for
   a. garages.
   b. homes.
   c. PUD buildings.
   d. condo buildings.

7. The most reliable approach to establishing values of single-family dwellings is the
   a. cost approach.
   b. income approach.
   c. gross multiplier.
   d. sales comparison approach.

8. When comparing properties with one that is being appraised, certain adjustments are made for differences in construction, quality, and other characteristics. In the event a comparable house is exactly the same as the subject house, except that the comparable is in better condition, the appraiser will
   a. deduct from the comparable.
   b. deduct from the subject property.
   c. make no adjustments.
   d. find that insufficient information is given to accurately determine the kind of adjustments required, if any.

9. The organization that publishes periodic summaries of sales in a designated area and available to real estate agents is
   a. Multiple Listing Service.
   b. County Recorder.
   c. County Assessor.
   d. Institute of Continuing Education.

10. Under the MDIA, disclosures must be delivered to loan applicants, with some exceptions, within
    a. 3 days of receipt of an application.
    b. 30 days of applying for a loan.
    c. 5 days of application.
    d. none of the above.

11. A dollar amount, subtracted from depreciation to arrive at the present value of the improvements, is used in the _____ approach to value.
    a. cost
    b. income
    c. market
    d. GRM

12. The location of a particular property is
    a. no longer considered a determinant of value as a result of redlining legislation.
    b. of considerable importance in determining the value of property.
    c. relevant only on commercial properties.
    d. relevant on all properties except owner-occupied SFDs.

13. When using the FHLMC/FNMA appraisal report form for single-family dwellings, appraisers
    a. normally use at least three comparable sales.
    b. make note of off-site improvements.
    c. consult available sources like Marshall & Swift to arrive at a cost per square foot.
    d. do all of the above.

14. FHA property standards
    a. are similar to conventional standards.
    b. require extensive repairs and improvements prior to issuing a loan.
    c. include suitability to meet specific needs of buyers.
    d. rely heavily upon appraisers to determine if a home meets property requirements.

15. Assume a property sells for $800,000 but is appraised for $650,000. Under HVCC, the final loan will be based
    a. midway between $650,000 and $800,000.
    b. on a maximum of $1,000,000 for joint borrowers.
    c. on $650,000.
    d. on $800,000.

16. Under the HVCC
    a. appraisers are hired to determine precise property values.
    b. the major objective is to determine if the value of the property is sufficient to serve as collateral for a given loan.
    c. the credit score of the borrower is secondary to the property value.
    d. a lender's property standards have no bearing on how much it will finance.

17. Regarding pest control reports
    a. any pest repairs work may be waived by an FHA loan applicant.
    b. they are required for every FHA appraisal.
    c. FHA appraisers are responsible for determining if a report should be ordered.
    d. compared to the FHA, VA loans do not require pest control clearance.

18. When a lender hires an appraiser, the lender is usually looking for the property's
    a. book value.
    b. market value.
    c. adjusted cost value.
    d. depreciated value.

19. Given an annual gross multiplier of 8 for a given rental market where the gross rents are $80,000 and the net operating income is $50,000, the indicated value of the property is
    a. $640,000.
    b. $400,000.
    c. $1,000,000.
    d. none of the above.

20. Which of the following regarding the income approach to value is true?
    a. The lower the capitalization rate, the lower the property value.
    b. The lower the gross rent multiplier, the higher the property value.
    c. The lower the capitalization rate, the higher the property value.
    d. The lower the net operating income, the higher the property value.

CASE & POINT

Appraisals and the New HVCC Rules

The appraisal process for conventional financing was, for many years, less complicated than that for FHA or VA loans. In May 2009, that process was severely impacted with the adoption of the *Home Valuation Code of Conduct (HVCC)*. Lenders (including mortgage brokers and other loan originators) were no longer able to order an appraisal from a selected local appraiser. Instead, a system of Appraisal Management Companies (AMCs) was established from which appraisal assignments would occur.

The motivation for these changes was to establish regulations to "enhance the quality and independence of the appraisal process." In other words, it was to protect the appraiser from coercive interference from lenders or real estate licensees, who were thought to have contributed to an invalid valuation process by accelerating home values during the heyday of subprime lending.

Critics immediately countered that the new process was a way to deflect attention away from the fact that the agencies did not provide sufficient oversight in the housing debacle. Plus, critics indicated that local appraisers did not create the market, but were most often caught in a spiral in which they were chasing home values as properties kept selling for ever increasing amounts. Ironically, the fraudulent case that spawned this regulation was conducted via an appraisal management company, the very same kind of entity that is now supposed to protect consumers from appraisal fraud.

Concerns that the new rules would impact how local appraisers, mortgage lenders, and realtors did business began to manifest themselves immediately as the new process was initiated. But worse still were the perceived negative impacts for the borrower/consumer. The increase in the cost of appraisals, while most noticeable, was the least of the impacts. More critical was that a lender had to be identified immediately in order to initiate the appraisal process. Previously, the borrower's application and documentation could be acquired along with the appraisal before selecting a lender. This allowed the loan originator to search for the best loan option, avoid guideline changes that could affect the borrower, and discuss any concerns with an appraiser before incurring a cost for an appraisal that might prove ineffective.

Lenders were also affected. They incurred additional costs as they had to establish procedures and commit staff to monitoring the process and developing quality controls with the AMCs. Most costly was devoting time to working out appraisal errors and valuation problems through a convoluted communication process that did not allow for direct contact with the appraiser. Complaints about errors, inappropriate comparison properties, inaccurately identified additions (requiring nonexistent building permits), and just plain bad appraisals mounted, especially during the first months of the new process. The mortgage originators had little access to the appraisal in order to identify valuation irregularities. Acquiring an appraisal copy only after it had been completed and delivered to the lender coupled with the prohibition to contact the appraiser directly eliminated any timely or easy way to correct problems.

As feared, many local appraisers, who best knew the market, were taken out of the process. It seemed that too many appraisers who were assigned were not only new and/or inexperienced, but seemed extremely conservative in their valuations. Complaints of receiving undervalued appraisals, compromising home sales, seemed numerous. Because the AMCs represented a third party that must be paid, appraisers received less money per appraisal. The result in some situations was a reduction of service (e.g., acquiring building permits when required). Advocates of the new process indicated that the complaints were exaggerated. Whether accurate or not, the perception that something was very wrong can and did often replace reality. The process was likely neither as bad as its critics suggested, nor did it perform as well as its advocates anticipated.

Although critics of the HVCC still abound, the industry has mostly accepted and adjusted to the process. Many of the most qualified local appraisers, after initially electing not to enroll in the AMCs, have now done so, and the quality of appraisals is now fairly consistent.

Some lenders now allow loan originators to recommend appraisers to their AMC from which appraisal assignments are made on a rotating basis. While not foolproof, originators are more apt to draw a recommended appraiser when an assignment occurs. This, in turn, has reduced the number of complaints regarding low-value or poorly prepared appraisals. The appraiser no-contact rule is now mostly interpreted by originators and appraisers as prohibiting conversation about value but allowing discussion about most other aspects of the appraisal.

Major criticisms continue to occur around the problem of rebutting any perceived irregularities in an appraisal. These perceived errors include, among others, questions about the selection of comparables, comments about the condition of the property, and inaccurate measurements. The process is unwieldy when the concern must be registered with the lender, referred to the AMC, who relays the question to the appraiser, and any answer is provided via the same referral system in reverse. The time delay is only one of the complications in this complaint process as unanswered concerns are not uncommon and frustrating for all concerned.

In some areas, time frames still impact the loan process, but most have adapted to how the process works. Appraiser fees initially reduced although the cost of the appraisals increased for the consumer. Fees have generally not improved for appraisers as the AMCs receive the payment via the Internet and after subtracting their fee remit the balance to the appraiser.

Appraisals have become more transferrable, especially in the government loan arena and with the more recent high-balance loan options. Conventional appraisals are still not readily transferred between lenders, resulting in borrowers having to sometimes pay a second appraisal fee if they switch lenders for any reason.

What many loan originators, lenders, and appraisers believe is that appraisers were made the scapegoats. It was suggested that they were responsible for the skyrocketing home value spiral, when in fact it was the unregulated easy credit with its lack of any buyer qualification that spawned the subprime debacle. The HVCC was originated on the premise that fraud was rampant within the appraisal process. Whether the HVCC process has reduced the perceived fraud within the valuation procedure is unknown and perhaps problematic, given the fact that the fraudulent case that spawned this regulation (as noted above) was conducted via an appraisal management company. But it is safe to say that the HVCC is here to stay, and the ability of the local loan originator to provide expertise or assistance in guiding the borrower's appraisal experience has mostly disappeared.

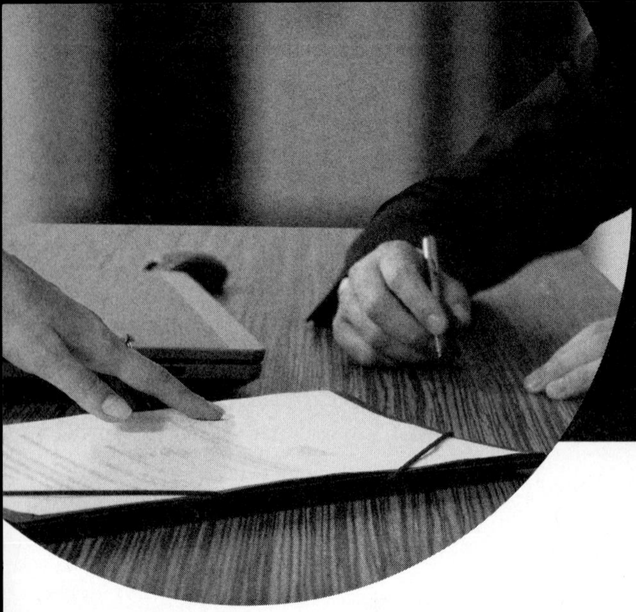

© Shutterstock

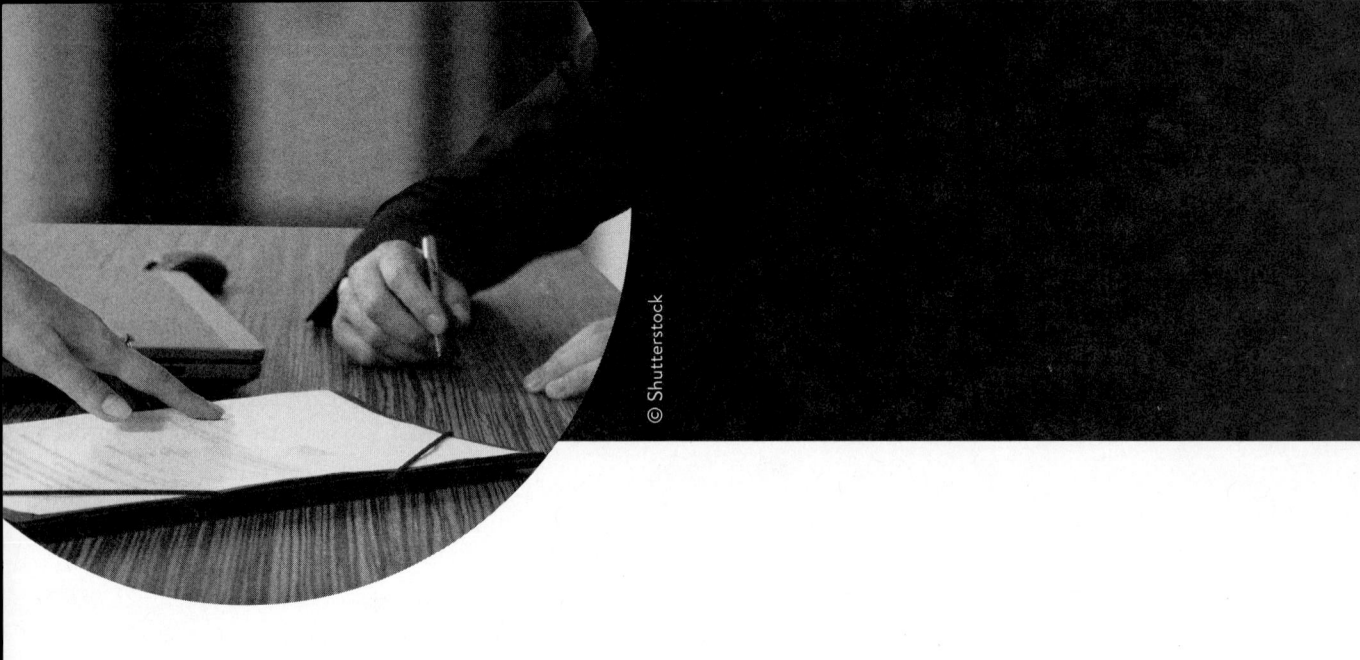

QUALIFYING THE BORROWER

OVERVIEW

The process of qualifying borrowers for real estate loans continues to change as does our market place. With the collapse of the subprime programs, we have gone from virtually no qualifying guidelines back to the standards of old, where lenders have traditionally looked at prospective borrowers and determined the 3 Cs of lending: Credit/Stability, Capacity/Ability, and Collateral—in other words, a credit file that indicates the likelihood of continued loan payments (using credit history as a guide), the ability and willingness to pay the loan (with income and reserve documentation), and a property with sufficient equity to protect the lender in the event of default.

In order to understand the qualifying guideline changes that have occurred, we need only review the relaxed standards that prevailed during the mid-2000s. Although the 3 Cs still applied, in many situations the focus had shifted primarily to promoting the idea of, "How can we qualify the buyer?"

As home values increased, lenders relaxed qualifying standards, resulting in a plethora of alternative loan instruments such as interest-only, stated income loans and negatively amortized option ARM loans. At the same time, lenders came to rely almost exclusively upon borrower credit scores as the primary measure of the likelihood of loan repayment.

While lenders likely recognized the risks involved in these alternative loan options, everyone wanted to believe that a borrower's good credit at least provided a good chance that the loan would be repaid, and that appreciation rates would protect them should the lender have to foreclose. Although it is unlikely that lenders deliberately made loans that might result in foreclosure, their dependence on the then rapid appreciation rates to protect them in case of default proved to be very wrong.

Despite the move toward the alternative mortgage instruments, many loans were still qualified under the more normal guidelines or the tried-and-true methods of evaluating a borrower's ability and willingness to pay a loan. As we continue, these are the guidelines we will apply when evaluating a borrower's ability to purchase. To compensate for the lack of qualifying standards, some say that the pendulum swung too far and qualifying guidelines had become so inflexible that some questioned if lenders wanted to approve any loans. Guidelines have relaxed a bit since those early days of recovery, but change is always occurring, and we can expect that the borrower qualifying process will continue to evolve.

After completing this chapter, you will be able to:

- Discuss income requirements to qualify for different types of loans.
- Explain what effect debts have on a prospective borrower's qualifications.
- Describe how lenders analyze stability of income.
- Explain why lenders are concerned about borrowers' credit history and credit score.
- Draw up a list of things that real estate agents can do to help clients obtain financing.

9.1 HOW LENDERS QUALIFY PROSPECTIVE BORROWERS

Interviewing a prospective borrower, a lender begins with determining the borrower's capacity and willingness to pay along with a mathematical calculation known as the loan-to-value percentage.

1. *Ability or Capacity to Pay.* To determine ability or capacity to repay loans, lenders seek answers to these questions: Do the borrowers earn enough to make the required payments? If so, is it a steady source of income? Do the borrowers have enough cash to buy the property? What other assets do they have?

2. *Desire or Willingness to Pay.* A person may have the ability to pay but lack the desire or willingness to do so. The desire to pay is just as important, but more difficult to measure. Lenders typically measure this with a credit score, but can also use a number of additional methods to determine a person's desire (as discussed later in the chapter).

Qualifying a borrower is not a strict, precise operation. It is a process that requires flexibility and judgment.

Qualifying guidelines, while meant to be somewhat flexible, had become fairly rigid. More recently, we note signs of returning to what used to be called "make sense underwriting" (mostly lost immediately following the economic downturn in 2008) in which the intended borrower is evaluated on his/her total economic profile. The loan review requirements include, among others, qualifying ratios being calculated, sufficient funds verified, credit scores checked and full documentation of every aspect of the process.

Qualifying Fannie Mae's Desktop Underwriting (DU) and Freddie Mac's Loan Prospector (LP) automated qualifying systems have made the qualifying process more objective and faster. Often forgotten in the ease of using the automated systems is that supporting documentation must be acquired and ultimately signed off by an underwriter. More importantly, it is not as easy as in the pre-recession days to explain any unusual aspects of a borrower's profile (e.g., recent credit difficulties, reduced savings record, the impact of recent health issues), as the computer is unsympathetic and underwriters are reluctant to override the computer result.

A third less arbitrary qualification and risk measurement is a mathematical calculation of the loan-to-value (LTV). Determined by dividing the loan amount by the purchase price or appraised value, whichever is lower, a higher LTV percentage is deemed a higher risk loan. For instance, a loan amount of $160,000 divided by the purchase price of $200,000 renders an 80 percent LTV. Considered the baseline for a lender's risk exposure, a higher LTV percentage generally requires an adjustment in the interest rate and sometimes the costs associated with the loan.

9.2 ABILITY OR CAPACITY TO PAY: A CASE HISTORY

A young mother contacted a loan officer in a local savings bank. Their conversation revealed the facts that her husband had recently died, and she wanted to buy a home to provide more permanent housing than a rental unit would furnish for herself and her three children, ages 6, 9, and 12.

The discussion further indicated that she had just returned to work for the first time in a dozen years, at age 38. The woman had a bachelor's degree in liberal arts and had been an executive secretary before having children. For the past 12 years, her husband had been the sole provider, but she had just been hired as an executive secretary with a gross monthly salary of $3,600.

She had found a small, but suitable home listed at $245,000. Her intent to put a 20 percent down payment would result in a loan of $196,000. A 30-year loan at 4.75 percent per annum would require monthly payments of $993.15 principal and interest, plus taxes and insurance of $308.80, for a total monthly payment of $1,301.95.

A quick computation demonstrates that her top housing payment ratio was 36.2 percent. Her long-term debt was approximately $275 per month, producing a bottom or overall debt ratio of 43.8 percent. While the overall ratio exceeds the current recommended maximum qualifying ratio, there are other factors that strengthen her overall loan profile.

In this case, compensating factors included that her credit was mostly combined with her deceased husband's and that her personal debt consisted of only two credit card accounts in her own name plus a $150 auto payment that would continue for four years. Her mid-credit score was 742. Other disclosures indicated that she had received $150,000 in life insurance policy proceeds. The couple had also accumulated $40,000 in the form of savings deposits, stock, and CD investments during their 14-year marriage.

In addition to the above compensating factors, the woman's employer indicated that her likelihood of continued employment was excellent. Her low credit debt demonstrated a commitment to retaining a low debt total. Her money in the bank represented more than the normally required amount of reserves, a financial cushion that would protect the lender from a threat of future loan default. And the substantial 20 percent down payment was viewed as protection for the lender.

The application was taken, and a fixed rate loan was approved.

What Does This Case Illustrate?

Lenders typically have guidelines upon which to base their lending decisions. Although expanded guidelines, as indicated in the Overview, have been used in the past, more recently, lenders have returned to more typical loan-qualifying guidelines. Thus, real estate licensees are urged to suggest to prospective buyers that lenders require stable income, sufficient assets, and acceptable credit. The days of easy-qualifying loans are over, at least for now.

Although compensating factors can be used under some circumstances, recognize that lenders mostly use these expanded guidelines to help an otherwise marginal buyer qualify by strengthening the buyer's file. No amount of compensating factors can overcome major deficiencies in a file (e.g., very low credit scores, lack of stable income).

Why Qualify Borrowers?

Some people ask, why bother to qualify borrowers? If the borrower doesn't make the payment, the lender can just take back the property! There are several reasons why a lender qualifies a borrower.

First, lenders are not in the business of foreclosing and taking back properties. Lenders are in the money business, not the real estate business. In most cases, when lenders foreclose they suffer a loss in both time and money.

In earlier years, when a much larger down payment was required, qualifying the borrower was not as important as it is today. With large down payments there was less need to worry about the borrower's qualifications. Few borrowers were willing to allow a loan to default and lose a large amount of equity.

With large equity, borrowers in financial trouble could simply sell the property, pay the lender, and salvage what they could or, if qualified, refinance the loan to lower the interest rate and/or loan payments. Today, the situation is different—lenders are still making reasonably high-ratio conventional loans up to 93 percent LTV or government-backed loans that require little, if any, down payment. With these loans, lenders must rely heavily on borrower qualifications because there is little, if any, equity in the property. Lenders believe the greater the equity, the greater the incentive to make mortgage payments and the less the equity, the less the incentive. In declining markets, values can actually drop below remaining loan balances. Known as being "upside down" or "underwater" on the mortgage, historic numbers of borrowers found themselves in this predicament by mid-2009. Short sales became commonplace as borrowers are unable to sell their properties for what they owed in loans. (Short sales are more fully discussed in Chapter 11.)

While lenders had for many years subscribed to the notion that it was a disservice to approve a loan beyond the borrower's financial capabilities, the subprime loan frenzy caused them to lose sight of that lending principle. We've previously discussed the difficulties that were created by excessively relaxing lending guidelines. Suffice it to say, we have returned to the belief that by turning down an unqualified buyer, the lender is actually doing the buyer a favor. It is obvious that *if a loan is not sound for the borrower, it is not sound for the lender, and vice versa*. In this regard, the creative financing options mentioned earlier created great hardships for some buyers and subsequently for lenders who have been forced to either foreclose or accept a short sale. The term "abusive lending practices" entered the vocabulary, and oversight agencies by 2012 began to seek penalties for some lenders who arranged financing for borrowers who were unable to comply with the loan's requirements, including excessive negative amortization and fast-rising mortgage payments, to name a few. Lending practices will undoubtedly continue to change and evolve as lenders determine not only what lending instruments the market may need but what actually works.

9.3 CAPACITY TO PAY

Whether the borrower earns enough to make the monthly payments on a loan is the first consideration in determining the applicant's ability or capacity to repay the loan. There is no one answer, because various lenders use different formulas depending upon the type of loan. Conventional lenders, the FHA, the VA, and Cal-Vet each have their own distinctive method of qualifying a borrower. To compare the qualifying methods used, we'll look at one set of borrowers. Figure 9.1 provides hypothetical information on the borrowers, a couple of whom we'll use as applicants for a conventional loan. We will then compare this type to FHA and VA requirements.

FIGURE 9.1 Basic information about sample borrowers.

Name	John and Janet Smith	
Dependents	Two, aged 4 and 6	
Employment		
John Smith		
Employer	Self-employed	
Position	Consultant	
Years on job	6 years	
Income	$3,200 per month	
Janet Smith		
Employer	County Assessor's Office	
Position	Administrative assistant	
Years on job	3 years	
Income	$2,100 per month	
Cash in bank	$60,000	
Debts:	Payment	Balance
Car	$300	$5,000
Furniture	75	1,000
Dept. Store	20	100
Loan Information:		
Purchase price of home	$300,000	
Loan amount	$250,000	
Interest rate	5.25%	
Term	30 years	
Monthly Payment:		
Principal and interest	$1,288	
Taxes	312	
Insurance	66	
Private Mortgage Insurance	104	
Total PITI	$1,770	

Source: © 2016 OnCourse Learning

Income Ratios

Lenders use the **monthly payment** on a property to determine a borrower's qualifications. The payment includes principal, interest, property taxes, and insurance—commonly referred to as **PITI**. Even if the borrowers are paying their own taxes and insurance (not impounded), the lender adds them all together for qualifying purposes. Private mortgage insurance (PMI) and/or Home Owner Association (HOA) dues must also be included in the calculation when applicable. For the FHA, both an Up Front Mortgage Insurance Premium (UFMIP) and Monthly Mortgage Insurance (MMI) are also included.

Lenders use ratios in qualifying borrowers. The housing ratio is quoted as the total monthly payment divided by the borrower's gross monthly income. The overall **qualifying ratio** is calculated by adding the housing expense plus all other credit debt divided by the borrower's gross monthly income.

The long-time accepted qualifying housing ratio used by the agencies is 33 percent, indicating that a borrower's monthly housing payments should not exceed 33 percent of his or her gross monthly income. Expressing it as a multiplier, we would say that the borrower should earn approximately three times the monthly payment. Qualifying ratios used by the agencies change depending upon various circumstances: as the cost of housing increases, borrowers must allocate more of their income to housing; compensating factors may allow an expansion of the ratios; and high credit score buyers are granted greater flexibility in their ratios. Thus, although the 33/43 ratios are identified in policy manuals, the agencies accommodate some flexibility. That flexibility reached unprecedented ratios accompanied by minimum documentation during the subprime loan era. Borrowers today, depending upon their down payment, credit scores, amount of consumer debt, and compensating factors, can exceed the guideline, but it is up to each individual lender to determine the compensating factors required to permit adjustments to the ratios. The following are some examples of when a lender might feel justified in approving a higher loan ratio.

- Borrowers have a substantial cushion/reserve. If the net worth is liquid, it can be used to make the mortgage payments, if necessary.
- Borrowers have a credit-worthy co-borrower with additional income. Co-borrower rules apply. Remember also that a co-borrower, regardless of how qualified, will not compensate for the bad credit rating of the main borrower.
- Borrowers have excellent potential for higher earnings due to education or training, and current income is stable. Recent graduates

fall into this category as they begin their careers, as do nurses and police officers.
- Borrowers are making a large down payment.
- Borrowers have no "payment shock," meaning that they have been making the change to their mortgage or rent payments at about the same level as the new loan payment.

Let's look at our sample borrowers, the Smiths from Figure 9.1, to determine how they qualify. Their monthly PITI payment is $1,770, and their monthly income is $5,300.

$$\frac{\text{Mortgage payment}}{\text{Gross income}} = \frac{\$1,770}{\$5,300} = 33.4\%$$

This ratio is frequently referred to as the housing ratio, top ratio, or front-end ratio. The Smiths would qualify based on current income guides.

Debts

So far, we have discussed only a borrower's housing ratio. Lenders must also take into account the borrower's debts. Lenders break debts down into two categories, short term and long term. The short-term debts are generally ignored, and only long-term debts are considered in qualifying a borrower. How are **long-term debts** defined? Conventional lenders follow the standards of Fannie Mae, Freddie Mac, the FHA, and PMI companies, which define a long-term debt as a debt that will take six months or longer to pay off. Child support payments are also considered long-term debts if they will continue for more than six months. Caveat: Because a significant monthly payment (e.g., a $650 car payment) could compromise the borrower during the first six months of new loan payments, such high monthly payments may be calculated into qualifying ratios even though only six months of payments remain.

Once long-term debts have been determined, the lender adds the total to the monthly payment. The two, added together, are called **total monthly expenses**. The total monthly expenses are divided by the borrower's gross monthly income, which results in another ratio, called the over-all ratio, bottom ratio, or **back-end ratio**. Conventional lenders use Fannie Mae and Freddie Mac most recent standards, which state that this ratio should not exceed 41 percent when PMI is included. Our borrowers, the Smiths, have three debts.

Their car and furniture payments will take more than one year to pay off. Therefore, these are long-term debts. The department store debt is a short-term debt. Long-term debts total $375 per month, which, added to the mortgage payment of $1,770, gives us a total monthly expense of $2,145.

$$\frac{\text{Total monthly expense}}{\text{Gross income}} = \frac{\$2,145}{\$5,300} = 40.5\%$$

On the basis of this back-end ratio, the Smiths also qualify, since their total monthly expenses are less than 41 percent. Borrowers must qualify on both tests. Some qualify on the first test but not on the second test because they have excessive debts. The second ratio is almost always the more important of the two. In fact, lenders will allow borrowers to exceed the typical housing ratio if their credit history demonstrates minimal consumer debt service. Figure 9.2 summarizes the qualifying procedure for conventional loans.

FIGURE 9.2 Summary of qualifying procedure for conventional lenders.

Income	
Allowable gross income	$5,300
Housing Payment and Expenses	
Principal and interest	1,288
Property taxes	312
Homeowner's Insurance	66
Private Mortgage Insurance	104
Total mortgage payment	$1,770
Long-term debts	375
Total monthly expenses	$2,145

Qualifying Guidelines:

1. $\dfrac{\text{Mortgage payment}}{\text{Gross income}} = \dfrac{\$1,770}{\$5,300} = 33.4\%$ (front-end ratio)

This ratio should not exceed 33% (under "perfect" ratio requirements)

2. $\dfrac{\text{Total monthly expense}}{\text{Gross income}} = \dfrac{\$2,145}{\$5,300} = 40.5\%$ (back-end ratio)

This ratio should not exceed 41% (under "perfect" ratio requirements or when PMI is required)

Source: © 2016 OnCourse Learning

9.4 QUALIFYING UNDER GOVERNMENT-BACKED LOANS

Federal Housing Administration (FHA)

The FHA uses the same qualifying procedure as conventional lenders, except that the FHA states that the front-end ratio should not exceed 29 percent, while the back-end ratio—the more important of the two qualifying tests—should not exceed 41 percent, including MMI. The 29/41 ratios are considered just right but, as in conventional financing, there is some flexibility allowed—especially when compensating factors are present. It has been suggested that the FHA adopt a "residual" component for qualifying borrowers. The residual method has been used with VA loans (reviewed in the next section) and proponents indicate that the result has been fewer loan defaults. So far, the FHA has considered the residual idea but insists that they do not intend to adopt it anytime soon.

Department of Veterans Affairs (VA)

The VA uses a two-phase qualifying procedure: (1) the **residual income** method and (2) the application of qualifying income ratio.

Figure 9.3 outlines the VA's procedure. The VA starts with **gross income** and subtracts federal and state income tax and Social Security or retirement payments to arrive at net take-home pay.

Phase 1: Residual Income Method

Housing expense consists of principal and interest, taxes, homeowner's insurance, maintenance, and utilities. The VA uses a maintenance fee calculation of 14 cents per square foot.

To the housing expense, the VA adds alimony, child support payments, and long-term debts. The VA defines a long-term debt as any debt that will take six months or more to pay off. Once again, this is not a hard and fast rule; the VA tries to be realistic. For example, if an applicant has a car payment of $400 a month with a balance of $1,500 and little cash reserve, it would probably count this debt, even though there are less than six months remaining on that loan. The VA considers the first few months of the loan critical. A large payment of $400 a month, lasting for four months, could naturally affect a buyer's ability to make loan payments during the first few months, and therefore the VA would count it in qualifying the borrower.

Another item that the VA includes is called a job-related expense. This mainly refers to babysitting expenses when both spouses work and have small children; travel and/or living expenses when employment requires commuting; or those jobs in which additional expenses are

FIGURE 9.3 Summary of VA qualifying procedure.

Allowable gross income	$5,300
Less: Federal income tax	677
State income tax	172
Social Security or retirement	382
Net take-home pay	$4,069
Housing payment and fixed obligations	
Principal and interest	$1,288
Property taxes	312
Homeowner's insurance	66
Total mortgage payment	$1,666
Maintenance/utilities	
(@14 cents/sq. ft.)	140
Total housing expense	$1,806
Alimony and child support	0
Long-term debts	$ 375
Job-related expense	0
Total housing and fixed obligations	$2,181
Analysis	
Net take-home pay	$4,069
Less: Housing and fixed expenses	2,181
Residual income	$1,888

This is an example only and figures have been rounded up and may differ slightly.
Source: © 2016 OnCourse Learning

likely to occur for uniforms, tools, etc. Police officers, firefighters, and construction workers, among others, fall into this category. There is no specific rule as to how much can be subtracted for job-related expenses. Schedule A of the 1040 tax returns generally identifies the amount of unreimbursed business expenses a borrower has incurred. This is the amount most often shown in the qualifying formula. The babysitting expenses can be lessened if one parent works at home or if a relative is available for child care. Commuting expenses can be reduced if an individual living away from home stays with a relative or if housing is paid for by the employer. In our example, because the husband is self-employed at home, we have not identified any babysitting costs.

Now that we have determined net take-home pay for the Smiths, along with their total expenses, we're ready to qualify them. The VA subtracts the total expenses of $2,181 from the net take-home pay of $4,069, leaving $1,888 as residual income. The next concern is,

"Is this residual income enough money to buy food and clothes, and provide for the other needs of the family?" To answer this, we must look at several significant factors:

1. *Family size.* It is obvious that one needs more money to feed and clothe six children than two children.
2. *Geographic area.* Cost of living varies according to area.
3. *Price of home and neighborhood.* The more expensive the house and neighborhood, the more it costs a family to live there.
4. *Borrowers' living pattern.* Not all borrowers are created equal. All have their own lifestyle. When considering the question, "Is this enough to live on?" we must consider how the particular family lives. An older couple with no children will likely require less income than a large family. To do a proper job of qualifying, we must consider these factors. It is easy to think about, but in practice difficult to apply, because it is not so simple to obtain the facts. However, there are clues that help. Looking at previous housing expenses and how much the borrowers were able to save is a good clue as to how they live. The number of debts and size of each also give a good indication of their lifestyle.

A number of factors affect how much money is needed to support a family. We have listed some basic ones, and you can probably think of more. The VA considers each case to determine how much a prospective home buyer will need. The Department of Labor provides statistics regarding cost of living for various family sizes.

Going back to our sample case, the Smiths have $1,888 left over to support their family. Based on the geographic area, we use guides provided by VA residual income tables, which vary by region. In the Western Region the residual table is as follows:

Family Size	Amount Needed
1	$491
2	823
3	990
4	1,117
5	1,158
6+	Add $80 for each additional family member up to 7

Using the guide, Mr. and Mrs. Smith with their two children need $1,117 a month to qualify. The amount needed is of course subject to periodic increases as cost of living increases. They actually have $1,888; therefore they would qualify under the residual income method.

Phase 2: VA Income Ratio Application

The income ratio is determined by taking the monthly housing expenses—principal, interest, property taxes, insurance, and long-term debts—and dividing this by the gross monthly income. If this ratio is 41 percent or less (considered the perfect ratio), the borrowers qualify. If the ratio is above 41 percent, then the VA underwriter, in order to justify the loan, must look at any compensating factors (see below for what constitutes compensating factors). The VA allows 41 percent ratios because it includes items other than those used by conventional lenders.

In the case of the Smith family, we show:

$$\frac{\text{Housing Payment and Long-Term Debt}}{\text{Gross Monthly Income}} = \frac{\$2,181}{\$5,300} = 41.2\%$$

Based on the general guideline of 41 percent or less, the Smiths would qualify, especially with compensating factors. On the other hand, if we were to add $250 a month for babysitting, this ratio would increase to 45.9 percent, which may be pushing the envelope for approval, even with compensating factors.

VA administrators stress that VA underwriting standards are guidelines and that they are willing to review individual veteran borrowers who do not automatically qualify, similar to the **compensating factors** considered by the FHA. Examples of compensating factors include larger-than-normal down payment, insignificant use of credit cards, no vehicle payments, substantial net worth, and stable work experience and history and more than the minimum required residual income, as in this case with the Smiths. The VA uses the tightest qualifying standards in lending due to the lack of initial equity.

Cal-Vet

The qualifying procedure used by Cal-Vet is as follows: From gross income, subtract federal and state income taxes and Social Security to arrive at **adjusted gross income**. Housing expense is arrived at by adding principal, interest, taxes, property and disability insurance, maintenance, and utilities. Next, long-term debts, which are any debts that will take longer than 10 months to pay off, are totaled and subtracted. The remaining income is then divided by the adjusted gross income to determine the relationship between that and the amount of money left over. This residual should be at least 50 percent of adjusted gross, though under some circumstances it can be less. This is merely a guide, since Cal-Vet looks closely at the balance of funds left over to determine if they are sufficient to support the family.

9.5 WHAT IS INCOME?

We have learned how a lender determines if a borrower earns enough to qualify for a loan. The next consideration is what income lenders include. There is no question that income from regular employment is included, but do lenders count income from overtime, part-time work, or sales commissions? To be counted as stable, income must normally be earned in the same or similar occupation for at least two years. This section covers how lenders look at a variety of income sources.

FNMA and FHLMC

The Federal National Mortgage Association (FNMA) and Federal Home Loan Mortgage Corporation (FHLMC) greatly influence the qualification process. First, they affect the sale and purchase of qualifying loans. While borrowers do not deal directly with either FNMA or FHLMC, these two agencies purchase, via the secondary market (discussed in Chapter 7), the bulk of conventional, and conforming loan limit loans.

Second, loans sold to either FNMA or FHLMC must comply with the qualifying ratios of the purchasing agency. Consequently there is greater standardization and uniformity in the lenders' qualifying process with the expectation of selling loans to either of the big players.

Fannie Mae loan limits were re-established in late 2013. The conforming limits had not changed in several years, but the high-balance limits did change from a high of $725,500 to the current maximums noted below. High balance mortgages are subject to unique eligibility requirements in preparation for sale to Fannie Mae.

Units	General Loan Limits	High Cost Area
1	$417,000	$625,500
2	$533,850	$800,775
3	$645,300	$967,950
4	$801,950	$1,202,925

Commissioned People and Tradespeople

Commissioned people do not earn a set figure each month. Since their income varies over the year, they must be judged on the basis of annualized earnings. Lenders usually look at the earnings over the last two to three years, as documented by tax returns. Some commissioned people incur expenses that are not reimbursed by the employer. These expenses, shown on Schedule A of the 1040 tax returns, must be subtracted from income to arrive at a true income figure. Lenders require income tax returns from commissioned people to verify incomes.

Tradespeople, such as carpenters and painters, are treated basically the same as commissioned salespeople. The lender determines the stability of income over the previous two years by means of W-2 forms and/or tax returns. If considerable variance in income occurred, the lender will often average the income over the past two years. Hourly rates are not used because employment may not have been regular and full time during the year.

Overtime and Bonus

Lenders are reluctant to include overtime because, in most cases, it is not consistent and dependable. If borrowers can prove that they will continue to work overtime in the future, lenders will consider overtime pay. In other words, the borrower must have had consistent overtime in the past two years and must have a job that demands overtime. A good example would be a police officer working as a detective, since the nature of the job consistently requires overtime. Other examples include firefighters, grocery clerks, truck drivers, and other utility employees.

Bonus income counts only if the lender believes it will continue in the future. A past record of consistent bonuses is the main way to prove it will continue and can be documented with past tax returns. How many years are required to show that a bonus is consistent? This is a matter of lender policy, though most lenders require at least two years of bonus pay before they include it as income.

Part-Time Work

At one time, earnings from part-time work were not counted by lenders. The Federal Equal Credit Opportunity Act specifically prohibits lenders from discounting income solely because it is part-time. For example, if a borrower works only 20 hours a week, the income must be counted if the job is stable. Many people work multiple jobs, some being part-time. In order to provide the benefit of this income, lenders will average part-time employment income over the past two years.

Spousal/Alimony and Child Support

Income from alimony and child support must be counted by the lender if the borrower can provide a court order and a history of consistent payments. However, as will be demonstrated in Chapter 10, under the Equal Credit Opportunity Act borrowers need not reveal such income, and lenders cannot ask about receipt of income from either child support or alimony. However, a lender can ask about payment of child support or alimony for long-term debt purposes.

Pensions and Social Security

Income from pensions and Social Security are counted if such sources are expected to continue on a steady basis. Copies of pension plans are required. Because this income may not always be fully taxable, lenders allow the amount to be grossed up using a 1.15 to 1.25 percent factor.

Military Personnel

Military personnel receive extra pay for quarters, clothing, and rations in addition to their base pay. When qualifying someone in the military, all of these extras are added to arrive at the true income. In addition, lenders take into account that military personnel receive free medical and other services.

Income from Real Estate

Lenders must determine if a rental property produces positive or negative cash flow. This is determined via a calculation in which the gross income times 75 percent less principal and interest payments, taxes, insurance, and any other operating expenses identifies the usable income for qualifying purposes. While the Schedule E of the tax returns can sometimes be used to determine cash flow, the predominant method is the 75 percent calculation. Positive cash flow is added to income, but negative cash flow is regarded as a long-term debt in determining qualifying ratios.

The cash flow generated by an investment in a single-family dwelling depends largely on the amount of down payment used in the purchase. Without a sizeable down payment, an investment in a single-family dwelling will most likely show a negative cash flow.

When a person wishes to buy and occupy a unit in a two-, three-, or four-unit building, knowing how the income from the rental units will be factored into the qualifying ratio is important.

The answer will vary by lender, but most lenders will count the income after subtracting a realistic figure for expenses and vacancy factor. Regardless of the type of financing, most lenders will require several months' reserves (e.g. additional liquid funds available at close of escrow) based upon the expected monthly payment debt for each unit. The reserve requirement is usually 6 months and sometimes 12 months times the expected debt. Units are a riskier investment and experience vacancy, and thus the reserves represent additional protection for the lender's loan.

FHA is slightly different. Although allowing the purchase of units, the borrower must occupy one of the units. The net rental income must cover the mortgage payment. Vacant units will require the appraiser to determine a rental survey, and borrower qualification will be based upon this market rent. The reserve requirement is three months of the total mortgage payment. These funds must be the borrower's own and cannot be gift money.

Self-Employment

A self-employed borrower can present a bit of a challenge for qualifying purposes. While balance sheets and profit and loss statements used to be required, lenders now rely upon tax returns to determine a borrower's capacity to buy. Lenders will review two or three years of returns, examining the Schedule C of said returns for net income after all business expenses have been deducted. A business should show a growth pattern over the examined years, whereas a decline in income from year to year would represent a concern for a lender. Under review, depreciation identified in the Schedule C as well as all depreciation on real estate (usually reported on Schedule E) is not considered a cash expense and therefore is usually added back to net income.

Often the Schedule C represents an aggressive approach by the self-employed borrower to write off as much as possible in expenses and thereby reduce the taxable income. Suddenly, when applying for a loan, the bottom line taxable income figure may be insufficient for qualifying purposes. Because of this conundrum, the old stated income loans for self-employed borrowers made sense as long as there was corroborating evidence of assets to support the stated income. When these loans became available to salaried employees, resulting in unsupported exaggerated stated incomes, they were quickly referred to as liar loans.

While rumblings occur regarding the re-introduction of such financing, we have yet to see stated income loans revived. In the meantime, self-employed borrowers can represent a challenge for qualifying purposes.

9.6 CO-BORROWING

The technical name lenders give a sole borrower is mortgagor. If there is more than one borrower, we have **co-mortgagors** (often a married couple), sometimes called co-borrowers. Co-mortgagors sign the note and deed of trust and their names go on the title together. It should be noted that **co-signers** are not the same as co-mortgagors: Co-signers sign the note as guarantors but are not on the title, do not sign the trust deed, and therefore are rarely acceptable to real estate lenders. Co-mortgagors, often non-occupants of the property being purchased, can help with income qualifying but, contrary to common belief, will not help cure bad credit or other deficiencies in the occupant's loan profile.

Lenders include all income and all debts from all parties to qualify for the loan. If one or more of the co-mortgagors is not to occupy the home, then things can get complicated. Some loan options (e.g. VA, USDA) require that all co-mortgagors occupy the home. Other lenders will try to work with the parties by counting some of the non-occupying co-mortgagor's income after deducting the co-mortgagor's own housing expenses and other monthly debts. Some lenders require the non-occupying co-mortgagor to be a close relative. Fannie Mae and Freddie Mac, however, have dropped the close relative requirement, but insist that the co-mortgagor not be the seller, builder, real estate broker, or any party who has an interest in the sales transaction. In short, the issue of non-occupying co-mortgagor is fluid and constantly changing and it is difficult to give any definitive guidelines.

All co-mortgagors, but particularly those who participate to strengthen the loan qualification of a primary borrower, need be aware of the credit ramifications that accompany co-borrowing.

9.7 AFTER INCOME, WHAT THEN?

Stability of Income

After a lender has determined whether a borrower earns enough money, the next step is to analyze the stability of that income. To accomplish this, lenders look at such things as:

1. *Length of time on the job.* Lenders apply flexibility and common sense in determining what represents sufficient time on the job.

The generally accepted criterion is a minimum of two years in the same job or line of work. College graduates with a degree and a new job in their field of study are considered to have had two years of experience, and the new position will be acceptable for qualifying purposes.

Another exception would be an engineer who has been on the job for one month, with prior work in another company for five years, also as an engineer. The new job was an advancement and it pays a higher salary. A lender would qualify this engineer because both jobs are in the same line of work and the new job is an advancement. In this case, the borrower may be required to provide a letter from the employer that the likelihood of continued employment is good.

2. *Type of job.* The type of work a person does also determines the stability of income. In the past, highly skilled individuals whose skills have been in demand, such as a physician, nurse, civil service position, or teacher typically did not have to worry about a job. As job losses mounted and unemployment levels increased starting in 2008 and 2009, lenders had to take a more cautious view of all employment. While not considered unstable, these traditionally safe jobs were lost along with traditionally non-stable jobs, like construction work.

Self-employed borrowers are also carefully scrutinized to determine their stability of income. Lenders look at the length of time they have been in business, the net income, the financial condition of the business, and the general prospects for the particular type of business.

3. *Age of the borrower.* Lenders at one time had a rule that said the age of the borrower plus the term of the loan could not exceed age 65, the normal retirement age. Lenders were understandably concerned about how the borrower was going to make the payments after retirement. This made the acquisition of a 30-year mortgage nearly impossible after the age of 35. Age discrimination is illegal, making it alone no longer a factor in the approval process. If the borrower is near retirement age a lender may seek retirement income information which is often a combination of pension, social security and/or investments. Age discrimination is illegal making it alone no longer a factor in the approval process.

Borrower's Assets

In addition to determining a borrower's income and the stability of those earnings, lenders analyze the borrower's assets. Identifying the source of the funds to be used for down payment and closing costs is important for two reasons:

1. To assure that there is no undisclosed debt for having borrowed money
2. To determine that the funds are legal

This "sourcing funds" became more complicated with the war on drugs campaign and the need to assure lenders that no funds were obtained from illegal activities. This latter requirement was especially critical in that the government ruled that "any property obtained with the use of illegal funds (mostly interpreted as having come from illegal drug activity) could be confiscated with no compensation of the mortgage debt to the lender."

For a time, the result was that every bank deposit was scrutinized and had to be explained and sourced. The rules more recently were relaxed and more common sense prevails with only larger deposits requiring to be explained. Funds from sale of property, liquidation of assets (e.g., stocks or bonds) and gift funds are all legitimate sources of funds.

Some buyers receive money for a down payment from their parents. The funds must be identified as a gift and not a loan and must be verified via a **"gift letter"** containing certain information, perhaps the most important being the phrase this is a gift and need not be repaid. In most cases, the borrower must document the gift with a cancelled check or other evidence showing that the funds came from the parents' account and were not borrowed. Most recent rules require a bank statement to verify funds available for gifting.

The down payment funds in most government loan options can be gift funds. Conventional loans now accept the initial down payment as gift and no longer require such funds to be seasoned in the borrower's account.

The amount and type of assets a borrower has will influence lenders. If the borrower has substantial liquid assets (called reserves), lenders feel more secure, realizing that, with ample assets, a borrower will be able to continue making the loan payments even if some problems arise. Borrowers with ample bank accounts or other assets are generally viewed as living within their means, conservative in financial affairs, and possessing the ability to accumulate and manage money.

9.8 DESIRE TO PAY

It was stated earlier that there are two major considerations in qualifying. One is the ability or capacity of the borrower to pay, which has been discussed. The other is the borrower's **desire (or willingness) to pay**. It is difficult to determine the borrower's desire to continue making payments once the loan has been granted. Although such desire is implied when applying for a loan, the lender seeks something more tangible than the borrower's *intent*. The following are some indicators with which lenders attempt to measure a borrower's desire.

Past Payment Record

People tend to develop specific credit patterns. How a borrower has paid debts in the past is usually a good indication of what can be expected in the future. If borrowers have paid debts on time in the past, they will likely continue paying on time. On the other hand, if they had problems paying debts in the past, chances are that they will have problems in the future. Reliance upon automated credit evaluation systems has made it much more difficult to "explain" credit blemishes. Loan underwriters, in the past, could ignore the occasional blemish, focusing instead on the overall credit history of the borrower. Credit scoring has mostly replaced this common sense method of credit evaluation.

If the borrower has owned a home before, the lender is particularly interested in the previous payment record. The reasoning has always been that past payment records on a previous mortgage loan are the best indication of what can be expected in the future. This may no longer be true. Historic levels of foreclosures resulting from numerous causes including, among others, an inability to meet rising loan payments because of loss of employment coupled with the inability to sell because of the loss of home equity resulted in loan defaults in otherwise very responsible borrowers.

In today's environment, credit challenged buyers face time frame obstacles in their quest to again obtain home financing. The guidelines for this path to recovery have been a moving target with revisions occurring regularly. Each type of loan option has its own requirements including numerous additional details to determine when a borrower recovering from a foreclosure, short sale, or bankruptcy will be eligible for a new home loan.

The current general rule for conventional loans is four years, and the government options are usually three years from the blemish until eligibility can be restored. While extenuating circumstances can reduce the wait period, this usually refers only to the death of the primary wage earner, long term uninsured illness, or other documented catastrophic occurrence. Agencies have hinted at considering a reduction in waiting period to two years and one year respectively for conventional and government loans. Most past problems were the result of the financial crises, and prospective buyers will be required to wait the full time periods.

Confusion occurred in the past when credit blemishes were identified as having occurred because of circumstances beyond the control of the borrower. Unfortunately, any of the above blemishes as a result of the financial crises are not classified as beyond the borrower's control. It should be noted that foreclosure or short sale, etc. as a result of divorce is not considered an extenuating circumstance.

By 2015, some of the early victims of the crises were becoming eligible but still found the approval process confusing and frustrating. Some felt that the rules denying potential borrowers who were clearly victims of an economic disaster (many with otherwise great credit) from purchasing sooner contributed to the slow housing recovery.

Of all the lending sources, FHA had introduced a refinance program for those borrowers in negative equity positions. Available through December 2016, the guidelines were detailed and the program has had questionable results.

People who have had bankruptcies are a special problem. They have had credit failures. It is possible for them to get another loan, but it is much more difficult because bankruptcy is usually regarded as an inability to accumulate and manage money.

In considering those who have had a bankruptcy, lenders want to know the type of bankruptcy. Was it a liquidation (Chapter 7) bankruptcy or a Chapter 13 bankruptcy? Under a Chapter 13 bankruptcy, also called the wage-earner's bankruptcy, the individual pays off all creditors in full under a schedule approved by the bankruptcy court. The debtor makes payments to a court-appointed trustee, who, in turn, makes the payments to the creditors over a two- to three-year period. Lenders look at someone who opted for a Chapter 13 bankruptcy with more leniency, and a borrower under some circumstances can acquire a loan while making payments on said bankruptcy as long as he or she can otherwise qualify.

Unfortunately, the credit scoring system no longer differentiates the reason for the bankruptcy. It makes no difference to the computer scoring whether it was due to circumstances beyond the borrower's control or due to poor financial management. While the answer used to be weighed in the lender's loan decision, that is no longer the case. This seems especially harsh in that statistics suggest that many borrowers absorbed greater debt and/or neglected some credit debt in their attempt to make mortgage payments. In too many cases borrowers were required to make decisions regarding which bills to pay with reduced income and mounting debt. Bankruptcy was the last resort.

The same three or four year period (or anticipated reduced time frame) noted above must elapse from the date of the discharge of the bankruptcy before eligibility for a new loan can be restored. Another requirement is that borrowers have established good credit since the bankruptcy.

Lenders want evidence that the buyer is paying existing debts on a timely basis. Missed payments on a credit obligation following a bankruptcy is often sufficient cause for a loan denial. Under a Chapter 13 bankruptcy, payments to the trustee would serve as a credit reference.

Credit Scoring—FICO

Credit scoring has become the accepted method of evaluating an applicant's credit history for the purpose of determining the probability of repayment of debts. The credit scoring method is usually referred to as FICO, from Fair Isaac Corporation. This type of credit analysis has been in use for many years by users of credit information for purposes other than real estate loans, such as automobile credit purchases.

Scoring ranges from about 300 to about 900, with the lower scores indicating a greater likelihood of default. During the subprime era, credit scores as low as 580 were common. In an effort to improve loan performance after the economic collapse, eligible scores increased to 660 and higher (580 credit scores are again loan eligible in some cases as of mid-2015). Risk-based pricing (see the Case & Point in Chapter 6) was introduced and credit scores became one of the criteria, along with loan-to-value and type of loan, that was evaluated for pricing a loan. Lower credit scores resulted in the borrower being penalized with having a higher interest rate to offset the risk.

The three major reporting agencies/repositories are *Equifax*, *Experian*, and *Trans Union*—and different scores can be disclosed by each of them, indicating differences in attitudes by the reporting companies. Also, various firms that extend credit to consumers may not report to all companies. The lender's copy of the report includes the scores from all three repositories. The borrower's middle score is used in determining loan eligibility. Borrowers now have the right to see their scores. Under the Federal Fair and Accurate Credit Transaction (FACT) Act, everyone is entitled to a free copy of their credit report once a year, thus helping to keep tabs on credit scores and guard against identity theft.

More than 30 underwriting factors are taken into consideration in arriving at a FICO score. The number of credit accounts is reviewed. Having either too many accounts, especially if opened in the past 12 months, or too few accounts is not considered good—the lender wants to know the ability of the borrower to manage credit payments.

If late payments turn up, such as 30, 60, or 90 days late within the preceding two years, if there are current delinquencies, or if credit has been used to its maximum allowance, scores drop. How long the credit has been established is important, since the lender must be in a position to evaluate its use.

If there are collections, judgments, or write-offs, they must be considered. A definite concern is bankruptcy, as well as the type of bankruptcy (Chapter 7 or Chapter 13) and how much time has lapsed since the filing. An older bankruptcy with clean credit for the past several years is acceptable as long as credit scores have sufficiently improved.

The number of credit inquiries, particularly recently, are taken into consideration in the ratings. Too many unused accounts with zero balances (called available credit) provide opportunities for use, which could be detrimental to the borrower's score.

The adoption of risk-based pricing models (see above) benefited the higher-scoring borrowers and accommodated the risk of lower scores in loan pricing. Whereas a 680 credit score had been considered quite good, by 2009 a 720 score was required to acquire the best loan terms and rates, and this later increased to 740 plus. As lenders have become more proficient at understanding what affects the computer scoring system, they can provide better guidance to prospective borrowers who want to improve low scores.

As of mid-2015, in its updated FICO scoring model, medical debt, under some circumstances, will be less impacting upon consumer credit scores. It was noted that medical bills can often go to collection while the consumer is waiting for insurance to pay the bill. Now, past paid medical debts, including those paid in collection, will not factor into the new scores. It has been determined that medical expenses are unique in that unpaid medical bills do not necessarily suggest that other bills will go unpaid. For that reason, unpaid medical debts will weigh less in the scoring protocol. While good news for consumers, we have yet to verify that the projected boost to scores actually occurs.

Motivation

When examining a borrower's desire to pay, we must also consider the borrower's motivation. Sometimes a strong desire on the part of the borrower to make the payments is one of the most important reasons for approving a loan. Among the things a lender considers when trying to determine motivation are the following:

1. *Down payment.* The amount of down payment heavily influences the borrower's desire to keep up loan payments. If you purchased a house for $300,000 and made a down payment of $100,000, you would do everything possible to maintain the payments.

If it became impossible to keep up the payments, you would sell the house. One way or another, you would not let the lender take your house by foreclosure: you would protect your $100,000 investment to the greatest extent possible.

On the other hand, if you had purchased the same property with little or no down payment, you would not be as motivated to maintain the payments. If you ran into financial problems, it might be easy to talk yourself into letting the lender take back the property. If you have no money invested in the property, you really have nothing to lose except your credit rating. You could easily decide to let the lender foreclose.

Lenders recognize the importance of the size of the down payment. As the down payment increases, the lender's risk decreases. The size of the down payment is one of the more important factors in determining whether a loan will be approved.

2. *Reason for buying.* When trying to determine the borrower's motivation, lenders also examine the reason for buying. Is the borrower buying the home for personal use or is the purchase an *investment* that is going to be rented? If the purchase is for personal use, the borrower is more likely to keep up the payments. If the purchase is an investment, the borrower may not have the same motivation.

9.9 WORKING WITH LENDERS

By now, you have learned that qualifying a borrower is not a precise mechanical function. A lender does not decide to say yes or no by looking at any one factor. The borrower's income, the stability of that income, and the credit record are all analyzed, and the decision is based on an overall impression of the borrower. While there are no hard and fast rules when it comes to qualifying, the inconsistencies among lenders' approval processes have been reduced considerably. Nevertheless, more than one person looking at the same loan and using the same qualifying standards can come up with different opinions. The human element cannot be fully eliminated—one must be able to recognize and learn how to work with it and learn the characteristics of the various lenders. While general guidelines are the same, some are more lenient than others, in the amount and type of documentation required. This is the main reason that loan originators use different lenders.

Every lender, if at all possible, would approve every loan submitted because it is not only more pleasant to approve loans than to reject them, but they make money only by making loans. Lenders prefer to say yes, but borrowers and real estate agents must make it easy for them to say yes.

What are some of the things that can make it easier to obtain a loan?

1. *Possibility.* Don't insult the lender with a loan that can't possibly be approved. For example, if the borrower declared bankruptcy a few months ago, don't try to force the loan through. You know what the answer will be. The lender will be irritated because you are wasting valuable time.

2. *Honesty.* Always be honest with the lender. If the borrower has had credit problems, he or she should level with the lender. If the borrower has a good reason, lenders will listen and try to help. If the borrower tries to hide credit problems, lenders will find out anyway after the credit report comes in.

3. *Cooperation.* Lenders ask for items that are necessary, so cooperate with them. Arguing with a lender as to why documents are needed does not get the loan approved. Different lenders may very well require different documentation.

4. *Lender input.* Do not be insulted if the lender says the borrower is not qualified for the loan. Ask the loan officer what you can do to make the borrower qualified. A good lender may have some helpful suggestions. For example, the loan officer may suggest a co-mortgagor, a larger down payment, or a reduction of long-term debt and may explore other ways of making the loan acceptable.

5. *Government-backed loans.* Most lenders today are FHA "direct endorsement" and VA automatic lenders that speed up the process as compared to when, in the past, loan packages had to be submitted directly to the agencies. It is rare today to have a loan submitted directly to the FHA or the VA. USDA loans have their own criteria, and the loan package, after underwriter review, is submitted to its own unique automated approval process. Sometimes the loan can be approved or disapproved depending on how well the information is presented. Be sure the lender you are working with has had experience processing FHA and VA loans.

6. *Exceptions and cover letters.* As with all loan submissions, a loan can sometimes be approved or denied depending upon how well the information is presented. If the borrower has loan weaknesses, loan officers must emphasize the borrower's strengths and be prepared to prove to the lender that the loan is a good risk. If one can present a convincing argument, backed up with written documentation, the borrower's chances of a loan approval may be enhanced.

Loan officers usually include a cover letter with the loan submission, in which the positives and the negatives and the reasons promoting loan approval are identified for the underwriter. A good cover letter, with accompanying documentation, can be persuasive when an underwriter begins the loan review. Rather than attempting to conceal loan weaknesses, the loan officer can tackle them head-on while explaining why they are not so important and/or why other aspects improve the quality of the loan submission.

Finally, if you are in doubt as to how to proceed with a particular loan, ask yourself this question: "If I were going to use my own money to make this loan, what would my attitude be?" You will be surprised at some of the answers. It will help you deal with lenders and understand them.

For additional information on how lenders view credit and what goes into a credit score, access the website of Fair Isaac through the link at www.myfico.com.

Chapter Summary

When qualifying a borrower, lenders try to answer the question "Will the borrower repay the loan on a timely basis?" Lenders qualify borrowers by analyzing their ability or capacity and their desire to pay.

An analysis of the ability to pay includes the amount and stability of income; the borrower's income is probably the most important factor in qualifying. Conventional lenders and the FHA use front- and back-end ratios when they qualify the borrower's income, while the VA uses an income ratio and residual methods. Cal-Vet looks for a residual or remaining income—after deducting for all housing debt, non-housing, long-term debt and disability insurance—that is at least 50 percent or more of adjusted income. The stability of income must also be considered. It is influenced by the length of time on the job and by the type of job.

Lenders measure a borrower's desire to pay partly by past credit performance. They also examine the borrower's motivation to continue making payments; the amount of down payment and credit score are the main measuring sticks.

One rule of thumb that applies to all lenders is that qualifying a borrower is a matter of applying guidelines with a great deal of judgment. Risk-based pricing models were introduced after the 2008 economic collapse.

Important Terms and Concepts

Adjusted gross income
Back-end ratio (bottom ratio)
Co-mortgagor
Compensating factors
Co-signer
Credit scoring
Desire to pay
Gift letter
Gross income
Long-term debt
Monthly payments
PITI
Qualifying ratio
Residual income
Total monthly expense

Reviewing Your Understanding

Questions for Discussion

1. What is the difference between "ability to pay" and "desire to pay"?
2. When trying to anticipate whether a borrower can be expected to make timely payments, what two questions must be answered for lenders?
3. Name the compensating factors lenders are most likely to consider when evaluating a borrower's risk level.
4. List four reasons why a borrower might have the income to qualify for a real estate loan but still be turned down by a lender.
5. How do real estate lenders count commissions? Part-time jobs? Alimony? Income from real estate investments?
6. Why are lenders concerned with a borrower's credit score? Will a past bankruptcy automatically disqualify a borrower from a real estate loan?

Multiple-Choice Questions

1. A monthly loan payment is called PITI. This stands for
    a. principal, interest, taxes, indebtedness.
    b. payments, including timed interest.
    c. past due, insurance, taxes, interest.
    d. principal, interest, taxes, insurance.

2. To arrive at adjusted gross income under Cal-Vet financing, the agency takes the gross income and subtracts
    a. long-term debts, including total housing expense.
    b. long-term debts, excluding housing expense.
    c. all voluntary payroll deductions.
    d. payroll taxes, including Social Security.

3. Given a gross income of $5,000, mortgage payments (PITI) of $1,400, and long-term monthly debts of $350, the monthly payment or front-end ratio is
   a. 15 percent.
   b. 28 percent.
   c. 35 percent.
   d. 41 percent.

4. Referring to Question 3, the back-end ratio is
   a. 35 percent.
   b. 28 percent.
   c. 7 percent.
   d. none of these.

5. Which of the following is considered a negative for credit-scoring purposes?
   a. A score of 800
   b. At least three current lines of credit
   c. No bankruptcy
   d. A former collection account paid in full

6. In qualifying a VA loan, the Department of Veterans Affairs deducts income taxes, Social Security, and retirement contributions from allowable gross income. The balance is called
   a. gross effective income.
   b. net effective income.
   c. net take-home pay.
   d. gross spendable income.

7. Which of these is likely to be the most important factor in qualifying a buyer for a loan?
   a. Amount of savings
   b. Type of job
   c. Number of dependents
   d. Adequacy and stability of income

8. You are applying for an FHA loan. Your gross income is $3,200 per month. The total monthly payment is $800. Another $600 is paid out monthly for long-term debts. The ratio of total mortgage payment to gross income is
   a. 32.8 percent.
   b. 25 percent.
   c. 43.8 percent.
   d. none of the above.

9. Using the data from Question 8, the total back-end ratio to gross income is
   a. 43.8 percent.
   b. 50 percent.
   c. 53.8 percent.
   d. none of the above.

10. In the process of making a loan, the loan officer will correlate the characteristics of the borrower, characteristics of the loan, and the characteristics of the property in making a decision to grant a loan. The most important consideration is
    a. property rental value.
    b. degree of risk.
    c. location of property.
    d. neighborhood.

11. The rules used by conventional lenders to qualify borrower-applicants
    a. are rigid and uniform throughout the industry.
    b. are all different with no two lenders being the same
    c. can be similar, with each lender setting its own flexible policies.
    d. are strictly governed by regulatory bodies.

12. In qualifying borrowers, conventional real estate lenders
    a. use ratios that relate monthly payments to income.
    b. generally will make loans if the circumstances appear reasonable.
    c. state that a loan is available to borrowers whose monthly payment does not exceed 50 percent of gross income.
    d. apply the 20 percent standard.

13. Income from overtime in regular occupations
    a. will not be considered by most lenders.
    b. is counted if it is stable and consistent.
    c. will be considered by a lender only to offset an equal amount of long-term debt.
    d. must be earned for at least three years before lenders will count it.

14. Income is considered stable by most lenders if
    a. it has been earned regularly for two years.
    b. the applicant has been in the same line of work for several years, even if he or she has been on a new job for one month.
    c. the type of occupation would normally warrant it.
    d. all of the above apply.

15. Regarding alternative loan options during the global crisis that had begun by 2005
    a. lenders were assured that loans granted to borrowers with good credit would be repaid.
    b. it was thought that escalating appreciation rates would protect lenders against foreclosure.
    c. most lenders deliberately made loans that might result in foreclosure.
    d. none of the above.

16. FNMA and FHLMC influence the borrower qualification process by
    a. buying qualifying loans.
    b. applying uniform qualifying ratios for all lenders.
    c. both (a) and (b).
    d. neither (a) nor (b).

17. When lenders are in the process of pre-approving a self-employed person for a loan, the lender will usually want to see
    a. two-three years of taxes including Schedule C.
    b. only the businesses last year of Profit and Loss Statements.
    c. the current Balance Sheet for the business.
    d. the W-2's of the potential client..

18. Each of the following is considered income except
    a. continuing spousal support.
    b. gifts from family members.
    c. positive cash flows from rentals.
    d. self-employment income.

19. Due to the subprime loan debacle, by 2009
    a. many borrowers were "upside down" or "under water," owing more than their homes were worth.
    b. short sales became commonplace.
    c. both (a) and (b) are correct.
    d. neither (a) nor (b) is correct.

20. Regarding loan qualification, risk-based pricing models include incentives predicated on
    a. loan-to-value ratio.
    b. whether property is to be used as a residence or investment.
    c. credit score.
    d. all of the above.

CASE & POINT

TILA-RESPA Integrated Disclosure (TRID) – New Forms Required

The primary purpose of the GFE accompanied by the Truth in Lending (TIL) form introduced in January 2010 was to provide clarity to borrowers regarding their estimated closing costs—in other words, to eliminate the last minute surprise regarding the fees and interest rate that too often accompanied home financing in the wild days leading up to the collapse in 2007–2008. By necessity, the new form addressed the yield spread premiums that became and continue to be popular. (See the Case & Point in Chapter 3 for YSP information.) Designed to promote easy borrower use in shopping for a loan offering the most attractive rate and fees, the form proved confusing for most consumers.

Many critics claimed that lumping all the brokerage closing costs into one amount allowed for easily misinforming the potential borrower. The lack of any margin for error on under-reporting estimated closing costs too often resulted in over-quoting, which also was misleading to consumers. (Note: over-disclosing as a protective device against under-quoting fees will no longer be allowed with the new regulations.) Loan originators developed their own methods for disclosing what they thought was a clearer representation of loan costs along with the required GFE form. Bottom line, borrowers had to trust the loan officer with whom they decided to work. The estimated costs, whether contained in a GFE or an estimated cost sheet, remained only as good as the veracity of the mortgage representative.

In response to the criticism, the CFPB is introducing a new three-page form called the Loan Estimate to replace the current initial GFE and TIL forms and an additional five-page Closing Disclosure replacing the final TIL and the current HUD-1 settlement statement. This integration of forms was implemented October 3rd, 2015. With a rule consisting of over 1,500 pages and representing numerous changes in the loan origination process, the expectation was that there would be initial confusion in adopting the new forms especially since there was originally no provision for any grace period allowing for unintentional errors in completing the new forms upon implementation. (In spite of the concerns, it should be noted that like previous rule changes, the industry is likely to adapt quickly and easily than expected.)

The new rule does not change the requirement for delivery of the initial Loan Estimate within three days of the acquisition of a loan application. The two critical elements identifying the receipt of a loan application which, in turn will trigger the three-day notice period, is denoting an address of the subject property along with an anticipated loan amount. The problem for mortgage originators is that they may not have sufficient other documentation to adequately declare the would-be borrower qualified to perform. In the past, many originators would not issue disclosures until they were in possession of most, if not all, documentation (i.e.; pay stubs, W2 forms, tax returns, bank statements, etc.) that confirmed a borrower's qualification. It made sense to wait until all borrower documentation was acquired before making a decision regarding the viability of the borrower's loan eligibility. Originators could now be compelled to issue a Loan Estimate without such confirmation of a borrower's ability to perform. A further complication is that the new rules prohibit over-disclosing of possible expenses as a protection against under-quoting fees.

Clarity around the reporting of the YSP to the buyer did not change with the newest forms. Although designed to promote easy borrower use in shopping for a loan offering the most attractive rate and fees, consumer confusion may still occur. As with the past GFE form, the rate of interest initially quoted with up-front disclosures may often not represent a locked-in rate. This will necessitate revised documentation when the rate is locked, identifying the revised terms. Since tolerance requirements are imposed in the regulations, while the rate could change, the accompanying fees may not be able to deviate, causing major concerns in paying the closing costs? The inability to over-quote the fees (noted above) to accommodate any such fee change may be a further complication.

The Mortgage Disclosure Improvement Act (MDIA) in which a waiting period between disclosure and incurring any cost, including an appraisal fee, is prohibited has not changed. This has the potential to delay the acquisition of an appraisal and thereby resulting in an unnecessary delay.

The *Change of Circumstance* form which was created by which changes to the loan amount, interest rate or a specific request by the borrower could be accommodated remains in place. Such changes most often include an increase or decrease in the appraised value or cost increases due to required repairs identified in the appraisal or inspection reports but can also include a change merely by borrower request. Any change must be documented, provided to the lender, and accompanied by a new disclosure. If a borrower was not confused initially by the forms, the issuance of several during the loan process, necessitated by any action noted above, could be greeted with consumer confusion.

Reluctant to proceed with loan processing without assurance that the borrower has ceased loan shopping upon receipt of the initial disclosure, the **Intent to Proceed** declaration form will be required. A **Certification of Receipt of the Loan Estimate** is a change wherein the past GFE form required no borrower signatures. For convenience, this certification is acceptable via e-consent.

To recap, the new Loan Estimate and Closing Disclosure do differ from the past disclosure forms. The timing of the disclosures, the reduction in fee tolerances for estimated costs and the fact that the Loan Estimate may be required prior to the acquisition of a borrower's fully documented loan request are the major changes. The Loan Estimate does appear more easily understood than the past GFE and TIL forms. But the TIL information is reduced to only two lines including the annual percentage rate (APR) and the total amount of interest to be paid over the loan term is designated as a percentage of the initial loan amount. It is this latter figure that may create the greater confusion for borrowers. At first glance, the amount of information, required under severe penalty to be accurate, seems daunting to both the lender and the consumer. Lenders and investors could face potential borrower law suits resulting from any misinformation. This will undoubtedly require all disclosure confirmation to be done via the lender/investor, further delaying the processing time for any loan request.

As with many new rules, regulations, and documentation, the industry adapted and these new rules will also be accommodated, but whether they merely create more unnecessary paperwork or really provide more clarity to consumers remains to be seen.

What is clear is that we have entered a lending phase that will continue to be impacted by additional regulation. It is laudable that authorities wish to promote better disclosure within the industry. The question is whether they will actually enforce the rules they have or continue to rely mostly upon the introduction of new forms in their efforts to mold industry behavior.

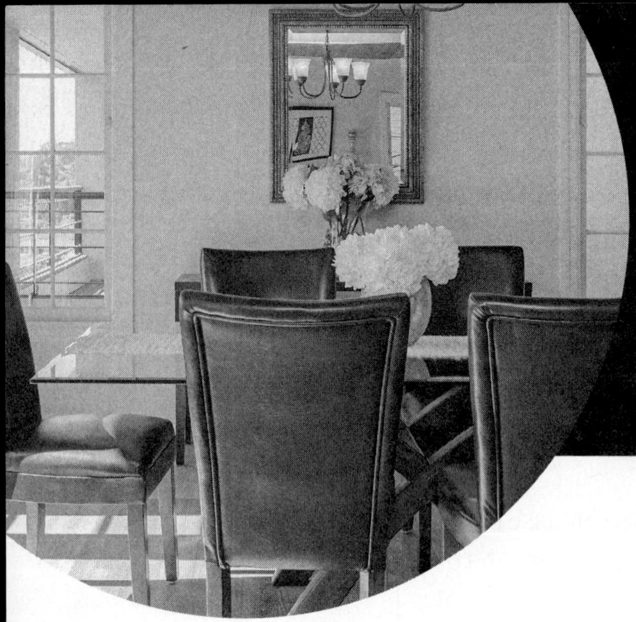

10

PROCESSING, CLOSING, AND SERVICING REAL ESTATE LOANS

OVERVIEW

This chapter describes how lenders process real estate loans using the loan application form and proceeding through a typical loan package. The loan approval process and the steps required to close the loan are discussed in detail. Finally, loan servicing, which occurs after the escrow closes, completes the discussion.

After completing this chapter, you will be able to:

- List the items that make up a loan package.
- Describe the process by which conventional, FHA, and VA loans are approved.
- List and explain borrowers' closing costs.
- Describe the difference between "assuming" a loan and taking the property "subject to" the loan.
- List rights that prospective borrowers have under the Fair Credit Reporting Act in the event that errors are shown in their credit reports.
- Cite the chief provisions of the Truth-in-Lending Law.

10.1 PROCESSING THE LOAN

Loan processing starts with the **loan application**. Most lenders use the FNMA/FHLMC standard application form shown as Figure 10.1.

After receiving the application and other requested documents, the lender can make a preliminary determination of the borrower's likelihood of qualifying for a loan. In many cases, the information is either forwarded to an underwriter or submitted to an automated qualifying program to acquire a preapproval. The preapproval identifies the conditions required from the borrower before final loan approval is obtained.

CHAPTER 10 Processing, Closing, and Servicing Real Estate Loans

FIGURE 10.1 FNMA/FHLMC residential loan application.

Uniform Residential Loan Application

This application is designed to be completed by the applicant(s) with the Lender's assistance. Applicants should complete this form as "Borrower" or "Co-Borrower," as applicable. Co-Borrower information must also be provided (and the appropriate box checked) when ☐ the income or assets of a person other than the Borrower (including the Borrower's spouse) will be used as a basis for loan qualification or ☐ the income or assets of the Borrower's spouse or other person who has community property rights pursuant to state law will not be used as a basis for loan qualification, but his or her liabilities must be considered because the spouse or other person has community property rights pursuant to applicable law and Borrower resides in a community property state, the security property is located in a community property state, or the Borrower is relying on other property located in a community property state as a basis for repayment of the loan.

If this is an application for joint credit, Borrower and Co-Borrower each agree that we intend to apply for joint credit (sign below):

_____ _____
Borrower   Co-Borrower

I. TYPE OF MORTGAGE AND TERMS OF LOAN

Mortgage Applied for:	☐ VA ☐ FHA	☐ Conventional ☐ USDA/Rural Housing Service	☐ Other (explain):	Agency Case Number	Lender Case Number
Amount $	Interest Rate %	No. of Months	Amortization Type:	☐ Fixed Rate ☐ GPM	☐ Other (explain): ☐ ARM (type):

II. PROPERTY INFORMATION AND PURPOSE OF LOAN

Subject Property Address (street, city, state & ZIP) — No. of Units

Legal Description of Subject Property (attach description if necessary) — Year Built

Purpose of Loan	☐ Purchase ☐ Refinance	☐ Construction ☐ Construction-Permanent	☐ Other (explain):	Property will be: ☐ Primary Residence ☐ Secondary Residence ☐ Investment

Complete this line if construction or construction-permanent loan.

Year Lot Acquired	Original Cost $	Amount Existing Liens $	(a) Present Value of Lot $	(b) Cost of Improvements $	Total (a + b) $

Complete this line if this is a refinance loan.

Year Acquired	Original Cost $	Amount Existing Liens $	Purpose of Refinance	Describe Improvements Cost: $	☐ made ☐ to be made

Title will be held in what Name(s) — Manner in which Title will be held — Estate will be held in: ☐ Fee Simple ☐ Leasehold (show expiration date)

Source of Down Payment, Settlement Charges, and/or Subordinate Financing (explain)

III. BORROWER INFORMATION

Borrower	Co-Borrower
Borrower's Name (include Jr. or Sr. if applicable)	Co-Borrower's Name (include Jr. or Sr. if applicable)
Social Security Number	Home Phone (incl. area code)	DOB (mm/dd/yyyy)	Yrs. School	Social Security Number	Home Phone (incl. area code)	DOB (mm/dd/yyyy)	Yrs. School
☐ Married ☐ Unmarried (include single, divorced, widowed) ☐ Separated	Dependents (not listed by Co-Borrower) no. ___ ages ___	☐ Married ☐ Unmarried (include single, divorced, widowed) ☐ Separated	Dependents (not listed by Borrower) no. ___ ages ___
Present Address (street, city, state, ZIP) ☐ Own ☐ Rent ___No. Yrs.	Present Address (street, city, state, ZIP) ☐ Own ☐ Rent ___No. Yrs.
Mailing Address, if different from Present Address	Mailing Address, if different from Present Address

If residing at present address for less than two years, complete the following:

Former Address (street, city, state, ZIP) ☐ Own ☐ Rent ___No. Yrs.	Former Address (street, city, state, ZIP) ☐ Own ☐ Rent ___No. Yrs.

IV. EMPLOYMENT INFORMATION

Borrower	Co-Borrower
Name & Address of Employer	☐ Self Employed	Yrs. on this job Yrs. employed in this line of work/profession	Name & Address of Employer	☐ Self Employed	Yrs. on this job Yrs. employed in this line of work/profession
Position/Title/Type of Business	Business Phone (incl. area code)	Position/Title/Type of Business	Business Phone (incl. area code)

If employed in current position for less than two years or if currently employed in more than one position, complete the following:

Uniform Residential Loan Application
Freddie Mac Form 65   7/05 (rev.6/09)   Page 1 of 5   Fannie Mae Form 1003   7/05 (rev.6/09)

FIGURE 10.1 (Continued)

Borrower	IV. EMPLOYMENT INFORMATION (cont'd)	Co-Borrower
Name & Address of Employer ☐ Self Employed	Dates (from – to)	Name & Address of Employer ☐ Self Employed	Dates (from – to)
	Monthly Income $		Monthly Income $
Position/Title/Type of Business	Business Phone (incl. area code)	Position/Title/Type of Business	Business Phone (incl. area code)
Name & Address of Employer ☐ Self Employed	Dates (from – to)	Name & Address of Employer ☐ Self Employed	Dates (from – to)
	Monthly Income $		Monthly Income $
Position/Title/Type of Business	Business Phone (incl. area code)	Position/Title/Type of Business	Business Phone (incl. area code)

V. MONTHLY INCOME AND COMBINED HOUSING EXPENSE INFORMATION

Gross Monthly Income	Borrower	Co-Borrower	Total	Combined Monthly Housing Expense	Present	Proposed
Base Empl. Income*	$	$	$	Rent	$	
Overtime				First Mortgage (P&I)		$
Bonuses				Other Financing (P&I)		
Commissions				Hazard Insurance		
Dividends/Interest				Real Estate Taxes		
Net Rental Income				Mortgage Insurance		
Other (before completing, see the notice in "describe other income," below)				Homeowner Assn. Dues		
				Other:		
Total	$	$	$	Total	$	$

* Self Employed Borrower(s) may be required to provide additional documentation such as tax returns and financial statements.

Describe Other Income   *Notice:* Alimony, child support, or separate maintenance income need not be revealed if the Borrower (B) or Co-Borrower (C) does not choose to have it considered for repaying this loan.

B/C		Monthly Amount
		$

VI. ASSETS AND LIABILITIES

This Statement and any applicable supporting schedules may be completed jointly by both married and unmarried Co-Borrowers if their assets and liabilities are sufficiently joined so that the Statement can be meaningfully and fairly presented on a combined basis; otherwise, separate Statements and Schedules are required. If the Co-Borrower section was completed about a non-applicant spouse or other person, this Statement and supporting schedules must be completed about that spouse or other person also.   Completed ☐ Jointly ☐ Not Jointly

ASSETS Description	Cash or Market Value	Liabilities and Pledged Assets. List the creditor's name, address, and account number for all outstanding debts, including automobile loans, revolving charge accounts, real estate loans, alimony, child support, stock pledges, etc. Use continuation sheet, if necessary. Indicate by (*) those liabilities, which will be satisfied upon sale of real estate owned or upon refinancing of the subject property.		
Cash deposit toward purchase held by:	$			
List checking and savings accounts below		LIABILITIES	Monthly Payment & Months Left to Pay	Unpaid Balance
Name and address of Bank, S&L, or Credit Union		Name and address of Company	$ Payment/Months	$
Acct. no.	$	Acct. no.		
Name and address of Bank, S&L, or Credit Union		Name and address of Company	$ Payment/Months	$
Acct. no.	$	Acct. no.		
Name and address of Bank, S&L, or Credit Union		Name and address of Company	$ Payment/Months	$
Acct. no.	$	Acct. no.		

Uniform Residential Loan Application
Freddie Mac Form 65   7/05 (rev. 6/09)

Page 2 of 5

Fannie Mae Form 1003   7/05 (rev.6/09)

FIGURE 10.1 (Continued)

VI. ASSETS AND LIABILITIES (cont'd)

Name and address of Bank, S&L, or Credit Union		Name and address of Company	$ Payment/Months	$
Acct. no.	$	Acct. no.		
Stocks & Bonds (Company name/ number & description)	$	Name and address of Company	$ Payment/Months	$
		Acct. no.		
Life insurance net cash value Face amount: $	$	Name and address of Company	$ Payment/Months	$
Subtotal Liquid Assets	$			
Real estate owned (enter market value from schedule of real estate owned)	$			
Vested interest in retirement fund	$			
Net worth of business(es) owned (attach financial statement)	$	Acct. no.		
Automobiles owned (make and year)	$	Alimony/Child Support/Separate Maintenance Payments Owed to:	$	
Other Assets (itemize)	$	Job-Related Expense (child care, union dues, etc.)	$	
		Total Monthly Payments	$	
Total Assets a.	$	Net Worth (a minus b) ▶ $	**Total Liabilities b.**	$

Schedule of Real Estate Owned (If additional properties are owned, use continuation sheet.)

Property Address (enter S if sold, PS if pending sale or R if rental being held for income) ▼	Type of Property	Present Market Value	Amount of Mortgages & Liens	Gross Rental Income	Mortgage Payments	Insurance, Maintenance, Taxes & Misc.	Net Rental Income
		$	$	$	$	$	$
Totals		$	$	$	$	$	$

List any additional names under which credit has previously been received and indicate appropriate creditor name(s) and account number(s):

Alternate Name	Creditor Name	Account Number

VII. DETAILS OF TRANSACTION

a.	Purchase price	$
b.	Alterations, improvements, repairs	
c.	Land (if acquired separately)	
d.	Refinance (incl. debts to be paid off)	
e.	Estimated prepaid items	
f.	Estimated closing costs	
g.	PMI, MIP, Funding Fee	
h.	Discount (if Borrower will pay)	
i.	Total costs (add items a through h)	

VIII. DECLARATIONS

If you answer "Yes" to any questions a through i, please use continuation sheet for explanation.

	Borrower	Co-Borrower
	Yes No	Yes No
a. Are there any outstanding judgments against you?	☐ ☐	☐ ☐
b. Have you been declared bankrupt within the past 7 years?	☐ ☐	☐ ☐
c. Have you had property foreclosed upon or given title or deed in lieu thereof in the last 7 years?	☐ ☐	☐ ☐
d. Are you a party to a lawsuit?	☐ ☐	☐ ☐
e. Have you directly or indirectly been obligated on any loan which resulted in foreclosure, transfer of title in lieu of foreclosure, or judgment? (This would include such loans as home mortgage loans, SBA loans, home improvement loans, educational loans, manufactured (mobile) home loans, any mortgage, financial obligation, bond, or loan guarantee. If "Yes," provide details, including date, name, and address of Lender, FHA or VA case number, if any, and reasons for the action.)	☐ ☐	☐ ☐

Uniform Residential Loan Application
Freddie Mac Form 65 7/05 (rev.6/09)   Fannie Mae Form 1003 7/05 (rev.6/09)

FIGURE 10.1 (Continued)

VII. DETAILS OF TRANSACTION		VIII. DECLARATIONS				
			Borrower		Co-Borrower	
		If you answer "Yes" to any question a through i, please use continuation sheet for explanation.	Yes	No	Yes	No
j.	Subordinate financing	f. Are you presently delinquent or in default on any Federal debt or any other loan, mortgage, financial obligation, bond, or loan guarantee?	☐	☐	☐	☐
k.	Borrower's closing costs paid by Seller	g. Are you obligated to pay alimony, child support, or separate maintenance?	☐	☐	☐	☐
l.	Other Credits (explain)	h. Is any part of the down payment borrowed?	☐	☐	☐	☐
		i. Are you a co-maker or endorser on a note?	☐	☐	☐	☐
m.	Loan amount (exclude PMI, MIP, Funding Fee financed)					
		j. Are you a U.S. citizen?	☐	☐	☐	☐
n.	PMI, MIP, Funding Fee financed	k. Are you a permanent resident alien?	☐	☐	☐	☐
o.	Loan amount (add m & n)	l. **Do you intend to occupy the property as your primary residence?** If "Yes," complete question m below.	☐	☐	☐	☐
p.	Cash from/to Borrower (subtract j, k, l & o from i)	m. Have you had an ownership interest in a property in the last three years?	☐	☐	☐	☐
		(1) What type of property did you own—principal residence (PR), second home (SH), or investment property (IP)?				
		(2) How did you hold title to the home— by yourself (S), jointly with your spouse (SP), or jointly with another person (O)?				

IX. ACKNOWLEDGEMENT AND AGREEMENT

Each of the undersigned specifically represents to Lender and to Lender's actual or potential agents, brokers, processors, attorneys, insurers, servicers, successors and assigns and agrees and acknowledges that: (1) the information provided in this application is true and correct as of the date set forth opposite my signature and that any intentional or negligent misrepresentation of this information contained in this application may result in civil liability, including monetary damages, to any person who may suffer any loss due to reliance upon any misrepresentation that I have made on this application, and/or in criminal penalties including, but not limited to, fine or imprisonment or both under the provisions of Title 18, United States Code, Sec. 1001, et seq.; (2) the loan requested pursuant to this application (the "Loan") will be secured by a mortgage or deed of trust on the property described in this application; (3) the property will not be used for any illegal or prohibited purpose or use; (4) all statements made in this application are made for the purpose of obtaining a residential mortgage loan; (5) the property will be occupied as indicated in this application; (6) the Lender, its servicers, successors or assigns may retain the original and/or an electronic record of this application, whether or not the Loan is approved; (7) the Lender and its agents, brokers, insurers, servicers, successors, and assigns may continuously rely on the information contained in the application, and I am obligated to amend and/or supplement the information provided in this application if any of the material facts that I have represented herein should change prior to closing of the Loan; (8) in the event that my payments on the Loan become delinquent, the Lender, its servicers, successors or assigns may, in addition to any other rights and remedies that it may have relating to such delinquency, report my name and account information to one or more consumer reporting agencies; (9) ownership of the Loan and/or administration of the Loan account may be transferred with such notice as may be required by law; (10) neither Lender nor its agents, brokers, insurers, servicers, successors or assigns has made any representation or warranty, express or implied, to me regarding the property or the condition or value of the property; and (11) my transmission of this application as an "electronic record" containing my "electronic signature," as those terms are defined in applicable federal and/or state laws (excluding audio and video recordings), or my facsimile transmission of this application containing a facsimile of my signature, shall be as effective, enforceable and valid as if a paper version of this application were delivered containing my original written signature.

Acknowledgement. Each of the undersigned hereby acknowledges that any owner of the Loan, its servicers, successors and assigns, may verify or reverify any information contained in this application or obtain any information or data relating to the Loan, for any legitimate business purpose through any source, including a source named in this application or a consumer reporting agency.

Borrower's Signature X	Date	Co-Borrower's Signature X	Date

X. INFORMATION FOR GOVERNMENT MONITORING PURPOSES

The following information is requested by the Federal Government for certain types of loans related to a dwelling in order to monitor the lender's compliance with equal credit opportunity, fair housing and home mortgage disclosure laws. You are not required to furnish this information, but are encouraged to do so. The law provides that a lender may not discriminate either on the basis of this information, or on whether you choose to furnish it. If you furnish the information, please provide both ethnicity and race. For race, you may check more than one designation. If you do not furnish ethnicity, race, or sex, under Federal regulations, this lender is required to note the information on the basis of visual observation and surname if you have made this application in person. If you do not wish to furnish the information, please check the box below. (Lender must review the above material to assure that the disclosures satisfy all requirements to which the lender is subject under applicable state law for the particular type of loan applied for.)

BORROWER	☐ I do not wish to furnish this information	**CO-BORROWER**	☐ I do not wish to furnish this information
Ethnicity:	☐ Hispanic or Latino ☐ Not Hispanic or Latino	**Ethnicity:**	☐ Hispanic or Latino ☐ Not Hispanic or Latino
Race:	☐ American Indian or Alaska Native ☐ Asian ☐ Black or African American ☐ Native Hawaiian or Other Pacific Islander ☐ White	**Race:**	☐ American Indian or Alaska Native ☐ Asian ☐ Black or African American ☐ Native Hawaiian or Other Pacific Islander ☐ White
Sex:	☐ Female ☐ Male	**Sex:**	☐ Female ☐ Male

To be Completed by Loan Originator:
This information was provided:
☐ In a face-to-face interview
☐ In a telephone interview
☐ By the applicant and submitted by fax or mail
☐ By the applicant and submitted via e-mail or the Internet

Loan Originator's Signature X		Date
Loan Originator's Name (print or type)	Loan Originator Identifier	Loan Originator's Phone Number (including area code)
Loan Origination Company's Name	Loan Origination Company Identifier	Loan Origination Company's Address

Uniform Residential Loan Application
Freddie Mac Form 65   7/05 (rev.6/09)   Page 4 of 5   Fannie Mae Form 1003   7/05 (rev.6/09)

FIGURE 10.1 (Continued)

CONTINUATION SHEET/RESIDENTIAL LOAN APPLICATION		
Use this continuation sheet if you need more space to complete the Residential Loan Application. Mark **B** f or Borrower or **C** for Co-Borrower.	Borrower:	Agency Case Number:
	Co-Borrower:	Lender Case Number:

I/We fully understand that it is a Federal crime punishable by fine or imprisonment, or both, to knowingly make any false statements concerning any of the above facts as applicable under the provisions of Title 18, United States Code, Section 1001, et seq.

Borrower's Signature X	Date	Co-Borrower's Signature X	Date

Uniform Residential Loan Application
Freddie Mac Form 65 7/05 (rev.6/09)

Page 5 of 5

Fannie Mae Form 1003 7/05 (rev.6/09)

FIGURE 10.1 (Continued)

INSTRUCTIONS

Uniform Residential Loan Application

The lender uses this form to record relevant financial information about an applicant who applies for a conventional one- to four-family mortgage. Roman numerals in these instructions correspond to the sections on the form.

Lenders must use the PDF dated 6/09 for mortgage loans applications taken on or after July 1, 2010.

Printing Instructions

We provide Form 1003 in an electronic format that prints as a letter size document. However, lenders may print Form 1003 as a legal size document or with different fonts or margins that may affect pagination; we have no specific standards for the number or size of pages the form may have. Consequently, the number and size of pages will not affect compliance with Fannie Mae requirements pertaining to use of the Uniform Residential Loan Application, provided that the content of the form has not been materially altered. When printing this form, you must use the "shrink to fit" option in the Adobe Acrobat print dialogue box.

Instructions

The lender may accept applications taken during a face-to-face interview, over the telephone, through the mail, or via the Internet. The lender should complete all blanks and attach any separate exhibits, details, or statements that are relevant to underwriting the mortgage. The borrower(s) must sign the original application at the time it is completed. If the application is taken over the telephone or via the Internet, the borrower(s) must sign the completed application as soon as possible thereafter. However, an electronic signature or facsimile of the borrower's signature is acceptable as indicated in the "Acknowledgment and Agreement" section of the application. The lender should retain the original application with the supporting information provided by the borrower(s). Before or at the loan closing, the borrower(s) must sign the final application that the lender prepares based on its verification of the information that the borrower(s) provided in the original application.

The instructions at the top of Form 1003 are consistent with the permissible inquiries that creditors are allowed to make under the Equal Credit Opportunity Act (ECOA). Although ECOA permits the lender in a community property state to obtain information regarding the liabilities of a borrower's spouse even though he or she is not applying for the mortgage and his or her income will not be considered for loan qualification purposes, we do not require the lender to obtain the information. This also means that in states where another person shares community property rights with the applicant, the lender does not need to include information on that person's liabilities if he or she is not an applicant.

Fannie Mae Form 1003 Instructions (Form Rev. 6/09, Instructions 12/13)

FIGURE 10.1 (Continued)

> Note: The following instructions highlight certain sections of the form.
>
> **Introductory Statement**
>
> We recognize that the introductory paragraph of Form 1003 differs slightly from the introductory paragraph in the Uniform Residential Loan Application found on Freddie Mac's website, Freddie Mac Form 65. However, because we have determined that these differences are not material, Fannie Mae will deem either version to comply with our requirements for use of the Uniform Residential Loan Application.
>
> **V. Monthly Income and Combined Housing Expense Information**
>
> Gross Monthly Income: If the net cash flow for an investment property is a positive number, it should be listed as "net rental income." If it is a negative number, it must be included in the applicant's monthly obligations. If the property is a two- to four-unit property for which the applicant occupies one of the units as a principal residence, the monthly rental income should be listed as "net rental income."
>
> Combined Monthly Housing Expense: The present monthly housing expenses for the borrower and the co-borrower should be listed on a combined basis. The proposed monthly housing expense for a two- to four-unit property in which the applicant will occupy a unit as a principal residence should reflect the monthly payment (PITIA) for the subject property. For all one- to four-unit investment properties the present monthly housing expense should reflect the applicant's principal residence.
>
> **VI. Assets and Liabilities**
>
> When the borrower's and co-borrower's assets and liabilities are not sufficiently joined to make a combined statement meaningful, a separate Statement of Assets and Liabilities (Form 1003A) should be completed for the co-borrower.
>
> **VII. Details of Transaction**
>
> The purchase price shown on Line "a" under the "Details of Transaction" should not include any discounts or rebates or other allowances paid or allowed to the purchaser. For refinancing, the amount being refinanced should be shown on Line "d" -- Refinance. The figure should include the total amount of all existing liens plus the costs of improvements that have been -- or will be -- made. Lines "a", "b", and "c" should not be used to describe a refinance transaction.
>
> **VIII. Declarations**
>
> Noncitizen Applicants: If an applicant indicates in his response to Question J that he is not a U.S. citizen, and also indicates in his response to Question K that he is not a permanent resident alien, the lender may wish to ask whether he is a nonpermanent resident alien or otherwise is lawfully present in the United States.
>
> Fannie Mae Form 1003 Instructions (Form Rev. 6/09, Instructions 12/13)

FIGURE 10.1 (Continued)

X. Information for Government Monitoring Purposes

This section is included to aid the federal government in monitoring compliance with equal credit opportunity, fair housing and home mortgage disclosure laws. Supplying this information is strictly voluntary on the part of the applicant, but lenders should ask all applicants to provide it, including those who apply by telephone and through the Internet, and should describe the reason for collecting this data. Race and ethnicity are separate categories, and although the lender should ask applicants to furnish information for both, applicants may furnish one but not the other. Note that there is no longer a place for applicants to indicate race as "Other" but applicants may check as many races as apply.

The Home Mortgage Disclosure Act and its implementing Regulation C generally require Lenders to collect sex, race, and ethnicity data on all applications.

When an application is taken in person and an applicant elects not to provide some or all of this information, federal law requires the lender to note the applicant's sex, ethnicity, and race on the form, based on the lender's visual observation or the applicant's surname. To aid in identifying applicants who may be of Hispanic ethnicity and who elect not to self-identify, the lender may wish to consult the list of Spanish surnames developed by the U.S. Bureau of the Census. Furthermore, the lender may wish to advise the applicant that he may complete or change the information in this section after the application is approved, at any time up until closing.

To Be Completed By Interviewer

The interviewer must complete this portion of the form to indicate the method used to take the application and to provide the name and telephone number of the interviewer, as well as his or her employer's name and address.

To Be Completed By Loan Originator (for PDF dated 06/09 for mortgage loans applications taken on or after January 1, 2010)

The loan originator must complete this portion of the form to indicate the method used to take the application and to provide the loan originator's name, ID, and telephone number, as well as his or her employer's name, company ID, and address.

Continuation Sheet/Residential Loan Application

Lenders may amend this section by including space to evidence intent to apply for joint credit. Other approaches, such as including this information on a separate document, are also acceptable to Fannie Mae, provided they meet the requirements of applicable law. Lenders should consult counsel to determine their alternatives.

Special Notice for Balloon Mortgages

For each balloon mortgage, the lender must insert a special notice regarding the nature of the balloon features on Form 1003 or in a separate attachment to the form.

Fannie Mae Form 1003 Instructions (Form Rev. 6/09, Instructions 12/13)

FIGURE 10.1 (Continued)

If an attachment is used, the borrower(s) must sign the attachment. The following language must be inserted, using capital letters:

"THIS LOAN MUST EITHER BE PAID IN FULL AT MATURITY OR REFINANCED TO A MARKET LEVEL FIXED-RATE MORTGAGE. YOU MUST REPAY THE ENTIRE PRINCIPAL BALANCE OF THE LOAN AND UNPAID INTEREST THEN DUE IF YOU DO NOT QUALIFY FOR THE CONDITIONAL RIGHT TO REFINANCE AS SPECIFIED IN THE NOTE ADDENDUM AND MORTGAGE RIDER. THE LENDER IS UNDER NO OBLIGATION TO REFINANCE THE LOAN IF QUALIFICATION CONDITIONS ARE NOT MET. YOU WILL, THEREFORE, BE REQUIRED TO MAKE PAYMENT OUT OF OTHER ASSETS THAT YOU MAY OWN, OR YOU WILL HAVE TO FIND A LENDER, WHICH MAY BE THE LENDER YOU HAVE THIS LOAN WITH, WILLING TO LEND YOU THE MONEY. IF YOU REFINANCE THIS LOAN AT MATURITY, YOU MAY HAVE TO PAY SOME OR ALL OF THE CLOSING COSTS NORMALLY ASSOCIATED WITH A NEW LOAN EVEN IF YOU OBTAIN REFINANCING."

For California Applications
California Civil Code 1812.30 (j) requires that credit applications clearly specify that the applicant, if married, may apply for a separate account. This requirement is not inconsistent with the language at the beginning of Form 1003.

Lenders may revise the description of the "Married" box in Section III for Borrowers and Co-Borrowers by adding "(includes registered domestic partners)." If lenders are unable to insert the language due to the format of the form, this language may be added to the continuation sheet or included as an attachment to Form 1003.

Fannie Mae Form 1003 Instructions (Form Rev. 6/09, Instructions 12/13)

Source: www.efanniemae.com

Armed with the preapproval, the lender starts the loan processing, which includes getting needed information to meet the lender's conditions, acquiring title and escrow information, and initiating the appraisal process (see the new Home Valuation Code of Conduct information in Chapter 8 Case & Point).

Qualifying the borrower continues as the lender receives the various required exhibits. Chapter 9 discussed the standards used to qualify a borrower. In this chapter, we will go step by step into how real estate lenders process and close loans.

Even though applications may vary in format and length, they generally ask the same basic questions regarding: (1) employment, (2) income, (3) assets, (4) debts, and (5) credit history. Many lenders use the FNMA 1003 form even if the loans are not intended to be sold in the secondary market.

Completing Loan Application Forms

The completed application form provides the lender with the borrower's financial and other information with which to make a loan decision. The completeness and accuracy of the information can affect whether a loan request is approved or rejected.

The prospective buyer's loan package that gets submitted to underwriting typically contains two applications, a handwritten one provided by the borrower and a typed application that often includes an expansion of the information originally supplied by the borrower. The typed application is the result of a personal interview and allows the lender and/or mortgage broker to fill in any gaps left by the handwritten application.

With the increase in financial fraud, the importance of the loan application, in the borrower's own handwriting, has taken on greater significance. In the Acknowledgement and Agreement section of the loan application (Figure 10.1, Section IX), the borrower confirms that the information provided is accurate and is warned that deliberate misrepresentation can result in severe punishment.

If the loan officer or mortgage correspondent's workload allows, there is a number of good reasons why it may be beneficial to have him or her present as a guide when the borrower completes the loan application.

- This gives the loan officer an opportunity to further interview the borrower and perhaps acquire additional information not asked for in the application.

For example, the borrower may be receiving a promotion or an increase in salary in the immediate future. If this information will help in qualifying the borrower, it can be added to the application.

- Many borrowers are applying for a real estate loan for the first time. They are not sure what to expect and have questions regarding the whole process. The loan officer can answer their questions and explain the process to them. If they understand what is involved, the entire transaction will go much more smoothly.

- If during the interview, the borrower seems unable to qualify, the loan officer or correspondent may be able to offer alternative loan options for which the borrower may be able to qualify. In some cases, the loan officer merely creates a "roadmap" by providing the prospective borrower with a list of what they must do regarding, income, assets, etc., to qualify for a loan.

A prospective borrower usually is provided with a basic list of items that the lender will need when the borrower applies for a loan. The list is a reminder of the information a lender will need to make a final loan decision. The list usually includes pay stubs, bank statements, tax returns, W-2 forms, etc. In the past, many borrowers were guided to the stated income or no documentation type of loan, not because it was the best loan option, but simply because the documentation requirements were much fewer.

Equal Credit Opportunity Act (ECOA)

The federal **ECOA** prohibits discrimination on the basis of race, color, religion, national origin, age, sex, or marital status, or on the grounds of receipt of income from a public assistance program. Since the act includes any person who regularly extends or arranges credit, it clearly applies to real estate lenders.

Some of the basic provisions of the act that affect real estate lenders are these:

1. Lenders cannot ask if the borrower is divorced or widowed. They may ask if the borrower is married, unmarried, or separated. For purposes of the law, unmarried means single, divorced, or widowed.

2. Lenders cannot ask about receiving alimony or child support unless the borrower is first notified that it need not be revealed. However, lenders may ask about obligations to pay alimony or child support.

3. Lenders cannot ask about birth control practices or childbearing intentions or capabilities.

4. Lenders must notify applicants in writing within 30 days as to what action has been taken on their applications. In case of disapproval, the reason must be given.
5. While borrowers may still provide information explaining blemishes, with the reliance upon automated credit scoring explanation, such letters have largely lost their persuasive ability. Divorce remains a major reason for blemished credit history on joint accounts. However, many lenders do not consider divorce as "beyond the control" of the borrower (unlike a job loss or medical complications), and this often does negatively impact a loan decision.

Real Estate Settlement Procedures Act (RESPA)

Known as **RESPA**, this law applies only to first loans on one- to four-unit residential properties. The main provisions of the act are as follows:

1. A lender must give the borrower a written estimate of the settlement or closing costs. This estimate is called a LE or Loan Estimate (see the Case & Point in Chapter 9). The estimate includes reserves collected for taxes, insurance, or prorations, if the loan is to be impounded. The estimate must be given or mailed to the borrower within three business days of the date of the loan application. New rules require that the borrower receive a Closing Disclosure (in place of the past HUD 1) at least three days prior to closing a loan.
2. Within the initial three business days, the borrower must be given the recently designed CFPB Know Before You Owe booklet that explains and gives information on closing costs.
3. Escrow and/or title companies are tasked with providing the required Closing Disclosure.
4. An anti-kickback provision prohibits real estate agents from generating unearned referral fees.

The Mortgage Disclosure Improvement Act (MDIA)

As a continuation of legislation designed to curb abusive lending practices, the MDIA rules went into effect on July 31, 2009. The new rules reemphasized the requirement that the original disclosures (the Mortgage Loan Disclosure and Loan Estimate) must be delivered to a prospective borrower within three days of receipt of the loan application. While the three-day rule has always been a lender requirement, the new legislation contained other important requirements.

Borrowers were relieved of the obligation to pay any fee (except a credit report fee) until the delivery of the disclosures. What represents "delivery" of the disclosures was clarified in the legislation. Only after the delivery period has elapsed are borrowers allowed to pay for the appraisal and other fees. This section of the rules can result in a delay the initiation of the appraisal portion of any conventional loan file by three to six days.

A loan lock period can also be impacted by this delay in ordering the appraisal. Locking a loan and then having to wait 6 days before ordering the appraisal and another 10 days before receiving the completed appraisal can use up 16 days of a 30-day lock period, increasing the difficulty in closing the loan within that short lock period.

Coupled with the Home Valuation Code of Conduct (HVCC), conventional appraisals must be ordered via the lender (originators are prohibited from selecting appraisers). Prior to ordering, a minimum broker's loan package consisting of a loan application, Loan Estimate and a credit report must be received; only then can the lender send its disclosures and initiate the opening timeframe. Brokers complain that this process—requiring the immediate selection of a lender— prohibits them from later choosing a lender that may have a better interest rate or program for their borrower. The recent relaxation in the ability to transfer appraisals from one lender to another and from one loan program to another is a welcome flexibility in providing customer service.

Following the original disclosure, if the annual percentage rate (APR) increases by more than 0.125 percent, a re-disclosed closing cost calculation (contained in the new Closing Disclosure form) must be provided to the consumer. Loan documents cannot be signed until three business days have elapsed from this newly disclosed calculation. Again, brokers point out that they are unable to change rates and terms, even those that are advantageous for their borrowers, because last-minute delays in the disclosure process result in the loss of rate lock-ins or cause unacceptable delays in escrow closing periods.

While critics of the MDIA legislation point out that the inherent delays in the loan process negatively impact borrowers, advocates praise the legislations as protecting consumers from abusive loan practices.

Verifying the Information on the Application

Following the completion of the loan application, documentation is acquired including (but not limited to) copies of pay stubs and W-2s, federal tax returns, checking and savings account statements, and other pertinent information. In increasingly rare cases, written verification in the form of a verification of employment (VOE) or verification of deposits (VOD) can be required. A credit report is acquired, which identifies, along with current credit accounts, any recorded judgments, divorces, or other liens. The report contains a credit score, representative of the borrower's total credit profile. This score is given considerable weight in the final loan approval. For borrowers with little credit use, an alternative credit qualification process, mostly used with government loan programs, can use current billings (e.g.; utility bills, insurance receipts) to create an acceptable credit profile. (See Chapter 9, Qualifying the Borrower, for more details.)

Because conventional lenders—with the development of risk-based criteria—depend more and more on credit scores for their approval decisions, to stay competitive, Fannie Mae, Freddie Mac, the FHA, the VA, and Cal-Vet have adopted an "alternative documentation" process for their loan-verification requirements. The most recent three months of bank statements and pay stubs plus the last two years of W-2 forms often are used as sufficient verification, especially for salaried borrowers with high credit scores. Tax returns are still required for self-employed borrowers or those who own rental real estate.

Loan Package

The loan officer or correspondent's next job is to assemble the **loan package**, which consists of all the forms, documents, and reports the lender needs to make a decision on the loan. If the loan officer does not have the authority to make the loan, the package is then given to a loan committee or to an underwriter who represents a lender.

A typical loan package might include: (1) borrower's loan application, (2) appraisal of the property, (3) verification of employment, (4) verification of banks statements, (5) credit report, (6) purchase contracts and amendments or counteroffers, (7) escrow instructions and preliminary title report, (8) documentation showing where the funds for the down payment and closing cost are coming from, which is often called "source of the funds," and (9) other supporting documents, such as tax returns, W-2 forms, and so on.

Experienced loan officers realize the importance of a loan package. They know that a complete and neat package is more likely to be approved. They also anticipate the questions or objections that a committee or underwriter may have and answer them in advance. For example, if the borrower has had a bankruptcy, the loan officer knows that there will be questions such as: Why did the borrower have a bankruptcy? When was it discharged? Has the borrower reestablished credit? Depending upon the severity of the information, the loan officer includes an explanation, usually in the cover letter submitted with the loan package.

With today's market conditions, the loan officer may more frequently advise a borrower regarding the things necessary to improve a credit score or otherwise prepare the file prior to submission.

10.2 HOW IS A LOAN APPROVED?

The loan approval process varies depending upon the lender. Conventional loans made by banks and thrift institutions are approved by authorized individuals or by a loan committee. If the approval is to be made by an individual, he or she will have the authority to approve loans up to a specific dollar amount. Any loan greater than the said dollar amount must be approved by a supervisor or a loan committee. Large banks and thrift institutions may have layers of committees with loan amount limitations at each level.

Technical advances now allow loan officers to submit a borrower's information directly to a Fannie Mae or Freddie Mac authorized automated loan analysis program. The complete loan file, including all supporting documentation, is then submitted for final approval to authorized underwriters. These underwriters, in turn, determine if any other documentation is required. These "conditions" must be satisfied before the loan can be completed. The automated systems have eliminated what used to be called personal or handwritten underwriting. As long as underwriters do not override the automated system with any personal decisions, they are protected from any responsibility in the case of the borrower's default.

Federal Housing Administration (FHA) and Department of Veterans Affairs (VA)

Criticism of the former practice of submitting all FHA- and VA-backed loan packages directly to these agencies led to the adoption of the **FHA Direct Endorsement System** and the **VA Automatic System**. Lenders approved to underwrite loans under these systems are labeled as either **supervised or non-supervised lenders**, with non-supervised lenders having the most latitude. Today, the majority of FHA- and VA-backed loans are approved by non-supervised lenders, such as mortgage companies.

To be approved as a non-supervised lender, companies must meet the guidelines set forth by FHA and VA. For example, a non-supervised mortgage company may be sponsored by an approved direct endorsement lender, to whom the mortgage company submits the

FHA-backed loan for final approval. In this case, FHA requires both the direct endorsement lender and the mortgage company to meet certain net worth requirements and to submit to an annual audit procedure. Note: See Chapter 6 wherein it is noted that FHA has recommended a significant change to this lender authorization and endorsement procedure.

Once the mortgage company submits the FHA or VA package to its sponsoring direct endorsement lender, and said lender approves the package, the loan is also automatically approved by the FHA or VA and sent to be insured or guaranteed by the appropriate agency. This in-house form of underwriting dramatically reduces the time required for FHA or VA loan approval and closing.

Fair Credit Reporting Act

The federal **Fair Credit Reporting Act** affects credit reporting agencies and users of credit information. If a loan is rejected because of information in a credit report, the borrower must be notified and given the name and address of the credit agency. The borrower then has the right to obtain from the agency the following:

1. All the information it has in its file on the borrower.
2. Sources of the information.
3. All the creditors to whom the agency has furnished reports within the last six months.

If an error is found, the credit agency must make the correction. If there is a dispute over any reported credit information, the borrower has the right to submit a Consumer Statement, which is generally limited to 100 words or less, explaining his or her side of the story. The credit agency must include this consumer statement in all subsequent credit inquires.

The reliance upon credit scoring has spawned a process by which, for a fee, consumers can accelerate a positive change in their credit scores by correcting inaccurate information quickly and then having the credit agency recalculate their new credit score to take advantage of a more favorable interest rate on their loan. Normally, a correction and recalculation of a credit score could take 60 days or longer. Called "rapid rescoring," this fee-based, special fast-track system might be able to reduce that time to just a day or two. But the cost can be substantial and in some situations could result in a less than anticipated score increase or, in rare, cases, even result in a lower score. The process should be used sparingly.

10.3 CLOSING THE LOAN

Once a loan has been approved, the next phase is called closing. Loan closings are usually handled by independent third parties, such as title and escrow companies. All the parties involved in the real estate transaction (buyer, seller, and lender) deliver their instructions, documents, and money to the escrow company. While a broker may deliver instructions to the escrow holder, it should be noted that the broker is not a party and does not directly control the closing. Exceptions arise, of course, when brokers act as principals.

In southern California, it is customary for escrows to be handled by independent escrow companies or the escrow departments of banks and title companies. In northern California, it is more common for escrow departments of title companies to handle the escrow. Some real estate companies, particularly the larger ones, have their own escrow departments. These companies close their own transactions, if approved by the lender to do so, and use the title company only for the title insurance. With the demand for more transparency and arm's length transactions, these in-house services are dwindling, especially with the current Qualified Mortgage (QM) requirements. Prior to the introduction of QM regulations, some lending institutions included their own escrow, title, and/or insurance affiliates. QM rules decree that maximum allowed fees include those of affiliated entities and consequently facilitated the independence of these entities. It is anticipated that there will be a relaxation in the affiliated entity rule in the future.

When all the instructions have been complied with, the escrow company instructs the title company to record the applicable deeds and notes. Escrow also prepares closing statements and disburses the money after recording has been confirmed. This final step of recording is when ownership changes hands.

Loan Documents for Escrow

The main loan documents prepared by the lender are:

1. Promissory note (Figure 10.2).
2. Deed of trust (Figure 10.3).
3. Closing Disclosure form

The promissory note outlines the financial terms of the loan: amount of loan, interest rate, monthly payments, date of first payment, and so on. The promissory note also lists other conditions such as late charges, prepayment privileges and penalties, and acceleration clauses.

A deed of trust is used to secure the repayment of the loan by creating a lien against the property. As explained in an earlier chapter, deeds of trust are used in California instead of mortgages because of the ease with which a lender can foreclose in case of a borrower's default.

FIGURE 10.2 Promissory note (partial).

NOTE

MIN 100033300091089113

[Date]   [City]   California [State]

[Property Address]

1. BORROWER'S PROMISE TO PAY
In return for a loan that I have received, I promise to pay U.S. $ _____ (this amount is called "Principal"), plus interest, to the order of the Lender. The Lender is _____.

I will make all payments under this Note in the form of cash, check or money order.

I understand that the Lender may transfer this Note. The Lender or anyone who takes this Note by transfer and who is entitled to receive payments under this Note is called the "Note Holder."

2. INTEREST
Interest will be charged on unpaid principal until the full amount of Principal has been paid. I will pay interest at a yearly rate of _____%.

The interest rate required by this Section 2 is the rate I will pay both before and after any default described in Section 6(B) of this Note.

3. PAYMENTS
(A) Time and Place of Payments
I will pay principal and interest by making a payment every month.
I will make my monthly payment on the 1st day of each month beginning on _____.
I will make these payments every month until I have paid all of the principal and interest and any other charges described below that I may owe under this Note. Each monthly payment will be applied as of its scheduled due date and will be applied to interest before Principal. If, on _____, I still owe amounts under this Note, I will pay those amounts in full on that date, which is called the "Maturity Date."
I will make my monthly payments at _____
_____ or at a different place if required by the Note Holder.

(B) Amount of Monthly Payments
My monthly payment will be in the amount of U.S. $ _____.

4. BORROWER'S RIGHT TO PREPAY
I have the right to make payments of Principal at any time before they are due. A payment of Principal only is known as a "Prepayment." When I make a Prepayment, I will tell the Note Holder in writing that I am doing so. I may not designate a payment as a Prepayment if I have not made all the monthly payments due under the Note.

I may make a full Prepayment or partial Prepayments without paying a Prepayment charge. The Note Holder will use my Prepayments to reduce the amount of Principal that I owe under this Note. However, the Note Holder may apply my Prepayment to the accrued and unpaid interest on the Prepayment amount, before applying my Prepayment to reduce the Principal amount of the Note. If I make a partial Prepayment, there will be no changes in the due date or in the amount of my monthly payment unless the Note Holder agrees in writing to those changes.

MULTISTATE FIXED RATE NOTE—Single Family—Fannie Mae/Freddie Mac UNIFORM INSTRUMENT   Form 3200 1/01
ITEM 1646L1 (0011)   (Page 1 of 3 pages)   GREATLAND ■
MFCD3002   To Order Call: 1-800-530-9393 □ Fax: 616-791-1131
                                                                                   9108911

Source: www.efanniemae.com

FIGURE 10.3 Deed of trust (partial).

After Recording Return To:
_____
_____
_____

_____ [Space Above This Line For Recording Data] _____

DEED OF TRUST

DEFINITIONS

Words used in multiple sections of this document are defined below and other words are defined in Sections 3, 11, 13, 18, 20 and 21. Certain rules regarding the usage of words used in this document are also provided in Section 16.

(A) "**Security Instrument**" means this document, which is dated _____, _____, together with all Riders to this document.
(B) "**Borrower**" is _____. Borrower is the trustor under this Security Instrument.
(C) "**Lender**" is _____. Lender is a _____ organized and existing under the laws of _____. Lender's address is _____. Lender is the beneficiary under this Security Instrument.
(D) "**Trustee**" is _____.
(E) "**Note**" means the promissory note signed by Borrower and dated _____, _____. The Note states that Borrower owes Lender _____ Dollars (U.S. $_____) plus interest. Borrower has promised to pay this debt in regular Periodic Payments and to pay the debt in full not later than _____.
(F) "**Property**" means the property that is described below under the heading "Transfer of Rights in the Property."
(G) "**Loan**" means the debt evidenced by the Note, plus interest, any prepayment charges and late charges due under the Note, and all sums due under this Security Instrument, plus interest.
(H) "**Riders**" means all Riders to this Security Instrument that are executed by Borrower. The following Riders are to be executed by Borrower [check box as applicable]:

☐ Adjustable Rate Rider ☐ Condominium Rider ☐ Second Home Rider
☐ Balloon Rider ☐ Planned Unit Development Rider ☐ Other(s) [specify] _____
☐ 1-4 Family Rider ☐ Biweekly Payment Rider

CALIFORNIA--Single Family--Fannie Mae/Freddie Mac UNIFORM INSTRUMENT   Form 3005 1/01 *(page 1 of 16 pages)*

Source: www.efanniemae.com

As shown in Figure 10.3, a deed of trust does not outline specific financial terms like the promissory note. A deed of trust shows only the loan amount, not the interest rate, monthly payments, or other information. The deed of trust shows that, if the debt it secures is not paid, the property may be sold to satisfy the debt. The deed of trust is recorded, while the promissory note is not. Recordation is notice to the world that there is a lien filed against the property, but to maintain confidentiality between the lender and borrower, the deed of trust shows only the amount of the loan, not the repayment terms. In addition, the deed of trust contains many other detailed agreements between the borrower and lender, identifying the rights of both.

Prior to recording the loan, escrow is tasked with preparing the final accounting for both buyer and seller in the form of a Closing Disclosure, which itemizes all incoming and outgoing items, thereby providing a financial picture of the closing transaction.

Truth-in-Lending Law (Regulation Z)

In 1968, Congress passed the **Truth-in-Lending Law**, known as TIL, in an effort to create a way for borrowers to compare loan costs from one lender to another as they shop for the best terms. A key feature of TIL was the requirement for lenders to calculate and present to the borrower a statement showing the **annual percentage rate (APR)**. The APR incorporates the interest rate on the loan, while also taking into account the total cost of acquiring the loan, which includes certain fees and other costs incurred to acquire the loan. The result is that the APR is usually higher than the note rate appearing on the promissory note.

As of October 2015, the TIL has been replaced by the Loan Estimate in which the APR calculation is reduced to a single block within the form. While simplified in the new form, consumers too often remain confused as to the definition accompanying APR as well as how it is calculated.

There continues to be confusion about the definition of APR and how it is calculated. To understand the APR, let's start with some definitions. A **prepaid finance charge** is a fee paid separately to a lender or a fee withheld from the loan proceeds. These prepaid finance charges typically include loan origination fees, prepaid interest, tax service fee, and mortgage insurance, to name a few. The amount financed is the loan amount minus the prepaid finance charges. The amount financed is the figure used to calculate the APR. Here is a simple example:

If a borrower applies for a $50,000 loan and the prepaid finance charges total $2,000, the amount financed is $48,000 ($50,000 − $2,000). The interest rate for the $50,000 loan is 7 percent amortized for 10 years; this results in a monthly payment of $580.54.

The calculations are as follows:

Total Payments	$69,665 [$580.54 × 120 months (10 yrs. × 12) = $69,664.80 round to $69,665]
Less: Loan Amount	$50,000
Total Interest	$19,665 (total interest to be paid over the life of the loan)
Plus: Prepaid Finance Charge	$2,000
Total Finance Charge	$21,665

Having calculated the amount financed, total payments, and the finance charge, we turn to the APR. Using a computer program or a programmed financial calculator, the APR would be determined to be 7.928 percent. Here is one way to think about APR: The monthly payment for borrowing $50,000 for 10 years at 7 percent is $580.54. If one borrowed only $48,000 ($50,000 minus the $2,000 fees), and retained the 10-year term and the same payment, the rate would be 7.928 percent. It stands to reason that if one borrows less money for the same term and payment, the rate will increase. Thus, the APR rate is higher than the note rate.

The APR does not determine the note interest rate but is a way of informing the borrower of the effective rate of interest when comparing loan costs. The bottom line is that, when shopping a loan, interest rate quotes can be deceiving when closing costs vary from lender to lender, so the APR is meant to serve as a guide to the borrower regarding the optimum selection of a loan option. This percentage could also be used when comparing what type of loan to get versus using a credit card, or getting a personal line of credit; it is a way to compare apples to apples. Since there is so much confusion and often lack of understanding about how the APR is calculated or what it means, borrowers are often advised to compare a list of actual loan costs rather than relying only upon the calculated APR.

In addition to disclosing the APR, the lender is required to disclose other information about the loan, such as the prepayment penalty, if any; late charge fees; and, if applicable, the three-day right to cancel on any refinance loan. These disclosures are regulated by the Federal Reserve under its **Regulation Z**.

Note: The new loan estimate form, introduced in October 2015, was designed to replace both the current good faith estimate (GFE) and the truth-in-lending (TIL) form by incorporation into a simplified three-page form. As part of the CFPB's "Know Before You Owe" campaign, the new loan estimate will mostly eliminate the current TIL (Figure 10.4) in an effort to make the information more easily understood by potential borrowers.

FIGURE 10.4 Sample closing cost.

Sales Price	$250,000
Loan Amount	$200,000
Loan Origination	$3,000
CLTA Title Policy	850
ALTA Title Policy	475
Escrow Fee	450
Credit Report	30
Appraisal Fee (POV)	(475)
Tax Service	125
Notary and Misc. Title Fees	300
Recording Fees	125
Pest Control Inspection	350
Total Nonrecurring Closing Costs	$5,705
Tax Proration	$275
Hazard Insurance Premium	650
Prepaid Interest	420
Total Recurring Closing Costs	$1,345
Combined Closing Costs	$7,050

Figures are example only
Source: © 2016 OnCourse Learning

Closing Costs

Calculating closing costs for a borrower is not a simple task. Real estate agents frequently estimate closing costs by using simple rules of thumb. Lenders must be more precise: they itemize each cost and provide an estimated total via the new Loan Estimate form.

Figure 10.4 lists the typical closing costs for the sale of a $250,000 home financed with a $200,000 loan at 5 percent interest, amortized for 30 years. Closing costs may vary according to custom and location.

Nonrecurring Closing Costs

Nonrecurring closing costs are one-time charges that the buyer-borrower usually pays at close of escrow. However, it must be stressed that the payment of closing costs is negotiable between the buyer and seller, and some (e.g., escrow and title fees) are often shared or split. Nonrecurring closing costs would include:

1. *Loan origination fee.* This fee compensates the lender for some of its expenses in originating the loan, preparing documents, and related work. The fee is usually a percentage of the loan, typically around 1.5–2 percent. It is common today for the originating lender to charge an additional processing fee of up to $500 to $600.

2. *Title policy.* Title policies are issued by title insurance companies, insuring buyers' and lenders' interests in the property against defects of title. There are two basic types of coverage in California—the California Land Title Association, or CLTA, and the American Land Title Association, or ALTA (sometimes referred to

as the buyer's or lender's policy). Most lenders require the ALTA policy because it provides additional coverage for the lender and is usually paid for by the buyer. The CLTA is often referred to as the seller's policy, as it assures the lender and borrower that the seller has a "good title" to convey. Who pays for the CLTA or standard title policy can vary by location and custom. For example, in southern California it is customary for the seller to pay; in central California it is often customary for the buyer to pay. There are other counties where the cost is split between the buyer and seller. However, it must be stressed that regardless of custom, the issue of who pays can always be negotiated. In our example, the buyer is paying for the policy.

3. *Escrow fee.* The escrow fee is charged for handling and supervising the escrow. As with title policies, custom also tends to dictate who pays the escrow fee. The buyer is paying the entire fee in our example, although in reality, escrow fees are often split in some fashion between buyer and seller. Remember that the veteran in a VA loan is prohibited from paying an escrow fee.

4. *Credit report.* The lender obtains a credit report in qualifying a buyer. The cost of the report is usually charged to the buyer.

5. *Appraisal.* The cost of the appraisal varies with the type of loan and property. With the introduction of the Home Valuation Code of Conduct (HVCC is discussed in the Case & Point in Chapter 8), this fee is nearly always paid when ordering the appraisal, usually via the buyer's credit card. The example shows the estimated $475 fee as Paid Outside the Contract (POC) and is therefore not included in the bottom line a cost to the buyer but in parenthesis to identify it will have been already paid.

6. *Tax service.* This one-time fee is paid to a tax service agency that, for the life of the loan, each year reviews the records of the taxing agencies. If a borrower fails to pay the property taxes, the agency reports this to the lender. If the lender is paying the taxes for the borrower, the agency also obtains the tax bill for the lender.

7. *Recording fees.* These cover the cost of recording the grant deed and deed of trust reconveyance.

8. *Notary fees.* Signatures on documents to be recorded, such as the grant deed, deed of trust, and reconveyances, must be notarized. Be aware that new fees surface from time to time.

9. *Pest control inspection fee.* The buyer or seller may pay this charge, depending on local custom. The charge varies from area to area but is always negotiable. VA loans require a pest control inspection whereas FHA and conventional loans rely upon the appraiser to

determine the need for such inspection. Requirements for completing any repairs identified in pest reports vary by type of loan. It has become the custom in many areas to sell "as is" in an effort to avoid pest control inspections and any subsequent work required. Caution should be exercised when selling a property in an "as is" condition. Sellers and/or real estate agents cannot escape the responsibility for disclosure via an "as is" sale and must report any known deficiencies. Other inspections often acquired, usually at the prospective buyer's expense, include a home inspection, roof inspection, etc.

Recurring Closing Costs

The buyer also pays **recurring closing costs**, which are the expenses that continue during the ownership of the property. In our example in Figure 10.5, the buyer will be paying property tax prorations, hazard insurance premium, and prepaid interest. In other transactions, these recurring closing costs could include additional items beyond our example (e.g., creating an impound account).

1. *Tax proration.* Most sales agreements provide for property tax prorations between the buyer and seller. This is calculated based upon the seller's current taxes and includes any prepaid or past due property taxes the seller may have paid or still owes. It is wise to remember that new taxes will be assessed based upon the sales price of a new purchase. Often the purchase price is substantially higher than the seller's current tax base and the buyer's taxes will be higher than the seller's previous taxes. In a market where foreclosure and short sales occur with regularity, the buyer's new taxes could be lower than the seller's current assessment. This new "supplemental tax" consequence, especially if it represents an increase, is not prorated at the close of escrow. The new buyer receives a supplemental tax bill typically between 60 to 120 days following the close of escrow.

    Note: Although homeowner taxes are a recurring cost, the initial proration of taxes between buyer and seller are technically a nonrecurring cost.

2. *Hazard insurance premiums.* Lenders require that the property be covered by insurance. In special flood zones, flood insurance is also required. Borrowers select their own insurance carriers and determine their coverage and premium cost. The buyer pays for the first-year premium at the close of escrow. Earthquake or other forms of protection can be obtained at the buyer's discretion but are not typically a lender requirement.

3. *Prepaid interest.* Depending upon which day escrow closes, the first loan payment may not be due on the first day of the next

month, but rather the following month. However, the lender is entitled to interest from the day of funding, which is usually the close of escrow. The escrow company collects interest from the buyer on behalf of the lender from the day escrow closes until the day the buyer's loan payments begin to cover the interest. This is called prepaid interest. Note: Whereas rent is paid in advance, interest is paid in arrears. In other words, when a borrower pays the mortgage payment, he or she is paying for the use of the funds for the previous month.

10.4 AFTER THE LOAN: RIGHTS AND RESPONSIBILITIES

Loan Payments

Loan payments are usually due on the first of each month. After the loan is closed, the borrower is notified as to how to make payments. There are basically three methods lenders use to collect payments. One is the *monthly billing system*. Before the first of each month, lenders mail a notice of payment due. Borrowers mail payments with the notice. The second method is the use of *coupons*. Each month, borrowers send in the monthly payment and enclose a coupon furnished by the lender. The third is the automatic monthly withdrawal from the borrower's checking account. Most lenders now also allow such payment methods as ACH automatic withdrawal, pay by phone, and online payments.

After the first of the year, most lenders give borrowers a yearly statement for the previous year. California law requires this accounting to be provided no later than January 31 of the new year. The statement shows the principal, interest, and taxes and insurance (if included in the payments) that were paid during the year. If taxes and insurance are included in the payment, a reserve analysis is also included. The analysis calculates the amount of tax and insurance reserve that should be in the reserve account.

If there is a shortage in the impound (reserve) account due to a tax or insurance increase, the lender may ask that the shortage be made up immediately. A more common practice is to spread the shortage over the next 12 months along with the required increase for the future. For example, assume a borrower had a shortage of $180 in the reserve account. Rather than demand the entire $180 immediately, the lender would increase the monthly payment by $15, which would make up the shortage in one year. In addition, an adjusted amount would be collected for any shortages expected in the following year. If there is a surplus in the account, the borrower may apply it to a future mortgage payment, ask for it in cash, or apply it against the principal. Some banks simply send a check to the borrower after this evaluation is done.

In addition to checking the reserve balances, the lender also analyzes the monthly payment. The payment may be increased or decreased if there has been a change in taxes or insurance premiums.

Late Charges

When borrowers fail to make payments on time, lenders may collect late charges. The amount of the late charge and when it is collected can vary depending upon the type of loan. Borrowers should consult their promissory note, deed of trust, or payment statement/coupon to determine the late fee agreement accompanying their specific loan.

While a payment is technically late one day after it is due, nearly all lenders have adopted a grace period of 15 days during which a payment will be considered on time. If the payment is due on the first of the month, it will be considered late on the sixteenth. The amount of the late fee can also vary but is more uniform now at 5 percent of the unpaid monthly payment amount. For example, if the principal and interest portion of the monthly payment is $1,000, the late fee would be $50 and charged on the sixteenth day after the payment was initially due.

Late payments are generally reported to credit bureaus when they are 30 days late. A mortgage payment late notification on the credit report is serious, and borrowers are urged to pay close attention to paying their mortgage on time.

Prepayment Privileges and Penalties

Most loan options allow borrowers to make extra payments on the principal balance without penalty. This is called a prepayment privilege. When a prepayment penalty does exist, typical conventional loans allow 20 percent of the original loan amount as a prepayment privilege per year as set forth in the civil code. This 20 percent includes all cumulative amounts paid toward principal reduction during the year. For example, if the original loan amount were $100,000, the borrower could make up to $20,000 in additional payments in any one year without penalty. FHA, USDA, and VA loans do not permit **prepayment penalties**.

QM standards apply to the majority of conventional loans originated today. Consequently, prepayment penalties have mostly disappeared. In order to comply with QM requirements, in late 2014 FHA eliminated its long-standing look back rule of interest charged for the full month regardless of when the loan closed (i.e., the old rule was if a loan closed on say the fifth of the month, interest was charged for the full month).

However, during times of high turnover due to frequent refinancing, lenders may still seek ways to discourage what is known as "churning" or the frequent refinancing a loan in pursuit of a lower rate, via some form of penalty.

10.5 HANDLING LOAN TAKEOVERS

Loan Assumptions/Subject to Transfers

Enforceable due-on-transfer (sale) clauses are included in most promissory notes in an effort to prevent the takeover of existing loans by another new owner without the lender's prior permission. Transferring property on a "subject to" basis is typically done without the lender's permission. There can be serious ramifications to both buyer and seller in either type of transfer, but these are beyond the scope of this text at this time. A short discussion on both forms of transfers is given below.

A real estate loan is assumed when the new borrower is approved by the lender and a formal assumption agreement is executed. When a loan is assumed, the original borrower—the seller—can be relieved of responsibility, provided release of liability is given.

In other words, if the original borrower wants to be relieved of liability, the new borrower must formally assume the loan and the original borrower must obtain a release of liability. This usually requires the new borrower to qualify for the loan. Unless there is a complete novation, both parties could be liable on a formal assumption. Loans can be formally assumed by applying to the lender.

Subject To's

Where property is purchased **subject to** the existing loan of record, the buyer does not agree to assume primary liability for the debt. Instead, the seller continues on the obligation; that is, although the buyer makes the payments directly to the lender, the seller remains responsible for any deficiency if a judgment is obtained.

As a practical matter, however, even though the buyer is not obligated to make the payments, the buyer will naturally continue the payments in order to keep the property. This is because the debt is secured by the property and the lender's security is held intact regardless of who makes the payments. Thus, if the buyer fails to make the payments, the lender proceeds against the property through foreclosure. The only time that the distinction between "assumption" and "subject to" becomes important is when the foreclosure results in a deficiency. If a deficiency judgment is obtained, the lender could proceed only against the maker of the note, the seller, if the buyer purchased subject to the existing loan. Had the buyer assumed primary liability for the debt, the buyer could be held liable for the deficiency. As for when a lender may or may not be able to obtain a deficiency judgment, see Chapter 11.

Chapter Summary

Loan processing starts with receipt of the loan application, which includes basic information regarding the borrower's employment, income, assets, and debts. The lender usually confirms the information by obtaining verifications of employment and bank deposits, and checks the borrower's credit. During this time an appraisal is ordered. Automated approval programs are now used extensively to determine if other documentation may be required. After a loan package is assembled, the loan is submitted to appropriate individuals, underwriters, or committees for approval. This function is now largely to assure that the required documentation has been acquired and that it is congruent with the original loan application submission.

Beginning in 2009, following the economic downturn of the previous years, sufficient disclosure, including the past truth-in-lending and good faith estimates, and since October 2015 the new Loan Estimate and Closing Disclosure have taken on added importance. The Mortgage Loan Improvement Act outlines the time table for such disclosures.

After the loan is approved, loan documents are prepared by the lender and sent to the escrow agent. Loan documents include a promissory note, deed of trust, and closing disclosure statement.

The closing costs paid by the borrower are broken down into non-recurring and recurring costs. Payments on loans are usually due on the first of the month. If the payments are late, the borrower owes a late charge. Prepayment penalties as we've known them in the past have mostly disappeared due to the Qualified Mortgage (QM) rules prohibiting them. FHA, VA, USDA, and Cal-Vet loans continue a long-held tradition and do not have a prepayment penalty. With the lender's permission, some loans may be formally assumed or they may be taken subject to an existing loan.

Important Terms and Concepts

Annual percentage rate (APR)
Equal Credit Opportunity Act (ECOA)
Fair Credit Reporting Act
FHA Direct Endorsement System
Loan application
Loan package
Nonrecurring closing costs
Non-supervised lender
Prepaid finance charge
Prepayment penalty
Real Estate Settlement Procedures Act (RESPA)
Recurring closing costs
"Subject to"
Supervised lender
Truth-in-lending law
Regulation Z

Reviewing Your Understanding

Questions for Discussion

1. Explain why many real estate lenders might qualify the buyer before appraising the property.
2. Briefly explain the purpose of the
   a. Equal Credit Opportunity Act,
   b. Real Estate Settlement Procedures Act (RESPA),
   c. Fair Credit Reporting Act, and
   d. Truth-in-Lending Law (Regulation Z).
3. List five forms, documents, or reports that are contained in a typical loan package.
4. Discuss how the procedures for approving a conventional real estate loan may differ from the procedures for approving an FHA-insured loan.
5. Define annual percentage rate (APR), prepaid finance charge, and loan origination fee.
6. Indicate who in your area customarily pays for the following closing costs: title insurance policy, escrow fee, pest control work, broker's commission, loan origination fee, discount points on an FHA or VA loan, pest control inspection fee, credit report, appraisal fee, and tax service.
7. What is the difference between recurring and nonrecurring closing costs? Give four examples of each.
8. What is the difference between assuming a seller's existing loan and purchasing subject to a seller's existing loan?

Multiple-Choice Questions

1. Which of the following would be the most important information sought by lenders about a potential borrower?
   a. Sex of the borrower
   b. Need for a loan
   ✓c. Credit history of the applicant
   d. Racial makeup of the area in which the property is located

2. Under the Equal Credit Opportunity Act, lenders are required to notify loan applicants on what action has been taken within a reasonable time period not exceeding
   a. two weeks.
   ✓b. 30 days.
   c. three months.
   d. any time mutually agreed to between borrower and lender.

3. Processing an application for a real estate loan may include verification of
   a. employment.
   b. bank deposits.
   c. debts.
   ✓d. all of the above.

4. Under the Fair Credit Reporting Act, an applicant who has been denied credit is entitled to receive which of the following information from the credit reporting agency?
   ✓a. Sources of the information
   b. The financial standing of the reporting agency
   c. All of the debtors to whom the agency has furnished reports
   d. Only the data that the agency provided the lender that rejected the loan

5. APR as used under Regulation Z stands for
   a. annuity percentage rate.
   ✓b. annual percentage rate.
   c. annual property return.
   d. amortized property return.

6. The last step in originating and processing loans is
   ✓a. a formal closing.
   b. qualifying the buyer.
   c. completing the application.
   d. qualifying the property.

7. A federal law that prohibits discrimination in lending solely on the basis of sex or marital status is the
   a. Equality in Sex and Marital Status Act.
   ✓b. Equal Credit Opportunity Act.
   c. Truth-in-Lending Law.
   d. Fair Credit Reporting Act.

8. Property taxes for the fiscal year, July 1 to June 30, are $3,600 and they have not been paid. Escrow closes August 1. The tax proration will be:
   a. credit the seller $300.
   b. debit the seller $3,300.
   c. debit the buyer $3,300.
   ✓d. credit the buyer $300.

9. For a typical home loan, the final approval or rejection rests with the
   a. real estate broker.
   b. mortgage broker.
   ✓c. underwriter.
   d. escrow officer.

10. Recurring closing costs include
    a. title fee.
    b. property taxes. ✓
    c. appraisal fee.
    d. credit report.

11. Under the Real Estate Settlement Procedures Act, lenders
    a. must comply with all requirements for income properties.
    b. must provide the applicant with a booklet on closing costs. ✓
    c. are required to provide exact closing costs.
    d. may not use their own escrow firms.

12. The loan committee of a conventional home lender
    a. is made up of at least three members.
    b. might be one individual with authority limited to a specific dollar amount. ✓
    c. typically meets only three days per week.
    d. has only limited authority to approve loans, since final authority for loan approval always rests with the chief managing officer of the lender.

13. In California, once a person has an owner-occupied home, any refinances or junior loans secured by a junior lien
    a. are illegal.
    b. are made only by private lenders.
    c. involve a three-day right of rescission. ✓
    d. are not made by institutional lenders.

14. Nonrecurring closing costs include which of the following items: I. Loan origination fees, II. Escrow fees, III. Hazard insurance fees, IV. Tax reserves, V. Recording fees
    a. I, II, and III only.
    b. II, III, and IV only.
    c. I, II, and IV only.
    d. I, II, and V only. ✓

15. Loan payments, whether required on the first of the month or another date
    a. may include reserves for taxes and insurance.
    b. are billed by the monthly billing system, the coupon method, or by automatic deduction from a checking account.
    c. may involve charges for a late payment.
    d. involve all of the above. ✓

16. The APR for a $100,000 loan at 7 percent amortized for 30 years, with no loan fees or financing charges of any sort is:
    a. 8.1 percent.
    b. 7.4 percent.
    c. 7.12 percent.
    d. 7 percent. ✓

17. Under the Truth-in-Lending Law, annual percentage rate refers to the
    a. nominal interest rate.
    b. effective interest rate. ✓
    c. stated interest rate.
    d. any of the foregoing.

18. Loan escrows may not close without full compliance with the written instructions of the
    a. lender and borrower. ✓
    b. escrow company and borrower.
    c. escrow company and lender.
    d. broker and borrower.
19. RESPA is specifically designed to
    a. reduce settlement costs.
    b. standardize settlement costs.
    c. accomplish both (a) and (b).
    d. accomplish neither (a) nor (b). ✓
20. Assumption of a loan is best illustrated when a
    a. property is sold subject to the loan.
    b. new owner of the property makes payments on a timely basis.
    c. takeover buyer signs a formal assumption and is approved by the lender. ✓
    d. seller agrees to let buyer assume the loan, subject to approval by buyer's agent.

CASE & POINT

A Typical Loan Process

1. Initial consultation (via phone, online, in person, or through the mail).
2. Initial file set up, obtain copies of client documentation.
3. Issue pre-qualification after reviewing documentation and obtaining credit report.
   a. FraudGUARD® protection will alert lender to any discrepancies.
4. After the offer is accepted, request updates to client documentation (if needed) and obtain the contract as well as escrow information/documentation. The Loan Estimate is now prepared.
5. Prepare initial loan file with all documentation from all required sources.
6. Locking in a rate will now be discussed with the borrower to determine if they prefer to lock a rate or "float the market." If the borrower elects to float the market, the loan rate may be locked at any time up to five days prior to anticipated closing date but before loan documents can be drawn.
7. Set up initial loan disclosure packet signing with client (via email, in person, or through the mail). A Loan Estimate must have been provided within three days of obtaining a dated loan application and confirmation to move forward from the borrower.
8. Once all disclosures have been signed and accepted by the lender, now FINALLY order the appraisal!
   a. Borrowers may wish to postpone until inspections have been reviewed.
9. While awaiting the appraisal, submit the full loan package to the lender for full underwriter approval.
10. Wait for conditional approval from the underwriter.
11. Review and communicate conditional loan approval with all parties, and request items that the underwriter required from each appropriate party.
12. Package and submit all prior to doc (PTD) conditions. The appraisal may be the only outstanding condition at this time.

13. Once the appraisal is obtained and reviewed for completeness, submit the appraisal and any other PTD conditions that may remain outstanding.
14. Wait for final documentation clearance to prepare loan document order via the underwriter and staff.
15. Loan documents ordered and obtained.
16. Review loan documents; coordinate with escrow to obtain any closing documents related to lender instructions and to determine that everyone is ready to proceed. Establish a time with the borrower to sign and notarize documents.
17. Final loan documents signed with the loan officer.
18. Escrow to prepare the document package according to the lenders instruction's and return them to the lender.
19. If any prior to funding conditions (PTF) remain un-cleared, obtain and return them with loan documents.
20. Submit said loan document package and any remaining PTF conditions to the funder.
    a. Last minute employment verification call made by funder.
21. Coordinate with the funder and escrow the close of escrow date and recording time.
22. The transaction is completed successfully!

Caveat: Many things can happen to interrupt the flow of the loan process:

    a. Borrower's delay in providing requested documentation
    b. Request to delay the appraisal
    c. Discovery of unexpected information—credit issues, less than sufficient funds to close, appraiser requiring inspections
    d. Inspection disclosures requiring more than anticipated work to be completed necessitating renegotiation

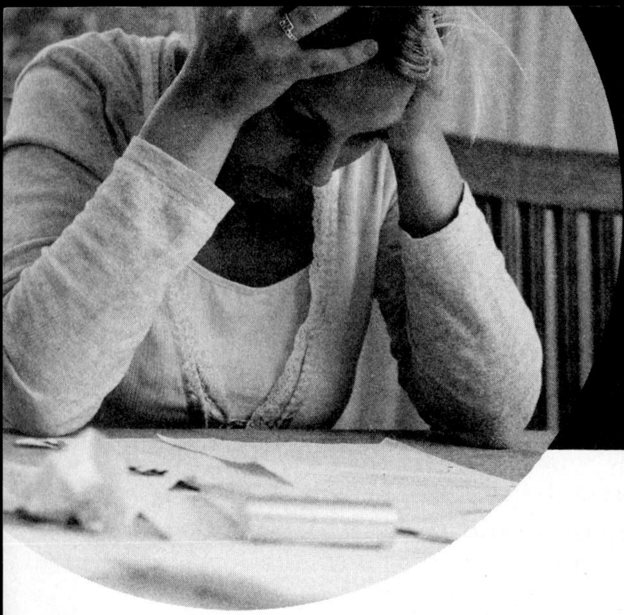

FORECLOSURES AND OTHER LENDING PROBLEMS

OVERVIEW

The basic responsibilities of the parties to a real estate loan appear very simple. In exchange for money loaned, borrowers agree to repay the loan according to the terms and conditions stipulated in the promissory note and deed of trust. However, in actual practice, there is much more to real estate loans than merely repaying principal and interest.

After completing this chapter, you will be able to:

- Explain the major provisions outlined in a typical promissory note and deed of trust.
- Outline the steps in a foreclosure procedure.
- Demonstrate why lenders in California prefer trust deeds over mortgages as security for their loans.
- List five ways a borrower and lender can minimize the possibility of a default and foreclosure.
- Discuss how private and government mortgage insurance has reduced the lender's risk in granting real estate loans.
- Understand the insurance coverage for PMI on loans over 80 percent LTV.
- Describe the controversial practice known as redlining.
- Explain the role of the Community Reinvestment Act (CRA).

11.1 COLLATERAL PROVISIONS OF DEEDS OF TRUST

Figure 11.1a is an example of the front page of a typical deed of trust, while Figure 11.1b is a list of major items in the complete document, which can run many pages, and contains several provisions designed to reduce the chance of default and foreclosure.

The deed of trust defines the rights and duties of the three parties to the loan—the trustor or borrower, trustee or title holder, and the beneficiary or lender. Even if the trustor is current with payments on the promissory note, the beneficiary can still foreclose should the trustor default in the performance of any of the other requirements—the collateral provisions of the trust deed—including the following:

1. *Maintenance of the property.* The typical trust deed requires the trustor to keep the property in good condition, to pay for labor and materials whenever improvements are made, not to lay waste

FIGURE 11.1a,b Partial deed of trust form.

RECORDING REQUESTED BY

AND WHEN RECORDED MAIL TO

SPACE ABOVE THIS LINE FOR RECORDER'S USE

DEED OF TRUST AND ASSIGNMENT OF RENTS

This Deed of Trust, made this ___ day of _____, between _____ herein called **Trustor**, whose address is _____, and _____, herein called **Beneficiary**, whose address is _____ and _____, A California corporation, herein called **Trustee**,

Witnesseth: THAT TRUSTOR IRREVOCABLY GRANTS, TRANSFERS AND ASSIGNS TO TRUSTEE IN TRUST, WITH POWER OF SALE, that property in _____ County, California, described as:

TOGETHER WITH the rents, issues and profits thereof, SUBJECT HOWEVER, to the right, power and authority given to and conferred upon Beneficiary by paragraph (11) of the provisions set forth below to collect and apply such rents, issues and profits.
For the Purpose of Securing: 1. Performance of each agreement of Trustor incorporated by reference or contained herein. 2. Payment of the indebtedness evidence by one promissory note of even date herewith, and any extension of renewal thereof, in the principal sum of $_____ executed by Trustor in favor of Beneficiary or order. 3. Payment of such further sums as the then record owner of such property hereafter may borrow from Beneficiary, when evidenced by another note (or notes) reciting it is so secured.

To Protect the Security of This Deed of Trust, Trustor Agrees:
  (1) That Trustor will observe and perform said provisions; and that the referenced to property, obligations, and parties in said provisions shall be construed to refer to the property, obligations and parties set forth in this Deed of Trust.
  (2) To keep said property in good condition and repair; not to remove or demolish any building thereon; to complete or restore promptly and in good and workmanlike manner any building which may be constructed, damaged or destroyed thereon and to pay when due all claims for labor performed and materials furnished therefore; to comply with all laws affecting said property or requiring any alterations or improvements to be made thereon, not to commit or permit waste thereof; not to commit, suffer or permit any act upon said property in violations of law; to cultivate, irrigate, fertilize, fumigate, prune and do all other acts which from the character or use of said property may be reasonably necessary, the specific enumeration's herein not excluding the general.
  (3) To provide, maintain and deliver to Beneficiary fire insurance satisfactory to and with loss payable to Beneficiary. The amount collected under any fire or other insurance policy may be applied by Beneficiary upon any indebtedness secured herein and in such order as beneficiary may determined or at option of Beneficiary the entire amount so collected or any part hereof may be released to Trustor. Such application or release shall not cure or waive any default or notice of default hereunder or invalidate any act done pursuant to such notice.
  (4) To appear in and defend any action or proceeding purporting to affect the security hereof or the rights or powers of the Beneficiary or Trustee; and to pay all costs and expenses, including cost of evidence of title and attorney's fees in a reasonable sum, in any such action or proceeding in which Beneficiary or Trustee may appear, and in any suit brought by Beneficiary to record this Deed.

PAGE 1

FIGURE 11.1a,b (Continued)

1. *Document number:* This is assigned to the document by the County Recorder's office. The book and page of the County Recorder's index books where the document is entered are shown adjacent to the document number.

2. *County recorder stamps:* The large stamp reflects the time and date of recording of the document as well as reference to the fee paid for recording. These stamps are placed on the document by the clerk in the Recorder's Office.

3. *Recording requested by:* This identifies the party requesting that the document be recorded and often shows the names of title companies when they submit groups of documents to the county for recording.

4. *When recorded mail to:* After recording, the document will be mailed by the county to the addressee shown in this section. This would be the lender who issued the loan.

5. *Title order no. and escrow no.:* On this line the title company order number will appear along with the customer escrow number if the document was recorded as part of a title order that culminated in the closing of an escrow.

6. *Date of execution:* This should be the date of the signing of the deed of trust by the trustor (borrower) and also can be the date the document is prepared.

7. *Trustor:* The name of the borrower, who is the record owner and identified as the trustor, is shown, as well as the borrower's status of record.

8. *Trustee:* The name of the entity that is being granted the property with legal title to exercise a power of sale if necessary is shown and is referred to as the trustee.

9. *Beneficiary:* The name of the lender is shown and is referred to as the beneficiary. This is the creditor to whom the debt is owing.

10. *Words of conveyance:* These are the words used by which legal title to the property is transferred from the trustor to the trustee with power of sale. On the sample the wording "grants, transfers, and assigns to trustee, in trust, with power of sale" satisfies this need.

11. *Legal description:* This identifies the property in question, which is usually by lot, block, and tract, by metes and bounds, or by government survey.

12. *Amount of indebtedness:* The amount shown in the promissory note.

13. *Signature of the trustor:* The signature of the trustor (borrower) will appear on the line in this section, and the name should be printed or typed beneath the signature.

14. *Acknowledgment:* In this area a formal declaration is personally made before a notary public by the borrower who has executed (signed) the document, that such execution is borrower's act and deed. (This is a requirement before the instrument can be accepted for recording.) The borrower signs before the notary public, who then completes the acknowledgment.

15. *Venue:* This identifies the state and county where the acknowledgment is taken.

16. *Notary seal or stamp:* In this section the official seal of the notary public must be affixed or stamped.

Source: © 2016 OnCourse Learning

to the property, and to comply with local building ordinances and other laws affecting the property—in short, to preserve the value of the property as security for the repayment of the loan.

2. *Hazard insurance.* To protect the security, the trustor agrees to maintain basic fire and windstorm insurance, with a loss payee clause in favor of the beneficiary. Under a loss payee provision, the lender may use any insurance proceeds to reduce the loan indebtedness, or turn over the funds to the owner to rebuild. When the trustor fails to maintain insurance satisfactory to the beneficiary, the latter may call the loan due and payable, but most often the lender obtains a policy and charges the cost to the trustor. The cost of lender-acquired insurance is very high and is paid by an increase to the monthly impound account payment or, for those not impounded, via a bill sent for payment to the borrower.

3. *Property taxes and other liens.* The trustor agrees to pay for property taxes, assessments, and all prior liens. Unless this is done, the beneficiary's interest can be eliminated by a tax sale, in which the state, after five continuous years of unpaid taxes, may sell the property. To help guard against this, the beneficiary may pay for these tax liens and then be reimbursed by the borrower. Depending on the lender, such advances may be billed to the trustor directly, with possible foreclosure action in the event of failure to repay, or the beneficiary may simply add the advances to the principal indebtedness. The loan is considered in default until the lender is reimbursed.

4. *Assignment of rents.* This clause is found in almost every trust deed. It provides that upon default by the trustor, the beneficiary may take possession of the property through a court-appointed trustee or receiver and collect the rents, applying them to the loan and to costs and expenses incurred. When there are sufficient sums collected from tenants in a property, it is possible that by applying them to the delinquent payments during the reinstatement period, default may be avoided. This is unlikely, however, because if the income from the property paid all the debts, there probably wouldn't be issues in the first place.

11.2 DEFAULT AND FORECLOSURE

Borrowers default on repayment of loans for a variety of reasons, some because of events beyond their control. Medical expenses, disability, death, and financial reversals such as loss of a job or business are some of the most common of these events. Other circumstances include divorce, bankruptcy, the excessive use of credit, and poor budgeting, although these circumstances are not considered beyond the control of the individual. Unless arrangements can be made with the lender to work out a satisfactory schedule for repayment following default, foreclosure is the ultimate price that the delinquent borrower must pay. However, most lenders try to avoid foreclosure wherever possible and use it only as a last resort, since most lenders are in the business of lending money and do not want to become involved in owning and managing real estate.

As foreclosures continued to mount in early 2009, new legislation was introduced to encourage lenders to take steps to help borrowers retain their homes. (See the Case & Point at the end of this chapter for details.)

As noted earlier, a borrower may be in default not only through delinquency on payments of principal and interest, but also when there is a violation of other terms of the trust deed agreement to maintain the property and pay other liens in a timely manner. Regardless of the violation, lenders in California must follow a prescribed procedure in removing the delinquent debtor. Foreclosure may be accomplished through either trustee's sale or judicial sale.

Note: The Ability to Repay (ATR) section of the Dodd-Frank Act provides for a borrower to assert a violation of this ATR section as a defense against foreclosure. In other words, the borrower may claim that he or she was not adequately informed regarding their ability to pay the mortgage. Although there is no time limit regarding the use of this defense, if successful, recovery is limited to no more than three years of finance charges and fees.

Trustee's Sale

Virtually all trust deeds contain a power of sale clause, which empowers the trustee, in the event of default by the trustor, to sell the property at public auction. While the provisions of the power of sale are a matter of contract and may vary from instrument to instrument, there are statutes that specifically regulate foreclosures through a **trustee's sale**, found in California's Civil Code. The statutory requirements are as follows:

1. *Notice of Default.* After notification and sufficient time for the trustor to satisfy any delinquent payments, the beneficiary will reach a point of being reasonably certain that a trustor is unable to make good on delinquent installment payments. The beneficiary

then delivers the note and trust deed to the trustee. The trustee is instructed to record a **Notice of Default** in the county where the property is located, and this filing starts the foreclosure clock. It must be recorded at least three months before a notice of sale can be advertised. An example of such notice is given in Figure 11.2. The notice must contain a correct legal description of the property, name of trustor, nature of the breach, and a statement to the effect that the party executing the notice of default has elected to sell the property in order to satisfy the obligation. While a trustor requests a Notice of Default through the Deed of Trust, under California law anyone may request a copy of the notice.

Within 10 days after filing the Notice of Default, a copy must be sent by registered or certified mail to anyone who has requested a copy of the NOD. These are typically second trust deed holders who filed a Request for Notice, but there may be others with a recorded interest who may be affected, for whom the time is extended to 30 days. This notice must be sent by the trustee.

During the three-month period preceding the advertising for sale, the trustor may reinstate the loan by paying all delinquent installments, costs, and trustee's fees. This **right of reinstatement**, or period of reinstatement, continues until five business days before the scheduled sale.

2. *Notice of Sale.* After expiration of the reinstatement period, which includes three weeks for advertising the time and place of the trustee's sale, the beneficiary is entitled to the entire unpaid balance of the note, plus costs and trustee's fees. The trustee records a **Notice of Sale**, similar to the sample shown in Figure 11.3. The Notice of Trustee's Sale must be recorded at least two weeks before the sale.

The notice must contain a correct identification of the property, such as the street address or legal description. It also must be published in a newspaper of general circulation in the county or jurisdiction in which the property is located. The publication must appear at least once a week for three weeks, not more than seven days apart. The notice must also be posted in a public place, such as a courthouse, and in some conspicuous place on the property, such as an attachment to a front door. Notice must be posted on the property no later than 20 days prior to sale. The sale must be held in a public place, during business hours, on a weekday, Monday through Friday. A copy of the Notice of Sale must also be mailed to those who had requested a copy of the notice of default.

3. *Final sale.* Any person, including the trustor and beneficiary, but not the trustee, may bid on the property through auction.

FIGURE 11.2 Sample notice of default.

RECORDING REQUESTED BY

WHEN RECORDED MAIL TO

Name

Street
Address

City &
State

		SPACE ABOVE THIS LINE FOR RECORDER'S USE
TITLE ORDER NO.	T.S. NO.	COMPUTER NO.
LOAN NO.	OTHER REF.	T.S. NO.

NOTICE OF DEFAULT AND ELECTION TO SELL UNDER DEED OF TRUST
IMPORTANT NOTICE
IF YOUR PROPERTY IS IN FORECLOSURE BECAUSE YOU ARE BEHIND IN YOUR PAYMENTS, IT MAY BE SOLD WITHOUT ANY COURT ACTION,

and you may have the legal right to bring your account in good standing by paying all of your past due payments plus permitted costs and expenses within the time permitted by law for reinstatement of your account which is normally five business days prior to the date set for the sale of your property. No sale date may be set until three months from the date this notice of default may be recorded (which date of recordation appears on this notice).

This amount is _____ as of _____ and will increase until your account becomes current.

While your property is in foreclosure, you still must pay other obligations (such as insurance and taxes) required by your note and deed of trust or mortgage. If you fail to make future payments on the loan, pay taxes on the property, provide insurance on the property, or pay other obligations as required in the note and deed of trust or mortgage, the beneficiary or mortgagee may insist that you do so in order to reinstate your account in good standing. In addition, the beneficiary or mortgagee may require as a condition to reinstatement that you provide reliable written evidence that you paid all senior liens, property taxes, and hazard insurance premiums.

Upon your written request, the beneficiary or mortgagee will give you a written itemization of the entire amount you must pay. You may not have to pay the entire unpaid portion of your account, even though full payment was demanded, but you must pay all amounts in default at the time payment is made. However, you and your beneficiary or mortgagee may mutually agree in writing prior to the time the notice of sale is posted (which may not be earlier than the end of the three-month period stated above) to, among other things, (1) provide additional time in which to cure the default by transfer of the property or otherwise; or (2) establish a schedule of payments in order to cure your default; or both (1) and (2).

Following the expiration of the time period referred to in the first paragraph of this notice, unless the obligation being foreclosed upon or a separate written agreement between you and your creditor permits a longer period, you have only the legal right to stop the sale of your property by paying the entire amount demanded by your creditor.

FIGURE 11.2 (Continued)

To find out the amount you must pay, or to arrange for payment to stop the foreclosure, or if your property is in foreclosure for any other reason, contact:

Name of Beneficiary or Mortgagee:

Phone:

If you have any questions, you should contact a lawyer or the Governmental agency which may have insured your loan.

Notwithstanding the fact that your property is in foreclosure, you may offer your property for sale, provided the sale is concluded prior to the conclusion of the foreclosure.

Remember, YOU MAY LOSE LEGAL RIGHTS IF YOU DO NOT TAKE PROMPT ACTION.

NOTICE IS HEREBY GIVEN: _____, a California Corporation, is duly appointed Trustee under a Deed of Trust dated _____ executed by _____ in favor of _____ as Trustor, to secure certain obligations _____, as beneficiary,

recorded _____ as instrument no. _____ in book _____ page _____

of Official Records in the Office of the Recorder of _____ County, California, describing the land therein as:

said obligations including _____ note(s) for the _____ sum of $ _____

that a breach of, and default in, the obligations for which such Deed of Trust is security has occurred in that payment has not been made of:

that by reason thereof, the undersigned, present beneficiary under such Deed of Trust, has executed and delivered to said duly appointed Trustee, a written Declaration of Default and Demand for Sale, and has deposited with said duly appointed Trustee, such Deed of Trust and all documents evidencing obligations secured thereby, and has declared and does hereby declare all sums secured thereby immediately due and payable and has elected and does hereby elect to cause the trust property to be sold to satisfy the obligations secured thereby.

Dated _____   _____

Source: © 2016 OnCourse Learning

FIGURE 11.3 Sample notice of trustee's sale.

Foreclosures

Notice of Trustee's Sale
Under Deed of Trust
TF 47739
Loan No. 277529
57831
BT

Notice is hereby given that SERRANO RECONVEYANCE COMPANY, A California corporation as trustee, or successor trustee, or substituted trustee pursuant to the deed of trust recorded November 10, 20XX in book T10686 page 822 of Official Records in the office of the County Recorder of Los Angeles County, California, and pursuant to the Notice of Default and Election to Sell thereunder recorded March 21, 20XX Instrument No. 77-281295 of said Official Records, will sell on August 16, 20XX at 11:00 A.M., at the Oxford Street entrance to the building located at 3731 Wilshire Boulevard, City of Los Angeles, County of Los Angeles, State of California, at public auction, to the highest bidder for cash (payable at the time of sale in lawful money of the United States) all right, title, and interest conveyed to and now held by it under said deed in the property situated in said County and State described as follows:

PARCEL 1:
Lot 11 of Tract 5852, in the City of Los Angeles, County of Los Angeles, State of California, as per map recorded in Book 61, Page 67 of Maps, in the office of the County Recorder of said County.

PARCEL 2:
That portion of Montevista, in the City of Los Angeles, County of Los Angeles, State of California, as per map recorded in Book 6, Page 324, of Miscellaneous Records, described as follows:
Beginning at Southeasterly corner of Lot 11 of Tract 5852, in the City of Los Angeles, as per map recorded in Book 61 Page 67 of Maps; thence along the Easterly line of said Lot 11, North 0 degrees 01' 40" West 40 feet to the Northeasterly corner of said Lot 11; thence Easterly along the Easterly prolongation of the Northerly line of said Lot 11 to a line that is parallel with and distant 10 feet Easterly, measured at right angles, from the Easterly line of said Tract 5852; thence South 11 degrees 16' 40" East to the intersection with the Easterly prolongation of the Southerly line of said Lot 11; thence Westerly along the Easterly prolongation of said Southerly line to the point of beginning.

Property Address purportedly known as: 10522 Frengien Av., Tujunga, CA 91042.

Said sale will be made, but without covenant or warranty, express or implied, regarding title, possession or encumbrances, to satisfy the indebtedness secured by said Deed, including the fee and expense of the trustee and of the trusts created by said deed, advances thereunder, with interest as provided therein, and the unpaid principal of the note secured by said deed; to wit: $23,000.00 with interest thereon from November 15, 20XX as provided in said note.

Dated: July 8, 20XX

SERRANO RECONVEYANCE
COMPANY,
as such Trustee
(213) 385-3321
By J.E. Cornwall,
President
Authorized officer

(J85505 Tues. Jul 19, 26, Aug 2)

Source: © 2016 OnCourse Learning

The holder of the debt may offset the amount owed, up to the amount of the debt. Others must pay cash or its equivalent. A trustee's deed, similar to the one illustrated in Figure 11.4, is issued to the highest bidder. Any surplus funds—that is, funds remaining after paying off all costs, fees, and expenses, along with all junior liens in order of their priority—are given to the trustor.

While no right of redemption exists after a trustee's sale, remember that the right of reinstatement, or period of reinstatement, continues until five business days before the scheduled sale. Then, at the time of sale, the purchaser acquires all rights

FIGURE 11.4 Sample trustee's deed for a foreclosure resale.

RECORDING REQUESTED BY:

AND WHEN RECORDED MAIL TO:

SPACE ABOVE THIS LINE IS FOR RECORDER'S USE

A.P.N.: _____ Order No.: _____ Escrow No.: _____

TRUSTEE'S DEED UPON SALE

_____ (herein called Trustee) does hereby grant and convey, but without covenant or warranty, express or implied, to _____ (herein called Grantee) the real property in the _____ County of _____, State of California, described as follows:

This conveyance is made pursuant to the authority and powers vested in said Trustee, as Trustee, or Successor Trustee, or Substituted Trustee, under that certain Long Form Security (Installment) Land Contract executed by _____, Vendor, and _____, Vendee, recorded _____, as Instrument No. _____, in Book _____, Page _____, of Official Records in the Office of the Recorder of _____ County, California; and pursuant to the Notice of Default recorded _____, as Instrument No. _____ in Book _____, Page _____, of Official Records of said County, Trustee having complied with all applicable statutory requirements of the State of California and performed all duties required by said Security Land Contract including, among other things, as applicable, the mailing of copies of notices or the publication of a copy of the notice of default or the personal delivery of the copy of the notice of default or the posting of copies of the notice of sale or the publication of a copy thereof.

At the time and place fixed in the Notice of Trustee's Sale, said Trustee did sell said property above described at public auction on _____ to said Grantee, being the highest bidder therefor, for $ _____ cash, lawful money of the United States.

Dated: _____

STATE OF CALIFORNIA
COUNTY OF _____

On _____, before me, _____
personally appeared
_____, who
proved to me on the basis of satisfactory evidence to be the person(s) whose name(s) is/are subscribed to the within instrument and acknowledged to me that he/she/they executed the same in his/her/their authorized capacity(ies), and that by his/her/their signature(s) on the instrument the person(s), or the entity upon behalf of which the person(s) acted, executed the instrument.

I certify under the PENALTY OF PERJURY under the laws of the State of California that the foregoing paragraph is true and correct.

WITNESS my hand and official seal.

_____
Trustee

_____
Assistant Secretary

_____ (Notary seal)
Signature

Mail Tax Statements to _____

Source: © 2016 OnCourse Learning

held by the former owner, becoming the successor in interest, and is entitled to immediate possession, subject to those having rights prior to the time when the trust deed was recorded (e.g., tenants' rights under a bona fide lease agreement). Lenders in California prefer the use of the Trustee's Sale under a Deed of Trust due to the fact that the procedures involved and the time required, which is approximately four months, are relatively easy to determine, whereas foreclosures under the judicial method and foreclosures involving mortgages entail court actions, with consequent uncertainty as to time. (See Figure 11.5.) If a trustee's sale is used instead of a judicial foreclosure, the lender cannot sue for a deficiency should one exist.

FIGURE 11.5 Deeds of trust versus mortgages.

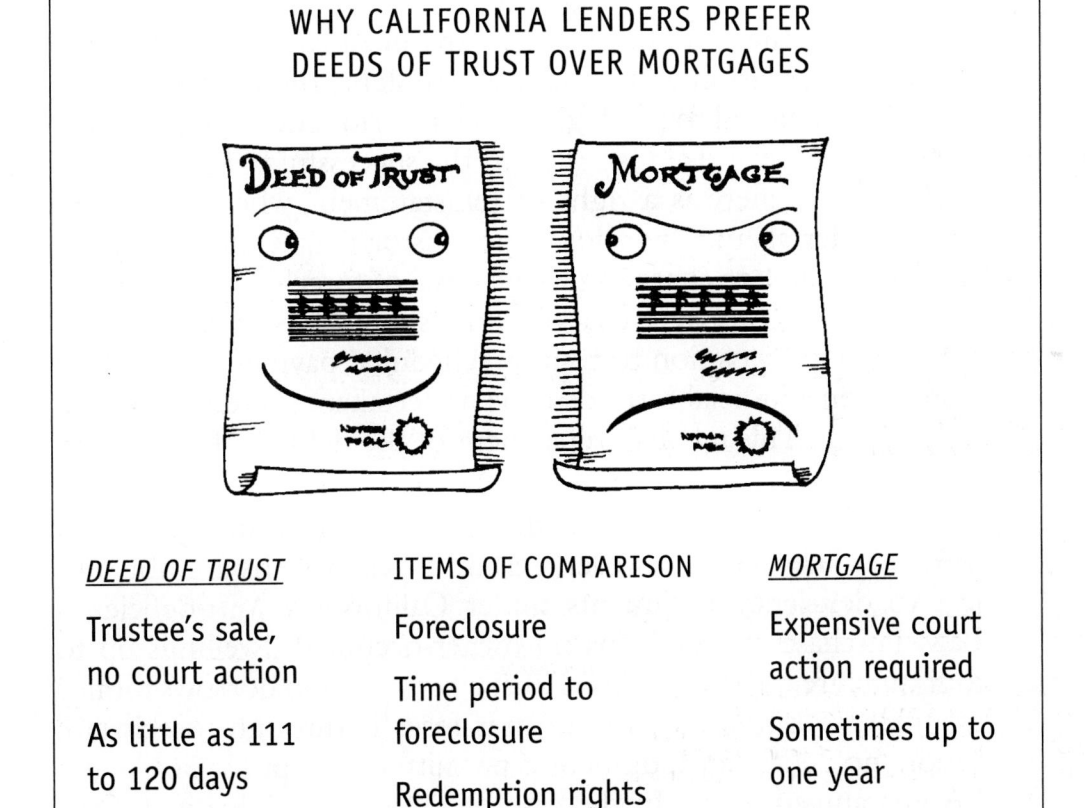

WHY CALIFORNIA LENDERS PREFER DEEDS OF TRUST OVER MORTGAGES

DEED OF TRUST	ITEMS OF COMPARISON	MORTGAGE
Trustee's sale, no court action	Foreclosure	Expensive court action required
As little as 111 to 120 days	Time period to foreclosure	Sometimes up to one year
No redemption rights	Redemption rights of the borrower after foreclosure	Right to redeem for up to one year

In short, it is quicker and cheaper to foreclose under a deed of trust than under a mortgage.

Source: © 2016 OnCourse Learning

Judicial Sale

Instead of a trustee's sale, a trust deed may also be foreclosed as a mortgage, that is, through court action. Court foreclosures of trust deeds are not common and usually occur only when the lender intends to seek a deficiency judgment.

1. *Procedure.* After serving a complaint upon the defaulting debtor, trial is held and a judgment is entered through a decree of foreclosure and order of sale by an officer of the court, such as a sheriff or marshal. Meanwhile, the debtor has the right to reinstate by paying all delinquent installments plus costs and attorney's fees.

2. *Sale.* A notice of the time, place, and purpose of the sale is posted and publicized. The court thereafter conducts a public auction sale. The highest bidder receives a Certificate of Sale.

    This conveys title to the property, subject to the debtor's right of redemption for a period of one year after the sale if there is a deficiency. If there is no deficiency, the deed is issued after three months. In addition to payment of the debt, the debtor is ordinarily also required to pay legal interest. If no redemption is made within this time, a deed is issued to the successful bidder.

    Note that there is a right of reinstatement when a trustee's sale is undertaken. This allows the trustor to pay all delinquencies, including late charges, plus all costs of foreclosure, including trustee's fees, recording charges, publishing costs, etc. The trustor is then in a position to resume scheduled payments under the loan. When a judicial foreclosure is undertaken, there is a right of redemption. This involves repayment of the debt.

3. *Deficiency judgments.* In the event that the sale does not bring enough funds to satisfy the debt, the creditor may obtain a **deficiency judgment**. However, certain types of loans are not subject to deficiency judgments under California's Anti-deficiency Law. Purchase money loans on owner-occupied dwellings up to four units are the exceptions. Thus, when a person borrows money to purchase a home and thereafter loses it through foreclosure action, no deficiency judgment is permitted, except for FHA- and VA-guaranteed loans. In the case of FHA and VA loans, federal law supersedes state law, and the FHA and the VA can but rarely do seek deficiency judgments.

The ability to obtain a deficiency judgment is one reason for lenders to seek a judicial foreclosure versus foreclosing via a trustee's sale. California is a state in which deficiency judgments, with rare exceptions, are unavailable to lenders. There are some general rules governing deficiency judgments, their tax consequences, and the rules under which they can be obtained.

Confusion can occur regarding whether the loan is categorized as recourse or non-recourse, the latter definition referring to residential property (one to four units), and purchase money loans (loans obtained to purchase a home, including owner financed loans). Refinanced loans or equity line loans wherein the proceeds are not for paying off purchase money loans and/or used in the renovation of the home are generally considered recourse loans, subject to deficiency judgments. While seldom exercised because of the costs involved in a deficiency judgment lawsuit, a sufficiently large unpaid loan debt might prompt a lender to proceed.

Since the financial crises in 2008, lenders' recourse should they seek a deficiency judgment is limited based upon the fair market value of the subject property. For example, if a home with an original $200,000 loan was sold via a short sale or foreclosed upon for $150,000, there would be a $50,000 deficiency. If the home's fair market value at the time of the short sale or foreclosure was $175,000, the lender would be entitled to only a $25,000 deficiency.

Short sales wherein qualified principal residence indebtedness is forgiven are mostly exempt from deficiency judgments in California. The difference between the amount owed and the eventual short sale results in what is known for tax purposes as the forgiveness of debt amount. The federal Mortgage Forgiveness Debt Relief Act of 2007 clarified that such forgiven debt was not taxable. The law expired in 2013 and not until very late in 2014 was legislation extended to include 2014 short sale sellers. The legislation was not extended beyond 2014, leaving many short sale sellers wary of the potential tax consequences of their forgiven debt during 2015 transactions and beyond. (Short sales are discussed in greater detail later in this chapter.)

Deed in Lieu of Foreclosure

To avoid the costly and time-consuming process of foreclosure, the lender may accept a voluntary conveyance from the defaulting borrower. Usually this is accomplished by a **Deed in Lieu of Foreclosure**, though it could be by grant or **quitclaim deed** which should be simultaneously recorded with a deed of reconveyance. Note, the lender is not required to accept a Deed in Lieu. One advantage of such a transaction for the borrower is that there won't be a deficiency judgment, with a judicial foreclosure. The downside is that lenders will not accept such a deed if there are other liens, such as unpaid real estate taxes, because lenders want to take property free and clear of any other claims. To be assured that the lender will not seek a deficiency judgment, the Deed in Lieu should contain a statement that it is in full satisfaction of the debt.

A Deed in Lieu requires cancellation of debt and reconveyance, while a quitclaim deed does not necessarily require this. Moreover, some future creditor may still view a Deed in Lieu of Foreclosure as a repossession and the borrower as a poor credit risk. The stigma and subsequent reduction in credit scores is much the same whether the loss of property is through a Deed in Lieu of Foreclosure or by foreclosure itself. There is also a serious question regarding liens not eliminated by a quitclaim deed, but this is better left to an attorney.

11.3 MINIMIZING LOAN DEFAULTS

It has been said that a loan that is not good for the lender is not good for the borrower. If the loan is marginal, as when the credit rating is poor, the borrower is more likely to default on payments, with the result that the lender will end up with a bad loan followed by foreclosure and, usually, the lender will take over the property. This section outlines a variety of ways to minimize or mitigate the chance of loss for both borrower and lender.

Impound Accounts

One way to reduce the possibility of default is through the establishment of an **impound account**. Under this concept, the borrower is required to pay, as a condition for receiving the loan, a pro rata portion of the annual property taxes and insurance each month. This effectively forces the debtor to budget each month amounts that would fall due in large sums if paid only once or twice a year. Requiring such payments 12 times a year by having borrowers add one-twelfth of the tax bill and insurance premiums to monthly payments of principal and interest reduces the chance of default. After all, even if the debtor is current on loan payments, the property may go into foreclosure because of default in payments on other property-related debts, in accordance with the terms of the trust deed.

In some areas an impound account is referred to as an **escrow account** or loan trust fund. Whatever its designation, it means the same. The lender deposits the tax and insurance portions of the installment payments into an escrow or impound account, forwarding payments to the tax collector and insurance company as they fall due. The lender is assured that these bills are paid, while the debtor is relieved of a large obligation falling due in one or two lump sums at a time when it may be inconvenient to pay. Borrowers may assume the responsibility for proper payments themselves, but an impound account is generally required with any loan over an 80 percent LTV.

Forbearance

By far, the most common default on real estate loans is for delinquent payments. When borrowers have legitimate reasons for their inability to pay, lenders will often make special arrangements to help such debtors retain their properties. Any arrangement that effectively delays or forestalls foreclosure action is referred to as **forbearance**. There are various ways in which lenders (through their loan administration efforts) can assist borrowers. These include a variety of moratorium schemes and recastings. (See the Case & Point at end of this chapter for information regarding various government intervention strategies to assist struggling home buyers.)

Moratorium

A **moratorium** is a temporary suspension or **waiver** of payments. It acts to delay or defer action for collection of a debt. Four types of moratoria are explained below.

1. *Waiver of principal payments.* One form of moratorium is the suspension of principal payments, allowing delinquent borrowers to regain their financial balance. Only interest is paid in such cases. Since the principal portion of the monthly payment is the smaller amount, especially during the early years of a mortgage, this option is often of little assistance to a struggling borrower.

    A variation of this moratorium is skipping the entire monthly payment of principal and interest. For instance, if P&I is $1,200 per month, and the lender permitted up to 10 months suspension, then $12,000 (10 × $1,200) would be added to the principal, which would result in higher payments once resumed.

2. *Deferring of interest.* Another form of moratorium is the suspension of interest payments. Interest is not forgiven but is added to the principal indebtedness, much like loans with negative amortizations. This can offer significant relief to the debtor whose installments are almost all interest, either because it is a relatively high-interest loan or because it is not a seasoned loan, or both.

    In the case of VA loans, interest that accrues during a period of forbearance becomes a part of the guaranteed indebtedness. Consequently, holders of VA mortgages can assist veterans through forbearance without incurring loss.

3. *Partial payments.* Lenders may also agree to accept partial payments. Indeed, the VA encourages holders of GI loans to extend such privileges so that veterans may be given every opportunity to retain their homes while awaiting financial recovery. This may result in negative amortization, but it's a way to preserve one's property from foreclosure. If by contrast payments were made because of special circumstances, such as temporary unemployment or disability, lenders may be persuaded to stop foreclosure proceedings if assurances can be made that an extra, say, $100 per month will be paid to repay the delinquent installments.

4. *Prepayments.* Prepayments credited to principal in the past may be reapplied for the purpose of curing a default or preventing a subsequent default. Similarly, some loans may have been credited with lump-sum payments derived from proceeds of a partial sale of property to highway departments, local municipalities, or private parties.

Note: A potential problem with all options is that borrowers may never recover financially and be able to restart full payments.

Recasting

Another form of borrower assistance is through **recasting** or loan modification. It actually involves a change in loan terms. In order to assist a delinquent borrower, the lender may agree to rearrange the loan in some fashion. This can be done at the outset, when the debtor first in default, or it may be done after a moratorium, in order to minimize the impact of having to repay both current and past installments.

The Department of Housing and Urban Development (HUD) adopted special forbearance regulations aimed at helping financially troubled homeowners save their houses. Under the relaxed rules, forbearance may be granted under any circumstances contributing to a default beyond the homeowner's control. For example, as the recession continued, monthly income was regularly affected by required pay reductions, imposed partial furloughs resulting in fewer hours worked, and other cost reduction measures taken by employers. Lost jobs resulted in employment in lesser paying positions from which some families have yet to recover. Here are four methods of recasting:

1. *Extended term.* If permitted by law or regulations, one way to recast a loan is to extend the original period of repayment, sometimes called reamortization. Extending to 30 years an existing loan that has, say, 15 years remaining of an original 25-year term will result in lower monthly payments. Some lenders may extract

a higher interest rate for this privilege, but the alternative might be foreclosure. Regulations may, however, prohibit institutional lenders from extending the term while a default exists.

2. *Increase of debt.* Though it's unlikely in situations where little or no equity exists, some lenders may increase the debt when they are satisfied that the debtor's dilemma will be solved, tiding over the debtor whose financial reversals are apparently temporary in nature. Again, the lender may exact a higher interest rate, but the new note can be extended for a longer term that may more than offset the increase in payments due to the higher rate. The proceeds of the new loan might be put in an assigned savings account for the borrower, which is then used to make the payments on both the old and new loans.

   Under VA-backed loans, advances may be made from the assigned account for maintenance, protective repairs, taxes, assessments, and hazard insurance. GI debtors may well save their homes when such funds are advanced.

3. *Reduction of interest.* Still another form of recasting a loan is a reduction of the interest rate, even if the reduction is only temporary. While most uncommon, a lender may be amenable to reducing the interest rate when the market warrants it. For example, an existing 6.0 percent rate might be reduced to 5.5 percent when the market is at, say, 4.75 percent.

4. *Reduction of principal amount owed.* The 2008–2009 negative equity dilemma introduced initially, but in extremely rare instances, loan modifications involving a reduction in principal loan amounts. After early government guidelines promoted the idea of principal reductions, support became tepid at best as the recession expanded and loss of equity via reduced values accelerated. Lenders resisted this option even as a last resort solution.

Recasting options during this time were made more difficult for three reasons:

1. Home values declined substantially in many areas, resulting in mortgage amounts far in excess of home values and causing the abandonment of all forms of recasting.
2. Recasting generally required the approval of the secondary market investors. With mortgages having been packaged and sold globally, this approval was difficult and, in some cases, impossible to acquire. Remember, many 100 percent loans had been made using an 80 percent LTV first trust deed followed by a 20 percent second TD. Secondary lenders resisted being wiped out as values declined.

3. HUD counseling centers, established to specifically assist homeowners determine their options to avoid foreclosure, were swamped with requests, and many borrowers found it difficult to get help.

Mortgage Guaranty Insurance

Insurance against loss through foreclosure is likely the best means of protecting the financial interests of lenders. This is accomplished through public and private mortgage insurance plans.

Government-Insured and Guaranteed Loans

With the introduction of Cal-Vet in 1923, the FHA program in 1934, and the VA program in 1944, many more buyers have been able to enter the housing market. This is because of the willingness on the part of lenders to extend loans with high loan-to-value ratios that are backed by insurance or a government guarantee.

Federal Housing Administration Options

As noted in an earlier chapter, risks to lenders can be eliminated through a federal insurance plan. The FHA is not the lender, but rather the insurer of the loan made by a qualified lender. Under the plan, the lender is assured that in case of foreclosure, the FHA will pay any loss in either cash or government debentures. Or the lender may, with prior FHA approval, assign the defaulted loan directly to the FHA before final foreclosure action in exchange for insurance benefits. Whichever way it acquires the property, the FHA sometimes repairs, refurbishes, and resells the property in order to minimize the losses to the FHA. In most cases, however, the FHA simply sells the property in an "as is" condition.

The cost of the insurance is borne by the borrower. Either the Mortgage Insurance Premium (MIP) is paid upfront in cash or, more often, it is financed as part of the loan and paid monthly. The MMI is paid with the monthly payments.

As efforts to help home owners find mortgage relief sputtered, FHA was enlisted as the agency to refinance troubled loans. The result was that FHA ended up with a greater default rate than anticipated. By June 3, 2013, in an effort to reduce emphasis on higher risk loans, FHA required a minimum 620 credit score (reduced again in late 2014 to 580 minimum score) and set 43 percent as the maximum debt to income for all borrowers. At the same time, FHA eliminated the automatic elimination of the Upfront Mortgage Insurance Premium (when the loan reached 78 percent LTV) in favor of a life-of-loan premium. The monthly mortgage insurance requirement remained intact for the life of the loan.

The FHA also offers a loan assignment program. For loans more than three months in default, and when the cause is not the fault of the borrower, the loan is assigned to HUD, which will pay off the lender. The homeowners, thereafter, make payments directly to HUD under a flexible schedule designed to meet their needs. The local FHA office is the source of additional information regarding the location of HUD counseling centers and HUD's pre-foreclosure program.

Department of Veterans Affairs Options

For qualified veterans, the VA guarantees lenders that, if the veteran defaults, the VA will satisfy at least part of the debt. Suppose, for example, that a 100 percent loan is made for the purchase price of $200,000. Assume the property thereafter goes on the auction block under foreclosure action and sells for $170,000. Finally, assume that there is $180,000 owing at the time of the foreclosure. How much will the VA be liable for? Recall from Chapter 6 that loans in excess of $144,000 have a maximum guarantee of 25 percent of the loan balance. Multiplying the $180,000 loan balance by 25 percent equals $45,000. Next we compare this figure with the actual loss (ignoring costs), which is $180,000 less $170,000, or $10,000. Hence, the VA's liability to the lender will be limited to $10,000 actual loss.

Veterans are charged an up-front funding fee for this guarantee. However, should a deficiency arise, the veteran is liable for any claim paid by the VA, which is said to have the right of **subrogation** for the amount paid. Suppose a veteran homeowner sells a property secured by a GI loan. How can the veteran be released from liability for any default caused by the new owner? There are two ways to do this: (1) pay off the existing loan in full from the proceeds of the purchaser's new loan, or (2) secure a written release from the Department of Veterans Affairs. Even though a buyer offers to assume the veteran seller's personal liability for the repayment of the loan, the veteran must still obtain written release from liability on the loan from the VA. Under most circumstances, a loan is assumed only if the rate is lower than what can be acquired via the current marketplace. The low interest rate market in recent years resulted in few, if any, loan assumptions occurring. To qualify for a release, four tests must be met:

1. A new purchaser must have requisite entitlement remaining.
2. The loan must not be delinquent.

3. The purchaser transferee must be acceptable to the VA from an income and credit standpoint.
4. The purchaser assumes the loan and the indemnity obligation signed by the veteran at the time the loan was originally made.

Like the FHA, the VA offers forbearance for vets in foreclosure. Once the veteran has missed three payments, the lender must notify the VA and provide a description of what it has done to remedy the default. The VA provides counseling and mediation services between lender and borrower.

Under the Soldiers and Sailors Civil Relief Act, various forms of relief are provided to active military members who get behind with their mortgage payments. Applicants are encouraged to double check with military lawyers to determine eligibility.

Federal Home Loan Mortgage Corporation (FHLMC)

Although mortgage lenders have wide discretion to extend relief to borrowers who encounter hardships, are cooperative, and have proper regard for fulfilling their obligations, too many struggling homeowners have found it difficult to acquire significant relief. The HAMP loan (see the Case & Point at the end of this chapter) was widely recommended but too often proved unavailable and/or ineffective.

California Veterans Farm and Home Purchase Act Assistance

The Cal-Vet plan, as this program is called, contains a life insurance feature that only indirectly benefits the lender, the Department of Veterans Affairs of the State of California, which holds legal title to the security. The veteran debtor is the party who benefits most from the insurance feature.

Qualified veterans under Cal-Vet financing must purchase life and disability insurance through its home protection plan. The plan insures the debtor's life for the amount of the unpaid loan balance at the time of death. A double indemnity clause is also included, until age 70, up to a maximum of $75,000. The monthly premiums for the home protection plan, including the optional benefits, are based on the age of the insured. The portion of the life insurance policy covering the remaining loan balance is paid to the California Department of Veterans Affairs.

Permanent and total disability benefits are included for veterans under age 65 and employed full-time, including full-time homemakers. Under the plan, the veteran's full loan payment is paid after the first three months of total disability and payments continue until the contract is paid off or for a maximum of three years, whichever occurs first.

Private Mortgage Insurance

As we discussed in Chapter 5, in addition to public insurance, private companies have devised insurance plans to reduce, if not eliminate, the risk of loss on conventional mortgages. Lenders protect themselves by generally requiring PMI coverage on loans in excess of 80 percent LTV. Prior to mid-2009, PMI-insured loans could be made up to 97 percent LTV. Reacting to the broadening foreclosure numbers accompanied by severe home value declines, PMI companies sought to reduce their risk by limiting their coverage to a maximum 90 percent loan-to-value and to borrowers with a minimum 720 FICO score. It was not until 2013 that 95 percent LTV loans were again available. In November 2014 Fannie Mae announced their intent to reintroduce a 97 percent LTV loan option (information is contained in Chapter 5). Private mortgage insurance does not insure the entire loan amount, only the top portion of the loan. Regulations governing how PMI coverage can be discontinued when the lender's equity is no longer endangered remain unchanged but are always subject to revision.

Private mortgage insurance is provided for conventional loans for one- to four-unit residential properties. Commercial and industrial property loans generally require a 20 percent or more down payment and thus mortgage insurance is not necessary.

Automatic Payment Plans

Another way to reduce the chance of default is through an **automatic mortgage pay plan** offered by many lenders. Under the plan, a system of preauthorized monthly mortgage payments is established. It relieves the homeowner of the chore of paying each month and protects the debtor against forgetting to make a payment. Borrowers simply authorize their banks to make an automatic monthly deduction from their checking accounts and to forward this amount to the real estate lender. This option is typically made available when signing loan documents but can be requested of most lenders at any time during the term of the loan.

Consumer Protection Laws and Regulations

Still another way to mitigate or reduce the chance of default is through consumer protection laws and regulations.

Public Regulations

A wide variety of laws and regulations protect real estate buyers in one way or another. Among these is the Truth-in-Lending Law (see Chapter 10). Also called the Consumer Credit Protection Act, this federal law prescribes full disclosure of all borrowing charges.

This calculation of the total cost of borrowing and the effective interest is called the APR. The federal government's anticipation is that borrowers can compare APR calculations to obtain the best loan terms when shopping for home financing. With certain kinds of loans, such as junior loans and refinancing, the borrower may rescind or cancel the credit arrangement within three business days after signing loan documents without declaring any reason for doing so. This right does not apply in the case of a first trust deed created or assumed for the purpose of financing the purchase of a dwelling in which the borrower expects to reside (See a more complete explanation of APR in Chapter 15). On the state level, an important law designed to protect consumers is the right to cancel home improvement contracts within three days of the time of their solicitation by a door-to-door salesperson. Even when such a contract is initiated by the homeowner, the truth-in-lending provisions allow cancellation within three business days if financing is involved. Thus, homeowners who change their minds for any reason may cancel during the first three days after signing any contract.

Home Warranties

Buyers of new or existing homes can encounter problems with major components of the home, resulting in financial hardship and difficulty in making their mortgage payments. Private industry over the years has offered a variety of home warranty programs in an effort to mitigate financial burdens at a time when borrowers can least afford such repairs. Most programs protect the new buyer for a specified time period, usually one year after close of escrow. Although warranties can differ, most cover the major home components, including plumbing, electrical system, heating and/or air conditioning, walls, roof, and foundation. Special components, like swimming pools, can be protected via the payment of additional policy fees. Sellers often provide and pay for a home warranty as a way to provide a benefit to the new buyer but also to protect themselves from being negatively impacted by unknown component difficulties after the close of escrow. Buyers may also purchase home warranties, but must do so before the close of escrow. During the warranty coverage period, homeowners pay an approximate $60 per service call fee as a deductible.

11.4 OTHER LENDING PROBLEMS

Usury

The cost of money is always related to the anticipated risk to the lender providing the financing. One way in which lenders may be compensated for any increase in potential loss is to charge higher interest rates. Those borrowers most susceptible to high interest rate loans are those who, for various reasons, have proven to be unable to acquire more conventional financing and/or are potential credit risks. However, there are state limitations on the amount of interest that can, regardless of the reason, be charged a borrower. The maximum rate that may be charged on loans made by nonexempt individuals, whether or not secured by real estate, is 10 percent, or 5 percent above the Federal Reserve discount rate, whichever is greater. Remember from Chapter 1 that the Federal Funds rate is the rate of interest one bank charges another for the overnight use of excess reserves. The low interest rates in recent years has, for the most part, resulted in a 10% maximum rate allowed for nonexempt lenders.

Regulated institutional lenders in California are not limited in the rate of interest they may charge, relying instead on the marketplace to restrain rates. Effective yields are increased through the use of points or discounts, as illustrated in Chapter 7. Sellers carrying back loans are exempt from usury laws, as are real estate brokers.

Borrowers who deal with noninstitutional lenders are perceived to require protection against usurious transactions. These lenders consist of private parties making hard money loans. This protection is reinforced with the disclosure requirements under Regulation Z of the Truth-in-Lending Act. As pointed out in Chapter 10, this federal law requires that borrowers receive a written statement of the total costs involved in any financial transaction. Truth-in-Lending does not prescribe limits on interest rates. But by requiring that the prepaid costs and expenses be translated into an annual percentage rate, it provides one way for borrowers to compare loan costs when shopping for their best loan terms.

Because of the increased risk for lenders providing junior trust deeds, there is usually an effort to maximize their rate of return. Borrowers making use of secondary or hard money loans can be more desperate for funding and thus more susceptible to lender schemes to circumvent the legal limits on interest rates.

The impact of usury statutes on money markets is a controversial subject. Proponents insist that borrowers need protection from unscrupulous lenders. Critics suggest that such limitations can reduce the money supply. Their argument is that by keeping interest rates down, at whatever levels, lenders naturally gravitate to those places where money can be put to more productive use. Thus, a lender might determine that the risk related to the limited return is too great and divert available funds from mortgage lending to other investments where the return is more commensurate with the risk. The net effect on potential home buyers would be a decrease in mortgage funds and a postponement of purchases.

Redlining

A serious problem at times in the past and that could occasionally resurface in real estate lending is redlining, the practice of systematic refusal to lend mortgage money in high-risk areas. These were usually older urban areas containing high minority concentrations, around which lenders placed red lines delineating such neighborhoods as off limits to mortgage credit. Little, if any, consideration was given to the creditworthiness of the individual borrower.

By limiting or refusing credit, the lender anticipated reducing its exposure to delinquencies and foreclosures. However, it has been demonstrated that the withholding of real estate financing hastens the decay of these neighborhoods. The so-called closed neighborhoods fall prey to speculators and absentee landlords, dubbed "slumlords" in some areas, who, some claim, drain the community, leaving deterioration and destruction in their paths. The few homes that are financed often end up abandoned and foreclosed, thus compounding the problem of redlining. Meanwhile, buyers in these neighborhoods find the money spigots turned off, with no place to turn for help. These buyers may be the very ones who place their savings into local financial institutions and then find themselves unable to borrow from these institutions while their deposits may be used to finance homes outside the redlined areas.

Both the federal and state governments have tried to resolve this dilemma. All federally regulated mortgage lenders are required to disclose publicly just where they make their mortgage loans. Also, the State of California has imposed guidelines relating to fair lending practices that prohibit denying credit or altering the terms of a loan solely because of neighborhood factors. When a person is denied a loan, the lender must notify the applicant, in writing, of the reasons for denial within 30 days of the application.

To help guard against the continued practice of redlining, state-chartered savings banks are required to file periodic reports with the California Department of Financial Institutions. Written details of how and where loans are being made are submitted so lending patterns can be determined. Many items must be included in the report: county and census tract; purpose of the loan and outcome—made, denied, purchased, or sold; amount of loan requested and amount issued; type of property, appraised value, year built, square footage; sales price; interest rate, and whether fixed or variable, discounts, fees charged; existing balance on loans refinanced and how the proceeds were used, such as for repairs or improvements; borrower's and total family income; race or ethnic makeup of the applicant, sex and age of borrower; data on co-borrowers and co-applicants; and information on whether neighborhood factors were considered in underwriting the loan.

Community Reinvestment Act (CRA)

To stop discriminatory practices, including redlining, Congress passed the **Community Reinvestment Act (CRA)**, which requires federally supervised financial institutions to disclose lending data in their lobbies and elsewhere. The Financial Institutions Reform, Recovery and Enforcement Act (FIRREA) requires lenders to report data on the race, gender, income, and census tract of people to whom they make loans. Its stated purpose is "to assist in identifying discriminatory practices and enforcing antidiscrimination statutes." CRA and FIRREA encourage lenders to offer mortgages for low and moderately priced housing and meet other credit needs for low- and moderate-income families. Lenders are required to make positive efforts to provide loans in areas from which savings are received. FIRREA requires evaluation reports and CRA ratings of lender practices to be made public for all institutions. In cooperation with other government agencies, it grades each institution on how well it:

- Knows the credit needs of its community.
- Informs the community about its credit services.
- Involves its directors in setting up and monitoring CRA programs.
- Participates in government-insured, guaranteed, or subsidized loans.
- Distributes credit applications, approvals, and rejections across geographic areas.
- Offers a range of residential mortgages, housing rehabilitation loans, and small business loans.

All of these criteria are designed to protect consumers against unlawful discrimination. A positive CRA rating is a prerequisite for institutions to open new branches and to engage in expansions, acquisitions, and mergers, since outside third parties can petition agencies to deny these activities to institutions with poor CRA grades.

Home Mortgage Disclosure Act (HMDA)

Mortgage lenders are required to provide an annual report regarding the borrowers who both applied for and acquired loans. Referred to as the HMDA report, the information is obtained via section X of the loan application. This section, entitled Information for Government Monitoring Purposes, seeks voluntary information from borrowers including ethnicity, race, and sex. Although the information is voluntary, borrowers are informed that "if you do not furnish ethnicity, race or sex, under federal regulations, this lender is required to note the information on the basis of visual observation and surname." Combating discrimination is critical in every aspect of the lending industry.

Short Sales

As property values continued to decline during the 2007–2009 period, more and more sellers were unable to sell their homes for prices sufficient to cover the outstanding loan balances and costs of selling (this is known as being upside down on their mortgage). Lenders were faced with either accepting less than what they were owed or foreclosing on the property. **Short sales** became an often recommended method of disposing of property under these circumstances.

Prior to 2007, short sales were not as popular because of the income tax consequences of such a sale. Called the phantom tax consequence, the loan relief or forgiveness portion of the lender's current mortgage amount was taxable. For example, if a borrower owed $200,000 but the short sale garnered only $150,000, the $50,000 of forgiven debt became taxable as income, even though the borrower had acquired no cash. Under these circumstances short sales were not popular, with many defaulting borrowers opting for foreclosure or deeds in lieu of foreclosure. The Mortgage Debt Forgiveness Act of 2007 was a welcome relief and made debt forgiveness retroactive for sales from January 2007. Greatly easing the problem on debt forgiveness for up to $2 million for a personal residence, it allowed the use of short sales to proliferate.

The act had been extended only through 2013, and many borrowers entering short sales in 2014 would have suffered serious tax complications if said legislation had not been passed at the last minute in the 2014 legislation designed to fund the government into 2015. Disappointed that the December 2014 extension did not include 2015, potential short sellers were left without assurance that the Mortgage Forgiveness Act would provide forgiveness of debt taxation from short sale transactions and loan modifications going into 2015 and the future. A pending bill in the legislature as of August 2015 had yet to be acted upon.

It should be noted that in California an IRS interpretation of state law seems to provide short sale forgiveness of debt tax relief without the extension of the Mortgage Forgiveness Act. There remains skepticism whether the IRS ruling also includes loan modifications wherein debt relief occurs. Tax counsel is, as always, advised in these kinds of situations.

While the seller can remain in possession of his or her home during the short sale process, the lender is the entity who has to agree to any terms of sale. Any offer to purchase is referred to the lender, who either accepts or counters the offer. Mounting short sale requests resulted in extraordinarily long time frames, often months, for any conclusion. Any transaction that involved a second mortgage became extremely difficult, and borrower frustration grew as the problems persisted and increased. At the same time, lenders began to lean toward foreclosure as a better remedy for them than the short sale route. The government made efforts to promote lenders' participation in helping borrowers with their declining home values. (See the Case & Point at the end of this chapter.)

The obvious result of the foreclosure and short sale explosion was the elimination of most of the risky loan options and a tightening of underwriting standards.

Web Help and Its Reliability

It is easy to turn to the Web for information about practically any subject, including all things financial. Borrowers seeking foreclosure, short sale, and other assistance seek information on the Web, as do those deciding to enter the real estate purchase market.

The reliability of the information must always be considered. Many of the websites that discuss this information are actually sales sites. Others simply have wrong data. Outdated and/or inaccurate information is not always easy to detect. Calculator sites are a good example. Unless one knows the internal formulas used to calculate estimated taxes or homeowners' insurance, the information is unlikely to be useful in every situation.

While you might use the Web to seek general information and to initiate your education in real estate finance, it is advised that you seek professional assistance when you are ready to proceed with any kind of real estate financing. With the ever-changing nature of the financial community, a do-it-yourself education via the Web may not be the best choice.

However, there are some sites that are kept updated and provide accurate information:

- www.hud.gov: The official site for FHA mortgage information includes home buying tips, information on how to avoid foreclosure, and abusive lending warnings.

- www.fanniemae.com: The Federal National Mortgage Association provides information on their Home Affordable program, tips on loan modification and refinance options, and a host of information for new and experienced homeowners.
- www.freddiemac.com: The Federal Home Loan Mortgage Corporation site addresses relevant buying and home owning issues.
- www.ftc.gov: The Federal Trade Commission site offers general information about current finance frauds, etc. The Consumer Information section has considerable lending information, including credit guidelines.
- www.mba.org: The Mortgage Bankers Association site features a Home Loan Learning Center along with up-to-date economic news and forecasts.

Chapter Summary

A deed of trust securing a promissory note requires more than simply repaying a loan. A default and possible foreclosure may result not only from delinquencies and nonpayment of the loan but also from noncompliance with many other provisions of the trust deed. These include proper maintenance of the property, carrying adequate hazard insurance, paying property taxes and other liens when due, and complying with all local building and safety ordinances.

A foreclosure action through a trustee's sale begins with the filing of a Notice of Default, followed by the publication of a Notice of Sale, and then the actual sale through auction. Liens are paid off in their order of priority, with remaining proceeds, if any, paid to the defaulting trustor. No redemptive rights exist thereafter. Foreclosure through judicial action is much more complicated and time consuming. Up to a one-year redemption period exists in favor of the defaulted trustor following final sale. Lenders therefore mostly resort to a trustee's sale, unless a deficiency judgment is sought, in which case court action is the only remedy.

Defaults can be largely minimized through establishment of an impound account; forbearance proceedings, including moratoriums and modifications or recasting; mortgage insurance, both public and private; automatic payment plans; repayment workouts; temporary indulgences; and an assortment of consumer protection laws and regulations.

Important Terms and Concepts

Automatic mortgage pay plan
Community Reinvestment Act (CRA)
Deed in Lieu of Foreclosure
Deficiency judgment
Escrow account
Forbearance
Impound account
Moratorium
Notice of Default

Notice of Sale
Quitclaim deed
Recasting
Right of reinstatement
Short sales
Subrogation
Trustee's sale
Waiver

Reviewing Your Understanding

Questions for Discussion

1. List four ways in which a borrower can default under the terms of a trust deed.
2. How does an assignment-of-rents clause operate to protect a lender?
3. What is meant by power of sale? Which party benefits from it, the beneficiary or trustor?
4. Contrast a Notice of Default with a Notice of Sale.
5. How does an impound account reduce against risk of loss?
6. List six ways that a lender's procedures can assist delinquent borrowers.
7. What is redlining? How does it affect lenders? Borrowers? Neighborhoods?

Multiple-Choice Questions

1. Reasons for defaulting on the repayment of a real estate debt are many and varied, including which one of the following?
   a. Marriage
   b. Increased earnings
   c. Judicious budgeting
   d. Disability

2. Following a foreclosure sale, surplus funds remaining after paying off all costs, fees, expenses, and liens are given to the
   a. successful bidder.
   b. trustee.
   c. beneficiary.
   d. trustor.

3. The successful bidder at a judicial sale of real estate property receives a
   a. Trustee's Deed.
   b. Certificate of Sale.
   c. Judicial Deed.
   d. Deed in Lieu of Foreclosure.

4. A temporary suspension or waiver of payments on a debt is termed
   a. forbearance.
   b. forestallment.
   c. wavering.
   d. recasting.

5. The MIP premium on FHA-insured loans
   a. must be paid at the end of the loan.
   b. can be added to the loan.
   c. is optional.
   d. is usually paid by the seller.

6. In the event of nonpayment of property taxes, the beneficiary may pay for the obligation directly, and thereafter
   a. bill the trustor directly.
   b. add the advances to the principal indebtedness.
   c. do either (a) or (b).
   d. do neither (a) nor (b).

7. Which of the following parties is not generally permitted to bid on a property offered at a foreclosure auction?
   a. Trustor
   b. Outside party
   c. Beneficiary
   d. Trustee

8. The right of redemption following a trustee's sale is good for
   a. one year.
   b. 90 days.
   c. three months.
   d. none of the above.

9. Assume that in a declining market, a small condo with an existing $119,000 GI loan sells for only $110,000 at a foreclosure sale. Ignoring foreclosure costs, the VA will reimburse the foreclosing lender
   a. $9,000.
   b. $21,000.
   c. $27,500.
   d. $30,250.

10. The trustor under a deed of trust became delinquent in his monthly payments, thereafter abandoning the premises and moving to another city. Which of the following actions is not part of the foreclosure procedure?
    a. Notify trustor of default
    b. Issue reconveyance deed
    c. Publish Notice of Sale
    d. Record Notice of Sale

11. If a borrower does not provide a real estate lender with proof of hazard insurance when required, the lender may
    a. purchase insurance coverage and add it to the principal balance of the loan.
    b. purchase insurance coverage and proceed with foreclosure if the borrower does not pay for it.
    c. institute foreclosure proceedings.
    d. do any of the above.

12. A trustee in a deed of trust may issue a trustee's deed upon a foreclosure sale as a result of
    a. violation of the due-on-sale clause.
    b. the power of sale contained in the deed of trust itself.
    c. provisions of the Business and Professions Code.
    d. the applicable sections of the Civil Code.

13. Proper foreclosure procedures include
    a. advertising in a newspaper of general circulation at least once a week for three months.
    b. posting a copy of the Notice of Sale on the property and in a public place.
    c. recording a copy of the newspaper advertisement.
    d. mailing a copy of the notice to the trustee by certified mail.

14. After the issuance of a Trustee's Deed at a foreclosure sale,
    a. all rights formerly held by the trustor are extinguished.
    b. the trustor has a one-year right of redemption.
    c. a successful bidder gets the full fee title, free of restrictions and with priority over the deed of trust foreclosed.
    d. the trustor has a three-month right of reinstatement.

15. Mortgage guaranty insurance, whether undertaken through government-backed or private sources,
    a. is designed to pay off the mortgage balance in the event of the death of a borrower.
    b. protects the lender against loss in the event of foreclosure.
    c. is paid for by the lender, since it is the lender that is protected.
    d. is a one-time charge paid for by borrowers.

16. The Community Reinvestment Act (CRA)
    a. prohibits redlining practices.
    b. requires posting of lending data for federally chartered lenders.
    c. may inhibit lender expansions and mergers.
    d. is involved in each of the above.

17. Recasting a loan may be accomplished by
    I. extending the term of the loan.
    II. increasing the debt.
    III. reducing the interest rate.
    IV. giving a Deed in Lieu of Foreclosure.
    a. I only.
    b. I and II only.
    c. I, II, and III only.
    d. I, II, III, and IV.

18. A homeowner fails to pay her special bond assessment due to loss of her job. The lender may
   a. pay the overdue tax and bill the homeowner.
   b. pay the overdue tax and add the amount to the loan.
   c. do either (a) or (b).
   d. do neither (a) nor (b).

19. A home with an original $140,000 VA loan nets $120,000 at a foreclosure sale. The amount owing at time of sale was $110,000. The borrower-trustor is entitled to
   a. $10,000.
   b. $20,000.
   c. $30,000.
   d. none of the above.

20. Should a borrower fail to maintain satisfactory property insurance, the lender's best cause of action would be to
   a. foreclose without any notice to the borrower.
   b. evict the borrower.
   c. sue the borrower for breach of contract.
   d. purchase a policy and add the premium to the loan.

> **CASE & POINT**
>
> **Foreclosure and Short Sales: Government Intervention Continues**
>
> The financial crisis that bloomed full bore by early 2008 was determined to be the result of the easy-qualifying conditions accompanied by the heavy reliance on adjustable rate mortgages (ARMs) that proliferated in the subprime mortgage era. Only later would it be learned that nearly 60 percent of the borrowers facing foreclosure had been eligible for a more stable loan option. Instead they opted for, or as some complained, had been sold an ARM product. Helping buyers attain the American dream of home ownership was the rationale continually heard for encouraging the ARM loan. Its low interest start rate accompanied by the lower monthly mortgage payment enabled borrowers to maximize their purchasing power or, as they later discovered, purchase beyond their ability to repay. At the time, double digit appreciation was expected to protect them from any erosion of equity

due to negatively amortized ARMs plus provide future profits as home values continued to climb. Everyone was wrong!

By January 2008, the rate of foreclosures was alarming. Borrowers who acquired loans starting in 2005 through June 30, 2007, were experiencing significant rate changes and projections were that millions more would soon be facing foreclosure. The 2008 Economic Recovery Act, known as the Stimulus Bill, was an effort to provide assistance to borrowers currently making on-time payments on loans still at their introductory rates but who were identified as unable to afford the soon-to-be-adjusted rates and accompanying payments. The information was unfortunately vague as to the procedure for determining eligibility. The broad guidelines addressed first loans only, seemingly eliminating buyers who used what had been a popular 80 percent first loan and 20 percent second loan with past 100 percent loan programs. Investor loans were deemed ineligible for modification, and the most glaring omission was no meaningful solution to the equity loss suffered by many homeowners.

Borrowers were further disillusioned when discovering that those who had already missed payments, thereby signaling that they were unable to make their adjusted payments, were not eligible for this remedy. Ironically, many of the borrowers who were now ineligible for assistance had been advised by these same institutions that the only way to receive any help was to actually go into default and possible foreclosure. Having taken that advice, they now found that having missed payments made them ineligible under the new guidelines.

Government plans remained unclear while proposals were tweaked and revised in an effort to find relief for a growing number of distressed homeowners. The process was complicated, as the very institutions/banks that had perpetrated the loan excesses were now being asked to voluntarily work to resolve the burgeoning foreclosure situation.

As is too often the case with new government plans, an overemphasis was placed on making sure that ineligible borrowers could not abuse the programs resulting in few being judged as eligible recipients. Plus, the lenders charged with voluntarily implementing the plans seemed not to fully embrace its lofty goals but instead to actually demonstrate a reluctance to really make them work. The result was constant revisions to eligibility and relatively few of the most desperate borrowers ultimately acquiring assistance.

The main thrust of the legislation to help homeowners in immediate risk of losing their homes to foreclosure was laudable, but success was hampered from the very beginning. Relying upon the voluntary cooperation of lenders and allowing each lender to determine the credit worthiness of the borrower and other aspects of each refinance/modification request resulted in inconsistency, long delays for borrowers, and disappointment. At the same time, lenders adopted a net present value calculation that in translation meant that they would compare the cost of a loan modification with a foreclosure and would implement whichever option provided the lesser cost or loss to the lender. This net present value calculation was performed by the lender without notification to the borrower, resulting in many borrowers being denied assistance without fully understanding why they didn't qualify for help.

This mostly failed help to borrowers was followed by millions losing homes even though lenders did not possess the appropriate documentation. Illegal foreclosures were conducted via what became known as the robo-signing scandal in which documents were fraudulently signed.

By early 2009 the Home Affordable Refinance Program (HARP) and the Home Affordable Modification Program (HAMP) were introduced among great expectations that consumers would finally acquire some meaningful assistance. Only borrowers who had acquired loans that were sold to the government-sponsored enterprises (GSEs) Fannie Mae and Freddie Mac were eligible for relief. Many borrowers had purchased with 100 percent financing, including both a first and second mortgage. These loans were mostly ineligible for either program. After considerable consumer disappointment, both programs have undergone numerous changes in an effort to reach and assist more homeowners, and the programs continue to this day.

HARP was designed for those borrowers who are current on their mortgage payments but because of a loss in home value are unable to acquire relief via a refinance loan. Initial emphasis was placed on borrowers who were "underwater" (owed more than their home was worth). The program was later expanded to include those whose equity position prohibited them from refinancing.

HAMP was envisioned as enabling borrowers to modify their mortgages to a more manageable long-term affordable rate. Only borrowers with loans with the GSEs were eligible, and again, the rules were complicated and confusing. The program's goals were laudable as they purported to include those who had lost employment, had second loans, and had missed mortgage payments.

The major lenders charged with implementing both programs (as noted above) demonstrated a reluctance to really make them work. The modification program, especially, was criticized by consumers as requiring mounds of paperwork (that kept getting lost by the participating lenders, requiring constant duplication) and long wait periods before ultimately determining the borrower ineligible. The original prediction that millions of homeowners would be helped proved overly optimistic.

In mid-2012, lenders were informed that they were to be evaluated on their participation in the programs, especially HARP, and were expected to make refinance loans. The program soon deteriorated into one in which borrowers were called and invited to do a HARP loan, at no out of pocket cost. Many of these borrowers were not experiencing difficulty with their mortgages, and the resulting refinance saved them little in the way of reduced monthly payments. Complaints continue that lenders seek borrowers who are not necessarily in need of relief while ignoring those for whom the programs were designed.

On the other hand, the lenders are able to point to the high volume of refinances being completed and the government powers, satisfied that the programs work, extended them until December 31, 2015. The guidelines have continually been relaxed, but many see the use for HARP and HAMP as having diminished. Even though millions have acquired this financing, the programs have not escaped the criticism of having been mostly bailout plans serving banks and other investors while failing to serve those most desperately in need of assistance.

By 2014 the number of foreclosures and short sales had declined and the housing market was perceived to be recovering, albeit slowly. Predictions for a robustly functioning housing market varied from occurring by the end of 2015 to mid-2017.

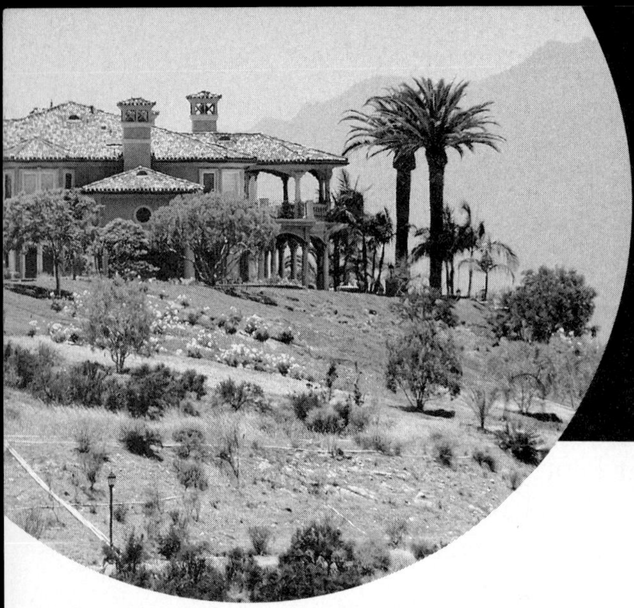

CONSTRUCTION LOANS

OVERVIEW

This chapter covers the field of financing construction projects. Topics in this chapter include sources and types of construction loans, loan costs, the construction loan process, and mechanic's liens.

After completing this chapter, you will be able to:

- List five types of construction lenders.
- List and define at least six technical words and terms that are common to the field of construction lending.
- Explain borrowers' costs under a construction loan.
- List the stages followed in processing a construction loan.
- Discuss the supporting documentation used in connection with construction financing.
- Outline the steps to take in filing mechanic's liens.
- Name three California laws that deal with assessments for the cost of construction of public improvements.

12.1 NATURE OF CONSTRUCTION LOANS

Construction financing is the provision of funds to pay for labor and materials that go into the construction of a new or existing property. The funds may come from two sources: (1) a general line of personal credit that a borrower has with financial institutions, materials suppliers, or subcontractors, and/or (2) a construction loan that is evidenced by a promissory note and secured by a deed of trust. The first involves the use of bank and commercial unsecured credit and is not classified as real estate credit. The second, the construction loan, is the subject of this chapter.

A *construction loan* is a short-term, interim, or temporary loan for building purposes, in contrast to permanent or long-term financing on already existing property. A typical construction loan for a single-family residence is usually for a term of 9 to 12 months and for a major project, such as an apartment house, a term of 18 months to two years may be normal. Apartment house construction loans generally allow sufficient time for completion and partial rental before full loan payments begin. Permanent loans on existing structures are written for longer terms, typically 15 to 30 years. When used in conjunction with a construction loan, a permanent loan is called a **take-out loan**. It is not unusual for a borrower to obtain a short-term construction loan from one lender, and then, when the project is completed, obtain a permanent or take-out loan from another lender to pay off the amount owed on the construction loan. Commercial banks favor interim construction loans, particularly where take-outs have been pre-approved, while savings banks prefer combination loans.

A construction loan is made for a specific dollar amount agreed upon before work begins. Construction funds are not paid to the borrower in a lump sum, but advanced in stages via a predetermined number of what are commonly referred to as draws as the construction process progresses. The permanent loan, in contrast, is placed after construction is completed and is paid over the loan term.

The construction loan is usually evidenced by a promissory note and secured by a deed of trust on the property under construction. The principal sum of the construction loan is non-amortized, though interest payments are periodically required from the borrower only on the money advanced.

Sources of Funds

Construction loans are made primarily by local financial institutions, mainly banks and credit unions.

The extent to which lenders are active in the construction loan market in a given area depends on several factors. Some lenders as a matter of policy do not make construction loans, whereas others may be in and out of the market as economic conditions change. Still others may make construction loans on a regular basis.

Kinds of Loans

There are two basic kinds of construction loans. The first is one that combines a construction loan with a permanent take-out mortgage, called a **combination loan.** These construction-to-permanent combination loans involve only one loan closing. The second type is the interim, short-term, straight construction loan, which is independent of the permanent loan, though the lender does anticipate that the proceeds of a permanent loan from some source will pay off the construction loan. Some banks will even allow a purchase loan-to-construction-to-permanent loan. This can be used for properties in need of repair or for a homeowner needing to remodel at the beginning of ownership. When using any of these options, the borrower must qualify for the payments of the final loan and any property will have to appraise for the future value, after work is complete.

Construction-to-Permanent Combination

Both the construction loan and the permanent loan originate in advance of construction and are secured under one instrument. The permanent loan begins according to the terms on the note at a predetermined time, designed to coincide with completion of construction. Two variations are common. The first variation is one in which advance payments are made to the contractor/builder as construction proceeds. The lender approves the borrower on the permanent mortgage and has the borrower sign the loan. Payments are made on the money as it is advanced during construction. This is frequently done in the financing of single-family homes built for an owner under contract with a builder for a custom home.

The second variation is also used in cases of single-family dwellings when the home is spec built—a common term used in construction—meaning that it is intended to be sold to a buyer (sometimes predetermined) upon completion. Here, the lender commits itself in advance of construction to make both the construction loan and permanent loan, but retains the right to approve the potential borrower, who is perhaps not yet known. The legal instruments are prepared so that the permanent loan can be assumed by the potential borrower. This kind of arrangement is in contrast with large-scale projects where lenders provide builders with construction money, perhaps a conventional blanket construction mortgage on an entire tract of land or subdivision, and the builders refer home buyers to the lender for permanent financing. The buyers usually have no obligation to place their loan through that particular lender.

The combination loan has potential advantages for both builder and potential buyer. In some cases there will be fewer expenses for the lender and these reductions or savings benefit the builder and buyer.

Short-Term Construction Loans

Interim, short-term, straight construction loans and separate take-out loans often involve two lenders and two sets of loan instruments compared with the single lender and instrument under the combination loan. The **short-term construction loan** can be made by a lender other than the lender making the permanent loan. The construction lender usually requires a commitment from the permanent take-out lender, unless the spec builder is well known to the lender, under which circumstances the original construction loan may be extended until a buyer is found. The loan is for a short term—say, one year—at which time it is due and payable. It is up to the borrower-builder to provide a take-out buyer during that time period or obtain permanent financing.

Loan Costs

The cost of a construction loan to the borrower consist of several items. Lenders may charge a flat fee, usually a percentage of the amount of the loan (such as 1, 2, or 3 percent) at the time the loan originates. These fees increase the effective rate of return on the loan to the lender, though a portion of the fee is used to cover the cost of originating the loan.

Charges may be made to cover the necessary items of expense in the origination and underwriting of the loan. Typical borrower's items would be charges for the appraisal report, credit report, survey, title insurance, legal fees, accrued interest, escrows, and premiums for hazard insurance and performance bond if required. Recall that these are similar to the nonrecurring costs discussed in Chapter 10 under closing costs for home loans. Lenders charge a flat fee, expressed in points, typically two to three, to cover all these items, or charge them in addition to their required origination points.

Construction loans, including combination loans, almost always involve higher fees than purchase money loans. This is due to higher overhead costs to the lender, such as onsite inspections, progress payments, and checking for mechanic's liens, and because of the higher risks involved. This is especially true if the home or project is being built on spec.

12.2 EVALUATION AND LENDING PROCESS

Lender Considerations for a Construction Loan

Before committing themselves to financing a construction project, construction lenders consider several factors.

Plans and Specifications

The construction lender will require a set of plans sufficiently detailed to determine room or space size, appropriateness of design features, proper use of lot topography, layout, and competitive amenities. The materials used in the project—and listed in the specifications (specs)—are viewed as to their durability, soundness, and appeal. A soil report is also required in some cases.

Cost Breakdown

On improvement projects, the lender usually likes to see at least two competitive bids. Evaluation of costs is of great concern to both construction lenders and title insurers who underwrite policies insuring the lender's priority position. This is especially true when construction costs are surging. Cost breakdowns list the cost to the builder of each component of construction.

Construction lenders differentiate between hard costs and soft costs. **Hard costs** are those used for the construction of the property materials, labor, etc., while **soft costs** include non-construction items permits, engineering, plan copies, etc. Some commercial lenders limit their construction loan offerings to the amount of the hard cost.

Construction Contract

The contract between the builder and owner should spell out in detail the segments of construction and performance standards for which the contractor will be responsible, the costs for such construction, the method of funding, disbursement schedule, and other provisions. The contract usually identifies an estimated completion date and may include a monetary penalty if said completion date is exceeded.

Source of Repayment

Loan repayment may take on many forms. The developer may request a combination loan, where the construction loan is combined with the permanent loan, using only one lender.

When government-insured or -guaranteed loans are used, commitments from the applicable agency are required in addition to a commitment to finance the potential purchaser's loan by an approved permanent lender. In the case of income property, the permanent loan, to be funded in the future, is obtained prior to arrangement for construction financing. A definite commitment for future permanent financing is termed a take-out commitment.

Financial Data

Supporting data will be required from the builder, owner, commercial tenants, and others who may have a financial interest in the project. Depending on the type and scope of construction, a lender might also require a narrative history of the builder's past experience, as well as a credit report furnished by a local Industry Credit Bureau (ICB). Other important aspects of the project, such as tract and condominium private deed restrictions, data from an economic and environmental point of view, rental and expense trends, lease provisions for income-producing properties, projected resale prices, and so on, would also have to be analyzed.

A financial analysis of the borrower is essential in order to assess his or her capacity to repay the loan. The following questions are often analyzed: How much does the borrower now have available to put into the project? How much income will the borrower have from other sources in the future, if there are problems? These questions are important because history suggests that construction project costs often exceed original estimates and borrowers must be able to carry the financial load ahead of draws. Note: Owner/builders are required to either have a contractor's license or they must hire a general contractor. The lender requires assurance that the construction will be overseen by someone with a valid license and who can be held accountable for the final product. Most construction loans will not allow an owner to do his or her own construction because of this liability. While most cities allow for an owner/builder, when paying someone more than $500 to do any work on your property, that worker must have a contractor's license.

Lending and Disbursement Procedures

There are many variables in financing, and no two lenders have the same standards for making construction loans. There are certain basic steps in the construction lending process that apply to most real estate lenders. These include:

1. Loan application with necessary accompanying data and documents, including plans and specifications, estimated costs for the proposed project, construction contract, credit data, and a financial statement of the borrower and builder.
2. Appraisal of the site and proposed construction, with an estimate of value upon completion determined from plans and specs and based on current market conditions.
3. Title examination, preparation of documents and legal instruments needed to secure the loan, and issuance of the commitment to make the loan.
4. Disbursement system for releasing money as construction progresses according to a predetermined schedule. The payout of

loan funds as construction progresses is one of the major distinguishing characteristics of a construction loan. This requires the establishment of a loan in progress account from which the lender pays the periodic construction expenses. Such an account is more easily monitored to assure that there will be sufficient funds to complete the project and make all required payments. An anticipated payout schedule is ordinarily incorporated into a **building loan agreement** between lender and borrower, an example of which is found in Figure 12.1.

A building loan agreement is a very important document that distinguishes a construction loan from other loans. It embodies the whole agreement between lender and borrower, and, if appropriate, a builder.

5. Escrow and settlement procedure.
6. Loan servicing system to assure loan repayment during the life of the loan.

The loan's payout schedule is a major characteristic of a construction loan. These payments are referred to by a variety of names: vouchers, **disbursements**, payouts, draws, **progress payments**, and advances. There are many types of payment systems but, regardless of the method used, the objective is to protect the lender in four matters:

1. The value of the work in place and materials delivered, plus the lot, will equal or exceed the total amount paid out.
2. Waivers of liens (debts owed to subcontractors, laborers, and material suppliers) will be obtained for each item of material work covered by the draw so as to avoid mechanic's liens.
3. The borrower and the lender will jointly authorize all draws.
4. There will always be sufficient funds in the possession of the lender to complete construction of the property.

With subdivision projects, a lot advance, an amount included in construction funds, may be made, so that a builder/borrower has funds sufficient to pay off any remaining balance on the vacant land being improved. Disbursement of funds can be made by a variety of methods: **draw system**, with payments made in stages as construction progresses; percentage of progress, involving incremental disbursement of construction completed based on 90 percent of work in place or delivered to the job on a monthly basis, with the remaining 10 percent retained for completion at the expiration of the mechanic's lien period; a **voucher system**, when money is disbursed on presentation of receipted bills by licensed building contractors, subcontractors, and material suppliers with appropriate lien waivers and releases; and

FIGURE 12.1 Sample partial building loan agreement.

Building Loan Agreement and Assignment of Account

This Agreement is executed for the purpose of obtaining a building loan from EASTERN NATIONAL BANK, and as a part of the loan transaction, which loan is evidenced by a Note of the undersigned for $ 500,000 of even date herewith, in favor of Bank, and is secured, among other things, by a Trust Deed affecting real property in the County of Los Angeles _____, State of California, described as:

Portion of Lot 10, Tract 10907, as shown on map recorded in Book 195, pages 1 and 2 of Maps, in the office of the county recorder.

Otherwise known as 13515 Addison Street, Sherman Oaks, California.

Upon recordation of the Trust Deed, the proceeds of the loan are to be placed by the Bank, together with the sum of $ 100,000 deposited by the undersigned, in special non-interest bearing Accounts with the Bank. Such deposit of the loan proceeds shall be deemed full consideration for the Note. Each of the undersigned hereby irrevocably assigns to the Bank as security for the obligations secured by the Trust Deed, all right, title and interest of the undersigned in said Accounts and all moneys to be placed therein. It is agreed that any funds deposited by the undersigned shall be disbursed in accordance with the terms of this Agreement prior to disbursement of the proceeds of the loan. By its acceptance of this Agreement the Bank agrees to use the moneys in said Accounts in accordance with the terms hereof.

The undersigned, jointly and severally, further agree as follows:

1. To commence construction of the improvements to be constructed on the property within 15 days after written notice has been given the undersigned by the Bank that it has received a satisfactory Policy of Title Insurance insuring that the Trust Deed is a first lien on the property. Should work of any character be commenced on, or any materials be delivered upon or to the real property or in connection with said improvement prior to receipt of said written notice from the Bank, the Bank at its sole option, may apply the funds in said Accounts to the indebtedness secured by the Trust Deed and to pay expenses incurred in connection with the transaction.

2. Construction shall be in accordance with plans and specifications approved by the Bank, and without change or alteration, except with the written consent of the Bank, and said construction shall be completed within **six** months from date hereof. All of the materials, equipment and every part of the improvement shall be paid for in full and become a part of the real property.

3. The terms of the Note notwithstanding, to pay to Bank on the first day of each calendar month interest at the rate of 10.00 % per annum on loan funds advanced, from the date of the respective advances to **December 21**, 20XX 20____; thereafter, interest on the entire principal amount of the Note shall be payable at the rate, at the time and in accordance with the terms stated in said Note. If such interest is not paid, the Bank may, at its option, pay the same to itself from the Accounts.

4. Subject to the provisions of this Agreement the proceeds of said Accounts are to be disbursed by the Bank as follows:
   A. To pay all costs and demands in connection with the closing of the loan transaction.
   B. To pay the sum of $ 500,000 in the proportions set out below to provide funds for the construction of the improvements, to any of the undersigned, or at the option of the Bank, to contractors, material-men and laborers, or any of them, and at such time as the construction, in accordance with the plans and specifications, has reached the following stages:

   1. 22% ($110,000) when foundation is complete, all ground mechanical systems are in place, sub floor installed, and all rough lumber is on the site.
   2. 21% ($105,000) when framing is complete, roof on, and all mechanical systems are roughed-in complete.
   3. 12% ($ 60,000) when interior drywall is complete, two coats on exterior and/or wood siding on and primed, including priming of all wood sash, door frames, etc., which contact drywall.
   4. 15% ($ 75,000) when sash and doors, cabinets and finish lumber are installed, flooring set (except hardwood finish, linoleum, or carpet).
   5. 20% ($100,000) when all improvements are complete (including flat concrete work, driveway and grading, plus removal of all debris), Bank has approved final inspection and a valid Notice of Completion has been recorded.
   6. 10% ($ 50,000) when the title company which issued the title policy insuring the lien of the Trust Deed will issue an endorsement or policy of title insurance with mechanics' lien coverage; and gives its written permission to release funds retained pursuant to an indemnity agreement, if any.

Source: © 2016 OnCourse Learning

through the use of a **builder's control service**, an outside third party that acts as an intermediary in the control and disbursement of funds.

A typical example of how the draw system operates is illustrated in Figure 12.2.

There are many variations in the amount and number of **advances** based on the percentage of construction completed at any given time. The five-draw plan shown in Figure 12.2, for instance, could be rearranged into three advances, or seven advances, and so on. Whatever system is used, the lender inspects the work at regular intervals before, during, and upon completion of construction. The purpose of these compliance or progress inspections is to make certain that the builder has followed the terms of the construction loan agreement and other

FIGURE 12.2 Example of a draw system for a construction loan.

Five-Draw Release Payments for a Construction Loan

Draw One—20% of loan amount upon completion of foundation, rough plumbing, and subfloor.

Draw Two—30% of loan amount upon completion of framing, roof, windows, and doors.

Draw Three—20% of loan amount upon completion of exterior and interior walls. Includes plumbing, wiring, and ducting.

Draw Four—20% of loan amount upon completion of finished floors, cabinets, trim, and all remaining aspects of construction. Notice of completion is recorded.

Draw Five—Final 10% of loan amount is released after the filing period for mechanic's lien has expired, or after issuance of a lien-free endorsement to the lender's ALTA title insurance policy. This is referred to as ***holdback***.

Source: © 2016 OnCourse Learning

documents; that construction is proceeding according to the plans, specifications, time schedules, and estimated costs; that a claimed stage of construction is actually in place; that there will be no disbursement of funds ahead of actual construction; and that the receipted bills for construction are verified.

Regardless of number of advances, the final draw is normally issued jointly to borrower and builder, so that the check cannot be cashed until the parties have all endorsed it and differences, if any, have been ironed out.

12.3 TAKE-OUT OR PERMANENT LOANS

As noted earlier, some construction lenders, as a prerequisite to making a construction loan, insist that the borrower have a firm take-out commitment from an approved permanent lender.

A take-out commitment is an agreement between the borrower and the permanent lender. It is essentially a promise by the permanent lender that, under stipulated conditions, it will issue a permanent loan upon satisfactory completion of the construction.

Take-out commitments vary depending on the credentials of the borrower, market conditions, property types, and policies of the lender. Certain provisions, however, are found in many take-out or permanent loan commitments, and they are an integral part of the terminology and practice of residential, commercial, and industrial construction financing.

Subordination Clauses

A **subordination clause** is an agreement to reduce the priority of an existing loan to a new loan to be recorded in the future. For example, a developer purchases vacant land by putting some money down and the seller carries the rest of the purchase price as first deed of trust. The developer then locates construction funds to develop the property but construction lenders usually insist they be the first deed of trust. Under a subordination clause, the seller who was originally the first trust deed holder agrees to voluntarily accept a second position to a newly recorded first trust deed. Upon recordation, the subordination deed is recorded followed by the new first trust deed. If the purchaser of vacant land or a lot intends to build on the property, they should consider drafting a subordination agreement at time of purchase if they can meet the requirements.

The provisions of sections 2953.1 through 2953.5 of the Civil Code require that deeds of trust containing subordination clauses, and separate subordination agreements, contain specified warning language. State judicial decisions require that a subordination clause or agreement be certain in its terms, and unless the maximum amount, maximum rate of interest, and terms of repayment of the loan secured by the future deed of trust are specified, the subordination clause or agreement will not be enforceable. Moreover, recent decisions clearly indicate that a subordination clause or agreement will not be enforceable unless it is fair and equitable to the beneficiary. An example of a subordination agreement is given in Figure 12.3.

Partial Release Clauses

Common to construction lending, is the **partial release clause**. This provision is used with a trust deed placed on more than one parcel of property, termed a **blanket trust deed**, such as in the development of a subdivision. As each individual lot is sold and the funds are delivered to the beneficiary, the lot is released from the blanket loan, the balance of which is correspondingly, but not necessarily proportionately, reduced. The release is accomplished when the lender issues a **partial reconveyance deed** on the individual lot being sold. Without a partial release clause, the trustor has no automatic right to receive a partial release.

The beneficiary (lender) requests that the trustee execute and record a partial reconveyance deed describing the portion of the property released from the blanket trust deed. The promissory note is usually endorsed to show that a partial release was given. When a series of such partial releases is contemplated, the deed of trust will usually provide that the trustee may receive the released proceeds for the beneficiary and give the partial reconveyance deeds without further demand or request from the beneficiary.

A partial release clause must be carefully examined with respect to such matters as these:

- Whether or not a trustor in default is entitled to partial releases.
- Restrictions on the selection of portions of the property to be released.
- The precise amount of the **lot release provision** and the method of computing the release price; payments for each release must be provided for in the agreement.
- Whether the release prices merely reduce the amount of the secured obligation or apply to past, current, and future installments due on the obligation.

FIGURE 12.3 Sample subordination agreement (partial).

RECORDING REQUESTED BY

AND WHEN RECORDED MAIL TO

NAME
ADDRESS
CITY
STATE & ZIP

SUBORDINATION AGREEMENT

NOTICE: THIS SUBORDINATION AGREEMENT RESULTS IN YOUR SECURITY INTEREST IN THE PROPERTY BECOMING SUBJECT TO AND OF LOWER PRIORITY THAN THE LIEN OF SOME OTHER OR LATER SECURITY INSTRUMENT.

THIS AGREEMENT, made this ____15th____ day of ____November____ ,20XX, by ____John Doe and Mary Doe____, owner of the land hereinafter described and hereinafter referred to as "Owner," and ____John Smith and Mary Smith____, present owner and holder of the deed of trust hereinafter described and hereinafter referred to as "Beneficiary":

WITNESSETH

THAT WHEREAS, ____John Doe and Mary Doe____ did execute a deed of trust, dated ____August 15, 20XX____, to ____ABC Title Insurance Company____, as trustee, covering:

(FULL LEGAL TITLE INSERTED)

to secure a note in the sum of $____$250,000____, dated ____August 14, 20XX____ in favor of ____John Smith and Mary Smith____, which deed of trust was recorded ____August 16, 20XX____, as instrument number ____1763____ Official Records of said county; and

WHEREAS, Owner has executed, or is about to execute, a deed of trust and note in the sum of $____$250,000____ dated ____August 14, 20XX____, in favor of ____LAST SAVINGS AND LOAN____, hereinafter referred to as "Lender," payable with interest and upon the terms and conditions described therein, which deed of trust is to be recorded concurrently herewith; and

WHEREAS, it is a condition precedent to obtaining said loan that said deed of trust last above mentioned shall unconditionally be and remain at all times a lien or charge upon the land hereinbefore described, prior and superior to the lien or charge of the security instrument first above mentioned; and

WHEREAS, Lender is willing to make said loan provided the deed of trust securing the same is a lien or charge upon the above described property prior and superior to the lien or charge of the security instrument first above mentioned and provided that Beneficiary will specifically and unconditionally subordinate the lien or charge of the security instrument first above mentioned to the lien or charge of the deed of trust in favor of Lender ; and

WHEREAS, it is to the mutual benefit of the parties hereto that Lender make such loan to Owner; and Beneficiary is willing that the deed of trust securing the same shall, when recorded, constitute a lien or charge upon said land which is unconditionally prior and superior to the lien or charge of the deed of trust first above mentioned.

NOW, THEREFORE, in consideration of the mutual benefits accruing to the parties hereto and other valuable consideration, the receipt and sufficiency of which consideration is hereby acknowledged, and in order to induce Lender to make the loan above referred to, it is hereby declared, understood and agreed as follows:

(1) That said deed of trust securing said note in favor of Lender, and any renewals or extensions thereof, shall unconditionally be and remain at all times a lien or charge on the property therein described, prior and superior to the lien or charge of the security instrument first above mentioned.

(2) That Lender would not make its loan above described without this subordination agreement.

(3) That this agreement shall be the whole and only agreement between the parties hereto with regard to the subordination of the lien or charge of the security instrument first above mentioned to the lien or charge of the deed of trust in favor of Lender above referred to and shall supersede and cancel any prior agreements as to such, or any, subordination including, but not limited to, those provisions, if any, contained in the deed of trust first above mentioned, which provide for the subordination of the lien or charge thereof to a deed or deeds of trust or to a mortgage or mortgages to be thereafter executed.

FIGURE 12.3 (Continued)

Beneficiary declares, agrees and acknowledges that

    (a) He consents to and approves (i) all provisions of the note and deed of trust in favor of Lender above referred to, and (ii) all agreements, including but not limited to any loan or escrow agreements, between Owner and Lender for the disbursement of the proceeds of Lender's loan;

    (b) Lender in making disbursements pursuant to any such agreement is under no obligation or duty to, nor has Lender represented that it will, see to the application of such proceeds by the person or persons to whom Lender disburses such proceeds and any application or use of such proceeds for purposes other than those provided for in such agreement or agreements shall not defeat the subordination herein made in whole or in party;

    (c) he intentionally and unconditionally waives, relinquishes and subordinates the lien or charge of the security instrument first above mentioned in favor of the lien or charge upon said land of the deed of trust in favor of Lender above referred to and understands that in reliance upon, and in consideration of, this waiver, relinquishment and subordination specific loans and advances are being and will be made and, as part and parcel thereof, specific monetary and other obligations are being and will be entered into which would not be made or entered into but for said reliance upon this waiver, relinquishment and subordination; and

NOTICE: THIS SUBORDINATION AGREEMENT CONTAINS A PROVISION WHICH ALLOWS THE PERSON OBLIGATED ON YOUR REAL PROPERTY SECURITY TO OBTAIN A LOAN A PORTION OF WHICH MAY BE EXPENDED FOR OTHER PURPOSES THAN IMPROVEMENT OF THE LAND.

_____   _____
_____   _____
            Beneficiary   Owner

STATE OF CALIFORNIA
COUNTY OF _____ } SS.
On _____ before me, _____,
personally appeared _____
personally known to me (or proved to me on the basis of satisfactory evidence) to be the person(s) whose name(s) is/are subscribed to the within instrument and acknowledged to me that he/she/they executed the same in his/her/their authorized capacity(ies), and that by his/her/their signature(s) on the instrument the person(s), or the entity upon behalf of which the person(s) acted, executed the instrument.

WITNESS my hand and official seal.

Signature_____   (This area for official notarial seal)

STATE OF CALIFORNIA
COUNTY OF _____ } SS.
On _____ before me, _____,
personally appeared _____
personally known to me (or proved to me on the basis of satisfactory evidence) to be the person(s) whose name(s) is/are subscribed to the within instrument and acknowledged to me that he/she/they executed the same in his/her/their authorized capacity(ies), and that by his/her/their signature(s) on the instrument the person(s), or the entity upon behalf of which the person(s) acted, executed the instrument.

WITNESS my hand and official seal.

Signature_____   (This area for official notarial seal)
                    (ALL SIGNATURES MUST BE ACKNOWLEDGED)
    IT IS RECOMMENDED THAT, PRIOR TO THE EXECUTION OF THIS SUBORDINATION AGREEMENT, THE PARTIES CONSULT WITH
                            THEIR ATTORNEYS WITH RESPECT THERETO

                         (CLTA SUBORDINATION FORM "A")   SUBAGMTA.DOC

Source: © 2016 OnCourse Learning

Rental Achievement Clauses

When the construction of commercial (and sometimes industrial) property is being financed, a **rental achievement clause** is common.

The granting of a construction loan for rental properties is usually contingent on the developer/borrower's ability to prelease a stated amount of space in the building. The developer usually provides a certified rent roll indicating who the tenants will be, the space to be leased, length of the leases, and the annual rents to be paid. The loan servicing agents then recertify that the developer's certified statements have been verified.

The rental achievement condition in the commitment for commercial property is of prime concern to construction lenders. Lenders do not want to finance construction projects and then discover that tenants are lacking for the rental space. Consequently, lenders are hesitant to advance any construction loan until the rental requirements of the take-out or permanent lender have been satisfied. It is typical for the permanent lender, in deference to the construction lender's concern, to provide that a certain portion of the loan be disbursed without any rental requirement and the balance, when rentals reach a stipulated level. The amount of the construction loan may be set at the lower amount, called the floor loan, at least until the necessary rentals have been achieved. Additional sums are then disbursed later as the rental schedule submitted with the loan application is met; however, this must be done within a specified time, usually one or two years after the closing of the floor loan.

There can be a gap between the higher amount and the floor amount, to which the permanent lender will commit if all rentals are achieved. The gap is usually 15 to 20 percent of the larger amount. The developer would like to obtain the full amount of the loan, that is, the full rental achievement commitment, in order to generate as much leverage as possible. Yet, the construction lender will usually commit itself only for the floor amount.

The construction lender may be willing, however, to commit for the full or larger amount if another lender will stand by or commit itself to provide the gap financing. The **gap commitment** guarantees that the borrower will have the difference between the floor loan and the upper level of the permanent loan if the rental achievement for the larger amount is not reached. A fee is charged for the gap commitment, and the interest rate is often higher because the loan, if made, would be a second mortgage. The developer does not expect to actually have to draw the funds from the gap commitment, and the gap lender does not expect it either.

Mechanic's Liens and Their Impact on Construction Loans

All construction lenders are wary about the possibility of mechanic's liens, that is, creation of liens against real estate by those performing the work. **Mechanic's liens** can arise if a builder does not complete the project or if the job is completed and the builder fails to pay material suppliers, subcontractors, and workers. The probability of a lien by one or more subcontractors and material suppliers is ever present, possibly jeopardizing the construction lender's priority position. This applies to all forms of real estate construction, including home improvement loans. An example of a mechanic's lien is given in Figure 12.4.

Mechanic's lien rights are protected by the state constitution and are granted to contractors, subcontractors, laborers, and material suppliers who have contributed to or worked on the property and have not been paid for their services. The law requires that in addition to a contract to do the work, a notice in the form of a notice of intent to lien, if provider is not paid, must be filed with the owner and construction lender's office within 20 days of commencement of each particular segment of work. The period for filing a lien varies from as few as 30 days to not more than 90 days after completion of a building or other work of improvement.

Notice of Completion

If a **Notice of Completion** (see Figure 12.5) is filed by the owner, not the contractor within 10 days after the job is substantially completed, the original contractor has 60 days in which to file a lien, while all other parties have 30 days. If no notice of completion is recorded, or if a notice of completion is faulty in any respect, all parties have 90 days from the date of **substantial completion**. To protect themselves, as well as the builder and lender, against mechanic's liens, owners can purchase **completion bonds**—extremely rare with home construction loans, but required for Cal-Vet construction loans, and always required for government construction jobs, usually costing 1.5 percent of hard costs.

Should a job not be completed due to acts of God, strikes, impossibility of performance, disagreements, work stoppage, or for any other reason, then a **Notice of Cessation of Labor** or **Notice of Abandonment** may be filed. These have time limits similar to those of a completion notice.

If any work of improvement started prior to recording the construction loan, a mechanic's lien may take priority over other liens that were placed on the property after the job was started. This is referred to as the **doctrine of relation back**. The financial interests of all others furnishing labor or materials are perceived to have begun from this

CHAPTER 12 Construction Loans

FIGURE 12.4 Sample mechanic's lien.

RECORDING REQUESTED BY
CHARLES L. LOAFER
WHEN RECORDED MAIL TO

Name: Charles L. Loafer
Street Address: 2432 Mountain Ave
City & State: Willow Springs, Calif.

1436

Recorded in Official Records of Oakdale County, Calif.
May 23, 20xx at 1:00p.m.
GEORGE L. FISH, County Recorder

FEE $3.00

(SPACE ABOVE THIS LINE FOR RECORDER'S USE)

MECHANIC'S LIEN

NOTICE IS HEREBY GIVEN that: Pursuant to the provisions of the California Civil Code, _____
Charles L. Loafer

hereafter referred to as "Claimant" (whether singular or plural), claims a lien upon the real property and buildings, improvements or structures thereon, described in Paragraph Five (5) below, and states the following:

(1) That demand of Claimant after deducting all just credits and offsets, is **$3,800**
together with interest thereon at the rate of **5** % per annum from **April 1**, **20xx**

(2) That the name of the owner(s) or reputed owner(s) of said property, is (are)
James M. Broke and Joanne S. Broke
(name, or state "unknown")

(3) That Claimant did from **March 25**, 20xx, until **March 28**, 20xx
perform labor and/or supply materials as follows: **Replacement of front main line, meter to**
(general statement of kind of work done or materials furnished, or both)
house. Replaced all valves and reconnected to sprinkler system with all valves up by porch, on a time and material basis. Material $800, sales tax $70, labor $2,900. Permit $30.

for the construction, alteration or repair of said buildings, improvements or structures, which labor, or materials, or both of them, were in fact used in the construction, alteration or repair of said buildings, improvements or structures, the location of which is set forth in Paragraph Five (5) below.

(4) Claimant furnished work and materials under contract with, or at the request of,
James M. Broke and Joanne S. Broke

(5) That the property upon which said lien is sought to be charged is situated in the City of **Harrisport**,
County of **Oakdale**, State of California, commonly known as
20436 S. Grand, Harrisport, California
(street address)
and more particularly described as **lot 306, tract 1415 as per map recorded in book 563 pages 21 to 25 inclusive of maps, in the office of the county recorder of said county.**
(legal description)

DATED: This **22nd** day of **May**, 20xx

Firm Name **Loafer Plumbing Service**
By **Charles L. Loafer**

(Verification for Individual Claim)

STATE OF CALIFORNIA,
County of **Oakdale** } ss.

Charles L. Loafer
being first duly sworn, deposes and says That ___ he is the
_____ Claimant
named in the foregoing claim of lien, that ___ he has read the same and knows the contents thereof, and that the statements therein contained are true, and that it contains, among other things, a correct statement of **his** demand, after deducting all just credits and offsets
Dated: this **22nd** day of **May** 20xx, at **Willow Springs**, Calif.
(City & State)

Charles L. Loafer
(Signature of affiant)

Subscribed and sworn to before me
May 22, 20xx
John Fairchild
Notary Public in and for said State.

OFFICIAL SEAL
JOHN FAIRCHILD
NOTARY PUBLIC — CALIFORNIA
PRINCIPAL OFFICE IN LOS ANGELES COUNTY
My Commission Expires Nov. 9,

(Verification for other than Individual Claim)

STATE OF CALIFORNIA,
County of _____ } ss.

_____ being first duly sworn, deposes and says That _____
the Claimant herein, is a _____
that affiant is ? _____
and for that reason he makes his affidavit on behalf of said _____
that he has read the same and knows the contents thereof, and that the statements therein contained are true, and that it contains, among other things, a correct statement of the demand of Claimant, after deducting all just credits and offsets.
Dated: this ___ day of 20 ___ at _____
(City & State)

_____
(Signature of affiant)

Subscribed and sworn to before me
_____, 19__

_____
Notary Public in and for said State.

MECHANIC'S LIEN—1024   8 pt. type or larger

Source: © 2016 OnCourse Learning

FIGURE 12.5 Sample notice of completion.

Source: © 2016 OnCourse Learning

initial date, even though they came on the scene subsequent to the creation of the trust deed. For this reason, lenders, and others making construction loans, carefully check to determine that no construction work has been started prior to the recordation of a loan; or lenders may require indemnity of an ALTA title policy protecting them against loss from mechanic's liens.

What constitutes start of construction? It could be delivering material, clearing the lot, setting grade stakes, grading, ditching, placing chemical toilets on the lot, setting power poles, setting location markers, marking chalk lines, clearing trees, and so on. In other words, start of construction is when the first action of the job starts, even if it's only the first shovel touching the dirt.

Anyone filing a mechanic's lien must institute a suit to foreclose the lien within 90 days after recording the lien. The suit is similar to a mortgage foreclosure, resulting in a court-ordered sale in order to satisfy the claims. In the event of insufficient funds following the sale, the court may award a deficiency judgment against the debtor for the balance. If no suit is filed, a mechanic's lien expires after 90 days.

Notice of Non-responsibility

Sometimes a lien is filed against property whose owner did not contract for the improvement, as when a tenant negotiates a contract for major repairs or alterations to a leasehold interest. To protect themselves, the owners may repudiate responsibility and liability by recording a Notice of Non-responsibility within 10 days of the time they acquired knowledge. A sample is shown in Figure 12.6. A copy of the notice must be posted on the property. The contractor would then have to look to the contract for remedy—that is, sue the contracting party for collection of money due. Most contractors check the ownership of property and will not contract with tenants to avoid this very issue.

Release of Mechanic's Liens

A mechanic's lien may be discharged by the running of the statute of limitations, after 90 days, if no foreclosure action is commenced:

- by written release, through the recording of a **Release of Mechanic's Lien** (illustrated in Figure 12.7);
- by the issuance of a bond to release the lien;
- by satisfaction of the judgment lien against the debtor;
- or by dismissal of the action when the court is convinced that a valid claim is not sustainable.

FIGURE 12.6 Sample notice of non-responsibility.

PUBLISHED AND DISTRIBUTED BY REAL ESTATE BUSINESS SERVICES, INC.

FORM NNR

Recording Requested By:

And When Recorded Mail To:

FOR RECORDER'S USE ONLY

CALIFORNIA ASSOCIATION OF REALTORS ®

NOTICE OF NONRESPONSIBILITY
(C.A.R. Form NNR, Revised 4/14)

TO: ______________________________
Notice is hereby given that:
1. ______________________ is the owner ☐ Other: ______________________ ("Non-Responsible Party" or "NRP") of real property described in paragraph 2 below and has a Fee (☐ Other: ______________________) interest in the Property.
2. The real property at issue is described as follows: ______________________
______________________, Assessor's Parcel Number ______________________ "Property".
3. NRP may be contacted at the following address: ______________________.
4. NRP first obtained knowledge of the work of improvement on the Property on ______________________.
5. A. The direct contractor's name and address is unknown at this time (or if known, is specified in 5C).
B. The construction lender's name and address is unknown at this time (or if known, is specified in 5C).
C. ______________________.
D. NRP will not be responsible for any claims arising from the work of improvement.

VERIFICATION: I, NRP, have read the Notice of NonResponsibility and have personal knowledge of all facts stated herein and such facts are true. I certify under penalty of perjury that the foregoing is true and correct.

NRP ______________________ Date ____________
Address ______________________ City ____________ State ______ Zip ________
Telephone ______________________ Fax ____________ E-mail ____________

This Notice shall be posted at a conspicuous place on the Property within ten (10) days after the person claiming the benefits of nonresponsibility has obtained knowledge of the work of improvement. Within this same ten day period, the Notice shall be recorded in the office of the county recorder of the county in which the Property, or some part thereof, is located.

ACKNOWLEDGMENT:

______________________ ("Declarant"), declares as follows:
The above Notice of Nonresponsibility is a true copy of a notice posted at ______________________, City of ____________, County of ____________, State of California on ____________, 20______.
Declarant is the person who signed the Notice or the agent of the person who signed the Notice and such agent has the authority to post and record the Notice. Declarant has read the Notice and knows the contents thereof. The facts stated in the Notice are true of Declarant's own knowledge.

______________________, ____________, 20______
(Declarant's Signature) (Date)
STATE OF CALIFORNIA, COUNTY OF ______________________, ON ____________ (Date) before me,
______________________ (Insert name and title of the officer)
personally appeared ______________________
______________________ (Name of Declarant),

who proved to me on the basis of satisfactory evidence to be the person(s) whose name(s) is/are subscribed to the within instrument and acknowledged to me that he/she/they executed the same in his/her/their authorized capacity(ies), and that by his/her/their signature(s) on the instrument the person(s), or the entity upon behalf of which the person(s) acted, executed the instrument.

I certify under PENALTY OF PERJURY under the laws of the State of California that the foregoing paragraph is true and correct.

WITNESS my hand and official seal.

(Notary's Signature) ______________________**(Seal)**

FOR NOTARY'S USE ONLY

SAMPLE

Published and Distributed by:
REAL ESTATE BUSINESS SERVICES, INC.
a subsidiary of the California Association of REALTORS®
525 South Virgil Avenue, Los Angeles, California 90020

Reviewed by ______ Date ______

EQUAL HOUSING OPPORTUNITY

NNR REVISED 4/14 (PAGE 1 OF 1) PRINT DATE

NOTICE OF NONRESPONSIBILITY (NNR PAGE 1 OF 1)

Source: © 2016 OnCourse Learning

FIGURE 12.7 Sample release of a mechanic's lien.

Release of Mechanic's Lien

RECORDING REQUESTED BY
JAMES M. BROKE & JAONNE S. BROKE

AND WHEN RECORDED MAIL TO
NAME: James M & Jaonne S Broke
ADDRESS: 20536 S Grand Ave.
CITY & STATE: Harrisport, California

SPACE ABOVE THIS LINE FOR RECORDER'S USE

That Notice of Mechanics Lien executed by Charles L. Loafer, naming as obligors (including the owners or reputed owners) James M Broke and Jaonne S Broke

Recorded May 23, 20XX, as Instrument No. 1436, in Book 5883, Page 25, Official Records of the County of Oakdale, State of California, upon that Real Property in said County and State described as:

Lot 306, Tract 1415 as per map recorded in Book 563, pages 21 to 25 inclusive of maps, in the office of the county recorder of said county.

Is hereby released, the claim having been fully paid and discharged.

Dated August 14, 20XX

Loafer Plumbing Service
By: Charles L. Loafer

STATE OF CALIFORNIA
COUNTY OF _____ } SS.

On August 14, 20XX before me, the undersigned, a Notary Public in and for said County and State, personally appeared Charles L. Loafer known to me to be the person(s) whose name(s) is (are) subscribed to the within instrument and acknowledged that he executed the same.

Robert J. Bond

OFFICIAL SEAL
ROBERT J. BOND
NOTARY PUBLIC - CALIFORNIA
LOS ANGELES COUNTY
My comm. expires JAN 31,

6511 Van Nuys Blvd, #12, Van Nuys CA 91401

Title Order No. _____ Escrow No. _____

Source: © 2016 OnCourse Learning

12.4 PUBLIC CONSTRUCTION

Often property owners are assessed for public construction projects that are proposed to improve the general health and welfare of the community. At the same time such public projects increase the value of properties of the affected owners in theory if not also in practice.

Assessment liens are imposed upon properties benefiting from capital projects that are classified as off-site improvements, such as street widening and installation of curbs, gutters, sidewalks, storm drains, sewers, and street lights. A number of state laws allow for the imposition of an assessment tax on the benefited properties, which share in the costs on a proportioned basis. The property owners may either pay the assessment in full within 30 days after completion—defined as final inspection and approval of the job by the applicable local regulatory agency—or pay the lien in installments over a period not to exceed 15 years through an assessment bond.

There are four significant state laws or improvement acts, as they are called, that provide for the construction and financing of capital improvements for which the property owner is assessed in whole or in part:

1. *Vrooman Street Act.* This law confers authority on city councils to grade and finish streets, construct sewers, and perform other improvements within municipalities or counties and to issue bonds secured and redeemed by tax levies. It also provides for the acquisition of public utilities by the local governing body. The act has been amended numerous times and continues to be challenged in some municipalities, with mixed legal results.

2. *Street Improvement Act of 1911.* The initial intent of this law was to allow communities to assess the costs of maintaining sidewalks. It was not until the 1940s that the law applied to a wider responsibility by community government. It was then that local government was presumed to have the duty to maintain, via the collection of taxes, roadways and easements. This law, with its amendments, provides that bonds may be issued by the municipality ordering the improvements and that the assessments may be paid in equal installments during the term of the bonds. The installments may be paid with property taxes over a 15-year period, but can be paid off at any time. The property owner must pay a share of the project within 30 days of its completion or bonds will be issued at an interest rate determined by the issuing local legislative body. The bonds will remain as liens against the property until paid in full.

3. *Improvement Bond Act of 1915.* This law, also as amended, provides for the activation of a special assessment district, usually related to

the construction of a new subdivision, to pay for street improvements, including sewer construction. The bond assessment and the accompanying interest are proportional against the property owners directly affected. While it can be paid at any time, the lien is usually paid with the taxes and depending upon its amount can be paid over as long as 40 years. Evidence of this debt is found in the preliminary title insurance report.

4. *Mello-Roos Community Facilities Act.* This 1982 law arose as a result of Proposition 13, passed in 1978, which restricts taxing districts from raising taxes upon the sale or transfer of property. The Mello-Roos CFA established another method whereby almost every municipal subdivision of the state may form a special, separate tax district to finance a long list of public improvements/facilities by the sale of bonds and finance certain public services on a pay-as-you-go basis. Initially developed to provide for new schools in newly constructed subdivisions, the program was expanded to encompass practically all necessary public services. Formed by local governments, the developer of a new project may impose the bonds and then market the properties, subject to individual lot assessments. For example, each purchaser of a home in such districts is assessed a pro rata share of the costs to put in the public facilities that can include freeway access routes and build and maintain roads, sewers, community centers, and even schools that serve the housing project. While initially used in new subdivisions, Mello-Roos districts have been established in older areas when the tax revenues are insufficient to accommodate the necessary infrastructure.

Chapter Summary

Construction loans are short-term or interim loans. Combination loans combine the short-term interim loan with the permanent or take-out loan. Some banks even allow a purchase-construction-take-out loan combination.

Construction lenders look for many things before finally committing themselves to fund a construction project. These include evaluation of the plans and specifications, detailed breakdown of the costs involved, analysis of the building contract, source of repayment, and supporting financial data required on the owner, builder, and others who may have a financial interest in the project. A construction loan contract may contain a variety of provisions that protect the lender and borrower, including a subordination clause, partial release clause, rental achievement clause, and others. Mechanic's liens protect those who improve real property by means of their labor, skills, services, and materials furnished for the job. Construction lenders must be on guard to see that their security is not impaired because of faulty construction, noncompliance with the building loan agreement, start of work before the construction trust deed is recorded, and other construction problems.

Important Terms and Concepts

- Advances
- Assessment lien
- Blanket trust deed
- Builder's control service
- Building loan agreement
- Combination loan
- Completion bond
- Disbursements
- Doctrine of relation back
- Draw system
- Gap commitment
- Hard costs
- Lot release provision
- Mechanic's liens
- Notice of Abandonment
- Notice of Cessation of Labor
- Notice of Completion
- Partial reconveyance deed
- Partial release clause
- Progress payments
- Release of Mechanic's Lien
- Rental achievement clause
- Short-term construction loan
- Soft costs
- Subordination clause
- Substantial completion
- Take-out loan
- Voucher system

Reviewing Your Understanding

Questions for Discussion

1. How do construction loans differ from take-out loans?
2. What is meant by progress payments?
3. List several methods of disbursing funds for construction projects.
4. What is a subordination clause? How does such a clause protect the construction lender?
5. Differentiate between a partial release clause and a rental achievement clause. For whose benefit are these provisions set up?

Multiple-Choice Questions

1. A lien filed by contractors due to the failure of an obligated party to pay for work of improvement is a
   a. contractor's lien.
   b. subordination lien.
   c. mechanic's lien.
   d. superior lien.

2. The payoff of a construction loan is normally accomplished through
   a. a take-out loan.
   b. cash flow generated from an income property.
   c. sale of the completed project.
   d. bonded indebtedness.

3. In a five-draw construction loan payment schedule, mechanic's liens are considered in (hint: see Figure 12.2)
   a. draw 4.
   b. draw 5.
   c. draw 1.
   d. draw 2.

4. The system of disbursements of construction funds upon presentation of receipted bills by contractors is called a
   a. percentage of progress.
   b. voucher.
   c. stage of completion.
   d. proof of billings.

5. An agreement between borrower and permanent lender relative to future delivery of a take-out loan upon completion is called a
   a. construction contract.
   b. building loan agreement.
   c. take-out commitment.
   d. tri-party agreement.

6. A contract between borrower, contractor, and lender establishing the obligations and duties of each party during the period of construction is a
   a. construction contract.
   b. building loan agreement.
   c. take-out commitment.
   d. bilateral agreement.

7. A construction loan may lose first-lien position to mechanic's lien claimants by
   a. commencement of work prior to recording of a construction loan.
   b. commencement of work prior to recording of a combination loan.
   c. either (a) or (b).
   d. neither (a) nor (b).

8. The largest number and volume of interim construction loans are generally made by
   a. local institutions.
   b. credit unions.
   c. real estate investment trusts.
   d. casualty insurance companies.

9. The document that is filed by the owner after a project is substantially completed is a
   a. Notice of Cessation of Labor.
   b. Mechanic's Lien.
   c. Notice of Non-responsibility.
   d. Notice of Completion.

10. When a mechanic's lien is filed against a property, the threat of loss of title rests with the
    a. lender.
    b. contractor.
    c. owner.
    d. subcontractor.

11. The costs of a construction loan to a borrower are greater than a regular purchase money loan because
    a. costs and interest rates are increasing daily.
    b. the lender knows that construction costs are constantly going up.
    c. the lender knows that values will have risen by the time the project is completed.
    ✓d. the lender has more overhead and greater risks.

12. In California, construction loans cannot be made
    a. unless a take-out loan has been committed by a responsible lender.
    b. for less than one year.
    c. except on an owner-occupied basis.
    ✓d. none of the above is correct.

13. The amount of a construction loan
    a. is paid out in a lump sum upon completion of construction.
    ✓b. normally is paid out in various stages.
    c. must be disbursed in no fewer than five draws.
    d. generally begins to be amortized as soon as the first disbursement is made.

14. A subordination clause in a deed of trust is most likely to be found in the case of
    a. a package deed of trust.
    b. a combination loan.
    c. a regular deed of trust.
    ✓d. land loans.

15. If a developer has signed a deed of trust covering all the lots in a subdivision, he or she will find that partial releases
    ✓a. cannot be required unless provided for specifically in the deed of trust.
    b. can always be obtained, even if not specifically provided for, upon payment of a pro rata amount of the principal balance due.
    c. can be obtained only if a subordination agreement is incorporated in the deed of trust.
    d. cannot be obtained until at least 50 percent of the lots in a subdivision are sold.

16. Which document separates a regular real estate loan from a construction loan?
    ✓a. Building loan agreement
    b. Promissory note
    c. Appraisal report
    d. Credit report

17. Which of the following is a direct result of Proposition 13?
    a. Mechanic's Lien Law
    b. Improvement Bond Act of 1915
    c. Street Improvement Act of 1911
    ✓d. Mello-Roos Community Facilities Act

18. A partial release clause is usually used in connection with a
    a. combination loan.
    ✓b. blanket loan.
    c. floor loan.
    d. standby loan.

19. Major alterations to a rental house were contracted for by the tenants. To disavow themselves from possible mechanic's liens against their property, the owners should file and post a
    a. Rental Achievement Clause.
    b. Notice of Completion.
    c. Notice of Non-responsibility. ✓
    d. Release of Mechanic's Lien.

20. Another name for an interim loan is
    a. a loan not amortized.
    b. progress loan.
    c. take-out loan.
    d. short-term loan. ✓

CASE & POINT

Tax Deferred Exchanges

Property exchanging can be a key element in developing an investment strategy. There are some very important terms used when describing all the aspects of tax deferred exchanges. A brief glossary of some of these important terms is at the end of this article.

Internal Revenue Code Section 1031 identifies the rules under which investment type real estate can be exchanged for like kind property and the payment of capital gain taxes deferred. While sometimes referred to as a tax free exchange, such words are a misnomer. Such a transaction merely defers tax by transferring the taxpayer's old cost basis to a newly acquired property. When this newly acquired property is in turn transferred, the full tax generated from both transfers will become due unless the latter transfer is also structured as a tax deferred exchange. The true power of exchanging is its ability to meet investment objectives without losing equity to taxation.

It is important to understand that the 1031 exchange rules do not apply to one's personal residence. More recent tax reform resulted in significant positive change in the ability to claim tax free home profits in the sale of a personal residence. Rules for the exchange of investment property via the 1031 section of the tax code have not been liberalized.

While most exchange transactions today are conducted on a delayed exchange basis, prior to 1979, an exchange was required to be a simultaneous exchange. A concurrent or simultaneous exchange is when both properties (the relinquished and replacement properties) are ready to close escrow and record the change of title the same day.

Now, the majority of exchanges are conducted via a professionally qualified intermediary (also known as an accommodator or facilitator) as it is the only safe way to conduct an exchange today. This third party becomes a part of the exchange agreement who acquires title to the property for the sole purpose of accommodating or facilitating the exchanger. It is critical that the sale proceeds from the relinquished property be held beyond the exchanger's constructive receipt by a third party intermediary. If the exchanger were to have access to the funds, tax consequences could result.

To make a completely tax-deferred trade, the cost of the rental or investment property acquired must equal or exceed the sales price of the relinquished property. Any consideration (i.e., cash, notes, personal property, or debt relief) received from the relinquished property sale is known as "boot" and is taxable.

The delayed exchange rules have been revised several times. In 1991, the regulations defining the identification requirements were enacted. The trickiest portion of the exchange process is often making certain that the required time periods are adhered to. The exchange period begins on the date the taxpayer transfers the relinquished property (closes escrow) and ends at midnight on the earliest of the 180th day thereafter OR the due date (including extensions) for the taxpayer's tax return for the taxable year in which the transfer of the relinquished property occurs. Depending upon the time of year in which the exchange occurs, the exchanger may not have the full 180-day period in which to consummate the transaction. Year-end exchanges can be affected when the April 15 tax filing date is less than the allowed 180 day period. Although a tax extension can be acquired, counsel is recommended.

Perhaps the more critical time period is the identification period. This period begins on the date the taxpayer transfers the relinquished property to the intermediary and ends at midnight on the 45th day thereafter. The taxpayer must find and notify the intermediary in writing of the replacement property to be received on or before the 45th day following the close of escrow on the relinquished property.

The property must be unambiguously described (generally a legal description or street address will suffice) and designated as replacement property in a written document signed by the taxpayer. Identification of the replacement property in the actual contract between the parties fulfills this requirement. Under most circumstances, no more than three potential replacement properties may be designated and total value requirements of the multiple designated properties prevail. Counsel is advised if more than one replacement property is to be identified.

Glossary of Exchange Terms

ADJUSTED COST BASIS: The cost basis with additions (i.e. improvements) and subtractions (i.e. depreciation) which subsequently becomes the value ascribed to the newly acquired property and from which future gain or loss is calculated.

BASIS or COST BASIS: Typically refers to the purchase price of the property when acquired by the exchanger, plus the cost of improvements and less any depreciation taken. The cost basis will thereafter serve as a base figure in determining gain or loss and can be transferred to other property via the tax deferred exchange process.

BOOT: The term used to describe unlike property received via the exchange. Cash, notes, personal property, reduction in mortgage (called debt relief) are all examples of boot and subject to tax. To avoid boot, an exchanger must trade across or up in two areas: equity and mortgage amount.

LIKE KIND PROPERTY: Refers to the nature or character of the property. Another way to describe eligible exchange property is the words "real for real," meaning that real property must be exchanged for other real property and cannot be exchanged for personal property. Under this definition, a rental home can be exchanged for another rental home, multiple units, apartment complex, commercial property, or unimproved property (land).

RELINQUISHED PROPERTY: The property that is being given up by the exchanger, sometimes referred to as the "down-leg" property.

REPLACEMENT PROPERTY: The property acquired by the exchanger in an exchange, sometimes referred to as the "up-leg" property.

400

CREATIVE FINANCING APPROACHES

13

OVERVIEW

During the subprime era the term "creative financing" was synonymous with easy-to-qualify financing. In this chapter the term is used to designate approaches to financing real property in ways that are not normally found through traditional sources. Many of these unique loan options involve seller participation. Unique lending practices usually surface when more traditional loan options are not readily available. The various techniques, a few of which are explained here, are limited only by one's imagination and knowledge.

In this chapter, we examine some creative methods used to solve both the difficult and not so difficult situations in which borrowers find themselves when they seek a real estate loan in a tight money market. These are not to be confused with the alternative mortgage instruments, or AMIs, discussed in Chapter 4. While AMIs are potentially very creative, they are variations on the basic fixed rate, fixed term, level payment, fully amortized loan that has been part of the permanent financing scene since 1934.

After completing this chapter, you will be able to:

- Differentiate between traditional and creative financing techniques.
- Identify at least five ways in which real estate can be financed through ways other than the traditional methods.
- Contrast the all-inclusive trust deed to the installment Contract of Sale, citing at least three differences.
- Apply the formula to calculate blended interest rates.
- Name the instruments required to close a sale using the creative techniques presented in this chapter.
- List at least six items that must be disclosed under the Creative Financing Disclosure Act.

CHAPTER 13 Creative Financing Approaches

13.1 SECONDARY FINANCING TECHNIQUES

Second Trust Deeds Carried by the Seller

Second trust deeds are sometimes referred to as gap loans carried back by sellers, who in effect help finance a portion of the selling price. The amount financed represents a part of the seller's equity. The difference between the down payment plus loan amount and the sale price leaves a gap that can be filled by the seller carrying back paper, the note secured by the second trust deed. The loan amount may be either a new loan commitment or an existing loan that the purchaser agrees to take over, whether under an assumption agreement or a "subject to" clause. Like first mortgages and trust deeds, seller carrybacks are referred to as **purchase money mortgages** because the seller's loan helps in the purchase.

Example: Assume that a property sells for $300,000 with a $30,000 down payment, and that an institutional lender has made a first trust deed commitment of $240,000 for 30 years at 6.5 percent interest per annum. The seller agrees to carry back the $30,000 balance in the form of a purchase money note with a second deed of trust. Terms of the second loan call for a straight, interest-only note with 7 percent interest per annum, all due and payable in four years. Ignoring closing costs, the buyer's position will appear as follows:

Sale price	$300,000
Cash down payment	−30,000
Balance needed to finance	$270,000
First trust deed	−240,000
Purchase money second (gap loan)	$ 30,000
Monthly interest-only payments	$ 175
Lump sum payment, end of 4 years	$ 30,000

The balance due at the end of four years, referred to as a lump sum payment, is $30,000 on a $30,000 second loan. In the event the buyer-borrower is unable to meet the lump sum payment, there are several options. He or she may: (1) renegotiate the note, if the beneficiary is willing to extend the term of the note; (2) secure a new loan from outside sources in order to pay off the debt; or (3) refinance the entire loan. The last alternative assumes, however, that enough equity has been built up during the four years to allow this. The new loan would pay off the remaining balance on the existing first, $228,143, plus the $30,000 due on the second. Thus, a net of $258,143 is needed, before points and other charges are paid from the loan proceeds.

There are risks involved in carrying back junior trust deeds. Figure 13.1 suggests ways in which sellers can minimize risks to themselves.

Note: The preceding information is for example purposes only. Second trust deeds, whether seller carried or an accompanying loan provided by the first trust deed lender, became popular for avoiding PMI. In our example, the borrower with a 10 percent down payment and a 10 percent seller carry second required only an 80 percent first trust deed and thereby avoided PMI coverage.

In mid-2009, institutional lenders eliminated second trust deed financing from the Fannie Mae and Freddie Mac loan programs, and it was not until mid-2014 that lenders relaxed their prohibition on secondary financing. Prior to the ban on second trust deed financing, lenders developed secondary loan guidelines including: (a) a five-year minimum term, (b) minimum interest-only payments, and (c) a requirement that the borrower qualify with the identified second trust deed payments. These guidelines were retained upon reintroduction of secondary financing.

Collateralizing Junior Loans

Using the previous example, what if the seller does not wish to carry a second trust deed? One solution to this problem is to obtain a collateralized loan using a seller-carryback note and second deed of trust as an asset. **Collateralization** is a process by which a note and deed of trust are pledged as collateral for a loan, usually through private parties, mortgage brokers, and commercial banks, for a percentage of the face value of said note, at a discounted value.

To illustrate its application, assume the same data as under the credit extension loan above.

Assume also that in order for the note to be accepted as collateral, it might be reduced to half its face value and a fee of ten discount points charged by the lender. With interest payable at 7 percent per annum on the note carried back by the seller and 10 percent payable on the collateralized note, the selling beneficiary's position will appear as follows:

Second loan carried by seller		$30,000
Collateral loan (50% from another lender)		−15,000
Deferred portion		$15,000
Interest seller is to receive on $30,000 second Deed of trust at 7% for 4 years		$8,400
Less: Interest paid on $15,000 collateral loan at 10% for 4 years	$6,000	
Less: Discount fee of 10 points (fee to lender for granting collateral loan)	1,500	7,500
Net Interest income over interest expense		$900

FIGURE 13.1 Protection devices for sellers.

> **PROTECTION DEVICES FOR SELLERS WHO CARRY BACK SECOND DEEDS OF TRUST**
>
> 1. Insert an alienation (due-on-sale) clause in the promissory note and deed of trust as a condition for granting the extension of credit.
>
> 2. File a request for copy of notice of default and sale on the existing first deed of trust.
>
> 3. Add the name of the beneficiary (seller) on the new buyers' fire insurance policy as second loss payee.
>
> 4. At the time of the sale ask the title company to issue a joint protection title insurance policy coinsuring both the new buyer and the beneficial interest of the seller.

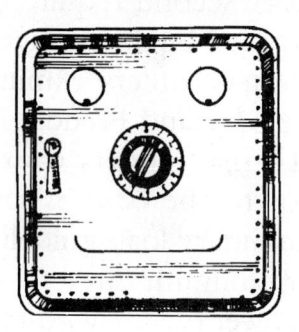

Source: © 2016 OnCourse Learning

First installment (lump sum) receivable at end of 4 years	$30,000
Final installment (lump sum) repayable at end of 4 years	15,000
Net payable to seller-borrower	$15,000

This technique is an alternative for the seller who wishes to retain an interest in the second trust deed but who also needs cash. In this example, the seller received use of $15,000 from the investor.

Collateralizing an existing note and second trust deed may or may not be advantageous, depending on the relationship between the terms and payout on the second loan owned by the seller and the terms and payout on the collateral loan. Collateralizing the note and deed of trust provides a means by which the borrower can obtain immediate cash of

$13,500 ($15,000 loan less $1,500 discount fee) and still keep control over an investment yielding 7 percent per year. The seller-borrower will receive interest income of $8,400 over the four-year period, or $2,100 annually, against a yearly payment of $1,500 in interest charges, netting $600 per year (plus the $1,500 discount fee). Then, at maturity, the seller-borrower will receive a lump sum of $30,000 from the purchaser of the property and pay out $15,000 on the collateralized note for net cash proceeds of $15,000.

Advantages of collateralizing to the seller-borrower include retention of the benefits of the original note; avoidance of loss through discounting of the note; and avoidance of additional debt, that is, the cash flow from seller's carryback note may more than offset the payments on the collateral note, as is true in the example above. Offsetting these would be the interest plus points paid and the time value of money.

As mentioned, such loans usually are obtainable through mortgage brokers, commercial banks, newspaper ads, and private parties. To save extra title insurance and escrow expenses, it would be more practical to arrange such a transaction during the sale escrow.

Seller Sells the Second Loan

Another solution is for the seller or real estate agent to arrange to sell the note and second trust deed that was carried back as part of the purchase price, in other words, to sell the junior lien. This will generate instant cash for the seller. However, selling junior liens almost always involves selling at a discount. This is particularly true in the case of a newly issued note, since there is no history of payments to establish any past record. Other factors that determine the amount of discount include interest rate, location and appraised value of the property, loan-to-value ratio, type and terms of the note, and the desired yield of the investor.

The amount of discount on the sale of a second note and trust deed depends on many variables, as explained in Chapter 3. Assuming the discount to be 25 percent and given the same facts outlined earlier, the application of discounting would appear as follows:

Face value, second trust deed note	$30,000
Less: 25% discount	7,500
Cash proceeds to seller	$22,500

The primary motivation for most **seller carrybacks** is to get the transaction done. The seller of the deed generally accepts a discount and sells at a loss only when there is no better option available (e.g., another offer with a larger down payment). The sale of notes secured by trust deeds is accomplished through the simple act of an assignment executed by the selling beneficiary, called the assignor, in favor of the purchaser, called the assignee. To protect the interest of the new holder of the note, the assignment form should be recorded. An illustration of a completed assignment of deed of trust form is shown in Figure 13.2. **Special note:** If the note is to be discounted and sold in the same escrow in which it is created, it must first be offered to the buyer-borrower on the same terms. If the buyer-borrower refuses the offer, written evidence should be maintained in the escrow files and the broker's files, since the California Department of Real Estate may investigate and the broker may be subject to license revocation for not making the offer to the buyer-borrower. If the note is sold after the escrow closes, this offer does not have to be made to the buyer-borrower.

Investors, buyers of seconds, can be found through escrow companies, loan brokers, holders of maturing junior trust deed loans, as disclosed by reconveyance deeds recorded at the County Hall of Records, classified ads, and, in the case of licensees, their own client files, particularly those disclosing previous sellers who carried back paper for part or all of the purchase price. Sellers are cautioned, of course, to look into a variety of criteria, and not just the amount of discount offered, before entering any transaction with any investor or investor entity.

Broker Participation

Another creative approach to solving real estate finance problems is to have the broker become a lender for part of the equity. Whatever the scheme, the broker effectively becomes a partner with the seller in the secondary loan by breaking down the note into two component parts. The seller is named the beneficiary but assigns part or the entire note to the broker as commission through a collateral agreement such as shown in Figure 13.3. As with the previous secondary loan variations, this plan is utilized when the seller of property needs more cash than is generated through a down payment that is less than the seller's equity, after allowance for the senior security. Under the plan, the note and second trust deed are assigned to the real estate agent. Caveat: Since you are taking on a partner, that person's attitudes must be considered in any action taken regarding the collateral.

FIGURE 13.2 Sample assignment of deed of trust.

RECORDING REQUESTED BY:

AND WHEN RECORDED MAIL TO:

Order No.:
Escrow No.:
APN:

SPACE ABOVE THIS LINE FOR RECORDER'S USE

ASSIGNMENT OF DEED OF TRUST

For value received, the undersigned hereby grants, assigns and transfers to

_____

all beneficial interest under that certain Deed of Trust dated _____, _____ executed

by _____, Trustor,

to _____, Trustee,

and recorded on _____, _____ as Instrument No. _____ of

Official Records in the office of the County Recorder of _____ County,

California, describing land therein as:

together with the note or notes as therein described or referred to, the money due and to become due

thereon with interest, and all rights accrued or to accrue under said Deed of Trust.

Dated: _____   _____

                                        _____

A notary public or other officer completing this certificate verifies only the identity of the individual who signed the document to which this certificate is attached, and not the truthfulness, accuracy, or validity of that document.

STATE OF CALIFORNIA   )
) SS.
COUNTY OF _____)

On _____ before me, _____, Notary Public, personally appeared _____,
who proved to me on the basis of satisfactory evidence) to be the person(s) whose name(s) is/are subscribed to the within instrument and acknowledged to me that he/she/they executed the same in his/her/their authorized capacity(ies), and that by his/her/their signature(s) on the instrument the person(s), or the entity upon behalf of which the person(s) acted, executed the instrument.

I certify under PENALTY OF PERJURY under the laws of the State of California that the foregoing paragraph is true and correct.

WITNESS my hand and official seal.

Signature_____

FOR NOTARY STAMP

Source: © 2016 OnCourse Learning

CHAPTER 13 Creative Financing Approaches

FIGURE 13.3 Sample installment note.

INSTALLMENT NOTE--COLLATERAL SECURITY

$ 18,000   Utopia, California,   July 6, 20xx

In installments as herein stated, for value received, Igot Stuck, Sellers promise to pay to Mrs. Broker and Mr. Salesman, or order, at Utopia, California the principal sum of Eighteen thousand ($18,000) and no/100 DOLLARS, with interest from date endorsed hereon on unpaid principal at the rate of Twelve (12%) per cent per annum; principal and interest payable in installments of Two hundred seventy ($270) and no/100 Dollars or more on the same day of each calendar month, beginning on the first (1st) day of September 20xx, and continuing until August 1, 20xx, at which time the entire unpaid balance of principal and interest shall become due and payable.

and continuing until said principal and interest have been paid. Should any installment of principal or interest not be so paid, then the whole sum of principal and interest shall immediately become due and payable at the option of the holder hereof; principal and interest payable only in lawful money of the United States. Should this note not be paid according to the terms hereof and suit be filed or an attorney employed or expenses incurred to compel payment of this note, or any portion hereof, I agree to pay a reasonable sum in in addition to attorney's fees. The makers and endorsers of this note hereby waive diligence, demand, presentment for payment, notice of non-payment, protest and notice of protest.

/s/ Mr. Igot Stuck
/s/ Mrs. Igot Stuck

As collateral security for the payment of this note and interest as stated therein and expenses which may accrue thereon we have deposited with Mrs. Broker, the following personal property of which we are sole owners, to-wit:
1. Note executed by Mr. & Mrs. Buyer, dated July 4, 20xx
2. Deed of Trust securing said Note, recorded July 5, 20xx
3. Duly executed Assignment of Trust Deed and Note by Mr. & Mrs. Stuck, recorded August 19, 20xx

And should the said note or any part thereof, or the interest, or the interest that may grow thereon, remain due and unpaid according to the tenor of said note, we hereby irrevocably authorize and empower said Mrs. Broker and Mr. Salesman, their heirs, executors, administrators or assigns, to sell and dispose of the above mentioned personal property, or any part thereof, at public or private sale, without any previous notice to us of any such sale, and from the proceeds arising therefrom to pay the principal and interest and all charges that shall then be due, and the costs of sale, and the balance, if any, to pay over to our or representatives upon demand. In case of deterioration of any of the above securities, or fall in the market value of the same we hereby promise and agree on demand to reduce the amount of said debt, or to increase the security in proportion to such deterioration or decrease of value, in default of which this note is to be considered due under the above stipulation. On the payment of this note and interest according to the terms of the same, and all charges, this agreement is to be void, and the above named securities to be returned to us.

Presentment, protest and notice of protest are hereby waived.

Dated August 19, 20xx

/s/ Mr. Igot Stuck
/s/ Mrs. Igot Stuck

NOTE—COLLATERAL SECURITY—INSTALLMENT—WOLCOTTS FORM 1426

Source: © 2016 OnCourse Learning

Example: Assume the sale of a home for $300,000 with a $240,000 first loan commitment. Assume further that the buyer has limited resources, say, a 10 percent down payment, or $30,000.

The commission rate is 6 percent, and the seller agrees to carry back a second loan, if enough cash can be generated so that the seller can in turn purchase another home. Suppose that the seller needs the cash and cannot afford to carry back the four-year note to maturity, yet the seller does not like the idea of collateralizing or selling at discount. The real estate agent can provide the solution by participating in the second trust deed loan, as follows:

Sale price		$300,000
Cash down payment		−30,000
Balance needed to finance		$270,000
First trust deed loan		−240,000
Junior financing for the balance	$30,000	
Broker's share at 6% of sales price	−18,000	
Seller's share for balance	$12,000	
Combined purchase money second trust deed		$30,000

The mechanics of this transaction are as follows: (1) A promissory note and trust deed are executed by the buyer of the property in favor of the seller for the full amount of the second deed of trust, $30,000. (2) Then an instrument similar to the installment note, the collateral security form in Figure 13.3, is executed by the sellers to the broker for the amount of commission, $18,000 in this case. The collateral agreement is, in effect, an assignment of the seller's note and trust deed for the portion representing the broker's interest. It states in so many words that for value received, the seller promises to pay to the broker the agreed amount at so much per month, including interest at so much per annum. In case of default, the broker would have a right to foreclose through either public or private sale of the collateral, the secured promissory note. When more than one licensee is taking part or all of the commission through this mechanism, like a selling salesperson and employing broker, both may be shown under the payee provision of the collateral note for the amount or percentage representing their respective commission interests. It is advisable to check with the lender and your broker to determine the acceptability of carrying one's commission.

Combination or Split Junior Liens

As a compromise to carrying back paper that the seller is unwilling to sell or collateralize, and when the broker is not willing to take a junior lien for all or part of the commission, the seller might be amenable to taking back a concurrent second and third trust deed, both carrying a 12 percent yield. The purchase money loan is split. Instead of one large second, the seller might agree to two smaller junior liens. Using the sales price and terms outlined in the original example, with a 10 percent down payment and assumed 70/30 split junior lien, the position of the junior trust deeds would appear as follows:

Sales price	$300,000
Cash down payment	−30,000
Balance needed to finance	$270,000
First trust deed	−240,000
Junior financing	$30,000
Second trust deed carried by seller	−21,000
Third trust deed carried by seller	$9,000

While both loans contain exactly the same terms, the advantage of such an arrangement is that it is easier to market a second of a smaller size, thus providing the seller with some immediate cash relief. Yet the seller is able to retain a relatively safe interest in the property at an attractive rate of return. The $30,000 junior financing may be divided into any portions that will allow the greatest flexibility to the seller. It may be a $21,000 second and $9,000 third as just illustrated, or a $15,000 second and $15,000 third, and so on. The buyer's costs are not substantially increased, since split loans require only two extra documents, one extra recording fee, and one extra reconveyance fee. Payoff terms can be adjusted to increase yield on the second or third that is to be sold.

13.2 ALL-INCLUSIVE TRUST DEED (AITD)

Definition

An AITD, for reasons that will soon become clear, is also referred to as a **wrap-around trust deed**. It may also be mistakenly referred to as a *blanket trust deed*, since it includes more than one trust deed loan within the framework of the instrument. A blanket trust deed encumbers more than one property (e.g., new developments), while an AITD usually covers just one property. An *all-inclusive trust* deed is always a *junior* deed of trust, often a purchase money deed of trust loan, given back to the seller, that includes in its scope the amount of the first encumbrance as well as any secondary liens. It normally contains a provision that the seller will pay off the senior loan or loans from monies the seller is to receive from the buyer. It is subject to, yet includes, encumbrances to which it is subordinate.

Since the concept essentially involves the seller as lender, it is most often used when money is tight or unavailable. Care and discretion must be exercised in its adoption, particularly when a real estate agent recommends its use.

An example of an all-inclusive deed of trust is shown in Figure 13.4. The instrument could be used on virtually any type of property where circumstances are appropriate. Brokers should not attempt to draft such trust deeds but should have them prepared by the parties' legal counsel and approved by the title company that is to insure them.

Uses for All-Inclusive Trust Deeds

The **all-inclusive trust deed** is used under a variety of circumstances. Some sellers will use it in lieu of an installment sales contract, the so-called land contract. It may also be used where a loan exists with a lock-in clause (not to be confused with lock-in-rate) that provides that the existing loan cannot be paid off before a certain date. A third use is when an owner is anxious to sell and a prospective purchaser will buy only under an all-inclusive device that incorporates features favorable to the buyer such as income tax benefits. Sellers may also offer this type of instrument when they have overpriced the property and creative financing may make the transaction attractive to a buyer. Low down payments may also tempt owners to sell this way.

Another type of transaction calling for a wrap-around is when there is a low-interest loan that the seller would prefer to keep, particularly when a buyer's credit is marginal, so that in the event of foreclosure by the selling beneficiary, the underlying low-cost loan is retained. When the seller is firm on price but not on terms, again its use may be justified.

Another circumstance is when a prospective buyer cannot qualify for required financing under a normal sale. When a seller would need to carry back a substantial junior loan, the all-inclusive may be more satisfactory. In cases involving heavy and burdensome prepayment penalties, buyers and sellers may resort to the AITD. In still another situation, an owner may need cash but the beneficiary under the existing trust deed will not commit itself to additional advances, forcing the seller to retain the prior lien or liens using an all-inclusive. Finally, when a severe money crunch hits the mortgage market, this device takes on added significance. After all, it is especially during periods of tight money that most creative financing techniques appear on the market.

Although we have advanced numerous reasons for using the all-inclusive deed of trust, sellers and buyers may, of course, be motivated

FIGURE 13.4 Sample all-inclusive deed of trust.

ALL INCLUSIVE PURCHASE MONEY PROMISSORY NOTE SECURED BY ALL-INCLUSIVE PURCHASE MONEY DEED OF TRUST
(INSTALLMENT NOTE, INTEREST INCLUDED)

$ 500,000   Van Nuys , California, April 15 , 20XX

In installments as herein stated, for value received, I/We ("Maker") promise to pay to James W. Johnson ("Payee") or order, at 6515-6517 Van Nuys Blvd, Van Nuys, CA the principal sum of Five hundred thousand and no/100 DOLLARS, with interest from date hereof on unpaid principal at the rate of twelve (12%) per cent per annum; principal and interest payable in installments of $5143.00 or more on the first (1st) day of each calendar month, beginning on the first (1st) day of June 20XX, and continuing until said principal and interest fully paid / June 1, 20XX, when the unpaid balance shall be due and payable.

Each installment shall be applied first on the interest then due and the remainder on principal; and interest shall thereupon cease upon the principal so credited.

The total principal amount of this Note includes the unpaid principal balance of the promissory note(s) ("Underlying Note(s)") secured by Deed(s) of Trust, more particularly described as follows:

1. (A) PROMISSORY NOTE:
   Maker: Newstate S & L and Allstate Mortgage Ltd.
   Payee: _____
   Original Amount: $300,000
   Date: _____

   (B) DEED OF TRUST:
   Beneficiary: _____
   Original Amount: _____
   Recordation Date: _____
   Document No. _____ Book _____ Page _____
   Place of Recordation: _____, County, California

2. (A) PROMISSORY NOTE:
   Maker: _____
   Payee: _____
   Original Amount: _____
   Date: _____

   (B) DEED OF TRUST:
   Beneficiary: _____
   Original Amount: _____
   Recordation Date: _____
   Document No. _____ Book _____ Page _____
   Place of Recordation: _____, County, California

By Payee's acceptance of this Note, Payee covenants and agrees that, provided Maker is not delinquent or in default under the terms of this Note, Payee shall pay all installments of principal and interest which shall hereafter become due pursuant to the provisions of the Underlying Note(s) as and when the same become due and payable. In the event Maker shall be delinquent or in default under the terms of this Note, Payee shall not be obligated to make any payments required by the terms of the Underlying Note(s) until such delinquency or default is cured. In the event Payee fails to timely pay any installment of principal or interest on the Underlying Note(s) at the time when Maker is not delinquent or in default hereunder, Maker may, at Maker's option, make such payments directly to the holder of such Underlying Note(s), in which event Maker shall be entitled to a credit against the next installment(s) of principal and interest due under the terms of this Note equal to the amount so paid and including, without limitation, any penalty, charges and expenses paid by Maker to the holder of the Underlying Note(s) on account of Payee failing to make such payment. The obligations of Payee hereunder shall terminate upon the earliest of (i) foreclosure of the lien of the All-Inclusive Purchase Money Deed of Trust securing this Note, or (ii) cancellation of this Note and reconveyance of the All-Inclusive Purchase Money Deed of Trust securing same.

Should Maker be delinquent or in default under the terms of this Note, and Payee consequently incurs any penalties, charges or other expenses on account of the Underlying Note(s) during the period of such delinquency or default, the amount of such penalties, charges and expenses shall be immediately added to the principal amount of this Note and shall be immediately payable by Maker to Payee.

Notwithstanding anything to the contrary herein contained, the right of Maker to prepay all or any portion of the principal of this Note is limited to the same extent as any limitation exists in the right to prepay the principal of the Underlying Note(s). If any prepayments of principal of this Note shall, by reason of the application of any portion thereof by Payee to the prepayment of principal of the Underlying Note(s), constitute such prepayment for which the holders of the Underlying Note(s) are entitled to receive a prepayment penalty or consideration, the amount of such prepayment penalty or consideration shall be paid by Maker to Payee upon demand, and any such amount shall not reduce the unpaid balance of principal or interest hereunder.

At any time when the total of the unpaid principal balance of this Note, accrued interest thereon, all other sums due pursuant to the terms hereof, and all sums advanced by Payee pursuant to the terms of the All-Inclusive Purchase Money Deed of Trust securing this Note, is equal to or less than the unpaid balance of principal and interest then due under the terms of the Underlying Note(s), Payee, at his option, shall cancel this Note and deliver same to Maker and execute a request for full reconveyance of the Deed of Trust securing this Note.

Should default be made by Maker in payment of any installments of principal, interest, or any other sums due hereunder, the whole sum of principal, interest and all other sums due from Maker hereunder, after first deducting therefrom all sums then due under the terms of the Underlying Note(s), shall become immediately due at the option of the holder of this Note. Principal, interest and all other sums due hereunder payable in lawful money of the United States. If action be instituted on this Note, I/we promise to pay such sums as the Court may fix as attorney's fees. This Note is secured by an ALL-INCLUSIVE PURCHASE MONEY DEED OF TRUST to Lawyers Title Insurance Corporation, a Virginia corporation, as Trustee.

_____ (Maker)   _Jack B. Quick_ (Maker) Jack B. Quick

The undersigned hereby accept(s) the foregoing All-Inclusive Purchase Money Promissory Note and agree(s) to perform each and all of the terms thereof on the part of Payee to be performed.
Executed as of the date and place first above written.

_____ (Payee)   _____ (Payee)

(THIS NOTE IS FOR USE ONLY IN PURCHASE MONEY TRANSACTIONS. IT IS RECOMMENDED THAT, PRIOR TO THE EXECUTION OF THIS NOTE, THE PARTIES CONSULT WITH THEIR ATTORNEYS WITH RESPECT THERETO.)

THIS FORM FURNISHED BY LAWYERS TITLE INSURANCE CORPORATION

Source: © 2016 OnCourse Learning

by a combination of two or more of these. Remember, an AITD cannot be used to get around an otherwise enforceable **due-on-sale clause.** Lenders can discover a concealed AITD when the homeowner's insurance policy is endorsed.

Comprehensive Application of AITD

As an example of an AITD, assume that a property is to sell for $600,000 and that it has an existing first trust deed loan of $236,000 payable at $2,360 per month, including interest at 8 percent per annum; and a second loan of $64,000 payable at $640 per month, including 10 percent annual interest. Deducting the $300,000 in loans from the $600,000 sale price leaves equity of $300,000. Suppose the parties agree to a one-sixth down payment, or $100,000. The balance of the purchase price, $200,000, is the remaining seller's equity that could be financed by carrying back either a third trust deed or an AITD. Since a substantial third would be involved, representing one-third of the sales price, such a step may not be advised. A better resolution may lie, therefore, with the wrap-around, if the existing loan(s) is assumable and/or the lenders agree to waive their due-on-sale rights. Schematically, the transaction would appear as follows:

SALE PRICE: $600,000			
$100,000 Down payment (Buyer's equity) interest	$500,000 All-inclusive trust deed, $5,143 per month at 12%		
	$236,000 First loan payable $2,360 per month at 8% annual interest	$64,000 Second loan payable $640 per month at 10% annual interest	$200,000 Seller's remaining equity

In the illustration, the seller's remaining equity is $200,000, and it is added to the existing liens under the banner of an AITD, payable at $5,143 per month including interest of 12 percent per annum.

Characteristics and Limitations

The AITD is characterized by a number of features. First, it can increase the seller's rate of return above what the rate would be under a traditional carryback loan. Second, it is a purchase money transaction, subject to, but still including encumbrances, to which it is subordinate. The buyer becomes a trustor-grantee, while the seller becomes a beneficiary-grantor. By virtue of its purchase money character, the transaction is subject to California's anti-deficiency statutes if it is a one- to four-unit, owner-occupied residential property, so that the buyer-trustor is held harmless in the event of a deficiency on the promissory note should foreclosure occur.

Legal title is actually conveyed, usually by grant deed, and may be insured by a policy of title insurance. Finally, in the event of default and foreclosure, the seller-beneficiary follows the same procedures that would apply in the foreclosure of any trust deed. However, the action is filed only against the seller's equity, representing the difference between the underlying liens and the overriding obligation, $200,000 in the preceding illustration. Again, the AITD is useful only if existing loans are assumable, or if the due-on-sale clause is waived by the prior lender.

Types of AITDs

The AITD may be one of two types:

1. *Equity payoff.* This takes place when the buyer, who is the trustor on the AITD, with the permission of the lender, takes over the prior loans after the seller's equity has been paid off. A deed of reconveyance is issued by the seller-beneficiary of the AITD. In the preceding example, once the buyer has paid off the difference between the $500,000 AITD and the $236,000 first trust deed plus the remaining due under the $64,000 second, the buyer steps into the shoes of the seller and makes payments on the prior notes directly to the beneficiaries of these senior liens.

2. *Full payoff.* Here the buyer-trustor is obligated to the seller until the entire balance of the AITD is paid off. Thus the seller-beneficiary continues to pick up the override, the difference between the 12 percent paid the seller and the lower rates due on the underlying notes (8 percent on the first, 10 percent on the second).

Benefits to Seller

There are a number of advantages to the seller in using the all-inclusive to solve financing problems. It may be the only practical way to dispose of a property when there is a lock-in clause. Furthermore, a broader market is created for the property when a seller is willing to carry back substantially all of the paper. A carryback by a seller does not incur loan fees and a variety of other financing charges. This attracts buyers and thereby increases the demand for the seller's property.

Moreover, the all-inclusive device affords flexibility so that the seller may be able to obtain a higher price due to the built-in financing terms. In effect, the seller has manufactured money by deferring the recapture of the seller's equity through this method. The seller retains the favorable terms of the existing loans in the event the seller is forced to repossess the property through foreclosure. During the holding period, the seller is able to increase the net yield on the overall trust deed. Recall that sellers' carryback purchase money mortgages and trust deeds are not subject to any interest rate limitations. Using the data from our previous example, if a simple interest rate were applied to each of the loans, the yield to the investor on the AITD would be almost 17.4 percent, computed as follows:

Interest income:	12% of $500,000 on AITD		$60,000
Interest expense:	8% of $236,000 on existing first deed	$18,880	
	10% of $64,000 on existing second deed	6,400	25,280
Net interest income over interest expense:			$34,720

$$\text{Yield} = \frac{\text{Seller's net interest income}}{\text{Seller's equity}} = \frac{\$34,720}{\$200,000} = 17.4\%$$

The effective yield is significantly greater than the 12 percent stated on the AITD note because the seller will collect 12 percent while paying only 8 percent and 10 percent on the existing notes, thereby earning an additional 4 percent on the first, and 2 percent on the second trust deed. The extra $10,720 interest is equivalent to another 5.4 percent return on the $200,000 remaining equity. That is,

$$\frac{(4\% \times \$236,000) + (2\% \times \$64,000)}{\$200,000} = 5.4\%$$

Adding this to the 12 percent buyer's contract rate produces a 17.4 percent effective rate to the seller. It should be noted that calculations using the foregoing formula are only approximations. They show the yield on a first year basis only and not over the life of the loan. Furthermore, they do not take into account other variables, including special features of the note, such as term, balloon payments, or variable rates; nor do they take into account income tax consequences and time value of money. Use the formula judiciously.

Another benefit might ensue in the event the seller-beneficiary had to cash out the all-inclusive note secured by a trust deed. A lower discount is commanded when a high effective yield is obtained. Even without a discount, when the purchaser could assume the underlying liens, in the previous example, the yield would be 17.4 percent.

A significant advantage to the seller is that this device makes the seller aware immediately of any buyer's default, in contract to taking back a junior deed of trust accompanied by the recording of a request for notice: months may pass before a senior lienholder files a notice of default should the trustor-buyer default in a prior loan, so that if the junior lienholder's own loan payments are current, such default would be unnoticed. When compared to a land contract of sale, the AITD may again be superior, because in case of foreclosure, a trustee's sale is speedier, surer, and absolute, while foreclosure under a land contract requires court action to become effective.

Finally, income tax advantages to the seller may be enhanced. For example, in a straight sale with conventional forms of financing, the entire gain is recognized in the year of sale. In contrast, in the AITD, the seller may declare only the actual receipts received each year, on a prorated basis over the term of the AITD note. This is because an AITD, since it is payable over more than one calendar year, is by its very nature an installment sale, as defined in the Internal Revenue Code, Section 453.

Benefits to Buyer

The AITD also offers many advantages to buyers. They may be able to acquire properties for which they may not otherwise qualify (for example, the purchaser who is retired and, although having substantial resources, has relatively little if any consistent income). When financing can be obtained, the buyer may acquire a larger property for the same low down payment, utilizing the principle of leverage. Moreover, one monthly payment will be required instead of a series of payments that comes when the buyer assumes the prior liens and executes another junior secured note in favor of the seller. Costs are reduced on appraisal fees, loan points, loan escrow fee, and other charges.

Greater flexibility may also be offered in the structure of the loan. When the seller is cooperative, the purchaser might be able to tailor the spendable income to his or her particular needs, such as through a lower debt service stretched over a longer period of time, and thus afford to pay more for the property by bargaining for better terms. There are no restrictions on lending, unlike institutional financing. Thus extra-long terms can be negotiated, with no points and no prepayment penalties as part of the bargain. And if the purchaser should pay more for the property, the basis will be thereby increased, with a subsequent lower capital gain or larger write-off in the event of a qualified sale at a loss.

Finally, when contrasted with a purchase under a land contract, the buyer gets a grant deed, or ownership in fee, up front, as opposed to a land contract, which gives legal title at the end of the contract, though it is also an insurable title.

Another advantage to both buyer and seller is that since the buyer will not ordinarily incur loan fees and a variety of financing charges, properly structured, this feature should attract more buyers and increase the demand for the seller's property.

Some Pitfalls of AITDs

Just as there are benefits to both buyers and sellers who structure the AITD correctly, precautions must be taken since this vehicle is not a cure-all for most housing transactions.

Precautions for Sellers

Both parties should take steps to guard against certain pitfalls that may arise in connection with the use of the wrap-around trust deed. For example, an impound account might be set up to cover taxes, insurance, and balloon payments on the prior liens. The seller might also have the installment payments on the wrap-around loan fall due at least a week before payments on the senior loan are due. This way, the seller will be using the buyer's money to make the payments on any senior loan.

A limit, if not an outright prohibition, might be imposed on further use of another AITD upon resale by inserting a due-on-sale clause in the AITD. Similarly, the seller should reserve the right to have the buyer refinance the property. The seller may wish to have the buyer refinance when the money market is more favorable, or when the lock-in period has expired, or when balloon payments are due on the senior debt. The seller should also make provision for the time when the purchaser may need to assume the existing loans, should such loans outlive the AITD.

Finally, when income-producing property is involved, the seller should reserve the right to approve all leases that might impair the value of the AITD. A shrewd buyer might, for example, lease the premises with substantial prepaid rents paid to the buyer, intending to milk the property, then walk away from it, leaving the seller stuck with the legal problems of dealing with the prepaid rents for each of the lessees, in addition to having to deal with the remaining lease terms, which may be economically unfavorable to the seller who must now step in to protect remaining interests. By reserving the right to prescreen all leases, the seller is protected against such problems in the AITD, since all subsequent leases are to be subordinated to the seller's superior interest as the beneficiary under the AITD.

Precautions for Buyers

The all-inclusive agreement should provide protections for the buyer in case the seller defaults on the loan or loans being wrapped.

The buyer might, for example, insert the right to make payments on the seller's underlying liens, and credit such payments toward the AITD. Payments might be made to a bank collection department, escrow, trust, or directly to the holder of the included encumbrances, stipulating that they be used in turn to reduce existing liens. The costs of setting up such machinery should be stipulated. If payments on the AITD are not sufficient to cover existing liens, provision should be made for seller's payment of any differences, such as through a bond. Further, the buyer might reserve the right to pay off part or all of the senior debts, assuming or retiring some or all of them.

All buyers should record a request for notice of default and notice of sale on the seller's senior liens to make sure they keep abreast of the status of these loans. If a notice of default is recorded, buyers will automatically receive notice.

Procedures in Setting Up an AITD

The procedures required in negotiating for and creating an AITD might follow these broad steps:

1. Examine existing trust deeds to determine whether there is an enforceable due-on-sale, alienation, or acceleration clause. If any exist, provision should be made either to pay off the loans or renegotiate them.

2. Outstanding balances, periodic payments, and balloon provisions should be ascertained so that a realistic payment schedule can be set up on the all-inclusive. For example, the new loan schedule may call for a longer or shorter period for payment, depending on the particular requirements of the respective parties. The AITD is recorded as a junior lien, subject to the existing liens. The purchaser may later, with the lender's permission, take over the senior loans, whereupon the seller would need to obtain a reconveyance of the AITD as a fully discharged instrument.

   A realistic payment schedule should be constructed to cover (a) periodic installments; (b) outstanding balances; (c) partial balloons on existing loans; and (d) any variations in payments, such as for adjustable or variable rates.

3. Decide who is to collect and disburse payments on the AITD and who is to pay the cost of establishing and administering the collection process. If the payments under the AITD are not sufficient to cover the senior loans, a system should be set up to see that the additional amounts are paid. Similarly, if there is an impound account for taxes, insurance, or other matters in the underlying note, it would be prudent to incorporate an impound account in the AITD note as well.

4. Spell out the conditions giving rise to default and what foreclosure procedure is to be followed. These are similar to those found in the standard trust deed, except that only the seller's remaining equity is affected.

5. Have the necessary agreements and documents drawn up, using essential phraseology to gain acceptance by title companies for insurance purposes. A joint protection policy of title insurance, insuring both the interests of the buyer as owner and the interests of the seller as lender and as to priority of lien, should be obtained.

6. Determine property insurance coverage so all parties are amply protected.

13.3 INSTALLMENT SALES CONTRACT

The **installment sales contract**, more popularly called a conditional sales contract, or land contract of sale, was popular in the 1970s during an extremely high interest rate period. The installment sale was resurrected in 2008 when home financing was difficult due to the lack of liquidity in the finance arena.

In an installment sale, a seller, called the vendor, sells to a buyer, the vendee, by financing the purchase. The vendor retains legal title until the terms and conditions of the contract are fulfilled. The owner-carried financing can include an existing mortgage, or the property can be free and clear. The latter situation is usually preferred as existing loans often contain acceleration and alienation clauses that could complicate the transaction. Reminder: An acceleration clause requires a borrower to immediately pay off a loan if certain conditions occur like failure to pay the mortgage. An alienation clause requires full payment of the mortgage balance if the property is sold or title transferred to another person. An underlying lender is often alerted to an installment sale when a new insurance policy is issued in the name of both the buyer and seller.

The issue of the transfer of title is an important difference between the installment sale and an AITD. The all-inclusive deed of trust permits a private sale of the property by the trustee in the event of default, eliminating the problems of a time-consuming and cumbersome judicial foreclosure. In contrast, the usual land contract may not contain a power of sale provision, so that a lawsuit is necessary for an effective foreclosure by the vendor. However, it may be noted that almost all title companies have produced contract forms that incorporate a power of sale provision. Figure 13.5 is an example of an Installment Land Sale Contract with Power of Sale.

Example: To illustrate the math involved in the sale of real property through a land contract, suppose a vacant lot sold for $100,000 and has an existing assumable 10 percent first trust deed loan of $60,000. The buyer is to make a down payment of 10 percent, or $10,000, and has agreed to execute an installment contract secured by the property for the balance of the purchase price. The contract is to be repaid at $966, rounded to the next dollar, per month, based on a 30-year amortization schedule including interest of 13 percent per annum, all due and payable in 15 years. Note that under such schedule the payments are reduced from the $1,138.72 that would be payable under 15-year amortization.

Sales price	$100,000
Down payment at 10%	−10,000
Balance payable $996 monthly at 13%	$ 90,000

The seller continues to make payments on the $60,000 first trust deed, at the more favorable 10 percent interest rate. Instead of a second trust deed of $30,000 ($90,000 less $60,000) at, say, 10 percent, the seller will receive more on a 13 percent loan on the entire unpaid balance of $90,000, meanwhile continuing with a 10 percent interest rate on the existing $60,000, yielding a differential of 3 percent on the full $60,000.

For all practical purposes, the vendee is the owner in that he or she has possession, has the right for quiet enjoyment and use, and can resell the property. In most instances, the buyer does not have to qualify for the loan (although the seller/vendor would be wise to seek at least a credit report), and the terms are fully negotiable including down payment, interest rate, and payment term. With the absence of lender fees, the costs are generally lower.

The vendor benefits by the ability to defer taxes (paying taxes only on the portion of capital gains each year) and obtains monthly income and often a rate of return in excess of market returns. The transaction usually can be completed more quickly than typical financial transactions, and it could be a way for selling and/or buying non-conforming

FIGURE 13.5 Installment land sale contract.

INSTALLMENT LAND SALE CONTRACT WITH POWER OF SALE

THIS INSTALLMENT LAND SALE CONTRACT WITH POWER OF SALE ("Agreement"), made and entered into this _____ day of _____, _____, by and between _____ [vendor's name and capacity] ("Vendor"), and _____ [vendee's name and capacity] ("Vendee"), whose address is _____ [address of vendee]; and _____ [trustee's name and capacity] ("Trustee").

Recitals

A. Vendor is now the owner of certain real property situated in the County of _____, State of California, commonly known as _____ [property street address], and described as follows: _____ [attach property description] (the "Property").

B. Vendor has agreed to sell and Vendee has agreed to buy the Property on the terms and conditions hereinafter set forth;

C. Vendor shall retain legal title to the Property as a security interest in the Property until the payment of the balance of the Purchase Price (as hereinafter defined) has been paid by Vendee to Vendor as set forth below.

NOW, THEREFORE, the parties hereto do hereby agree as follows:

Section 1. Purchase Price.

Vendor agrees to sell, and Vendee agrees to buy the Property for the sum of _____ ($_____) (the "Purchase Price"), lawful money of the United States, as hereinafter more fully set forth.

Section 2. Payment of Purchase Price

Vendee shall pay the Purchase Price as follows:

(a) Vendee shall pay to Vendor the sum of _____ Dollars ($_____) (the "Down Payment") as a down payment.

(b) The balance of Purchase Price of _____ ($_____) shall be paid by Vendee to Vendor with interest at the rate of _____ percent per annum on any balance unpaid. Said sum shall be paid in installments of _____ ($_____) on the _____ day of each month commencing _____ and continuing thereafter until _____.

Each payment shall be credited first to interest, with the balance to principal. This Agreement will require _____ years and _____ months to complete payment in accordance with its terms. Vendor shall make payment of any installments on existing first, second and/or third deeds of trust in accordance with paragraph (c) below.

Total Monthly payment is to include the following:
    Principal and interest $_____
    Tax and Fire Insurance Impounds $_____
    Service Charges $_____
                         $_____
    Total Payment $_____

[Optional provision:]

(If multiple mortgages are involved, language will be inserted here identifying the terms and conditions under which they shall be paid.)

FIGURE 13.5 (Continued)

      (c) Vendor under this Agreement shall make due and timely payments of installments in the amount of $_____ principal and interest
on the first deed of trust and note in the original amount of $_____ in favor of _____, current unpaid balance of which is _____ with interest paid to _____.

      Vendor hereby indemnifies and agrees to save Vendee harmless from any default in connection with the obligation or obligations secured by the above first or se cond deeds of trust. In the event any such installment payments on the obligations secured by said deeds of trust shall be in default, Vendee under this Agreement may make payments thereof at its option and credit such payments to the obligation herein secured. In the event Vendee makes a payment upon the deeds of trust that is in excess of the amount required to be made under this Agreement, such excess shall be credited on the next installment or installment payments that may become due under this contract, and Vendee shall not be required to pay such excess in addition to the regular payment of monthly installments under this Agreement.

      (d) Upon recordation of this Agreement, Vendor and Vendee will obtain policies of title insurance from _____, with cost to be borne by _____.

      (e) The basis upon which the tax estimates in this Agreement are made is the tax billed for the fiscal year.

      (f) At any time after the calendar year in which this Agreement is recorded, Vendee may prepay without penalty all or any portion of the balance due Vendor or due on any other encumbrance on the property when the terms of such encumbrance so provides. In such event any payments made by Vendee shall be credited against the balance of the obligation owed by Vendee to Vendor as set forth in (c) above. Any prepayment penalty shall be paid by Vendee and shall not reduce the balance owed to Vendor.

                     Section 3. Appointment and Powers of Trustee.
Upon recordation of this Agreement, Vendor and Vendee irrevocably grant, transfer, and assign their respective rights, titles, and interests to the Property herein to Trustee in trust for purposes of securing Vendor's and Vendee's obligations herein, and confer upon Trustee the following powers:

      (a) Power to convey to Vendee legal title upon full satisfaction of Vendee's obligation to Vendor, upon instructions from Vendor or his or her successor in interest.

      (b) power to foreclose under power of sale below, and issue a deed upon foreclosure and sale. Said deed shall convey title without covenant or warranty, expressed or implied, and any recitals contained therein of any matters or facts shall constitute proof of the truthful ness thereof. Any person, including Vendor, Vendee or Trustee may purchase at such sale. The parties do not intend hereby to alter in any manner their rights as Vendor or Vendee, but rather to vest the Trustee with title so as to create powers coupled with an interest, and Vendor and Vendee shall retain the rights and obligations imposed upon them by California Civil Code Section 2985 and all other applicable laws and statutes

Source: © 2016 OnCourse Learning

property that cannot easily be financed. The purchaser must recognize that the same inability to finance condition may prevail when he or she wishes to sell the property.

The vendee is advised to obtain an appraisal and the vendor should acquire a buyer's credit report. Both may wish to arrange to have payments collected from the buyer and for said company to make payments to any underlying loans. It is likely that installment sales will remain a little-used option for real estate purchases because of some of the challenges noted above. In addition, a major potential problem for the buyer is the seller's inability to deliver marketable title after the buyer has made all the payments and met all the conditions. A potential problem for the seller, in some states, is the difficulty of evicting a defaulting buyer who claims an equitable interest in the property.

As noted above, there can be tax advantages to the seller and perhaps to the buyer as well. Check with a tax consultant for further details. Incidentally, a land contract can be used for any type of real estate, including vacant land.

Lease with Option to Purchase

When interest rates are low or home values are reduced but poised to appreciate in the future, buyers are increasingly anxious to purchase a home. Lacking the necessary down payment or sufficient credit rating to proceed immediately, a **lease with option to purchase** can be viewed as a way to buy at today's price, while having time to accumulate the necessary down payment or improve a credit rating to consummate a transaction.

A lease with option to purchase is an agreement between a seller and a buyer to sell a property for a specific dollar amount within a specified period of time, typically 12 to 18 months. The parties agree to a deposit (option amount) from the lessee (buyer), a monthly rent amount, and any other concessions. Problems can occur if the agreements are not acceptable to a lender at the time the buyer decides to exercise his or her option to purchase.

While a seller must be highly motivated to enter a lease option, a good question to ask of the buyer is, "What will be different in 12 to 18 months that will allow you to purchase then that prohibits you from purchasing right now?" The answer to this question will determine if the parties should enter into a lease option agreement.

There are several considerations for both buyer and seller in a lease option.

1. The seller may not contribute down payment funds or other cash to the buyer to facilitate the purchase. The seller may make some contributions as long as they meet lender guidelines (i.e., paying a portion of the buyer's closing costs, etc.).

2. Since all moneys provided by the buyer for down payment, loan costs, or cash reserves must be documented as acceptable sources of funds, it should be determined at the very beginning of the transaction how this documentation will be accomplished. Cancelled checks, current bank statements, or gift letters should be obtained immediately. All documentation with the contract and deposit receipt should be retained. It is easier to obtain this data at the origination of the agreement than 12 to 18 months later.

3. It is critical that everyone understands the rent credit portion of the contract. The only amount of the rent payment that can be credited toward the buyer's eventual down payment funds is the portion that exceeds fair market rent. An appraiser will have to determine the fair market rent, and the buyer may be required to supply cancelled checks verifying the actual rent payments made over the option period.

4. Determining the purchase price can require compromise. While the buyer may prefer to lock in a price at today's reduced value, the seller may expect values to increase and want to set a purchase price anticipating some appreciation during the option period. The final appraisal conducted when the option is exercised can cause confusion, particularly if market values have declined and the amount of loan the buyer can acquire is adversely affected. The alternative is that the property value may increase beyond the seller's expectations, causing the seller to have second thoughts regarding selling.

5. Buyers can be surprised that they must provide a non-refundable option payment, usually several thousand dollars, for the privilege of holding the property available during the option period. This money is forfeited if the buyer fails to exercise the lease option within the agreed upon time limit.

A lease option can be more complicated than it first appears. Underlying loans present the same consequences noted in the above installment loan section. Real estate commissions are often not paid until a final consummation of the transaction. Because of the numerous potential difficulties, lease options are not generally highly promoted by lenders or real estate licensees.

Note: Recent new rules and regulations have rendered the following financial arrangements as more likely to be used by corporate-like borrowers.

13.4 LENDER PARTICIPATIONS

A **participation** is the sharing of an interest in the property by a lender. When money is tight, or available only at high interest rates, or both, the lender will insist on a higher yield to itself to compensate for the greater risk involved. Without this, the lender may not be motivated to commit funds. This is especially true of large projects for which equity participation provides a means by which substantial investment capital could be raised.

Participation can be created in a variety of ways and may be classified according to the following categories:

1. *Lender participation in the revenue of the project.* For example, if a project costs $1 million to develop, in order to maximize leverage and yield on return, the developer will want to obtain the largest possible loan. But lenders may not be content with a fixed rate of return. One alternative would be to offer a piece of the action through a participation in the income. This may be either a percentage of gross revenue or a percentage of net revenue. For instance, an institutional lender might finance 75 percent of the project at 10 percent interest per annum, payable over 25 years, with the provision that the lender is to also receive 20 percent of the net income, before depreciation and income taxes. If net income amounted to $50,000, the lender would receive $10,000 in addition to the 10 percent on the $750,000 loan—an effective yield of approximately 11.33 percent. Of course, to make the venture attractive to the developer, the project would have to produce an overall yield equal to or exceeding 11.33 percent per annum return.

2. *Equity participation.* In the previous example, instead of a percentage of profits, the lender may insist on a certain percentage of ownership. If 20 percent were agreed upon, the lender would have a direct title interest in 20 percent of the equity in the real property (or stock or other ownership interest) as a condition for making the loan. Assuming again a $250,000 equity in the development, after a $750,000 commitment on a $1 million project, the lender would thus have a $50,000 ownership interest (20 percent × $250,000), or 5 percent of the entire property. The lender would thus be entitled to 5 percent of all income, in addition to all of the other benefits of ownership, such as depreciation

write off and capital gain. Of course, the lender would also be burdened by 5 percent of all expenses and costs of operation, just as with any real property ownership.

3. *Fees and discounts.* The lender could also increase the loan yield by charging a fixed interest rate but, in addition, requiring a one-time fee or points as a condition of making the loan. In effect, the loan is discounted by the amount of points charged at the front, much as government-backed loans are when the buyer or seller is charged a loan commitment fee.

4. *Profit participation.* Instead of sharing in the income, the lender may opt for a participation in the profits of a venture. Thus, when a lender believes that a project is expected to increase in value, it may prefer to share in capital gains at time of sale or exchange, rather than in the income during the holding period. For example, if the parties agreed to a 25 percent participation, and the $1 million development were subsequently sold for a net of $1.4 million, the lender would be entitled to 25 percent of the $400,000 gain, or $100,000. This is a less likely form of participation in as much as large projects are less frequently liquidated.

5. Multiple lenders. This involves the purchase of a portion of loans made by other lenders. It is similar to the concept of reinsurance, when two or more insurance companies participate in a high-risk project. Similarly, in mortgage lending, large loans may be underwritten by more than one lender. Such schemes are common in corporate loans for large capital projects.

13.5 SALE-LEASEBACK

The **sale-leaseback** is also referred to as a purchase and lease-back, a purchase-lease, a sale-lease, a lease-purchase, and so on. But whatever its designation, it is characterized by a sale of one's property to another party, usually a large financial institution, which, in turn, leases it back to the seller. The property could consist of land only (ground lease), improvements only, or both land and improvements. This technique is a popular financing vehicle among strongly rated companies with excellent credit. Although it can be used with the sale and purchase of homes, our primary focus in this section is on nonresidential transactions.

Procedure

The mechanics of a sale-leaseback encompass four essential steps:

(1) Investors buy property that they desire. This may be improved or unimproved. (2) If unimproved, the investor develops the land

to its specifications. A large grocery chain, for example, may wish to build a 50,000-square-foot grocery store on a parcel of land it now owns. (3) The owner sells the land or improvements to a major investor, such as a life insurance company, pension fund, trust, or even a nonprofit organization. (4) The investor-purchaser leases the property back to the seller at an agreed rent under a long-term lease.

The seller becomes the lessee, and the buyer becomes the lessor. No specific form is used. An offer to purchase is a contract that describes the terms and conditions of sale accompanied by a mutually acceptable lease agreement between the parties to the transaction.

Potential Advantages to Seller

Among the possible advantages and benefits to the seller-lessee are the following:

- Lease payments are fully tax deductible for business and investment properties. This includes rents paid on both land and improvements, which in most instances will result in a greater write-off than interest payments on a loan or depreciation on just the value of the improvements.
- Rent may be lower than loan payments. During an inflationary period, a fixed rental schedule favors the lessee. Furthermore, the lease term can be made longer than the loan term, leases may run for as long as 99 years in some cases.
- Improvements made by the lessee can be deducted through depreciation write-off.
- When only the land is sold and leased back, not only are the ground rent payments deductible but depreciation on the improvements is deductible as well.
- Capital that would otherwise be tied up in equity is freed for other uses. More capital can normally be raised in this way than by borrowing.
- Since long-term leases are not ordinarily shown as a long-term liability, the balance sheet of the seller-lessee will appear stronger, thereby enhancing the credit position of the lessee.
- By selling the development at a profit, the lessee is able to obtain cash today but repay with constantly inflating dollars. Additionally, the time value of money, due to the return on invested capital, works to the lessee's advantage.

- The owner may structure the sale so as to provide a buy-back privilege through a repurchase option.

Potential Disadvantages to Seller

Obviously the seller may find some drawbacks to a sale-leaseback arrangement, including the following:

- The seller-lessee is committed to a lease contract that may run for a considerable length of time.
- Any increase in the value of the property will not accrue to the lessee's benefit.
- Fixed rental schedules may prove cumbersome, if not fatal, in times of economic distress. Even in normal times, the rents may be higher than payments on a fully amortizing loan.
- The expiration of the lease period may come at an inopportune time, with either no provision for renewal, or renewal only at excessively high rents. This might occur, for example, after the seller-lessee, who is using the property, has developed the business to a very successful level that may be due in large measure to the specific location of the property.
- When land only is sold and leased back, the costs to the seller-lessee of constructing improvements may absorb the bulk of the capital generated from the sale of the land.

Possible Advantages to Buyer

Among the possible benefits or advantages to the buyer-lessor are the following:

- The sale-leaseback may return a higher yield than is available through a trust deed investment. Furthermore, there are none of the risks of a premature payoff that are associated with early retirement of a secured debt either through sale or refinancing of property. Hence, the investor-lessor will not need to be concerned with seeking alternative good-quality investments when suddenly confronted with a large amount of cash. This is one of the reasons that lenders charge prepayment penalties on premature loan payoffs. Also, the lessor has better control of the property through ownership than is gained through a security interest in a deed of trust.
- Any increase in value through appreciation will accrue to the lessor-owner.

- In the event of the lessee's default, the lessor may proceed against other assets of the lessee. When the lessee has a high credit rating, these assets may be substantial.
- Lease payments may be sufficiently large to recover the original investment several times over, in the case of long-term leases, and still leave the lessor with the fee title to the property. Moreover, by continued leasing, regardless of how long the leasehold period may extend, a capital gains tax is avoided.
- Depending on the arrangement, the lease could specify that the lessee is to pay for all repairs, maintenance, insurance, utilities, taxes, and operating expenses, so that the lessor is left with a care-free investment (such an arrangement is termed a **triple net lease**).
- A buyer in need of cash may be able to resell yet retain the same lessor interests through a second sale-leaseback arrangement.

Possible Disadvantages to Buyer

- Lease payments to the lessor, including the first month's payment, and perhaps the last two months' payments, are fully taxable as ordinary income, after deducting lessor-incurred operating expenses.
- Unless carefully structured, the leasehold term may, in a time of inflation, favor the lessee, whose contractual rents in time may be less than the economic rent. A shrewd lessor will guard against such a prospect by inserting a clause that would tie the rents to an index, such as the Consumer Price Index (CPI) or the Producer's Price Index (PPI), a wholesale price index.
- If the lessee defaults, the buyer will have to operate the property. This may occur at an economically depressed time and could lead to substantial negative economic consequences for the buyer.
- When only a ground lease is involved, the buyer-lessor will not be entitled to the benefits of depreciation deductions when the land is subsequently improved by the lessee.
- Capital that could otherwise be used in the buyer-lessor's business is tied up in equity.
- In the event of insolvency of the seller-lessee, the buyer-lessor's rights are restricted to those of a lessor only, and not to those of a secured creditor, for the balance owed on account of the purchase price.
- Though the lessee may be strong at the execution of the lease, the lessee may cease to flourish at a later date. If the lessee improves

the property in a special way and then files for bankruptcy, the lessor may be left with a special-purpose development that is not able to be sold or leased.

- In times of inflation, the lessor is paid rents with constantly deteriorating dollars.
- When a repurchase option, which can be tied to an index, is inserted in the contract, the lessee may be allowed to profit at the expense of the lessor should the agreed repurchase price be significantly less than the value existing at the time the repurchase option is exercised.

13.6 OPEN-END TRUST DEED

In most deeds of trust, no provision is made for the borrower to secure additional funds. Thus, in order to obtain additional money to finance repairs or improvements, a borrower would need to refinance the property or seek other sources of funds. This could prove very expensive, not only because of the prepayment penalties and other costs incurred in such a transaction, but because of the added burden incurred when market rates are higher than the interest rate currently being paid on the note. Homeowners are particularly vulnerable, since dwellings cannot generate revenue as is the case with income-producing properties. Secondary financing may not be the answer because it is unavailable or very expensive.

The solution is to find a loan at the very outset that will include an open-ended clause, permitting a borrower, at the lender's option, to add to the loan amount at periodic intervals. In addition to borrowing the amount repaid through amortization, the debtor could, in some cases, arrange to have the loan increased to reflect the appreciated value of the property. Such arrangements are more readily realized during times when demand for funds is sluggish, while the supply is abundant and property values are rising.

Under the open-end mortgage or trust deed, the new loan is added to the old one. Monthly payments can be increased to absorb the differential, or the term for repayment can be extended so that the combined loan will be amortized through monthly installments. Such clauses are permitted in government-backed as well as conventional loans. The procedure is to fill out an application, sign a new note, and record a notice of additional advance. The new note is still secured by the original deed of trust. The original note continues to carry the original interest rate and terms, while the new note can carry any interest rate and terms agreed by the parties. These do not merge into one debt. Moreover, the notice of additional advance does not have to be recorded to be valid, but it should be recorded to avoid possible situations where priority could be disturbed. This procedure dates back to the days when institutional lenders could not legally make loans secured by second deeds of trust unless they also held the first. Lenders can now legally make second mortgages, but since the popularity of the home equity line of credit (HELOC), the open-ended clause is used today almost exclusively with large loans and projects.

13.7 PERSONAL LOAN

A non-institutional way of financing real estate is through an unsecured personal loan. A personal loan is usually of short duration and is ordinarily limited to borrowers known to the lender and who possess substantial assets. Reliance is placed on the credit of the borrower or other security. The amount and terms of the loan are based on the income and credit standing of the borrower, along with the availability of funds. While proceeds from a straight bank loan of this type can be used to purchase real estate or to finance home improvements, other secured loan options are generally recommended and more available.

If the prospective borrower is interested only in financing home improvements, a home improvement loan or HELOC may be more advisable.

A third use for personal loans is in the area of equity buying. Investors who specialize in purchasing at foreclosure and other forms of involuntary sales are required to pay all cash. After the property has been successfully acquired, repaired, and marketed, proceeds from the resale can in turn be used to pay off the personal loan.

13.8 STOCK EQUITY/PLEDGED ASSET LOANS

A **stock equity** loan, another type of personal loan, is obtainable most commonly through a securities brokerage firm or commercial bank. Securities owned by the borrower are pledged as collateral. These include common and preferred stock, bonds, and debentures. Like the straight bank loan, the proceeds from the note can be used to purchase real estate, to finance desired improvements, or most likely for further investment. Like the personal loan, after the property's value is enhanced as a consequence of installing improvements, the appreciated value of the property will likely justify a significantly larger mortgage in time to pay off the short-term note at maturity.

13.9 BLENDED-RATE LOANS

As an alternative to all-inclusive or other forms of seller carryback, the buyer-borrower may consider approaching a lender for a **blended-rate loan**, also called blended-yield. Under this plan the buyer, with the lender's knowledge and consent, would not take over an existing low-interest-rate loan, because it may have too low a balance. Instead, a new loan for a higher amount is negotiated with the existing lender, providing an interest rate that is based upon a weighted average of the relatively low existing rate and the relatively high rate charged on the added funds needed to complete the purchase of a property.

The central idea is to combine the low existing contract rate and the high new market rate into a blended rate that accomplishes two objectives: (1) increases the loan amount and (2) blends the two interest rates into one single rate that is higher than the existing rate but lower than the market rate. Such an approach is especially important if the existing loan is callable, that is, if the alienation clause is enforceable.

The method for determining the blended yield, or weighted average between the old and new interest rates, is as follows:

$$\text{Blended yield} = \frac{(\text{Existing rate} \times \text{Existing loan balance}) + (\text{Market rate} \times \text{Net new money})}{\text{Total financing}}$$

In the numerator we have essentially the total annualized interest cost. In the denominator, total financing consists of both the old loan and the amount added thereto, so we could call this combined figure the new loan amount. While the interest rates are exaggerated, an example will help clarify.

Example: Assume that interest rates skyrocket during a credit crunch and you are buying a $225,000 property that has an existing loan of $80,000 at 10 percent. You need a total of $180,000, however, after the 20 percent ($45,000) down payment. Assume that the existing lender is charging 15 percent for new loans. What will be the probable charge under a blended rate?

$$\text{Blended yield} = \frac{(10\% \times \$80,000 + 15\% \times \$100,000)}{\$180,000}$$

$$\text{Blended yield} = \frac{\$80,00 + \$15,000)}{\$180,000}$$

$$\text{Blended yield} = 12.78\%$$

The 12.78 percent rate, which may be rounded up to 12 7/8 (12.875) percent by the lender, is higher than the 10 percent on the existing loan, but lower than the 15 percent market rate.

Benefits of the Blended Rate

- Buyers receive a below-market rate.
- Although a marginal benefit, the borrower might qualify more easily, since the loan is based upon a lower rate.
- The seller is not required to carry back as much paper.
- The lender has an opportunity to increase its effective yield on old low-rate loan balances. The blended rate need not necessarily be a fixed rate but can be a variable or adjustable blended rate.
- The blended-yield loan can be made even more creative through seller participation when financing is tight. Referring to the previous example, suppose the existing lender is willing to offer total financing of only $150,000, and not $180,000, and that the seller is willing to accept a note secured by a second trust deed for the balance of $30,000 at 12 percent per annum. What is the effective or blended rate? Table 13.1 summarizes the data and provides the answer. The blended rate for the three separate rates is 12.28 percent, or 0.5 percent less than the blended rate of 12.78 percent in the previous case, where the seller did not participate in the financing.

13.10 CREATIVE FINANCING DISCLOSURE ACT

For the protection of both sellers and buyers when sellers are to carry back loans in the sale of properties of from one- to four-dwelling units, certain disclosures must be made. These usually involve small investors

TABLE 13.1 Blended yield with seller carryback of junior trust deed.

	Loan Amount	×	Interest Rate	=	Annualized Interest Cost
Existing loan balance	$80,000		10%		$8,000
Net new money	70,000		15%		10,500
Second trust deed	30,000		12%		3,600
Totals	$180,000				$22,100

$$\text{Blended yield} = \frac{\$22,100}{\$180,000} = 12.28\%$$

Source: © 2016 OnCourse Learning

or individuals dealing with private homes, who are less likely to understand the obligations and difficulties involved with creative financing. The law requires that arrangers of credit, usually real estate brokers, involved in the sale of the property, must disclose the following items for the benefit of the buyer-borrower:

1. Description of the terms of the loan taken back by the seller.
2. Description of any other financing on the property.
3. A warning that if refinancing of the seller's existing loan is required because of negative amortization, such financing might be difficult or impossible to obtain.
4. If an AITD is involved, information about who is responsible for potential problems with senior trust deeds.
5. Terms of any balloon payments involved in the transaction.

The law also requires disclosures by agents for the seller's benefit, including:

6. Credit information about the buyer, including occupation, employment, income, debts, and the like. In the alternative, a written statement may be made that no representation as to the creditworthiness of the buyer is being made by the credit arranger.
7. Warnings to the seller about deficiency limitations available to the seller in case of the buyer's default, if applicable.

Additional provisions of the law include requirements for balloon payments. Holders of such loans on one- to four-unit dwellings must give written notices to the debtor not less than 90 days, no more than 150 days, before the balloon payment is due, with date due, amount, and a description of the rights of the borrower to refinance the balloon. Failure to provide the notice does not excuse the liability, but the holder cannot collect the payment until 90 days after proper notice is made. See Figure 13.6 for the creative financing disclosure form most commonly used in California.

13.11 IMPUTED INTEREST

The **imputed interest** rule was included as part of the 1984 tax act in order to stop tax avoidance by people making loans at artificially low interest rates. This often still occurs between family members or other closely related persons in which extremely low or zero interest is charged. The IRS requires that an **applicable federal rate (AFR)** be applied to all loans of six or more months in duration, with the specific minimum rate determined by the term of the mortgage instrument. The AFR that applies is the published rate for the month in which any

FIGURE 13.6 Sample seller financing disclosure statement.

CALIFORNIA ASSOCIATION OF REALTORS®

SELLER FINANCING ADDENDUM AND DISCLOSURE
(SEE IMPORTANT DISCLOSURE ON PAGE 4)
(California Civil Code §§2956-2967)
(C.A.R. Form SFA, Revised 11/13)

This is an addendum to the ☐ Residential Purchase Agreement, ☐ Counter Offer, or ☐ Other _____, ("Agreement"), dated _____
On property known as _____ ("Property"),
between _____ ("Buyer"),
and _____ ("Seller").
Seller agrees to extend credit to Buyer as follows:

1. **PRINCIPAL; INTEREST; PAYMENT; MATURITY TERMS:** ☐ Principal amount $ _____, interest at _____%
   per annum, payable at approximately $ _____ per ☐ month, ☐ year, or ☐ other _____,
   remaining principal balance due in _____ years.

2. **LOAN APPLICATION; CREDIT REPORT:** Within 5 (or ☐ _____) Days After Acceptance: (a) Buyer shall provide Seller a completed loan application on a form acceptable to Seller (such as a FNMA/FHLMC Uniform Residential Loan Application for residential one to four unit properties); and (b) Buyer authorizes Seller and/or Agent to obtain, at Buyer's expense, a copy of Buyer's credit report. Buyer shall provide any supporting documentation reasonably requested by Seller. Seller, after first giving Buyer a Notice to Buyer to Perform, may cancel this Agreement in writing and authorize return of Buyer's deposit if Buyer fails to provide such documents within that time, or if Seller disapproves any above item within 5 (or ☐ _____) Days After receipt of each item.

3. **CREDIT DOCUMENTS:** This extension of credit by Seller will be evidenced by: ☐ Note and deed of trust; ☐ All-inclusive note and deed of trust; ☐ Installment land sale contract; ☐ Lease/option (when parties intend transfer of equitable title); OR ☐ Other (specify)
   THE FOLLOWING TERMS APPLY ONLY IF CHECKED. SELLER IS ADVISED TO READ ALL TERMS, EVEN THOSE NOT CHECKED, TO UNDERSTAND WHAT IS OR IS NOT INCLUDED, AND, IF NOT INCLUDED, THE CONSEQUENCES THEREOF.

4. ☐ **LATE CHARGE:** If any payment is not made within _____ Days After it is due, a late charge of either $ _____, or _____% of the installment due, may be charged to Buyer. **NOTE:** On single family residences that Buyer intends to occupy, California Civil Code §2954.4(a) limits the late charge to no more than 6% of the total installment payment due and requires a grace period of no less than 10 days.

5. ☐ **BALLOON PAYMENT:** The extension of credit will provide for a balloon payment, in the amount of $ _____ plus any accrued interest, which is due on _____ (date).

6. ☐ **PREPAYMENT:** If all or part of this extension of credit is paid early, Seller may charge a prepayment penalty as follows (if applicable): _____. Caution: California Civil Code §2954.9 contains limitations on prepayment penalties for residential one-to-four unit properties.

7. ☐ **DUE ON SALE:** If any interest in the Property is sold or otherwise transferred, Seller has the option to require immediate payment of the entire unpaid principal balance, plus any accrued interest.

8.* ☐ **REQUEST FOR COPY OF NOTICE OF DEFAULT:** A request for a copy of Notice of Default as defined in California Civil Code §2924b will be recorded. If Not, Seller is advised to consider recording a Request for Notice of Default.

9.* ☐ **REQUEST FOR NOTICE OF DELINQUENCY:** A request for Notice of Delinquency, as defined in California Civil Code §2924e, to be signed and paid for by Buyer, will be made to senior lienholders. **If not,** Seller is advised to consider making a Request for Notice of Delinquency. Seller is advised to check with senior lienholders to verify whether they will honor this request.

10.* ☐ **TAX SERVICE:**
    A. If property taxes on the Property become delinquent, tax service will be arranged to report to Seller. **If not,** Seller is advised to consider retaining a tax service, or to otherwise determine that property taxes are paid.
    B. ☐ Buyer, ☐ Seller, shall be responsible for the initial and continued retention of, and payment for, such tax service.

11. ☐ **TITLE INSURANCE:** Title insurance coverage will be provided to **both** Seller and Buyer, insuring their respective interests in the Property. **If not,** Buyer and Seller are advised to consider securing such title insurance coverage.

12. ☐ **HAZARD INSURANCE:**
    A. The parties' escrow holder or insurance carrier will be directed to include a loss payee endorsement, adding Seller to the Property insurance policy. If not, Seller is advised to secure such an endorsement, or acquire a separate insurance policy.
    B. Property insurance **does not** include earthquake or flood insurance coverage, unless checked:
       ☐ Earthquake insurance will be obtained; ☐ Flood insurance will be obtained.

13. ☐ **PROCEEDS TO BUYER:** Buyer will receive cash proceeds at the close of the sale transaction. The amount received will be approximately $ _____, from _____ (indicate source of proceeds). Buyer represents that the purpose of such disbursement is as follows: _____.

14. ☐ **NEGATIVE AMORTIZATION; DEFERRED INTEREST:** Negative amortization results when Buyer's periodic payments are less than the amount of interest earned on the obligation. Deferred interest also results when the obligation does not require periodic payments for a period of time. In either case, interest is not payable as it accrues. This accrued interest will have to be paid by Buyer at a later time, and may result in Buyer owing more on the obligation than at its origination. The credit being extended to Buyer by Seller will provide for negative amortization or deferred interest as indicated below. (Check A, B, or C. CHECK ONE ONLY.)
    ☐ **A.** All negative amortization or deferred interest shall be added to the principal _____
    (e.g., annually, monthly, etc.), and thereafter shall bear interest at the rate specified in the credit documents (compound interest);
    OR ☐ **B.** All deferred interest shall be due and payable, along with principal, at maturity; _____
    OR ☐ **C.** Other _____.

*(For Paragraphs 8-10) In order to receive timely and continued notification, Seller is advised to record appropriate notices and/or to notify appropriate parties of any change in Seller's address.

Buyer's Initials (_____)(_____)   Seller's Initials (_____)(_____)

The copyright laws of the United States (Title 17 U.S. Code) forbid the unauthorized reproduction of this form, or any portion thereof, by photocopy machine or any other means, including facsimile or computerized formats. Copyright © 1997-2013, CALIFORNIA ASSOCIATION OF REALTORS®, INC. ALL RIGHTS RESERVED.

Reviewed by _____ Date _____

SFA REVISED 11/13 (PAGE 1 OF 3) Print Date

SELLER FINANCING ADDENDUM AND DISCLOSURE (SFA PAGE 1 OF 4)

FIGURE 13.6 (Continued)

Property Address: _____ Date: _____

15. ☐ **ALL-INCLUSIVE DEED OF TRUST; INSTALLMENT LAND SALE CONTRACT:** This transaction involves the use of an all-inclusive (or wraparound) deed of trust or an installment land sale contract. That deed of trust or contract shall provide as follows:
  A. In the event of an acceleration of any senior encumbrance, the party responsible for payment, or for legal defense is: ☐ Buyer ☐ Seller; OR ☐ **Is not** specified in the credit or security documents.
  B. In the event of the prepayment of a senior encumbrance, the responsibilities and rights of Buyer and Seller regarding refinancing, prepayment penalties, and any prepayment discounts are: _____ ; OR ☐ **Are not** specified in the documents evidencing credit.
  C. Buyer will make periodic payments to _____ (Seller, collection agent, or any neutral third party), who will be responsible for disbursing payments to the payee(s) on the senior encumbrance(s) and to Seller. NOTE: The Parties are advised to designate a neutral third party for these purposes.

16. ☐ **TAX IDENTIFICATION NUMBERS:** Buyer and Seller shall each provide to each other their Social Security Numbers or Taxpayer Identification Numbers.

17. ☐ **OTHER CREDIT TERMS** _____

18. ☐ **RECORDING:** The documents evidencing credit (paragraph 3) will be recorded with the county recorder where the Property is located. If not, Buyer and Seller are advised that their respective interests in the Property may be jeopardized by intervening liens, judgments, encumbrances, or subsequent transfers.

19. ☐ **JUNIOR FINANCING:** There will be additional financing, secured by the Property, junior to this Seller financing. Explain: _____

20. SENIOR LOANS AND ENCUMBRANCES: The following information is provided on loans and/or encumbrances that will be senior to Seller financing. NOTE: The following are estimates, unless otherwise marked with an asterisk (*). If checked: ☐ A separate sheet with information on additional senior loans/encumbrances is attached

		1st	2nd
A.	Original Balance	$ _____	$ _____
B.	Current Balance	$ _____	$ _____
C.	Periodic Payment (e.g. $100/month):	$ _____	$ _____ / _____
	Including Impounds of:	$ _____	$ _____ / _____
D.	Interest Rate (per annum)	_____ %	_____ %
E.	Fixed or Variable Rate:	_____	_____
	If Variable Rate: Lifetime Cap (Ceiling)	_____	_____
	Indicator (Underlying Index)	_____	_____
	Margins	_____	_____
F.	Maturity Date	_____	_____
G.	Amount of Balloon Payment	$ _____	$ _____
H.	Date Balloon Payment Due	_____	_____
I.	Potential for Negative Amortization? (Yes, No, or Unknown)	_____	_____
J.	Due on Sale? (Yes, No, or Unknown)	_____	_____
K.	Pre-payment penalty? (Yes, No, or Unknown)	_____	_____
L.	Are payments current? (Yes, No, or Unknown)	_____	_____

21. BUYER'S CREDITWORTHINESS: (CHECK EITHER A OR B. Do not check both.) In addition to the loan application, credit report and other information requested under paragraph 2:
  A. ☐ No other disclosure concerning Buyer's creditworthiness has been made to Seller;
OR **B.** ☐ The following representations concerning Buyer's creditworthiness are made by Buyer(s) to Seller:

  Borrower _____ Co-Borrower _____
  1. Occupation _____ 1. Occupation _____
  2. Employer _____ 2. Employer _____
  3. Length of Employment _____ 3. Length of Employment _____
  4. Monthly Gross Income _____ 4. Monthly Gross Income _____
  5. Other _____ 5. Other _____

22. ADDED, DELETED OR SUBSTITUTED BUYERS: The addition, deletion or substitution of any person or entity under this Agreement or to title prior to close of escrow shall require Seller's written consent. Seller may grant or withhold consent in Seller's sole discretion. Any additional or substituted person or entity shall, if requested by Seller, submit to Seller the same documentation as required for the original named Buyer. Seller and/or Brokers may obtain a credit report, at Buyer's expense, on any such person or entity.

Buyer's Initials (_____)(_____)   Seller's Initials (_____)(_____)

Copyright © 1997-2013 CALIFORNIA ASSOCIATION OF REALTORS®, INC.

SFA REVISED 11/13 (PAGE 2 OF 4)   Reviewed by _____ Date _____

SELLER FINANCING ADDENDUM AND DISCLOSURE (SFA PAGE 2 OF 4)

FIGURE 13.6 (Continued)

Property Address: _____ Date: _____

23. CAUTION:
   A. If the Seller financing requires a balloon payment, Seller shall give Buyer written notice, according to the terms of Civil Code §2966, at least 90 and not more than 150 days before the balloon payment is due if the transaction is for the purchase of a dwelling for not more than four families.
   B. If **any** obligation secured by the Property calls for a balloon payment, Seller and Buyer are aware that refinancing of the balloon payment at maturity may be difficult or impossible, depending on conditions in the conventional mortgage marketplace at that time. There are no assurances that new financing or a loan extension will be available when the balloon prepayment, or any prepayment, is due.
   C. If **any** of the existing or proposed loans or extensions of credit would require refinancing as a result of a lack of full amortization, such refinancing might be difficult or impossible in the conventional mortgage marketplace.
   D. In the event of default by Buyer: (1) Seller may have to reinstate and/or make monthly payments on any and all senior encumbrances (including real property taxes) in order to protect Seller's secured interest; (2) Seller's rights are generally limited to foreclosure on the Property, pursuant to California Code of Civil Procedure §580b; and (3) the Property may lack sufficient equity to protect Seller's interests if the Property decreases in value.

If this three-page Addendum and Disclosure is used in a transaction for the purchase of a dwelling for not more than four families, it shall be prepared by an Arranger of Credit as defined in California Civil Code §2957(a). (The Arranger of Credit is usually the agent who obtained the offer.)

Arranger of Credit - (Print Firm Name) _____ By _____ Date _____
Address _____ City _____ State ____ Zip ____
Phone _____ Fax _____

BUYER AND SELLER ACKNOWLEDGE AND AGREE THAT BROKERS: (A) WILL NOT PROVIDE LEGAL OR TAX ADVICE; (B) WILL NOT PROVIDE OTHER ADVICE OR INFORMATION THAT EXCEEDS THE KNOWLEDGE, EDUCATION AND EXPERIENCE REQUIRED TO OBTAIN A REAL ESTATE LICENSE; OR (C) HAVE NOT AND WILL NOT VERIFY ANY INFORMATION PROVIDED BY EITHER BUYER OR SELLER. BUYER AND SELLER AGREE THAT THEY WILL SEEK LEGAL, TAX AND OTHER DESIRED ASSISTANCE FROM APPROPRIATE PROFESSIONALS. BUYER AND SELLER ACKNOWLEDGE THAT THE INFORMATION EACH HAS PROVIDED TO THE ARRANGER OF CREDIT FOR INCLUSION IN THIS DISCLOSURE FORM IS ACCURATE. BUYER AND SELLER FURTHER ACKNOWLEDGE THAT EACH HAS RECEIVED A COMPLETED COPY OF THIS DISCLOSURE FORM.

Buyer _____ Date _____
(signature)
Address _____ City _____ State ____ Zip ____
Phone _____ Fax _____ E-mail _____

Buyer _____ Date _____
(signature)
Address _____ City _____ State ____ Zip ____
Phone _____ Fax _____ E-mail _____

Seller _____ Date _____
(signature)
Address _____ City _____ State ____ Zip ____
Phone _____ Fax _____ E-mail _____

Seller _____ Date _____
(signature)
Address _____ City _____ State ____ Zip ____
Phone _____ Fax _____ E-mail _____

THIS FORM HAS BEEN APPROVED BY THE CALIFORNIA ASSOCIATION OF REALTORS® (C.A.R.). NO REPRESENTATION IS MADE AS TO THE LEGAL VALIDITY OR ADEQUACY OF ANY PROVISION IN ANY SPECIFIC TRANSACTION. A REAL ESTATE BROKER IS THE PERSON QUALIFIED TO ADVISE ON REAL ESTATE TRANSACTIONS. IF YOU DESIRE LEGAL OR TAX ADVICE, CONSULT AN APPROPRIATE PROFESSIONAL.
This form is available for use by the entire real estate industry. It is not intended to identify the user as a REALTOR®. REALTOR® is a registered collective membership mark which may be used only by members of the NATIONAL ASSOCIATION OF REALTORS® who subscribe to its Code of Ethics.

Published and Distributed by:
REAL ESTATE BUSINESS SERVICES, INC.
a subsidiary of the California Association of REALTORS®
525 South Virgil Avenue, Los Angeles, California 90020

Reviewed by _____ Date _____

SFA REVISED 11/13 (PAGE 3 OF 4)
SELLER FINANCING ADDENDUM AND DISCLOSURE (SFA PAGE 3 OF 4)

FIGURE 13.6 (Continued)

Property Address: _____ Date: _____

IMPORTANT SELLER FINANCING DISCLOSURE - PLEASE READ CAREFULLY

The Dodd-Frank Wall Street Reform and Consumer Protection Act (Dodd-Frank) has made significant and important changes affecting seller financing on residential properties. Effective January 10, 2014, sellers who finance the purchase of residential property containing 1-4 units may be considered "loan originators" required to comply with certain Truth In Lending Act ("TILA") requirements. Even under Dodd-Frank however, the following two exemptions exist:

1. The seller finances only **ONE** property in any 12 month period and:
   a. The seller is a natural person, a trust or an estate, and
   b. The seller did not construct the property, and
   c. The financing has a fixed rate or does not adjust for the first 5 years, and
   d. The financing does not result in negative amortization.

OR

2. The seller finances no more than **THREE** properties in any 12 month period and:
   a. The seller is a natural person or organization (corporation, LLC, partnership, trust, estate, association, etc.), and
   b. The seller did not construct the property, and
   c. The loan is fully amortized, i.e., no balloon payment, and
   d. The financing has a fixed rate or does not adjust for the first 5 years, and
   e. The borrow has the reasonable ability to repay the loan.

Sellers who finance the purchase of residential property containing 1-4 units meeting either of the two exemptions are not subject to the TILA requirements above may continue to, and are required by California Law to, use the Seller Financing Addendum.

Sellers who finance the purchase of residential property containing 1-4 units who do not meet either of the two tests above should still complete the Seller Finance Addendum and speak to a lawyer about other TILA disclosures that may be required.

Sellers who finance the purchase of residential property containing 5 or more units, vacant land, or commercial properties are not subject to the TILA disclosures nor are they required to use the Seller Financing Addendum.

A seller who originates a single extension of credit through a mortgage broker and additionally meets the definition of a "high-cost" mortgage under Dodd-Frank may be subject to the Truth in Lending Act's requirement to verify the borrower's ability to repay.

Buyer's Initials (_____)(_____)   Seller's Initials (_____)(_____)

Copyright ©1997-2013, CALIFORNIA ASSOCIATION OF REALTORS®, INC.

SFA REVISED 11/13 (PAGE 4 OF 4)   Reviewed by _____ Date _____

SELLER FINANCING ADDENDUM AND DISCLOSURE (SFA PAGE 4 OF 4)

Source: Reprinted with permission of California Association of REALTORS®

applicable loan is created. The old rule of thumb was that the seller had to carry at 9 percent interest or the AFR, whichever was lower. In recent years, the AFR has been in the 5 percent or less range and has had less effect on seller-carryback financing than in the past.

Why is the IRS concerned with the interest rate on these seller carry loans? The IRS is aware that a seller who carries at a very low interest rate might be able to increase the sales price. The increase in sales price would be taxed at a low capital gain tax rate, escaping the higher ordinary rate that applies to interest income. This imputed interest rule is complicated and, if necessary, counsel should be sought from a CPA or directly from the IRS at www.irs.gov.

Special note: This imputed interest provision does not apply to seller carryback loans in which buyers use the property as their principal residence.

The whole idea of imputed interest rates is to prevent sellers from converting interest income on deferred payments from ordinary income tax rates to the lower capital gains tax rate by making interest a part of an increased purchase price without specifying it as interest. Thus, if a seller carryback fails to specify any interest, or provides for an unreasonably low rate, the IRS may step in and read into the agreement its own interpretation of what it should be, thereby restructuring the transaction in a way that converts some of the capital gain into ordinary income.

Chapter Summary

Secondary financing techniques include notes secured by second trust deeds carried back by sellers, representing the gap between sales price and liens now on the property or to be placed thereon. Collateralizing junior loans is a method by which existing loans are pledged as security for a loan without giving up legal title to the junior trust deed. Brokers may resort to a variety of techniques to put together transactions when the money market is tight.

All-inclusive deeds of trust are used in a variety of ways. They may be used in lieu of land contracts or when a lock-in clause is enforceable by a beneficiary. Low down payments, especially with an overpriced listing, make the AITD a mutually attractive vehicle. Care must be exercised to structure the AITD properly, including minimum interest rates that must be charged under the imputed interest rules, so as to protect both seller and buyer.

Lenders may increase their yields through participations or equity kickers. They can participate in the revenue of a project, take a percentage of the equity, charge fees or discounts, or participate in the profit.

Sale-leaseback, open-end trust deeds, stock equity, and personal loans are further examples of financing that can be affected through other-than-traditional approaches. Indeed, financing schemes are limited only by the knowledge, creativity, and ingenuity of the people involved. It should be noted that with the 2009 changes in home financing enacted by Fannie Mae and Freddie Mac, these lending techniques are more suited to larger loan transactions, which often involve corporate borrowers.

Important Terms and Concepts

- All-inclusive trust deed (AITD)
- Applicable federal rate (AFR)
- Blended-rate loan
- Collateralization
- Commercial loan
- Creative Financing Disclosure Act
- Due-on-sale clause
- Imputed interest
- Installment sales contract
- Lease with option to purchase
- Participation
- Personal loan
- Purchase money mortgages
- Sale-leaseback
- Seller carryback
- Stock equity
- Triple net lease
- Wrap-around trust deed

Reviewing Your Understanding

Questions for Discussion

1. How does collateralization of a junior loan provide for retention of the legal title by the junior holder?
2. In what ways may a broker use junior liens to put together a real estate transaction when money is tight?
3. Describe five ways in which an all-inclusive trust deed can be more effectively used instead of the traditional junior trust deed transaction.
4. Describe the positives and negatives when using a lease with option to purchase transaction.
5. State the basic purpose of the Creative Financing Disclosure Act. Do you think this law is accomplishing what it was intended to accomplish?

Multiple-Choice Questions

1. Jayne Buyer is unable to meet a balloon payment on a junior lien now that it came due. Among her remedies might be to
   a. renegotiate the junior loan.
   b. secure a new loan from outside sources.
   c. refinance the entire loan.
   d. seek out any of the foregoing remedies.

2. A purchase money junior lien, given back to a seller, that includes the amount of the first encumbrance as well as any secondary liens, is called
   a. a hold-harmful lien.
   b. a wrap-around loan.
   c. a due-on-encumbrance lien.
   d. an overextension loan.

3. Retention of legal title by the seller in the financing of property is accomplished through the use of which one of the following instruments?
   a. All-inclusive trust deed
   b. Mortgage instrument
   c. Installment land contract
   d. Exchange agreement

4. Assume a property is to sell for $160,000. It has an existing first loan of $78,000 and a second lien of $20,000. If a purchaser pays 15 percent as a down payment and an all-inclusive deed of trust is to be used to finance the transaction, the seller's remaining equity at close of escrow will amount to
   a. $38,000.
   b. $58,000.
   c. $62,000.
   d. $116,000.

5. A lender holding a junior trust deed, who wants to be informed when defaults and foreclosures occur on senior liens, should record:
   a. Assignment of Note and Trust Deed.
   b. Request for Notice of Default and Notice of Sale.
   c. Disclosure Statement.
   d. Collateral Security Agreement.

6. A variation of the secondary financing approach to solving real estate finance problems, wherein a junior trust deed is assigned to the licensee for part or all of his commission, is referred to as
   a. a broker participation loan.
   b. an assignment loan.
   c. a split junior lien.
   d. an open-end trust lien.

7. An all-inclusive trust deed is characterized by which one of the following statements?
   a. The seller-trustor under the existing liens becomes the beneficiary under the all-inclusive deed of trust.
   b. It is a senior encumbrance that includes all of the underlying liens.
   c. Legal title is retained until the terms and conditions of the lien are satisfied.
   d. Title insurance is not issued at the time of the sale.

8. Under the Creative Financing Disclosure Act, the written disclosure is prepared by the
   a. buyer.
   b. seller.
   c. insurer.
   d. agent.

9. Lenders may take participation interests in a property on which they are making a loan in a variety of ways. Which of the following would be the least likely method of participating in a lending transaction?
   a. A one-time initial points charge
   b. Open-end provisions
   c. Participation in the equity
   d. Revenue sharing

10. Creative financing refers to techniques that are
    a. insured or guaranteed.
    b. used by institutional lenders to avoid banking regulations.
    c. legally used to finance a property in a nontraditional manner.
    d. commonly used on most home loans.

11. If you collateralize a note secured by a second deed of trust, it means that
    a. the note and deed of trust is sold at a discount.
    b. a third party lends money using the note and second deed of trust as security.
    c. the beneficiary's interest therein has been fully transferred.
    d. an additional junior lien has been created on the secured property.

12. An all-inclusive trust deed cannot be used to
    a. increase the seller's yield.
    b. lower the buyer's closing costs.
    c. help generate a higher sales price.
    d. avoid an enforceable due-on-sale clause.

13. A disadvantage found in a sale-leaseback transaction is that
    a. the seller-lessee can take full tax deduction for lease payments.
    b. the buyer-lessor gets a steady tenant.
    c. the seller-lessee can write off depreciation on improvements he or she adds.
    d. payments to buyer-lessor are taxed as ordinary income.

14. A $100,000 loan at 10 percent interest with payments of $800 per month appears to be
    a. fully amortized.
    b. partially amortized.
    c. negatively amortized.
    d. fundamentally sound.

15. Assume a new loan amount of $180,000 under a blended-rate arrangement. The existing loan has an $80,000 balance at 10 percent interest per annum. The rate the lender seeks for new loans is 15 percent. The blended rate will compute at
    a. 10.722 percent.
    b. 13.33 percent.
    c. 12.5 percent.
    d. 12.778 percent.

16. Legal title is transferred to the buyer by a deed when the property is financed by using
    a. an installment sales contract.
    b. an all-inclusive trust deed.
    c. a land contract.
    d. an agreement of sale contract.

17. You sold your home for $300,000. The buyers pay 15 percent down and secure a first trust deed for 80 percent of the purchase price. The amount needed to fill in the gap will be
    a. $30,000.
    b. $45,000.
    c. $22,500.
    d. $15,000.
18. Under the Creative Financing Disclosure Act, the agent must disclose the drawbacks of creative financing to
    a. all subagents to a transaction.
    b. buyers only.
    c. sellers only.
    d. both buyers and sellers.
19. The imputed interest rules found in the Internal Revenue Code apply to
    a. certain seller carryback loans.
    b. assumptions of existing loans.
    c. loans at 10 percent or greater interest rate.
    d. new loans granted by institutional lenders.
20. A creative financing scheme is best illustrated by
    a. seller carrying back a first trust deed loan for 25 percent of the sale price.
    b. seller carrying back under an all-inclusive trust deed.
    c. buyer paying 10 percent down, obtaining the balance through a PMI loan.
    d. buyer paying 50 percent down and getting a private hard-money loan for the balance.

CASE & POINT

Fraud Enforcement and Recovery Act (FERA)

The Fraud Enforcement and Recovery Act (FERA) became law in May of 2009. Its focus was on mortgage fraud; it was in response to a congressional perception that rampant mortgage fraud was a major cause of the mortgage crises. Additionally, the perception was that mortgage brokers and those lenders not federally regulated purposefully participated in predatory lending practices to misguide borrowers and that all parties intentionally encouraged borrowers to acquire loans that they could not afford and that later could not refinance.

Although the legislation was initiated in response to the 2008 economic collapse, it became more broad based in its attempt to create prosecution tools to combat fraud at all levels in an effort to protect the public from future fraudulent acts. Within its lofty goals, there were several specific actions that related to mortgage fraud. It amended the definition of a mortgage lending business, which broadened the range of companies that would now come under its jurisdiction. Private mortgage companies were specifically named as a part of this expansion of oversight.

Among its other mortgage related provisions were increased penalties for mortgage fraud, including amending existing fraud and money laundering statutes. In addition to these fraud and tougher regulation aspects specifically addressing monetary policy, the legislation addressed accounting practices, capital requirements, the concept of too-big-to-fail institutions, compensation structures, and other Wall Street excesses.

Misrepresentation and falsification of borrower information and documentation have always been federal offenses. While seemingly focused on mortgage brokers and unregulated entities, FERA proved to be mostly a paper tiger as offending banks escaped any repercussions for their part in promoting and ultimately lying about the integrity of the subprime loan options. Shortly after the big bank bailout of 2008 and 2009, Wall Street compensation was not curbed as huge bonuses were paid to Wall Street bankers. The efforts of the Consumer Financial Protection Bureau (CFPB) to reign in excesses were mostly postponed by a Congress beholden to the big banks. A final blow fell in December 2014 when passage of a last minute government funding bill contained a provision whereby the CFPB, created by the Dodd-Frank Act, was no longer authorized to oversee bank derivatives and swaps, the very instruments that were widely held to be accountable for the economic collapse. For some, this suggested that history was poised to repeat itself, again at the expense of the American consumer.

Returning to the portion of the legislation specifically related to mortgage loans, the law addressed primarily two areas of loan origination:

1. Blatant falsification of mortgage application and documentation information.
2. The use and abuse of reduced-documentation loan programs mostly introduced in the subprime market and referred to as stated-income or no-income documented loans.

Anticipation was that the legislation would have little impact upon most lenders who had performed honestly and without participation in predatory lending practices. As indicated, legislation failed to recognize that the offending loan instruments were introduced to mortgage brokers by major lender representatives. These loan reps promoted these easy-to-acquire loan options and, in many cases, instructed brokers in how to submit their loans for easy underwriting approval. Most of these methods included exaggerating borrowers' income or not reporting it at all.

This emphasis on what became known as liar loans was accompanied by several often-used mantras at the time:

- It is the new wave of lending and everyone is doing it.
- I am helping borrowers acquire the American dream of homeownership.
- There is no way to lose, with home values escalating. If the borrower cannot make future adjusted payments, they can always sell the home for a big profit.

None of the rationalizations can excuse the fact that some brokers willingly took part in fraudulent practices, knowing that they were putting borrowers into untenable loan options. Perhaps the most egregious rationale was "if I don't give the buyer this loan, someone else will": in other words, tacitly acknowledging that it was not a good loan but being willing to do it anyway.

While somewhat weakened in its initial oversight anticipation, FERA did pave the way for the adoption of the Home Value Code of Conduct (HVCC) that continues to affect the lending business (see the HVCC Case & Point at the end of Chapter 8).

The message for all lenders, including mortgage brokers, who want to protect themselves against unintended complications related to oversight is to concentrate on the basics of loan file documentation. In other words, return to the old-fashioned common sense method of documentation. In addition to guarding against consumer fraud, it is important to develop a zero tolerance policy for originator and processor shortcuts. The result will be to re-instill consumer confidence in the loan process as well as to protect the licenses of loan originators and avoid any and all inferences of fraud or other criminal allegations. If this is accomplished, FERA will have been successful.

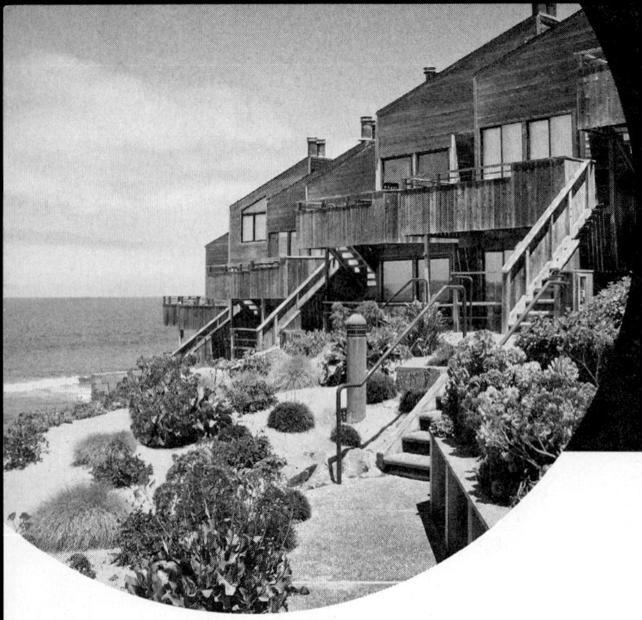

14

FINANCING SMALL INVESTMENT PROPERTIES

OVERVIEW

A popular investment strategy in the past was to leverage, or acquire the maximum loan with as little down payment as lenders would allow, utilizing the tax advantages while allowing the property to appreciate in value. This investment style worked well during the period when real estate appreciation rates were skyrocketing and lenders were much less risk adverse than today.

While real estate still represents a viable wealth building vehicle, the economic collapse beginning in 2008 did alter how lenders and investors viewed real estate investments. Real estate investment financing is now impacted by required larger down payments and risk-based pricing concerns (see the Chapter 6 Case & Point).

In this chapter we examine the financing characteristics of various residential investment properties—single-family dwellings, two- to four-unit dwellings, and large apartment houses—and review the financing aspects along with the advantages and disadvantages of owning each type of investment. Finally, we introduce the financing of commercial and industrial properties.

After completing this chapter, you will be able to:

- Describe financing alternatives for residential income, commercial, and industrial properties.
- List and briefly explain advantages and disadvantages to investing in each of the categories of investment property.
- Calculate and apply break-even analysis to income-producing properties.
- Discuss how financing conditions affect prices of income-producing properties.
- Compute debt-coverage ratios.

14.1 THE SINGLE-FAMILY HOUSE AS INCOME PROPERTY

Key Characteristics

There is usually a sufficient supply of single-family properties on the market from which to make a selection, and management is usually easier than practically any other type of residential property. A single-family residence (SFR) generally has an active resale market, thus offering a higher degree of liquidity for investors, since it can sell faster than other types of property.

A key element in real estate investment strategy is the use of the 1031 Tax Deferred Exchange rules wherein real estate can be sold outright or exchanged, with taxes deferred, for other *like-kind* property. Under this definition, a rental home can be exchanged for another rental home, multiple units, apartment complex, commercial property, or unimproved property (land). (See Chapter 12 Case & Point for full details of the 1031 Tax Deferred Exchange.)

Kinds of Financing Available for Non-owner-Occupied Single-Family Dwellings

A non-owner-occupied conventional loan of 75 percent of the lower of appraised value or the purchase price is the most often available loan from the majority of lending institutions. Fannie Mae and Freddie Mac will make financing available up to the 80 percent loan-to-value level, but the cost of the lender's perceived risk in exchange for this extra 5 percent loan balance is considerable. Plus, a lower down payment can result in inordinate negative cash flow, making it difficult for the borrower to qualify for the loan. FNMA/FHLMC's rule requiring a borrower to have at least one year's experience as a landlord to be eligible for non-owner financing was eliminated by late 2015. The three to six month reserve requirement at close of escrow was retained. Lenders use a 75 percent rule wherein only 75 percent of the total amount of existing rental income less the debt service (PITI) is the amount used when qualifying the borrower for the loan.

Seller financing is also possible, though unlikely unless the seller owns free and clear or possesses only a small remaining loan balance. In that case, a seller might be persuaded to participate in an installment sale, but the goal for most sellers is to cash out or exchange.

Interest Rate and Other Loan Terms for Rental Houses

Conventional lenders generally ask for a quarter to one-half percent more interest on a loan for a rental home than if the same home were owner occupied. Of all residential rental properties, the single-family home allows for the lowest interest rate and the best overall terms.

Term of loan, late charges, and other provisions are generally the same as on owner-occupied, single-family homes. Higher loan-to-value ratios and adjustable rate loans were popular, but as the economy worsened in 2007, fixed rate financing became and remains the loan of choice for both lenders and investors.

Generally there are no prepayment penalties with fixed rate loans. Qualified Mortgage (QM) rules enacted with the Dodd-Frank Act and enforced via the CFPB disallows, with few exceptions, prepayment penalties. In the rare circumstances when a prepayment penalty might occur, they are usually limited to no more than three years and the lender must meet other fairly strict conditions. Rules change, and borrowers should pay attention to their specific loan terms.

Note: As the real estate market is cyclical, there have been and are likely to be again times when home values escalate rapidly. The last time excessive appreciation in home values occurred, the term "flipping" was introduced to the lending world. Investors purchased a home with the express purpose of holding it for a short period of time during escalating prices and selling it for an immediate profit. Investors entered long escrow periods, during which the property would appreciate, and then would often sell the property prior to having closed their original escrow. When the market suddenly changed during the recent recession and home values declined, investors found that they were holding homes which they could no longer sell, let alone sell for a profit. When many investors simply walked away from these home investments, the market response was a significant period during which lenders were reluctant to loan on non-owner-occupied property. Underwriting guidelines toughened along with higher down payment and borrower credit score requirements.

Regardless of market conditions, some investors look for underpriced property or foreclosures to flip. Although less frequent in these times, these investors primarily use all-cash purchases and may not even do any repairs on the property. But if the new buyer seeks a loan, rules now require the investor to have owned the property a period of time before a resale with a loan to the borrower will be permitted. These new rules, accompanied by slower home appreciation rates, have resulted in many fewer flips occurring.

Advantages of the Single-Family Home as an Investment Vehicle

1. A larger selection of properties is usually available.
2. Management can be easier than on other types of income properties.
3. The investment is more liquid than other forms of real property.

4. Tenants usually pay for all utilities and do the gardening and minor repairs, in contrast to larger properties where these services are furnished by outside employees or a property manager.
5. The ratio of improvements to overall investment may be high, giving a greater **depreciation** write-off, generally from 70 percent to 80 percent. This gives a greater tax shelter to the investor, since improvements are depreciable while investments in raw land are non-depreciable.
6. Tenants usually remain longer in single-family homes than in apartments. These tenants are often families, who may also be more financially stable.
7. Passive loss rules apply to rental houses, allowing investors to deduct up to $25,000 of losses against certain other taxable income, such as wages, salary, interest, dividends, etc.
8. Few people build single-family homes for investment, so there is little danger of glutting the market with competitive rentals. Thus vacancy factors in single-family homes are lower than in any other type of residential investment.
9. Home prices tend to rise more quickly and at a greater rate in inflationary years than for any other class of investment property, thereby giving investors a good hedge against inflation.
10. Investors are able to **leverage** (e.g., purchase with minimal down payment) single-family homes to a greater degree than most other investment type properties.
11. A single-family dwelling that is rented can be exchanged for other rental property or raw land under section 1031 of the Internal Revenue Code.

Disadvantages of the Single-Family Home as an Investment Vehicle

1. *Cash flow*. Even with lower home prices, increasing rents, and possibly lower interest rates, it can be difficult to leverage a home investment that will not generate a **negative cash flow**, that is, where the income is less than the outgo, even after an allowance for a tax shelter. Any negative cash flow must be accommodated as an expense in the borrower's qualifying ratios.
2. *Square footage*. Homes tend to have more square footage than apartments; the larger the unit, the less the rent per square foot in comparison.
3. *Vacancy*. When a home is vacant, 100 percent of the rent is lost until it has been rented again. Stated differently, since only one

tenant is living in the house at any given time, the vacancy factor will be either 0 percent or 100 percent.

4. *Management.* The investor may elect to personally manage the property, but professional management firms are available at a typical fee of 10 percent of the monthly rent. Although personal management can maximize the rental income, some homeowners are not temperamentally fit to handle all such responsibilities. Particularly troublesome are calls from tenants, especially when complaints are made at inopportune times. Meeting would-be tenants can be inconvenient and having to evict a tenant can be unpleasant, making professional management more attractive.

5. *Repairs.* If the owner cannot do minor repair work himself, the cost of hiring plumbing, electrical, mechanical, and other contractors may increase to the point when one repair can represent a substantial proportion of the monthly rent.

6. *Economy of operations.* As an investor acquires more houses, especially in scattered locations, more money and time are required for travel and other expenses than if the units were all under one roof, as in an apartment building.

7. *Tax deductions.* The U.S. government continues to use the tax code, especially as it relates to housing, for the purpose of social engineering. Thus, the rules and accompanying benefits of owning rental housing change periodically and often unexpectedly.

14.2 THE TWO- TO FOUR-UNIT RESIDENTIAL INCOME PROPERTY

Key Characteristics

An alternative to an SFR rental especially for the first time investor is the two- to four-unit residential income property. This type of property is still relatively easy to manage, possesses good salability, and residential financing is available, whereas five-plus units are considered commercial property, and financing options change. Laws that apply to up to four units are enforced because borrowers of these properties are perceived as less sophisticated than those purchasing commercial designated real estate.

Kinds of Financing Available on Two- to Four-Unit Dwellings

Leveraged financing (e.g. minimal down payment) is generally no longer available, and lenders now require a minimum of 25 percent down payment on two- to four-unit property. The reluctance to accept higher loan-to-value ratio loans is mostly due to lenders' desire to minimize the amount of negative cash flow. For the same reason, lenders are usually not accepting of seller-carried secondary financing. As with a single-family home used as a rental, lenders use the 75 percent rule (e.g., 75 percent of monthly rental income less PITI debt service) when considering rents in offsetting monthly payments.

Seller financing for the first loan is generally unlikely since fewer sellers own these type properties free and clear and may more often be participating in a 1031 Tax Deferred Exchange. With the restoration of lenders' acceptance of secondary financing there may be circumstances under which some sellers may carry second loans behind new first loans, if lenders allow such financing.

Owner-occupied financing is available if a buyer chooses to live in one unit while renting the others. Conventional lenders mostly still require 25 percent down payment, but FHA financing with as little as their current 3.5 percent down payment is available.

Interest Rates and Other Terms on Two- to Four-Unit Properties

Much like a single family residential property, a two- to four-unit lender first looks at the buyer and how much the buyer can afford to purchase. Then, the lender qualifies the property, including its income and expenses. These loans are also priced based upon the perceived risk to the lender. Depending upon the borrower's credit score and loan to value, a conventional loan can charge from 0.375 percent to 0.75 percent higher interest than on owner-occupied single-unit dwellings. Borrower loan fees sometimes run higher than on owner-occupied houses.

Advantages of Two- to Four-Unit Dwellings as Investment Vehicles

Two- to four-unit properties can be found in most communities. The owner can manage the property without being required to have a resident manager. Tenants often pay their own utilities and do minor repairs. Units can be rented without furnishings and a refrigerator, but most landlords provide a stove. If the owner desires to delegate some of the management duties, such as gardening, sweeping, and laundry room cleanup, one of the tenants may often do such work for a nominal fee, saving the owner time and expense. This party may also show vacant units to prospective tenants.

For tenants, two- to four-unit properties are very popular and will often rent while large multi-unit apartment complexes remain vacant.

Two- to four-unit properties offer more privacy, with fewer people above or below a tenant's own apartment. In spite of market changes, the loan-to-value ratios and down payment requirements provide sufficient incentive for investors. Generally there is a high ratio of improvements to overall investment, ranging from 70 percent to 80 percent of building to total value, offering a maximum depreciation basis and tax shelter.

Disadvantages of Two- to Four-Unit Dwellings as Investment Vehicles

Because of the added income, compared to an SFR and the lower amount of required down payment (compared to five-plus units), two- to four-unit properties are desirable and may demand higher prices because of the greater competition between potential buyers. As prices climb, the yield to the investor will not always be sufficient to meet operating costs and debt service, requiring owners to "feed the property" because of negative cash flow. With a higher purchase price, a lender may have added liability. Because of this, a buyer will have to be more qualified with more reserves or possibly higher credit scores.

With any investment property, the possibility of surprise repairs and unit turnovers requires that reserves should be put aside. An owner who fails to set aside reserves could end up short of funds for needed repairs at inconvenient times. The owner may need to pay for utilities, such as water, outside lights, and laundry room utilities, thereby creating more expense than in single-unit investments where the tenant pays all. When there is a high vacancy factor or a rise in uncollectible rents, owners may be forced to keep rents lower than the break-even point in order to compete with other units on the market. Owners prefer to keep rents advancing at the same rate of increase as their taxes and other operating costs, but are constantly affected by the market costs of units in the area.

14.3 THE FIVE-PLUS UNIT RESIDENTIAL INCOME PROPERTY

Whether a well located apartment building is a better buy than the two- to four-unit property depends upon the capacity of the buyer, the availability of financing, and the overall economic conditions in the local community. Apartment complexes are usually acquired by what are considered more sophisticated and/or more experienced borrowers. The larger down payments required can put these units out of reach for some investors.

A popular concept is that the larger down payments required coupled with the more complicated qualifying guidelines results in fewer potential buyers and some control on values. The economic downturn beginning in 2008, however, resulted in a significant reduction in apartment construction. The subsequent lack of new product has enhanced the value of existing apartment complexes because of the supply to demand consequence. Economics played a large part in this reduction in construction but community land use decisions also impact builder decisions. The availability of appropriate vacant land, local planning and land density guidelines, length of time and cost of the permit process, new energy and insulation requirements, and the local need for new apartments are all considerations.

While location remains an important selection criteria, the value of larger properties is determined mostly based upon their ratio of income to expense. Although attention must be paid to property condition, tenant turnover, and the above mentioned income versus expense figures, many buyers still opt for what they perceive as the better neighborhood. The concept is that the nicer units will attract more reliable tenants, will allow for future rent increases, and may require less maintenance if tenants view the well-kept units favorably.

As short sales and foreclosures exploded after 2008, rents climbed dramatically in all forms of housing as former homeowners were required to rent. By mid-2014, rents began to level off with subsequent future rent hikes projected to be less severe through 2015 and beyond. Some rent pressure may be exacerbated as multiple unit construction also began to occur. Future buyers will need to be realistic in their rent projections in regards to valuing larger units. Families still prefer single family homes and smaller unit projects to the large apartment facilities.

Financing Options for Five-Plus Units

To purchase a five-plus unit building, unlike a two- to four-unit building, a bank first looks at the property and the income it generates. If the property is qualified, the buyer is then approved. Usually the minimum down is 30 percent, but depending upon the property's income and the buyer's ability, the lender may require less of a down payment but more likely, a larger one. No matter the percentage down, there are fewer banks that will lend on larger apartment buildings. In the final analysis, LTV ratios are governed by the property's cash flow and the income break-even point, or debt coverage ratio (discussed in detail toward the end of this chapter).

Interest rates and loan fees are driven by economic conditions and availability of funds and will always be higher than for single units. Loan programs usually have 30-year terms but have a shorter term during which the rate is fixed. For example, the loan may have a 1, 3, 5, 7, or 10-year fixed rate. After this initial fixed rate expires, the borrower must pay off the loan, refinance, or accept conversion to its previous variable amount. The loan terms, rates, index, and margin are determined at origination.

Even though the borrower's credit scores are sufficient, income is stable and adequate, the appraisal confirms the value, and the property income versus expense calculations are acceptable, the lender may still be concerned about the borrower's ability to manage a large apartment complex. This will especially be true if the borrower has no landlord experience at the level the subject will require.

The current rents of a subject property used to evaluate the value of the projected borrower's purchase can be deceptive. The lender will conduct its own calculations, usually using the market rents confirmed in the appraisal. For example, if present rents from the apartment are abnormally high related to the market rent schedule in the appraisal, lenders may use the average market rents for similar units in the area as being a realistic long-term trend and reduce the projected value of the project proportionately. On the other hand, if the project is currently rented below market, the lender may opt to determine value on current rents as opposed to what the higher market rents would justify. If the property is furnished, lenders may deduct all of the rental income attributable to furniture and use the **capitalized income stream** from the unfurnished unit to determine the loan value. Thus, a $5 million furnished building may be valued at $4,500,000 on an unfurnished basis, resulting in a smaller overall loan and a greater down payment.

When money becomes tight, lenders often make apartment loans only to exceptionally qualified borrowers. Even those who do qualify may have to pay excessive interest rates, and perhaps even points, to obtain any type of loan. When conventional loans are unavailable, many of the creative financing techniques discussed in Chapter 13 can be used, either on an interim basis until conventional financing is again available or on a permanent basis.

Advantages of Investing in Five-Plus Units

Since housing is a basic need, there is a constant demand for housing, regardless of the ups and downs of the business cycle. Therefore, apartment investments tend to be more desirable and perhaps safer than other real estate investments, like commercial property, retail centers, etc.

Management is concentrated in one location rather than diffused over a wide area for the same number of small units. A relatively inexperienced investor can acquire an apartment building and, with some personal effort, learn the business of apartment management. The owner can hire a resident manager to handle the day-to-day work of managing the property, such as showing units, maintaining grounds, and collecting rent. This resident manager usually will have a reduction in rent for these services. The owner can then supervise the property overall and set up management policies. In California, apartment complexes of 16 units or more must have a resident manager, unless the owner resides on the premises.

There is also the option of hiring a professional management company to handle all the aspects of management. This company collects rent, schedules repairs, screens tenants, organizes evictions, and prints monthly accounting statements. For this service, an owner usually pays 5 to 7 percent of the gross income. As you own more property or negotiate fewer services, this fee can stay closer to 5 percent, in contrast to closer to 10 percent for the management of an SFR.

With five-plus units, the cost of operation is usually less per unit than in scattered properties. For instance, the cost of a new, inexpensive roof on a 1,200-square-foot SFR might run up to $5,000. This is the cost per unit, as there is only one unit. The cost of reroofing a three-story apartment house containing 24 units might be $24,000, so the cost per unit is only $1,000, because the one roof covers three stories.

Large apartment buildings can provide an excellent tax shelter, since typically 80 percent of the value is in improvements that can be fully depreciated, usually over a straight line schedule of 27.5 years (an equal amount of depreciation each year for 27.5 years). The cost of personal property (such as carpets, drapes, appliances, or furnishings) may be written off (deducted) on a 200 percent declining balance basis, typically ranging from five to seven years. The accelerated method of depreciation is enticing, but all depreciation is recaptured at the time of resale and thus should be discussed with appropriate tax counsel. Depreciation formulas, of course, are subject to change as tax laws change.

While there has been reduced inflation in recent years, the shortage of new apartment construction has tended to build some equity through appreciation, similar to other types of residential real estate. In addition, the rent paid by tenants goes toward reducing the principal balance (loan), which also helps acquire more equity.

Disadvantages of Investing in Five-Plus Units

Inexperienced investors often do not realize the true expenses of owning an apartment house, gloss over maintenance costs, do not set aside reserves for carpet and appliance replacements, and can wind up with a negative cash flow. Unless investor capital can be added to meet the cash outflow, the investor can wind up having to sell the building at a sacrifice price, especially at times when financing has become more difficult. As noted above, this is exactly why lenders are more selective when qualifying a buyer of the properties.

Changing neighborhood patterns and encroachments of heavy business or industrial buildings may cause building values to decrease. As neighborhoods decline, rents often decline or higher vacancies occur which may not be mitigated even via higher inflation. A combination of high vacancies, bad debts, and difficulty of financing make for a downward spiral in value. As pride of ownership dissolves, more damage often results, further making a sale of the building almost impossible. However, it is said that every property will sell at the right price.

New consumer laws pertaining to owner-tenant relationships and the eviction process can lead to rent-collection problems and increasing legal fees. The cost of evicting tenants for nonpayment of rent, when they exercise their legal rights to defend against such an action, can be significant, including attorney fees, legal papers, and other eviction costs. This is in addition to lost rent and any refurbishing costs if a tenant has damaged an apartment.

As apartment vacancy rates go down, rents usually accelerate and there is an insufficient supply of housing where demand exceeds supply. A solution posed by local jurisdictions sometimes includes **rent control** laws that limit the amount of rental increases (see Figure 14.1). Such laws tend to decrease the yield from an apartment, since allowable rental increases might lag behind operating costs. Investment capital would flow to other uncontrolled types of investments or to cities with no rent control, making it difficult to sell an apartment building.

Many owners do not have the temperament to deal with problems of management or with the multiplicity of tenant requests for services. Patience, tolerance, and the ability to deal with people tactfully are absolutely vital to operate apartment buildings successfully.

14.4 BREAK-EVEN ANALYSIS

Both lenders and investors are interested in the viability of investments based upon financing considerations. One tool to help assess cash flow

FIGURE 14.1 Argument Against Rent Control.

RENT CONTROLS—DO THEY MAKE SENSE?

LANDLORD   TENANT

Rent control is a controversial topic, with emotions and misconceptions running rampant on both sides of the issue.

From a purely economic point of view, rent controls make little sense. The issue has been repeatedly studied by both liberal and conservative economists, and most agree that rent controls do not solve housing problems. Rents are high because demand for apartment housing is high and supply is inadequate. The solution is to either decrease demand for rental units, increase the supply, or a combination of both.

Rent controls do neither. Rent controls artificially depress rent levels, which in turn stimulates rather than reducing demand. Rent controls reduce returns and yields on apartment investments, thereby discouraging the construction of new units or the conversion of large homes into apartments.

In the long term, rent controls can actually cause landlords to defer needed maintenance resulting in a property's deterioration. An often overlooked result of long-term rent control is the departure of investors in rental property altogether. If investors are unable to make a reasonable return on any specific type of investment, they will abandon it as an investment vehicle. The result over time is likely to be an ever decreasing number of available rental opportunities for tenants. Finally, never fully explored or understood is the psychological hostage-like situation that is established for tenants unwilling to move from their rent controlled apartments. Artificially maintained low rents can cause tenants to defer moving to areas where market rents prevail even when such a move may be to their overall economic benefit. In short, rent controls tend to perpetuate the ill they are supposed to cure!

Source: © 2016 OnCourse Learning

and the profitability of an investment property is a **break-even analysis**. Figure 14.2 shows the number of apartment units, though the process can apply to any property, both real and personal, that would need to be rented in an apartment project to break even—that is, the point at which the revenue exactly equals the outgo.

FIGURE 14.2 Monthly break-even analysis.

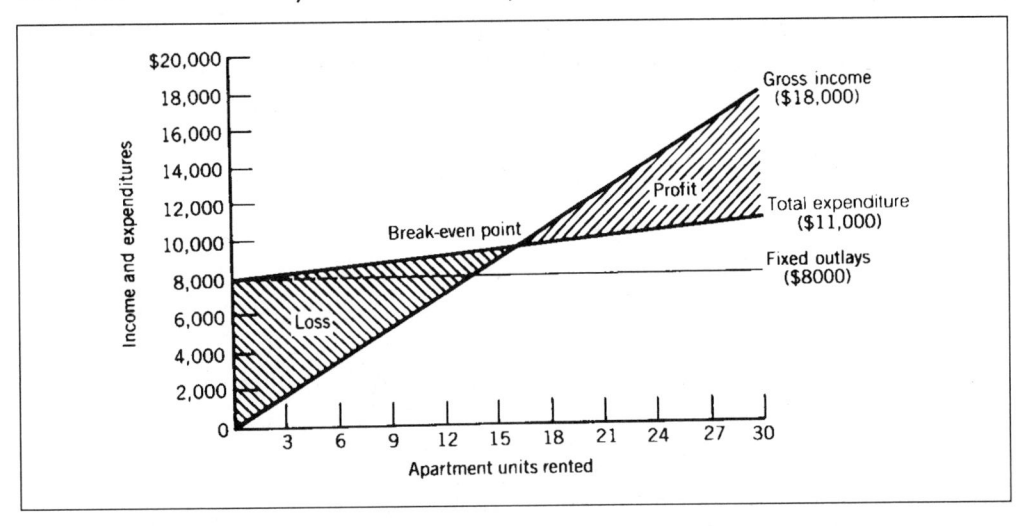

[Graph: Monthly break-even analysis showing Income and expenditures (y-axis, $0 to $20,000) vs. Apartment units rented (x-axis, 0 to 30). Shows Gross income ($18,000), Total expenditure ($11,000), Fixed outlays ($8000), with Break-even point, Loss region, and Profit region marked.]

Source: © 2016 OnCourse Learning

In the example below, assume a 30-unit apartment building, at $600 monthly rent per unit. Fixed outlays for taxes, insurance, debt service, licenses, and so on equal $8,000 per month. Variable costs, including management, maintenance, repairs, and utilities, are estimated at $100 per month per unit. We must then ask ourselves, given the amount of rent per unit, the fixed expenses that continue regardless of the number of units rented, and the variable expenses that are tied to the number of units actually rented, at what point does income equal the costs and expenses?

The vertical bar represents the dollar amount of income and expenses. The horizontal bar represents the number of units rented. Since the fixed expenses are $8,000, a straight horizontal line is drawn at the $8,000 level to represent fixed outlay. Then, as each unit is rented, $100 of variable expenses is added, thus adding to the $8,000 figure. We simultaneously plot the income figures at increments of $600 for each unit rented. Finally, where the total expenses equal gross income, we arrive at the break-even point. In the example, this point is at 16 units. Here, the income totals $9,600 and the expenses, including debt service (loan payments), equal $9,600. This is arrived at by charting the fixed expenses at $8,000 and superimposing thereon $100 per unit, cumulatively, for each rented unit. Since we know that each rented unit is $600 per month, simply add $600 for each additional unit, cumulatively, for all 30 units as if each were occupied. Where the two lines intersect, this is the break-even point.

Break-even analysis is simply a condition for prudent lending and investing; both the lender and investor need to know exactly what the risks and rewards are, and at which point. The prudent lender is aware of the level below which the property is not carrying itself, and therefore increasing the risk of delinquency and foreclosure; the prudent investor is aware of the level above which the property is profitable, or above which he or she need not feed the property from outside income. As shown in Figure 14.2, the area below the break-even point is labeled the loss zone, where there is a negative cash flow; that is, expenses exceed revenues. In contrast, the area above the break-even point is labeled the profit zone, where there is **positive cash flow**; that is, revenues exceed expenses.

The number of units rented and plotted on the horizontal axis could, just as conveniently, be labeled occupancy-vacancy ratio, expressed as percentages. Thus, the break-even point would be 16/30, or 53.3 percent. So, 16 of the 30 units, or just over 53 percent of the total number of available units, would need to be rented to break even.

It should be emphasized that the analysis shown here for apartments also holds true for any type of occupancy-vacancy ratios. Thus, the analyses have equal application to commercial properties as well. It is not uncommon for lenders on commercial properties, for instance, to hold back a portion of the projected loan until a minimum percentage of occupancy, agreed upon by lender and borrower, is reached in the rentals. The minimum is called the floor amount, and could be as high as 70 percent of the total loan amount.

14.5 FINANCING STARTS WITH THE LISTING

Why Sell Your Apartment Building?

As there are many and varied reasons for selling, it is important to know the owner's motivation for doing so. If there are negative circumstances like lots of deferred maintenance, declining rents, or liens coming due, these can affect the overall value. If a seller is facing financial difficulty, including a possible foreclosure, a shortened marketing time can impact value. On the other hand, if there are no known negative circumstances and the seller does not intend to purchase another property, financing options may include seller participation, some of which were discussed in Chapter 13. Or, current financing may lend itself to financing options including loan assumptions, etc.

If the seller intends to exchange into another property, the time frame for finding the replacement property will need to be accommodated. Knowing the reasons for seeking replacement property can assist in making a reasonable assessment regarding finding the appropriate property. (The Case & Point in Chapter 12 provides exchange information.)

Obviously, the listing appointment will cover any known code violations, current vacancies, unpermitted additions, or anything that should be disclosed to a prospective buyer. After securing the listing, an agent should investigate it with the local planning division, determine taxes are paid to date, check permits for any additions, etc. The more information obtained, the better prepared one will be to market the property.

Obtain Financing Information on the Building

When you take a listing, it is important to know what financing is available within the community for potential buyers. Knowing this information at the start of your market can assist qualified investors and limit your wasted time on unqualified buyers. Obtaining all financial information, including a current mortgage statement from the seller, can assist in knowing what the current balance is, what the interest rate is, and if the current lender will participate in an assumption. If there is more than one loan, the agent should find out similar information for each.

In the event of a short sale (see Chapter 11), having this information from your seller early on can help the process go more smoothly. If need be, and with signed approval from your seller, you can contact the bank directly to assist with the required paperwork and contracts.

Plan for Probable Financing of Sale

If an assumption is allowed by the lending institution, it is helpful to know what they are looking for: a minimum credit score, amount of down payment, fees, etc. If not assumable, will the existing bank create a new loan for the buyer? This can sometimes reduce fees or allow a smoother or faster sale, since the existing bank is already familiar with the property.

When interest rates are low, new financing may represent a more attractive situation than assuming a seller's loan. Determine what special terms the new loan will contain with respect to the interest rate, term of the loan, prepayment penalty, acceleration clause, loan fee, and other requirements. What down payment will be required? Will the lender allow a second loan? Will the new lender require an impound account for taxes or will this be waived? If a new first loan can be obtained for a higher amount than the present one, ascertain how much the holder of the second loan, if one exists, will require for a complete payoff. Will the second loan holder take some payoff and allow an assumption of the remaining portion of the loan on the property, and subordinate to the new first loan? As an agent, you can introduce this information to a potential buyer, but to avoid any misunderstanding it might be best to allow your buyer to discuss these points of interest directly with his or her lender.

If the current financing market is poor, and both buyer and seller are willing to be creative, perhaps the owner can carry back a first loan or an all-inclusive loan with a provision that whenever the finance market improves, the owner can present the buyer with new financing at rates not in excess of the current rate being paid. The buyer may then be obligated to take out such new loan and pay off to the owner all or a portion of the seller carry back loan. This gives the buyer time to obtain conventional financing when the market is stronger and allows the seller to sell the building at a time when poor financing is available to the buyers. When a buyer is obligated to perform a future refinance, make certain the terms under which such refinance will be sought are clear to everyone. Additionally, determine that the buyer will be qualified to acquire the necessary future financing.

How Market Financing Conditions Affect Property Prices

The value of a property can be affected by the current interest rate environment in which financing is being acquired. When interest rates go up, the net income after interest expenses decreases unless the rents can be raised or the expenses reduced. Since rents and expenses cannot always be easily changed, the net result of an increase in interest rates usually results in a reduction in yield and a lower market value. When interest rates decrease, yields are increased, which tend to raise the value of a property.

Some investors may use the capitalization rate (cap rate) method for measuring the value at which a property should be purchased. The cap rate is determined by dividing the net operating income (NOI) by the potential sales price. The NOI divided by the asking price of a property will provide the cap rate. From the buyer's perspective, the higher the cap rate the better. Sometimes used as a check against the market comparable approach to assessing value, it is good to remember that the cap rate calculation is merely another measurement tool in obtaining a rough estimate of value.

Given that the success of any investment often lies with the initial cost, the use of multiple approaches to valuing a real estate asset can be desirable. Cap rate calculations allow for an easy comparison tool, but only one, when considering various income producing properties. The savvy investor must also assess other risk factors including the term of any leases, the location and quality of construction of the property, the credit worthiness of tenants, and overall market conditions.

In difficult financing markets, existing low-interest assumable loans should be preserved if at all possible. There may be such loans, including insurance company loans, private loans, and so on. The balances on these loans may be low if they have been in existence for many years, so the sellers may have a large amount of equity. If the buyers put down only 15 or 20 percent, the sellers may have to carry an excessively large second loan, and if they need cash, over and above the down payment, they cannot sell such a loan because of its size. In this event, the agent can structure the sale so that the sellers' remaining equity could be split. For example, if the equity were $150,000, it could be split into a $50,000 second loan and $100,000 third loan. The sellers could then sell the second loan at the prevailing discount, receive some cash, and hold a $100,000 third loan until its due date or until the refinance clause can be invoked. This solution is similar to the creative options seen in Chapter 13.

Economic Principles versus Tax Shelter

An error too often made by inexperienced investors is to evaluate an investment only by its **tax shelter** capacity. Tax laws change, the interest deduction decreases with each mortgage payment, and depreciation allowance will likely be recaptured at some future time when the investment is liquidated.

Therefore, an investment must also meet economic investment principles including such aspects as cash flow, appreciation expectation, property condition, and likelihood of future sale. The management of multi-unit property can require greater attention to tenant turnover, need to more frequently refurbish units, more time used to show units and interview possible tenants, and depending upon the size, the expense of hiring a resident manager. For these reasons, apartment complexes generally require a higher rate of yield, sometimes expressed via the cap rate, to entice buyers. Sellers sometimes need to be reminded of this when preparing to sell.

Marketability will be enhanced when a property is listed at an acceptable price, reasonable financing is available, perhaps with seller assistance, and the transaction is structured as a win-win for both buyer and seller.

14.6 INTRODUCTION TO COMMERCIAL AND INDUSTRIAL PROPERTIES

Financing requirements for commercial and industrial properties are more strict than for residential property. As a result the tenant's financial stability is critical with lenders preferring a major corporation with good credit standing and the likelihood of long-term occupancy. Similar to five-plus unit apartment buildings, lenders look at the financial performance, positive or negative, of the property in determining their willingness to financially participate. Location can factor into the lender's decision. For instance, in shopping centers, a new freeway may bypass a community or otherwise alter travel patterns, encouraging the construction of competing centers. Suburbs may develop with home owners preferring closer shopping centers. Many things change in a community over time, any of which could result in losses to older centers. To mitigate such risk, many lenders prefer multipurpose office buildings and multipurpose retail buildings as security for loans. Special purpose facilities, such as bowling alleys, theaters, gyms, restaurants, and so on generally are not considered the most attractive security for real estate loans.

Commercial Properties

A partial list of commercial property types consist of the following:

- Neighborhood stores, including strip malls, that is, stores running parallel to and fronting the street—"along the strip"
- Free-standing commercial buildings, either single purpose or multipurpose
- Neighborhood convenience centers, including clusters of stores around a minimarket, usually with some off-street parking
- Community shopping centers, consisting of a larger group of stores surrounding a major supermarket
- Department stores
- Service stations
- Garage buildings
- Franchise outlets
- Fast-food chain stores, either in a free-standing building or as part of a center, including automotive franchise buildings
- Motels, hotels, mobile-home parks
- Office buildings, including ground floor and multi-story, such as medical-dental buildings

- Rest homes and convalescent hospitals
- Special-purpose buildings, such as built-to-order drive-in banks

Industrial Properties

Industrial properties can be classified into three categories:

1. *Small industrial properties.* These are free-standing single buildings in industrially zoned areas of a city. Such buildings may be from 10,000 to 100,000 square feet, often divided into many small individual units that can be rented to many different tenants.
2. *Larger industrial properties.* These are large industrial buildings leased to one tenant on a long-term lease.
3. *Industrial parks.* These are planned parks where developers can buy land and develop individual buildings to the specifications of the master plan. They usually have landscaped areas surrounding the buildings.

The larger the industrial property, the greater the need for transportation options including proximity to freeways for trucking ability, rail facilities, or other means of transporting products.

Office Parks

An **office park** is an area for which a master plan of development is adopted and in which all buildings are designed for office occupancy. There are off-street parking areas and often landscaping to give a park-like setting. In many areas, the master plan of such a park allows restaurants and shops to be located in certain areas to serve the persons working in the office park. Hotels and motels may also be situated within the area to allow conferences. Examples of this type of development can frequently be found around airports and freeway interchanges.

Advantages of Investing in a Commercial or Industrial Property

If the property has a long-term lease with a strong tenant, there is a high likelihood of steady income. When compared with residential income properties, commercial and industrial ownership offers the advantage of greater stability of lessees as well as potentially low vacancy factors, in some markets. Sometimes the lessee will need to make major capital improvements to the property to make it suitable for its business and at the same time adding to the value of the owner's property.

Most commercial and industrial rents are on a net, net, net (triple net) basis in which the tenant pays all taxes, insurance, and maintenance (including repairs and utilities). The trade off to the owner is to potentially accept a slightly lower rent amount because the tenant is burdened with all the expenses.

Most commercial leases contain either a cost-of-living increase clause or a **percentage lease** in the case of retail establishments. This allows an owner to realize increased rents as operating costs increase. If the property is in a prime commercial location, the successful operation of the business tenant will result in a high percentage of the gross income, thereby providing overall rent of more than just minimum base rent.

The growth of the city creates greater demand for commercial properties, giving the owner increased rents. For the commercial investor, there is little risk of rent control, as rules are seldom approved by city government officials for commercial properties. Additionally, some investors prefer to deal with what is presumed to be a more professional approach from business tenants. Finally, lease insurance is available to protect both landlord and tenant in case of business interruption due to specified hazards outlined in the insurance policy, such as the destruction of part or all of the premises through fire, windstorm, earthquake, and the like.

Disadvantages of Investing in a Commercial or Industrial Property

Just as city growth can enhance the success of this type of real estate investment, a downturn in city circumstances can affect profitability. In periods of over-building, the market is flooded, at least temporarily, with unused commercial space resulting in lower rents and poor investment returns. During the accelerated market downturn in 2008 and 2009, owners of commercial property suffered significant loss of revenues via increased vacancies due to poor business climate and failing businesses.

Investments in older types of commercial buildings, such as older Main Street stores, can affect profitability as city limits expand to the suburbs, making shopping in town inconvenient for many customers. As leases expire, tenants may move to newer centers as they are created resulting in vacancies that may take a long time to fill. Succeeding businesses may be of lower quality and not able to pay as high a rent. Changing neighborhood patterns may result in an entire commercial area becoming less desirable, with entire blocks of stores remaining vacant and subject to vandalism.

Some tenants may have long-term leases with fixed rental rates, thereby freezing the owners into fixed income while taxes and other expenses rise.

City requirements related to retrofitting rules often force owners to add expensive improvements to safeguard occupants and the public. For instance, a hotel may have to install new fire doors, outside fire escapes, or different elevators to conform to fire, safety, and disability requirements. This can require owners to spend a substantial amount of capital.

Looking Ahead

We noted previously that lender liquidity became a limiting factor in purchasing real estate following the economic crises of 2008. Access to funds for all real estate transactions was affected, but residential unit property fared better than commercial real estate. Qualifying guidelines for non-owner single family homes tightened and two- to four-unit purchases slowed dramatically. Apartment lending along with commercial loans became very difficult to acquire.

Financing for residential units up to four became available by 2010, although still requiring tough qualifying standards. It was not until mid to late 2014 that commercial lending began a significant turnaround. Much of the commercial and industrial property that had been abandoned via business failures had been absorbed, and vacancy rates fell. Businesses began to flourish again, and the demand for office space accelerated.

While admitting that much still had to occur before the commercial/industrial real estate sector could safely be considered in full recovery, expectations for 2015 and beyond were positive. Growth projections were encouraging for increased need for office space, and industrial development seemed also to be on the upswing.

The reports of continued growth in job creation and employment in 2015 added to the perception that we were on the road to recovery. Increasing rents and less supply of suitable real estate space spurred the growth of enthusiasm among investors wanting to get in early on what promised to be a resurgence in this real estate sector. Alarmingly, foreign investment also appeared on the horizon and seemed poised to provide competition to local investors. Although competition is typically good for the market in general, the concern at this time is whether too much development, too soon will result in a glut of space and another downturn in the commercial/industrial arena.

Once again, we will witness market forces at work and wait to see the result.

14.7 DEBT COVERAGE RATIO

After carefully analyzing the borrower's qualifications, income property appraisal, and cash flow forecast, the loan underwriter frequently does a debt coverage ratio analysis. The property's annual **net operating income (NOI)** is divided by the property's annual debt service to compute the **debt coverage ratio (DCR)**.

$$\text{Debt coverage ratio} = \frac{\text{Annual net operating income}}{\text{Annual debt service}}$$

Annual net operating income is the annual estimated rents, less vacancies and operating expenses; annual debt service is the required monthly loan payments × 12 months, which is labeled loan constant.

Example: On a small income property, the figures might be as follows:

Gross rent estimate	$100,000
Less vacancy (10%)	−10,000
Gross operating income	$ 90,000
Less operating expenses (taxes, insurance, repairs, management, etc.)	−30,000
Net operating income	$ 60,000

The potential borrower has applied for a $500,000 loan at 9 percent amortized for 30 years with payments of $4,023 per month; multiplied by 12 this equals $48,276 annual debt service.

$$\text{Debt coverage ratio} = \frac{\$60,000}{\$48,276} = 1.24$$

The loan underwriter would then compare this debt coverage ratio with the company policy guidelines to determine if the property's net income justifies the loan. If the debt coverage ratio is acceptable and the borrower's qualifications and the appraisal are acceptable, then the income property loan is approved. If the debt coverage ratio is too low, the loan may be denied until either the net operating income is increased or the annual debt service is reduced (or both) to bring the debt coverage ratio into line.

A lender's debt coverage ratio requirements will vary by property types, market conditions, and portfolio requirements. A call to your local loan representative can give you the current requirements. In today's real estate market, most lenders want a debt coverage ratio of 1.1 or better.

Few, if any, lenders will accept a debt coverage ratio that breaks even or is negative, where income will not cover loan payments. Here, the bank will require more down payment to off-set the loan amount and lower the debt coverage ratio. The main consideration for an income property lender is the amount of net operating income (gross annual rents, less vacancies and operating expenses). Income property lenders know that the money for the loan payments comes from the net income of the property. If the property has a negative cash flow, net income will not cover the loan payments. From this discussion, you can see why income property lenders place such importance on a property's net operating income and debt coverage ratios. However, it must be understood that an excellent net operating income and debt coverage ratio will not guarantee an approved loan if the borrower has questionable qualifications and the property appraisal is too low. Income property lenders insist upon good borrowers and adequate appraisals, but tremendous emphasis is placed on the property's net operating income.

Chapter Summary

Houses that are used as rentals are not financed under the same terms as owner-occupied property. Some speculators simply buy property for short-term gain, renting out the house until an opportunity for a favorable resale arises. In cases where they believe that a house is being purchased by a speculator, lenders have been known to (1) reduce the loan-to-value ratio, (2) increase the interest rate, (3) adjust loan fees (points) upward, or, in extreme cases, (4) refuse the loan altogether. Apartment buildings are generally financed from 60 percent to 75 percent of the lender's appraised value. For oversold properties, where the rental income does not cover all expenses and loan payments, often the lender's estimate of value will be below the actual sales price. This is because lenders reason that a project must be economically sound. Negative cash flows invite problems that may lead to subsequent delinquencies and defaults. Interest rates for apartments are higher than single-family homes because of the higher risk involved. More favorable terms can be negotiated if the property and the borrower's credit are both sound. Financing of commercial and industrial properties requires specialized knowledge of market conditions, management, quality of property and tenants, and other factors. There is no uniform lending pattern, though institutional lenders tend to shy away from loan-to-value ratios exceeding 70 percent. The key for commercial and industrial properties is an adequate debt coverage ratio (DCR). If a property's income does not cover the debt, a larger down payment will be required to offset the risk.

Important Terms and Concepts

Break-even analysis
Capitalized income stream
Debt coverage ratio
Depreciation
Leverage
Negative cash flow
Net operating income (NOI)
Office park
Percentage lease
Positive cash flow
Rent control
Tax shelter

Reviewing Your Understanding

Questions for Discussion

1. List two advantages and two disadvantages of investing in
   a. apartment houses.
   b. commercial properties.
   c. industrial properties.
2. Discuss the risks involved in over-financing or overleveraging, that is, too much borrowing against a property.
3. From a marketing viewpoint, why is it important to determine the motivation of owners who desire to sell their properties?
4. What is meant by the expression "feeding the property"?

Multiple-Choice Questions

1. The main advantage of a single-family rental, as compared to other real estate investments, is its
   a. liquidity.
   b. higher interest rates.
   c. fewer choices.
   d. difficulty of management.

2. Which of the following statements concerning the financing of large apartment projects is correct?
   a. The larger the size of a building, the lower the loan-to-value ratio.
   b. Loan fees for large complexes are usually lower than for single dwellings.
   c. Loan terms seldom exceed 15 years.
   d. Lenders ignore debt service in assessing the loan collateral.

3. If an owner is required to feed the property to meet operating costs and debt service, it is always due to
   a. positive cash flow.
   b. negative cash flow.
   c. excellent management.
   d. excess depreciation write-off.

4. Most apartment properties are financed by
   a. private loans.
   b. government loans.
   c. conventional loans.
   d. foreign loans.

5. The ability to assume an existing loan is determined by the
   a. method of taking title to the property.
   b. existence of a due-on-sale clause.
   c. amount of taxes.
   d. title insurance required by the lender.

6. Buying real estate with little down payment and with maximum financing is called
   a. equity buying.
   b. leverage.
   c. progression.
   d. regression.

7. The California Civil Code limits prepayment penalties on certain types of real estate loans to the first three years. Which of the following transactions qualifies for the limitation?
   a. Owner-occupied single-family residence
   b. A house purchased for rental
   c. Houses purchased on speculation
   d. A vacant lot

8. Break-even analysis refers to
   a. debt coverage ratio.
   b. use of very low leverage.
   c. positive cash flow.
   d. the point at which income equals outgo.

9. If the yield on a property is 9 percent, but the buyer must pay 11 percent interest, the net effect is termed
   a. negative leverage.
   b. positive leverage.
   c. neutral leverage.
   d. trading on the equity.

10. Which of the following properties is most likely to be subject to rent control ordinances?
    a. Commercial
    b. Industrial
    c. Parking lots
    d. Apartments

11. Buyers of non-owner-occupied single-family rentals
    a. are generally charged more interest than for owner-occupied homes.
    b. will never pay a higher loan origination fee than on an owner-occupied home.
    c. cannot be required to pay a prepayment penalty for an early payoff.
    d. are considered safer than equally qualified owners who occupy the premises.

12. The financing of a non-owner-occupied duplex generally means that
    a. lenders will never loan more than 70 percent of value.
    b. interest rates are higher than on owner-occupied single family dwellings.
    c. new loans are not available.
    d. rental management is not required.

13. With respect to apartment complexes, the experienced investor knows that
    a. a resident manager or owner is required by California law for 16 or more units.
    b. management of apartment units is scattered, rather than concentrated.
    c. the cost of operation per unit is greater for apartment units than in scattered properties.
    d. none of the above are true.

14. While the issue of rent controls is a controversial one, we find that
    a. the imposition of rent controls actually enhances rental income.
    b. yields on apartment houses increase under rent controls.
    c. rent controls discourage construction of apartment houses, leading to diminished supply and greater demand.
    d. rent controls tend to increase the capitalized value of apartment houses.

15. Special-purpose properties (restaurants, franchise fast-food outlets, and the like)
    a. are usually considered the best security by most lenders.
    b. are considered too risky by most lenders as security for loans.
    c. normally command lower interest rates than most other commercial properties because of their history of financial success.
    d. are favored by lenders because of their relatively easy conversion to other uses.

16. Which of the following statements concerning the financing of large apartment projects is true?
    a. Lenders usually don't bother with the borrower's credit for income-producing properties.
    b. In general, the larger the size of the project, the lower the loan-to-value ratio.
    c. Lenders usually ignore debt service in qualifying the loan.
    d. Loan fees are lower than for smaller properties.

17. Operating expenses for an apartment complex include
    a. interest payments.
    b. principal payments.
    c. depreciation write-offs.
    d. management fees.

18. Investors in two- to four-rental units find that
    a. lenders qualify both the borrower and the property.
    b. loan assumptions are commonplace.
    c. no secondary financing is permitted if there is negative cash flow.
    d. government-backed financing is in abundance.

19. From a real estate agent's perspective, thoughts about financing should always begin with the
    a. offer.
    b. acceptance.
    c. listing.
    d. appraisal.

20. Investing in commercial property
    a. requires less down payment than apartment projects.
    b. requires a debt coverage ratio of less than 1.
    c. may involve the use of percentage leases.
    d. is less sophisticated than investing in rental homes.

CASE & POINT

Some Things to Know About Investing

The most often asked questions from individuals preparing to invest in property are:

- What is the cash flow?
- What will be the return on my investment?

Becoming familiar with several basic investment principles will reassure you that you are receiving appropriate answers to your questions.

Let's look first at cash flow. Positive cash flow is most often a direct result of the amount of down payment. For example, if one pays all cash for an income producing property, it will produce a positive cash flow. Should one purchase the same property via maximum leverage (using minimum down payment funds), it will most likely result in negative cash flow.

Depreciation Makes a Difference

Don't be too quick to condemn a negative cash flow position. The most often made mistake by investors is their failure to examine after-tax benefits. Experienced investors recognize that a major consideration in every investment is the depreciation allowance. Depreciation is a non-cash expense that can be claimed each year without spending a cent to offset it. Thus, depreciation does not reduce the property's cash flow.

On the other hand, depreciation can make a dramatic difference in sheltering your cash flow in the investment by providing a paper loss. The typical real estate straight line depreciation schedule is 27.5 years. The land portion of the property's cost is not depreciable and is deducted from the purchase price before calculating the depreciation schedule.

Figuring the Return

A distinction must be made between various returns on investment property. Most people first think of before-tax cash flow, which is determined by first deducting the overall cash outlays (e.g., mortgage expense, taxes, insurance, and operating expenses) from the gross income. The percent of return is then determined by dividing the resulting cash flow by the amount of cash invested, resulting in a before-tax consequence return.

More important to most investors is the after-tax return, taking into consideration the tax shelter benefits of depreciation. Calculate depreciation (27.5 years) by multiplying the improved portion of the property value by the factor of 0.0363. There are various analysis worksheets available that will identify the return following all the allowable deductions in calculating the after-tax return on actual cash invested.

Leverage is also Important

Leverage involves the use of other people's money (typically a lender) with which to purchase the property. Thus, the smaller the down payment, the higher the leveraged position in the ownership. While leverage is good, the investment can be jeopardized by attempting to leverage too much. Careful analysis is required, taking into consideration the investor's goals, comfort zone (with negative cash flow), ability to find appropriate financing, etc., when determining down payment amounts.

Determining Value

A common phrase heard in the investment arena is "the project is made at the time of purchase." Translated, this means that if one pays too much (over market value) for the investment, it will impact the return on yield on the investment over time. At the same time, it is important to remember that good investments are lost because someone wanted to make a "killer deal." Another adage to remember is "buy at market and sell at market and one will generally make money."

These are some rules of thumb that have been used to provide a guide to value (e.g.: gross rent multipliers, cap rate calculations, etc.). Each method has its deficiencies and must not be relied upon totally in the decision making process. There are also very sophisticated methods of evaluating an investment, most of which provide so many numbers and statistics that most investors can not make sense of them or become so confused that they end up making no decision.

Trust Your Instincts (And Your Team of Advisors)

There comes a time in the investment process that, after evaluating all of the information, you end up relying upon your gut instinct . . . does the venture feel right or not? Seek some consensus from your team of advisors . . . your real estate representative, mortgage lender, attorney and/or accountant. Then make a decision and move forward.

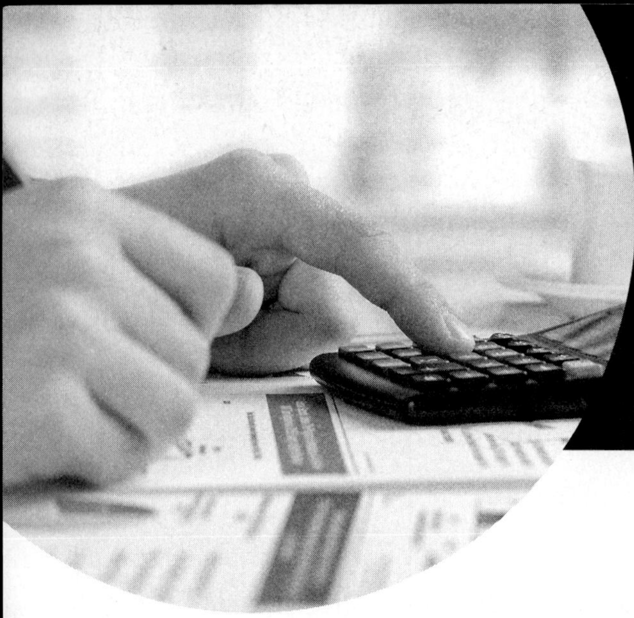

© Shutterstock / Zadorozhnyi Viktor

BASIC MATHEMATICS OF REAL ESTATE FINANCE

OVERVIEW

In this, our final chapter we depart a bit from the format of the previous chapters. A basic understanding of the mathematics of real estate is vital to the agent, consumer, lender, and investor. The good news, especially for those agents who are concerned about math, is that agents are now expected to provide mostly very basic math information. New legislation emphasizes that all professionals are accountable for the information provided consumers.

Although having the knowledge to calculate the annual percentage rate (APR) for a loan might be important for the agent, it may, in today's lending climate, be advisable to leave that kind of calculation and the accountability for its accuracy to the lender. On the other hand, the agent will be expected to calculate estimated mortgage payments on various loan amounts, estimate interest and principal breakdown for payments, develop estimated closing costs for sellers, and perhaps a few other basic calculations.

A financial calculator is a must for anyone doing real estate mathematics. We will discuss the most often used real estate industry calculator and a few of the basic calculations. We will then conclude this final chapter with what we will call "tip sheets" addressing topics that are important in the real estate financial arena but did not lend themselves easily to inclusion in the preceding chapters. Finally, we will discuss behavior and ethics as they apply to real estate and mortgage practices.

Before engaging in the math, we should review the components of a real estate loan.

15.1 REVIEW OF THE BASIC COMPONENTS OF A REAL ESTATE LOAN

1. Interest is the charge or price, expressed as dollars, paid for the use of money. Much like a tenant pays rent for the use of living space, a borrower pays interest for the use of money. A borrower can be viewed as a tenant, renting money for an agreed period of time,

returning the rented funds with an additional charge for their use. The interest rent may be paid either at the end of the period—the maturity date—or, more commonly, at periodic intervals, such as monthly payments.

2. **Principal** is the amount of money borrowed. It is the initial amount that appears on the promissory note.
3. **Rate** is the percentage of interest charged on the principal and is usually expressed as an annual rate.
4. The **term** denotes the length of the loan and the frequency of payments. The term is usually expressed as years, with the payment due monthly.

Review of Promissory Notes

Straight Note (Interest-Only Payments)

The **straight note** usually calls for interest-only payments, with the entire principal due in a lump sum at a future date. The interest is usually paid monthly, but some notes may call for other payment intervals such as quarterly or annually.

Example: Assume a $100,000 straight note at 8 percent interest per annum, payable monthly, all due in five years. What is the monthly interest payment?

Solution: $100,000 principal × .08 = $8,000 interest for the year ÷ 12 months = $666.67 per month, with the entire $100,000 principal due and payable at the end of five years.

Amortized Loan

An **amortized loan** calls for installment payments that include both principal and interest. Two main types are:

1. *Installment Note—Fully Amortized.* This is the most common note found in real estate financing transactions. Each payment remains constant, with interest computed on the unpaid balance of the note, which is defined as simple interest. Hence, each payment decreases the principle owed and, therefore, decreases the amount of interest due. Since the installments continue in equal amounts until the entire obligation is repaid, this type is referred to as a fully amortized note.
2. *Installment Note—Partially Amortized with a Balloon Payment.* This note calls for payments of interest and principal, but not enough principal to completely pay off the loan by the due date.

The payments remain constant until a stated date, at which time the outstanding balance, called a balloon payment, is due. As described in Chapter 1, a *balloon payment* is defined as any payment at least twice the size of the normal payment.

Why Amortized Loans Are Used

Prior to the Great Depression of the 1930s, many real estate loans made no provision for the reduction of the principal through periodic payments. In those days, if a person borrowed $10,000 at, say, 8 percent interest, the buyer was expected to pay only the annual interest of $800, in monthly installments, without reducing the principal. Then at some time in the future, the entire principal of $10,000 would become due and payable. Borrowers were often unable to make the balloon payment, resulting in the loan being extended time after time with little expectation of it ever being paid. During the Great Depression, people lost their jobs and could not make even the monthly interest payments let alone pay the principal loan amount when it came due. The massive number of resulting foreclosures exposed the weakness of this interest-only payment plan. Lending reforms, led by several government agencies, resulted in the current practice of monthly payments that include principal reduction.

How to Compute Amortized Loan Payments

To determine the required payments on a loan, one can use an amortization table, a financial calculator, or an online calculator. The **amortization table** contains tables that show the amounts needed to pay off (a) varying amounts of loans, (b) at specified rates of interest, and (c) for specified periods (or terms). A sample page from an amortization table is shown in Table 15.1.

To use Table 15.1 to find monthly payments at 12 percent interest, merely locate the amount of the loan, then the term or number of years of the loan. At the point of intersection the monthly payment is given. For example, an $80,000 loan at 12 percent for 30 years will require an $822.90 monthly payment.

30- Versus 40-Year Amortization

Lenders occasionally promote 40-year amortized loans and the accompanying lower payments as a way to more easily qualify buyers. Let's examine the practicality of this using Table 15.1 and comparing a 30-year versus a 40-year loan.

TABLE 15.1 Monthly loan amortization payments at 12 percent.

Amount	\multicolumn{8}{c}{TERM (YEARS)}
	3	5	10	15	20	25	30	40
80,000	2657.17	1779.56	1147.85	960.18	880.90	842.60	822.90	806.80
81,000	2690.38	1801.80	1162.19	972.18	891.91	853.13	833.19	816.89
82,000	2723.61	1824.04	1176.54	984.18	902.92	863.66	843.47	826.97
83,000	2756.82	1846.29	1190.89	996.19	913.93	874.19	853.76	827.06
84,000	2790.05	1868.53	1205.24	1008.19	924.94	884.73	864.05	847.14
85,000	2823.22	1890.78	1219.59	1020.19	935.95	895.26	874.33	857.23
86,000	2856.44	1913.02	1233.94	1032.19	946.96	905.79	884.62	867.31
87,000	2889.65	1935.27	1248.28	1044.20	957.98	916.32	894.90	877.40
88,000	2922.88	1957.51	1262.63	1056.20	968.99	926.86	905.19	887.48
89,000	2956.10	1979.76	1276.98	1068.20	980.00	937.39	915.48	897.57
90,000	2989.29	2002.00	1291.33	1080.20	991.01	947.92	925.76	907.65
91,000	3022.42	2024.24	1305.68	1092.20	1002.02	958.45	936.05	917.74
92,000	3055.69	2046.49	1320.02	1104.21	1013.03	968.99	946.34	927.82
93,000	3088.89	2068.73	1334.37	1116.21	1024.04	979.52	956.62	937.91
94,000	3122.09	2090.98	1348.72	1128.21	1035.05	990.05	966.91	947.99
95,000	3155.36	2113.22	1363.07	1140.21	1046.06	1000.58	977.19	958.08
96,000	3188.55	2135.47	1377.42	1152.22	1057.08	1011.12	987.48	968.16
97,000	3221.75	2157.71	1391.76	1164.22	1068.09	1021.65	997.77	978.25
98,000	3255.00	2179.96	1406.11	1176.22	1079.10	1032.18	1008.05	988.33
99,000	3288.22	2202.20	1420.46	1188.22	1090.11	1042.71	1018.34	998.42
100,000	3321.43	2224.44	1434.81	1200.22	1101.12	1053.25	1028.62	1008.50

Source: © 2016 OnCourse Learning

The monthly payment difference between the 30- and 40-year loans (see the last two figures on the bottom line) is $20.12 a month whereas the difference between a 15- and 30-year loan is $171.60 a month. While the $20.12 will not result in the buyer being able to borrow any significant additional loan amount, the borrower will pay over the 40 years an additional $121,020 ($1,008.50 times 10 additional years or 120 months) if the loan were to be paid to term. The message here is that extending a loan term over 30 years results in little benefit to a borrower.

Another type of amortization table is shown in Table 15.2. This table shows the amount of payment per $1,000 of loan amount at interest rates from 6 percent to 15 percent, and repayment terms from 3 to 40 years.

To use Table 15.2, assume a $100,000 loan to be repaid in 30 years, in equal monthly installments, including interest of 8 percent per annum. What is the monthly payment?

TABLE 15.2 Monthly payments needed to amortize a $1,000 loan at various interest rates.

Term (Years)	RATE OF INTEREST (%)									
	6	7	8	9	10	11	12	13	14	15
3	30.42	30.88	31.34	31.80	32.27	32.74	33.22	34.18	34.67	37.17
5	19.34	19.81	20.28	20.76	21.25	21.75	22.25	22.76	23.79	26.50
6	16.58	17.05	17.54	18.03	18.53	19.04	19.56	20.08	21.15	23.96
7	14.61	15.10	15.59	16.09	16.61	17.13	17.66	18.75	19.30	22.21
8	13.15	13.64	14.14	14.66	15.18	15.71	16.26	17.38	17.95	20.96
9	12.01	12.51	13.02	13.55	14.08	14.63	15.19	16.34	16.93	20.03
10	11.11	11.62	12.14	12.67	13.22	13.78	14.35	15.53	16.14	19.33
15	8.44	8.99	9.56	10.15	10.75	11.37	12.01	13.32	14.00	17.57
20	7.17	7.76	8.37	9.00	9.66	10.33	11.02	12.44	13.17	16.99
25	6.45	7.07	7.72	8.40	9.09	9.81	10.54	12.04	12.81	16.79
30	6.00	6.66	7.34	8.05	8.78	9.53	10.29	11.07	12.65	16.72
35	5.71	6.39	7.11	7.84	8.60	9.37	10.16	11.76	12.57	16.69
40	5.51	6.22	6.96	7.72	8.50	9.29	10.09	11.72	12.54	16.68

Source: © 2016 OnCourse Learning

First, locate 30 in the number of years column in Table 15.2. Then look across, to the entry under the column headed 8 percent. Here we find the number 7.34. This means that the monthly payment, including principal and interest, is $7.34 for each $1,000 of loan amount. Multiplying 7.34 by 100, since we are looking for a monthly payment for a $100,000 loan, results in $734 (rounded to the nearest dollar). It should be understood that this table shows the payments based on so much per thousand, though realistically the figures would typically be rounded to the nearest penny only after carrying them out to at least six places. The actual payment, using a financial calculator, is $733.76 per month.

15.2 THE REAL WORLD OF FINANCIAL CALCULATORS AND COMPUTERS

The computation of loan payments, interest rates, principal and interest allocations, discount yields, remaining balances, balloon payments, and many other mathematical real estate problems are no longer solved by using complicated tables. Instead, professionals use **financial calculators** and computers. Although surrounded by a world of computers, a real estate professional in the field frequently still needs the convenience of a financial calculator. The ability to use a financial calculator and quickly compute loan payments, qualifying ratios, and other numbers is essential in today's competitive real estate market. With the growth of technology, many cell phones also have downloadable applications to assist with these calculations.

Financial calculators should not be confused with the simple four-function calculators sold at variety stores. Nor should they be confused with scientific calculators. Financial calculators are pre-programmed to handle the time value of money, and can therefore compute most real estate finance and investment problems without the need for amortization tables. In addition, there is no need to memorize complicated formulas, as financial calculators are programmed to handle all the mathematics internally.

Several calculators have been popular over the years, but the Calculated Industries' Qualifier Plus IIIx was introduced several years ago and remains an industry favorite. There is no "right" calculator, but one must be comfortable with and learn the full functionality of one's selection. For our purposes, we will demonstrate a few of the more useful mathematic computations using the Qualifier Plus IIIx.

15.3 ILLUSTRATED USE OF CALCULATED INDUSTRIES QUALIFIER PLUS IIIX REAL ESTATE CALCULATOR

All financial calculators have five special keys that deal with the time value of money (TVM). On the Qualifier Plus IIIx real estate calculator, the five financial keys are as follows:

Term	This refers to the length of time. The period could be years, months, or days.
Int	This refers to the interest rate. Here you enter the interest per period, be it annual, monthly, or daily interest.
Loan Amt	Here is where you enter the loan amount.
Pmt	This is the key you push to solve for payment, be it an annual, monthly, or daily payment.
Shift **Loan Amt** (FV)	

This stands for future value. This combination of keys is used when you wish to find a financial answer that lies in the future, such as a future balloon payment. For all real estate loan problems you are given three elements to enter into three of these keys, then you push a fourth key to obtain your answer. Usually one key—the fifth—is not needed. Your job is to figure the three elements you know and enter them, then from the two remaining keys, select the one that will calculate the information you seek. For example, a real estate loan payment has four elements: the term (number of payments), interest rate, loan amount, and payment.

15.3 Illustrated Use of Calculated Industries Qualifier Plus IIIx Real Estate Calculator

If you enter any three elements, the Qualifier Plus IIIx solves for the fourth unknown element. The order in which you enter the known information does not matter.

Loan Payments

The Qualifier Plus IIIx can compute any type of loan payment. It does not matter if the payment is annual, semiannual, quarterly, monthly, biweekly, weekly, or daily. The thing to remember is that all of the financial keys must be in the same time frame!

Example: On a $100,000 loan at 10 percent for 30 years, what is the monthly payment?

Description	Keystrokes	Display
Clear Calculator	On/C On/C	0.00
Enter loan amount	1 0 0 0 0 0 Loan Amt	LA 100,000.00
Enter Term	3 0 Term	ANN TERM 30.00
Enter Interest	1 0 Int	ANN INT 10.00 %
Find monthly P & I payment	Pmt	P+I 877.57 PMT

You can enter any element in any order. You do not need to enter the loan amount first, then the interest, then the payments. Any order is acceptable to all financial calculators.

Caution: Clear the calculator between each calculation to assure that no leftover numbers remain in the financial keys that could distort the correct answer in your next calculation. Make sure that FV (future value) is always shown as 0.00 (zero) when entering computations.

Making Larger Loan Payments

How fast will a loan be paid off if larger monthly payments are made?

Example: Using the same figures as above:

Description	Keystrokes	Display
Clear Calculator	On/C On/C	0.00

(Continued)

Description	Keystrokes	Display
Enter loan amount	1 0 0 0 0 0 [Loan Amt]	LA 100,000.00
Enter Term	3 0 [Term]	ANN TERM 30.00
Enter Interest	1 0 [Int]	ANN INT 10.00 %
Find monthly P & I payment	[Pmt]	P+I 877.57 PMT

If the borrower paid $900 per month, how long would it take to pay off this loan?

Description	Keystrokes	Display
Enter new payment amount	9 0 0 [Pmt]	P+I 900.00 PMT
Solve for new Term	[Term]	ANN TERM 26.14

If the borrower paid $1,000 per month, how long would it take to pay off this loan?

Description	Keystrokes	Display
Enter new payment amount	1 0 0 0 [Pmt]	P+I 1000.00 PMT
Solve for new Term	[Term]	ANN TERM 17.99

The lesson here is that a borrower can make larger payments and greatly reduce the total amount of interest paid and the length of time it takes to pay off a loan.

Interest and Principal Allocation

People often want to know how much of a payment is interest and how much is principal. Or after borrowers have made a series of payments, they may want to know the breakdown of each payment into interest and principal, and what the remaining balance is.

The Qualifier Plus IIIx easily does this using the [Term] key (amortization).

Example: Assume a $100,000 loan at 10 percent for 30 years. What is the monthly payment? What is the remaining loan balance? How much of the first payment is principal? Interest?

Description	Keystrokes	Display
Clear Calculator	[On/C] [On/C]	0.00
Enter loan amount	1 0 0 0 0 0 [Loan Amt]	LA 100,000.00
Enter Term	3 0 [Term]	ANN TERM 30.00
Enter Interest	1 0 [Int]	ANN INT 10.00 %

(Continued)

15.3 Illustrated Use of Calculated Industries Qualifier Plus IIIx Real Estate Calculator

Description	Keystrokes	Display
Find monthly P & I payment	**Pmt**	P+I 877.57 PMT
Enter number of payments	**1** **Shift** **←** **Amort**	AMRT 1 – 1 PER
Find Interest of first payment	**Amort**	AMRT 833.33 TTL INT
Find total principle of first payment	**Amort**	AMRT 44.24 TTL PRIN
Find remaining balance	**Amort** **Amort**	BAL 99,955.76

Principal and Interest Allocation for 12 Months

Example: Using the Qualifier Plus IIIx, assume a $100,000 loan at 10 percent for 30 years. What is the monthly payment? What is the remaining loan balance after 12 payments? What is the principal paid for 12 months? What is the interest paid after making 12 monthly payments?

Description	Keystrokes	Display
Clear Calculator	**On/C** **On/C**	0.00
Enter loan amount	**1** **0** **0** **0** **0** **0** **Loan Amt**	LA 100,000.00
Enter Term	**3** **0** **Term**	ANN TERM 30.00
Enter Interest	**1** **0** **Int**	ANN INT 10.00 %
Find monthly P & I payment	**Pmt**	P+I 877.57 PMT
Find monthly	**Pmt**	P+I 877.57 PMT
Enter Year 1	**1** **Amort**	AMRT 1 – 12 PER
Find total interest in year 1	**Amort**	AMRT 9,974.98 TTL INT
Find total principle in year 1	**Amort**	AMRT 555.88 TTL PRIN
Find remaining balance	**Amort** **Amort**	BAL 99,444.12

This calculation is handy for estimating interest for annual income tax deductions.

Balloon Payments

Balloon payments are also called remaining loan balance and outstanding loan balance. To solve for the balance on a loan after a series of payments, all four parts of a loan must be in the calculator:

Term, **Int**, **Loan Amt**, and the payment in the **Pmt** key

If the payment is missing, you first must solve for payment; then the balloon payment can be found by correctly using the future value function.

Example: Use the Qualifier Plus IIIx for a $100,000 loan at 10 percent amortized for 30 years, but due in five years. What will be the balance after five years?

Description	Keystrokes	Display
Clear Calculator	On/C On/C	0.00
Enter loan amount	1 0 0 0 0 0 Loan Amt	LA 100,000.00
Enter Term	3 0 Term	ANN TERM 30.00
Enter Interest	1 0 Int	ANN INT 10.00 %
Find monthly P & I payment	Pmt	P+I 877.57 PMT
Enter parameter and solve for balance	5 Shift Amort	BAL 96,574.32

What will be the balance after 10 years?

Enter parameter and solve for balance	1 0 Shift Amort	BAL 90,938.02

More Complicated Calculations

The preceding examples are the major calculations that real estate licensees are most likely to be expected to perform. The following calculations are more complicated and may be best left to loan officers and lenders to perform. The financial calculators can be programmed to accommodate the local tax and insurance factors and should you wish to do so, determine the factors used by local mortgage lenders. Determining a buyer's qualification ratios or the amount for which he or she might be qualified is dependent upon the type of loan and a multiple of variables, including whether mortgage insurance will be a part of the equation. Determining these things is the reason for urging the buyer to become prequalified with a lender.

15.3 Illustrated Use of Calculated Industries Qualifier Plus IIIx Real Estate Calculator

Given this information, you may wish to skip ahead to the Biweekly Loan Payment section. Again, you may prefer to introduce the concept to your buyer and urge him or her to explore the idea with a mortgage lender.

Calculating Loan Payments That Include PITI (Principal, Interest, Taxes, and Insurance)

Example: A buyer is interested in a home that is listed for $500,000. An 80 percent loan of $400,000 at 7.5 percent for 30 years is available to qualified buyers. What would be the monthly PITI required to buy this home?

Solution: First, key in the typical property tax and insurance percentage for the area. Let's say property taxes in a high-cost area run 1.5 percent of the purchase price and high-quality personal liability and homeowner's insurance is 0.5 percent of the purchase price. The keystrokes using the Qualifier Plus IIIx real estate model are:

Description	Keystrokes	Display
Clear Calculator	On/C On/C	0.00
Enter property tax	1 . 5 Tax	ANN TAX 1.50%
Enter property insurance rate	. 5 Ins	ANN INS 0.50%
Enter sale price	5 0 0 0 0 0 Price	PR 500,000.00
Enter Term	3 0 Term	ANN TERM 30.00
Enter annual interest	7 . 5 Int	ANN INT 7.50 %
Enter down payment %	2 0 Dn Pmt	DN PMT 20.00 %
Find P & I payment	Pmt	P&I 2,796.86 PMT
Find PITI payment	Pmt	PITI 3,630.19 PMT

Calculating Monthly Income Needed to Qualify for a Loan

Example: A buyer is interested in a home that is listed for $500,000. An 80 percent loan at 7.5 percent for 30 years is available if the buyers have a 20 percent down payment. The buyers have monthly long-term debts of $500. What would be the monthly income required to buy this home?

Description	Keystrokes	Display
Clear Calculator	On/C On/C	0.00

(Continued)

Description	Keystrokes	Display
Enter annual interest	7 • 5 [Int]	ANN INT 7.50 %
Enter term in years	3 0 [Term]	ANN TERM 30.00
Enter tax rate	1 • 2 5 [Tax]	ANN TAX 1.25 %
Enter insurance rate	• 3 [Ins]	ANN INS 0.30 %
Enter sale price	5 0 0 0 0 0 [Price]	PR 500,000.00
Enter insurance rate	• 3 [Ins]	ANN INS 0.30 %
Enter down payment %	2 0 [Dn Pmt]	DNPMT 20.00
Enter monthly debt	5 0 0 [Debt]	MO DEBT 500.00
Find loan amount	[Dn Pmt]	LA 400,000.00
Find P&I payment	[Pmt]	P&I 2,796.86
Find PITI payment	[Pmt]	PITI 3,442.69

Then key in typical loan qualifying ratios used by lenders, such as 28 percent for total monthly housing expense and 36 percent for total monthly housing and debt expense. Qualifier Plus IIIx [Qual 1] default stored value is 28%:36% ratio.

Description	Keystrokes	Display
Display qualifying ratios	[Qual 1]	ENT 28.00 – 36.00
Find annual income required	[Qual 1]	REQ 147,543.92
Find monthly income required	÷ 1 2 =	12,295.33

Note: These standards are flexible.

Calculating What a Buyer Can Afford to Borrow and the Price Range of Homes

Rather than looking at a home and then computing what income is needed to qualify as in the previous example, here we know the buyers' income and debts and we are trying to figure out what price range of homes, given current loan terms, the buyers are qualified to purchase.

Example: The buyers have combined monthly income of $8,000 and monthly debts of $400. Assume an 80 percent loan at 7.5 percent for 30 years is available if the buyers have a 20 percent down payment. What loan amount and price range of homes do the buyers appear to qualify for?

Description	Keystrokes	Display
Clear Calculator	[On/C] [On/C]	0.00

(Continued)

15.3 Illustrated Use of Calculated Industries Qualifier Plus IIIx Real Estate Calculator

Description	Keystrokes	Display
Enter term in years	3 0 Term	ANN TERM 30.00
Enter annual interest	7 . 5 Int	ANN INT 7.5%
Enter tax rate	1 . 2 5 Tax	ANN TAX 1.25 %
Enter insurance rate	. 3 Ins	ANN INS 0.30 %
Enter monthly income	8 0 0 0 Shift Inc	INC MO 8,000.00
Enter monthly debt	4 0 0 Debt	MO DEBT 400.00
Enter down payment %	2 0 Dn Pmt	DMPMT 20.00
Display qualifying ratio	Qual 1	ENT 28.00 – 36.00 %
Find qualifying loan amount	Qual 1	MAX LA 260,261.49
Find price	Price	PR 325,326.87
Find monthly P&I	Pmt	P&I 1,819.79
Find down payment required	Dn Pmt Dn Pmt	DNPMT 65,065.37

This is a handy series of keystrokes to estimate what price range of homes to show buyers, and what will be the loan amount, monthly payment, and down payment requirements.

Finding Price or Yields When Buying Existing Notes and Deeds of Trust

Some people prefer to invest in notes and deeds of trust secured by real estate rather than purchase the real estate itself. They are attracted by the rates of return and do not wish to deal with the problems of being a landlord. Financial calculators make it easy to compute price and **yields** when negotiating for the purchase of notes and deeds of trust.

Finding the Price of a Note When You Know the Desired Yield

Example: A $79,000 note at 8.5 percent is amortized for 30 years but due in 7 years. An investor wishes buy this note at a price that will yield 18 percent. What price should the investor pay?

Description	Keystrokes	Display
Clear Calculator	On/C On/C	0.00

(Continued)

Description	Keystrokes	Display
Enter loan amount	7 9 0 0 0 [Loan Amt]	LA 79,000.00
Enter term in years	3 0 [Term]	ANN TERM 30.00
Enter annual interest	8 • 5 [Int]	ANN INT 8.50%
Find P&I payment	[Pmt]	P+I 607.44 PMT
Find balloon payment	7 [Term] [Shift] [Loan Amt]	73,532.45 FV
Enter desired yield	1 8 [Int]	ANN INT 18.00 %
Find purchase price	[Loan Amt]	LA 49,955.09
Enter desired yield	1 8 [Int]	ANN INT 18.00 %
Find purchase price	[Loan Amt]	LA 49,955.09

Calculating the Yield When You Know the Discount Price of the Note

Example: A $79,000 note at 8.5 percent is amortized for 30 years but due in seven 7 years. An investor can buy this note for $49,955.09. What will be the investor's yield?

Description	Keystrokes	Display
Clear Calculator	[On/C] [On/C]	0.00
Enter loan amount	7 9 0 0 0 [Loan Amt]	LA 79,000.00
Enter term in years	3 0 [Term]	ANN TERM 30.00
Enter annual interest	8 • 5 [Int]	ANN INT 8.50%
Find P&I payment	[Pmt]	P+I 607.44 PMT
Find balloon payment	7 [Term] [Shift] [Loan Amt]	73,532.45 FV
Find purchase price	4 9 9 5 5 • 0 9 [Loan Amt]	LA 49,955.09
Enter desired yield	[Int]	ANN INT 18.00 %

Biweekly Loan Payments

Occasionally, some real estate borrowers are given the option of making biweekly instead of monthly loan payments. **Biweekly loan payments** are made every two weeks (26 payments per year), instead of once a month (12 payments per year). Many times this better matches the borrower's paycheck (paid on the job every two weeks). In short, a biweekly program takes a monthly payment then divides it in half, and this amount is paid 26 times per year.

A payment every two weeks is equal to approximately 13 monthly payments per year instead of the usual 12 monthly payments. Making biweekly loan payments can save on interest paid and reduce the time it takes to pay off a loan. The Qualifier Plus IIIx and some other financial calculators are pre-set to easily compute biweekly payments.

Example: Using the Qualifier Plus IIIx, for a $100,000 loan at 10 percent for 30 years, what are the biweekly payments?

Description	Keystrokes	Display
Clear Calculator	On/C On/C	0.00
Enter loan amount	1 0 0 0 0 0 Loan Amt	LA 79,000.00
Enter interest	1 0 Int	ANN INT 10.00%
Enter term	3 0 Term	ANN TERM 30.00
Find Bi-Weekly term	Shift Term	BI ANN TERM 20.96
Find Bi-Weekly P&I	Pmt	P&I BI PMT 438.79
Find the interest Saved	Term Term	SVG BI TTL INT 76,816.82

This illustrates the savings under a biweekly payment system as compared with the normal monthly payment program.

15.4 ANNUAL PERCENTAGE RATES

Under the federal Truth-in-Lending Law, most commercial lenders must disclose the total cost of real estate financing. The disclosure includes the total interest paid, the estimated costs of acquiring the financing, and the annual percentage rate (APR). The impetus for the past mandated Truth-in-Lending (TIL) form was to provide consumer protection by requiring lenders to disclose the cost of borrowing with a standardized form. It was intended to make it easy for borrowers to compare lenders, loan options, and the effective rate of interest or true cost of borrowing. With this form from multiple lenders, it was anticipated that a borrower would be able to compare apples to apples to see the best cost. As of late 2015 the TIL has been replaced with the Loan Estimate (LE) form. (We discuss the LE and the APR in detail in Chapter 10.)

Disclosure of Total Interest Paid

Borrowers are generally unaware of the cost of borrowing, in the form of interest paid, and are surprised to discover the total cost of their loan if held to term. Assume a $100,000 loan at 8 percent interest for 30 years with a monthly payment of $733.76. The total interest on the actual loan, excluding any financing fees, can easily be calculated with a financial calculator:

Total scheduled to be paid over 30 years ($733.76 × 360 months)	$264,155.25
Less: Original loan amount	−100,000.00
Total interest paid over scheduled life of the loan	$164,155.25

Disclosure of Annual Percentage Rate

When there are charges other than interest, some of these charges must be considered in determining the annual percentage rate (APR). The additional financial charges on real estate loans, other than interest, include loan fees and certain other miscellaneous finance fees. The APR calculation must take into consideration loan fees and these other miscellaneous finance fees, as well as the note's interest rate. Below is a simplified version of calculating APR.

Example: Assume a $100,000 loan at 8 percent interest for 30 years, and the lender charges 1.5 points, plus $1,000 in other financing fees covered by the Truth-In-Lending Law. What is the APR?

Description	Keystrokes	Display
Clear Calculator	On/C On/C	0.00
Enter loan amount	1 0 0 0 0 0 Loan Amt	LA 100,000.00
Enter term in years	3 0 Term	ANN TERM 30.00
Enter annual interest	8 Int	ANN INT 8.00%
Find monthly P&I payment	Pmt	P+I Pmt 733.76
Recall loan amount	Rcl Loan Amt	LA 100,000.00
Find point cost	× 1 . 5 % =	1,500.00
Add fees and find total	+ 1 0 0 0 =	2,500.00
Find APR	Shift Int	"run" APR 8.27%

New regulations impose a greater accountability upon those providing this disclosure. The intention is to require the figures provided a potential borrower to be within a limited allowable change from the beginning of the loan to its conclusion. Fines for violations could be severe, suggesting that the APR calculation is best done by the mortgage lender.

Chapter Summary

Real estate mathematics is used to clearly communicate the cost of a loan. Real estate promissory notes come in a variety of forms, and the interest and principal calculations depend on the specific type of note used. The two basic types are: (1) the straight note, which is payable interest-only with the principle entirely due on the due date, and (2) the amortized loan, which contains payments of both principal and interest. The amortized loan can be either fully or partially amortized. If partially amortized, a balloon payment will be owed on the due date. Financial calculators and computers have simplified all real estate lending arithmetic. In addition to calculating loan payments, principal and interest allocation and balloon payments, financial calculators and computers can calculate price and yields on notes, biweekly payments, annual percentage rates (APR), and much more. Finally, most financial calculations in a real estate transaction are for the buyer. A lender will be doing most of these for the loan, but it is always helpful for an agent to know the basics as well. Monthly payment calculations, balloon payment balances, and loan qualifying calculations are a few of the examples demonstrated. For the most part, a seller is concerned with how much he or she will have after the sale closes. This calculation doesn't necessarily require a financial calculator, as an agent will typically provide an Estimated Net Sheet.

The following tip sheets address what some might think of as peripheral issues related to real estate financing. But knowledge of these less obvious finance areas will make a difference in how you are best able to serve your buyers. The following are in tip format, which will allow you to reproduce them for use with customers should you wish to do so. Be aware, however, that the world of real estate financing remains in flux, and make sure that any information you share remains current and appropriate.

This section includes the following:

1. The Financing Partnership—what to look for when seeking to partner with a lender.
2. Loan Pre-Approval Letters—when should you use them; how reliable are they?
3. Shopping Rates—information you can share with buyers.

4. Locking the Rate—when can a loan rate be locked in? The commitment from the buyer?
5. Understanding Your Credit Report
6. Credit Scoring
7. Don't Let Closing Costs be a Surprise—these are often more than expected.
8. Title Insurance—agents need to know that the property they are representing can be financed.
9. Internet Lenders—what to look for when your buyer is acquiring a loan via the Internet.
10. Behavior Accompanying Being Your Best— the ethics surrounding real estate sales and financing.

THE FINANCING PARTNERSHIP

When a home buyer is recommended to a loan officer by a sales agent, it is easy to become a bit confused as to whose client the buyer is. When a buyer enters into a loan process with a lender, the buyer becomes the lender's client. The buyer is owed confidentiality and total focus on what is best for the client. Although both the real estate agent and the lender have a separate client relationship, they are united in their desire to have the transaction close successfully, have the buyer pleased, and to behave in the client's best interest. Communication is essential between the lender and the real estate agent during this time.

A real estate licensee's first concern is whether the buyer is qualified to buy and at what purchase price. The pre-approval letter should have already been obtained from the lender prior to the real estate licensee showing the buyer any property.

By making appropriate initial inquiries, real estate licensees can get an idea regarding the buyer's ability to acquire a loan.

Here are a few key questions that can be asked of the loan officer:

1. At what purchase price should I show property?
2. Can you tell me the kind of loan the buyer might acquire?
3. Is it likely that the seller may need to be asked to assist with closing costs?
4. Have you reviewed the credit report?
5. Have you identified sufficient down payment funds?
6. Have you identified sufficient income for qualification purposes?
7. Has the loan been approved via the Direct Underwriting System?
8. What is the anticipated time schedule for loan submission?

A loan officer cannot provide any confidential information but can only answer the above inquiries in the broadest of terms.

A pre-approval letter is often requested, and some of the above items might be addressed in said letter. Often, the information upon which the pre-approval letter is based will need to be updated, and things do change during the loan process.

There are some things that you can do to expedite the transaction with buyers and sellers.

- Encourage the buyer to submit ALL requested information immediately.
- Make sure the lender is in possession of ALL counter offers/amendments that have been fully executed.
- Have the buyer arrange for homeowner's insurance as soon as escrow is opened.
- Arrange for ALL inspections as soon as practicable, and make sure the lender is aware of any item that will impact the transaction (e.g. change in purchase price, seller concessions, outcome of inspections).
- Recommend that the buyer inspect any and all permits provided by seller, or if not provided by seller, check with the city regarding any permits.

The loan qualification process seems to always be changing. Even the most seemingly qualified borrower may have an obstacle emerge. Remember, the real estate licensee is partners with the lender. Approach any hurdle ready to resolve the issue rather than trying to find blame. Last minute delays can occur in spite of the most diligent attention from the loan officer and the real estate licensee. Don't blame each other or any other participant in the process (e.g. escrow, title, appraiser). Make everyone a partner in seeing that the process reaches a successful conclusion.

The loan officer does not always have total control of the timing of submissions, underwriter approval, and ordering appraisals. The key is to have reasonable and appropriate expectations of when the various loan aspects will be accomplished. Appraisals can be unpredictable. Underwriters do provide last minute, sometimes unexpected, conditions that to the borrower, agent, and loan officer seem irrelevant. Don't argue and get upset; acquire the information if possible. If not, explain the situation and the inability to provide what is sought, and see if the underwriter can provide an alternative. The underwriter's predicament is making sure the loan is salable in the secondary market while the real estate licensee is focused on getting the loan approved and completed.

While loan denials represent a small portion of the total financing arena, they cause a disproportionate amount of frustration. Often, denial is temporary and only requires that the prospective buyer clarify a credit issue, be on the job for a while longer or save additional money for down payment or closing costs. It is important to keep the client positive while determining this kind of road map to eventual home ownership. For example: must be on the job for a few more months, save additional money for closing and/or down payment, etc.

On the other hand, sometimes it is futile and everyone has to simply let go and move on to the next possible client.

When all is said and done, if the partners remain calm and focused on what needs to be done to reach the finish line, the loan transaction, in most cases, will be successful.

LOAN PRE-APPROVAL LETTERS

It has become commonplace to request a pre-approval letter to accompany the presentation of an offer to purchase. The perception is that a letter of confirmation of the buyer's ability to acquire a loan can be critical in the seller's willingness to accept the purchase offer.

In the past, lenders differentiated between pre-approval and pre-qualification letters. The latter was generally provided when, upon review of a prospective borrower's documentation, a loan officer would indicate the borrower was pre-qualified. A pre-approval letter was issued only after submission of the borrower's loan file and approval from an underwriter. The difference has been blurred in recent years as licensees and sellers preferred only the assurance of a pre-approval.

Occasionally in the past, a pre-qualification letter might have been prepared after having only had a conversation with the prospective borrower, relying solely on information acquired without any written confirmation. While mostly abandoned as a practice, the unreliability of such borrower assessments have likely led to the current insistence upon pre-approval.

It is important to recognize exactly when a loan is reliably deemed approved. The first step is usually the acquisition of information. An experienced loan officer can, with reasonable certainty, determine if a borrower is likely to be approved. The reliability of this determination depends upon the information provided. Preferably, the lender will have acquired a credit report, verified income, and identified the cash required in the transaction. At the very least, it is recommended that the lender will have also acquired pay check stubs, bank statements, and other easily provided information with which to render an opinion. The information is prepared for submission to an underwriter.

Typically, it is at this point that the elusive pre-approval letter is requested. In most cases, a loan file is not submitted to a lender for underwriting until all the information has been gathered and a purchase contract has been acquired. It makes sense that without an identified property and an approved purchase contract price and terms, no borrower approval has yet been acquired. Common sense suggests that any letter provided at this stage, regardless of its title, usually represents the loan officer's opinion that the borrower will be approved.

With today's automated underwriting capacity, a quick approval (known as a direct underwriting approval) can be acquired, but it is still critical that the information inserted into the automated process be accurate as the final loan file must be signed-off by an underwriter. While an automated approval is not a guarantee of a buyer's capacity to perform, it is often perceived as such, and this second step often results in a more reliable sense of pre-approval.

The third step in the process, a pre-approval by a required underwriter, occurs only after a full borrower's loan file has been submitted to the lender. This loan submission will include the previous identified documentation plus title and escrow information. The underwriter provides a Conditional Approval, identifying if there are any other conditions or information required. All that is generally necessary to close the transaction, following the underwriter's approval, is the property appraisal. Only now do we have an approved loan.

Understanding this final approval process sequence, experienced licensees know that the letter attending the presentation of an offer may say pre-approval but that it is unlikely that the borrower's file has been underwritten or an underwriter's opinion yet acquired. Thus any pre-approval letter is only as reliable as the information upon which the opinion was based as well as the experience, competency, and truthfulness of the lender providing the information.

There are conflicting philosophies as to exactly when any letter should be presented to the seller. Some prefer to have a letter available at the time of original presentation of the purchase offer. In the absence of an agreed upon purchase price, this letter often does not identify the actual loan amount for which the buyer is qualified, but rather is of a more general nature. Others prefer to finalize the transaction with the understanding that a letter will be acquired within 24 hours of the acceptance of the offer. In this latter situation, the letter is more likely to confirm that the buyer is qualified for the actual loan amount identified in the purchase contract.

Let's examine the timing for presenting the pre-approval letter in a bit more detail. Let's assume a purchase contract with an offer to purchase of $250,000 with an anticipated 95 percent loan-to-value ratio loan of $237,500. If the offer to purchase includes a pre-approval letter indicating that the borrower is approved for a $237,500 loan, does it help or hinder the process? For instance, what if the seller is unwilling to accept the $250,000 offer and wants to counter offer at a higher price? Would the seller be reluctant to do so, perhaps believing that the $237,500 pre-approval amount is the maximum available to the buyer? Would this disadvantage the buyer?

Or, there is another possibility. The buyer is actually pre-approved for a total loan amount of $250,000 but wants to make an offer, as indicated above, with only a $237,500 loan amount. If a seller sees a pre-approval letter for a $250,000 loan amount, is it likely that the seller will want to counter an offer at a higher price, recognizing that the buyer can obviously afford it? Doesn't this have the potential to disadvantage the buyer?

An alternative to the above scenarios could be to indicate to a seller that a pre-approval letter will be forthcoming within 24 to 36 hours of the signing of the purchase contract. This delay might additionally provide the time necessary for the automated submission of the borrower's file and the acquisition of an actual system approval (noted above), which would provide greater assurance that the borrower can proceed.

So there is a strategy to when to provide a pre-approval letter and determining exactly what it should include as well as what it really means. Lenders want to assist with the transaction and gladly provide such pre-approval letters. But experienced lenders often refer within the letters to the actual data upon which they based their opinion and may otherwise qualify the approval if they have not at least been able to access the automated approval process.

SHOPPING RATES: A FEW COMMENTS

Often the first question asked by a potential borrower is, "What is today's interest rate?" Interest rates change regularly and sometimes very rapidly. The actual rate you may expect depends on the type of loan ultimately acquired. With the introduction of risk-based pricing (discussed in the Case & Point at the end of Chapter 6), rates are adjusted based on a borrower's credit scores, the loan-to-value ratio, and other loan aspects that impact the interest rate obtainable. In other words, loan pricing is complicated and confusing.

Buyers are advised to shop rates and negotiate the fees. The media suggests that mortgage representatives will likely inflate both the rate and fees when given an opportunity. The problem for most buyers is how would they know if someone is taking advantage of them?

The reality is that the buyer must ultimately determine if the person from whom they intend to acquire financing is trustworthy.

SHOPPING RATES AND POINTS. These are the two loan aspects that are perhaps most easily understood by prospective borrowers. But there are numerous other considerations when acquiring home loan financing. Lenders make loans based upon their risk level and the yield on the mortgage over a period of time. Points (one point equals 1 percent of the loan amount) are the cost for acquiring a loan and are a part of the lender's yield calculation. For instance, one might acquire a loan at 4.25 percent with a one point loan cost or 4.125 percent with a 1.5 point fee. The lender's yield will be the same over a predetermined period of time. Because this can be confusing, mortgage representatives could quote lower points as a "come on" and compensate for the yield with a higher rate and/or fees.

The fact is that all lenders have the same loan programs at the same costs. The difference is whether the lender is charging an overage in the fees, a higher origination fee, etc. Pricing depends on how long it might take to close the loan transaction. If you are calling for loan quotes, be sure that you are comparing apples with apples. For instance, if one lender is quoting a 15-day rate (remember, it is highly unlikely that you will close a transaction from start to finish in 15 days) and the next lender is quoting a more realistic 30- or 45-day rate, the more honest loan representative will be at a disadvantage. So think about the fact that you are not only shopping rates but need also to concentrate on shopping service, knowledge, expertise, and the capacity to get the loan completed with the least hassle for you, the borrower.

It can be a mistake trying to reach every lender—at most, select only a few lenders. A good rule of thumb is when you have called several lenders and received very comparable quotes, be very skeptical of the one fantastically low quote from some lender. Remember the saying, *"If it sounds too good to be true, it probably is."* While you may feel that the higher rate quote is not competitive, it might just be the more honest approach to letting you know what to realistically expect.

Potential buyers have become more suspicious of what they sometimes view as "bait and switch" quotes. More local lenders try hard to quote as accurately as possible, based upon your individual loan needs and your current credit situation and the risk-based factors that have to be considered. The more legitimate lenders will most likely tell you that they are unable to quote reliably without having your documentation information, including income information, bank statements, credit report, etc. Only then can a dependable rate quote be provided.

DON'T RELY UPON THE INTERNET. The Internet is notorious for misinformation. There is little accountability by Internet lenders, so they can quote super rates. Unfortunately, stories are numerous about those borrowers who, upon receiving their loan documents, find the rate higher than that originally quoted. Although the borrower may be unhappy about any of a number of reasons provided for the rate increase, the transaction is often too far along to cancel and start over.

CONSIDER SERVICE. It's an overused word but critical to any buyer. Will the lender

- help the buyer consider all the available options (interview and counsel)?
- get the loan completed in a timely fashion?
- keep the buyer informed throughout the process?

Buyers who shop too much

- can "shop until they drop" with confusion and as a result often do nothing.
- can be dazzled by the fast footwork of some lenders, promising rates and terms that are impossible. The result is the loan takes longer or sometimes cancels.

BE SMART! TRUST YOUR INTUITION. Acquiring an interest rate quote is not as simple as it appears. When you find a mortgage lender who you trust, stay with them. Stop shopping rates and enjoy the loan experience.

LOCKING THE RATE

A rate lock is a lender's commitment to loan money at a predetermined interest rate and fee and to hold such commitment for a predetermined time period. It is also a commitment from the borrower to complete the loan with the agreed upon terms. When interest rates trend upward, borrowers are more concerned about protecting themselves by locking in their loan rate.

The primary factor that determines pricing is the length of time for the lock period. A lender, for instance, might guarantee a borrower a 4.25 percent interest rate at a cost of 1 point origination/discount fee as long as the loan transaction is completed within 45 days. If the lock period were for a shorter period of time (i.e. 15 days), perhaps the rate or the fee would adjust downward. Should the loan transaction not be completed within the lock period, it will expire. The typical rule upon expiration is that the borrower would be required to accept (within 30 days following the lock expiration) either the lock rate or current market rate, whichever is higher. This is to discourage borrowers from merely letting a lock commitment expire just prior to closing escrow with the expectation of acquiring a lower rate.

Obviously, borrowers would prefer a rate lock system that allowed them to protect themselves from upward motion of interest rates but take advantage of any rate reduction that might occur during their lock period. Called a "float down," these arrangements are generally not available anymore, but most lenders will consider renegotiating the rate should a significant reduction unexpectedly occur.

Rate lock periods vary, usually 15, 30, 45, or 60 days. When the lender is expected to hold the rate for more than the 15-day period, the origination/discount fee usually increases slightly depending upon the length of the lock, market conditions, and the consequent risk to be absorbed by the lender. Any additional cost can also depend upon the type of loan acquired (i.e., fixed, conventional, FHA, or VA). Adjustable rate loans are generally not locked until near ready to close.

Most loans can be locked at the time of application or at any time during the loan processing period. Some jumbo loans (i.e., those loan amounts in excess of $417,000) can be locked only for a maximum of 45 days, or, in some instances, may be locked only after lender/underwriter approval.

Potential home buyers who regularly compare rates by calling lenders for their daily quote can be confused when they are given varied rates because each lender may be quoting for a different lock-in period. Be certain that one is obtaining true comparison quotes when shopping rates. It is advised that borrowers schedule a free pre-qualification interview rather than merely shop rates. An interview will let the lender suggest the appropriate loan product to meet the borrower's particular financial need(s). At the same time, the lender can provide some guidance as to the best time frame for locking your loan.

The alternative to locking in the rate is to allow the loan to "float the market" during the loan processing period. The borrower can elect at any time during this float period to lock their loan, or the loan can continue to float toward the final stages of the loan process. The question then is, should one lock or float? This is usually the borrower's decision alone and can seem like a bit of a gamble. While no one can know for sure what interest rates are likely to do over any particular period of time, consultation with the lender and realtor(s) is always available to assist in trying to acquire the best rate possible.

One final thought: after deciding to lock your loan, don't second guess your decision. Remember, you selected the rate, you can't change it, stop worrying about it. An eighth of a percent is likely to make little difference in your payment anyway, so don't make yourself crazy over having missed that very lowest rate.

UNDERSTANDING YOUR CREDIT REPORT

With the increased emphasis on credit scoring, it is important to understand what is involved in an individual's credit history. The following represent some of the most frequently asked questions.

What kind of information does my file contain? Personal data such as name, address, Social Security number, and employment for you and a spouse (if married). Credit lines including bank loans, credit cards, department store charge accounts, finance company loans, gasoline credit card accounts, as well as mortgage accounts. Collection accounts, including those that have been paid. Legal items such as judgments, tax liens, foreclosures, and bankruptcies.

How does the lender evaluate the credit history? Stability is the key word for lenders when reviewing credit history, particularly employment and payment history. For some transactions, a lender may require sufficient credit history—usually a minimum of three credit lines—proving that the borrower can manage their credit usage. Obviously, a lender also prefers income stability as evidence of the ability to pay the debt (e.g. employment).

How can I find out what is contained in my credit file? You can contact the local credit bureau and for a small fee obtain a copy of your credit report. Your request will probably have to be in writing. Check in advance to determine that the report will include all three repositories and credit scores. If you are denied credit, you are entitled to a free credit report, which should explain the reason(s) for the denial.

NOTE: The Fair Credit Reporting Act (FCRA) requires each of the nationwide credit reporting companies — Equifax, Experian, and TransUnion — to provide you with a free copy of your credit report, at your request, once every 12 months.

Why do I need to access all three major credit repositories? Various creditors may choose to report to only one or two of the repositories rather than all three. One can guarantee all of the reported credit history only by accessing all three repositories and comparing the information. One bureau may be sufficient if the credit history is limited or to merely obtain an idea of what your credit looks like.

What if I find information I believe to be incorrect? In some circumstances the credit bureau will re-verify any data you feel is in error. If you are unsure if the information is erroneous, the report provides addresses and phone numbers for the creditors, allowing you to contact them directly to clarify reported information.

You may dispute a delinquency reported by a creditor. If the creditor does not respond within a reasonable period of time (typically 30 days), the item in question can be deleted from the credit file. It is important to note that sometimes a delinquent item is deleted because a creditor delays their response, only to find that the creditor responds later resulting in the delinquent item being reinstated in the credit report. You are allowed under all circumstances to add a consumer statement of 100 words or less to your file related to any specific delinquent item. If the information is determined to be inaccurate, your credit score will ultimately change. For more information, check the FTC website at www.consumer.ftc.gov.

FACT: Avoid credit fix invitations, most of which are scams. In spite of enticing advertisements suggesting that your credit report can immediately be enhanced, if the adverse information is accurate it cannot just be expunged. Credit counseling organizations can help if you find yourself in what seems an unfixable credit situation. Such counseling services have some limitations and should not be entered into without serious consideration and need for assistance.

How long does adverse information remain on file? Most adverse information will generally remain on record for seven years, although a creditor can choose to remove a delinquent item prior to the seven year maximum. Exceptions to this rule include judgments, which remain for 10 years and can be renewed by creditors.

How frequently do creditors update information to the credit repositories? While this depends upon the individual creditor, the general rule is that updates are recorded every 30 to 60 days for active accounts. As indicated above, the credit scoring system is under considerable criticism for what is considered by many to be long delays in adjusting credit scores. A "rapid score" process, while costly, can be effective in situations that cannot wait the time period for credit scores to adjust more normally. Caution: This is not necessarily a quick fix and sometimes the result is that scores decline.

What steps can I take to improve my credit profile or to make certain that I retain the best possible profile? Obviously the most critical thing to do is pay all bills on time. Two prominent misconceptions for consumers include:

- one cannot make up for a missed payment one month by sending two monthly payments the next month.
- partial payments will not prevent adverse ratings.

FACT: Not all creditors are created equally. Some creditors impact a score, favorably and unfavorably, more than others. Consistent installment debt payments usually affect a score more favorably than revolving credit, and national credit card accounts generally are better for score ratings than local department stores.

Make sure that all the creditors to whom you are making timely payments are reporting to all the credit repositories. If you discover that they are not, ask that they report your good account status. Not reporting good status is a favorite ploy of creditors who wish to keep a borrower paying higher interest on their current debt service. Department stores and finance companies are the most frequent abusers.

It is advised that before seeking a major purchase, you determine your credit situation in advance. This will allow you to take care of any problems and/or discrepancies that appear in your credit file. Always retain copies of reports, letters, or other written correspondence with creditors and/or credit repositories. Retain notes regarding any phone conversations, including the names of persons with whom you speak and the date and time of conversations. Ask for written confirmation of agreements.

Finally, remember that your credit report is a reflection of the way you handle credit responsibilities. Lenders will not be receptive to either excuses for late payments or the promise to do better in the future. Lenders will require you to prove your ability to handle credit via a demonstration of on-time payments for a minimum of a 12-month period.

CREDIT SCORING: HOW IT WORKS

The Fair Isaac Credit Bureau Scores, known as FICO scoring, has been available in all types of lending for a number of years. It is the process of examining the past credit history of a borrower to determine the likelihood of timely future payments on any new credit debt.

This scoring not only assesses how likely a borrower is to pay back a loan, but also measures the degree of risk a borrower represents to the lender. Scores range from 300 to 900, the higher score indicating better credit quality.

In measuring the relationship between credit scores and default records, lenders have learned that there are many more dimensions to credit than just reviewing and explaining a late payment record.

There are 33 variables, grouped into five categories, gathered for a borrower's credit profile. Some of the items include:

1. **Previous Credit Performance:** Examining late payments, judgments, collections, etc. and how recently they occurred.
2. **Current Level of Debt:** Number of outstanding account balances versus the credit limit.
3. **Pursuit of New Credit:** Review of the number of inquiries made by creditors and new accounts opened during the past year.
4. **The Time Credit Has Been Used:** Examination of how old the accounts are.

5. **Types of Credit in Use:** Are the accounts bank, gas, entertainment, department store credit cards, personal loans, automobile, or installment loans? Installment debt and low balances on bank cards result in the higher scores

Most recent indications of the "weight" given to scoring goes like this:

1. Late Payment History   35%
2. Current Level of Debt   30%
3. Pursuit of New Credit   10%
4. Length of Credit   15%
5. Type of Credit   10%

Here is one way in which you might interpret the above information:

1. Pay on time, all the time. Making up missed payments doesn't work.
2. Don't exceed 30 percent of any revolving credit limit.
3. Keep some revolving accounts open. While some lenders, as evidence of a borrower's ability to use credit, prefer to see several credit lines, outstanding balances need not be maintained. Avoid excessive inquiries by not applying for credit unless you need it. Inquiries during the past 12 months are reviewed and can negatively impact a score.
4. Retain long-standing cards. They do not have to be used regularly but if used, pay off the balance each month to build a higher credit score.
5. Avoid finance company credit in favor of using bank credit and installment financing.

FACT: Today's practice of constantly transferring account balances to lower interest rate bearing cards, while a good business decision, could result in lowering a score.

Should a consumer be denied credit due to a low score, clues as to why might be found by reviewing the four most significant reasons for the low score as provided by the credit provider. These are generally the four most important factors that affected the score and kept it from being higher.

You can get an idea regarding what your credit looks like by accessing one of the repositories. The Equifax site is recommended as the most user-friendly by many, but here are all three sites:

www.equifax.com
www.transunion.com
www.experian.com

While the above sites will likely assess a fee, there are now websites that promote free reports. The report you receive is likely to represent only one credit repository (out of a total of three repositories) but may provide insight regarding your credit profile. The three most reliable free sites are:

www.creditkarma.com
www.quizzle.com
www.annualcreditreport.com

These sites will attempt to sell you more services than you need. Do not be tempted. Proceed with obtaining a free credit report. After examination for any errors, you can consult your home mortgage lender for assistance in interpreting the report and help in correcting errors and/or improving your credit score.

Our credit reporting system can be error prone, and consumers are charged with proving any error is inaccurate. Maintaining good credit requires discipline and attention to how you use your credit. There are no shortcuts, but the good news is, with competent guidance, most credit histories can be improved over time if you are willing to put in the work required.

DON'T LET CLOSING COSTS BE A SURPRISE

Many buyers are most often concerned with the amount of down payment that will be required for their proposed purchase. It is easy to forget or underestimate the amount of closing costs that will also be required. These expenses mount up quickly and can be a shock to the buyer. If these costs have not been anticipated, they can result in the cancellation of the purchase simply for the lack of sufficient funds. So, here are the costs that need to be considered in a purchase transaction.

1. ORIGINATION FEE: This represents the lender's charge for making the loan, commonly called "points." One point represents 1 percent of the loan amount. The origination fee reflects the lender's income in the loan. New rules eliminate the practice, prevalent in the subprime loan era, of charging more points if the borrower's credit scores are low (because of blemished credit) or some other greater than normal risk factor exists. Today's "no points" or "no cost" loan is simply the acceptance of a higher interest rate in exchange for rebate pricing with which the fees are paid. The ability of borrowers to use this option to reduce closing cost fees has been severely impacted by the newly enacted

regulations. (See the explanation of yield spread premium at the end of the article.)

2. DISCOUNT POINTS: These are mostly connected to what are called "buy downs" and are a reflection of the yield anticipated by the investor who will ultimately purchase the loan. A buyer can buy down the interest rate via the payment of discount points. For example, instead of accepting a 5.25 percent interest rate loan at a 1 percent loan cost, the buyer could choose a 5.125 percent rate at a 1.5 percent loan cost. The additional one-half percent loan fee would enable the buyer to acquire a one-eighth percent lower interest rate. Before deciding to buy-down the rate, buyers are encouraged to discuss the savings versus the cost factors with their mortgage lender. The decision to pay additional points will depend upon a number of factors including how long you intend to own the property, the actual cost of any buy-down, and who is actually paying the fee.

3. LENDER/ADMINISTRATION FEES: While these can vary depending upon the type of loan, typical lender fees generally do not exceed $1,200 and include:

   - Tax service fee
   - Wire transfer fee
   - Loan documents preparation
   - Underwriting
   - Flood certification

   In addition, a processing fee ranging from $400 to $600 is usually charged by the lender/broker. Many real estate authors point to these costs as the "garbage" fees and encourage that they be negotiated and/or eliminated in the transaction. The reality is that the fees have to be paid, and they will either be fully disclosed or hidden within the pricing structure. Know that the fees will be paid and opt for full disclosure.

4. TITLE INSURANCE: The payment of title fees is determined via contract agreement and is usually guided by what is common or customary for the area. Who will pay which fees is by agreement identified in the purchase agreement. There are two title insurance fees usually involved in a purchase transaction. The more costly CLTA fee is to assure the transfer of clear title. The ALTA fee, or lender's coverage, is to insure extended coverage for the lender. The ALTA is often paid by the buyer and the CLTA can be paid exclusively by the seller or it can be split between buyer and

seller. (Note: Make sure you understand title insurance coverage when you purchase).

5. ESCROW FEE: This fee is most often split equally between buyer and seller but can be paid in full by either according to the contract. In VA loans, the seller is charged the total escrow fee as the veteran is prohibited from paying this fee. Additionally, estimate several hundred dollars for such items as recordation fees, federal express charges, and other miscellaneous escrow costs.

6. HOMEOWNER'S INSURANCE: The buyer is required to purchase a one year homeowner's insurance policy paid for in escrow, with the cost depending upon the home value and coverage acquired. Buyers are urged to seek insurance early in the purchase process. Be aware that flood insurance will be required if the property is located in a flood zone. Earthquake insurance, in California, is not required by lenders.

7. TAX PRORATIONS: Buyers and sellers will be assessed their appropriate portion of the existing property taxes to be prorated in escrow. Depending upon the date of close of escrow (COE) and the assessed taxes, this can be a significant sum. While not a closing cost required in escrow, buyers will want to educate themselves as to the impact of supplemental taxes that will likely come due 90 to 120 days after close of escrow.

8. IMPOUND ACCOUNTS: When a loan represents a sufficient risk (typically above an 80 percent LTV), the lender imposes an impound requirement. This means that the monthly payment will include an amount for taxes and insurance as well as the normal principal and interest payment. There will be an initial assessment to start the impound account. This amount will vary depending upon the month in which the loan closes escrow.

9. INTEREST ON NEW LOAN: Loan payments are due on the first day of each month. The interest owed on the loan is always paid in arrears (i.e., the payment made on June 1 is in payment for the use of the money in May). This necessitates a proration of interest on the new loan from the day it funds to the end of the month. The first loan payment is generally not due for a month or more after the close of escrow. Depending upon the day of the month the loan is funded, this amount can be nearly a full month of interest and be substantial. The first loan payment is then due (in this scenario) on July 1.

10. APPRAISAL & CREDIT REPORT: These fees are collected by some lenders at the time the loan application is submitted. In most cases, new rules around appraisals now result mostly ordering them

via the borrower's credit card. Credit reports are often acquired initially at the lender's expense but are reimbursed in escrow. These fees vary by area, but the borrower cannot be charged more than the actual cost. Expect appraisal fees on conventional loans for non-owner occupied type loans to be more expensive.

While this is not intended as an exhaustive list of loan costs, it does represent the basic fees. The costs can become rather substantial depending upon the loan circumstances. To avoid surprises, you may find it beneficial to discuss the type of loan you wish to acquire and secure an estimate of the closing costs from your lender early in the loan process. Lenders are making some assumptions when first calculating these anticipated closing costs. That is why they are called "estimated." A more accurate closing cost estimate is provided after obtaining all the information, including the purchase contract, which will identify the payment of title and escrow fees, any seller paid fees, or other concessions.

The closing costs for refinance transactions differ somewhat but are still often more than borrowers anticipate. Again, it is advised that you thoroughly investigate the estimated closing costs before proceeding with your loan. And, make sure you acquire an accounting of all the expected costs. Refinancing can be expensive, so it is usually not a good idea to enter into a loan option that will automatically require you to refinance within a couple of years.

Asking sellers to pay all or some of the buyer's closing costs has become more frequent in recent years. Most loan options allow a seller to pay buyer's closing costs, at least up to 3 percent (and often up to 6 percent) of the purchase price. This has become a popular way to assist buyers who may be short of cash for closing costs.

Calculating closing costs can be a challenge. As with any financing arrangement, to avoid unwelcome surprises, meet with your trusted mortgage loan officer and make certain that you understand the process completely.

We mentioned yield spread premium (YSP) in the origination fee discussion above. When a lender acquires a loan at an interest rate above the market rate, a rebate is generated that can now be used by the borrower to help pay closing costs. During the subprime era, YSP was often abused by steering buyers into higher interest rate loans in order to generate more income for lenders. Any generated rebate today will generally be disclosed in the initial Loan Estimate and confirmed in the Closing Disclosure (discussed in the Case & Point at the end of Chapter 9) and will be used to offset buyer closing costs, including, in many cases, the lender's origination fee. Buyers are urged to ask their mortgage lender about YSP and how it might be used for the borrower's benefit. (YSP is discussed in the Case & Point at the end of Chapter 3.)

TITLE INSURANCE: BASIC INFORMATION

Title insurance, while seldom used for claim purposes, provides considerable protection for a homeowner at a bargain price. While it is unlikely that one can acquire a home mortgage without title insurance, it is widely accepted that every home loan borrower, even if not required, should avail themselves of this protection. Unlike other forms of insurance, title insurance requires only one premium payment at the time of purchase or refinance, and the coverage continues as long as you own the property.

Title insurers research all of the records affecting the property to be purchased or refinanced and determine if they can insure marketable title. If the title is found to be defective or questionable, the title insurer will either decline to insure or will insure with exceptions. A lender/investor will then review the policy exceptions to determine if they will provide a loan.

Title insurers devote nearly 90 percent of insurance premiums on researching titles before insuring them in the attempt to avoid major risks. Title risks can involve anything from minor recording errors and copying and indexing snafus to the more serious forged signature on a deed, unpaid tax or other liens, etc.

There are two forms of title insurance. The California Land Title Association (CLTA) policy, known as the owner/lender policy, typically insures the lender and guarantees the priority of the lender's loan (i.e. that the lender's loan is in first position in the recordation process). Additionally, it identifies that the current owner (seller) of the property has good title to convey. This coverage is usually based upon the amount of the mortgage loan, and the amount of coverage decreases as the mortgage is paid.

The American Land Title Association (ALTA) policy, sometimes known as the lender/buyer's insurance, typically protects the owner's equity in the property. The ALTA basic policy generally covers Insuring Provisions, Exclusions from Coverage, Conditions and Stipulations, and finally Schedule A and Schedule B comments. It is important that the borrower read and understand the coverage provisions and exclusions.

The decision regarding who pays for title insurance can be a matter of local custom, but the original purchase contract between buyer and seller usually identifies the agreement for payment. Everyone is urged to be clear as to the decision(s) being made regarding title insurance costs.

Every title insurer has the authority to issue policy endorsements, usually resulting in additional coverage/protection and, of course, at an additional cost. The rule is, inquire about anything you don't understand and be sure you are comfortable with the answers you receive.

Various Ways to Hold Title

How you choose to take title to your new home purchase depends upon your specific needs and situation. The four primary methods of holding title are joint tenancy, community property, tenancy in common, and the newer community property with right of survivorship. Following is a brief description of each form of ownership.

JOINT TENANCY: The property is owned in common by two or more people, with right of survivorship. In other words, a deceased joint tenant's interest passes automatically to the remaining joint tenant(s) without having to go through probate. This process usually requires only the filing of an Affidavit of Death of Joint Tenancy to satisfy the change of ownership. This was for a long time the preferred method of holding title in California.

Each person is deemed to own an equal undivided percentage interest in the property, in common with the other co-tenants. Each tenant may transfer his or her interest at any time, but to do so severs the joint tenant's interest. The new co-owner will be a tenant in common with the remaining joint tenants. At the time of death, only the deceased's percentage interest in the property acquires a stepped-up basis to its fair market value at the date of the joint tenant's death.

Before moving on to the next form of ownership, let us discuss what "step-up in basis" means. Let's assume for a moment that two joint tenants acquire a piece of property worth $100,000. Each joint tenant is assumed to own a $50,000 interest in the property. At the time of death of one joint tenant, let us assume the property has appreciated to $200,000. Again, each joint tenant is assumed to own a half interest or $100,000. Upon the death of the joint tenant, the deceased's portion of the property "steps up" to its current value (i.e. $100,000). The value to the remaining joint tenant remains at the original value, and should he or she sell the property, capital gain would be due only on the increased value in this portion, in this case $50,000 (the difference between the original $50,000 half value and the current $100,000 half value of the remaining joint tenant). This can be confusing, and you may require tax counsel to clarify this aspect of ownership.

COMMUNITY PROPERTY: The property is owned in common by a married couple, usually acquired during the course of the marriage. Each spouse is deemed to own an undivided one-half interest in the entire property (in some states known as an interest in the entirety) in common with the other spouse.

Title cannot be transferred separately, requiring both spouses to join in the transfer via deed. In the event of the death of one spouse, the deceased spouse's interest passes according to his or her will. In the absence of a will, the entire interest passes to the surviving spouse. This transfer is typically accomplished via probate. A probate proceeding can be lengthy and costly depending upon the size of the estate. Living trusts have become a popular vehicle for retaining property and can circumvent the expense and time of a probate process. You are advised to seek legal counsel regarding such trusts and whether it is a vehicle that would benefit your specific circumstances.

The ENTIRE property acquires a step up in basis to its fair market value at the date of the spouse's death. This is in contrast to joint tenancy in which only the deceased's property interest is stepped up in basis. There are obvious tax consequences related to this step up basis process, and borrowers are advised to seek legal counsel before selecting the method of holding title.

TENANCY IN COMMON: The property is owned in common by two or more people without the right of survivorship. Each person is deemed to own a divisible percentage interest in the property, in common with the other co-tenants. This is typically the choice of ownership when several unrelated persons purchase together. This is particularly true when the amount of dollar investment from each owner varies as this is the only form of ownership in which the co-tenants may own unequal percentages of the entirety.

Each tenant has a separate title interest that can be transferred separately at any time by its owner. The new co-owner then becomes a tenant in common with the remaining tenants in common. A deceased tenant's in common interest passes via probate per the deceased's will or via the laws of intestacy. Only the deceased's percentage interest in the property acquires a stepped-up basis to its fair market value at the date of the tenant in common's death.

COMMUNITY PROPERTY WITH RIGHT OF SURVIVORSHIP: This newest form of holding title became law in 2001 and seems to provide the best of all worlds to married couples as it provides the probate avoidance benefits of joint tenancy and the tax benefits of community property. This form of ownership requires the signature or initials of the parties on the face of the document or on some other document to demonstrate the clear intention of the parties to take the identified property as community property with right of survivorship.

The reason for this requirement for affirmatively requesting this new form of ownership stems from the often misunderstood concept known as the "community property presumption," that is that property acquired by spouses during marriage and which is held in joint form is community property. This presumption, however, applies only for purposes of division of property upon dissolution of marriage or legal separation. If one party dies, the language of how title is held in the deed is controlling, not the community property presumption. So, while people are often under the misperception that because they acquired a home during marriage, the home will be treated as community property with the appropriate tax advantages, this is simply not the case. This new form of taking title is designed to clarify both buyer options and intent of ownership.

OTHER CONSIDERATIONS: Every situation differs depending upon whether spouses have been previously married, how the funds were contributed for the purchase, and/or how a deceased owner may wish his or her interest dispersed after death. Thus, it is always recommended that tax and/or legal counsel be sought prior to any final decisions regarding title.

INTERNET LENDERS: APPROACH WITH CAUTION!

If the TV ads are to be believed, home loans are not only easy to acquire but practically anyone is eligible for home ownership. This constant promotion urges consumers to apply for their home mortgages via the Internet. More and more, borrowers have been disappointed with this method of acquiring a home loan. Too often, borrowers are surprised toward the end of the transaction to discover that their loan documents are significantly different than they thought they had been promised over the phone.

When a borrower compares the fees provided by an Internet lender versus a local lender, the discrepancy can be significant. This confusion is generally a misunderstanding of the phrase, "Our fees are only $____." The quote from the Internet may represent only the lender's fees (typically the loan fee, appraisal, credit report) whereas the more accurate fee usually includes all the fees you are likely to see at the close of escrow. These include such items as escrow and title fees, tax prorations, impound accounts, etc. The key when using the Internet lender is to ask for an estimate of costs that will include all of the fees likely to be required at close of escrow. Now you will be comparing apples and apples.

It is well known that the Internet lenders are seeking the best quality borrowers: those with high credit scores, low qualifying ratios, and plenty of reserves (money left after close of escrow). They have had little patience or time for the more marginal buyer. A fair percentage of borrowers require credit counseling, either to clarify an error or to improve credit scores. It is important for a would-be borrower to understand credit scoring and what it means to their ability to acquire particular financing.

It is doubtful that most Internet lenders are versed in the loan options that might be somewhat specific to a local area. This particularly applies to some of the government loan options. Equally unlikely is that any counseling occurs to assist a borrower determine what the best loan option might be for a specific situation (i.e., length of time expected to occupy the home, lender paid loan fees, etc.).

Internet lenders have neither the inclination nor the methods in place to perform these important counseling functions for borrowers. They generally have a loan to sell and that is the sole purpose, whereas local lenders provide such service on an everyday basis.

There is no denying the anonymity and the ease of applying for a loan afforded by Internet lending sources. But one can't beat the service and personal attention acquired via a local lender.

BEHAVIOR ACCOMPANYING BEING YOUR BEST!

Providing super service or becoming the best in a profession are subjects written about and talked about endlessly but about which little is actually done. It can be likened to the diet that will one day be started. But, today's real estate environment is finally demanding that we recommit ourselves to becoming the best in our profession and mean it.

Just as important as understanding the nuts and bolts of real estate financing and of qualifying buyers/borrowers is recognizing the obligations that accompany our representation. Functioning from one's best self requires an examination of what some would call ethics. Ethics can't be taught or regulated. But how we behave and function with our customers/clients will ultimately affect our success and our ability to develop those critically important relationships based on trust.

Trust is that intangible upon which every relationship, personal or business, relies to guarantee its continuation. Without it, relationships fail. It requires a lot of effort to develop but can be undone in an instant. Trust means one functioning always from one's best self and always with high regard for the interests of the other person(s) in the relationship.

Take, for instance the 2009 congressional hearing with Wall Street CEOs wherein each of the company leaders claimed that they didn't see the financial problems coming, relied upon inaccurate computer models, and each indicated, "We pledge to do everything necessary to regain the trust of our investors and the American public." Who among us believed that they did not function out of greed and knew exactly what they were doing? They followed that testimony by providing excessive bonuses to Wall Street operators using the bailout funds provided by the American public. The incongruity and deceit in their statements didn't bode well for the development of future trust, and the ensuing years have demonstrated their inability to regain that public trust. To this day many view Wall Street with distain and distrust.

Perhaps we shouldn't have been surprised that many subscribe to what they deem to be situational ethics in which each act is considered unique and is judged on a case by case basis rather than on a more absolute moral standard related to right and wrong. Ethics are very personal and fluid. Such flexible guidelines can come in handy. We usually can recognize a breach of ethics if committed by someone else, but they may become more difficult to recognize when we, ourselves, step over the line—whatever the line is that we've drawn for ourselves.

So what does one do to become known not only as an expert in real estate but the person possessing the character with whom fellow licensees and the public wants to work? There are gurus willing to sell all kinds of plans from books to training events, which mostly result in giving away a lot of money for minimal, if any, results. That isn't to say that there isn't good reading material and some terrific teachers from whom we can all learn. But it doesn't require deep analysis to determine how to treat those with whom we do business and with whom we want to develop trust relationships.

Developing trust relationships and always functioning from one's best self is very personal. But here are a few thoughts as you determine how you intend to stand out as one of the best and most highly regarded in the industry.

Clients First Attitude: Buyers and sellers can easily spot when someone merely wants to make a sale. Seeming to be interested only in the commission to be earned suggests a desperateness that many clients will view with suspicion. Instead, always function from the position of doing what is best for the client. That doesn't mean that you can't differ in your opinion or that the client is always right. But it does mean that everything you say to a client and every action you take is motivated genuinely for the best interest of the client. People will "get it" and trust you and tell everyone about you.

Own Your Mistakes: We have all experienced situations where people have not wanted to take responsibility for their decisions and/ or mistakes. We all forget to dot an i or cross a t on occasion. Own up to your errors, the sooner the better. Once something starts to unravel, it seldom gets better. Don't blame others even when something may have been out of your control. Let your client know that something has glitched but "we are working hard to fix it." Your client doesn't care whose fault it was but just wants to know everything will work out.

Your Word Is Your Bond: People used to acknowledge agreements by handshake. Their word was their bond, and they didn't need a multiple page contract to make sure they met their obligations. Times have changed, and it would be foolish in these litigious times not to have agreements in writing, but persons need to be able to rely upon our word. If you say you'll do something, do it. No excuses! Remember that adage about service: "under promise and over deliver."

Don't be Afraid of Evaluation: Each person must find his or her own evaluation method. We grow and improve by constant evaluation of what we've done. Live by the adage that "I don't have to be bad to get better." Be open to criticism (as long as it isn't mean spirited) and adopt those suggestions that make sense.

Bottom line: Ethical behavior is pretty simple. Always behave in a way that will never cause you to be embarrassed by what you've done. Behave as if the customer were going to take out a full-page ad in the newspaper describing the experiences he or she has had with you. One person exclaimed that when he is faced with a decision, one that may cause him to step over a self-imposed ethical line, he asks himself, "When I go home today, do I want my wife and sons to know what I did?" If the answer is no, he shouldn't do it. Each person must find his or her own evaluation method, but if you are at ease at the end of each day with that, it is likely that you are doing pretty well, and that your trust relationships are in good shape.

Important Terms and Concepts

Amortization table	Financial calculator
Amortized loan	Straight note
Biweekly loan payment	Yield

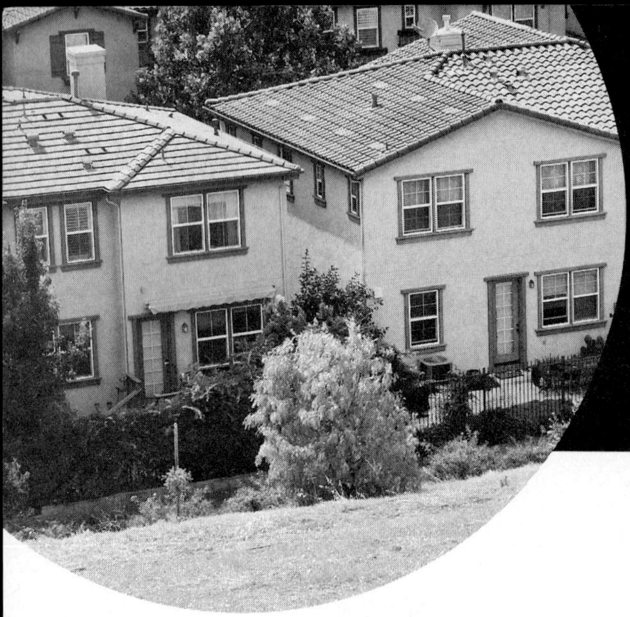

APPENDIX A

THE INTERNET INFLUENCE

Our reliance upon the Internet as a source of information continues to grow. We can check credit scores, search property values, apply for a home mortgage, calculate loan qualifying ratios, and find up-to-date information on nearly every subject, including home loan financing. However, there are some limitations to the Internet, and users are cautioned to remain skeptical of its credibility.

Acquiring a Loan Using the Internet

Just a few years ago, it was predicted that the Internet would revolutionize the financial arena. It was thought that one would be able to shop for the lowest interest rate and/or loan costs very quickly— saving money.

Internet lenders (deservedly) soon acquired the reputation that they only accommodate trouble-free transactions. Those borrowers who exhibit a need for credit counseling, or who may be short of cash, require a co-borrower, or need help with any number of other aspects of home loan financing often find themselves without assistance from Internet lenders. Recognizing the growing complexities of real estate financing, there may be compelling reasons for *not* securing a loan via the Internet.

With the disappearance of the subprime loans and the reduced use of adjustable rate financing, fixed rate financing is back in vogue. Fixed rate loans today are priced to meet the requirements of the investor who will ultimately purchase the loan from the originating lender. In most cases, that investor is either Fannie Mae (Federal National Mortgage Association) or Freddie Mac (Federal Home Loan Mortgage Corporation). All lenders (including those who function on the Internet) typically quote a daily rate related to these investors' requirements for purchase. Thus, during any specific period, a borrower should receive the same quote of rate and fees from every lender polled. If one lender is quoting a rate significantly better than all other lenders, a borrower should be suspicious: some lenders, even on the Internet, employ bait-and-switch quotes.

The lender must gather sufficient borrower documentation before providing any reliable rate quotes. Credit scores, the loan-to-value amount based on the down payment available, and the type of property being purchased or refinanced are all factored into any quoted interest rate. Quoted rates on the Internet and in most publications represent what may be available to the most qualified or preferred borrower. The rates seldom reflect rates that would be offered to the more challenged borrower.

It is also important for borrowers to become educated in regards to the loan process and procedures. Many borrowers require assistance in obtaining a loan, clearing negative credit items, developing a strategy for securing the necessary funds, or attaining a co-borrower. This kind of guidance is usually available through a local lender. Lenders on the Internet are basically unaccountable, whereas a local lender is more likely to feel that it must deliver on its promises, whether they involve quoted rates, costs, or a time period for closing the loan.

It would be unfair to suggest that a borrower cannot acquire a loan via the Internet. However, given that it is unlikely that the loan interest rate and costs acquired via the Internet will be any better than what can be acquired locally, most borrowers would be better served doing business with a lender whom they know. As the borrower is more likely to receive personal attention throughout the loan process, it may make sense for borrowers to function locally. This is the best way for a borrower to remain in charge of the process, knowing that it is proceeding in a timely fashion, and having the assurance that there will be no surprises at the last minute.

MORTGAGE CALCULATORS: ARE THEY RELIABLE?

Web-based mortgage calculators that allow borrowers to test various financial scenarios are now available. While they are entertaining to experiment with, borrowers need to be cautious about relying upon their results. Few mortgage calculators are accompanied by an explanation of what assumptions are used in their calculations. Most calculator programs identify the typical qualifying ratios that prospective borrowers should meet to be eligible for a loan.

There are numerous variables that must accompany any calculation. For instance, does the calculation to determine a borrower's home buying qualification include mortgage insurance, or property taxes and insurance calculation for an impound account when required? The more questions that the borrower is asked before clicking "calculate," the more reliable the outcome.

With the advent of automated qualifying systems accompanied by the continued reliance upon risk-based scoring (i.e., taking into consideration the borrower's credit score, the amount of down payment, the type of property, etc.), the normal qualifying ratios often do not apply. Add to this the varying private mortgage insurance (PMI) requirements and the continuing changes in conventional, FHA, and VA loan qualifications, and it is clear that there is no way for a programmed calculator to account for all the possible variables existing in today's qualification matrix.

Borrowers using a real estate Web calculator may mistakenly believe that they qualify for a real estate loan—or they may incorrectly believe that they do not qualify and miss their home ownership opportunity. The best that some calculators can do is to identify a worst-case scenario. While useful up to a point, the reliability of the results depends upon the calculator's internal assumptions and formulas coupled with the accuracy of the user-entered information. It is easy to see that reliable results are unlikely.

With few exceptions, potential buyers will be better served by a face-to-face consultation with a competent loan officer who can assess the best loan option for their particular situation and determine their ability to qualify for a loan.

Credit and the Internet

The Fair Isaac Credit Bureau scores (known as FICO scoring) were introduced to mortgage lending nearly two decades ago. To arrive at the score, a borrower's credit history is examined to determine the likelihood of timely future payments on a new mortgage. This analysis has proven remarkably accurate but does undergo periodic adjustments. The most recent change is the modification of how medical debt is evaluated, as it has been learned that it had a highly negative effect on borrower scores. The system not only assesses how probable a borrower is to pay back a loan, but also measures the degree of risk a borrower represents to the lender. Scores range from 300 to 900, the higher score indicating better credit quality.

Consumers can check their credit profiles using the Internet, and it seems logical that they would do so in preparation for home loan financing. Although many sites indicate that one can acquire a free credit report, this can be somewhat misleading. In addition to checking if the information contained in one's credit report is accurate, the credit score is important when acquiring a home loan. When visiting most Web sites, one is urged to upgrade the report, at a cost, in order to acquire the credit score. The "free" option is generally sufficient to provide a glimpse of the borrower's credit profile. Thirty-day free trials are popular, but usually unnecessary.

All three credit repositories (listed at the end of this Appendix) have Web sites through which borrowers can obtain good credit information and a score at a cost of $8.50–$14 per report. When applying for a home loan, the lender requires a report from all three repositories. Acquiring the reports individually costs more money, and the reports are not usable by an eventual lending source. Nevertheless, it may be useful for a borrower to get an idea of what his or her credit looks like by accessing one of the repositories. Equifax is recommended as the most user-friendly.

There is yet another possible complication in acquiring credit information over the Internet. Consumers may find it difficult to interpret the information. There are 33 variable criteria that influence a credit score. A borrower may get a clue as to what affects his or her score by reviewing the four most significant reasons given by the credit provider. These are generally the four most important factors affecting the score and perhaps keeping it from being higher. Lenders are trained in interpreting the credit report results and in recommending actions required to improve the scores. It usually costs $20–$35 for a three-merged report, depending upon whether it is for a single person or a married couple.

Using the Internet as a Tool

It is always tempting to acquire information from the Internet, but use caution. Many sources are mostly promotional rather than focused on consumer information. With rapid changes occurring in the financial arena, sites can be out-of-date and their information inaccurate.

With this in mind, we offer some sites (grouped by interest and/or specific information) that may prove helpful. In most cases, we have listed the sites alphabetically. Inclusion on the list should not be construed as a recommendation.

Government Sites (consumer information and specific loan data)
www.cdva.ca.gov (California VA loan information)
www.hud.gov (FHA loans)

www.fanniemae.com (conventional loans)
www.freddiemac.com (conventional loans)

Loan rates via the Internet (mostly promotional)
(See tip sheet section in Chapter 15 and Appendix regarding use of the Internet in acquiring a loan.)
www.ditech.com
www.eloan.com
www.lendingtree.com
www.quickenloans.com

Consumer Education (Many of these sites promote sales and or request subscriptions—use accordingly.)
www.aarp.org (senior information, especially reverse mortgages)
www.inman.com (well-known commentator's site)
www.hrblock.com (tax tips)
www.mbaa.org (Mortgage Bankers Association)
www.nolo.com (legal information)
www.responsiblelending.org (abusive lending alerts)

Credit Score Information (credit information and credit reports, usually for a fee)
www.equifax.com www.experian.com www.transunion.com

Free Credit Report Information (usually selling upgraded credit reports for credit scores—the free report is usually sufficient)
www.annualcreditreport.com
www.creditkarma.com www.credit.com
www.myfico.com
www.quizzle.com

Media Sites (financial news and articles)
www.bloomberg.com www.kiplinger.com www.thinkglink.com

Real Estate Calculators (see information in Appendix about Internet calculator sites)
www.aarp.org
www.kiplinger.com
www.mortgagecalc.com (one of the better sites)
www.mortgageprofessor.com
(After entering some of these sites, search for real estate calculators as some sites can be difficult to navigate.)

APPENDIX A

Home Valuation (relying upon Internet home valuations can be dangerous, as the information can be outdated)
www.homegain.com (the report ultimately comes from a realtor)
www.zillow.com

Finally, national bank sites (e.g., Bank of America, Chase, Wells Fargo) and real estate companies (e.g., Century 21, Coldwell Banker, RE/MAX) offer a plethora of information. Recognize that the information may be outdated and that the sites are often mostly promotional in their focus.

ANSWERS TO MULTIPLE-CHOICE QUESTIONS

Chapter 1

1. b
2. c
3. a
4. c
5. d
6. d
7. b
8. a
9. d
10. d
11. c
12. a
13. b
14. a
15. c
16. b
17. d
18. b
19. d
20. d

Chapter 2

1. a
2. d
3. a
4. c
5. d
6. d
7. d
8. c
9. c
10. c
11. a
12. c
13. b
14. b
15. c
16. a
17. d
18. a
19. d
20. d

Chapter 3

1. b
2. d
3. c
4. b
5. d
6. d
7. a
8. c
9. b
10. b
11. d
12. b

13. d
14. a
15. c

16. a
17. a
18. a

19. b
20. b

Chapter 4

1. d
2. d
3. a
4. b
5. c
6. c
7. d

8. c
9. b
10. d
11. c
12. d
13. c
14. b

15. a
16. a
17. c
18. d
19. b
20. a

Chapter 5

1. c
2. a
3. a
4. a
5. b
6. c
7. d

8. a
9. b
10. a
11. d
12. c
13. c
14. b

15. b
16. c
17. b
18. b
19. c
20. c

Chapter 6

1. a
2. d
3. c
4. b
5. d
6. c
7. b

8. d
9. b
10. b
11. a
12. c
13. d
14. d

15. a
16. a
17. b
18. b
19. b
20. d

Chapter 7

1.	b	8.	d	15.	d
2.	c	9.	a	16.	d
3.	b	10.	d	17.	b
4.	c	11.	b	18.	b
5.	b	12.	b	19.	b
6.	b	13.	d	20.	a
7.	b	14.	c		

Chapter 8

1.	b	8.	a	15.	c
2.	b	9.	a	16.	b
3.	a	10.	a	17.	c
4.	c	11.	a	18.	b
5.	d	12.	b	19.	a
6.	a	13.	d	20.	c
7.	d	14.	d		

Chapter 9

1.	d	8.	b	15.	b
2.	d	9.	a	16.	c
3.	b	10.	b	17.	a
4.	a	11.	c	18.	b
5.	d	12.	a	19.	c
6.	c	13.	b	20.	d
7.	d	14.	d		

Chapter 10

1.	c	4.	a	7.	b
2.	b	5.	b	8.	d
3.	d	6.	a	9.	c

10. b	14. d	18. a
11. b	15. d	19. d
12. b	16. d	20. c
13. c	17. b	

Chapter 11

1. d	8. d	15. b
2. d	9. a	16. d
3. b	10. b	17. c
4. a	11. d	18. c
5. b	12. b	19. a
6. c	13. b	20. d
7. d	14. a	

Chapter 12

1. c	8. a	15. a
2. a	9. d	16. a
3. b	10. c	17. d
4. b	11. d	18. b
5. c	12. d	19. c
6. b	13. b	20. d
7. c	14. d	

Chapter 13

1. d	8. d	15. d
2. b	9. b	16. b
3. c	10. c	17. d
4. a	11. b	18. d
5. b	12. d	19. a
6. a	13. d	20. b
7. a	14. c	

Chapter 14

1.	a	8.	d	15.	b
2.	a	9.	a	16.	b
3.	b	10.	d	17.	d
4.	c	11.	a	18.	a
5.	b	12.	b	19.	c
6.	b	13.	a	20.	c
7.	a	14.	c		

Chapter 15

1.	b	8.	c	15.	a
2.	a	9.	d	16.	a
3.	b	10.	a	17.	b
4.	d	11.	a	18.	a
5.	b	12.	b	19.	b
6.	c	13.	b	20.	c
7.	b	14.	a		

GLOSSARY

A

Ability/Capacity to Pay The position of a borrower relative to repaying a loan, based on income and other assets.

Ability to Repay A rule requiring the mortgage originator to make a good faith determination of the borrower's ability to qualify for and repay a mortgage loan.

Acceleration Clause Clause in trust deed or mortgage giving a lender the right to all sums owing to be immediately due and payable upon the happening of a certain event, such as a loan default.

Accrued Depreciation The difference between the cost of replacement of building new, as of the date of the appraisal, and the present appraised value. Depreciation that has accumulated over a period of time.

Adjustable Rate Mortgage (ARM) A loan pegged to an index; as the index goes up or down, the borrower's interest rate follows according to contractual limits, spelled out in the note and trust deed.

Adjusted Cost Basis The cost basis with additions (i.e.; improvements) and subtractions (i.e.; depreciation) which subsequently becomes the value ascribed to the newly acquired property and from which future gain or loss is calculated.

Adjusted Gross Income Gross income less federal and state income taxes and Social Security.

Adjustment Interval The time between changes in the interest rate or monthly payments for an ARM, typically six months to one year.

Adjustments As part of an appraisal, the subtractions from the replacement cost of a property to allow for any loss in value due to age, condition, and other factors; also the additions to and subtractions from the values of comparable properties.

Advances Money advanced by the beneficiary under a trust deed to pay real estate taxes or other items to protect the lender's interest under the trust deed. Also refers to additional funds loaned under an open-end trust deed or mortgage. Also, periodic payments to the builder as construction progresses.

Alienation Clause A special type of acceleration clause that gives the lender the right to demand payment of the entire loan balance upon a sale or transfer of title. Also known as a due-on-sale clause.

All-Inclusive Trust Deed (AITD) A deed of trust that includes the amount due under a senior trust deed or deeds on the same property. Also known as a wrap-around.

Amortization Tables A table that shows amounts needed to pay off different loan amounts at specified interest rates for specified terms.

Amortization Book A book with information for determining monthly payment amounts, loan yields, and other financial calculations now more readily acquired via the use of a financial calculator.

Amortized Loan A loan that is completely paid off, interest and principal, by a series of regular payments that are equal or nearly equal. Also called *level-payment loan.*

Annual Percentage Rate (APR) Under the Truth-in-Lending Law, the APR is used to disclose the total cost of a loan to a borrower and is converted to the so-called effective rate.

Annuity A series of equal or nearly equal payments to be made over a period of time. The installment payments due to a landlord under a lease or installment payments due to a lender are examples of annuities.

Antideficiency Legislation Legislation that prohibits a lender from obtaining a judgment for money against a defaulting borrower under a note and deed of trust when the value of property foreclosed upon is not adequate to satisfy the debt. See *Deficiency Judgment.*

Applicable Federal Rate The rate used for imputed interest in a seller-financed transaction, equal to the rate on federal securities with a similar term.

Appraisal An estimate or opinion of value.

Appraisal Management Company (AMC) An organization through which all conventional appraisals must now be ordered.

Assessment Lien A lien against property for public construction projects that benefit the property, such as street improvements or sewers.

Assignment of Deed of Trust An instrument that transfers the security interest under a deed of trust from one lender to another.

Assignment of Rents Clause A clause in a trust deed that gives the beneficiary the right under limited circumstances to collect rents of the property if the borrower defaults.

Assumption Fee A lender's charge for changing and processing records for a new owner who is assuming an existing loan.

Assumption of Deed of Trust or Mortgage Taking over responsibility and liability for the payment of the existing deed of trust loan from the seller.

Automatic Payment Plan A plan whereby the borrower authorizes deduction of monthly payments from a checking account rather than sending payments.

B

Back-End Ratio (Bottom Ratio) A ratio representing the sum of the borrower's mortgage payment and long-term debts, divided by gross income.

Balloon Payment One installment payment on an amortized note that is at least double the amount of a regular installment. This is frequently a final payment on the due date.

Basis or Cost Basis Typically refers to the purchase price of the property when acquired by the exchanger, plus the cost of improvements and less any depreciation taken. The cost basis will thereafter serve as a base figure in determining gain or loss and can be transferred to other property via the tax deferred exchange process.

Beneficiary A lender under a note secured by a deed of trust.

Biweekly Loan Payments Real estate loan payments made every two weeks. A monthly payment is divided by two and paid 26 times per year.

Blanket Trust Deed A single trust deed covering more than one parcel of real estate.

Blended-Rate Loan An interest rate that is less than market rate, but greater than the existing contract rate. Sometimes offered as an alternative to a new buyer who wishes to assume an existing loan and needs additional funds.

Boot The term used to describe unlike property received via the exchange. Cash, notes, personal property, reduction in mortgage (called debt relief) are all examples of "boot" and subject to tax.

Break-Even Analysis Calculation of the point where the income and expenses for a proposed project would be equal.

Bridge Loan A loan that bridges the gap between two other loans, usually for a short term. See *Swing Loan*.

Broker Participation A plan in which part of a seller's interest in a trust deed is assigned to the real estate broker to pay the commission on the sale, making the broker a partner with the seller on the loan.

Broker's Loan Statement A statement signed and received by the borrower at the time of a loan transaction, indicating the costs and deductions, including commissions, of a loan negotiated by a real estate licensee.

Builder's Control Service An outside third party that acts as an intermediary in the control and disbursement of funds to the builder in a building project.

Building Loan Agreement A document that contains the agreement between the lender, builder, and borrower concerning a construction project, including the schedule of disbursements to the builder.

Buy-Down Loan The purchase of a reduced interest rate, usually by home builders, allowing the borrower to qualify at a lower income level.

C

CalHFA Loans provided via the California Housing Finance Agency.

Cal-Vet Loans Loans made to eligible veterans by the Department of Veterans Affairs of the State of California for the purchase of real estate, utilizing a contract of sale.

Cap Upper limit on adjustable or variable interest rate loans on a periodic basis during life of loan.

Capital Gains Gains on the sale of property, as qualified by statute.

Capitalization In appraising, a method used to determine value of a property by dividing annual net operating income by a desirable capitalization rate.

Capitalization Rate The rate that is believed to represent the proper relationship between the value of the real property and the net operating income generated from the property.

Capitalized Income Stream Valuation approach to income-producing property measured by converting the income into a single present value.

Cash Equivalency Price in terms of cash versus other assets, such as trust deed, stocks, and bonds that may be worth less than their face amount.

Cash Flow The pattern of income and expenditures, which affects investment properties.

Certificate of Eligibility A certificate issued by the Department of Veterans Affairs that shows the amount of the veteran's entitlement.

Certificate of Reasonable Value (CRV) A document issued by the Department of Veterans Affairs that shows the appraised value of the property.

Certified Appraisal Report A written communication of an analysis, opinion, or conclusion relating to the value of real property certified according to state and federal requirements.

Closing Costs Costs paid by the borrower when borrowing for the purchase of a property. Costs paid by buyers and sellers on the sale of a property.

Cost of Funds Index (COFI) Adjustable-rate mortgage with rate that adjusts based on cost of funds index, after the 11th District Cost of Funds.

Collateralization The hypothecating of property, as security for a loan.

Collateralized Mortgage Obligation (CMO) A security issued by FNMA that is designed to limit the investor's risk that borrowers will prepay the loans early.

Combination Loan One loan combining a construction loan and permanent take-out loan after construction is completed.

Commercial Bank A financial institution chartered by a state or the federal government to receive, lend, and safeguard money and other items of value.

Commercial Loan Nonmortgage method of financing real estate through a personal loan from a commercial bank.

Commitment Agreement by a lender to lend mortgage money at a future date, subject to compliance with stated conditions.

Community Home Buyer's Program An FNMA/FHLMC program for purchasers with lower incomes that features 97 percent financing, with reduced closing costs and cash reserve requirements.

Community Reinvestment Act Federal law requiring financial institutions to lend in communities served, including low- and moderate-income areas, consistent with considerations of safety and soundness.

Co-Mortgagor A person who signs a note and deed of trust in addition to the primary borrower to give extra security to the loan. The co-mortgagor is jointly liable for the repayment of the loan, and is in title to the real estate.

Comparables Recently sold properties near the property being appraised and similar to it.

Comparative Market Analysis An opinion on a property's value prepared by a real estate licensee rather than a certified appraiser.

Compensating Factors Positive factors that are considered by lenders to approve loans to otherwise marginal borrowers.

Completion Bond A bond that the owners of a project can purchase to protect themselves, builders, and lenders from mechanic's liens.

Computerized Loan Originations (CLO) Accessing lender loan programs via computer.

Conditional Commitment The FHA appraisal, issued by an independent fee appraiser on the property, that includes any conditions such as repairs the FHA will require before insuring a loan.

Conditional Sale Contract A contract for the sale and purchase of property stating that delivery and possession is to be given to the buyer- vendee, but that legal title is to remain with the seller-vendor until the conditions of the con- tract have been fulfilled.

Condominium A form of ownership in which separate units of three-dimensional air-space are owned by individual owners. The individual owners also jointly own an undivided interest in the common areas such as hallways, swimming pools, and land. Sometimes referred to as a vertical subdivision.

Conduit Purchase of loans from mortgage bankers and commercial banks, then collateralizing them with mortgage-backed securities.

Conforming Loan Maximum loan amount purchased by FNMA and FHLMC.

Constant Debt Service payments as a percentage of the original loan amount.

Construction Loan Loan made for the construction of improvements. Usually funds are disbursed at periodic intervals as the work progresses.

Consumer Financial Protection Bureau Agency designated to oversee consumer financing activities and promote consumer awareness of financial endeavors. Created legislatively via the Dodd-Frank Wall Street Reform and Consumer Protection Act of 2010.

Contract of Sale See *Conditional Sale Contract*.

Conventional Loan Any loan that is not insured or guaranteed or made by a government agency.

Co-Op Similar to a long-term lease, but with right to sole and exclusive possession of the unit for an indefinite period.

Correspondent An abbreviated term meaning mortgage loan correspondent. Applies when a mortgage company originates a loan for an investor.

Co-Signer One who signs a note as guarantor but whose name is not on the title to the property.

Cost Approach A method in which the value of a property is derived by estimating the replacement cost of the improvements, then deducting the estimated depreciation, then adding the market value of the land.

Cost of Funds Costs incurred by lenders to obtain capital.

Creative Financing Any financing out of the ordinary, such as seller carrybacks wraparounds and sub prime loans.

Creative Financing Disclosure Act California law that requires disclosure of specified terms to the buyer-borrower in a seller carryback financing situation covering one to four dwelling units.

Credit History Summary of applicant's credit accounts that includes repayments, past due accounts, judgments and foreclosures.

Credit Life Insurance A form of declining term life insurance that will pay all or part of the mortgage if the borrower dies.

Credit Report Credit history of a person or business issued by a company in the credit reporting business, used to help determine creditworthiness.

Credit Scoring A method of evaluating an applicant's credit history for the purpose of determining the probability of repayment of debts. Also called *FICO score*.

Credit Union Cooperative organization of members of a particular group who agree to save money and make loans to its members.

D

Debenture Bonds issued without security, backed only by the credit standing and earning capacity of the issuer.

Debt Ceiling A legislative mechanism to limit the amount of national debt that can be issued by the Treasury by limiting how much money the government may borrow.

Debt Coverage Ratio (DCR) Net operating income divided by annual debt service. Used by lenders when analyzing income property loans.

Debt Service Another term for the principal and interest payments on a loan. Widely used for commercial and industrial properties.

Debt-to-Income Ratio Borrowers' monthly payment obligations as a percentage of their income.

Deed in Lieu of Foreclosure A voluntary conveyance to the lender from the defaulting borrower that avoids the foreclosure process.

Deed of Reconveyance Upon the repayment of a promissory note secured by a trust deed, trustee transfers legal title back to the trustor (borrower), thereby releasing the lien.

Deed of Trust Instrument by which title to real estate is transferred to a third-party trustee as security for repayment of a real estate loan. Used in California instead of a mortgage.

Default Failure to fulfill a duty or promise. Failure to make the payments on a real estate loan.

Deferred Interest See *Negative Amortization*.

Deficiency Judgment A judgment given when the security pledged for a loan does not satisfy the debt upon foreclosure. Certain conditions must be met.

Delinquency Failure to make timely payments on loans.

Demand Deposit Checking account or transaction deposit withdrawable upon demand, as opposed to time deposit.

Department of Veterans Affairs (DVA) Federal government agency that guarantees approved lenders against foreclosure loss on loans made to eligible veterans.

Deposit Receipt A form used to accept earnest money to bind an offer for the purchase of real property. When accepted by the seller, it creates a sale contract.

Depreciation A loss of value in real property brought about by age, physical deterioration, or functional or economic obsolescence. Broadly, a loss in value from any cause. Also called *write-off*.

Desire to Pay The predisposition of a borrower to repay a loan, suggested by prior credit history, size of down payment, and reason for buying.

Desktop Originator (FNMA) A program of the Federal National Mortgage Association that allows loan agents to take applications and prequalify borrowers immediately.

Development Loans Loans that finance the acquisition of land and the installation, prior to building, of utilities, sewage systems, roads, and so on. Sometimes called *land loan*.

Direct Private Lender Individual who invests directly in loans without going through an intermediary and expects to receive higher interest rate yields.

Disbursements Periodic payments as construction progresses.

Discount An amount deducted in advance from the loan before the borrower is given the money. Also referred to as Points. In secondary market sales, a discount is the difference between the sale price and the principal balance on the note. Contrast *Premium*.

Discount Rate The interest rate that the Federal Reserve Bank charges local member banks for funds they borrow.

Discount Tables Tables used by lenders and investors to show how much a given value is, called the discounted value, based upon various interest rates and terms of maturity.

Discrimination by Effect Lending practices that have a discriminatory effect against protected groups. Prohibited unless shown to be required to achieve a legitimate business purpose.

Disintermediation Relatively sudden outflow of funds from a financial intermediary when depositors can obtain higher returns elsewhere.

Doctrine of Relation Back The principle that if work on a project begins before the trust deed is recorded, all who furnish labor or materials thereafter may file mechanic's liens that have precedence over the trust deed.

Down Payment The difference between the sale price of the property and the loan amount.

Draw System An arrangement by which a builder receives periodic payments as construction proceeds.

Due-on-Sale Clause Clause in a trust deed that allows lenders to demand immediate payment of the loan balance if borrower sells or transfers an interest in the property.

DVA Department of Veterans Affairs, a federal agency (not Cal-Vet). Formerly VA.

DVA Automatics Approvals of DVA loans by certain lenders qualified to use in-house underwriters.

DVA-Guaranteed Loan A loan for veterans under which the Department of Veterans Affairs guarantees to reimburse the lender a specified maximum amount in case of foreclosure.

E

Earnest Money Money paid with an offer to purchase, given to bind a sale.

Easy Money Loose money policy of the Federal Reserve Board, indicating increased availability of money in circulation.

Economic Life The period during which an improvement on a parcel of land can be used for any beneficial purpose.

Economic Obsolescence A loss in property value caused by forces outside the property, such as adverse zoning or neighborhood nuisances.

Effective Age The age assigned to the improvements by the appraiser, not necessarily the chronological age.

Effective Interest Rate The percentage of interest actually being paid by the borrower for the use of the money, including certain expenses for obtaining the loan. See *Annual Percentage Rate (APR)*.

Endowment Funds The invested funds that are received as gifts by institutions such as colleges and charities.

Entitlement The maximum amount that the DVA will pay if the lender suffers a loss on a DVA loan.

Equal Credit Opportunity Act (ECOA) Federal law prohibiting discrimination in the extension of credit.

Equifax One of three major credit reporting repositories, along with Experian and TransUnion.

Equity The interest or value that an owner has in real estate over and above liens against the property. The difference between market value and the existing indebtedness.

Equity Financing Lender finances high-ratio loan in exchange for a percentage of ownership and the right to share in the property's cash flow.

Equity Participation When a lender receives partial ownership interest in the project in order to increase its return on the loan.

Escalation Clause Refers to rent increases or decreases tied to an appropriate index.

Escrow A neutral depository, where a third party carries out instructions for the lender, buyer, and seller and is responsible for handling the paperwork and disbursing funds needed to transfer the property.

Escrow Account See *Impound Account*.

Experian One of three major credit reporting repositories, along with Equifax and TransUnion.

Extended Term Recasting of a loan by extending the remaining term, thereby lowering monthly payments.

F

Fair Credit Reporting Act Federal law that gives a rejected borrower the right to inspect and correct his or her credit agency file.

Fair Market Value (FMV) The price in terms of money that a parcel of property will bring on the open market when neither buyer nor seller is under any compulsion to act.

Federal Deposit Insurance Corporation (FDIC) Insures accounts at member banks up to $250,000.

Federal Fair & Accurate Credit Transaction Act (FACT) A seven-provision act wherein the two most important provisions are the establishment of procedures to help protect against identity fraud and allowing consumers to request a free credit report every 12 months from each of the three major credit repositories.

Federal Funds Rate The rate one bank charges another bank for overnight use of excess reserves.

Federal Home Loan Bank (FHLB) Provides credit reserves systems for member state and federal savings banks.

Federal Home Loan Mortgage Corporation (FHLMC) An agency known as Freddie Mac, which provides a secondary market for savings banks and other institutions.

Federal Housing Administration (FHA) Division of the U.S. Department of Housing and Urban Development that insures residential mortgage loans made by approved lenders against loss through foreclosure.

Federal Housing Finance Board (FHFB) Federal agency that regulates the 12 Federal Home Loan Banks.

Federal National Mortgage Association (FNMA) Popularly known as Fannie Mae, a private corporation whose primary function is to buy and sell mortgages in the secondary mortgage market.

Federal Reserve Bank Board (FRBB) An agency that oversees the Federal Reserve System, regulates commercial banks, and regulates the flow of money and credit.

Federal Reserve System Central banking system of the United States consisting of 12 Federal Reserve districts and the Federal Reserve Board, which sets monetary policy.

FHA Direct Endorsement An automatic approval system that allows FHA loan approvals by an in-house underwriter.

FHA-Insured Loan A loan made by a bank or mortgage company with insurance from the FHA against loss to the lender in the event the loan must be foreclosed.

FHA 203(b) Program The basic loan insured by the FHA for financing one- to four-unit dwellings.

FICO Score See *Credit Scoring*.

Finance Charge Charges paid separately or withheld from the proceeds of the loan, such as loan origination fees or mortgage insurance premiums.

Finance Company A firm involved in lending usually to high-risk borrowers at high interest rates.

Financial Calculator An electronic calculator that is designed to compute loan payments, interest rates, and other calculations used in real estate financing.

Financial Institutions Reform, Recovery, and Enforcement Act (FIRREA) Federal law that restructured deposit insurance funds and regulatory system for thrifts.

Financial Intermediary A depository that pools funds of clients and depositors and invests them into real estate loans.

Finder's Fee A fee paid by a lender or broker for referring a borrower to a certain lending institution or real estate office, often paid to a nonlicensee.

First Deed of Trust or Mortgage The first recorded loan; it takes precedence over junior loans and encumbrances. Also called *senior lien* or *primary lien*.

Fiscal Policy Programs by the federal government that are intended to influence economic activity by making changes in government expenditures and taxation, implemented by the U.S. Treasury.

Five-Step Financing Process The process of borrowing money that includes making application, qualifying the borrower and property, processing documents, closing, and servicing the loan.

Fixed Rate Loans Loans with constant fixed rates that will not change over the life of the loan.

Flipping A real estate investment strategy in which property is purchased with the intent to resell quickly for a profit generated usually via minimal renovations during a very active or hot market. Sometimes considered a predatory practice.

Floor Loan A minimum amount that a permanent lender will provide for construction until the developer can secure all the planned tenants for the project.

Forbearance An arrangement that delays foreclosure action by restructuring and/or temporary postponement of monthly payments.

Foreclosure Process whereby property pledged as security for a real estate loan is sold to satisfy the debt if the borrower defaults.

Fractional Reserve Banking Money "created" by the banking system through monetary policy.

Front Money The money required to get a real estate project started.

Front-End Ratio (Top Ratio) A ratio representing the borrower's mortgage payment divided by gross income.

Functional Obsolescence Poor structural design or unusual floor plans that could affect marketability and value of a property.

G

Gap Commitment A lender's commitment to provide the difference between the floor amount that a developer will receive for a project and the full amount to be received when all rentals are achieved.

GI Loans Common term for loans guaranteed by the Department of Veterans Affairs for qualified veterans. Also known as DVA loans.

Gift Deed Deed for which no consideration is given except love and affection.

Gift Letter Verification that a gift to a borrower for a down payment is not an undisclosed a loan.

Government Mortgage Insurance Government programs that eliminate risk of loss to lenders from default on loans, thereby making the loans more attractive.

Government National Mortgage Association (GNMA) A federal corporation popularly known as Ginnie Mae. It is mainly involved in the administration of the mortgage-backed securities program and other federal programs.

Government-Backed Loans Loans obtained with the help of government agencies such as FHA, Department of Veterans Affairs, Cal-Vet, or other programs.

Government-Sponsored Enterprise (GSE) Collective title for the secondary market entities consisting of the FNMA, FHLMC, GNMA.

Graduated-Payment Mortgage (GPM) Fixed interest rate loan on which the scheduled monthly payments start low, but rise later, then level off. Produces negative amortization.

Gross Income Total stable income before deductions.

Gross Operating Income (GOI) Gross scheduled income less a reasonable vacancy factor and rent collection losses.

Gross Rent Multiplier (GRM) A rule of thumb method of appraising income property that provides a "ballpark" figure only. It is an appropriate factor, usually determined by an appraiser, which, when multiplied by monthly or annual rents, estimates property value.

Gross Scheduled Income Total income from property before deducting any expenses.

Growth Equity Mortgage (GEM) Loan with fixed interest rate and scheduled annual increases in monthly payments, resulting in shorter maturity.

H

Hard Costs Costs for which the builder must pay out money.

Hard Money Loan Loan usually from a private lender. Actual money loaned and secured by a deed of trust as opposed to a loan carried back by a seller, in which no money passes.

Hazard Insurance Covers dwelling and contents for fire, wind, and water damage, theft, and other specified losses.

Holdback Final percentage of construction loan amount released after the filing period for mechanic's liens has expired.

Housing Economic Recovery Act Legislation whereby banks were encouraged to voluntarily assist struggling homeowners via established guidelines for modifying home loans. The Act also led to the establishment of minimum standards for all residential mortgage brokers and lenders, leading to the initiation of new disclosure rules.

Home Valuation Code of Conduct (HVCC) Legislation that established regulations to ensure the quality and independence of the appraisal process by protecting the appraiser from coercive interference from lenders or real estate licensees.

Home Warranty A protection policy to repair and/or replace major home components should such occur after the close of escrow.

HUD An abbreviation for the U.S. Department of Housing and Urban Development.

Hypothecate To give a thing as security without the necessity of giving up possession; for example, when real estate is used as security for a loan.

I

Impound Account Funds retained in a special account by a lender to cover property taxes and hazard insurance. Also called *escrow account* or *loan trust fund*.

Improvement Bond Act of 1915 California law that provides for issuance of bonds for subdivision street improvements, to be paid from proportional assessments against affected property owners.

Imputed Interest A minimum interest rate that is applied to all seller-financed transactions to prevent sellers from treating interest income as capital gains in order to pay less in federal tax.

Income Approach One of three methods in the appraisal process, which analyzes income and expenses, then uses a capitalization rate to arrive at value.

Income Ratio The monthly payment on a loan (including principal and interest, taxes, and insurance) divided by the borrower's monthly gross income.

Indirect Lender Individual who invests in loans through a mortgage broker in order to benefit from the broker's expertise.

Inflation Sharp increase in prices for goods and services resulting from too much money in circulation and/or rising costs of materials and labor.

Installment Note A loan providing for payment of the principal in two or more installments.

Installment Sales Contract A sale in which legal title to the property remains with the seller until terms agreed upon have been satisfied.

Institutional Lender A savings bank, commercial bank, or insurance company that deals in real estate loans.

Interest Change Clause Provision in an adjustable rate mortgage that the interest rate can change at specified intervals according to changes in a specified index.

Interest Rate The charge made for a loan of money expressed as a percentage of the principal.

Interest-Only Note A straight nonamortizing loan, in which only interest is paid. Interest can be paid periodically or at maturity, when principal is paid in a lump sum. Also called *straight note*.

Interim Loan Any short-term financing, such as a Swing Loan, or a loan used to finance construction, due at the completion of the construction, which is usually paid off with the proceeds of a Take-Out Loan.

Intermediate-Term Loans Temporary short-term loans—ordinarily 3 to 10 years—that include home improvement loans, consumer loans, or loans for the purpose of permitting a developer to delay longer-term financing until more favorable loan terms become available.

Intermediation When a financial institution acts as go-between for saver-depositors and borrowers.

J

Joint Note A note signed by two or more persons who have equal liability for payment. Usually expressed as "joint and several," which includes individual liability.

Judicial Sale A sale of property by court proceedings to satisfy a lien.

Jumbo Loan Loan exceeding the maximum amount purchased by FNMA and FHLMC. Also called *nonconforming loan.*

Junior Mortgage A subordinate or inferior lien.

L

Land Contract of Sale See *Conditional Sale Contract.*

Late Charge An additional charge a borrower is required to pay as a penalty for failure to pay a regular installment when due, after the grace period expires.

Lease A contract between an owner and tenant, setting forth conditions upon which a tenant may occupy and use the property.

Letter of Credit Letter from a bank asking that the holder be allowed to withdraw money from the recipient bank or agency that will be charged back to the first bank.

Leverage The relationship between an owner's equity and total debt on a property. The higher the leverage, the higher the debt in relation to the value of the property.

Lien A form of encumbrance that makes the property security for the payment of a debt. Examples include deeds of trust, mortgages, judgments, and mechanic's liens.

Life Insurance Company A business that collects a person's savings by selling contracts (policies) paid for through periodic premiums and providing cash payment upon death.

Lifetime Cap Ceiling for rate increases over the life of an ARM, expressed either as a particular percentage rate or as so many points over or under the initial rate.

Like-Kind A phrase used to identify an appropriate property for an exchange in a 1031 Tax Deferred Exchange transaction.

Like Kind Property Refers to the nature or character of the property. Another way to describe eligible exchange property is the words "real for real" ... meaning that real property must be exchanged for other real property and cannot be exchanged for personal property. Under this definition, a rental home can be exchanged for another rental home, multiple units, apartment complex, commercial property or unimproved property (land).

Liquidity of Investment The ease with which investments can be readily converted into cash.

Loan Application The written form submitted by the borrower, usually the standard form of FNMA/FHLMC.

Loan Assumption The lender's approval of a new borrower who takes over an existing loan.

Loan Closing When all conditions of the loan have been met, the lender authorizes the recording of documents.

Loan Commitment Agreement by a lender to make a loan subject to certain conditions being met, covering a specific period of time.

Loan Committee A committee or one individual in a lending institution that reviews loan packages and either approves or disapproves.

Loan Correspondent See *Correspondent.*

Loan Origination Steps involved in the loan application process prior to close of escrow.

Loan Origination Fee A charge, usually measured by points, made by a lender for originating the loan. Included in nonrecurring closing costs.

Loan Package Documentation consisting of all the forms, documents, and reports the lender needs in order to make a decision on the loan.

Loan Underwriting The process of approving or disapproving loan applications.

Loan-to-Value Ratio The amount of loan, ex-pressed as a percentage of a property's value or sales price, whichever is lower.

Lock-in Clause A provision that prohibits paying off a loan before a specified date.

Lock-in Loan Lender's written guarantee that the rate quoted will be available for a specific period of time.

Long-Term Debt How long a term outstanding debt is to last, the precise term varying by lenders and agencies.

Lot Release Provision The release of an individual lot from the blanket trust deed covering a subdivision. Provides for a deed of partial reconveyance.

Low Down Payment Conventional Loans Loans offered through programs of FNMA and FHLMC that relax the usual down payment requirements for purchasers with lower incomes and excellent credit.

Lump Sum Payment of the entire principal amount due at maturity on a straight note.

M

Market Data Approach An appraisal method in which the value of a property is estimated by means of comparing it with similar properties recently sold.

Market Price Amount paid for property, regardless of motives, knowledge, and so on.

Market Value See *Fair Market Value*.

Maturity Date The date upon which a real estate note or other negotiable instrument becomes due and payable.

Mechanic's Lien A claim against the property by contractors, laborers, or material suppliers who have not been paid for their contributions to a building project. A summary right.

Mello-Roos Community Facilities Act California law that authorizes setting up a taxing district that can issue bonds, initially to build new schools but now often used to pay for a housing development's improvements, such as roads, sewers, and community center.

MIS Mortgage Information System.

Monetary Policy Policies of the Federal Reserve System that increase or decrease the supply of money in an effort to achieve designated economic goals.

Monthly Payments These always include principal and interest, and may also, depending upon lender or loan, include taxes and insurance.

Moratorium A temporary waiver or suspension of payments on a loan.

Mortgage A two-party instrument in which the borrower-mortgagor retains legal title during loan term while the real estate serves as collateral for the loan.

Mortgage Banker The packaging of real estate loans to be sold to a permanent investor often with servicing retained for a fee. Mortgage bankers act as correspondents for investors.

Mortgage Brokers Differ from mortgage bankers in that they invest no capital: their prime function is to bring together borrowers and lenders, for which they are paid a fee.

Mortgage Company A firm that may represent other investors in arranging and servicing real estate loans. May also invest its own funds.

Mortgage Correspondent See *Correspondent*.

Mortgage Loan Disclosure Statement A legally required written statement to the borrower concerning estimated costs of a loan and the net amount to be received.

Mortgage Revenue Bonds Tax exempt bonds issued by units of government to finance mortgages at rates below market rate.

Mortgage-Backed Securities Investment securities similar to bonds, representing an interest in a pool of mortgages.

Mutual Savings Bank A savings bank originated in the New England states in which the depositors place their savings with the right to borrow money for home loans. There are no mutual savings banks in California.

N

Negative Amortized Loans Loans in which the required payment relative to the interest rate charged is insufficient to pay all of the interest due each month, resulting in negative amortization.

Negative Cash Flow The situation where income from investment property is less than outgo, so that money must be added to make the venture solvent.

Negotiable Instrument A promissory note or other instrument that meets certain legal requirements, allowing it to circulate freely in commerce.

Neighborhood A group of properties relatively similar in land use and value. It can be large or as small as a single block or street.

Net Operating Income (NOI) Gross annual income less vacancies, uncollectible rents, and other operating expenses.

Net Spendable Income Net operating income less debt service and income taxes on the property's taxable income.

Nominal Interest Rate The interest rate that appears on the real estate promissory note. Also called *note rate*.

Nonconforming Loan See *Jumbo Loan*.

Noninstitutional Lender Lenders on real estate loans other than commercial banks, insurance companies, and savings banks.

Nonrecurring Closing Costs Costs that are one-time charges paid at the close of escrow.

Nonsupervised Lender Mortgage company that must be approved in advance by DVA to make automatic approvals of borrowers.

Note A signed instrument acknowledging a debt and a promise to repay per the terms outlined.

Notice of Abandonment A notice filed in case a construction project is abandoned before completion.

Notice of Cessation of Labor A notice filed in case construction is not completed due to various reasons.

Notice of Completion A notice filed by the owner of a new construction project within 10 days after the job is completed, starting a period during which liens may be filed by conractors and other parties.

Notice of Default Recorded notice that a default has occurred under a deed of trust and that the beneficiary intends to proceed with a trustee's sale.

Notice of Sale Notice that property in default will be sold to pay off the loan. It must be advertised in a newspaper and posted at the property and in a public place.

NOW Accounts Stands for Negotiable Order of Withdrawal, a checking account permitted for savings banks.

O

Obligatory Advances Disbursements of money that the lender is required to make under the terms of a construction loan.

Office of Thrift Supervision (OTS) A branch of the U.S. Treasury that regulates all federally insured savings banks.

Office Park Planned development for office buildings and related services.

Online Loan Refers to ability to apply for a real estate loan through the Internet.

Open-End Deed of Trust A deed of trust containing a clause that permits the borrower to obtain additional advances of money secured by the same deed of trust, if the lender permits, but not necessarily under the same terms.

Open-Market Operations Federal Reserve actions to influence the money supply by selling or buying government securities.

Operating Costs The owner's expenses in operating investment property, such as utilities, repairs, and replacement of furnishings.

"Or More" Clause A clause in a note that permits extra payments on principal of the loan without penalty.

Origination Fee A charge for arranging and processing a real estate loan. See *Loan Origination Fee.*

P

Package Loan Loan secured by both real and personal property, often appliances and other fixtures.

Paper Term used by real estate agents, investors, and others to designate promissory notes, usually secured by deeds of trust.

Par The face amount of a loan with no premium or discount.

Partial Amortization A repayment schedule that does not pay back enough principal to completely pay off a loan by the due date, leaving a balloon payment.

Partial Entitlement The amount of additional entitlement allowed to a veteran who had previously used an entitlement when maximum amounts were lower.

Partial Reconveyance Deed A deed used to reconvey a portion of the land encumbered by a deed of trust.

Partial Release Clause A clause in a deed of trust that provides for release of part of the property from the deed of trust upon payment of a specific portion of the debt.

Participation When a lending institution sells a part interest in a block of loans to another institution or agency. Also, when a lender receives part of the income from a property to increase its return on the loan. Also see *Equity Participation.*

Pass-Through Securities Securities backed by a pool of FHA and DVA mortgages, issued by the Government National Mortgage Association.

Passive Loss Rules that apply to rental properties, especially houses, which allow investors to take a tax deduction for losses against certain other taxable income, such as wages, salary, interest, dividends, etc.

Payout Schedule The predetermined system of releasing money to the builder as construction progresses.

Pension Funds Public and private retirement savings funds held in trust, which can be invested in real estate loans, stocks, or government securities.

Percentage Lease A commercial lease in which the owner gets a percentage of the tenant's gross receipts.

Performance Bond A bond furnished to guarantee that a builder will perform in accordance with the contract terms and that the property at completion will be free of mechanic's liens.

Permanent Financing See *Take-Out Loan.*

Physical Depreciation Deterioration of property caused by wear and structural problems.

PITI An abbreviation for principal, interest, taxes, and insurance, commonly used when referring to the monthly loan obligation.

Planned Unit Development (PUD) A land-use design that combines private fee ownership of a parcel and joint undivided ownership of common facilities such as grounds, parking, and recreational facilities.

Plans and Specifications Architectural and engineering drawings and specifications for construction of a building, including description of materials and manner in which they are to be applied.

Points Amount paid by the borrower or the seller, which increases the effective yield for a lender. Each point equals 1 percent of the loan.

Portfolio Loan Any loan retained by the lender, as contrasted with selling it in the secondary market.

Positive Cash Flow The situation where income from investment property is greater than outgo, so that a profit is made.

Predatory Lending Term applying to all acts construed as having taken advantage of a borrower's naiveté related to the charging of excessive fees or interest rate.

Premium An amount, usually measured in points, in excess of the loan balance owing, paid for the purchase of a note and deed of trust.

Prepaid Finance Charge Charges paid separately or withheld from the proceeds of the loan, such as loan origination fees or mortgage insurance premiums.

Prepaid Items Expenses paid by buyer-borrower at closing, such as taxes, insurance, and interest. See *Recurring Closing Costs*.

Prepayment Penalty A charge for the payment of a mortgage or deed of trust note before maturity.

Prepayment Privilege Allows borrowers to make certain extra payments on the principal balance without penalty.

Price The amount for which a lender will sell a loan to an investor, equal to the face value of the loan minus the discount or plus a premium.

Primary Mortgage Market The market in which loans are made directly to the borrowers.

Prime Rate Interest rate individual banks charge their most creditworthy preferred corporate customers.

Principal The face amount on a real estate loan, the amount upon which interest is calculated.

Private Lender Individual who invests his/her own funds into real estate loans, directly or through mortgage brokers.

Private Mortgage Insurance (PMI) Insurance written by a private company, protecting the mortgage lender against specified loss in case of foreclosure.

Processing Preparation of loan application and supporting documents for consideration by a lender or insurer; all procedures up to close of escrow.

Progress Payments Periodic payments to the builders as construction proceeds.

Promissory Note See *Note*.

Purchase Money Deed of Trust A trust deed securing a note given as part or all of the purchase price. Examples: carryback by a seller or a new loan from a lender.

Purchase Money Mortgages The term applied to loans, particularly those carried by sellers, in assisting in a purchase transaction.

Q

Qualified Mortgage A loan that limits mortgage originators' compensation, establishes maximum qualifying ratios, and clearly identifies the fees and costs allowing for greater understanding by the consumer.

Qualified Mortgage Bond Program Use of low interest rate revenue bonds for targeted first-time home buyers under the Cal-Vet program.

Qualifying Ratio A lender's policy on how much income a borrower should have in order to make the payments of principal, interest, taxes, and insurance on the desired loan; for example, payments not exceeding 28 percent of gross income.

Quitclaim Deed A simple conveyance of rights in property without warranty.

R

Rate Lock See *Lock-In Loan*.

Real Estate Investment Trust (REIT) A corporation, trust, or association in which investors pool funds for investments in real estate but avoid double taxation as a corporation.

Real Estate Settlement Procedures Act (RESPA) A federal law that requires lenders to provide borrowers with certain information on settlement (closing) costs.

Real Property Land and buildings as opposed to personal property.

Real Property (Mortgage) Loan Law A California statute that governs real estate loan brokers, limiting commissions, requiring disclosure to the borrower, and regulating balloon payments and insurance requirements.

Recasting A change in loan terms to assist the borrower, such as by extending the term or reducing the interest rate.

Reconveyance See *Deed of Reconveyance*.

Recurring Closing Costs Repeating expenses paid by the borrower at close of escrow, such as tax reserves, hazard insurance, and prepaid interest. See *Prepaid Items*.

Redlining The illegal practice of refusing to lend mortgage money in certain areas without regard to the creditworthiness of the individual borrower.

Refinance To renew or replace the existing loan with additional financing, or to secure a loan on a free and clear property already owned by the borrower.

Regulation Z See *Truth-in-Lending Law/Regulation Z*.

Reinstate To cure a default under a note secured by a deed of trust.

Reintermediation Return of savings to thrift institutions from previously higher-paying investment outlets.

Release of Liability An agreement by the lender to terminate the personal obligation of the borrower.

Release of Mechanic's Lien The lifting of a mechanic's lien, usually by written release, issuance of a bond, or satisfaction of a judgment.

Relinquished Property The property that is being given up by the exchanger, sometimes referred to as the "down-leg" property.

Rent Control Local laws that limit the amount of increase in residential rents.

Rental Achievement Clause The provision in a loan agreement that the developer will secure tenants in advance for a new commercial or industrial project.

Replacement Cost Amount required to replace improvements of comparable quality, at today's prices. An appraiser's estimate of amount needed to rebuild an existing property at today's prices using cost approach.

Replacement Property The property acquired by the exchanger in an exchange, sometimes referred to as the "up-leg" property.

Request for Notice of Default and Notice of Sale A recorded notice made by anyone requesting that he or she be notified in the event that foreclosure proceedings are instituted or that time and place for the sale has been set.

Reserve Requirement The amount of reserve funds that banks and thrift institutions must set aside in order to protect depositors; it may be raised or lowered by the Federal Reserve.

Residual Income DVA's calculation resulting from the deduction of taxes, housing payment, and fixed expenses, such as child support and long-term debts from gross income. Also used by Cal-Vet.

Reverse Annuity Mortgage Stream of monthly payments provided to senior homeowners through an annuity purchased by a loan against the owners' accumulated equity in their home.

Right of Reinstatement The trustor's right to reinstate a loan by paying all delinquent payments, late charges, and foreclosure fees. Starts with recording of notice of default and lasts up to five business days before scheduled sale.

Risk Rating A process used by lenders to determine the soundness of offering a loan.

Rollover Loan that may extend beyond certain intermediate maturities.

S

Sale-Leaseback Land and/or buildings may be sold at 100 percent of value and then leased back by the seller. This is an alternative form of financing.

Sales Comparison Approach See *Market Data Approach to Value.*

Savings and Loan Association Deposit-type savings institution that lends in the residential field. The name/title has been virtually replaced by "Savings Bank."

Savings Association Insurance Fund (SAIF) Administered by the FDIC to insure deposits at savings banks and federal savings banks.

Savings Bank Savings and loan association using newly permitted designations.

Secondary Financing A loan secured by a junior trust deed.

Secondary Mortgage Market The purchasing and selling of existing notes secured by deeds of trust which promotes a constant flow of funds allowing lenders to continue to provide new loans to ready borrowers.

Securitization Debt issuance backed by mortgage portfolios or other types of assets.

Seller Carryback The seller's agreement to take payments on a note secured by a trust deed to help the buyer finance all or a portion of the purchase price.

Servicing Supervising and administering a loan after it has been made. This involves such things as collecting payments, keeping records, property inspections, and foreclosing on defaulted loans, and any process after close of escrow.

Short Sale Lender agreement to compromise a debt when the value of the security property is less than the debt owed.

Short-Term Construction Loan An interim loan that covers the construction of a building and can be paid off by a take-out loan.

Sight Deposit See *Demand Deposit.*

Soft Costs Costs of a builder for such noncash items as profit, overhead, and supervision.

Split Junior Loan (or Lien) Seller financing divided into second and third trust deeds, which may be easier to resell than one larger second lien.

Stability of Income The stability of the borrower's income, based on such things as length of time on the job and type of job.

Standardization Refers to the use of the same borrower and property standards accompanied by the same forms for loans acquired by investors in the secondary mortgage market.

Standby Commitment A contract—usually between FNMA/ FHLMC and a lender—to buy a pool of loans in the future from a lender at a specified yield.

Stock Equity Pledge of stock as collateral for the purchase of real estate, usually nonresidential.

Straight Note See *Interest-Only Note.*

Street Improvement Act of 1911 California law that allows assessments for street improvements to be paid off during the term of the bonds that are issued for them.

"Subject To" The taking of real property "subject to" an existing loan is done without being personally liable to the existing lender. This is in contrast to assuming a loan, when the buyer assumes responsibility and liability for the loan.

Subordination Clause An agreement under which a senior trust deed is made subordinate to an otherwise junior lien. Often used when a land loan subordinates to a new construction loan.

Subrogation Assignment of rights.

Substantial Completion The point from which a period for filing liens on a completed construction project is counted if a proper Notice of Completion is filed or not filed.

Supervised Lender Institution such as a commercial bank or savings bank that is supervised by an agency of the state or federal government and can approve DVA borrowers automatically, if qualified.

Swing Loan Used to assist in purchase of replacement house before sale of original house is completed. See *Bridge Loan*.

Syndication Investors pooling their resources to purchase real estate, usually through a limited partnership.

T

Take-Out Commitment The terms involved when lenders agree to lend on a specified property to a specified borrower for a certain length of time at a certain interest rate.

Take-Out Loan A permanent loan that pays off the existing construction loan.

Tax Service A one-time fee paid to a tax service agency that each year reviews the records of taxing bodies and reports any delinquencies to the lender and borrower. The fee is usually paid by the borrower.

Tax Shelter A strategy for investment that should result in reduced tax liability.

Tax-Deferred Exchange A method of deferring capital gains taxes by exchanging one or more properties for other like property.

Terms Refers to all conditions involved in a loan. The word term often also refers to the number of years over which the loan is repaid.

Thrift Institution Savings bank and other institutions that invest principally in real estate trust deeds.

Tight Money A situation in which the demand for money exceeds the supply, causing interest rates to increase and borrower qualifications to be tightened.

Time Deposit Savings account with a fixed maturity, as opposed to demand deposit.

Title Insurance Insurance written by a legal title insurance company to protect property owners and lenders against loss due to certain title defects.

Total Monthly Expense In qualifying for a loan, this is the addition of mortgage payments plus nonmortgage long-term debts. Used by FHA, DVA, Cal-Vet, USDA and Conventional lenders.

Townhouse A residential unit connected to other similar units. Often a two-story structure. A style of architecture.

Trade Association Group that promotes the interests of the firms in their memberships and provide them with research and information.

Transaction Accounts Accounts used to make payments or transfers to others, such as checking accounts.

TransUnion One of three major credit reporting repositories, along with Equifax and Experian.

Triple Net Lease A lease arrangement in which the lessee pays for all repairs, maintenance, taxes, and operating expenses.

Trust Deed Deed from a borrower to a trustee who holds title for security purposes until loan terms are satisfied. See a *Deed of Trust*.

Trustee An entity or person who holds the title to property for the benefit of another.

Trustee's Deed A deed given to the successful bidder at a trustee's sale (foreclosure).

Trustee's Sale Sale of property in foreclosure by the trustee, rather than through a judicial sale.

Trustor A borrower under a trust deed, who deeds property to trustee as security for the repayment of the debt.

Truth-in-Lending Law (Regulation Z) A federal law designed to show a borrower the total cost of a loan. The annual percentage rate (APR) is the term used to disclose the effective rate of interest.

U

Underwriting Evaluation by lenders of loan applicant's ability to repay a real estate loan.

Unrestricted Funds A Cal-Vet program for qualified veterans with wartime service.

Unsecured A loan that is not secured by a deed of trust, mortgage, or other property.

U.S. Treasury Cabinet-level agency that manages the federal government's spending and taxing policy.

Usury The charging of interest in excess of that permitted by law.

Usury Law The legislation that identifies what represents an unlawful rate of interest. In California, the greater of 10 percent or 5 percent over the Federal Reserve Board's discount rate at any given time; however, regulated lenders, such as banks, savings banks, and life insurance companies, are exempt from the usury law. Also exempt are loans arranged by licensed real estate brokers and sellers who carry back.

V

VA (Veterans' Administration) See *Department of Veterans Affairs (DVA)*.

Variable Interest Rate An interest rate that can go up or down according to an independent index, as contrasted with a fixed interest rate that stays the same over the life of the loan.

Verification of Deposit (VOD) Form sent to a loan applicant's bank to verify funds for down payment and closing costs.

Verification of Employment (VOE) Checking on the accuracy of the applicant's information, usually by mailing forms directly to the employer, or by original pay stubs and W-2s.

Vesting The names of owners of real estate and the method or manner in which title is held.

Voucher System A plan to pay for construction costs upon presentation of receipted bills and lien waivers by licensed building contractors, subcontractors, and material suppliers.

VRM Variable Rate Mortgage See *Adjustable Rate Mortgage (ARM)*.

Vrooman Street Act California law that authorizes city councils to issue bonds secured by tax levies for street construction.

W

Waiver Suspension of principal payments on a loan in order to help debtors.

Warehousing Temporary storage of loans pending sale to investors.

Wrap-Around Trust Deed See *All-Inclusive Trust Deed (AITD)*.

Y

Yield The actual interest earned by the lender on the money loaned. Also called *rate of return*, it is usually expressed as a percentage.

INDEX

A

adjustable rate mortgages (ARMs)
- adjustable rate loan rider, 112–113
- advantages of, 111, 113
- assumability of, 108, 114
- disadvantages of, 114
- disclosure requirements, 111, 113
- fixed rate hybrid with, 114
- issues to consider with, 113
- negatively amortized, 4, 106–107, 127
- objectives and rationale for, 105–107
- option ARM, 4, 106, 111, 122, 127, 366
- Section 245(2) FHA, 171
- terminology associated with, 107–108

alimony, 280, 310

all-inclusive trust deed
- buyer issues, 416–417, 418
- characteristics and limitations of, 411, 413
- comprehensive application of, 413
- defined, 410
- disadvantages/precautions of, 417–419
- procedures for setting up, 418–419
- sample, 412
- seller issues, 414–416, 417–418
- types of, 414
- uses for, 411

American Bankers Association, 63

amortization
- amortization tables, 482–483
- amortized loans, 27–28, 481–483
- negative, 4, 27–28, 106–107, 128

annual percentage rates (APR), 319–320, 493–494

applicable federal rate, 434

applications, loan, 31, 52, 95, 227, 299–310, 312–313, 374–376

appraisals
- appraisal management companies, 228, 254, 260–262
- appraiser licensing, 251, 253–254
- Certificates of Reasonable Value, 178, 183, 226
- comparable market data for, 241–248, 254, 255
- construction loan requirements, 376
- cost approach, 245
- cost of, 322
- FHA requirements, 225–227, 250–251
- final market value, 247–248
- Freddie Mac/Fannie Mae influence, 224, 225
- Home Value Code of Conduct, 226, 226, 227, 260–262, 445
- income approach, 245–248
- location/neighborhood impacting value, 229–230, 238–239
- of planned unit developments/ condominiums, 248–251, 252, 253
- property characteristics impacting value, 237, 239–241
- purpose of, 227–228
- qualifying the property, 223–227
- sales comparison approach, 241–248
- sales price *versus* fair market value, 247–248
- time frame for, 228
- underwriting, 248
- Uniform Residential Appraisal Report form, 231–237
- VA requirements, 225–226
- working with appraisers, 254–255

APR. *See* annual percentage rates (APR)

ARMs. *See* adjustable rate mortgages (ARMs)

assessment tax, 391–392

assets, loan qualification based on, 283–284

assignments
- of deed of trust, 407
- of loans, 353
- of rents, 338

assumability of loans, 108, 178–179, 180, 326–327

automatic payment plans, 355

B

balloon payment fixed rate loans, 115
balloon payments, 27, 89–90, 115, 488–489
Bank Insurance Fund, 59
Bank of America Corporation, 213
bankruptcy, 286–287
banks/lenders. *See also* institutional lenders; non-institutional lenders
   appraisals for (*See* appraisals)
   bank failures, 60, 144–146, 212
   borrower qualifying (*See* loan qualification)
   classifications of, 42
   commercial banks, 46–52
   cost characteristics of mortgage market, 22–27
   discount rate, 17–18
   discriminatory lending practices, 50, 146–149, 223, 229, 357, 359
   endowment funds, 93–94
   fair lending regulations for, 146–149
   federal funds rate, 18–19, 201
   finance companies, 94
   financing by (*See* loans; mortgages; real estate financing)
   fiscal policy and, 19–20
   foreclosures by/loan defaults to (*See* foreclosures/defaults)
   government regulatory agencies for, 57–59
   interest rates (*See* interest rates)
   legislation impacting, 50–52, 54, 58, 69–70, 78, 81–90, 94, 146–149
   lender participation, 426–427, 515–516
   lending characteristics of, 44–45, 46–47, 52–53, 55, 77, 80–81
   licensing of, 44, 46, 52, 63, 69–70, 81
   life insurance companies, 52–54
   loan origination fees to, 95, 116, 136, 181, 186, 321, 373
   monetary policy and, 14–19, 25–26
   mortgage entities, 80
   mutual savings banks, 54
   number in California, 26
   open-market operations, 16–17
   pension and retirement funds, 55–57, 93
   personal loan, 431
   predatory lending practices, 83–84, 444–446
   private mortgage insurance protecting, 148–154, 355
   private party lenders, 30–31, 73–77, 357, 402–426, 433–439
   real estate investment trusts, 91–92
   reserve requirements, 15–16, 213
   savings banks, 43–45, 47, 54
   selecting, 135–140, 184
   sellers as private lenders, 30–31, 76, 77, 357, 402–426, 433–439
   syndications, 90–91
   trade associations, 62–64
   utilized forms, 53–54
   underwriting by, 248, 470–471
biweekly loans payments, 119–122, 492–493
blanket trust deed, 381, 410
blended interest rates, 386–388, 432–433
bonds, 208, 214
bonus income, 279–280
borrower qualifying. *See* loan qualification
break-even analysis, 459–462
bridge loans, 47. *See also* gap loans
brokers. *See* real estate brokers
buy-down loans, 140–142

C

Calculated Industries Qualifier Plus IIIx financial calculator, 483–493
calculations
   all-inclusive trust deed, 411, 413, 415
   amortized loan, 481–483
   annual percentage rate, 319–320, 493–494
   ARM payment, 400–401
   balloon loans/balloon payment, 488–489
   biweekly loan payment, 492–493
   blended interest rate, 386–388, 432–433
   break-even analysis, 459–462
   debt coverage ratio, 470–471
   effective interest rate, 202–203
   financial calculators/computers for, 483–493
   gross rent multiplier, 217
   income appraisal approach, 247–248
   income ratio, 490
   interest and principal allocation, 486–488
   interest rate, 319–320, 432–433, 493–494
   loan amount/price range, 169–170, 490–491
   loan payment, 485–486, 489–490
   PITI, 489–490
   unpaid loan balance, 392–393
   yield, 202–203, 205, 206–207, 415, 491–492
California
   California Department of Business Overnight (DBO), 61
   California Department of Financial Institutions, 61
   California Housing Finance Agency Program (CalHFA), 188–189

Cal-Vet loans, 30, 90, 107, 131–134, 185–188, 190, 277, 354
  fair lending regulations, 146–149
  licensing requirements in, 69, 82
  mortgage market, unique characteristics in, 26–27
  Office of Real Estate Appraisers, 251, 254
  PERS (Public Employees Retirement System), 55, 93
  STRS (State Teachers Retirement System), 55, 93
  title companies in, 26, 316
  usury law, 78
Cal-Vet loans
  adjustable rates for, 107, 186
  advantages/disadvantages of, 188
  comparison of government-backed loans, 190
  conventional *versus* government-backed loans, 131–134
  eligibility for, 185–186
  general information about, 186–188
  insurance requirements, 90, 187, 354
  land contract of sale, 25, 187
  late charges on, 325
  loan amounts, 132, 186
  loan qualification requirements, 278
  prepayment penalties, 325–326
capitalization rate, 246
ceiling rates, 108
certificates
  Certificate of Eligibility, 180
  Certificate of Reasonable Value, 178, 183, 226
  mortgage-backed security certificates, 209–210
  'd support, 280, 310

closing. *See* closing costs; escrow closing costs
  FHA requirements on, 168
  nonrecurring, 321–323
  recurring, 323–324
  VA requirements on, 178, 179–180, 158
Closing Disclosure, 311, 312, 319
co-borrowers/co-mortgagors, 282
collateral. *See also* security collateralized mortgage obligations, 211
  collateralizing secondary financing, 403–405, 406–409
  deed of trust collateral provisions, 335–338
  institutional lender requirements, 45, 46–47
commercial banks, 46–52
commercial/industrial property, 466–469
commissions, 75, 82, 88, 279
Community Home Buyer's Program, 143–144
Community Mortgage Banking Project (CMBP), 63–64
Community Reinvestment Act, 49–50, 359
comparable market data, 241–248, 254, 255
computerized loan origination, 95
condominiums, 248–251, 254
construction loans
  building loan agreement, 376, 378
  Cal-Vet requirements, 187
  construction-to-permanent loans, 45
  costs of, 373–374
  disbursement procedures, 372, 376–380
  evaluation and lending process, 374–380
  from institutional lenders, 45, 46–47, 52
  lender considerations, 374–376

  mechanic's liens impacting, 385–391
  nature of, 371–374
  notice of completion, 385, 387–388
  notice of non-responsibility, 388–389
  partial release clauses, 381
  public construction, 391–392
  rehabilitation mortgages *versus*, 171
  rental achievement clauses, 384
  sources of, 372
  subordination agreements, 380–381, 382–383
  take-out/permanent loans, 372, 380–391
  types of, 372–374
Consumer Financial Protection Bureau (CFPB), 8, 57, 158–160
consumer protection laws/regulations, 355–356
contracts
  construction, 375
  installment sales, 30, 187, 419–425
conventional loans advantages/disadvantages of, 131–134
  borrower qualifications, 137
  buy-down loans, 140–142
  government-backed *versus*, 131–134
  income property, 450–452, 453–454, 456–457
  interest rates on, 136, 141–142, 450–452, 454, 456–457
  late charges on, 325
  lender policy updates, 138–140
  loan amounts/limits, 132, 135–136
  loan fees, 136
  loan-to-value ratio, 132, 135
  low down payment conventional loans, 142–143
  mortgage-backed security backed by, 210–211

prepayment penalties, 325–326
sources of, 135–137
types of loans, 137
costs
   closing, 168, 178, 179–180, 184, 320–324
   construction loan, 373–374
   cost appraisal approach, 245
   cost characteristics of mortgage market, 22–27
   Good Faith Estimate of loan costs, 202, 295–297, 311
   loan origination fees, 95, 117, 136, 181, 186, 321–324, 373
   mortgage broker, 89
   reverse annuity mortgage incurring, 117, 118
   yield-spread premiums, 201–202, 295
Creative Financing Disclosure Act, 433–434
credit. *See also* loans; mortgages; real estate financing
   credit history, 284–288, 312, 314–315, 322
   credit report, 504–506
   credit scoring, 287–288, 316, 506–508
   Fair Credit Reporting Act, 315
   Federal Fair and Accurate Credit Transaction (FACT) Act, 287
   money *versus*, 9
   credit cards, 45
   credit life insurance, 151
   credit unions, 47. *See also* savings banks
   lending characteristics, 47–48

D

debt coverage ratio, 470–471
debts, loan qualification considering, 272–274, 470–471
deeds
   all-inclusive trust deed, 410–419
   blanket trust deed, 381, 410
   deed in lieu of foreclosure, 347–348
   deed of trust, 26, 28–29, 318–319, 335–338, 339–348, 407
   open-end trust deed, 430–431
   partial reconveyance deed, 381
defaults, loan. *See* foreclosures/defaults deposits
   demand *versus* time, 46
   insurance on, 58–59, 144–146
   savings, 198–199
Deposit Insurance Fund (DFI), 58–59
depository institutions
   types of, 42
disclosure
   of annual percentage rate, 493–494
   ARM requirements, 111, 113
   Community Reinvestment Act disclosure requirements, 49
   Creative Financing Disclosure Act, 433–434
   Home Mortgage Disclosure Act, 50–52, 359–360
   Mortgage Disclosure Improvement Act, 84, 227, 311–312
   Mortgage Loan Disclosure Statement, 84–87
   seller financing disclosure statement, 435–438
   of total interest paid, 493
   Truth-in-Lending, 84, 111, 319–320, 355, 356–358, 493
   of yield-spread premium, 202, 295
discount points defined, 201
   price and, 204–205
   reasons for using, 202–203
   secondary financing and, 205–207, 405–406
   yield and, 202–207, 492
discount rate, 17–18

discrimination
   California fair lending regulations, 146–149
   Community Reinvestment Act on, 49, 359
   foreclosures/defaults and, 357–360
   redlining, 146–149, 223, 229, 358–359
disintermediation, 9, 13–14, 25, 198
divorce, 286, 311
documentation requirements
   construction loan, 374–376
   conventional loan, 132
   loan application, 310, 312–313
   loan document for escrow, 316–319
down payments
   CalHFA requirements, 188–189
   Cal-Vet requirements, 186
   conventional loan requirements, 135, 142–143
   FHA requirements, 167, 169
   loan qualification considering, 268, 269, 271, 278, 284, 288
   low down payment conventional loans, 142–143
   savings bank requirements, 44
   VA requirements, 177–178, 182–183
due-on-sale rights, 413

E

easy money, 25–26
economy
   appraisals impacted by, 245
   circular flow of the economy, 11–14
   economic crisis, 5–9, 19, 26, 37–39, 60, 83, 111, 122, 128–129, 144–146, 171, 207–209, 219–221, 366–369, 444–446
   economic stimulus, 127–129, 171, 219–221, 366–369

fiscal policy, 19–20
monetary policy and, 14–21, 25–26
real estate cycle interaction with, 8–9, 11–14, 37–39
effective interest rates, 202–203
employment, loan qualification considerations, 276, 278–281, 282–283
endowment funds, 93–94
Equal Credit Opportunity Act (ECOA), 310
equity
equity participation, 53, 425
home equity loans, 4
reverse annuity mortgage borrowing against, 116–119
stock equity/pledged asset loans, 431
escrow
closing costs, 168, 178, 179–180, 184, 320–324, 508–511
closing the loan, 316–323
escrow fee, 322–323
escrow (impound) accounts, 348–349
loan documents for, 316–319

F

Fair Credit Reporting Act, 315
fair lending regulations, 146–149
fair market value (FMV), 228
Fannie Mae (Federal National Mortgage Association)
conservatorship of, 60, 219
conventional loan standard guidelines, 135–137
HomeStyle Construction-Permanent Mortgage, 380
income property financing, 450–451
lender property standards influence, 224
loan amount limits, 211
loan applications, 52

loan qualification requirements, 278–279
low down payment loans, 142–143
mortgage insurance requirements, 150–151
reverse annuity mortgage programs, 117, 118–119
role of, 60
secondary mortgage market role, 60, 199, 207–209, 210, 213, 219–221
FDIC (Federal Deposit Insurance Corporation), 59, 144–146
Federal Fair and Accurate Credit Transaction (FACT) Act, 287
federal funds rate, 18, 201
federal government. See government
Federal Home Loan Mortgage Corporation. See Freddie Mac
Federal Housing Administration (FHA)
advantages of FHA-insured loans, 167–169
appraisal/property standards, 225–226, 250–251
conventional versus government-backed loans, 131–134
FHA-insured loans, 163–175, 190, 209, 225–226, 250–251, 274, 314, 325–326, 352–353
future changes, 171–175
Homeowner's Armed with Knowledge (HAWK), 165–167
late charges by, 325
loan approval process, 314
loan qualification requirements, 274
loan refinancing through, 161, 171–175
mortgage insurance, 150, 165–167, 352–355
pest inspections requirements, 168, 226
prepayment penalties, 325

reverse annuity mortgage programs, 117, 118–119
role of, 163–167
Federal Housing Finance Agency, 59
Federal Housing Finance Board, 44, 60
Federal National Mortgage Association. See Fannie Mae
Federal Open Market Committee, (FOMC), 60
Federal Reserve System
discount rate, 17–18
federal funds rate, 18–19, 201
Federal Reserve Bank Board, 15, 60
monetary policy, 14–21, 25–26
open-market operations, 16–17
reserve requirements, 15–16
FHA. See Federal Housing Administration (FHA)
FICO (Fair Isaac Corporation) credit scoring, 287–288
fifteen-year mortgages, 119, 121
finance companies, 94
financial calculators, 483–493
financial crisis. See economy: economic crisis
financial institutions. See banks/lenders Financial Institutions Reform, Recovery, and Enforcement Act (FIRREA), 58, 359
financing. See loans; mortgages; real estate financing
fiscal policy, 19–20
five-plus unit residential property, 455–459
fixed rate loans
adjustable rate hybrid with, 114–115
balloon payment fixed rate loans, 115
CalHFA 30-year fixed rate loan program, 189
flood insurance, 240, 323
forbearance, 349–352

foreclosures/defaults
  assumable *versus* subject to loans and, 326–327
  automatic payment plans, 355
  consumer protection laws/regulations, 355–356
  credit history impacted by, 286
  deed in lieu of foreclosure, 347–348
  deed of trust *versus* mortgage, 28–29, 318, 346
  deficiency judgments, 346
  discriminatory lending practices and, 357–360
  economic crisis and, 37, 127–129, 366–369
  final sale, 340, 343, 346
  forbearance, 349–352
  impound accounts, 348–349
  judicial sale, 346–348
  minimizing loan defaults, 348–358
  mortgage insurance triggered by, 148–154, 165–167, 352–355
  notice of default, 339–340, 340, 346
  notice of sale, 340, 346
  option ARM role in, 118
  recasting loan terms, 350–351
  redlining and, 358–359
  reinstatement period, 340, 343, 346–347
  short sales, 360–361, 366–369
  trustee's sale, 339–343
  usury and, 356–358
  Web site help, 361–362
Fraud Enforcement Act (FERA, 2009), 444–446
Freddie Mac (Federal Home Loan Mortgage Corporation)
  conservatorship of, 60, 219
  conventional loan standard guidelines, 135–137
  foreclosure/default alternatives, 354
  income property financing, 450
  lender property standards influence, 224
  loan amount limits, 211
  loan applications, 50
  loan qualification requirements, 278–279
  low down payment loans, 142–143
  mortgage insurance requirements, 150–151
  role of, 60
  secondary mortgage market role, 59, 199, 207–209, 210, 213, 219–221

G

gap loans, 47, 402
Ginnie Mae (Government National Mortgage Association), 207–210
Glass-Steagall Act of 1933, 56
Goldman Sachs, 213
Good Faith Estimate, 202, 295–297, 311
government. *See also* legislation; taxation; *federal entries; U.S. Department entries*
  economic crisis programs, 127–129, 171, 219–221, 366–369
  fiscal policy, 19–20
  government-backed loans, 131–134, 163–195 (*See also specific programs by name*)
  monetary policy, 14–21, 25–26
  public construction, 391–392
  regulatory agencies, 58–62
  securities, 16–17
Government National Mortgage Association (Ginnie Mae), 207–210
gross rent multipliers, 245

H

hazard insurance, 240, 323, 338

Hewlett Packard Model 12C financial calculator, 484
home equity. *See* equity home improvement loans, 430–431
Home Keeper Program, 118–119
Home Mortgage Disclosure Act, 50–52, 359–360
Homeowner's Armed with Knowledge (HAWK), 165–167
homeowner associations, 248–251
Homeowner's Protection Act (1998), 152
Home Value Code of Conduct (HVCC), 226, 227, 227, 260–262
home warranties, 356
Housing and Economic Recovery Act (HERA, 2008), 59
Housing Discrimination Act (Anti-Redlining Law), 146–149
HUD. *See* U.S. Department of Housing and Urban Development (HUD)
hybrid loans, 114–115

I

impound accounts, 348–349
Improvement Bond Act (1915), 391–392
imputed interest, 434, 439
income
  alimony as, 280, 310
  commission as, 75, 82, 88, 279
  income appraisal approach, 245–248
  income ratio for loan qualification, 271–272, 277–278, 490
  overtime/bonuses, 279–280
  real estate/rental property, 244–246, 280–281, 452, 455–456, 457, 458–459, 461, 468–471
  residual income method of loan qualification, 274–277, 278
  sources of income, 278–281
  stability of, 282–283

income property. *See also* rental property
  advantages of, 451–452, 454, 457–458, 467
  break-even analysis, 459–462
  commercial/industrial property as, 466–469
  debt coverage ratio, 470–471
  disadvantages of, 452–453, 455, 459, 468–469
  financing and interest rates for, 450–452, 453–454, 456–457, 463–464, 470–471
  five-plus unit residential property as, 455–459
  income from, 452, 455–456, 457, 458–459, 461, 468–471
  listing for sale, 462–466
  price of, 450–453, 454–456, 458–459, 464–466, 468
  property management of, 452, 454, 457–458
  rent controls, 459, 462, 460, 468
  single-family house as, 450–453
  tax issues with, 450, 453, 458, 460, 466
  two-to-four-unit residential property as, 453–455
index, adjustable rates based on, 107–108
individual retirement accounts (IRAs), 56
inflation, 21, 24
installment notes, 408
installment sales contracts, 30, 187, 419–425
institutional lenders
  commercial banks, 46–52
  future impact, 48–49
  government regulatory agencies for, 58–60
  legislation impacting, 50–52, 54, 58, 69–70
  lending characteristics of, 44–45, 46–47, 52–53, 55
  licensing of, 44, 46, 52, 69–70

life insurance companies, 52–54
loan maturity dates/ terms, 44–45, 47, 53
loan-to-value ratios, 44–45, 46–47, 53, 54, 55
mutual savings banks, 54
pension and retirement funds, 55
savings banks, 43–45, 54
trade associations, 62–64
utilized forms, 53–54
insurance
  Cal-Vet requirements, 90, 187, 354
  credit life insurance, 151
  FDIC, 58–59, 144–146
  FHA-insured loans (*See* Federal Housing Administration)
  flood, 240, 323
  hazard, 240, 323, 338
  impound accounts, 348–349
  life insurance/life insurance companies, 52–54, 151, 354–355
  mortgage insurance, 148–154, 165–167, 352–355
  PITI payments including, 271, 489–490
  real property loan law on, 90
  title, 322, 512–515
interest payments
  allocation of, 486–488
  calculations of (*See* calculations)
  deferred, 4, 27–28, 106–107, 129, 349
  defined, 480
  interest-only loans, 480–481
  PITI payments including, 271, 489–490
  prepaid, 323–324
  promissory notes including, 27–28
interest rates
  adjustable, 4, 105–107, 171
  amortization tables of, 483
  annual percentage rate, 319–320, 493–494

  applicable federal rate, 434
  blended, 386–388, 432–433
  buy-down loan, 141–142
  calculations of, 319–320, 432–433, 493–494
  CalHFA loan, 188–189
  Cal-Vet loan, 186
  causes of change in, 23–24
  ceiling rates, 108
  conventional loan, 136, 141–142, 450–452, 454, 456–457
  cost of mortgage money and, 22–23
  defined, 480
  discount rates and, 17–18
  effective, 202–203
  federal funds rate, 18, 201
  fiscal policy impact on, 19
  fixed, 114–116, 188–189
  imputed, 434, 439
  income property financing, 450–452, 454, 456–457, 463–464
  inflation and, 23–24
  institutional lender, 45, 52
  maturity date impacting, 118, 120
  non-institutional lender, 76, 77
  reduction of, 351
  subprime loans and, 83–84
  usury law on, 78, 356–358
  VA loan, 181–182
  yield-spread premiums and, 201–202, 295
Internal Revenue Service, 434, 439. *See also* taxation
investment bankers, 212–213
investment property. *See* income property; rental property
investing, 476–477

J

judicial sale, 346–348
jumbo loans, 212
junior loans. *See* secondary financing

K
Keogh plans, 56

L
land contract of sale, 30, 187, 419–425
late charges, 325
legislation
    Community Reinvestment Act, 49, 359
    Creative Financing Disclosure Act, 433–434
    Equal Credit Opportunity Act, 310
    Fair Credit Reporting Act, 315
    Federal Fair and Accurate Credit Transaction Act, 287
    Financial Institutions Reform, Recovery, and Enforcement Act, 59, 359
    Fraud Enforcement Act (FERA, 2009), 444–446
    Home Mortgage Disclosure Act, 50–52, 359–360
    Homeowner's Protection Act (1998), 152
    Housing and Economic Recovery Act (HERA, 2008), 59
    Housing Discrimination Act (Anti-Redlining Law), 146–149
    Improvement Bond Act (1915), 391–392
    Mello-Roos Community Facilities Act, 392
    Monetary Control Act, 54
    Mortgage Debt Forgiveness Act (2007), 360
    Mortgage Disclosure Improvement Act, 84, 227, 311–312
    Real Estate Settlement Procedures Act (RESPA), 311
    Recovery Act (2008), 81
    Regulation Z, 111
    Secure & Fair Enforcement for Mortgage Licensing Act, 69–70
    Soldiers and Sailors Civil Relief Act, 354
    Street Improvement Act (1911), 391
    Tax Reform Act (1986), 453
    Truth-in-Lending, 84, 111, 319–320, 355, 356–358, 493
    Vrooman Street Act, 391
Lehman Brothers, 213
lender participation, 425–426
lenders. *See* banks/lenders
liar loans, 4, 444–446
licenses
    appraiser, 251, 253–254
    institutional lender, 44, 46, 52, 69–70
    non-institutional lender, 81
life insurance, 151, 354–355
life insurance companies, 51–54
lines of credit, 118
loan qualification
    appraisals for (*See* appraisals)
    assets, 283–284
    capacity to pay, 267–285
    co-borrowing, 282
    conventional lender guidelines, 137
    credit history, 285–288, 311, 314–315, 322
    debt considerations, 272–274, 470–471
    desire to pay, 267, 285–289
    down payment considerations, 268, 269, 271, 278, 284, 288
    employment-related considerations, 276, 278–281, 282
    fair lending regulations impacting, 146–149
    Fannie Mae/Freddie Mac influence on, 278–279
    FHA requirements, 274
    historical overview, 4, 37
    income ratios, 271–272, 277–278, 490
    income sources considered, 278–281
    methods of qualification, 266–267
    reasons for qualifying borrowers, 268–269
    residual income method, 274–277, 278
    stability of income, 282–283
    VA requirements for, 178, 180, 274–278, 353–354
    working with lenders, 289–290
loans. *See also* banks/lenders; loan qualification; mortgages
    amortized, 27–28, 481–483
    applications for, 31, 52, 95, 227, 299–310, 312–313, 374–376
    approval process, 314–315, 374–376
    assignment of, 353
    assumable, 108, 178–179, 180, 326–327
    automatic payment plans, 355
    balloon payment fixed rate, 115
    balloon payments, 27, 89, 115, 488–489
    biweekly payments, 119–122, 492–493
    blended-rate, 386–388, 432–433
    buy-down, 140–142
    calculations on (*See* calculations)
    CalHFA, 188–189
    Cal-Vet, 30, 90, 107, 131–134, 185–188, 190, 277, 354
    closing the loan, 316–323
    computerized loan origination, 95
    construction, 45, 46–47, 52, 171, 187, 371–392
    conventional, 131–144, 210–211, 325–326, 450–452, 453–454, 456–457 (*See conventional loans for details*)

defaulting on (*See* foreclosures/defaults)
disclosure of terms (*See* disclosure)
discriminatory practices (*See* discrimination)
down payments for (*See* down payments)
Department of Veterans Affairs for detail)
FHA-insured, 163–175, 190, 209, 225–227, 250–251, 274, 314, 325–326, 352–353 (*See Federal Housing Administration for detail*)
financing process, 31–32, 496–498
fixed rate, 114–115, 189
gap, 47, 402
Good Faith Estimate of loan costs, 202, 295–297, 311
government-backed, 131–134, 163–195 (*See also specific programs by name*)
government sponsored, 199–200
home equity, 4
home improvement, 430–431
hybrid, 114–115
income property, 450–452, 453–454, 456–457, 463–464, 470–471
insurance requirements (*See* insurance)
interest-only, 480–481
interest rates on (*See* interest rates)
jumbo, 212
junior (*See* secondary financing)
late charges on, 325
legislation impacting (*See* legislation)
liar loans, 4, 444–446
loan amounts/limits, 132, 135–136, 169–170, 182, 186, 211, 490–491, 430–431

loan correspondents, 53, 80–81
Loan Estimate, 84, 102, 159, 295, 311, 319, 321, 493
loan origination fees, 95, 116, 136, 181, 186, 321, 373 (*See also* points)
loan package, 313
loan payments, 324–325, 485–486, 489–490
loan takeovers, 326–327
loan-to-value ratios, 44–45, 46–47, 52, 54, 55, 132, 135, 150–151, 189, 224
low down payment conventional loans, 142–143
online, 96
payday, 79–80
personal, 431
pre-approval letters, 498–500
prepayment of (*See* prepayment of principal)
private party, 30, 73–77, 357, 402–426, 433–439
processing the loan, 31, 299–313, 332–333, 374–380
promissory notes, 27–28, 317, 480–481
real property loan law, 83–90
refinancing (*See* refinancing loans)
savings relationship to, 11, 11–14
secondary financing (*See* secondary financing)
security on (*See* security)
seller carry back, 30, 76, 77, 357, 402–410, 419–426, 433–434
shopping, 500–502
stock equity/pledged asset, 431
subordination agreements, 380–381, 382–383
subprime, 83–84
swing, 47
take-out, 372, 380–391
term of, 44–45, 47, 48, 53, 77, 94, 118, 141, 350–351, 480
U.S. Department of Agriculture (USDA), 175–176

VA-guaranteed, 131–134, 190, 209, 225–227, 274–278, 314, 325–326, (*See U.S.*
veterans (*See* Cal-Vet loans; U.S. Department of Veterans Affairs)

M

margin, defined, 108
marital status, 286, 310
market value determination. *See* appraisals
mechanic's liens, 385–391
Mello-Roos Community Facilities Act, 392
Merrill Lynch, 213
Monetary Control Act, 54
money. *See also* income
   accumulation of, 10–11
   cost of mortgage money, 22–23
   creation of, 9–10
   credit *versus*, 9
   defined, 9
   federal control of money supply, 14–21
   flow of, into mortgage market, 11–14
   sources of, in mortgage market, 42 (*See also* banks/lenders)
   tight *versus* easy, 25
Morgan Stanley, 213
mortgage bankers, 63, 81, 199
Mortgage Bankers Association of America, 63
mortgage brokers commissions of, 75, 81, 89
   costs and expenses of, 89
   mortgage bankers *versus*, 81
   mortgage loan broker law, 84–90
   predatory lending practices of, 444–446
   private lender relationship with, 74–75, 76
   trade association of, 64
mortgage entities, 80

Mortgage Debt Forgiveness Act (2007), 360
Mortgage Disclosure Improvement Act, 84, 227, 311–312
Mortgage Loan Disclosure Statement, 84–87
mortgages. *See also* loans
    adjustable rate mortgages, 4, 105–107, 122, 127, 171, 366
    California mortgage market, 26–27
    collateralized mortgage obligations, 211
    cost characteristics of mortgage market, 22–27
    deeds of trust *versus*, 28–29, 318, 345
    fifteen-year, 119, 121
    junior (*See* secondary financing) mortgage-backed securities, 205–206, 219–221
    mortgage crisis (*See* economy: economic crisis)
    mortgage insurance, 148–154, 165–167, 352–355
    mortgage market, overview of, 9–27
    mortgage revenue bonds, 208, 214
    negatively amortized adjustable rate mortgages, 4, 106–107
    rehabilitation, 171
    reverse annuity, 116–119
    secondary mortgage market (*See* secondary mortgage market)
    as security, 27–28, 207–213, 219–221
mutual savings banks, 54

N

National Association of Mortgage Brokers, 63
National Association of Professional Mortgage Women (NAPMW), 64
Nationwide Mortgage Licensing System (NMLS), 8
negative amortization
    negatively amortized adjustable rate mortgages, 4, 106–107
    negatively amortized promissory notes, 27–28
    endowment funds, 93–94
    finance companies, 93–94
    legislation impacting, 78, 81–90, 96
    lending characteristics, 77, 81–83
    licensing of, 82
    loan maturity dates/terms, 77, 95
    mortgage entities, 80
    pension funds, 93
    private party lenders, 30, 73–77, 357, 402–426, 433–439
    real estate brokers' role, 94–95
    real estate investment trusts, 91–92
    real property loan law, 83–90
    syndications, 90–91
    usury law on, 78
notary fees, 322
notices
    notice of completion, 385, 387–388
    notice of default, 339–340, 340, 346
    notice of non-responsibility, 388–389
    notice of sale, 340, 346

O

Office of Comptroller of the Currency, 58
Office of Thrift Supervision, 58, 210
office parks, 467
online loans, 96
open-end trust deed, 430–431
open-market operations, 16–17
Option ARM, 4, 106, 111, 122, 127, 366
overtime income, 279–280

P

partial reconveyance deeds, 381
partial release clauses, 381
payday loan, 79–80
pension and retirement funds, 55, 93, 280
pest inspections, 168, 184, 226, 228, 322
PITI (principal, interest, taxes and insurance), 271, 489–490
planned unit developments (PUD), 248–251, 253
points, 201. *See also* discount points; loans: loan origination fees
predatory lending practices, 83–84, 444–446
premiums. *See* yield-spread premiums
prepayment of principal
    ARMs' suitability for, 107
    through biweekly loan payments, 119–122, 492–493
    default minimization by applying, 349
    prepayment penalties, 46, 108, 134, 136–137, 169, 325–326, 450
    secondary mortgage market issues with, 211
price
    of income property, 450–453, 454–456, 458–459, 464–466, 468
    price range calculations, 490–491
    sales price *versus* fair market value, 247–248
    of secondary loan sales, 204–205
principal
    allocation of, 486–488
    balloon payment of, 27, 89, 115, 488–489
    biweekly payment of, 119–122, 492–493

calculation of payments
(*See* calculations)
deferred interest added to, 4, 27–28, 106–107, 349
defined, 480
forbearance measures altering, 349, 358
PITI (principal, interest, taxes and insurance), 271, 489–490
prepayment of, 46, 107, 108, 119–122, 134, 136–137, 169, 211, 325–326, 492–493, 450
promissory note payment of, 27–28, 317, 480
private mortgage insurance, 148–154, 355
private party lenders, 30, 73–77, 357, 402–426, 433–439
promissory notes, 27–28, 317, 480–481
property management, 452, 454, 457–458
property qualifying, 223–227. *See also* appraisals
property taxes, 338
proposition 13, 392
public construction, 391–392

Q

qualified mortgage, 8, 74
qualifying for loans. *See* loan qualification
qualifying the property, 223–227. *See also* appraisals
quantitative easing, 19

R

real estate brokers
financial advisory role of, 94–95
secondary financing participation by, 406–409
real estate financing. *See also* banks/lenders; interest rates; loans; mortgages
cost characteristics of mortgage market, 22–27
economic impact of, 7–8, 11–13, 37–39
federal control of money supply, 14–21, 24–25
financing process, 31–32
flow of money and credit, 11–13
history of, 4, 37–39
instruments of, 27–31
language of, 31
meaning of money, 9–11
mortgage market overview, 9–27
savings relationship to, 10, 11–13
real estate investment trusts (REITs), 91–92
Real Estate Settlement Procedures Act (RESPA), 311
real property loan law, 83–90
recasting, 350–351
recording fees, 322
Recovery Act (2008), 81
redlining, 146–149, 223, 229, 357–359
refinancing loans
Cal-Vet requirements, 187
economic crisis and, 4, 37, 83, 111,
FHA requirements, 161, 171–175
recasting loan terms, 350–351
VA requirements, 181
Regulation Z, 111
rehabilitation mortgages, 171
rental property
advantages as investment vehicle, 451–452, 454, 457–458, 467
assignment of rents, 338
break-even analysis, 459–462
commercial/industrial property as, 466–469
debt coverage ratio, 470–471
disadvantages as investment vehicle, 452–453, 455, 459–459, 468–469
financing and interest rates for, 450–452, 453–454, 456–457, 463–464, 470–471
five-plus unit residential property as, 455–459
income from, 244–246, 280–281, 452, 455–456, 457, 458–459, 461, 468–471
listing for sale, 462–466
price of, 450–453, 454–456, 458–459, 464–466, 468
property management of, 453, 454, 457–458
rental achievement clauses, 384
rent controls, 459, 462, 460, 468
sale-leaseback arrangements, 426–430
single-family house as, 450–453
tax issues with, 450, 453, 458, 460, 466
two-to-four-unit residential property as, 453–455
reserves/reserve requirements, 16–19, 213
retirement funds, 55, 93, 280
reverse annuity mortgages, 116–119

S

sale-leaseback, 426–430
savings, 10, 11–13, 198–199
Savings Association Insurance Fund (SAIF), 59, 60
savings banks, 43–45, 48, 54
secondary financing
all-inclusive trust deed, 410–419
broker participation in, 406–409
collateralizing secondary financing, 403–405, 406–409
combination or split junior liens, 409–410
discounts on, 205–207, 405–406

government-backed loan requirements on, 183–184, 186–187
installment sales contracts, 30, 187, 419–426
lender participation, 425–426
sale of second loan, 405–406
secondary mortgage market *versus*, 197–198
seller carrybacks as, 30, 76, 77, 357, 402–410, 419–426, 433–434
secondary mortgage market
additional sources for, 199
collateralized mortgage obligations, 211
Fannie Mae role in, 60, 199, 207–209, 210, 213, 219–221
federal funds rate, 201
Freddie Mac role in, 60, 199, 207–209, 210, 213, 219–221
Ginnie Mae role in, 207–209
investment bankers in, 212–213
methods of funds shifting in, 199
mortgage-backed securities, 207–213, 219–221
mortgage revenue bonds, 208, 214
pension funds in, 93
points and discounts in, 201–207
purpose of, 198–199
secondary financing *versus*, 198
standardization in, 214
Secure & Fair Enforcement for Mortgage Licensing Act (SAFE, 2009), 69–70
security
bonds, 208, 214
collateral, 45, 46–47, 211, 335–338, 403–405, 406–409
deed of trust as, 27, 28–29, 318–319, 335–338, 339–348, 407
government securities, 16–17

mortgage-backed securities, 207–213, 219–221
mortgages as, 28–29, 207–213, 219–221
secured credit cards, 45
self-employment, 281, 284
seller financing
all-inclusive trust deed with, 410–419
installment sales contracts, 30, 187, 419–426
sale-leaseback, 426–430
seller carrybacks, 30, 76, 77, 357, 402–410, 419–426, 433–434
seller financing disclosure statement, 435–438
shares/stocks, 44, 431
short sales, 360–361, 366–369
single-family income property, 450–453
Soldiers and Sailors Civil Relief Act, 354
stock equity/pledged asset loans, 431
stocks, 44, 431
Street Improvement Act (1911), 391
subdivisions, 381
subject to transfers, 326, 327
subordination agreements/clauses, 380–381, 382–383
subprime loans, 83–84
swing loans, 47. *See also* gap loans
syndications, 90–91

T

take-out loans, 372, 380–391
taxation
assessment tax, 391–392
fiscal policy on, 19–20
impound accounts, 348–349
imputed interest rate and, 434, 439
income property and, 450, 453, 458, 460, 466
PITI payments including taxes, 271, 489–490,

property taxes, 338
REITs and, 91
short sale tax issues, 360
tax proration, 323
tax service fees, 322
Tax Deferred Exchanges, 396–398
Tax Reform Act (1986), 453
thrift institutions. *See* mutual savings banks; savings banks
tight money, 25–26
TILA-RESPA Integrated Disclosure (TRID), 295
title companies
in California, 27, 316
escrow involvement of, 316
title insurance policies, 321–322
trade associations, 62–64
trustee's sale, 339–343, 344
Truth-in-Lending, 84, 111, 319–320, 355, 356–358, 493
two-to-four-unit residential property, 453–455

U

underwriting, 248, 314–315, 470–471
Uniform Residential Appraisal Report form, 231–237
Upfront Mortgage Insurance Premium (UFMIP), 165
U.S. Department of Housing and Urban Development (HUD). *See also* Federal Housing Administration (FHA)
forbearance regulations, 350
Ginnie Mae program, 207–210
HUD-1 Form, 101
loan assignments to, 353
website of, 169
U.S. Department of Veterans Affairs (VA)
appraisal/property standards, 225–227
conventional *versus* government-backed loans, 131–134

deferred interest guarantees, 349
late charges by, 325
loan approval process, 315
loan qualification requirements, 178, 180, 274–278, 353–354
mortgage insurance requirements, 353–354
pest inspection requirements, 184, 228
prepayment penalties, 325–326
VA-guaranteed loans, 131–134, 176–185, 190, 183, 198–200, 274–278, 277, 325–326, 349–350, 353–354

U.S. Treasury, 19–20, 58, 210
usury law, 78, 356–358

V

valuation of property. *See* appraisals
veterans loans. *See* Cal-Vet loans; U.S. Department of Veterans Affairs
Vrooman Street Act, 391

W

warranties, 356
websites
    foreclosure/default information, 361–362

U.S. Department of Housing and Urban Development, 169
wrap-around trust deed. *See* all-inclusive trust deed

Y

yield, 202–207, 491–492, 415
yield-spread premiums, 201–202, 295

Z

zoning, 239–240